"The book does a terrific job of explaining the tax code. The tax advice . . . is on target and has depth. Smart chapters — not just thumbnail sketches — for filling out forms."

—Gannett News Service

"Among tax advice books is far and away the best. *Taxes 2022 For Dummies* is fun to read and teaches about the tax system itself. The book also provides excellent advice about dealing with mistakes — created by you or the Internal Revenue Service. And it talks about fitting taxes into your daily financial planning. In other words, it's a book you can use after April 15, as well as before."

—Kathy M. Kristof, *Los Angeles Times*

"The best of these books for tax novices. Substitutes simple English for tax-code complexities."

—*Worth* magazine

"User-friendly income-tax preparation and sound financial advice you can use throughout the year."

—*The Seattle Times*

"This book is the most accessible and creative. It's also the best organized of the lot, presenting information in the order you need it to complete your tax forms."

—*USA Today*

"*Taxes 2022 For Dummies* will make tax preparation less traumatic . . . It is a book that answers — in plain English, and sometimes with humor — many puzzling questions that arise on the most commonly used tax forms."

—Stanley Angrist, *The Wall Street Journal*

"This is a lot of book for the money, filled with good examples . . . and level-headed advice. It follows the line-by-line format but also has year-round reference value for taxpayers who plan ahead . . . A human heart beats in this highly intelligent tax tome."

—Michael Pellecchia, syndicated columnist

"$$$$ — Highest rated among the annual tax guides . . . superb writing and friendly organization."

—*Publishers Weekly*

More Bestselling For Dummies Titles by Eric Tyson

Investing For Dummies®

The complete guide to building wealth in stocks, real estate, mutual funds, and small business. With updated coverage on everything from internet brokerages to information sources, this friendly guide shows you how to assess your situation, gauge risks and returns, and make sound investments. Also check out the latest edition of Eric's *Mutual Funds For Dummies!*

Personal Finance For Dummies®

Discover the best ways to establish and achieve your financial goals, reduce your spending and taxes, and make wise personal finance decisions. *Wall Street Journal* bestseller and winner of the Benjamin Franklin best business book award.

Home Buying For Dummies®

America's #1 real estate book includes coverage of online resources in addition to sound financial advice from Eric Tyson and frontline real estate insights from industry veteran Ray Brown. Also available from America's best-selling real estate team of Tyson and Brown — *House Selling For Dummies* and *Mortgages For Dummies*.

Real Estate Investing For Dummies®

Real estate is a proven wealth-building investment, but many people don't know how to go about making and managing rental property investments. Real estate and property management expert Robert Griswold and Eric Tyson cover the gamut of property investment options, strategies, and techniques.

Small Business For Dummies®

Take control of your future and make the leap from employee to entrepreneur with this enterprising guide. From drafting a business plan to managing costs, you'll profit from expert advice and real-world examples that cover every aspect of building your own business. Also take a look at Eric's *Small Business Taxes For Dummies*.

Taxes 2022

Taxes 2022

by Eric Tyson, MBA Financial consultant, bestselling author

Margaret Atkins Munro, EA Tax advisor

David J. Silverman, EA Tax advisor

for dummies®

A Wiley Brand

Taxes 2022 For Dummies®

Published by
Wiley Publishing, Inc.
111 River St.
Hoboken, NJ 07030-5774
www.wiley.com

Copyright © 2022 by Eric Tyson, David J. Silverman, and Margaret Atkins Munro

Published by Wiley Publishing, Inc., Indianapolis, Indiana

Published simultaneously in Canada

For general information on our other products and services, please contact our Customer Care Department within the U.S. at 877-762-2974, outside the U.S. at 317-572-3993, or fax 317-572-4002. For technical support, please visit https://hub.wiley.com/community/support/dummies.

Wiley publishes in a variety of print and electronic formats and by print-on-demand. Some material included with standard print versions of this book may not be included in e-books or in print-on-demand. If this book refers to media such as a CD or DVD that is not included in the version you purchased, you may download this material at http://booksupport.wiley.com. For more information about Wiley products, visit www.wiley.com.

Library of Congress Control Number: 2021950181

ISBN 978-1-119-85845-4 (pbk); ISBN 978-1-119-85847-8 (ebk); ISBN 978-1-119-85846-1 (ebk)

SKY10033438_022322

Contents at a Glance

Table of Contents

Introduction

Welcome to *Taxes 2022 For Dummies* — the latest up-to-date revision of our annual best-selling book (the first edition of which was published in 1994) by your humble co-authors — Eric Tyson, Margaret Atkins Munro, and David J. Silverman. These pages answer both your tax-preparation and tax-planning questions in plain English and with a touch of humor.

About This Book

Our book can help you make sense of the tax laws, especially the newest ones. We promise to help relieve your pain and misery (at least the tax-related portion), legally reduce your income tax bill, and get you through your tax return with little discomfort.

We also help you keep your mind on your taxes while you plan your finances for the upcoming year. As you probably know, Congress and political candidates engage in never-ending discussions about ways to tinker with the nation's tax laws. Where appropriate throughout the book, we highlight how any resulting changes may affect important decisions you'll need to make in the years ahead.

In addition to helping you understand how to deal with federal income taxes, we explain how to handle and reduce some of those pesky and not-so-insignificant taxes slapped on by states and other tax-collecting bodies.

We also show you how to steer clear of running afoul of tax laws. The fact that Congress keeps changing the tax rules makes it easy for honest and well-intentioned people to unknowingly break those laws. We explain how to clear the necessary hurdles to keep the taxing authorities from sending threatening notices and bills. But if you do get a nasty letter from the tax police, we explain how to deal with that frightful situation in a calm, levelheaded manner so that you get the IRS off your back.

Throughout this book, we provide line-by-line and step-by-step instructions on how to fill out various tax forms and give examples of what these forms look like. If ever you need to look up a form or print one out, simply go to www.irs.gov and type the form name in the search box.

Foolish Assumptions

At their worst, some annual tax-preparation books are as dreadful as the IRS instruction booklets themselves — bulky, bureaucratic, and jargon-filled. In particular cases, preparation books simply reproduce dozens of pages of IRS instructions! At their best, these books tell you information you can't find in the IRS instructions — but the golden nuggets of tax information often are buried in massive piles of granite. *Taxes 2022 For Dummies* lays out those golden nuggets in nice, clean display cases so that you won't miss a single one. There's still plenty of granite, but we don't use it to bury you — or key insights!

Among the three of us, we have more than nine decades of experience providing personal financial and tax advice to real people just like you. We understand your tax and financial concerns and know how to help solve your quandaries!

Most people's tax concerns fall into three categories: filling out their forms properly, legally minimizing their taxes, and avoiding interest and penalties. *Taxes 2022 For Dummies* addresses these concerns and helps take some of the pain and agony out of dealing with taxes.

We've made some assumptions on how you may want to use this book. Here are the various practical ways that we figure you will use *Taxes 2022 For Dummies* to complete your forms, legally reduce your taxes, and avoid penalties:

>> **As a reference:** For example, maybe you know a fair amount about your taxes, but you don't know where and how to report the dividends you received from some of your investments. Simply use the table of contents or index to find the right spot in the book with the answers to your questions. On the other hand, if you lack investments — in part because you pay so much in taxes — this book also explains legal strategies for slashing your taxes and boosting your savings. Use this book before and after April 15.

>> **As a trusted advisor:** Maybe you're self-employed and you know that you need to be salting money away so that you can someday cut back on those long workdays. Turn to Chapter 22, and find out about the different types of retirement accounts, which one may be right for you, how it can slash your taxes, and even where to set it up.

>> **As a textbook:** If you have the time, desire, and discipline, by all means go for it and read the whole shebang. And please drop us a note and let us know of your achievement!

Icons Used in This Book

TIP

This target marks recommendations for making the most of your taxes and money (for example, paying off your nontax-deductible credit-card debt with your lottery winnings).

TAX CUT

The info by this friendly sign is useful if you want to discover ways to reduce your taxes — and all the suggestions are strictly legit.

REMEMBER

This icon is a friendly reminder of stuff we discuss elsewhere in the book or of points we really want you to remember.

WARNING

This alert denotes common, costly mistakes people make with their taxes.

TECHNICAL STUFF

This nerdy guy appears beside discussions that aren't critical if you just want to know the basic concepts and get answers to your tax questions. However, reading these gems can deepen and enhance your tax knowledge. And you never know when you'll be invited to go to a town meeting and talk tax reform with a bunch of politicians!

NEW STUFF

Throughout this book, we highlight new tax provisions with this icon. Although searching for and reading passages marked with this icon quickly tells you what's new, don't overlook the many tax-reducing strategies and recommendations throughout the rest of the book.

SEEK ADVICE

Some tax problems are too complex to be handled in any one book. If you're one of the unlucky ones who's in a tax situation that can spell big trouble if you get it wrong, consult a tax advisor to be on the safe side. We tell you how to select one in Chapter 2.

Beyond the Book

In addition to the material in the print or e-book you're reading right now, this product also comes with some access-anywhere info on the web. Go to www.dummies.com and type in "Taxes 2022 For Dummies Cheat Sheet" in the search box to discover some tax-wise pointers.

Where to Go from Here

There are numerous different ways that readers tell us that they use our book. If you're on a deadline to complete your Form 1040 U.S. income tax return, you can turn to those chapters in Parts 2 and 3. If you've got an audit or other notice from the IRS and want advice on that — see Part 4. If you'd like a good overview on the tax system and are trying to make wise year-round tax decisions, check out the other Parts, especially Part 5.

Beyond the Book

Where to Go from Here

1

Getting Ready to File

Chapter **1**

Understanding the U.S. Tax System

M ost people — including your humble authors — find taxes to be tedious. First, everyone faces the chore of gathering various complicated-looking documents to complete the annual ritual of filling out IRS Form 1040 and whatever form your state may require.

You may need to become acquainted with some forms that are new to you. Perhaps you need to figure out how to submit a quarterly tax payment when you no longer work for a company and now receive self-employment income from independent contract work. Maybe you sold some investments (such as stocks, mutual funds, or real estate) at a profit (or loss), and you must calculate how much tax you owe (or loss you can write off).

Unfortunately, too many people think of taxes only in spring, when it comes time to file that dreadful annual return. Throughout this book, you can find all sorts of tips, suggestions, and warnings that help you discover the important role that your taxes play in your entire personal financial situation year-round. In fact, we devote Part 5 of the book to showing you how to accomplish important financial goals while legally reducing your taxes.

We hope that you include our book as an understandable resource you can count on. *Taxes 2022 For Dummies* helps you discover how the tax system works and how to legally make the system work for you. You'll quite possibly be bothered by some of the things this book shows you that don't seem fair. But getting angry enough to make the veins in your neck bulge definitely won't help your financial situation or your blood pressure. (We don't want to see your medical deductions increase!) Even if you don't agree with the entire tax system, you still have to play by the rules.

Figuring Out the U.S. Tax System

Whenever money passes through your hands, it seems that you pay some kind of tax. Consider the following:

>> When you work and get paid, you pay federal, state, and local taxes (on top of having to deal with the migraines your bosses and difficult customers give you).

>> After paying taxes on your earnings and then spending money on things you need and want (and paying more taxes in the process), you may have some money left over for investing. Guess what? Your reward for being a saver is that you also pay tax on some of the earnings on your savings.

You'll pay more in taxes than you need to if you don't understand the tax system. Unfortunately, when you try to read and make sense of the tax laws, you quickly realize that you're more likely to win the lottery than figure out some parts of the tax code! That's one of the reasons that tax attorneys and accountants are paid so much — to compensate them for their intense and prolonged agony of deciphering the tax code!

A BRIEF HISTORY OF U.S. INCOME TAXES

Federal income taxes haven't always been a certainty. In the early 20th century, people lived without being bothered by the federal income tax — or by televisions, microwaves, computers, smartphones, and all those other complications. Beginning in 1913, Congress set up a system of graduated tax rates, starting with a rate of only 1 percent and going up to 7 percent.

This tax system was enacted through the 16th Amendment to the Constitution, which was suggested by President Teddy Roosevelt, pushed through by his successor (President William H. Taft), and ultimately ratified by two-thirds of the states.

In fairness, we must tell you that the 1913 federal income tax wasn't the first U.S. income tax. President Abraham Lincoln instituted a Civil War income tax in 1861, which was abandoned a decade later.

Prior to 1913, the vast majority of tax dollars collected by the federal government came from taxes levied on goods, such as liquor, tobacco, and imports. Today, personal income taxes, including Social Security taxes, account for about 85 percent of federal government revenue.

In 1913, the forms, instructions, and clarifications for the entire federal tax system would have filled just one small three-ring binder. (And we're not even sure that three-ring binders existed back then.) Those were, indeed, the good old days. Since then, thanks to endless revisions, enhancements, and simplifications, the federal tax laws — along with the IRS and court clarifications of those laws — can (and should) fill several dump trucks.

But here's a little secret to make you feel much better: You don't need to read the dreadful tax laws. Most tax advisors don't read them themselves. Instead, they rely upon summaries prepared by organizations and people who have more of a knack for explaining things clearly and concisely than the IRS does. Wolters Kluwer — the organization responsible for technically reviewing this fine book — has compiled a *Federal Tax Reporter* publication that details and explains all federal tax laws. This publication now has in excess of 80,000 pages!

Even if your financial life is stagnant, recent tax law changes may require you to complete some new forms and calculations. And, if you're like most people, you're currently missing out on some legal tax reduction tactics.

You can reduce your taxes

REMEMBER

The tax system is built around incentives to encourage desirable behavior and activity. Home ownership, for example, is considered good because it encourages people to take more responsibility for maintaining properties and neighborhoods. Therefore, the government offers numerous tax benefits (*allowable deductions*) to encourage people to own homes (see Chapter 25). But if you don't understand these tax benefits, you probably don't know how to take full advantage of them, either.

Even when you're an honest, earnest, well-intentioned, and law-abiding citizen, odds are that you don't completely understand the tax system. This ignorance wreaks havoc with your personal finances because you end up paying more in taxes than you need to.

Adding insult to injury, you may step on a tax land mine. Like millions of taxpayers before you, you can unwittingly be in noncompliance with the ever-changing tax laws at the federal, state, and local levels. Your tax ignorance can cause mistakes that may be costly if the IRS and your state government catch your errors. With the proliferation of computerized data tracking, discovering errors has never been easier for the tax cops at the IRS. And when they uncover your boo-boos, you have to pay the tax you originally owed, interest, and possibly penalties. Ouch!

REMEMBER

So don't feel dumb when it comes to understanding the tax system. You're not the problem — the complexity of the income tax system is. Making sense of the tax jungle is more daunting than hacking your way out of a triple-canopy rain forest with a dinner knife. That's why, throughout this book, we help you understand the tax system, and we promise not to make you read the actual tax laws.

You should be able to keep much more of your money by applying the tax-reducing strategies we present in this book. Here are some things to consider:

>> You may be able to tax shelter your employment earnings into various retirement accounts such as 401(k) and SEP-IRA plans. This strategy slashes your current income taxes, enables your money to grow tax-free, and helps you save toward the goal of retirement.

>> The less you buy, the less sales tax you pay. You can buy a less costly, more fuel-efficient car, for example. (You'll spend less on gasoline, including gasoline taxes, as well.)

>> When you invest, you can invest in a way that fits your tax situation. This strategy can make you happier and wealthier come tax time. For example, you can choose tax-friendly investments (such as tax-free bonds) that reduce your tax bill and increase your after-tax investment returns.

Beyond April 15: What you don't know can cost you

Every spring, more than 100 million tax returns (and several million extension requests) are filed with the IRS. The byproduct of this effort is guaranteed employment for the nation's more than 1 million accountants and auditors and 2 million bookkeeping and accounting clerks (not to mention more than a few tax-book authors and their editors). Accounting firms rake in tens of billions of dollars annually, helping bewildered and desperately confused taxpayers figure out all those tax laws. So that you can feel okay about this situation, keep in mind that at least some of the money you pay in income taxes actually winds up in the government coffers for some useful purposes.

Given all the hours that you work each year just to pay your taxes and the time you spend actually completing the dreaded return, on April 16, you may feel like tossing the whole tax topic into a drawer or closet until next year. Such avoidance, however, is a costly mistake.

During the tax year, you can take steps to ensure not only that you're in compliance with the ever-changing tax laws, but also that you're minimizing your tax burden. If your income — like that of nearly everyone we know — is limited, you need to understand the tax code to make it work for you and help you accomplish your financial goals. The following case studies demonstrate the importance of keeping in mind the tax implications of your financial decisions throughout the year.

The costs of procrastination

Consider the case of Sheila and Peter, the proud owners of a successful and rapidly growing small business. They became so busy running the business and taking care of their children that they hardly had time to call a tax advisor. In fact, not only did they fail to file for an extension by April 15, but they also didn't pay any federal or state income taxes.

By August, Peter and Sheila finally had time to focus on the prior year's income taxes, but by then they had gotten themselves into some problems and incurred these costs:

>> A penalty for failure to file, which is 5 percent per month of the amount due, up to a maximum of 25 percent (for five months).

>> Interest on the amount due, which at that time was running about 3 percent per year. (*Note:* This rate is adjusted over time based on current interest rate levels.)

>> A larger tax bill (also caused by lack of planning), which turned out to be far more expensive than the first two expenses. Because they had incorporated their business, Peter and Sheila were on the payroll for salary during the year. Despite the high level of profitability of their business, they had set their pay at too low a level.

A low salary wouldn't seem to be a problem for the owner and only employee of a company. The worst that you'd think could happen to Peter and Sheila is that they may have to eat more peanut butter and jelly sandwiches during the year. But because they received small salaries, the contributions they could make to tax-deductible retirement accounts were based on a percentage of only their small salaries.

The rest of the business profits, however, had to be taken by Sheila and Peter as taxable income, because they had their company set up as an S Corporation. (We explain the different types of corporations and their tax consequences in Chapter 23.) This gaffe caused Sheila and Peter to pay thousands in additional taxes, which they could've legally — and easily — avoided.

>> Loss of future investment earnings, which means that over time Sheila and Peter actually lost more than the additional taxes. Not only did Peter and Sheila miss out on an opportunity to reduce their taxes by making larger deductible contributions to their tax-sheltered retirement accounts, but they also lost the chance for the money to compound (tax-deferred) over time.

The consequences of poor advice

WARNING

Getting bad advice, especially from someone with a vested interest in your decisions, is another leading cause of tax mistakes. Consider the case of George, who sought counsel about investing and other financial matters. When he received a solicitation from a financial advisor at a well-known firm, he bit. The polished, well-dressed lad was actually a broker (someone who earns commissions from the financial products that they peddle) who prepared a voluminous report complete with scads of retirement projections for George.

Part of the advice in this report was for George to purchase some cash-value life insurance and various investments from the broker. The broker pitched the insurance as a great way to save, invest, and reduce George's tax burden.

Through his employer, George can invest in a retirement account on a tax-deductible basis. However, the broker conveniently overlooked this avenue — after all, the broker can't earn fat commissions by telling people like George to fund their employers' retirement accounts. As a result, George paid thousands of dollars more in taxes annually than he needed to, not to mention those fat, and unnecessary, commissions.

Funding the life insurance policy was a terrible decision for George, in large part because doing so offered no upfront tax breaks. When you contribute money to tax-deductible retirement accounts, such as 401(k) plans, you get to keep and invest money you normally would've owed in federal and state income taxes. (See Chapter 22 to find out more about retirement accounts and check out Chapter 24 for the other reasons why life insurance generally shouldn't be used as an investment.)

Understanding Your Income Tax Rates

Many people remember only whether they received tax refunds or owed money on their tax returns. But you should care how much you pay in taxes and the total and the marginal taxes that you pay, so you can make financial decisions that lessen your tax load.

Although some people feel happy when they get refunds, you shouldn't. All a refund indicates is that you overpaid your taxes during the previous year. When you file your income tax return, you settle up with tax authorities regarding the amount of taxes you paid during the past year versus the total tax that you actually are required to pay, based on your income and deductions.

Adding up your total taxes

The only way to determine the total amount of income taxes you pay is to get out your federal and state tax returns. On each of those returns, well before the end, is a line that shows the total tax. Add the totals from your federal and state tax returns, and you probably have one of the largest expenses of your financial life (unless you have an expensive home or a huge gambling habit).

You need to note that your taxable income is different from the amount of money you earned during the tax year from employment and investments. Taxable income is defined as the amount of income on which you actually pay income taxes. You don't pay taxes on your total income for the following two reasons. First, not all income is taxable. For example, you pay federal income tax on the interest that you earn on a bank savings account but not on the interest from municipal bonds (loans that you, as a bond buyer, make to state and local governments).

A second reason that you don't pay taxes on all your income is that you get to subtract deductions from your income. Some deductions are available just for being a living, breathing human being. For tax year 2021, single people receive an automatic $12,550 *standard deduction*, heads of household qualify for $18,800, and married couples filing jointly get $21,100. (People older than 65 and those who are blind get slightly higher deductions.) Other expenses, such as mortgage interest and property taxes, are deductible to the extent that your total itemized deductions exceed the standard deductions.

REMEMBER

A personal budget or spending plan that doesn't address your income taxes may be doomed to failure. Throughout this book we highlight strategies for reducing your taxable income and income taxes right now and in the future. Doing so is vital to your ability to save and invest money to accomplish important financial and personal goals.

Following your marginal income tax rate

Marginal is a word that people often use when they mean small or barely acceptable. Sort of like getting a C– on a school report card (or "just" an A– if you're from an overachieving family). But when we're talking taxes, *marginal* has a different meaning. The government charges you different income tax rates for different portions of your annual income. So your *marginal tax rate* is the rate that you pay on the last dollars you earn. You generally pay less tax on your *first*, or lowest, dollars of earnings and more tax on your *last*, or highest, dollars of earnings. This system is known as a *graduated income tax*, a system noted in Greece as far back as 2400 B.C.

Our advice is to keep an open mind, listen to all sides, and remember the big picture. Back in the 1950s (an economic boom time), for example, the highest federal income tax rate was a whopping 90 percent. And whereas during most of the past century the highest income earners paid a marginal rate that was double to triple the rate paid by moderate income earners of the time, that gap was reduced during the past generation. Still, the highest income earners continue to pay the lion's share of taxes. In fact, using the latest IRS data, the Tax Foundation recently found the top 1 percent of all income earners pay about 40 percent of all federal taxes (while earning 21 percent of all income). The top 10 percent pay about 71 percent of the total individual income taxes collected (while earning 48 percent of all income).

The fact that not all income is treated equally under the current tax system isn't evident to most people. When you work for an employer and have a reasonably constant salary during the course of a year, a stable amount of federal and state taxes is deducted from each of your paychecks. Therefore, you may have the false impression that all your earned income is being taxed equally.

Table 1-1 gives the 2021 federal income tax rates for singles and for married people filing jointly.

Table 1-1   2021 Federal Income Tax Brackets and Rates

Federal Income Tax Rate	Single Filers Tax Brackets	Married Couples Filing Jointly Tax Brackets
10%	Up to $9,950	Up to $19,900
12%	$9,951 to $40,525	$19,901 to $81,050
22%	$40,526 to $86,375	$81,051 to $172,750
24%	$86,376 to $164,925	$172,751 to $329,850
32%	$164,926 to $209,425	$329,851 to $418,850
35%	$209,426 to $523,600	$418,851 to $628,300
37%	$523,601 or more	$628,301 or more

REMEMBER

Remember that your marginal tax rate is the rate of tax that you pay on your last, or so-called highest, dollars of taxable income. So, according to Table 1-1, if you're single and your taxable income during 2021 totals $46,000, for example, you pay federal income tax at the rate of 10 percent on the first $9,950 of taxable income. You then pay 12 percent on the amount from $9,950 to $40,525 and 22 percent on income from $40,525 up to $46,000. In other words, you effectively pay a marginal federal tax rate of 22 percent on your last dollars of income — those dollars in excess of $40,525.

After you understand the powerful concept of marginal tax rates, you can see the value of the many financial strategies that affect the amount of taxes you pay. Because you pay taxes on your employment income and on the earnings from your investments other than retirement accounts, many of your personal financial decisions need to be made with your marginal tax rate in mind. For example, when you have the opportunity to moonlight and earn some extra money, how much of that extra compensation you get to keep depends on your marginal tax rate. Your marginal income tax rate enables you to quickly calculate the additional taxes you'd pay on the additional income.

Conversely, you quantify the amount of taxes that you save by reducing your taxable income, either by decreasing your income — for example, with pretax contributions to retirement accounts — or by increasing your deductions.

Actually, you can make even more of your marginal taxes. In the next section, we detail the painful realities of income taxes levied by most states that add to your federal income burden. If you're a middle-to-higher income earner, pay close attention to the section later in this chapter where we discuss the Alternative Minimum Tax. And as we discuss elsewhere in this book, some tax breaks are reduced when your income exceeds a particular level — here are some examples:

>> **Education tax breaks:** There are numerous education tax deductions and credits, the rules for which continue to evolve and change. All of these helpful tax breaks, however, are subject to income limitations well below $200,000 (see Chapter 26 to plan ahead and get more specifics).

>> **Saver's credit:** The saver's credit rewards lower-income earners with federal income tax credits on Form 8880 (Credit for Qualified Retirement Savings Contributions). This credit phases out in 2021 for single taxpayers with adjusted gross income (AGI) above $33,000 and for married couples filing jointly at AGIs above $66,000.

>> **Rental real estate losses:** If you own rental real estate, you may normally take up to a $25,000 annual loss when your expenses exceed your rental income. Your ability to deduct this loss begins to be limited when your AGI exceeds $100,000.

>> **Roth IRA contributions:** Your eligibility to fully contribute to Roth individual retirement accounts (IRAs; see Chapter 20) for 2021 depends on your modified AGI being less than or equal to $140,000 if you're a single taxpayer or $208,000 if you're married. Beyond these amounts, allowable contributions are phased out.

REMEMBER

Your marginal income tax rate — the rate of tax you pay on your last dollars of income — should be higher than your average tax rate — the rate you pay, on average, on all your earnings. The reason your marginal tax rate is more important for you to know is that it tells you the value of legally reducing your taxable income. So, for example, if you're in the federal 24 percent tax bracket, for every $1,000 that you can reduce your taxable income, you shave $240 off your federal income tax bill.

States want in on the income tax action, too

Note that your *total marginal rate* includes your federal and state income tax rates. As you may already be painfully aware, you don't pay only federal income taxes. You also get hit with state income taxes — that is, unless you live in Alaska, Florida, Nevada, South Dakota, Tennessee, Texas, Washington, or Wyoming. Those states have no state income taxes. As is true with federal income taxes, state income taxes have been around since the early 1900s.

TIP

You can look up your state tax rate by getting out your most recent year's state income tax preparation booklet. Alternatively, we've been crazy — but kind —enough to prepare a helpful little (okay, not so little) table that can give you a rough idea of your state tax rates (see Table 1-2). This table reflects state individual income taxes. Some states impose other taxes, such as local, county, or city taxes, special taxes for nonresidents, or capital gains taxes, which aren't included in this table.

Table 1-2   State Marginal Tax Rates

State	Single Tax Filers		Married Filing Jointly	
	Rates	Brackets	Rates	Brackets
Alabama	2.00%	>$0	2.00%	>$0
	4.00%	>$500	4.00%	>$1,000
	5.00%	>$3,000	5.00%	>$6,000
Alaska	none		none	
Arizona	2.59%	>$0	2.59%	>$0
	3.34%	>$27,272	3.34%	>$54,544
	4.17%	>$54,544	4.17%	>$109,088
	4.50%	>$163,632	4.50%	>$327,263
	8.00%	>$250,000	8.00%	>$500,000
Arkansas	2.00%	>$0	2.00%	>$0
	4.00%	>$4,000	4.00%	>$4,000
	5.90%	>$8,000	5.90%	>$8,000
California	1.00%	>$0	1.00%	>$0
	2.00%	>$8,932	2.00%	>$17,864
	4.00%	>$21,175	4.00%	>$42,350
	6.00%	>$33,421	6.00%	>$66,842
	8.00%	>$46,394	8.00%	>$92,788
	9.30%	>$58,634	9.30%	>$117,268
	10.30%	>$299,508	10.30%	>$599,016
	11.30%	>$359,407	11.30%	>$718,814
	12.30%	>$599,012	12.30%	>$1,000,000
	13.30%	>$1,000,000	13.30%	>$1,198,024
Colorado	4.55%	>$0	4.55%	>$0
Connecticut	3.00%	>$0	3.00%	>$0
	5.00%	>$10,000	5.00%	>$20,000
	5.50%	>$50,000	5.50%	>$100,000
	6.00%	>$100,000	6.00%	>$200,000
	6.50%	>$200,000	6.50%	>$400,000
	6.90%	>$250,000	6.90%	>$500,000
	6.99%	>$500,000	6.99%	>$1,000,000
Delaware	2.20%	>$2,000	2.20%	>$2,000
	3.90%	>$5,000	3.90%	>$5,000
	4.80%	>$10,000	4.80%	>$10,000
	5.20%	>$20,000	5.20%	>$20,000
	5.55%	>$25,000	5.55%	>$25,000
	6.60%	>$60,000	6.60%	>$60,000
Florida	none		none	
Georgia	1.00%	>$0	1.00%	>$0
	2.00%	>$750	2.00%	>$1,000

(continued)

Table 1-2 (continued)

State	Single Tax Filers Rates	Brackets	Married Filing Jointly Rates	Brackets
	3.00%	>$2,250	3.00%	>$3,000
	4.00%	>$3,750	4.00%	>$5,000
	5.00%	>$5,250	5.00%	>$7,000
	5.75%	>$7,000	5.75%	>$10,000
Hawaii	1.40%	>$0	1.40%	>$0
	3.20%	>$2,400	3.20%	>$4,800
	5.50%	>$4,800	5.50%	>$9,600
	6.40%	>$9,600	6.40%	>$19,200
	6.80%	>$14,400	6.80%	>$28,800
	7.20%	>$19,200	7.20%	>$38,400
	7.60%	>$24,000	7.60%	>$48,000
	7.90%	>$36,000	7.90%	>$72,000
	8.25%	>$48,000	8.25%	>$96,000
	9.00%	>$150,000	9.00%	>$300,000
	10.00%	>$175,000	10.00%	>$350,000
	11.00%	>$200,000	11.00%	>$400,000
Idaho	1.125%	>$0	1.125%	>$0
	3.125%	>$1,568	3.125%	>$3,136
	3.625%	>$3,136	3.625%	>$6,272
	4.625%	>$4,704	4.625%	>$9,408
	5.625%	>$6,272	5.625%	>$12,544
	6.625%	>$7,840	6.625%	>$15,680
	6.925%	>$11,760	6.925%	>$23,520
Illinois	4.95%	>$0	4.95%	>$0
Indiana	3.23%	>$0	3.23%	>$0
Iowa	0.33%	>$0	0.33%	>$0
	0.67%	>$1,676	0.67%	>$1,676
	2.25%	>$3,352	2.25%	>$3,352
	4.14%	>$6,704	4.14%	>$6,704
	5.63%	>$15,084	5.63%	>$15,084
	5.96%	>$25,140	5.96%	>$25,140
	6.25%	>$33,520	6.25%	>$33,520
	7.44%	>$50,280	7.44%	>$50,280
	8.53%	>$75,420	8.53%	>$75,420
Kansas	3.10%	>$0	3.10%	>$0
	5.25%	>$15,000	5.25%	>$30,000
	5.70%	>$30,000	5.70%	>$60,000
Kentucky	5.00%	>$0	5.00%	>$0
Louisiana	2.00%	>$0	2.00%	>$0

State	Single Tax Filers Rates	Brackets	Married Filing Jointly Rates	Brackets
	4.00%	>$12,500	4.00%	>$25,000
	6.00%	>$50,000	6.00%	>$100,000
Maine	5.80%	>$0	5.80%	>0
	6.75%	>$22,450	6.75%	>$44,950
	7.15%	>$53,150	7.15%	>$106,350
Maryland	2.00%	>$0	2.00%	>$0
	3.00%	>$1,000	3.00%	>$1,000
	4.00%	>$2,000	4.00%	>$2,000
	4.75%	>$3,000	4.75%	>$3,000
	5.00%	>$100,000	5.00%	>$150,000
	5.25%	>$125,000	5.25%	>$175,000
	5.50%	>$150,000	5.50%	>$225,000
	5.75%	>$250,000	5.75%	>$300,000
Massachusetts	5.00%	>$0	5.00%	>$0
Michigan	4.25%	>$0	4.25%	>$0
Minnesota	5.35%	>$0	5.35%	>$0
	6.80%	>$27,230	6.80%	>$39,810
	7.85%	>$89,440	7.85%	>$158,140
	9.85%	>$166,040	9.85%	>$276,200
Mississippi	3.00%	>$4,000	3.00%	>$4,000
	4.00%	>$5,000	4.00%	>$5,000
	5.00%	>$10,000	5.00%	>$10,000
Missouri	1.50%	>$107	1.50%	>$107
	2.00%	>$1,073	2.00%	>$1,073
	2.50%	>$2,146	2.50%	>$2,146
	3.00%	>$3,219	3.00%	>$3,219
	3.50%	>$4,292	3.50%	>$4,292
	4.00%	>$5,365	4.00%	>$5,365
	4.50%	>$6,438	4.50%	>$6,438
	5.00%	>$7,511	5.00%	>$7,511
	5.40%	>$8,584	5.40%	>$8,584
Montana	1.00%	>$0	1.00%	>$0
	2.00%	>$3,100	2.00%	>$3,100
	3.00%	>$5,500	3.00%	>$5,500
	4.00%	>$8,400	4.00%	>$8,400
	5.00%	>$11,300	5.00%	>$11,300
	6.00%	>$14,500	6.00%	>$14,500
	6.90%	>$18,700	6.90%	>$18,700
Nebraska	2.46%	>$0	2.46%	>$0

(continued)

Table 1-2 (continued)

State	Single Tax Filers		Married Filing Jointly	
	Rates	Brackets	Rates	Brackets
	3.51%	>$3,340	3.51%	>$6,660
	5.01%	>$19,990	5.01%	>$39,990
	6.84%	>$32,210	6.84%	>$64,430
Nevada	none		none	
New Hampshire	5.00%	>$0	5.00%	>$0
New Jersey	1.400%	>$0	1.400%	>$0
	1.750%	>$20,000	1.750%	>$20,000
	3.500%	>$35,000	2.450%	>$50,000
	5.525%	>$40,000	3.500%	>$70,000
	6.370%	>$75,000	5.525%	>$80,000
	8.970%	>$500,000	6.370%	>$150,000
	10.750%	>$1,000,000	8.970%	>$500,000
			10.750%	>$1,000,000
New Mexico	1.70%	>$0	1.70%	>$0
	3.20%	>$5,500	3.20%	>$8,000
	4.70%	>$11,000	4.70%	>$16,000
	4.90%	>$16,000	4.90%	>$24,000
	5.90%	>$210,000	5.90%	>$315,000
New York	4.00%	>$0	4.00%	>$0
	4.50%	>$8,500	4.50%	>$17,150
	5.25%	>$11,700	5.25%	>$23,600
	5.90%	>$13,900	5.90%	>$27,900
	5.97%	>$21,400	5.97%	>$43,000
	6.33%	>$80,650	6.33%	>$161,550
	6.85%	>$215,400	6.85%	>$323,200
	8.82%	>$1,077,550	8.82%	>$2,155,350
North Carolina	5.25%	>$0	5.25%	>$0
North Dakota	1.10%	>$0	1.10%	>$0
	2.04%	>$40,125	2.04%	>$67,050
	2.27%	>$97,150	2.27%	>$161,950
	2.64%	>$202,650	2.64%	>$246,700
	2.90%	>$440,600	2.90%	>$440,600
Ohio	2.850%	>$22,150	2.850%	>$22,150
	3.326%	>$44,250	3.326%	>$44,250
	3.802%	>$88,450	3.802%	>$88,450
	4.413%	>$110,650	4.413%	>$110,650
	4.797%	>$221,300	4.797%	>$221,300
Oklahoma	0.50%	>$0	0.50%	>$0
	1.00%	>$1,000	1.00%	>$2,000

State	Single Tax Filers		Married Filing Jointly	
	Rates	Brackets	Rates	Brackets
	2.00%	>$2,500	2.00%	>$5,000
	3.00%	>$3,750	3.00%	>$7,500
	4.00%	>$4,900	4.00%	>$9,800
	5.00%	>$7,200	5.00%	>$12,200
Oregon	4.75%	>$0	4.75%	>$0
	6.75%	>$3,650	6.75%	>$7,300
	8.75%	>$9,200	8.75%	>$18,400
	9.90%	>$125,000	9.90%	>$250,000
Pennsylvania	3.07%	>$0	3.07%	>$0
Rhode Island	3.75%	>$0	3.75%	>$0
	4.75%	>$66,200	4.75%	>$66,200
	5.99%	>$150,550	5.99%	>$150,550
South Carolina	0.00%	>$0	0.00%	>$0
	3.00%	>$3,070	3.00%	>$3,070
	4.00%	>$6,150	4.00%	>$6,150
	5.00%	>$9,230	5.00%	>$9,230
	6.00%	>$12,310	6.00%	>$12,310
	7.00%	>$15,400	7.00%	>$15,400
South Dakota	none		none	
Tennessee	none		none	
Texas	none		none	
Utah	4.95%	>$0	4.95%	>$0
Vermont	3.35%	>$0	3.35%	>$0
	6.60%	>$40,350	6.60%	>$67,450
	7.60%	>$97,800	7.60%	>$163,000
	8.75%	>$204,000	8.75%	>$248,350
Virginia	2.00%	>$0	2.00%	>$0
	3.00%	>$3,000	3.00%	>$3,000
	5.00%	>$5,000	5.00%	>$5,000
	5.75%	>$17,000	5.75%	>$17,000
Washington	none		none	
West Virginia	3.00%	>$0	3.00%	>$0
	4.00%	>$10,000	4.00%	>$10,000
	4.50%	>$25,000	4.50%	>$25,000
	6.00%	>$40,000	6.00%	>$40,000
	6.50%	>$60,000	6.50%	>$60,000
Wisconsin	3.54%	>$0	3.54%	>$0
	4.65%	>$12,120	4.65%	>$16,160
	6.27%	>$24,250	6.27%	>$32,330

(continued)

Table 1-2 (continued)

State	Single Tax Filers		Married Filing Jointly	
	Rates	Brackets	Rates	Brackets
	7.65%	>$266,930	7.65%	>$355,910
Wyoming	none		none	
District of Columbia	4.00%	>$0	4.00%	>$0
	6.00%	>$10,000	6.00%	>$10,000
	6.50%	>$40,000	6.50%	>$40,000
	8.50%	>$60,000	8.50%	>$60,000
	8.75%	>$350,000	8.75%	>$350,000
	8.95%	>$1,000,000	8.95%	>$1,000,000

The second tax system: Alternative Minimum Tax

There's actually a second federal income tax system (yes, we groan with you as we struggle to understand even the first complicated tax system). This second system may raise your income taxes higher than they'd otherwise be.

In 1969, Congress created a second tax system — the *Alternative Minimum Tax* (AMT) — to ensure that higher-income earners with relatively high amounts of itemized deductions pay at least a minimum amount of taxes on their incomes.

If you have a bunch of deductions from state income taxes, real estate taxes, certain types of mortgage interest, or passive investments (such as limited partnerships or rental real estate), you may fall prey to the AMT. The AMT is a classic case of the increasing complexity of our tax code. As incentives were placed in the tax code, people took advantage of them. Then the government said, "Whoa, Nelly! We can't have people taking that many write-offs." Rather than doing the sensible thing and limiting some of those deductions, Congress created the AMT instead.

The AMT restricts you from claiming certain deductions and requires you to increase your taxable income. So you must figure the tax you owe under the AMT system and under the other system and then pay whichever amount is higher (ouch!). Unfortunately, the only way to know for certain whether you're ensnared by this second tax system is by completing — you guessed it — another tax form (see Chapter 8).

Noting the Forever Changing Tax Laws

Since tax law changes are passed by Congress, they change as the makeup of Congress changes. The most recent major piece of tax legislation was the Tax Cuts and Jobs Act of 2017, which took affect for tax years 2018, and beyond. There have been some smaller pieces of legislation since, addressing retirement accounts and savings and the COVID-19 pandemic. This section provides the highlights for this more recent legislation and associated tax law changes.

The Tax Cuts and Jobs Act of 2017

For most individuals, the biggest change from the Tax Cuts and Jobs Act bill was the lowering of tax rates. The lower tax brackets were lowered by three full percentage points (for example, from 15 percent down to 12 percent, from 25 percent down to 22 percent), and the next income bracket up from that was cut four full percentage points from 28 percent down to 24 percent, which produced substantial tax savings for lower- and moderate-income earners. The highest income earning taxpayers saw smaller reductions in their tax brackets.

According to Brian Riedl, a senior fellow at the Manhattan Institute, a greater share of the individual income tax benefits from this bill went to lower- and moderate-income earners.

Here are some of the other major changes in this tax bill:

>> **Increased standard deduction and eliminated personal exemption:** Proponents of the bill liked to talk about how the standard deduction nearly doubled. This amount is deducted from your income before arriving at your taxable income, so a larger standard deduction reduces your taxable income and tax bill. However, Congress also eliminated personal exemptions, which offset much of this change. Ultimately, though, far more taxpayers can simply claim the standard deduction, which is a time-saver when it comes to completing the annual federal 1040 tax form.

>> **Increased child tax credit:** The child tax credit was doubled by this legislation, and up to 70 percent of that credit was made refundable for taxpayers not otherwise owing federal income tax. Also, the incomes at which this credit starts phasing out was more than tripled for married couples and more than doubled for non-married filers.

>> **State and local taxes deduction capped at $10,000:** This also includes property taxes on your home, and for homeowners in high cost-of-living areas with high state income taxes (for example, metro areas such as San Francisco, Los Angeles, New York, and Washington D.C.), this cap poses a modest or even significant negative change. Because these taxes are itemized deductions, only being able to take up to $10,000 (previously unlimited) caused some taxpayers to no longer be able to itemize. Also, by reducing the tax benefits of home ownership, this change effectively raises the cost of home ownership, especially in high-cost and highly taxed areas.

>> **Mortgage-interest deduction for both primary and second homes capped at $750,000 borrowed:** This represents a modest reduction from the previous $1 million limit on mortgage indebtedness deductibility.

The Tax Cuts and Jobs Act also brought some long overdue corporate tax reform. For too long, the United States had way too high a corporate tax rate, which caused increasing numbers of companies to choose to do less business in the United States.

The SECURE ACT of 2019

Retirement accounts and retirement savings rules were ripe for revisions and improvement. Some of those happened with the SECURE (Setting Every Community Up for Retirement Enhancement) ACT of 2019. Here are the highlights:

» Small-business owners are eligible for up to $5,000 in tax credits when starting a retirement plan. This credit applies to new 401(k), profit sharing, SEP, and SIMPLE plans for small employers with up to 100 employees.

» More part-time workers can participate in company 401(k) plans. Previously, you had to work at least 1,000 hours per year to take part in a company's 401(k) plan. Now, workers who achieve at least 500 hours over three consecutive years may participate.

» You can withdraw up to $5,000 per parent penalty-free from your retirement plan for a "qualified birth or adoption distribution" for the birth or adoption of a child. This new provision waives the normal 10 percent early withdrawal penalty and allows you to repay the withdrawn money as a rollover contribution.

» 529 funds can be used to pay down up to $10,000 in student loans and pay for qualifying apprenticeship programs.

» Required minimum distributions (RMDs) from retirement accounts begin at age 72, not 70½. This gives you more options and flexibility, but delaying required distributions that are based upon your life expectancy may or may not be in your best long-term interests. It's impossible to know for sure, but you and/or your tax advisor may want to crunch some numbers, which requires making some assumptions, to see what the optimal age is to begin your RMDs.

» You can make traditional IRA contributions past age 70½ so long as you continue earning employment income. This brings the contribution rules for these accounts into alignment with those for Roth IRAs and 401(k)s.

» Inherited retirement accounts must now be tapped and emptied through distributions generally within a decade. Before when folks inherited a retirement account, the inheritor could stretch their distributions and associated tax payments out over their life expectancy. For retirement accounts now inherited from original owners who have passed away in 2020 or later years, most beneficiaries must complete withdrawals from the account within ten years of the death of the account holder. There are some exceptions to this ten-year rule for retirement accounts left to a surviving spouse, a minor child, a disabled or chronically ill beneficiary, and beneficiaries who are less than ten years younger than the original retirement account owner.

Possible upcoming changes

Congress continually tinkers with our nation's tax laws. Bigger changes tend to occur when the same party controls both chambers of congress as well as the presidency. As this book goes to press in late 2021, we have been through a lengthy period where there has been lots of talk of tax increases by the Democrats, the party currently in control of congress and the presidency, but that has largely been blocked to date due to their super-slim majorities in both the House and Senate. However, the Democrats have turned to the budget reconciliation process to draft comprehensive tax legislation that is expected to become law by the end of the year. (Any changes passed and signed into law late in 2021 would impact 2022 and beyond and are highly unlikely to impact 2021.)

With the 2022 congressional mid-term elections on the horizon, history suggests that the most likely outcome for those elections will be divided government, which will mean even more gridlock and less likelihood for tax increases or tax changes in general. That said, here's a short list of changes that have been discussed and that have the highest likelihood of being part of a tax package within the next year, if one ever passes:

>> Higher federal income tax rates on high-income earners

>> Some elimination of the step-up cost basis at death for investors in the highest tax brackets

>> Expansion of the state and local income tax deduction from $10,000 to some higher amount or a temporary repeal (a two-year repeal has been most frequently mentioned)

>> Increased corporate federal income tax rate

>> Higher federal capital gains tax rate for those in the highest federal income tax brackets

>> Reduction in the federal estate exemption amount

>> Application of the Social Security tax to more income for the highest income earners

Chapter **2**

Tax Return Preparation Options and Tools

B y the time you actually get around to filing your annual income tax return, it's too late to take advantage of many tax-reduction strategies for that tax year. And what can be more aggravating than, late in the evening on April 14 when you're already stressed out and unhappily working on your return, finding a golden nugget of tax advice that works great — if only you'd known about it last December!

REMEMBER

Be sure to review Part 5, which covers the important tax-planning issues that you need to take advantage of in future years. In the event that you've waited until the last minute to complete your return this year, be sure to read Part 5 thoroughly after you file your return so you don't miss out next year.

If you're now faced with the daunting task of preparing your income tax return, you're probably trying to decide how to do it with a minimum of pain and taxes owed. You have several options for completing your return. The best choice for you depends on the complexity of your tax situation, your knowledge about taxes, and the amount of time you're willing to invest.

Going it Alone: Preparing Your Own Return

You already do many things for yourself. Maybe you cook for yourself, do home repairs, or even change your car's oil. You may do these tasks because you enjoy them, because you save money by doing them, or because you want to develop a particular skill.

Sometimes, however, you hire others to help you do the job. Occasionally, you may buy a meal out or hire someone to make a home improvement. Plenty of folks have a service garage change the oil in their car and perform other needed services. And so it can be with your annual income tax return — you may want to hire help, but you may end up, like most people, preparing your own return.

REMEMBER

Doing your own income tax return is an especially good option if your financial situation does not change much from year to year. You can use last year's return as a guide. You may need to do some reading to keep up with the small number of changes in the tax system and laws that affect your situation (and this book can help). Given the constant changes to various parts of the tax laws, you simply can't assume that the tax laws that apply to your situation are the same from one year to the next just because your situation is the same.

A benefit of preparing your own return includes the better financial decisions that you make in the future by using the tax knowledge you gain from learning about the tax system. Most tax preparers are so busy preparing returns that you probably won't get much of their time to discuss tax laws and how they may apply to your future financial decisions. Even if you can schedule time with the preparer, you may rightfully worry about paying for the personal tutorial you're sitting through.

Last, but not least, doing your own return should be your lowest-cost tax-return-preparation option. Of course, we're assuming that you don't make costly mistakes and oversights and that the leisure time you forego when preparing your return isn't too valuable!

You bought this book, which was a smart move. You're confident enough to tackle the tax forms yourself, and you're savvy enough to know you need expert guidance through the thicket of annual tax law changes. Give our advice a try before throwing in the towel and paying hundreds (perhaps thousands) of dollars in tax-preparation fees. And if you stay alert while preparing your return, reading the list of deductions that don't apply to you may motivate you to make changes in your personal and financial habits so that you can take some of those deductions next year.

Taking Advantage of IRS Publications

In addition to the instructions that come with the annual tax forms that the good old Internal Revenue Service (IRS) provides you with every year, the IRS also produces hundreds of publications that explain how to complete the myriad tax forms various taxpayers must tackle. These booklets are available in printed form or through the IRS's website (www.irs.gov; see the section "Internal Revenue Service" later in this chapter for more on what the site has to offer) or by mail if you simply call and order them from the IRS (800-829-3676). Additionally, the IRS provides answers to common questions through its automated phone system and through live representatives.

If you have a simple, straightforward tax return, completing it on your own using only the IRS instructions may be fine. This approach is as cheap as you can get, costing only your time, patience, photocopying expenses, and postage to mail the completed tax return.

Unfortunately (for you), IRS publications and employees don't generally offer the direct, helpful advice that we provide in this book. For example, here's something you don't see in an IRS publication:

> STOP! One of the most commonly overlooked deductions is. . . . You still have time
> to . . . and slash hundreds — maybe thousands — of dollars from your tax bill!
> HURRY!

WARNING

Another danger in relying on the IRS staffers for assistance is that they have been known to give wrong information and answers. When you call the IRS with a question, be sure to take notes about your phone conversation, thus protecting yourself in the event of an audit. Date your notes and include the name of the IRS employee (and office location and employee number) with whom you spoke, what you asked, and the employee's responses. File your notes in a folder with a copy of your completed return.

In addition to the standard instructions that come with your tax return, the IRS offers some pamphlets that you can request by phone such as the following:

>> **Publication 17:** *Your Federal Income Tax (For Individuals)* is designed for individual tax-return preparation.

>> **Publication 334:** *Tax Guide for Small Business (For Individuals Who Use Schedule C or C-EZ)* is for (you guessed it) small-business tax-return preparation.

These guides provide more detail than the basic IRS publications. To access or request these free guides, visit the IRS website at www.irs.gov or call them at 800-829-3676. (Actually, nothing is free. You've already paid for IRS guides with your tax dollars!)

The IRS also offers more in-depth booklets focusing on specific tax issues. However, if your tax situation is so complex that this book (and Publications 17 and 334) can't address it, you need to think long and hard about getting help from a tax advisor or from one of the other sources recommended in the "Hiring Help" section later in this chapter.

TIP

IRS publications present plenty of rules and facts, but they don't make it easy for you to find the information and advice you really need. The best way to use IRS publications is to confirm facts that you already think you know or to check the little details. Don't expect IRS publications and representatives to show you how to cut your tax bill.

Perusing Tax-Preparation and Advice Guides

Privately published tax-preparation and advice books are invaluable when they highlight tax-reduction strategies and possible pitfalls — in clear, simple English. We hope you agree with the reviewer comments in the front of this guide that say *Taxes For Dummies* is top of the line in this category. Such books help you complete your return accurately and save you big money. The amount of money invested in a book or two is significantly smaller than the annual cost of a tax expert.

Taxes For Dummies covers the important tax-preparation and planning issues that affect the vast majority of taxpayers. A minority of taxpayers may run into some nit-picky tax issues caused by unusual events in their lives or extraordinary changes in their incomes or assets. This book may not be enough for those folks. In such cases, you need to consider hiring a tax advisor, which we explain how to do later in this chapter (see the section "Hiring Help").

Using Software

If you don't want to slog through dozens of pages of tedious IRS instructions or pay a tax preparer hundreds of dollars to complete your annual return, you may be interested in tax preparation software that can help you finish off your IRS Form 1040 and supplemental schedules. If you have access to a private computer, tablet, or even a smartphone, tax-preparation software can be a helpful tool.

Tax-preparation software also gives you the advantage of automatically recalculating all the appropriate numbers on your return if one number changes — no more painting out math errors with a little white brush or recalculating a whole page of figures because your dog was sleeping on some of the receipts. (Just don't let your cat walk on your keyboard or another family member use the computer before saving your return!) The best tax-preparation software is easy to install and use on your computer, provides help when you get stuck, and highlights deductions you may overlook.

WARNING

Before plunking down your hard-earned cash for some tax-preparation software, know that it has potential drawbacks. Here are the big ones:

>> **Garbage in, garbage out.** A tax return prepared by a software program is only as good as the quality of the data you enter into it. Of course, this drawback exists no matter who actually fills out the forms; some human tax preparers don't probe and clarify to make sure that you've provided all the right stuff, either. Tax software programs also may contain glitches that can lead to incorrect calculating or reporting of some aspect of your tax return.

>> **Where's the beef?** Some tax software gives little in the way of background help, advice, and warnings. This lack of assistance can lull you into a false sense of security about the completeness and accuracy of the return you prepare.

>> **Think, computer, think!** Computers are good at helping you access and process information. Remember that your computer is great at crunching numbers but has a far lower IQ than you have!

TIP

TurboTax, H&R Block, TaxAct, TaxSlayer, and Jackson Hewitt Online are the leading programs, and they do a reasonable job of helping you through the federal tax forms. One way to break a tie between good software options is considering price — you may be able to get a better deal on one software package. (TurboTax and H&R Block carry higher suggested retail prices.)

Procrastinating also offers some benefits, because the longer you wait to buy the software, the cheaper it generally gets — especially when you buy it after filing for an extension. (You may also want to examine whether the tax software you buy can import the data from the checkbook software you've been using to track your tax-deductible expenses throughout the year.)

Accessing Internet Tax Resources

In addition to using your computer to prepare your income tax return, you can do an increasing number of other tax activities via the internet. The better online tax resources are geared more to tax practitioners and tax-savvy taxpayers. But in your battle to legally minimize your taxes, you may want all the help you can get! Use the internet for what it's best at doing — possibly saving you time tracking down factual information or forms.

TIP

On the internet, many websites provide information and discussions about tax issues. Take advice and counsel from other internet users at your peril. We don't recommend that you depend on the accuracy of the answers to tax questions that you ask in online forums. The problem: In many cases you can't be sure of the background, expertise, or identity of the person with whom you're trading messages. However, if you want to liven up your life — and taxes make you mad — a number of political forums enable you to converse and debate with others. You can complain about recent tax hikes or explain why you think that the wealthy still don't pay enough taxes!

The following sections describe some of the better sites out there.

Internal Revenue Service

When you think of the Internal Revenue Service — the U.S. Treasury Department office charged with overseeing the collection of federal income taxes — you probably think of the following adjectives: bureaucratic, humorless, and stodgy. Difficult as it is to believe, the IRS website (www.irs.gov) is reasonably well organized and relatively user-friendly.

The IRS site also has links to state tax organizations, convenient access to IRS forms (including those from prior tax years), and instructions. To view and download forms from the IRS site, start browsing at www.irs.gov/forms-instructions.

You can complete your tax forms online at the IRS site. The IRS site even features a place for you to submit comments on proposed tax regulations, with a statement that, "Although we cannot respond individually to each email, we do appreciate your feedback and will consider your comments as we revise our tax products." Is this the IRS we know and love?

GOING PAPERLESS AND PAYING YOUR INCOME TAXES ELECTRONICALLY

It's "old school" to keep paper records and paper copies of your income tax returns.

It's "old school" to mail in your completed income tax returns and to send in a paper check if you owe income taxes quarterly and/or when it's time to submit your complete annual returns to the federal government and state government if you live in a state with a state income tax.

If you like doing things the "old-school" way, that's a good enough reason to keep doing them that way.

There is an alternative. The IRS and state governments allow you to register on their income tax websites and have an account through which you can pay your income taxes and obtain records as needed. And there are many ways today to submit completed income tax returns electronically.

The benefits of going the electronic route include no papers to keep track of and organized or possibly perused by nosy people in your home or office. It's also quicker to file and pay that way and get your refund if you're due one.

Just be sure that if you're submitting payments electronically, you are on the relevant official federal or state website. Beware of scams and fraudsters!

There are plenty of other useful things you can do on the IRS website such as the following:

>> Create an online account to access your tax information and historical data (including via transcripts).

>> Make online payments, such as quarterly estimated tax payments. The lowest cost way to do this is through an electronic payment from your bank account (no charge) or via a debit card ($2.55). Do not pay your taxes with a credit card because you will get whacked with a near 2 percent service charge of the tax amount paid.

>> Check your refund status and access other recent tax perks. This includes being able to tap your COVID-19 relief payments and the advance child tax credit if you qualify.

Research

TECHNICAL STUFF

Most tax research sites have information that is of greater interest to tax and other financial professionals. That said, here are some tax websites that may be of some interest or use to you:

>> **Tax Foundation:** For lots of insightful research and data on taxes, visit taxfoundation.org/

>> **Congressional tax doings:** If you really have nothing better to do with your time, check the government sites with updated information on tax bills in Congress: The Joint Committee on Taxation (www.jct.gov/) and the Ways & Means Committee (waysandmeans.house.gov).

Tax preparation sites

A number of websites enable you to prepare federal and state tax forms and then file them electronically. Many of these sites allow you to prepare and file your federal forms for free if you access their site through the IRS website. Just go to www.irs.gov and click on any link for "Free File" to see if you qualify. If you access a tax preparation site directly instead, you may have to pay a fee for a service that would be free through the Free File program.

If you don't want to use "Free File," a reasonably priced alternative worth your consideration can be found at eSmart Tax's website (www.esmarttax.com/), where you enter data on interview forms and calculate your tax. For $44.95, you can print your completed return and electronically file your tax return with the IRS and any state that accepts electronic returns.

Remember that if you're simply after the tax forms, plenty of the sites mentioned in this section offer such documents for free, as do public libraries and post offices.

Hiring Help

Because they lack the time, interest, energy, or skill to do it themselves, some people hire an auto mechanic to handle the servicing of their car. And most people who hire an auto mechanic do so because they think that they can afford to hire such a person.

For some of the same reasons, some people choose to hire a tax preparer and advisor. By identifying tax-reduction strategies that you may overlook, competent tax practitioners can save you money — sometimes more than enough to pay their fees. They may also reduce the likelihood of an audit, which can be triggered by blunders that you may make. Like some auto mechanics, however, some tax preparers take longer, charging you more, and not delivering the high-quality work you expect. As with an auto mechanic, you may not even be aware that the person you've hired to help with your income taxes isn't very competent or ethical because you're not an expert in their area.

Deciding whether you really need a preparer

Odds are quite good that you can successfully prepare your own income tax return. Most people's returns don't vary that much from year to year, so you have a head start and can hit the ground running if you get out last year's return, which hopefully you retained a copy of!

Preparing your own return may not work as well whenever your situation has changed in some way — if you bought or sold a house, started your own business, or retired, for example. In such an event, start by focusing on the sections of this book in Parts 2 and 3 that deal with those preparation issues. If you want more planning background, check out the relevant chapters in Part 5.

Don't give up and hire a preparer just because you can't bear to open your tax-preparation booklet and get your background data organized. Even if you hire a tax preparer, you still need to get your stuff organized before a consultation.

TIP

As hard and as painful as it is, confront preparing your return as far in advance of April 15 as you can so that if you feel uncomfortable with your level of knowledge, you have enough time to seek help. The more organizing you can do before hiring a preparer, the less having your return prepared should cost you. Avoid waiting until the last minute to hire an advisor — you won't do as thorough a job of selecting a competent person, and you'll probably pay more for the rush job. If you get stuck preparing the return, you can get a second opinion from other preparation resources we discuss in this chapter.

If you decide to seek out the services of a tax preparer/advisor, know that tax practitioners come with various backgrounds, training, and credentials. One type of professional isn't necessarily better than another. Think of them as different types of specialists who are appropriate for different circumstances. The four main types of tax practitioners are unenrolled preparers, enrolled agents, certified public accountants, and tax attorneys.

Unenrolled preparers

Among all the tax practitioners, *unenrolled preparers* generally have the least amount of training, and more of them work part-time. H&R Block is the largest and most well-known tax-preparation firm in the country. In addition, other national firms such as Jackson Hewitt and plenty of mom-and-pop shops are in the tax-preparation business.

The appeal of preparers is that they're relatively inexpensive — they can do basic returns for $150 or so. The drawback is that you may hire a preparer who doesn't know much more than you do! As with financial planners, no national regulations apply to tax-return preparers, and no licensing is required, although this may change in the near future. Currently, though, in most states, almost anybody can hang out a tax-preparation shingle and start preparing. Most preparers, however, complete some sort of training program before working with clients.

TIP

Preparers make the most sense for folks who don't have complicated financial lives, who are budget-minded, and who dislike doing their own taxes. If you aren't good about hanging onto receipts or don't want to keep your own files with background details about your taxes, you definitely need to shop around for a tax preparer who's going to be around for a few years. You may need all that paperwork stuff someday for an audit, and some tax preparers keep and organize their clients' documentation rather than return everything each year. (Can you blame them for keeping your records after they go through the tedious task of sorting them all out of the shopping bags?) Going with a firm that's open year-round may also be safer, in case tax questions or problems arise. (Some small shops are open only during tax season.)

Enrolled agents (EAs)

A person must pass IRS scrutiny to be called an *enrolled agent* (EA). This license enables the agent to represent you before the IRS in the event of an audit. The training to become an EA is longer and more sophisticated than that of an unenrolled preparer. Continuing education also is required; EAs must complete at least 24 hours of continuing education each year to maintain their licenses, which are renewed every three years.

Enrolled agents' prices tend to fall between those of a preparer and a certified public accountant (we discuss CPAs in the next section). If you require tax return preparation and related advice and representation, and nothing more (no corporate audits or production of financial reports), an enrolled agent can provide the expertise you need for a reasonable cost.

TIP

The main difference between enrolled agents and CPAs and attorneys is that EAs work exclusively in the field of taxation, which makes them more likely to stay attuned to the latest tax developments. Not all CPAs and attorneys do. In addition to preparing your return (including simple to complex forms), good EAs can help with tax planning, represent you at tax audits, and keep the IRS off your back. You can find names and telephone numbers of EAs in your area by contacting the National Association of Enrolled Agents (taxexperts.naea.org). NAEA members have an even higher standard for continuing education requirements, totaling 30 hours per year.

Certified public accountants (CPAs)

Certified public accountants (CPAs) go through significant training and examination to receive the CPA credential. To maintain this designation, a CPA must complete at least 40 hours' worth of continuing education classes every year.

As with any other professional service you purchase, CPA fees can vary tremendously. Expect to pay more if you live in an area with a high cost of living, if you use the services of a large accounting firm, or if your needs are involved and specialized.

TIP

Competent CPAs are of greatest value to people completing some of the more unusual and less user-friendly tax forms/schedules, such as K-1 for partnerships. CPAs also are helpful for people who had a major or first-time tax event during the year, such as the childcare tax-credit determination. (Good EAs and other preparers can handle these issues as well.)

WARNING

Whenever your return is uncomplicated and your financial situation is stable, hiring a high-priced CPA year after year to fill in the blanks on your tax returns is a waste of money. A CPA once bragged to Eric (your humble coauthor of this book) that he was effectively making more than $500 per hour from some of his clients' returns that required only 20 minutes of an assistant's time to complete.

Paying for the additional cost of a CPA on an ongoing basis makes sense if you can afford it and if your financial situation is reasonably complex or dynamic. If you're self-employed and/or file many other schedules, hiring a CPA may be worth it. But you needn't do so year after year. If your situation grows more complex one year and then stabilizes, consider getting help for the perplexing year and then using other preparation resources discussed in this chapter or a lower-cost preparer or enrolled agent in the future.

If you desire more information about CPAs in your area, we suggest you contact the local organization of CPAs in your state. To locate your state's group, visit the American Institute of Certified Public Accountants listing of state CPA associations and useful state tax links at www.aicpa.org/advocacy/state/statecontactinfo.html. If you're considering hiring a CPA, be sure to ask how much of the person's time is spent preparing individual income tax returns and returns like yours.

WHO'S BEST QUALIFIED — EA, CPA, OR PREPARER?

Who is best qualified to prepare your return? That really depends on the individual you want to hire. The CPA credential is just that, a credential. Some people who have the credential will try to persuade you not to hire someone without it, but don't always believe this advice.

Some tax-preparation books perpetuate the myth that only a CPA can do your taxes. In one such book, in a chapter about choosing a tax preparer, entitled "How to Prepare for Your Accountant," the authors say, "Choosing an accountant isn't something that should be done casually. There are more than 300,000 certified public accountants." These authors then recommend that you ask a potential preparer, "Are you a certified public accountant?" (As you may have guessed, the firm behind the book is a large CPA company.)

What about all the non-CPAs, such as EAs, who do a terrific job helping prepare their clients' returns and tax plans throughout the year?

If you can afford to and want to pay hundreds of dollars per hour, hiring a large CPA firm can make sense. But for the vast majority of taxpayers, spending that kind of money is unnecessary and wasteful. Numerous EAs and other tax preparers are out there doing outstanding work for less.

Tax attorneys

Unless you're a super-high-income earner with a complex financial life, hiring a *tax attorney* to prepare your annual return is prohibitively expensive. In fact, many tax attorneys don't prepare returns as a normal practice. Because of their level of specialization and training, tax attorneys tend to have high hourly billing rates — $300 to $400-plus per hour isn't unusual, and some attorneys in a major metropolitan area have crossed the $1,000-per-hour threshold.

Tax attorneys sometimes become involved in court cases dealing with tax problems, disagreements, or other complicated matters, such as the purchase or sale of a business. Other good tax advisors also can help with these issues.

The more training and specialization a tax practitioner has (and the more affluent the clients), the higher the hourly fee. Select the one who best meets your needs. Fees and competence at all levels of the profession vary significantly. If you aren't sure of the quality of work performed and the soundness of the advice, get a second opinion.

Finding Tax Preparers and Advisors

TIP

The challenge for you is to locate a tax advisor who does terrific work, charges reasonable fees, and thus is too busy to bother calling to solicit you! Here are some resources to find those publicity-shy, competent, and affordable tax advisors:

>> **Friends and family:** Some of your friends and family members probably use tax advisors and can steer you to a decent one or two for an interview.

>> **Coworkers:** Ask people in your field what tax advisors they use. This strategy can be especially useful if you're self-employed.

>> **Other advisors:** Financial and legal advisors also can be helpful referral sources, but don't assume that they know more about the competence of a tax person than you do. Beware of a common problem: Financial or legal advisors may simply refer you to tax preparers who send them clients.

>> **Associations:** EAs and CPAs maintain professional associations that can refer you to members in your local area. See the relevant sections earlier in this chapter.

Never decide to hire a tax preparer or advisor solely on the basis of someone else's recommendation. To ensure that you're hiring someone who is competent and with whom you will work well, please take the time to interview at least two or three prospective candidates. In Chapter 31, we list key questions that you need to ask prospective tax advisors before hiring them. Because you've gone to the trouble and expense of tracking down this book, please make use of it — you've got many more chapters to check out. The more you know before you seek a tax advisor's services, the better able you'll be to make an informed decision and reduce your expenditures on tax preparers.

Chapter 3

Getting and Staying Organized

D o you want to make your tax preparation easier and make sure you claim every deduction you're entitled to? Would you like to survive an IRS audit and not pay additional tax, interest, or penalties? Do you want to save money by not paying tax preparers $50 to $200 or more an hour to organize your stuff?

Then, keep good records!

WARNING

If you're like most people, you probably aren't a good bookkeeper. But without good records, you may be in trouble, especially if you're ever audited. Furthermore, some tax preparers and accountants love to see you walk into their offices with shoeboxes full of receipts. Knowing that they can charge you a hefty hourly fee and then turn around and pay someone else $20 an hour to organize your receipts brightens their day and fattens their firm's bottom line.

Compiling tax records is one of life's many challenges, but it doesn't need to be one of the awful ones. Look at this step as an opportunity to connect with your past — you may find not only tax records for the most recent year, but you may also find old report cards or to-do lists from five years ago (that still have unfinished business). Taking the time to rummage is often worth it. You may finally be able to itemize your deductions this year, but you first need to be able to produce those charitable receipts, medical bills, and mortgage and real estate tax bills.

In this chapter, you discover tried and proven ways of keeping track of everything you need to survive — not only this tax-preparation season, but also in future tax situations.

Maintaining the Burden of Proof

Perhaps you can easily imagine yourself the night before an IRS audit wondering how you're going to support your claim for all those business entertainment costs. Do you know what happens when you're audited and you can't document your claims? First, you get socked with additional tax and interest. Then come the penalties — and the IRS has a lengthy list of them.

But enough horror stories! You know that you must take some steps now to avoid the misery associated with not keeping good records. Although resurrecting your records for this current tax return may be impossible, it isn't too late to establish good habits for next year.

TIP

To deal effectively with the IRS, you need documentation, because the tax laws place the burden of proof primarily on the taxpayer. Do you think this policy means that you're guilty until proven innocent? Unfortunately, it does, but don't let that depress you. Remember that you need to produce documentation only if you're audited. Even if you're not being audited, you still need to organize your records now.

If you are audited and lack the tax records that you need to support your case, don't throw in the towel. This chapter shows you how to overcome such a problem — just in case you failed Record-Keeping 101.

WARNING

As a result of the IRS horror stories, Congress shifted the burden of proof when taxpayers and the IRS end up in court. But don't get too excited over this provision. The fine print is murder. You still have to present credible evidence and be cooperative (Boy Scouts to the head of the line). Shifting the burden of proof doesn't mean that you can sit back and say, "Prove it." Remember, too, that few cases go to court. The Taxpayer Bill of Rights in Chapter 20 explains the fine print.

Keeping Good Records

Tax records pose a problem for many people because the IRS doesn't require any particular form of recordkeeping. In fact, the IRS recommends, in general terms, that you keep records only to file a "complete and accurate" return. Need a bit more detail? Read on.

Ensuring a complete and accurate tax return

In case you don't feel like flipping through countless pages of government instructions on what constitutes a "complete and accurate" return, we thought you may want to check out several common problem areas at a glance and the types of records normally required.

>> **Itemized deductions:** Receipts, receipts, who's got the receipts? If you're planning on itemizing your deductions on Schedule A (see Chapter 11 for more information), you need the numbers to calculate your deductions and to prove your claims in case you're audited. Here's a list of expenses you'll want to have proof that you paid in the order you'll find them on Schedule A:

- **Medical expenses:** Keep all your receipts, and make sure you get receipts for all services that you receive during the year, including cab fares to and from the doctor's office. The list of allowable medical deductions is long and fairly inclusive, and as healthcare costs continue to rise faster than most people's salaries, more and more people will find they can take a medical deduction.

- **Mortgage interest payments:** You should receive a record of these payments, which are documented on Form 1098, from the bank that holds your mortgage.

- **Real estate taxes:** Keep a copy of your real estate tax bill, and either the canceled checks, a receipt from your city or town, or a line item on your Form 1098 (if your mortgage company pays your taxes for you).

- **Personal property taxes:** Keep a receipt for your excise tax bill.

- **State and local income taxes:** Hang on to copies of your canceled checks if your bank still gives you back your checks. If you pay your state income taxes electronically, the state's website will have an electronic record of your payments.

- **Charitable deductions:** For donations in excess of $250 (per donation), keep a written receipt or letter from the charity that states the amount and nature of your donation. For donations under $250 (per donation), make sure you have a credit card receipt, canceled check, notation on a bank statement, or a receipt from the charity if you want to claim that deduction.

- **Casualty or theft losses:** You just never know when your number will come up in the burglar lottery, or you'll drop your diamond ring down the garbage disposal. If you don't have your receipts, don't despair, though; you have other ways to prove this deduction. Check out the "Casualty losses" section later in this chapter.

- **Unreimbursed job expenses, safe deposit box fees, tax preparation fees, and other miscellaneous itemized deductions:** Once again, keeping your receipts makes these deductions easy to prove.

You may be rejoicing to find that you don't have enough deductions to itemize in 2021, so you can trash all your receipts now. And, you may also be assuming that the same will be true in 2022. Keep in mind, though, that your finances — and your tax situation — can do funny things from year to year; be sure to hang on to your 2022 receipts so that you keep all your deduction options open down the road.

» **Dependent expenses:** If you plan to claim someone other than your qualifying child as a dependent, you need to be able to prove (if you're audited) that you provided more than 50 percent of that person's total support. The length of time that you provide the support doesn't mean anything — it's the total cost that matters. So be ready to show how much you paid for your dependent's lodging, food, clothes, healthcare, transportation, and any other essential support stuff. (See Chapter 4 for the rules for claiming dependents and the definition of a qualifying child.)

» **Car expenses:** If, for the business use of your car, you choose to deduct the actual expenses rather than the standard mileage rate (which is 58 cents per mile for 2021), you need to be able to show the cost of the car and when you started using it for business. You also must record your business miles, your total miles, and your expenses, such as insurance, gas, and maintenance. You need a combination of a log and receipts, of course!

>> **Home expenses:** If you own your home, you not only need to keep track of your mortgage and real estate tax payments, but you also need to keep records of your purchase price and purchase expenses, plus the cost of all the improvements and additions you make over time (save your receipts, please!). Although you may not be selling your house this year, when you do, you'll be thankful you have all your receipts. (Chapter 14 discusses house sales in detail.) If you rent a portion of your house, or you run a business from it, you'll also need your utility bills, general repair bills, and housecleaning and lawn-mowing costs in order to calculate your net rental income or your home office expense. (See Chapter 13 for more information on the home office deduction and Chapter 15 for how to calculate net rental income.)

>> **Business expenses:** The IRS is especially watchful in this area, so be sure to keep detailed proof of any expenses that you claim. This proof can consist of many items, such as receipts of income, expense account statements, and so on. So make sure that you hang on to the bill or receipt for every expense you incur. (See Chapter 13 if you're self-employed and Chapter 11 if you're an employee.)

Setting up a record-keeping system

The tax year is a long time for keeping track of records that you'll need (and where you put them) when the filing season arrives. So here are some easy things you can do to make your tax-preparation burden a little lighter:

>> Invest in an accordion file. You can buy one with slots already labeled by month, by category, or by letters of the alphabet, or you can make your own filing system with the extra labels — all this can be yours for $10 to $15.

>> If $10 to $15 is too much, you can purchase a dozen or so of those manila file folders for about $5. Decide on the organizational method that best fits your needs, and get into the habit of saving all bills, receipts, and records that you think you can use someday for your tax purposes and for things that affect your overall financial planning. This basic advice is good for any taxpayer, whether you file a simple tax return or a complicated Form 1040 with numerous supplemental schedules. Remember that this plan is only minimal, but nevertheless is much better than the shoebox approach to recordkeeping.

>> If your financial life is uncomplicated, then each new year you can set up one file folder that has the year on it (so in January 2022 you establish your 2022 file). During the year, as you receive documentation that you think you'll use in preparing your return, stash it in the folder. In January 2023, when you receive your dreaded Form 1040 booklet, or the address label they sometimes send instead, toss that in the file, too. Come springtime 2023, when you finally force yourself to sit down and work on your return, you have everything you need in one bulging file.

>> If you're a 1040 user and a real perfectionist, you can arrange your records in a file according to the schedules and forms on which you'll report them. For example, you can set up folders such as these:

• **Schedule A:** Deductible items (such as mortgage interest, property taxes, charitable contributions, and job-related expenses)

- **Schedule B:** Interest and dividend income stuff
- **Schedule D:** Documents related to buying, selling, and improving your home, and the sale and purchase of investments such as stocks and bonds

You 1040 filers have so many options that you truly need to take the time to figure out your return — we can help you there — so that you can anticipate your future tax needs.

Tracking tax information on your computer

A number of financial software packages enable you to keep track of your spending for tax purposes. Just don't expect to reap the benefits without a fair amount of upfront and continuing work. You need to figure out how to use the software, and you need to enter data for it to be useful to you come tax time. Don't forget, though, that you still need your statements/receipts to back up your claims; in an audit, the IRS may not accept your computer records without verifying them against your statements/receipts.

TIP

If you're interested in software or an app, consider Quicken or GoodBudget. Or you may want to explore a more business-oriented program, such as QuickBooks, Xero, or FreshBooks for your small-business accounting. Whichever software or app you choose, make certain it allows you to do everything you need to, such as keep track of your stock portfolio, pay your bills, balance your checking account, and best of all, get help with tabulating your tax information. Just remember that the package tabulates only what you enter. So if you use the software to pay your monthly bills but neglect to enter data for things you pay for with cash, for example, you won't have the whole picture.

Deciding when to stash and when to trash

REMEMBER

One of the most frequently asked questions is how long a taxpayer needs to keep tax records. The answer is easy — a minimum of three years. That's because the statute of limitations for tax audits and assessments is three years. If the IRS doesn't adjust or audit your 2018 tax return by April 15, 2022 (the three years starts running on April 15, 2019), it missed its chance. On April 15, 2022, feel free to celebrate another auditless year with a "Shredding the 2018 Tax Year" party. (If you filed after April 15 because you obtained an extension of time to file, you must wait until three years after the extension due date rather than the April 15 tax date. The same is true when you file late — the three-year period doesn't start until you actually file your return.)

TIP

However, we must add one point to the general three-year rule: Save all records for the assets that you continue to own. These records can include purchase records for stocks and bonds, automobiles, your home (along with its improvements), and expensive personal property, such as jewelry, video cameras, or computers.

Some taxpayers take the practical step of videotaping their home and its contents, but if you do, make sure that you keep that record outside your home. Uploading such files to the cloud or emailing them to yourself would do the trick.

WARNING

In situations where the IRS suspects that income wasn't reported, IRS agents can go back as far as six years. And if possible tax fraud is involved, forget all time restraints!

Reconstructing Missing Tax Records

The inscription above the entrance to the national office of the Internal Revenue Service reads

Taxes are what we pay for a civilized society.

But any taxpayer who has ever had a tax return examined would probably enjoy a little less civilization!

Our experience shows that the number-one reason why taxpayers must cough up additional tax when they're audited is lousy recordkeeping. They don't get themselves into this situation by fabricating deductions, but rather because most taxpayers aren't very good bookkeepers and they fail to produce the records that properly substantiate the deductions they have a right to claim.

TIP

When taxpayers misplace tax records or simply don't save the ones that they need to be able to claim the deductions they're allowed under the law, all is not lost. Other ways exist for gathering the evidence that establishes what was actually spent, but obtaining the necessary evidence may prove time-consuming. And yet, when you consider the other option — paying additional tax, interest, and penalties on disallowed deductions from an audit where you can't prove what you spent — your time and energy are typically amply rewarded. The following sections describe some ways to reconstruct lost or forgotten records. (You may also want to look at Chapters 18 and 19, which tell you how to fight back against an IRS audit when it comes to tax records.)

Property received by inheritance or gift

The starting point for determining whether you made or lost money on a sale of a property is the property's *tax basis*. (Remember, to the IRS, *property* can be more than just real estate; it also includes stocks, bonds, cars, boats, and computers.)

Tax basis is an IRS term for cost. Your basis usually is what you paid for something.

However, the rules for determining the tax basis for property you inherited or received as a gift are different. Because you don't know the cost of the inheritance, the tax basis for determining the taxable gain or loss of the property you inherited is the fair market value of the property on the date of the titleholder's death. For property received as a gift, the tax basis is either the donor's cost or the fair market value on the date you received the gift (see Chapter 14).

The best time for determining your basis in either a gift or an inheritance is when you receive that gift or inheritance, not years later after people who may have that information have long since forgotten or even died. If you know the basis of the property you've received, either through a gift or an inheritance, because you have access to either the Gift Tax Return (Form 709), the Estate Tax Return (Form 706), or because your Uncle Joe told you upfront what your basis is in this property, great! When you sell the property, you're all set with your initial basis information, and calculating your gain or loss will be a matter of simple math.

If, on the other hand, Uncle Joe hasn't been so accommodating, and the relevant estate or gift tax returns aren't available, you're not out of luck, but you'll need to do some research on your own.

If there has been no estate tax return prepared for an estate, you're responsible for establishing the date-of-death value for your inheritance. You can use four methods to compute your tax basis: newspaper ads, local real estate board and broker records, the property's assessed value, and the *Consumer Price Index* (CPI). (You know the CPI: It tells you that what cost $10 five years ago this past month costs $50 this month. Seriously, it probably costs $10.02, and the CPI is an official government measure that tells how much prices increase over time.)

CHALLENGING THE ESTABLISHED VALUES

When you inherit something, don't automatically assume that its fair market value as reported on the estate tax return is correct, especially where real estate and art are concerned. The IRS constantly challenges the value placed on an item for estate tax purposes, and so can you. If, using a reasonable method for valuation, you arrive at a value different than on the estate tax return, chances are good that the IRS will accept your valuation. Remember, though, that your "reasonable method" needs to be just that, and you need to be able to provide substantiation, in the event of an audit, for how you arrived at your value.

If an estate tax return has been filed for the estate and you decide to challenge the value placed on your inheritance, beware! The estate's executor has likely placed as low a value on the property as possible in order to minimize the estate taxes, and you probably want as high a value as possible in order to minimize your capital gain when you sell the property. When you successfully argue for an increased value, you'll lower your income taxes, but you may raise the amount of estate tax the estate pays. Generally speaking, estate tax rates are substantially higher than income tax rates, so your success on the income tax side of this equation will only cost you (and your family) more on the estate tax side. Think twice before you challenge an estate tax valuation!

Researching newspaper ads

The internet is also a wonderful resource for current and prior values. Most newspapers allow you to access their archives online. Local libraries often have such access and necessary subscriptions if that would be easier or less expensive for you. What you're seeking is to find a copy of the newspaper published on the approximate date for which you're trying to establish the value.

TIP

If a piece of real estate exactly like yours wasn't offered for sale at that time, you may have to find an ad for one as close as possible in description to yours and simply estimate the price. For example, suppose that you're trying to figure out how much Aunt Jessica's farm was worth when she left it to you in 1990. You now want to sell the 100-acre farm and farmhouse, and you're searching for its value in 1990. You check out some 1990 ads from the *Daily Bugle* and find

>> An ad showing a house and 50 acres for $75,000

>> An ad showing a house and 60 acres for $85,000

Because the farm with ten more acres was selling for $10,000 more, assume that an acre was worth around $1,000. The IRS, should you ever be audited, would likely find your assumption reasonable. Therefore, Aunt Jessica's farm has 40 more acres than the one selling for $85,000, so you can figure that the value of the farm in 1990 was about $125,000 ($85,000 + $40,000).

TIP

If you do get audited, the IRS won't generally accept the statement that you looked up this information. Remember, IRS agents act as if they come from Missouri (the Show Me state — in case you were absent from school the day your fifth-grade teacher lectured on state nicknames). If you go to all the trouble to visit the library, make sure you come away with a photocopy of the paper's real estate section and the real estate pricing data we just discussed. The IRS requires documentation, especially when you use an alternative method to establish something's value.

Consulting local real estate board and broker records

If your trip to the library or local newspaper office comes up short, try the local real estate board or a real estate broker (one may owe you a favor or want your business). Individual brokers or local real estate boards usually keep historical data on property sold in their respective areas. Again, you may have to estimate selling prices if you don't find a property exactly like yours.

Obtaining assessed values

The assessed-value method may uncover the most accurate estimate of a property's value. Because property taxes are collected on the basis of assessed values, try to obtain the property's assessed value on the date you're interested in. With that information and the percentage of the fair market value that the tax assessor used in determining assessed values, divide the percentage into the assessed value to come up with the market value.

TIP

You can obtain assessed values for property (and the percentage of the fair market value of property assessed in its vicinity) from the government office that receives or collects property taxes, which you can usually find in the courthouse of the county where the property is located. Don't forget to get a copy of this information. For example, if the assessed value was $2,700 and the percentage of the fair market value at which the property was assessed was 30 percent, the fair market value was about $9,000 ($2,700 ÷ 30 percent).

Using the Consumer Price Index (CPI)

Unlike baseball, when you're assessing the value of real estate, you're not out on three strikes. When all else fails, use the CPI method. For example, say you sold a tract of land for $300,000. If the CPI has tripled since you inherited it, your tax basis would be about $100,000.

REMEMBER

Determining the property's acquisition date depends on how you acquired the property. If you inherited it, the acquisition date is the date of the previous owner's death. If the property was a gift, the acquisition date is the date the property originally was purchased by the person who gave you the gift.

CPI data is available on the internet at the Consumer Price Index page of the Bureau of Labor Statistics website (www.bls.gov/cpi/home.htm).

WARNING

If you use the CPI to value real estate, don't be surprised if the IRS doesn't accept your valuation without some further adjustment. That's because historically real estate prices have risen at higher rates than the CPI in many major metropolitan areas.

Securities received by inheritance or gift

Establishing a stock or a bond's price on a particular date is much easier than coming up with the value of other property, especially if the stock or bond is traded on a major securities exchange.

When you inherit a stock or bond, your tax basis usually is the value of the stock or bond on the deceased's date of death. Sometimes an estate — to save taxes — uses a valuation date that is six months after the date of death. If you receive the security as a gift, you often have the added task of establishing the date when the donor acquired the security, because you normally must use the value on that date (including any commission expense). Not to confuse you, but sometimes you must use the value on the date you received the gift. We explain all this information in Chapter 14. You can contact the transfer agent to find out when the stock was acquired. The transfer agent is the company that keeps track of the shares of stock that a company issues. Your investment brokerage firm can tell you how to locate the transfer agent, or you can consult the *Value Line Investment Survey*, which you can find at most local libraries.

A number of investing websites such as Yahoo! Finance (finance.yahoo.com/) provide free historical stock pricing data going way back. Also, consider checking with the investment firm where the securities were (or are still) held. The firm may be able to research this information — maybe even for free.

Improvements to a residence

How many homeowners save any of the records regarding improvements that they make, even when those expenditures are substantial? Not nearly enough. Why? Because improvements to a home quite often are made during a multi-year and sometimes even multi-decade span, and saving records for that many years is a lot to ask of anyone. For example, landscaping expenditures — one tree or bush at a time — can really add up.

The point of counting every tree and bush and other improvement to your home sweet home is to raise the basis, or total investment, that you have in your residence so that you can reduce your taxable profit when you sell. (See Chapter 14 for details.)

Although the tax laws eliminated the fiendish record-keeping requirements for sales in which a profit of $500,000 or less for couples filing jointly and $250,000 for singles is realized, for sales above these amounts you still need records to prove, for example, that you didn't make more than these threshold amounts ($500,000/$250,000). And if you buy a house today, say for $350,000, you don't know what the sales price will be in 10, 20, 30, or more years when you finally sell it. Here's hoping it's $1 million. So tax records are still important.

TIP

Before you estimate how much you spent on residential improvements, you first have to determine what improvements you spent the money on. This step is necessary because if you can't document the amount spent, you at least can establish that an improvement was made. Your financial records for your bank and credit card accounts likely document payments made to home improvement contractors you likely hired over the years. Photos you've taken over the years may also document important improvements you've made to your home and property.

Obtaining a Certificate of Occupancy

TIP

If you can't get a receipt from the contractor who made improvements to your home, hike down to the county clerk's office to obtain a copy of the Certificate of Occupancy (the house's birth certificate, so to speak), which shows what your house consisted of when it was built. Records at the county clerk's office also reveal any changes in the house's assessed value as the result of improvements you made, along with any building permits issued. Any of these documents can clearly establish whether improvements were made (assuming, of course, that you did obtain the proper permits for these improvements).

Getting an estimate

When original invoices, duplicate invoices, or canceled checks aren't available, obtain an estimate of what the improvement would cost now, and then subtract the increase according to the CPI (as explained in "Using the Consumer Price Index" earlier in this chapter). This procedure can help establish a reasonable estimate of what the improvement originally cost.

Casualty losses

A casualty loss is probably the most difficult deduction to establish. Few people consistently save receipts on the purchase of personal items, such as jewelry, clothing, furniture, and so on. If the casualty loss occurred because of a fire or hurricane, any receipts that you may have had were probably destroyed along with your property. Although a police, fire, or insurance company report establishes that a casualty loss was sustained, how do you establish the cost of what was stolen or destroyed? The answer: with a little bit of luck and hard work.

For example, the value of an expensive necklace that was stolen was once established by using a photograph that showed the taxpayer wearing the necklace. The taxpayer then obtained an appraisal from a jeweler of the cost of a similar necklace.

TIP

Although you can prove to the IRS that you have enough money to afford the lost or stolen item, the IRS also needs proof that you had the item in your possession. For example, suppose that your $10,000 Rolex watch is stolen (we feel for you). To make the IRS folks happy, you must prove two things:

>> That you can afford the Rolex, which your total income from your tax return can prove.

>> That you had the Rolex, which can be established by a statement from a friend, a relative, or an acquaintance asserting that you actually owned the item. If the Rolex was a gift, a statement from the giver also helps. Perhaps you had your watch repaired or cleaned in recent years but lack a receipt for that — the store that performed the service can document your ownership.

You can use an appraisal from the Federal Emergency Management Agency (FEMA) if you obtained a disaster loan as evidence for tax purposes to claim a casualty loss.

Business records

If business records have been lost or destroyed, you can often obtain duplicate bills from major vendors. You shouldn't have a great deal of trouble getting copies of the original telephone, utility, rent, credit card, oil company, and other bills. Reconstructing a typical month of automobile use can help you make a reasonable determination of the business use of your automobile. If that month's use approximates an average month's business use of an auto, the IRS generally accepts such reconstructed records as adequate substantiation.

Using duplicate account statements

If all your business income was deposited in a checking or savings account or investment firm account, you can reconstruct that income from those bank or investment firm statements. Although banks usually don't charge for copies of bank statements, they do charge for copies of canceled checks. You can generally access your account records online without charge.

Understanding the Cohan Rule

Before we end this discussion about undocumented claims, we must tell you about the case of George M. Cohan and the resulting Cohan Rule. It's the story of one person's victory over the IRS, and it may inspire you to defend your own rights as a taxpayer. Even if some of the rights that taxpayers earned because of his victory have been eroded over the years, Cohan's battle for the right to estimate deductions still has repercussions today.

In 1921 and 1922, George M. Cohan deducted $55,000 in business-related travel and entertainment expenses. The IRS refused to allow him any part of these entertainment and travel deductions on the grounds that it was impossible to tell how much Cohan spent because he didn't have any receipts to support the deductions he claimed.

Cohan appealed to the Second Circuit Court of Appeals, and, in 1930, the court established the rule of approximation. The court instructed the IRS to "make as close an approximation as it can, bearing heavily, if it chooses, upon the taxpayer whose inexactitude is of his own making." (Isn't "inexactitude" a lovely way of saying "no records"?)

For more than 30 years, the Cohan Rule enabled taxpayers to deduct travel and entertainment expenses without having to substantiate what they spent. Taxpayers had only to establish that it was reasonable for them to have incurred travel and entertainment expenses in the amount they claimed they spent.

WARNING

Congress changed the law regarding travel, use of a car, and entertainment expenses in the early 1960s. Since that change, taxpayers no longer can deduct travel or entertainment expenses without adequate substantiation.

The Cohan Rule still applies, however, to other expenses whose records aren't available. Under the Cohan Rule, the Tax Court routinely allows deductions based on estimates for the following deductions:

>> Petty cash and office expenses

>> Delivery and freight charges

>> Tips and business gifts

>> Cleaning and maintenance expenses

>> Small tools and supplies

>> Taxi fares

>> Casualty losses (fire, flood, and theft losses)

For some expenses, obtaining receipts for what you spend is impractical, if not downright impossible. Petty cash and tips are just two examples of such expenses.

WARNING

The Cohan Rule doesn't mean that you can stop keeping receipts and simply use estimates. You must have a valid reason for relying on the Cohan Rule, such as impracticability or lost or destroyed records. In fact, taxpayers have had penalties assessed against them for not attempting to obtain duplicate records that were lost when they moved, and for periodically destroying all business records immediately upon the filing of their tax returns. One court held that the unexplained loss of corporate records carries a strong presumption that the records would have prejudiced the taxpayer's position.

In case you're scratching your head and wondering if any of this will work, the question you have to ask yourself is this: If you were sitting on a jury and saw this evidence, would you believe it? If the answer to this question is yes, guess what? You're most likely going to prevail.

Chapter **4**

What Kind of Taxpayer Are You?

You have to make some key decisions before grabbing those good ol' tax forms and marking them up. Even though you're anxious to begin, read the relevant portions of this chapter first. We explain some important issues you must resolve each tax year before you knuckle down to complete your return.

What Rendition of 1040 Shall We Play?

The days of the so-called "long form" (Form 1040), "short form" (Form 1040-A), and the ever-popular Form 1040-EZ are gone, and new forms have replaced them. No, the size of a tax return hasn't shrunk down to a postcard — politicians almost never make tax forms simpler; the new forms have fewer lines but more confusion, and if you're filing on paper, the information is spread over more sheets of paper. There was one positive on the simplification front with these changes: The standard deduction was greatly increased so far more taxpayers are claiming that and far fewer people now need to complete Schedule A for Itemized Deductions.

Form 1040

Unless you or your spouse is over age 64, this new rendition of Form 1040 is the one most U.S. taxpayers will use. It's filled with all the biographical information you've come to know and love that inhabits every tax form you've ever filed, including your name (and your spouse's, if you have one of those), address, Social Security numbers for you and your spouse, and your list of dependents and their Social Security numbers.

The Form 1040 then starts listing out different forms of income, such as wages, interest, dividends, IRA distributions, pensions and annuities, Social Security benefits, and capital gains or losses. It's only after you get to this point in your return that the fun and games really begin, with the introduction of Schedules 1, 2, and 3.

You may feel a bit intimidated by these Form 1040 schedules, but don't be: All the IRS has done is moved much of the information that used to be on the long Form 1040 off the Form 1040 itself, and it has now taken up residence on these three schedules, which were introduced in the 2019 tax filing season.

If your financial situation isn't particularly complex, you may not need to use any of these schedules, but if you need to use any or all of them, here's what they include:

>> **Schedule 1, Additional Income and Adjustments to Income:** Here is where you now report things like taxable state tax refunds, alimony received, business income or loss, other gains or losses, income or losses from rental real estate, royalties, partnerships, S Corporations, estates and trusts, farm income or loss, unemployment compensation, net operating losses, gambling income, cancellation of debt, the foreign earned income exclusion, taxable distributions from Health Savings Accounts, Alaska Permanent Fund distributions, jury duty pay, prizes and awards, and income from hobbies. Actually, the list goes on even longer, but we won't bore you with all that now. If you have received some other form of income, please check out Chapter 6 to get the full picture of all the types of income that show up here.

The second page of Schedule 1 is where you put all your deductible adjustments to income, which run the gamut from educator expenses to alimony paid, IRA, HSA and Archer MSA deductions; student loan interest deduction; the 50 percent deduction for self-employment tax; the deduction for the cost of health insurance for self-employed people; and so on. Once again, the list of adjustments is long, and we cover it more fully in Chapter 7.

>> **Schedule 2, Additional Taxes:** Our annual tax return filings not only cover income taxes, but also a plethora of additional taxes to which you may be subject, and Schedule 2 is where you report them. The most popular ones include self-employment tax, additional taxes paid on non-qualified distributions from IRA and other tax-favored accounts, household employment taxes, additional Medicare taxes for high-income individuals, and the net investment income tax. Just like with Schedule 1, we're just scratching the surface with these additional taxes here, but you'll find the full story regarding Schedule 2 in Chapter 8.

>> **Schedule 3, Additional Credits and Payments:** This is the schedule you may adore if you qualify for some of these credits. These credits include the child tax credit, the foreign tax credit, education credits, retirement savings credits, residential energy credits, and an entire cornucopia of additional nonrefundable and refundable tax credits to which you may be entitled. Because credits offset tax liability, and refundable credits can actually generate cash in your pocket in the form of a refund if you have more credits than you have tax, you're going to want to flip to Chapter 9 to see all the types of credits that are available to you this year.

CAN I ITEMIZE? SHOULD I ITEMIZE? AND WHAT THE HECK ARE ITEMIZED DEDUCTIONS?

Deductions are just that: You subtract them from your income before you calculate the tax you owe. (Deductions are good things!) To make everything more complicated, the IRS gives you two methods for determining the total of your deductions: itemized and standardized deductions. You get to pick the method that leads to the best solution for you — whichever way offers greater deductions. If you can itemize, you should, because it saves you tax dollars.

The first method — taking the standard deduction — requires no thinking or calculations. For most people, taking the standard deduction is generally the better option. And the good news is that far more people now can and do claim the standard deduction because it was nearly doubled by the Tax Cuts and Jobs Act which took effect in 2018.

Some deductions — some moving expenses, the penalty for early withdrawal from savings, and so on — are available even if you don't itemize your deductions. We tell you how to do this in Chapter 11.

If you are paying on a large mortgage, have high medical expenses, or give a substantial amount to charity, you may be better off itemizing your deductions. Recent tax legislation eliminated some itemized deductions, so if you were used to itemizing because of large payments you made to investment advisors, or you had unreimbursed employee business expenses, we're so sorry, but those are no longer deductible. Neither is the cost of this book, although we still think you'll find it helpful even without the deduction.

TIP

If English isn't your first language but Spanish is, and if you feel intimidated by dealing with the forms and instructions in English, you'll be happy to know that more and more forms and instructions have been translated into Spanish by the IRS. Form 1040, 1040-SR, and Schedules 1, 2, and 3 are all available in Spanish.

Form 1040-SR

If you or your spouse is age 65 or older, you no longer file the standard Form 1040; now, the IRS has created a form especially for you, Form 1040-SR (U.S. Tax Return for Seniors). Instead of a two-page form, you now get the exact same form but with larger print so it takes up three pages. Those of us with diminishing eyesight would like to thank the IRS for their consideration.

As with Form 1040, once you move beyond very basic forms of income, you need Schedules 1, 2, and/or 3 to complete all the parts of your return.

Form 1040-NR

Form 1040-NR (U.S. Nonresident Alien Income Tax Return) gets a little trickier, and it doesn't apply to most of us. This form is only used by people who are nonresident aliens with U.S.-sourced income from a trade or business, or who are filing for someone who is a nonresident alien. So, a Canadian citizen, for example, who owns rental real estate in Florida would be required to file Form 1040-NR to report the rental income or loss from that property. So would that same Canadian who works for a company across the border in a border state, such as Minnesota, Washington, or North Dakota.

Once again, Schedules 1, 2, and/or 3 can be used with Form 1040-NR if your circumstances warrant it.

Don't try to use Form 1040-NR if you are a U.S. citizen or green card holder who lives outside the U.S. If you fall into that category, your form of choice will be either Form 1040 or Form 1040-SR.

Choosing a Filing Status

When filing your return, you must choose the appropriate filing status from the five filing statuses available. You select a status by checking the appropriate box directly below your name on page 1 of Form 1040, where it says "Filing Status":

>> Single

>> Married filing jointly

>> Married filing separately

>> Head of household

>> Qualifying widow(er) with dependent child

Each filing status has its own tax rates. As a general rule, you pay the lowest tax if you're able to file jointly or as a qualifying widow(er). Those individuals who are married filing separately pay tax at the highest rate. However, like every rule, a few circumstances exist in which married filing separately saves couples money, as we explain later in this section. In addition, you can select a different filing status every year. For example, because you filed jointly last tax year doesn't mean you automatically have to file that way this tax year.

Single

Most people who aren't married file as *single*. The IRS doesn't recognize couples living together as being married for filing purposes.

However, if you were widowed, divorced, or legally separated by the end of the tax year (December 31, 2021) and provided support to dependents, such as children or an elderly parent, you may be able to save yourself some tax dollars by filing as *head of household* or as a *qualifying widow(er)*. You can find out more in the upcoming section "Head of household" or "Qualifying widow(er) with dependent child."

Married filing jointly

If you're married, you probably share many things with your spouse. One of the more treasured tasks you get to share is the preparation of your annual tax return. In fact, this may be the one time during the year that you jointly examine and combine your financial information. Let the fireworks begin!

For your 2021 return, you're considered married if you got married by or were still married as of the end of the tax year — December 31, 2021. In some rare instances, married folks can save money by filing their taxes as *married filing separately.* This somewhat oddball status can be useful for couples who have large differences between their two incomes and can claim more itemized deductions by filing separately. See the section "Married filing separately" later in this chapter to determine whether you can save money by filing separately.

REMEMBER

If you file a joint return for 2021, you may not, after the due date for filing, amend that return to change to a married filing separately filing status. You're "jointly" stuck!

You can file jointly if you meet any of the following criteria:

>> You were married as of December 31, 2021, even if you didn't live with your spouse at the end of the year.

>> Your spouse died in 2021, and you didn't remarry in 2021.

   If your spouse died during the year, you're considered married for the entire year, providing you didn't remarry. You report all your income for the year and your spouse's income up to the date of their death.

>> Your spouse died in 2022 before you filed a 2021 return. If you're filing jointly in 2021, but your spouse died in either 2021 or before you managed to file your return in 2022, you're exempt from the "both must sign" rule. Only you are required to sign the return. After your name, write the words, "surviving spouse."

You and your spouse may file jointly even if only one of you had income or if you didn't live together all year. However, you both must sign the return, and you're both responsible for seeing that all taxes are paid. That means if your spouse doesn't pay the tax due, you may have to.

TIP

If you've signed that joint return, but are either unaware of what's on it, or someone (your spouse) has exerted pressure on you to sign that return, you may be a candidate for the *Innocent Spouse Rule* (see Chapter 20). This rule can, in some instances, relieve a spouse who was unaware of their spouse's shenanigans from sharing joint responsibility for what is owed.

A couple legally separated under a divorce decree may not file jointly. On the other hand, if one spouse lived away from the home during the entire last six months of the tax year (July 1, 2021, through December 31, 2021), the remaining spouse, if taking care of dependents, may be able to file under the more favorable head of household status (see "Head of household" later in this chapter).

SPOUSES WHO ARE NONRESIDENT ALIENS OR DUAL-STATUS ALIENS

If one spouse is a nonresident alien and doesn't pay U.S. income taxes on all of their income, regardless of the country (or countries) in which it's earned, then the couple may not choose the married filing jointly tax status.

The same is true when your spouse is a dual-status alien — that is, if during the year, your spouse is a nonresident as well as a resident. You may file jointly under these circumstances:

- If you were married as of December 31, 2021, even if you didn't live with your spouse at the end of 2021.

- If your spouse is a nonresident alien, or if either of you are dual-status aliens, you can make a special election to file jointly. IRS Publication 519 (*U.S. Tax Guide For Aliens*) explains how to make this election.

TIP

Although this suggestion is decidedly unromantic, if you're considering a late-in-the-year wedding, especially in December, you may want to consider the tax impact of tying the knot so soon. A considerable number of couples pay higher total taxes when they're married versus when they were single. On the other hand, what spells commitment more than sending money to the IRS with the one you love?

Some couples have been known to postpone their weddings until January and use the tax savings to pay for the cost of their honeymoons! Others choose not to marry, and they cohabit instead. Although we don't want to criticize or condone such decisions, it's unfortunate that such a high tax cost of getting married exists for a sizable minority of couples.

Married filing separately

The vast majority of married couples would pay more taxes if they chose to file separate returns. The IRS won't stand in the way of your filing separate returns. However, by filing separately, you may be able to avoid the marriage penalty and save on your combined tax bill. To determine whether filing separately is to your benefit, figure your tax both ways (married filing jointly and married filing separately).

TIP

Besides saving money, another reason you may choose to file separately is to avoid being responsible for your spouse's share of the joint tax bill whenever you suspect some kind of monkey business (for example, your spouse is underreporting taxable income or inflating deductions).

If your marriage is on the rocks, married filing separately may be the way to go. Remember, if you both sign that tax return, you're both on the hook for any amounts due. Even if the tax owed may be solely due to your soon-to-be ex-spouse's income, if said spouse refuses to pay the bill, you may have to. This is a case where paying a little more upfront can save you a whole lot down the road.

TIP

Even though married filing separately on your federal return may work out to be the same as filing jointly, don't overlook the possibility that by filing that way you may save state taxes.

If you file separately, be aware that the following restrictions may apply:

>> You can't take the standard deduction if your spouse itemizes deductions. Both spouses must itemize their deductions, or both must claim the standard deduction.

>> You can't claim the credit for child and dependent care expenses in most cases. The amount of income you can exclude under an employer dependent care assistance program is limited to $2,500 instead of the $5,000 by filing jointly.

>> You can't claim a credit for qualified adoption expenses.

>> You can't take the earned income credit.

>> You can't exclude from your taxable income the interest you earned from series EE U.S. Savings Bonds issued after 1989, even if you paid higher education expenses in 2021.

>> You can't take the credit for being elderly or disabled unless you lived apart from your spouse for all of 2021.

>> You may have to pay more tax on the Social Security benefits you received in 2021.

>> You usually report only your own income, exemptions, deductions, and credits. Different rules apply to people who live in community property states.

>> You can't deduct interest paid on your student loan.

>> You may have a lower Child Tax Credit than you would have if you filed jointly. The Child Tax Credit in 2021 is now worth up to $3,600 per "qualifying child," depending on the child's age, and it's now refundable, which means if you don't have enough tax to use the full amount of your credit against your tax liability, you'll get a check for the balance (you may have been receiving monthly checks since July 2021 as a partial prepayment of the credit, in which case, you're going to have to reconcile the amounts you received during 2021 with the amount you are entitled to on your 2022 Form 1040. (See "Defining Who Is a Qualifying Child" later in this chapter for specific information on which children qualify.)

>> If you own and actively manage real estate, you can't claim the passive loss exception (see the particulars in Chapter 15).

>> You can't claim the American Opportunity Credit, the Hope Scholarship Credit, and the Lifetime Learning Credits.

>> You can't claim the $6,000 IRA deduction for a nonworking spouse. And you may not be able to deduct all or part of your own $6,000 IRA contribution if your spouse is covered by a retirement plan.

>> You can't transfer funds from a traditional IRA to a Roth IRA.

>> Your capital loss limit is $1,500 instead of $3,000.

>> Income levels at which itemized deductions start being reduced are half the amount for joint filers.

Instead of filing separately, you may be able to file as a head of household if you had a child living with you and you lived apart from your spouse during the last six months of 2021. See the "Head of household" section later in this chapter for more information.

For many, the choice between filing jointly and filing separately comes down to a simple matter of dollars and cents — which leads you to pay the least tax? For many married couples, the fact that you're married means that you're paying higher taxes than if you and your spouse shacked up and filed as single taxpayers. Welcome to the so-called *marriage penalty*, which is the annual additional tax you pay for being married.

If you and your beloved fall into the marriage penalty category, you may be able to limit the amount of your penalty by filing as married filing separately. Take the time to prepare three returns — two separate and one joint — and see which filing status produces a lower tax bill for you and your honey. We know it's a time sink, so you may want to purchase a computerized tax program that does the number crunching for you. (See Chapter 2 for our software recommendations.)

Married couples most likely to save tax dollars filing separately are those who meet both of the following criteria:

>> Couples who have two incomes

>> Couples who have hefty deductions for medical expenses, miscellaneous itemized deductions, or casualty losses

If you fall under this umbrella, by all means complete the three tax returns to determine which filing status works best for you.

Table 4-1 shows an example of how the same income and the same deductions can be used to obtain a very different result when you compare a joint return with two separate returns. In this example, you earn $75,000, your spouse earns $65,000, and your spouse has a casualty loss (see Chapter 11) of $13,000. If you file a joint return, the two of you lose that deduction because casualty losses can't be deducted until they exceed 10 percent of your income, in this case $14,000. But if you and your spouse file separate returns, your spouse is entitled to a $6,500 deduction, because the loss is $6,500 greater than 10 percent of your spouse's income ($13,000 − $6,500 = $6,500). For the purpose of this illustration, the $100 nondeductible portion of casualty loss and the rate reduction credit aren't being considered.

Amounts may vary slightly depending on whether you use the tax tables or the rate schedules.

Filling out both joint and separate returns and comparing them is worth doing the numbers. For example, in Table 4-1, the sample couple saves a total of $4,335 by filing separately. Their combined separate tax bill comes to only $13,672 instead of $18,007.

Table 4-1   Filing Jointly versus Separately: A Sample Couple

	Jointly	Husband	Wife
Gross income	$140,000	$75,000	$65,000
Casualty loss	$13,000	$0	$13,000
Less 10 percent of income	($14,000)	($0)	($6,500)
Deductible casualty loss	$0	$0	$6,500
Taxes (state, local, real estate, personal property, and so forth)	$5,000	$3,000	$2,000
Mortgage interest	$9,500	$9,500	$0
Charitable contributions	$5,000	$5,000	$0
Total itemized deductions	$19,500	$17,500	$8,500
Taxable income	$120,500	$57,500	$56,500
Tax	$18,007	$6,946	$6,726

FILING SEPARATELY IN COMMUNITY PROPERTY STATES

Community property states are Arizona, California, Idaho, Louisiana, Nevada, New Mexico, Texas, Washington, and Wisconsin. If you and your spouse live in one of these states, you have to follow your state's law in determining what is community income and what is separate income, if you want to file separately.

In a community property state, each spouse, as a general rule, must report one-half of the joint income. However, this step isn't necessary if

- You and your spouse lived apart for the entire year.

- You and your spouse filed separately.

To qualify, at least one of you must have salary, wages, or business income — none of which was transferred between you and your spouse. Child support isn't considered a transfer. You can also disregard the community property rules and file a separate return without having to report any portion of the community property income where your spouse fails to inform you of the income and acts as if the income was exclusively theirs. Nor does the IRS require you to include an item of community property income on your separate return where you didn't know of the income, had no reason to know of it, or where it would be unfair to make you pay tax on income. This is an area where you should either read IRS Publication 555 *(Federal Tax Information on Community Property)* or consult a tax advisor.

REMEMBER

If you think you could have saved money in a previous year by filing separately, sorry. There's nothing you can do about it now. After you file a joint return, you can't turn back the clock and change it to separate returns. On the other hand, if you and your spouse filed separately, you can (within three years from the due date of your return or two years from the date the tax was paid) file an amended return and switch to filing jointly. You may want to do this if, when audited, some of the deductions you and your spouse claimed were disallowed, or if you get an insurance recovery greater than you expected, reducing the amount of the casualty loss. If you're making estimated tax payments during the year, it doesn't matter whether you make joint or separate payments. You can still file your actual return however you choose and divide the estimated tax payments in accordance with the rule for joint refunds in Chapter 20.

Head of household

The rules for who may file as a head of household are fairly straightforward, extremely specific, and only apply if you were unmarried, or separated and considered unmarried at the end of the year, and you paid more than half of the cost of maintaining a home (see Table 4-2 to compute that figure) that either

>> Was your parent's main home for the entire year, provided you can claim your parent as your dependent. Unlike every other dependent relationship, your parent doesn't have to live with you in your own home to qualify as your dependent, but can still be in their own residence, whether it's the old family homestead, an apartment of their own, an assisted living situation, or even a nursing home.

>> You lived in for more than half of the year (temporary absences, such as for school, vacation, or medical care, count as time lived in your home) with any of the following:

- Your qualifying child (which we explain in "Defining Who Is a Qualifying Child" later in this chapter).

- Any other person you can claim as your dependent.

- Your qualifying married child, but only if that child doesn't file a joint income tax return with their spouse, and only if that child is a U.S. citizen, U.S. national, or a resident of the United States, Mexico, or Canada (an exception is made for certain adopted children).

You can't claim head of household status on the basis of a person who is your dependent only because they lived with you for the entire year, or because you're entitled to claim that person as a dependent under a multiple support agreement. (Check out "Dependent Exemptions" later in this chapter for more information.)

WARNING

Emotional estrangement doesn't qualify as living apart for head of household status. In a Tax Court case on this topic, a couple became estranged but continued to reside in the same dwelling. The court rejected the idea that emotional estrangement equated to actual separation. Living apart requires geographical separation and living in separate residences.

In the case of a birth or death of a dependent, you must have provided more than half the cost of keeping up a home that was that person's home for more than half the year; if the person wasn't alive that long, they must have been a member of your household during the period of the tax year that they were alive.

Table 4-2 How to Compute the Cost of Maintaining a Home

	Amount You Paid	Total Cost
Property taxes	$_____	$_____
Mortgage interest expense	$_____	$_____
Rent	$_____	$_____
Utility charges	$_____	$_____
Upkeep and repairs	$_____	$_____
Property insurance	$_____	$_____
Food consumed on the premises	$_____	$_____
Other household expenses	$_____	$_____
Totals	$(a)_____	$(b)_____
Subtract Total (a) from Total (b) and enter here		($_____)

Note: If you paid more than half of the total cost of maintaining a home, you qualify for head of household status.

WARNING

The cost of keeping up a home doesn't include clothing, education, medical expenses, vacations, life insurance, or transportation. These are personal support items that are taken into account to determine whether you're entitled to claim the larger standard deduction for the support of a dependent.

THE MARRIAGE PENALTY VERSUS THE MARRIAGE BONUS

One of the most common changes in the first year of marriage is the different result you get from filing a joint tax return for the two of you, as opposed to single tax returns for each of you. Many people find that their combined taxes have risen, while others find that their overall tax burden drops.

Briefly, the marriage penalty occurs when the tax liability for a married couple exceeds what the total tax liability would have been for each of them had they been single. And the marriage bonus is the opposite: You're now paying less tax together than you were when you were single. The good news is that most couples find that their joint tax bill is less. This often happens when one spouse doesn't earn any income or when both partners have a modest income.

If you're part of a couple that earns a higher wage, that is collecting Social Security, that owns their home instead of rents, has high medical expenses, or you have capital losses, you may find yourself subject to the marriage penalty, Why? Because U.S. tax brackets are graduated, and the highest income bracket is not double that of filing single. So, if you jointly have taxable income in excess of $628,300, you're going to find yourself paying more on a joint return than you would if you were single.

(continued)

(continued)

This is the most obvious example of the marriage penalty, but marriage penalties are littered throughout the tax code. For example, if you have capital losses, you can deduct up to $3,000 from your ordinary income, no matter whether you're single, head of household, or married filing joint. And if you're married filing separately, you can only deduct $1,500.

Likewise, if you have high medical expenses, your deduction is going to be limited to 7.5 percent of your adjusted gross income, whether you're single or married. 7.5 percent of your combined income is going to be higher than 7.5 percent of each of your incomes singly.

In the same vein, with the deduction for state and local taxes now capped at $10,000 for everyone (except for $5,000 for married filing separately), you're obviously going to lose more of this deduction, especially if you live in a high tax state.

And Social Security? Well, your Social Security begins to be taxed when 50 percent of your benefit plus all your other income is greater than $25,000 if you're single, but only $32,000 if you're married. These numbers have never even been adjusted for inflation since taxing Social Security benefits came into existence in 1984, so not only are you dealing with an inequitable formula for calculating the amount of Social Security being taxed, but you're also faced with non-inflation-adjusted dollars over the past 36 years. And if you think that's nothing, realize that inflation adjusted Social Security benefits have risen by 90.5 percent since 1984. Compounded, these inflation adjustments have taken $100 of Social Security benefits in 1984 to $235.40 in 2020.

Can you do anything about it? In a small number of cases, married couples can cut their tax bills simply by filing separately.

Some people opt for another approach — not marrying at all or getting a divorce. By living together as unmarrieds, you and your significant other each pay taxes at the individual rate. We're not advising this course, but it's simply what we hear and see. You also need to know that you can't divorce in December just to save on your taxes and then remarry the next year. Taxpayers who've tried this scam in the past have been slapped with penalties in addition to the extra taxes they would've owed if they'd stayed away from divorce court.

If you decide not to stay married for the long haul just to save on income taxes, be warned that unmarried couples aren't eligible for any of the significant survivor's Social Security benefits if one partner passes away or splits. A person who doesn't work is particularly vulnerable; if that person is married and their spouse passes away or divorces them, the nonworking spouse qualifies for Social Security benefits based on the working partner's income history and Social Security taxes paid. If you aren't married and you don't work, you aren't entitled to Social Security benefits if your partner leaves you.

Congress has tried recently to address the inequities of the marriage penalty, and it has had some limited success. Standard deductions for married couples are now double what they are for individuals, and the amount of income eligible for all but the highest tax bracket is now exactly twice as large as it is for singles. It remains to be seen whether Congress will continue to whittle away at this penalty or will look to increase the penalty as it does under a proposal in the House of Representatives at the time of this writing.

Qualifying widow(er) with dependent child

If you meet all five of the following tests, you can use the tax table for married filing jointly:

» Your spouse died in 2019 or 2020, and you didn't remarry in 2021.

» You have a child, stepchild, adopted child, or foster child whom you can claim as a dependent.

» This child lived in your home for all of 2021. Temporary absences, such as for vacation or school, count as time lived in your home.

» You paid more than half the cost of keeping up your home for this child.

» You could have filed a joint return with your spouse the year your spouse died, even if you didn't actually do so. (But you can't claim an exemption for your deceased spouse.)

If your spouse died in 2021, you may not file as a qualifying widow(er) with a dependent child. But see whether you qualify for filing jointly and refer to the "Filing a Return for a Deceased Taxpayer" section near the end of this chapter. And if you can't file as a qualifying widow(er) with a dependent child, see whether you can qualify as a head of household. If you don't meet the rules for a qualifying widow(er) with a dependent child, married filing a joint return, or head of household, you must file as single.

For example, suppose that a mother with children died in 2018, and the husband hasn't remarried. In 2019 and 2020, he kept up a home for himself and his dependent children. For 2018, he was entitled to file a joint return for himself and his deceased wife. For 2019 and 2020, he may file as a qualifying widow(er) with dependent children. After 2020, he may file as head of household if he qualifies. If he doesn't qualify, he files as single.

Counting your dependents

The number of dependents you have, whether qualifying children or other dependents, can impact a slew of income tax credits you may be entitled to take, including the child tax credit, the additional child tax credit, the earned income tax credit, and all the education credits (American Opportunity Credit, Lifetime Learning Credit, and Hope Credit). Your dependent's deductible expenses can also impact the tax you pay, since you're the one actually paying that person's medical bills.

If you're a traditional family with both parents married to each other, and minor children, and you're all living together in the United States, this calculation is easy — your minor children are your dependents. In the middle of the first page of your Form 1040, in the section marked "Dependents," enter their full names, Social Security numbers, and their relationship to you, and tick the appropriate box for either qualifying for the child tax credit or the credit for other dependents. Presto, you're done.

If you're part of a nontraditional family, you may have to work a little harder to determine who is, and who isn't, your dependent (see the next section). But please, persevere — each dependent that you claim can put money into your pocket in the form of refundable credits.

Deciding who is your dependent

You can claim a dependent if the person in question is your qualifying child (see the section "Defining Who Is a Qualifying Child" later in this chapter). You're also allowed to claim a qualifying relative as your dependent if you provide more than half of that person's support, if they can't be claimed as a dependent on anyone else's tax return, and if they pass the five dependency tests. (Don't forget that if you claim someone, that person can't claim a personal exemption on their own tax return.)

TIP

Qualifying relative is a pretty broad term and can include people who are not related to you by blood or marriage. If, for example, a friend lives with you, has no income of their own, and you provide all their support, you may find that they qualify as your dependent. Run through all the rules in the following sections to see if they pass the tests. And to make it even easier, there is a terrific Interactive Tax Assistant (ITA) on the IRS website at www.irs.gov/help/ita/whom-may-i-claim-as-a-dependent.

Okay, you may open your booklets and begin the tests now. In order for a person other than your qualifying child to be your dependent, he or she must meet all five of the following tests:

Test 1: Member of your household or relative

Your dependent must either live with you for the entire year as a member of your household or must be related to you by blood or marriage. The required relationships are very specific, so that your parents' siblings qualify on the relationship part of this test, but their children, your cousins, need to live with you for the entire year.

If you file a joint return, you don't need to show that a dependent is related to both you and your spouse. The dependent only needs to be related to one of you.

REMEMBER

Temporary absences are ignored. If a person is placed in a nursing home for constant medical care, the absence is also considered temporary.

Here are some more details you may need to consider:

>> **Death or birth:** A person who died during the year but was a member of your household until death meets the member of your household test. The same is true for a child who was born during the year and was a member of your household for the rest of the year. A child who was born and died in the same year qualifies, but a stillborn child doesn't. The child must have been born alive — even if for just a moment — to qualify as a dependent.

>> **Violation of local law:** A person doesn't meet the member of your household test if your relationship violates local law.

>> **Adoption:** Before the adoption is legal, a child is considered your child if they were placed with you for adoption by an authorized adoption agency (and the child must have been a member of your household). Otherwise, the child must be a member of your household for the entire tax year to satisfy this test.

>> **Foster care:** A foster child or adult must live with you as a member of your household for the entire year to qualify as your dependent. However, if a government agency makes payments to you as a foster parent, you may not list the child as your dependent.

>> **Employees:** Your nanny or live-in housekeeper doesn't qualify for this test. Living with you may be a requirement of their job, but it doesn't meet the member of the household test.

Test 2: Married person

If your dependent is married and files a joint return, unless the purpose of filing that return is to claim a refund, you can't take this person as an exemption.

Test 3: Citizen or resident

The dependent must be one of the following:

>> A U.S. citizen or U.S. resident alien

>> A resident of Canada or Mexico

>> Your adopted child who isn't a U.S. citizen but who lived with you all year in a foreign country

You can't claim a person who isn't a U.S. citizen or resident and lives abroad (in a country other than Canada or Mexico) as a dependent.

Test 4: Income

The dependent's gross income must be less than $4,300. Gross income counts all taxable income, but doesn't include nontaxable income, such as welfare benefits or nontaxable Social Security benefits. Income earned by a permanently and totally disabled person for services performed at a sheltered workshop school generally isn't included for purposes of the income test.

Of course, there are exceptions. Your qualifying relative can have a gross income of $4,300 or more under one of the following conditions:

>> The person was under the age of 19 at the end of 2021.

>> The person was under the age of 24 at the end of 2021 and was also a student.

REMEMBER

Your qualifying relative is considered a student if they're enrolled as a full-time student at a school during any five months of 2021. A school includes technical, trade, and mechanical schools. It doesn't include on-the-job training courses or correspondence schools.

WARNING

Students just graduating college (or high school if they choose to work full-time after that) generally want to claim themselves on their tax returns in the year they leave school. But beware! For people graduating at any time from May through December, that dependency claim rightly belongs with the parent, not the child. Be sure to remind your graduating senior that they're still your dependent this one last year.

CHILDREN OF DIVORCED OR SEPARATED PARENTS

The parent who had custody of the child for the largest number of nights is the one entitled to claim the child as a dependent — provided that both parents together paid more than half of the child's support.

A noncustodial parent can claim the child if any of the following apply:

- The custodial parent gives up the right to claim the child as a dependent by signing Form 8332, Release of Claim to Exemption for Child of Divorced or Separated Parents. The form allows for the release of a child for a single year, a number of years, or all future years. The noncustodial parent must attach this form to the return.

- A decree or separation agreement signed after 1984 provides that the noncustodial parent is unconditionally entitled to claim the child as their dependent, and the custodial parent isn't. You must list the child's name, Social Security number, and the number of months the child lived in your home. You also must attach a copy of the cover page of the decree or agreement with the custodial parent's Social Security number written next to their name, along with the page that unconditionally states that you can claim the child as a dependent. Don't forget to attach a copy of the signature page of the decree or agreement.

- A decree or separation agreement signed before 1985 provides that the noncustodial parent is entitled to the exemption, and that this parent provided $600 or more toward the child's support.

- In the extreme right column on line 6 of your 1040 where you list your total exemptions, you must list the number of dependents who didn't live with you separately from the number who did.

Note: If you fail to pay child support in the year it's due but pay it in a later year, it isn't considered paid for the support of your child in either year.

Even if you can't claim a child because your ex-spouse is claiming the child, you still can claim the child's medical expenses, and you're entitled to the Child and Dependent Care Credit if you're the custodial parent. When the child reaches the age of majority, the custodial parent rules no longer apply. The parent who provides more than 50 percent of the child's support is entitled to the exemption.

Note: The special rules for divorced or separated parents also apply to parents, whether married or not, who lived apart at all times during the last six months of the year. In such situations, you either have to provide more than half the support of the child or enter into a multiple support agreement (Form 2120).

Also, be aware that most storefront tax preparation services fail to ask all the questions they should or explain what the questions mean, so if your student has filed their return through one of these services, chances are good that they've tried to claim themselves. When you attempt to file your return electronically, it will be rejected if someone has already claimed that Social Security number; to fix this, you'll have to file your return on paper, and your dependent will have to amend their return.

Test 5: Support

You must have provided more than half of your qualifying relative's total support in 2021 to claim that person as your dependent. If you file a joint return, support can come from either spouse. If you remarried, the support provided by your new spouse is treated as support coming from you. For exceptions to the support test, see the sidebar "Children of divorced or separated parents."

Support includes food, a place to live, clothing, medical and dental care, and education. It also includes items such as a car and furniture, but only if they're for the dependent's own use or benefit. In figuring total support, use the actual cost of these items, but figure the cost of a place to live at its fair rental value. Include money the person used for their own support, even if this money wasn't taxable. Examples are gifts, savings, Social Security and welfare benefits, and other public assistance payments. This support is treated as not coming from you.

Total support doesn't include items such as income tax and Social Security taxes, life insurance premiums, or funeral expenses. A person's own funds aren't considered support unless they're actually spent for support. For example, your mother received $2,400 in Social Security and $400 in interest. She paid $2,000 for rent and $400 for recreation. Even though her income was $2,800, she spent only $2,400 for her own support. If you spent more than $2,400 for her support, you can claim her as a dependent because you provided more than half her support.

TIP

Even if you didn't pay more than half of a dependent's support, you may still be able to claim this person as a dependent if all five of the following apply:

>> You and one or more eligible persons paid more than half of the dependent's support. An *eligible person* is someone who could have claimed the dependent but didn't pay more than half of the dependent's support.

>> You paid more than 10 percent of the dependent's support.

>> No individual paid more than half of the dependent's support.

>> Dependency tests 1 through 4 are met.

>> Each eligible person who paid more than 10 percent of support completes Form 2120, Multiple Support Declaration, and you attach this form to your return. The form states that only you will claim the person as a dependent for 2021.

Securing Social Security numbers for dependents

You must list a Social Security number for every dependent in the "Dependents" section on the face of Form 1040, column (2). If your dependent was born and died in 2021 and didn't have a Social Security number, write "Died" in column (2). No Social Security number, no deduction, and no right to claim head of household status. Check out Chapter 26 for the ins and outs of how to get your child a Social Security number.

TIP

If you're in the process of adopting a child who is a U.S. citizen or resident and can't get a Social Security number until the adoption is final, you can apply for an adoption taxpayer number (ATIN) that you can use instead of a Social Security number. To get one, file Form W-7A, Application for Taxpayer Identification Number for Pending U.S. Adoptions.

Filing for Children and Other Dependents

Even if you're able to claim someone else (your child, your grandchild, and so on) as a dependent on your return, that person may have to file their own income tax return in the following circumstances:

>> The dependent had unearned income (generally, income other than wages, income from self-employment, and tips), and the total of that income exceeds $1,100.

>> The dependent had earned income in 2021 on which income tax has been withheld.

>> The dependent had no unearned income but had earned income that exceeds $12,550.

>> The dependent had both earned and unearned gross income that exceeds the larger of (a) $1,100 or (b) the earned income up to $12,250 plus $350.

For example, suppose that your teenager has interest income of $600 and salary from a summer job of $4,500. This dependent doesn't need to file because the total income was less than $12,550, and their unearned income (interest) is less than $1,100. If your teenager had no unearned income but earned $2,000 from a summer job, they wouldn't have to file either because the earned income was under $12,550, unless income tax was withheld, and they wanted to request a refund.

TIP

But here's an important point: Your dependent, who isn't going to have a tax liability in the first place, doesn't need to have income tax withheld from their paycheck. Instead, have that dependent claim an exemption from income tax when completing Form W-4. If the dependent didn't claim an exemption on Form W-4, they must file to get back the tax that was withheld from their paychecks. Remember, though, when they reach $12,550 in income, withholding will have to start, and a new W-4 must be filed with the employer.

You may encounter another wrinkle in the IRS rules for this exemption from withholding to apply — the teenager's investment income (interest) can't exceed $350. If it does, they can't claim an exemption from withholding if their total income exceeds $1,100. There's no such thing as being too young when introducing your kid to convoluted tax laws.

TIP

A new Form W-4 needs to be filed for each year your child is exempt, and once your child is no longer exempt, a fresh Form W-4 should be filed, indicating the number of exemptions they will be claiming for withholding purposes.

Congress continues to fiddle with the *kiddie tax* (tax on a child's income that's taxed at their parents' highest marginal tax rate) that applies to all children under age 19 and to children who are full-time students under the age of 24 unless they're earning more than half of their own support. The kiddie tax kicks in once your child hits $2,200 of unearned income in 2021. Chapter 10 gives you more information on this wonderful tax law nuance, and Chapter 17 gives you all the specific rules for 2021.

Defining Who Is a Qualifying Child

In case you were wondering, there is a uniform definition for who, exactly, is a qualifying child for the following tax benefits:

» Dependency exemptions

» Head of household filing status

» The earned income credit (EIC)

» The child tax credit

» The credit for child and dependent care expenses

For your child to qualify for any of these benefits, they need to meet the age test, the relationship test, the residency test, and the support test. If they don't meet the requirements of all these tests, unfortunately they aren't your qualifying child in the eyes of the IRS.

Age test

For your child to qualify under the age test for dependency exemptions, head of household filing status, and the earned income credit, they must be under the age of 19 at the end of the year or under the age of 24 if a full-time student for some part of each of five months during the year (not necessarily consecutive). No age test applies for a child who is permanently and totally disabled.

NEW STUFF

To qualify for the child tax credit, your child must be under age 18 by the end of the tax year.

To be eligible for the child and dependent care credit, your child must be under age 13, or permanently and totally disabled. For the purpose of this credit only, expenses you incur *and* pay for that child in the year of their 13th birthday before that birthday can be used to claim the credit; expenses incurred after that birthday can't, even if you made payment before their 13th birthday.

Relationship test

The child must either be your child, adopted child (even if the adoption isn't yet final), stepchild, eligible foster child (any child placed with you by an authorized placement agency, or by a judgment, decree, or any other court order), brother, sister, stepbrother, stepsister, or the descendent of one of these relatives.

Residency test

Your qualifying child must live with you for more than half of the year. Although the days don't have to be consecutive, they do need to add up to at least 183. Temporary absences for school, vacation, military service, medical reasons, or for detention in a juvenile detention center don't count as time away from you.

TECHNICAL STUFF

"Days" actually doesn't mean days at all; instead, you need to count the number of nights they spend with you.

An exception is made for children who are born during the tax year, provided that they lived with you for the entire period they were alive. So, a child who is born on December 30, 2021, is your qualifying child, even though they may not make it home from the hospital until January 1, 2022. An exception is also made for a child who dies during the year and for a child who is kidnapped, provided that the kidnapper isn't related.

Finally, the children of divorced or separated parents qualify under the rules set out in the sidebar in this chapter entitled "Children of divorced or separated parents."

Support test

To meet the standards of this test, your child must not have provided at least half of their own support. Calculate how much your child spent on their share of housing costs (including rent, utilities, furnishings, and repairs, but not mortgage interest, insurance, or real estate taxes), on clothing, on food, on education, and on medical and dental bills not reimbursed by insurance. Also add vacations and travel, and any other miscellaneous expenses that your child paid for their benefit. Then compare this number against the total cost of that child's share of these items. If the amount your child paid is less than 50 percent, you meet this test.

TIP

If you're having some difficulty in figuring out whether your child qualifies under the support test, use the nifty worksheet in IRS Publication 501 *(Exemptions, Standard Deduction, and Filing Information)*.

Filing a Return for a Deceased Taxpayer

When someone dies, a separate taxpaying entity is created — the decedent's estate. If the estate has more than $600 in income or has a beneficiary who is a nonresident alien, the executor or administrator for the estate (the person responsible for winding up the decedent's financial affairs) must file Form 1041, U.S. Income Tax Return for Estates and Trusts. This filing is in addition to the decedent's final tax return.

Suppose the decedent died before April 15, 2022, without having filed their 2021 tax return. The executor is responsible for filing a tax return for that individual for 2021 (a complete year) and for 2022, which isn't due until April 15, 2023. For example, if someone died on April 1, 2022, a return must be filed for 2021, and a final return for 2022 must be filed by April 15, 2023, reporting all the deceased's income and deductions for the period January 1, 2022, through April 1, 2022.

If a decedent died in 2021, you must allocate their income based on what was earned and received prior to and including the date of death, and what was received after the date of death. Income received prior to death is reported and taxed on the decedent's final Form 1040; after the date of death, all income received is reported on the Form 1041 for the estate. The good news is that even though you report only part of the year's income on the Form 1040, you get to deduct the full amount of the decedent's standard deduction if you're not itemizing.

If the surviving spouse didn't remarry in the same year as the death, a joint return can be filed. The surviving spouse reports their income and deductions for the entire year and the deceased's up to the date of death. If you remarry in the same year that your spouse dies, you can file jointly with your new spouse, but not with your deceased spouse. Your deceased spouse's filing status will revert to "Married Filing Separately."

Medical expenses paid within one year of the decedent's death must be deducted on the decedent's final return; an estate can't take this type of deduction on its Form 1041. If you've already filed that last return, and then you pay more bills (within the one-year time limit), you may amend that final return (by filing IRS Form 1040X), take the larger medical deduction, and receive a refund.

If the deceased owned E or EE Savings Bonds and chose not to report the interest during their lifetime, the tax on the interest must be paid by the survivor unless an election is made to report the interest on the decedent's final return. Doing so may make sense if the deceased died early in the year and had little income and large deductions.

Either the surviving spouse or the executor can sign the deceased's final personal income tax return. Write "DECEASED," the decedent's name, and the date of death at the top of page 1 of the 1040. If you are using tax software, make sure to include the date of death in the program so the return produces the appropriate diagnostics.

TIP

Please be aware that, while the IRS encourages us all to file our tax returns electronically, when you are dealing with the final 1040 for a deceased person, even if it is joint with their spouse, that return, including any extension, may have to be filed on paper. Please make sure that, when you mail the return to the appropriate IRS office, you send it via Certified Mail. You want to make certain that, if the IRS loses that return, you have proof that you timely filed it.

If the deceased's final Form 1040 isn't joint with the surviving spouse and a refund is due, the person who is receiving the refund must also file Form 1310, aptly named "Statement of Person Claiming Refund Due a Deceased Taxpayer." Who said the IRS wasn't any good with words?

Check out Peggy's book, *Estate & Trust Administration For Dummies,* coauthored with Kathryn A. Murphy, Esq. (Wiley), for complete information on how to fill out the decedent's final Form 1040 and prepare Form 1041 for the estate.

Must I File?

Yes, you must file a tax return when your income exceeds the amount for your age and filing status, as shown in Table 4-3.

Table 4-3   When You Must File

Marital Status	Filing Status	Age*	Filing Required When Gross Income Exceeds
Single, divorced, legally separated	Single	Under 65	$12,550
		65 or older or blind	$14,250
		65 or older and blind	$15,950
	Head of household	Under 65	$18,800
		65 or older or blind	$20,500
		65 or older and blind	$22,200
Married with a child and living apart from spouse during last six months of 2021	Head of household	Under 65	$18,800
		65 or older or blind	$20,500
		65 or older and blind	$22,200
Married and living with spouse at end of 2021 (or on date of spouse's death)	Married (joint return)	Under 65	$25,100
		65 or older (one spouse)	$26,400
		65 or older (both spouses)	$27,700
		65 or older and blind (one spouse)	$27,500
		65 or older (one spouse) and older and blind (one spouse)	$29,000
		65 or older and blind (both spouses)	$30,300
	Married (separate return)	Under 65	$12,550
		65 or older	$14,250
		65 or older and blind	$15,950
Married and not living with spouse at end of 2021 (or on date of spouse's death)	Married (joint or separate return)	Under 65	$12,550
		65 or older	$14,250
		65 or older and blind	$15,950
Widowed before 2021 and not remarried in 2021	Single	Under 65	$12,550
		65 or older or blind	$14,250
		65 or older and blind	$15,950
Qualifying widow(er) with dependent child		Under 65	$25,100
		65 or older	$26,400
		65 or older and blind	$27,700

If you turn 65 on January 1, 2022, you're considered to be age 65 at the end of 2021.

When to file

If you don't file by April 18, 2022 (or April 19, 2022, if you're a resident of Maine or Massachusetts), you'll have to pay penalties and interest. If you live or work outside the United States, your filing deadline is June 15, 2022.

If you know that you can't file by April 18 or 19, depending on where you live, you can get an automatic six-month extension of time to file — until October 16, 2022 — by filing Form 4868, Application for Automatic Extension of Time to File U.S. Individual Income Tax Return. Keep in mind that you must file this form by April 15, 2022. If you pay all or a portion of what you think the balance due is using either the IRS Direct Pay, the EFTPS (Electronic Federal Tax Payment System), or a credit or debit card to pay the balance owed for 2021, you don't have to separately file Form 4868; it's done automatically for you when you choose "extension payment" as the type of payment you're making. We explain how to pay by credit card in Chapter 10. You can also obtain extensions of time to file by using your personal computer and a tax software program. The choices are endless, so don't blow the April 15 filing date.

If you're living outside the country, you're not required to file Form 4868 until June 15, 2022, which is the due date of your return. Form 4868 for taxpayers living abroad extends the due date to October 16, 2022.

WARNING

Filing an extension of time to file doesn't extend the time to pay. You'll be charged interest and a late payment penalty of 0.5 percent a month on your unpaid balance if you don't pay at least 90 percent of your tax by April 18, 2022 (April 19, 2022, for residents of Maine and Massachusetts).

If you don't file

You can end up crushing rocks. Remember, Al Capone didn't go to prison for running rackets; he went to the big house for tax evasion. Realistically, though, it's more likely that you'll be assessed penalties that make crushing rocks seem like a stroll in the park. Annually, the IRS prosecutes only 5,000 individuals (you can't call them taxpayers) for tax evasion. Some 80 percent are members of organized crime or drug dealers, and the balance is made up of high-profile individuals and others. You don't want to be one of the others. Even though the government currently is interested in high-profile CEOs and movie actors, you never know who the IRS may decide to take an interest in. The IRS moves in mysterious ways.

If you don't file, based on the information reported to the IRS by your employers, the IRS either prepares a substitute return and assesses a late filing penalty of 25 percent, a late payment penalty of 0.5 percent a month to a maximum of 25 percent plus interest (and possibly a 75 percent fraud penalty), or issues a summons for you to appear with your tax records so that the IRS can use those records to prepare a more accurate return. Interest and penalties are charged whichever way the IRS decides to proceed.

Where to file

The IRS website (www.irs.gov/filing/where-to-file-paper-tax-returns-with-or-without-a-payment) lists all the addresses to which you can send your forms. So does your instruction booklet. Just look for the "Where To File" link in the "Resources" section.

How to file

Okay, so this whole book is supposed to be about this subject. But what we mean in this short section is that you have a couple of ways to get the forms — and the check, if necessary — to IRS Central: You can file the old-fashioned way through the U.S. Postal Service, or you can file electronically.

Electronic filing

Although electronic filing became the most popular form of tax filing for the first time in 2005, we still need to define it, especially for that last 10 percent who insist on doing it the old-fashioned way, on paper and by mail (in 2019, about 92 percent of all individual returns were filed electronically). You or the company that offers this service files your return securely and encrypted over the internet. All you need is a computer and a modem.

REMEMBER

Through a link on the IRS web page (www.irs.gov/filing/free-file-do-your-federal-taxes-for-free), a group of software companies are offering free online tax filing. Why are they doing this? To ensure that the IRS doesn't jump into the online tax filing market with a competitive product. If free electronic filing sounds too good to be true, you're probably right. We have experienced that when someone offers something for nothing, usually a gimmick is involved. Some companies may have something up their sleeves and try to solicit you for their financial services or products. Others only offer a stripped-down version of their regular software for free — if your taxes are more complicated, they're happy to sell you the necessary software to prepare your return (the electronic filing remains free). Another catch we noticed is that, although they'll file the federal return for free, you need to pay a fee to file your state return.

Each participating software company has set its own eligibility requirements for free filing. Generally, those requirements are based on age, adjusted gross income (AGI), eligibility to claim the Earned Income Credit, state residency, and active-duty military status (if applicable). Each company has a description of the criteria for using its free service.

The advantage of electronic filing is that you may get your hands on your hard-earned refund in about ten days, which is approximately three weeks faster than by mail. Also, you can have your refund deposited directly into your bank account. Your state return gets filed along with your federal return at the same time. One transmission does it all.

Some tax preparation firms not only prepare and electronically file your return, but they also loan you money based on the projected amount of the refund. These clever loans are called *refund anticipation loans*.

REMEMBER

Our principal objection to these refund anticipation loans is that they're too pricey. Here's why: According to the IRS, the average refund taxpayers received in 2020 was $2,707. Some tax preparation firms can arrange for an on-the-spot loan for the amount of your refund. According to the Consumer Federation of America and the National Consumer Law Center, the effective interest rate on the typical loan for the average refund was at an almost 40 percent annual percentage rate. This is the result of the loan being repaid within ten days when the refund is deposited into a special account set up by the lender. A class action suit was once settled against H&R Block involving deceptive business practices concerning their refund loans.

Filing by mail or other private delivery service

Face it, many taxpayers, whether by choice or through necessity, still do it the old-fashioned way, with a trip to the post office on April 18 or April 19, depending on where you live. If you're one of those taxpayers who feels the job isn't done right without that postmark on the upper right-hand corner of the envelope, you need to consider the following:

>> Make sure you have proof of mailing. For the post office, that means a certified mail receipt.

>> If you choose to use a private delivery service, you need to know that only certain types of deliveries (such as DHL, FedEx, and UPS) provide you with adequate proof (in the form of dated receipts) should the IRS question whether you have timely filed.

A Final Bit of Advice

TIP

Here's an old saying from a wise man — the father of one of us. He said, "Son, there are two kinds of payments in the world you should avoid: too early and too late." That kind of advice also applies to filing your taxes. Filing taxes late leads to IRS interest and penalties; paying your taxes too early, or withholding too much, is simply an interest-free loan to the federal government. Thanks for the advice, Dad.

Tackling the Main Forms

2

Chapter **5**

All The Form 1040s: Income Stuff

S urely you remember the old war slogan "Divide and conquer!" (We think Alexander the Great, or some other real famous warrior said it.) Well, that's our strategy here. We break down each section and each line of Form 1040 and pound each one into submission.

Note: All Form 1040s are created somewhat equal, so whether you're filing the regular version of Form 1040, the nonresident taxpayer Form 1040-NR, or the Form 1040-SR for seniors age 65+, almost all the line references will be the same. We'll let you know where the differences lie as you get to them. If we don't tell you that a reference we make is to either Form 1040-NR or Form 1040-SR, you can assume that all three forms are asking for the same information.

So, welcome to Chapter 5, where the fun and games really begin.

Starting at the Very Beginning: The Top of 1040

When you first look at any version of Form 1040, the first thing you'll notice at the top of page 1 is all the biographical information you're requested to provide, things like your name and address. Check out Figure 5-1 for a visual. But wait, there's more there, and if you're not careful, you might miss some or all of it.

Choosing your filing status

We'd be remiss if we didn't start right at the top of page 1 of Form 1040, which begins with your filing status. If you're unsure of your filing status (single, married filing separately, married filing jointly, head of household, or qualifying widow[er]), flip back to Chapter 4. We explain it all there. All you need to do here is check the correct box, and you're good to go, except if you've just ticked the "Married filing separately" box, in which case you need to add your spouse's name and Social Security number on the lines below that ask for that information. Oh, and if you've checked either the "Head of Household" or the "Qualifying Widow(er)" status, you need to enter the name of the child that qualifies you for that status if that child is not your dependent.

FIGURE 5-1: The biographical section of Form 1040 tells the IRS who you are and how you're choosing to file.

Source: Internal Revenue Service

TIP

Filing statuses are tricky, even for those of us who do this for a living. If, even after reading about filing statuses in Chapter 4, you're still confused, the IRS has a handy questionnaire for you to complete which will tell you what filing status you should use. Check out www.irs.gov/help/ita/what-is-my-filing-status.

Adding your name(s), address and Social Security number(s)

Once you've selected your filing status, you're going to need to tell the IRS who you are and who else you're filing for. So go ahead; fill out the biographical information they ask for, and please make sure that you enter all Social Security numbers accurately. It's incredibly easy to switch two numbers around, and that will cause your return to be rejected for processing, whether you're filing electronically or on paper.

Electing to give to the next presidential campaign

Under the box for yours and your spouse's Social Security numbers, there's a question asking if you'd like to contribute $3 to the Presidential Election Campaign Fund. Checking this box "yes" will not change the amount you owe or the size of your refund; it's just to let the IRS know whether to take $3 of your taxes and send them over to that fund. This may be the only place in the entire tax code that we get to choose where our tax dollars go, so choose wisely here.

Disclosing virtual currency transactions

Finally, just above the box marked "Standard Deduction," there's a question regarding virtual currency. Virtual currency is a digital representation of value that functions as a medium of exchange, a unit of account, and/or a store of value, according to the IRS. Among the most popular cryptocurrencies, you'll find Bitcoin, Dogecoin, Ethereum, Litecoin, and Polkadot (okay, we find these names funny). Virtual currencies and cryptocurrencies are a relatively new phenomenon, and new ones are being invented almost daily, so if we haven't listed it here, that's because we don't have enough space or time to list them all.

We discuss more about virtual currency in Chapter 14 since most people who are buying and selling virtual currency are going to incur either capital gains or losses. For now, though, know that if you've been playing in the virtual currency world, you should check this box.

Calculating your standard deduction

No, honestly, we're not asking you to actually add up how much your standard deduction is, especially if you're using a computer to prepare your return. We just want to make sure that you're using the correct amount of a standard deduction, because this is certainly not a one-size-fits-all number. Refer to Chapter 4 if you're preparing your return on paper, and figure out where you fit in Table 4-3, which is not just the amount you need to earn to not file, but also the default standard deduction for all those categories.

If you're preparing your return using a computer, though, just answer the following questions, and the computer will calculate the standard deduction for you:

>> Can anyone claim you as a dependent?

>> Can anyone claim your spouse as a dependent?

>> Did your spouse itemize on a separate return?

>> Are either you or your spouse a dual-status alien?

If you're not sure how to answer the first two questions, look back at Chapter 4 to see if you or your spouse qualifies as someone else's dependent. Question 3 will only apply if you and your spouse are filing using the "Married filing separately" status, and the last question only applies to people who are not U.S. citizens or resident aliens (also known as green card holders), who may have lived in the U.S. for a portion of the year and outside of the U.S. for the rest of the year.

Listing your dependents

Just below where you calculate the amount of your standard deduction, you need to list everyone who is your dependent on this return. You don't need to enter yourself or your spouse; you've already accounted for the two of you up above. For everyone else who qualifies, either as a qualifying child or a qualifying relative or member of your household, enter each person's first and last names, their Social Security numbers, and their relationship to you. Check the box next to each name if that dependent qualifies for the child tax credit, and if they don't, check the box for the credit for other dependents right next to it.

REMEMBER

You must have a valid Social Security number for each dependent; without one, the IRS will disallow that dependent.

If you're not clear on whether someone is or isn't your dependent, or whether they qualify for the child tax credit or the credit for other dependents, check out Chapter 4 for all the dependency rules and regulations.

Finally, you're not limited to just four dependents, even though the forms only give you space for four. If you have more than four dependents, check the box to the left of those four lines, and list their information on a separate page if you're filing on paper. If you're filing electronically, your computer will do this for you.

Lines 1-9: Income

Income is, in brief, something of value that you receive regardless of whether you work for it or you have an investment that works for it (think interest on your bank account, dividends from a corporation, or rental income from a house you own), and it's usually paid in the form of money. Most people know that wages earned from toiling away at jobs are income. But income also includes receipts of alimony, certain interest, dividends, profits on your investments, and even your lottery winnings or prizes won on *Wheel of Fortune.*

TIP

Gifts of money or other property are not income. If someone gifts you something, they have given up "all right, title, and interest" in the property without receiving anything of value from you in return. If, on the other hand, you're helping your elderly parent, for example, by assisting them in paying their bills, doing odd jobs around the house, or taking them to appointments, the money they give you can be construed as income, since you are performing services in exchange for the money.

In this chapter, you discover the meaning of all those little slips of paper you receive from your employer, your bank, your investment firms, Social Security, your state government, and anyone else who may have paid you some money during the year. We show you how to use all this information to complete lines 1 through 9, the "Income" section of Form 1040. Check out Figure 5-2. You can round off to the nearest dollar, so you don't have to fiddle with pennies. It only takes a minute or two; we promise.

FIGURE 5-2:
The income
section of
Form 1040 lists
how much you
made in 2021.

Attach Sch. B if required.	1	Wages, salaries, tips, etc. Attach Form(s) W-2			1		
	2a	Tax-exempt interest	2a	b Taxable interest	2b		
	3a	Qualified dividends	3a	b Ordinary dividends	3b		
	4a	IRA distributions	4a	b Taxable amount	4b		
	5a	Pensions and annuities	5a	b Taxable amount	5b		
Standard Deduction for— • Single or Married filing separately, $12,550	6a	Social security benefits	6a	b Taxable amount	6b		
	7	Capital gain or (loss). Attach Schedule D if required. If not required, check here ▶ ☐			7		
	8	Other income from Schedule 1, line 10			8		
	9	Add lines 1, 2b, 3b, 4b, 5b, 6b, 7, and 8. This is your **total income** ▶			9		

Source: Internal Revenue Service

Line 1: Wages, salaries, tips

If you work for an employer, you'll receive the famous Form W-2, Wage and Tax Statement, which your employer is required to deliver to you no later than January 31, 2022. The requirement is that this form be mailed to you, but your employer may also provide a secure portal where you can access a digital copy of Form W-2. However you receive it, hang onto it when you get it; without it, it will be impossible to accurately complete your Form 1040. Form W-2 tells you the amount you earned during the year and how much your employer withheld from your wages for taxes.

You need to have your Form W-2 in front of you in order to fill in an amount on line 1 (see Figure 5-3). You may notice that you have three or four pages of the same W-2, or that you have multiple copies on the same page. Why? If you use regular mail, attach Copy B to your federal return and Copy 2 to your state return; you file Copy C and any other copies your employer gave you with your neat and organized tax records. If you are filing electronically, keep all the copies in your files with a copy of your completed tax return. In case you're wondering, your employer has already sent Copy A to the folks at the Social Security Administration. If you look at the lower-left corner of your W-2s, you see what to do with each copy.

FIGURE 5-3:
Form W-2
shows how
much you
earned and
various taxes
you paid.

a Employee's social security number					
b Employer identification number (EIN)			**1** Wages, tips, other compensation	**2** Federal income tax withheld	
c Employer's name, address, and ZIP code			**3** Social security wages	**4** Social security tax withheld	
			5 Medicare wages and tips	**6** Medicare tax withheld	
			7 Social security tips	**8** Allocated tips	
d Control number			**9**	**10** Dependent care benefits	
e Employee's first name and initial Last name Suff.			**11** Nonqualified plans	**12a** See instructions for box 12	
			13 Statutory employee ☐ Retirement plan ☐ Third-party sick pay ☐	**12b**	
			14 Other	**12c**	
				12d	
f Employee's address and ZIP code					

15 State Employer's state ID number	16 State wages, tips, etc.	17 State income tax	18 Local wages, tips, etc.	19 Local income tax	20 Locality name

Form **W-2** Wage and Tax Statement   **2021**   Department of the Treasury—Internal Revenue Service

Copy B—To Be Filed With Employee's FEDERAL Tax Return.
This information is being furnished to the Internal Revenue Service.

Source: Internal Revenue Service

Safe, accurate, FAST! Use IRS e-file   Visit the IRS website at www.irs.gov/efile   OMB No. 1545-0008

If you're self-employed and you don't receive a W-2, you get to skip this line, but you're going to end up doing tons more work completing Schedule C so you can fill in Schedule 1, line 3, of the 1040. For farmers, it's Schedule F and Schedule 1, line 6. Retirees can skip 'em both — one of the many perks of retirement!

TIP

Check the information contained on your W-2 carefully, including your name, address, and Social Security number. If any item on your W-2 is wrong, contact your employer to have it corrected as soon as possible. Otherwise, you'll pay too much or too little tax — and you would not want to do that. An incorrect Social Security number will prevent the IRS computers from matching the information you report with what they've received from your employer, so you may not get the credit you deserve for taxes you've paid. If you didn't receive your W-2, call your employer. If your employer doesn't give you a corrected Form W-2 by the end of February 2022, file Form 4852, Substitute for Form W-2, Wage and Tax Statement, or Form 1099-R, Distributions from Pensions, Annuities, Retirement or Profit-Sharing Plans, IRAs, Insurance Contracts, Etc., which is a substitute for missing W-2s (and missing 1099-Rs). The magnanimous IRS allows you to estimate your salary and the amount of tax withheld on this form. You then attach Form 4852 to your tax return. The easiest way to access a copy of Form 4852 is through your tax software or downloading it from the IRS website at www.irs.gov. If you get no joy from either of those methods, you can always call the IRS toll-free at 800-829-1040. Be patient; it often takes hours to reach an agent, but perseverance will pay off in the end, and they will mail you a copy.

What those W-2 boxes mean

Each of the numbered boxes on your W-2 contains either welcome information (like your gross income, which momentarily makes you feel rich) or the type of information that surely will have you shaking your head in disbelief (such as the total amount of different types of taxes that you paid throughout the year, which effectively makes you feel poor again). If you notice in this discussion that we're skipping over some of those little boxes, rest assured that we explain them when we need to in later chapters.

Box 1: Wages, tips, and other compensation

Your taxable wages, tips, other compensation, and taxable fringe benefits are listed here. This box is a biggie. Everything but the kitchen sink was thrown into box 1. Common examples are your salary, your tips, and the taxable portion of any fringe benefits like the personal-use part of your company car. Other stuff that your employer tossed into box 1 includes disability pay, back pay, bonuses, commissions, severance or dismissal pay, and vacation pay.

Because box 1 is a catchall, the figure in it may be larger than your actual cash salary. Get it over with — fill in the amount on Form 1040, line 1. If you have one or more W-2s, add 'em up and put in the total.

Box 8: Allocated tips

If you worked in a restaurant and didn't report all your tip income to your employer, box 8 includes the difference between your share of at least 8 percent of the restaurant's income and what you reported. This amount doesn't mean that you're entitled to this money. Your employer figures what 8 percent of the restaurant's income amounts to. This is the minimum amount of tip income the employees have to pay tax on. Your employer then computes your share, which doesn't let you off the hook. The IRS can always audit the restaurant's books and determine, for example, that the tip rate was in fact 15 percent. Ouch! This income shown in box 8 isn't reported in box 1 — it's in addition to the income in box 1. Therefore, you must add it to the amount on Form 1040 (line 1). You must also enter this amount on Form 4137, Social Security and Medicare Tax on Unreported Tip Income. You get an earful about this form in Chapter 8.

Box 10: Dependent-care benefits

If your employer has a daycare plan or provides daycare services, this box includes the reimbursement from your employer for daycare costs or the value of the daycare services that your employer provides. If you have elected to put up to $5,000 into a Section 125 (cafeteria plan) to pay qualified dependent care expenses, the amount you put into that plan will also be included here. Any amount over $5,000 is taxable to you and has been included in box 1 — don't report it again!

You need to fill out Form 2441, Child and Dependent Care Expenses, if you're filing a Form 1040. This form is used for two reasons:

» To find out if you qualify for the child and dependent care credit (and how much that will be)

» To see if any portion of the dependent care benefits shown in box 10 of your Form W-2 is taxable

Take a look at Chapter 16 to discover how to complete these forms. They're not difficult, but you do need to gather some information beforehand.

If your box 10 shows less than $5,000, but your Form 2441 (or Schedule 2) indicates that a portion of the amount you had deducted for dependent care is taxable, add that amount to line 1 of your 1040 (or 1040A), and write "DCB" (dependent care benefits) next to it.

Box 12: See instructions for box 12

This cryptic message is meant to direct you to the instructions on the reverse side of your W-2 to find out what the symbols in this box mean. This box includes your 401(k) or 403(b) contributions, the premium on group life insurance of more than $50,000 (that amount also is included in box 1), nontaxable sick pay, employer contributions to your medical savings account, and uncollected Social Security and Medicare taxes on tips that you reported to your employer (and that your employer wasn't able to collect from you — the letter A will be next to the amount). Uncollected Social Security tax is added to your final tax bill and is reported on Schedule 2, line 5, and then transferred to Form 1040, line 17, with any other taxes you might owe. A list of codes, A through HH, on the back of your W-2 explains what each code stands for in box 12. Some of the items entered in boxes 12a through 12d also are entered in box 1 (Wages); others aren't. If an amount in box 12 of your W-2 is already included in box 1, make sure that you don't enter it again on line 1 of your 1040. You don't want to pay more tax than you have to, do you? A silly question, but we thought we'd ask it anyhow.

DIFFERENT DEFINITIONS OF WHAT YOU EARNED

Many of the boxes on your W-2 include wage information that you don't need to include on your Form 1040. Think of them as FYI boxes. They simply show you the different ways that the IRS computes income for assessing different taxes.

For example, box 3, "Social Security wages," reports the amount of your wages for the tax year that is subject to Social Security taxation (not the benefits that the Social Security Administration is paying you!). Your Social Security wages may differ from your wages as reported in box 1 because some types of income are exempt from income tax but aren't exempt from Social Security tax. For example, if you put $3,000 in a 401(k) retirement plan in 2021, box 3 is going to be $3,000 higher than box 1.

Box 5, "Medicare wages and tips," reports the amount of your wages that is subject to Medicare tax. For most people, their wages that are subject to Medicare equal their total wages that are reported in box 1. Although the amount of your wages that is subject to Social Security tax is 6.2 percent up to $142,800, there is no maximum on wages subject to the 1.45 percent Medicare tax.

Box 7, "Social Security tips," is the amount of tips that you received and reported to your employer. This amount is included in box 1, so don't count it again!

Box 11, "Nonqualified plans," pertains to retirement plans in which you can't defer the tax. Distributions to an employee from a nonqualified or a nongovernmental Section 457(b) (Deferred Compensation Plan) are reported in box 11 and in box 1. Distributions from governmental Section 457(b) plans are reported on Form 1099-R. Be thankful that this box applies to only a few people.

Box 12, "See instructions for box 12," is for entering things like 401(k) contributions (code D), excludable moving expenses for members of the military (P), non-taxable combat pay (Q), adoption benefits (T), employer contributions to your Health Savings Account (W), designated Roth contributions under Section 401(k) (AA) and 403(b) (BB), and the cost of employer-sponsored health coverage (DD). Taxable fringe benefits, such as your personal use of a company car and reimbursed employee business expenses, are included in box 1 of your W-2 and not here.

The first $5,250 of employer-paid educational expenses is tax-free. Although benefits above that amount are taxable, see Chapter 9, lines 21–27, to determine whether you can claim a deduction for any portion of the taxable amount. The exclusion now applies to graduate-level courses. Aren't you glad you went back to school so that you can understand all this stuff? Up to $270 per month of employer-provided parking and $270 per month for the total of commuter transit passes and commuter van pools are considered tax-free fringe benefits (these are the 2021 amounts). If, however, you opt for the cash, they're taxable.

Box 13: Statutory employee

Full-time life insurance salespeople, agents, commission drivers, traveling salespeople, and certain homeworkers can file as self-employed rather than as employees. This status enables them to deduct their business expenses on Form 1040, Schedule C (Profit or Loss From Business).

If you want to deduct your business expenses on Schedule C and "Statutory Employee" is checked in box 13 of your W-2, report the amount of your W-2's box 1 on Schedule C, not line 1 of your Form 1040. By doing it this way, you can deduct all your travel, auto, and other business-related expenses instead of having to claim them as itemized deductions. (See Chapter 13 for loads of Schedule C stuff.) Line 1 of Schedule C has a box to check if you're claiming business expenses as a statutory employee.

If the statutory employee box is checked, congratulations! Since miscellaneous itemized deductions are no longer deductible, being able to deduct your business expenses on Schedule C means you won't lose them, unlike your friends who don't have the statutory employee box checked.

Line 2a: Taxable interest income

Add up all of your interest income from boxes 1 and 3 of all of your Form 1099-INTs, and boxes 1, 2, and 6 of any Form 1099-OIDs you may have (for any so-called zero-coupon bonds you may own) — if the total is $1,500 or less, enter that amount on this line. If this amount is more than $1,500, you must complete Schedule B. No biggie! Schedule B is easy to complete, with the exception of a couple of questions regarding foreign accounts at the bottom of Schedule B. For more information, you have permission to cruise to Chapter 12 to dive further into that schedule. When you get the total, come back and fill it in. Except for interest from municipal bonds, all the interest that you earn is taxable. If you need examples, the IRS publications have pages of them. But don't report the interest that you earn on your traditional IRA or other tax-deferred retirement account; any money you earn in those accounts is taxed only when you withdraw the funds.

If you keep lots of your money in bank accounts, you may be missing out on free opportunities to earn higher interest rates. Chapter 24 discusses money market funds, a higher yielding alternative to bank accounts, and shows you ways to keep more of your investment income.

Line 2b: Tax-exempt interest

In the past, because municipal bond interest wasn't taxable, you didn't receive a 1099 showing the tax-exempt interest you received. Now box 8 of Form 1099-INT and box 11 of Form 1099-OID list the municipal bond interest paid to you, and Form 1099-INT, box 9, gives you the portion of the box 8 number that comes from so-called private activity bonds, or municipal bonds that are actually funding joint public-private projects, such as privately owned utilities or football stadiums.

Even though you may not have to pay tax on tax-exempt interest, these numbers are important in figuring out how much of your Social Security benefits may be subject to tax and in allocating itemized deductions between taxable and tax-exempt income. Interest from private activity bonds is listed because it's taxable under the dreaded Alternate Minimum Tax.

Surprisingly, some people who invest money in tax-exempt bonds actually shouldn't. These people often aren't in a high enough income tax bracket to benefit. If your taxable income isn't at least $40,525 and if you're filing as a single (or $81,050 if married filing jointly), you shouldn't invest heavily in tax-exempt bonds. You'd be better off moving at least some of your money into taxable bonds or stocks (where gains can be taxed at rates as low as 5 percent,

10 percent, or 15 percent). See Chapter 24 for more information about investments that are subject to more favorable tax rates.

Line 3a: Ordinary dividends income

In 2003, dividends were much in the news as President George W. Bush pushed through tax changes that reduced the income tax rate on corporate dividends to 15 percent for most people, and a princely 0 percent for taxpayers in the 10 or 12 percent brackets in 2021. So, this change must mean that when you receive your Form 1099-DIV, Dividends and Distributions, everything on it will be taxed at no more than 12 percent. Right? Wrong! The current rates now max out at 20 percent (plus an additional 3.8 percent for higher income earners).

Box 1a of your Form 1099-DIV includes the amount of all the ordinary dividends (not capital gains), whether qualified for the lower rate or not. If you have more than one 1099-DIV, add together all the amounts in box 1a, and plop the total on line 9a of your Form 1040. If you're using Schedule B because your total dividend income is greater than $1,500, you'll carry the number from line 6 of those schedules over to line 8a of your 1040. Easy as pie!

Form 1099-DIV includes all kinds of dividends and distributions from all sorts of companies, credit unions, real estate investment entities, and so forth. Some of these may qualify for the special "qualified dividends" tax rates; others don't. If you have an entry in box 1b of your 1099-DIV, make sure you check out Chapter 12, which explains everything to do with dividends in much greater detail.

TIP

Although you aren't required to file 1040 Schedule B when your dividend income is less than $1,500, if you have more than a couple of Form 1099-DIVs arriving in your mailbox, you may want to anyway. One of the most common reasons for the IRS to contact you is because what you report on your return doesn't match the information they've gathered about you from other sources. The more detail you can give on your return, the easier it is to find the discrepancies when they occur. These schedules are probably the easiest IRS forms ever devised, and you'll have absolutely no problems completing them. Again, check out Chapter 12 to find out how to complete Schedule B.

Line 3b: Qualified dividends

It would be really easy for us to tell you to just add together all the amounts in box 1b of your 1099-DIV and write that number onto line 3b of your Form 1040. Oh, if only life were that simple.

Companies who can attest to whether or not their dividends qualify for the special rates fill out Form 1099-DIVs; what they don't know is whether or not you've held the stock for the required period of time so that your period of stock ownership qualifies. Remember, in order for a dividend to be eligible for these lower rates, not only does the type of dividend payment matter, but also the length of time you've owned the security. Not all dividends reported to you on line 1b qualify; only you can make that determination. Check out the rules in Chapter 12 regarding qualifying dividends.

WARNING

If you're manually preparing your return and you do finally end up with a number on line 3b of your 1040, be sure to calculate your tax using the tax computation worksheet that we provide at line 16 in Chapter 10. In this instance, relying on the tax tables is a sure way to overpay your tax. Of course, if you have only $10 of qualified dividends, and you don't have a tax software program that automatically calculates your tax, we understand when you decide that making the computations necessary for your $10 to be taxed at the lower 0 percent or 12 percent rates is hardly worth the hassle.

Because we've been talking about the 1099-DIV extensively here, just a quick heads up — long-term capital gains distributions that have been paid to you from either a mutual fund or from a corporation during 2021 are reported to you on Form 1099-DIV, lines 2a through 2f. If you have no other capital gains or losses for 2021, you can list these gains shown on Form 1099-DIV, line 2a only on Form 1040, line 7 and check the box next to the line; you don't need to bother with completing Schedule D. If you have any items on Form 1099-DIV, lines 2b through 2f, or you have other capital gains or losses to report, you're going to have to fill out Schedule D first. Sorry!

Lines 4a and 4b: Total IRA distributions

One of the benefits from all those years of hard work and diligent savings is that someday, hopefully, you'll be able to enjoy and live off the fruits of your labor. When you take distributions from your Individual Retirement Account (IRA), you'll receive a Form 1099-R, Distributions from Pensions, Annuities, Retirement or Profit-Sharing Plans, IRAs, Insurance Contracts, etc.

If you withdrew money from an IRA in 2021, your bank or broker will send you Form 1099-R (see Figure 5-4).

		CORRECTED (if checked)	
PAYER'S name, street address, city or town, state or province, country, ZIP or foreign postal code, and telephone no.	**1** Gross distribution $	OMB No. 1545-0119 **2021** Form **1099-R**	**Distributions From Pensions, Annuities, Retirement or Profit-Sharing Plans, IRAs, Insurance Contracts, etc.**
	2a Taxable amount $		
	2b Taxable amount not determined ☐	Total distribution ☐	**Copy B**
PAYER'S TIN	RECIPIENT'S TIN	**3** Capital gain (included in box 2a) $	**4** Federal income tax withheld $	**Report this income on your federal tax return. If this form shows federal income tax withheld in box 4, attach this copy to your return.**
RECIPIENT'S name		**5** Employee contributions/ Designated Roth contributions or insurance premiums $	**6** Net unrealized appreciation in employer's securities $	
Street address (including apt. no.)		**7** Distribution code(s)	IRA/ SEP/ SIMPLE ☐	**8** Other $ %	
City or town, state or province, country, and ZIP or foreign postal code		**9a** Your percentage of total distribution %	**9b** Total employee contributions $	This information is being furnished to the IRS.
10 Amount allocable to IRR within 5 years $	**11** 1st year of desig. Roth contrib.	**12** FATCA filing requirement ☐	**14** State tax withheld $ $	**15** State/Payer's state no.	**16** State distribution $ $
Account number (see instructions)		**13** Date of payment	**17** Local tax withheld $ $	**18** Name of locality	**19** Local distribution $ $

Form **1099-R** www.irs.gov/Form1099R Department of the Treasury - Internal Revenue Service

FIGURE 5-4: Form 1099-R tells you about distributions made from your retirement accounts.

Source: Internal Revenue Service

As a general rule, distributions made from a traditional IRA are fully taxable unless you made nondeductible contributions to the IRA, which we explain in the upcoming instructions for box 2a of the 1099-R. Here's a rundown of the important boxes that you need to read on your 1099-R to report an IRA distribution on Form 1040.

WARNING

If you turned 72 in 2021, you now must begin taking required minimum distributions (RMDs). The old rule of being able to wait until the year following the year in which you turn 70½ has been changed for anyone who turned age 70 after June 30, 2019; the age to begin taking RMDs has been increased to 72, but you now must begin taking that first required distribution by April 1 of the year after the year you turned that age. If you wait until the beginning of the year following your 72nd birthday, you'll also have to take a second distribution in that same year, by December 31.

Box 1: Gross distribution (Form 1099-R)

This box represents the amount of money that you withdrew from your IRA and that was reported to the IRS. Make sure that it's correct by checking to see whether the figure matches the amount withdrawn from your IRA account statement. If you made a nondeductible contribution to an IRA — that's an IRA contribution for which you didn't take a tax deduction and thus filed Form 8606, Nondeductible IRAs — write the number from box 1 on line 4a of your Form 1040. The taxable portion of your IRA that you computed on Form 8606 is entered on line 4b. See Chapter 17 for information about how to fill out the form. However, if your IRA distribution is fully taxable (see the next section), don't make an entry on line 4a; write the number on line 4b instead.

Box 2a: Taxable amount

This box contains the taxable amount of your IRA distribution. However, the payer of an IRA distribution doesn't have enough information to compute whether your entire IRA distribution is taxable. Therefore, if you simply enter the amount reported in box 1 on Form 1040 (line 4b) as being fully taxable, you'll overpay your tax if you made nondeductible contributions to your IRA. If you made nondeductible contributions, you must compute the nontaxable portion of your distribution on Form 8606. And you must attach Form 8606 to your return. We show you all you need to know about this form in Chapter 17.

Box 7: Distribution code

A number code is entered in this box. Here are some of the most popular:

>> **Code 1:** Early distribution, no known exception. You may know of an exception that you qualify for, but if you didn't notify the company that holds your account, they will apply this code to your distribution. You do have the ability to correct this on your tax return with the exception that applies.

>> **Code 2:** Annuity exception

>> **Code 3:** Disability exception

>> **Code 4:** Death exception

>> **Code 7:** Indicated in box 7 if you're at least 59½ years old. That way the IRS knows that the 10 percent penalty for an early distribution doesn't apply.

›› Code G: Direct rollover from a qualified plan to another qualified plan. The IRS says that, if you made a so-called "trustee-to-trustee" transfer (you never saw the money; instead, the original company that held the accounts sends the money directly to the new company that will be holding the account), you don't need to report this transfer on your Form 1040. However, in our experience, its best to include this as a nontaxable distribution on line 4a, Form 1040, so that all reporting information in the IRS's systems matches up exactly with what is on your return.

COMPUTING REQUIRED RETIREMENT ACCOUNT WITHDRAWALS

If you reached age 72 in 2021, you had to begin withdrawing at least a minimum amount from your retirement accounts. The minimum amount you must withdraw at 72 is computed by using the IRS life-expectancy table in this sidebar. An important exception to using this life-expectancy table benefits those of you with spouses who are more than 10 years younger than you. You can use a more advantageous life-expectancy table. Using this other life-expectancy table means that you're not required to take out as much as with the standard life-expectancy table.

Here's an example of how to compute the minimum amount that must be withdrawn: If you turn 72 in 2021, divide the value of your account on the preceding December 31 — say it was $200,000 — by the number of payout years next to your age in the life-expectancy table. In your case, it's 25.6 years. So, by April 1, 2022, you must withdraw at least $7,812,50 ($200,000 ÷ 25.6). Then, on or before December 31, 2022, you divide the balance in the account on December 31, 2021, by 24.7, and withdraw at least that amount from your account.

Minimum Distribution Life Expectancy Table (Uniform Lifetime)

Age	Payout Years	Age	Payout Years	Age	Payout Years
70	27.4	77	21.2	84	15.5
71	26.5	78	20.3	85	14.8
72	25.6	79	19.5	86	14.1
73	24.7	80	18.7	87	13.4
74	23.8	81	17.9	88	12.7
75	22.9	82	17.1	89	12.0
76	22.0	83	16.3	90	11.4

Single Life Expectancy Table, Appendix B, IRS Publication 590-B can be found at www.irs.gov/publications/p590b#en_US_2020_publink100035552

The IRS Table goes to age 115 and older. Supplement to Publication 590, *Individual Retirement Arrangements (IRAs),* contains the entire table all the way to age 115 (it's Table III), and the life-expectancy table for someone whose spouse is more than 10 years younger (it's Table II). If you're 72, and your spouse is 45, instead of having to use 25.6 years as your life expectancy, Table II in Supplement to Publication 590 enables you to use 39.3 years.

(continued)

(continued)

You can find three lifetime-expectancy tables in the Supplement to Publication 590. Table III (illustrated in this sidebar) is the Uniform Lifetime Table that IRA owners use when they're required to start making withdrawals. Table I (referred to as the Single Life Table) is for beneficiaries of an inherited IRA. IRA owners whose spouses are more than 10 years younger can use Table II.

Note: If you have more than one IRA, you don't have to take a minimum amount out of each account. Tally the total of all your IRAs before computing the minimum amount you must withdraw. You can take that amount from any of your IRAs. With other types of retirement accounts (non-IRAs), you have to withdraw the minimum from each account.

Your bank or broker is required to notify the IRS on Form 5498, IRA Contribution Information, (with a copy to you) that a minimum distribution from your IRA was required. On the 2021 form, box 11 will be checked to indicate that a minimum distribution is required in 2022. They're also obliged to compute the required minimum amount whenever asked to do so. But please be careful — they're only aware of accounts they hold, not the total amount you have in all your IRA accounts. Make sure you add up all the minimum distributions amounts from all accounts to be certain you're taking enough out in any given year.

TAX CUT

If you turned 72 in 2020, you're going to want to read this, as you may have missed it in the waves of significant legislation and changes that have occurred in the last two years. If you normally would have had an RMD required in 2020, you may be aware that 2020 RMDs were suspended under the CARES Act. Fair enough, but 2020 is done and dusted. Except that it's not. If your 72nd birthday happened in 2020, and you were required, under ordinary circumstances, to take your first RMD by April 1, 2021, that first RMD has also been suspended. You are required, though, to take the RMD distribution that must happen by December 31, 2021. We thought you'd like to know.

TIP

Make sure that you read the terms of your IRA agreement that you signed when you opened your account so that you understand all your withdrawal options.

Distributions before 59½

If you withdraw money from your IRA before you turn 59½, not only do you have to include that amount in your income, but you may also owe a 10 percent additional tax on the taxable amount that you withdrew (your nondeductible contributions aren't subject to the 10 percent additional tax). The additional tax is computed on Form 5329, Additional Taxes on Qualified Plans (Including IRAs) and Other Tax-Favored Accounts. Attach the form to your return and carry over the additional tax to Schedule 2, Form 1040, line 8. The additional tax doesn't apply to IRA distributions that are paid because of death or disability, paid over your life expectancy, or rolled over to another IRA.

The 10 percent additional tax also doesn't apply to withdrawals from an IRA used to pay medical expenses in excess of 7.5 percent of your income. Additionally, anyone receiving unemployment for 12 consecutive weeks can withdraw money to pay health insurance premiums without paying the additional tax. Self-employed people out of work for 12 weeks also can make penalty-free withdrawals to pay their health insurance premiums.

TIP

The 10 percent additional tax doesn't apply to distributions paid over your lifetime or the joint lives of you and your beneficiary. You can switch out of this method after you reach 59½ and after you've used it for five years — for example, you're 56 years old and need some dough. You start taking out annual amounts based on your life expectancy. Read the IRS Supplement to Publication 590 (*Individual Retirement Arrangements*) and then follow the illustration we provide in the sidebar "Computing required retirement account withdrawals" for the amount you have to withdraw every year. After receiving distributions based on your life expectancy for at least five years, you can switch out of this method. At age 61, you can withdraw the remaining balance or any part of it if you want to. You don't have to make this election for all your IRAs. You can use it with the IRA that has the largest or smallest balance.

TIP

Penalty-free (but taxable) withdrawals are allowed for the purchase of a first home and to pay college expenses. This exception to the additional tax includes the first home of you and your spouse, child, or grandchild. Penalty-free withdrawals for higher education also apply to you and education expenses of your spouse, child, or grandchild. Withdrawals for graduate school also are penalty-free. No limits are placed on amounts that you withdraw for college expenses. What expenses qualify? Tuition fees, books, and room and board — as long as the student is enrolled on at least a half-time basis.

A first home doesn't mean your first ever — it simply means that you didn't own one within two years of the withdrawal. For example, you sold your home, lived in a rented apartment for three years, and then purchased a new home — this purchase qualifies for the $10,000 penalty-free withdrawal. The homebuyer's exception has a limit of $10,000, but you can stretch the withdrawals over several years. For example, if you withdraw $3,000 in December, you can withdraw $7,000 the following January. You must, however, use the funds within 120 days of withdrawal to buy, build, or rebuild a "first home." Your lifetime limit is $10,000; so, after you take out $10,000, that's it.

A married couple can each withdraw up to $10,000, penalty-free, from their respective IRAs. For example, David and Betsy have their own IRAs; they can take out $10,000 from each account, but they can't take $20,000 from one account.

WARNING

The rules for withdrawals from a traditional IRA and a Roth IRA are dramatically varied and different from one another. Chapter 7 has the lowdown on Roth IRAs.

Transfers pursuant to divorce

TECHNICAL STUFF

The transfer of an IRA account as a result of a divorce or maintenance decree isn't taxable to you or your former spouse, nor is it subject to the 10 percent additional tax penalty provided your divorce decree requires that you transfer all or part of your IRA to your former spouse, even if one or both of you are younger than 59½.

You can take two approaches to making sure there is no 10 percent additional tax assessed when you transfer your IRA to your ex-spouse.

>> Your ex-spouse can open their own IRA, and you can then make a so-called trustee-to-trustee transfer between the accounts.

>> In the case of a total transfer, you may decide just to rename the account you already have, putting your spouse's name and Social Security number on it instead of yours.

WARNING

Don't allow your current IRA custodian to hand you a check and then you attempt to sign it over to your ex-spouse. One hapless taxpayer discovered this mistake the hard way. He withdrew the funds from his IRA and endorsed the check over to his ex-spouse. Although the transfer was required by his separation agreement, he ran afoul of the requirement that he didn't transfer his interest in his IRA account. The Tax Court sided with the IRS in determining that his interest in his IRA was extinguished when he withdrew the funds.

Also, please make sure that, if you are transferring all or any part of an IRA to your soon-to-be ex, the divorce decree includes an order for a Qualified Domestic Relations Order (QDRO). With a QDRO in place, your ex is responsible for any taxes owed on the transfer; without it, you not only have to pay the money to your ex, but you're on the hook for all the taxes, too.

Inherited IRAs

When you inherit an IRA, you usually have the option of either withdrawing the money and paying tax on the amount withdrawn or taking the money out in dribs and drabs so the IRA can continue sheltering the balance in the account from tax. We say "usually," because in some instances the IRA owner predetermines whether upon their death the account will be paid out all at once or over time. The 10 percent additional tax that normally applies to withdrawals made to someone before reaching 59½ doesn't apply to beneficiaries.

Determining how the money is taken out of the IRA and over what period of time is based on whether the account was left to a spouse (spouses have two additional choices that we explain in the next section) or to someone else. The SECURE Act of 2020 significantly changed the rules regarding how beneficiaries who inherit an IRA are required to take the money out of the account, and over what period of time. It created three categories of beneficiaries: eligible designated beneficiary (which includes the surviving spouse, although the rules for surviving spouses are a little different than for everyone else), designated beneficiary, and all others.

According to the SECURE Act of 2020, there are now three main categories of beneficiaries (see Table 5-1):

>> Eligible designated beneficiaries, which include the surviving spouse, minor children, disabled beneficiaries, chronically ill beneficiaries, and any individual who is not more than ten years younger than the decedent

>> Designated beneficiaries, which include every other natural person who the decedent may have named as a beneficiary of the account(s)

>> Non-designated beneficiaries, including the decedent's estate, trust, or charity

Table 5-1 shows how the eligible designated beneficiaries and non-designated beneficiaries may take distributions, over what time period, and governed by whose age.

Table 5-1   Designated Beneficiary

	Eligible Designated Beneficiary: Spouse Only	Eligible Designated Beneficiary: Non-Spouse	No Designated Beneficiary (including an estate, charity, or some trusts)
IRA owner dies on or after required beginning date	Spouse may treat as their own **or** Distribute over spouse's life using Table I* • Use spouse's current age each year **or** Distribute based on owner's age using Table I* • Use owner's age as of birthday in year of death • Reduce beginning life expectancy by 1 for each subsequent year • Can take owner's RMD in year of death	Distribute using Table I • Use younger of 1) beneficiary's age or 2) owner's age at birthday in year of death • Determine beneficiary's age at year-end following year of owner's death • Use oldest age of multiple beneficiaries • Reduce beginning life expectancy by 1 for each subsequent year • Can take owner's RMD for year of death	Table I • Use owner's age as of birthday in year of death • Reduce beginning life expectancy by 1 for each subsequent year • Can take owner's RMD for year of death • Distributions must be completed within 10 years of the death of the owner
IRA owner dies before required beginning date	Spouse may treat as their own **or** Take entire balance by end of 10th year following year of death **or** Distribute based on Table I • Use spouse's current age each year • Distributions do not have to begin until owner would have turned 72	Take entire balance by end of 10th year following year of death **or** Distribute based on Table I • Use beneficiary's age at year-end following year of owner's death • Reduce beginning life expectancy by 1 for each subsequent year	Take entire balance by end of 10th year following year of death, unless the owner died in a year ending before 2020, or is not an individual, in which case the entire balance must be withdrawn by the end of the 5th year.

* *Table 1 - Single Life Expectancy, Appendix B, IRS Publication 590-B can be found at* www.irs.gov/publications/p590b#en_US_2020_publink100035552

Determining who is an eligible designated beneficiary

It's pretty clear that, if you're the surviving spouse, you qualify as an eligible designated beneficiary, and the rules in the first column of Table 5-1 apply to you.

But if you're not the surviving spouse, you may be unclear whether you qualify as an eligible designated beneficiary, or only as a designated beneficiary. And the difference here can be significant on your tax return.

Other than the surviving spouse, here are the categories of eligible designated beneficiaries for inherited IRA accounts under the SECURE Act of 2020, and the distribution rules associated with them:

>> **Minor child:** A minor child, as described in the Internal Revenue Code and the regulations, is someone who has not reached the age of majority, or someone who has not completed a "specific course of education" and is under age 26. During this period, the child may use the life expectancy rules shown in Table 5-1 to determine the annual RMDs. Once the child reaches age 26, they revert to the rules for a designated beneficiary, and the remaining funds in the account now must be taken out over the next ten years.

>> **Disabled person:** Someone who is unable to engage in any substantial gainful activity by reason of a medically determinable physical or mental impairment, which can be expected to result in death or to be of long-continued and indefinite determination. This person must be able to prove their disability and is allowed to use the life expectancy rules shown in Table 5-1.

>> **Chronically ill person:** Someone who is unable to perform at least two activities of daily living for a period of at least 90 days due to loss of functional capacity, or having a disability that aligns with that, and that requires substantial supervision to keep the person safe due to cognitive impairment. Like the disabled person, this person may use the life expectancy rules shown in Table 5-1.

>> **Any person who is not more than ten years younger than the decedent:** Such a person may also use the life expectancy rules shown in Table 5-1.

Designated beneficiaries and the ten-year rule under the SECURE Act of 2020

If you can't find yourself described in the eligible designated beneficiary categories outlined previously and you're not the surviving spouse, the SECURE Act of 2020 changed the distributions rules for inherited IRAs in a major way: It states that all funds in either a traditional or Roth IRA must be distributed within ten years after the decedent's date of death. So, if you inherit an IRA from your grandparent who died in 2021, for example, you are now required to take enough distributions between your grandparent's date of death in 2021 and 2031, and of course, pay any taxes owed on those distributions.

But wait, there's more. The IRS has recently come out with guidance that indicates that you're also not allowed to take distributions in years one through nine, but instead you are required to take RMDs in each of the first nine years and then empty whatever is left in the account in the tenth year. As with every newish piece of legislation, there are kinks to be worked out here. The IRS has not issued any proposed regulations yet, so it's not clear if the IRS's interpretation of the SECURE Act is correct, or merely wishful thinking on their part. However, in the interest of trying to prepare a return that won't generate a ton of notices from the IRS, it's probably safe to assume that you're going to want to take annual distributions based on the life expectancy tables referenced in Table 5-1 in years one through nine or at least until the IRS comes out with some definitive guidance.

Non-designated beneficiaries

Not everyone can be designated. There are many people who fail to write a Last Will and Testament, or who don't ever get around to naming beneficiaries on their accounts, especially their retirement accounts. There are as many reasons for failing to cross the t's and dot the i's in an estate plan as there are grains of sand on the beach, and we won't go into them here. If you fall into this category, you may already know that all the rules and regulations mentioned in this chapter don't apply to you. And you'd be correct.

One of the purposes of the SECURE Act of 2020 was to create a federal tax revenue generator without actually raising tax rates. And the way this was accomplished was by shortening the time frame under which you had to empty out inherited retirement accounts. The old rules allowed you to stretch them out over the course of your lifetime; clearly, even designated beneficiaries have now had that shortened to ten years if they are unable to use the life expectancy tables. But for you, the rules are even more dire: If the original owner of the IRA was not yet required to take distributions and died before January 1, 2020, you must empty out the account within five years. If the owner died after December 31, 2019, you're eligible for the ten-year payout plan if you're a person. If the deceased IRA owner was already taking required distributions, however, you catch a break — you are allowed to use the original owner's life expectancy as a guide to your annual RMDs, as shown in Table 5-1.

There are many beneficiaries who aren't people, though, and we'd be wrong if we didn't go into the rules for them. If the decedent failed to designate a beneficiary, or even worse, designated their estate or trust, the estate or trust is required to pay out the entirety of the account by December 31 of the fifth year after death. So, if the decedent dies on April 15, 2021, for example, the full amount of the IRA must be distributed no later than December 31, 2026.

TIP

This rule also applies to IRAs that are given to charity, but in this case, there is no tax consequence to the charity and no danger that the charity will be pushed into a higher tax bracket. It's a charity, and its income isn't subject to income tax.

WARNING

Although an estate can be named as a beneficiary, it isn't considered a *designated beneficiary* under the minimum distribution rules because an estate doesn't have a life expectancy. If the account passes to someone under state law (next-of-kin rule), the IRA also is considered not to have a named beneficiary. However, if the terms of the IRA permit, a beneficiary can be named in a will or by some other election — a letter or note, for example.

Withdrawal of nondeductible contributions

If you made nondeductible contributions to your IRA, or if you inherited an IRA from someone who made nondeductible contributions, use Form 8606 to compute the taxable portion of your withdrawal. You don't have to pay tax on nondeductible contributions that you withdraw — you already have. The total of your IRA distributions is entered on line 7 of Form 8606; enter that same total on line 4a of Form 1040. Carry over the figure from line 15c of Form 8606 to line 4b of the 1040. That's the taxable portion.

Loss on an IRA

TIP

You can deduct losses on Roth and nondeductible IRAs. Say that you invest $2,000 in a Roth. The value drops to $1,500. You decide to minimize your losses and withdraw the $1,500. Deduct your $500 loss as a miscellaneous itemized deduction on line 23, Schedule A, Form 1040. To report a loss in a Roth, you have to liquidate all your Roths. This liquidation rule also applies to losses on nondeductible contributions to a traditional IRA.

Lines 5a and 5b: Total pensions and annuities

Here's where you report your retirement benefits from your taxable pension, profit-sharing, 401(k), SEP, or Keogh plans. How these plans are taxed depends on whether you receive them in the form of an annuity (paid over your lifetime) or in a lump sum.

The amounts that you fill in on lines 5a and 5b are reported on a Form 1099-R that you receive from your employer or your plan's custodian. If the amount that you receive is fully taxable, complete only line 5b and leave line 5a blank.

TIP

Just like with IRAs, the age at which you're required to start taking distributions from your annuity pension, profit-sharing, 401(k) plan, SEP, or Keogh plans has been increased from 70½ to 72 for people who reached age 70½ after December 31, 2019.

Pensions and annuities

If you didn't pay or contribute to your pension or annuity using money you already paid tax on — or if your employer didn't withhold part of the cost from your pay while you worked — then the amount that you receive each year is fully taxable. The amount that you contributed, for which you received a deduction — such as tax-deductible contributions to a 401(k), SEP, IRA, or Keogh — isn't considered part of your cost.

If you paid part of the cost (that is, if you made nondeductible contributions or contributions that were then added to your taxable income on your W-2), you aren't taxed on the part that you contributed, because it represents a tax-free return of your investment. The rest of the amount that you receive is taxable. To compute this amount, you can use either the Simplified Method or the General Rule.

Simplified Method

TIP

You must use the *Simplified Method* for figuring the taxable amount of your pension or annuity if the starting date for your pension or annuity occurred after November 18, 1996, and the payments were from a qualified employee plan, a qualified employee annuity, or a qualified tax shelter annuity. The word *qualified* is tax jargon for a retirement plan approved by the IRS. You can't use this method if you were 75 or older at the starting date and if your payments were guaranteed for more than five years at the time the payments began. Who came up with this one? In case you're wondering whether you can use the Simplified Method if your pension began on or before November 18, 1996, the answer is yes — unless, that is, you're required to use the General Rule that we explain in a moment.

FAILING TO TAKE REQUIRED IRA DISTRIBUTIONS

If you haven't yet started withdrawals from your IRA and are getting to the age where you should, we must share some important information with you. (IRAs come in three varieties: deductible, nondeductible, and Roth IRAs. See Chapters 6 and 22 for more on these investment vehicles.)

If you turned 72 in 2021 and you haven't begun taking distributions from your IRA yet, you must take your first distribution by April 1, 2022. In addition, because you're now required to take annual distributions from your IRA, in 2022 you'll be making two distributions to yourself — one for 2021 (when you turned 72) and one for 2022.

Failure to take required distributions from a traditional IRA is a costly mistake because the IRS assesses a 50 percent penalty on the amount that you should have taken out. For example, when you forget to take a $4,000 required distribution, you'll owe a cool $2,000 in penalties. Ouch! If you've been stashing your retirement funds in a Roth (instead of a traditional) IRA, you can relax; minimum withdrawal rules don't apply to Roths because distributions from them are nontaxable anyway. So, should you choose, you can keep your Roth IRA intact and growing for as long as you want.

It is possible to have minimum distribution penalties reduced, but you need to act promptly. If you discover you should have been taking distributions, start now! The longer you delay, the higher the penalty, and the harder to convince the IRS to see the facts your way. After you've begun taking your distributions, you can start trying to talk your way out of the penalties. You need to attach a statement to your Form 5329, Additional Taxes on Qualified Plans (Including IRAs) and Other Tax-Favored Accounts, to explain why you didn't make the required distributions and why you shouldn't be penalized for that. Some good reasons are math errors or illness. Be contrite (I'm sorry, this won't happen again, and I've fixed my mistake), and be convincing. The "dog ate my address book" probably won't work here, but an unanticipated family upheaval probably will.

Even though the IRS instructs you to explain why the penalty should be excused and what steps you have taken to correct the error and to attach that explanation to Form 5329, the IRS nevertheless requires that you pay the penalty as computed on lines 52-55 of Part IX, Form 5329. If the IRS believes that you made your case, it will refund the penalty.

Because not parting with your money in the first place is a whole lot nicer, try this suggestion: On lines 52–55 of Form 5329, write "See attached explanation of why the penalty should be excused for reasonable error." Call it our version of "Go now and pay only when you have to." The only downside to taking this step: If the IRS doesn't waive the penalty, you'll have additional interest to pay.

Under the Simplified Method, the IRS allows you to declare as nontaxable part of the money that you receive from a certain number of payments made to you or to your beneficiary, based on your age when your pension or annuity started. The nontaxable portion is your after-tax contributions, if any, to the pension. Divide the amount of your contribution to the pension by the number of payments that the IRS allows. Use Table 5-2 to arrive at the nontaxable amount of each payment if your pension is based on one life or if it is based on two life expectancies and the pension starting date was before January 1, 1998. If your pension started before January 1, 1998, and it is based on two lives, use the age of the primary beneficiary, which usually is the employee.

Table 5-2   Simplified Method — One Life

Combined Age at Annuity Starting Date	Divide By	After 11-18-96
55 and under	300 payments	360 payments
More than 55 and under 60	260 payments	310 payments
More than 60 and under 65	240 payments	260 payments
More than 65 and under 70	170 payments	210 payments
More than 70	120 payments	160 payments

For reasons that we can't explain, Congress won't make it simple and pick the beginning of a year as the date for making a change. If you started receiving payments after November 18, 1996, you must use the payment schedule in the right-hand column of Table 5-2.

Here's another midstream change. If your retirement began in 1998 or in later years and your pension or annuity is being paid over the life expectancies of two or more retirees — for example, the life expectancies of you and your spouse — you have to use Table 5-3. What's your life expectancy? The IRS determines everything, so send for IRS Publication 575 (*Pension and Annuity Income* or access it online at https://www.irs.gov/pub/irs-pdf/p575.pdf.

Table 5-3   Simplified Method — Two Lives

Combined Age at Annuity Starting Date	Divide By
110 and under	410 payments
More than 110 and under 120	360 payments
More than 120 and under 130	310 payments
More than 130 and under 140	260 payments
More than 140	210 payments

Suppose that you retired at age 65 and began receiving $1,000 per month under a *joint and survivor annuity* with your spouse (that is, an annuity that pays a benefit to you or your spouse as long as one of you is still living). Your spouse is 60, and you contributed $31,000 to the pension. Divide the $31,000 by 310 (the amount for your combined age of 125). The resulting $100 is the monthly amount that you receive tax-free. If you live to collect more than the 310 payments, you'll have to pay tax on the full amount of your pension that you receive beyond that point. Your contribution includes amounts withheld from your paycheck and any contributions made by your employer that were reported as additional income.

If you die before you receive 310 payments, your spouse continues to exclude $100 from each payment until the number of payments received, when added to yours, totals 310. If your spouse dies before the 310 payments are made, a miscellaneous itemized deduction on your spouse's final tax return is allowed for the balance of the 310 payments remaining to be paid, multiplied by $100. If your spouse dies with 40 payments yet to be made, a $4,000 deduction would be allowed (40 × $100).

If your annuity starting date was after July 1, 1986, but before January 1, 1987, you can take the exclusion as long as you're receiving payments. You don't need to stop at the total number of payments you determined in Table 5-2.

General Rule

You must use the *General Rule* to figure the taxability of your pension or annuity that you receive from a *nonqualified* (not approved by the IRS) employee plan, or a private or commercial annuity, or from a qualified (IRS-approved) plan if you were 75 or older at the starting date and your payments were guaranteed for more than five years at the time they began. You can use the General Rule for a qualified plan that began on or before November 18, 1996 (but after July 1, 1986), if you do qualify or don't choose to use the Simplified Method.

Under the General Rule, a part of each payment is nontaxable because it's considered a return of your cost. The remainder of each payment (including the full amount of any later cost-of-living increases) is taxable. Finding the nontaxable part is extremely complex and requires you to use actuarial tables. For a full explanation and the tables you need, get IRS Publication 939 (*General Rule for Pensions and Annuities*) or consult a tax advisor.

The nontaxable amount remains the same under the General Rule even if the monthly payment increases. If your annuity starting date was after July 1, 1986, and before 1987, you continue to exclude the same nontaxable amount from each annuity payment for as long as you receive your annuity. If your annuity starting date is after 1986, your total exclusion over the years can't be more than your cost of the contract, reduced by the value of any refund feature. This means that you can't exclude more from tax than you contributed.

TAX CUT

If you (or a survivor annuitant) die before the cost is recovered, a miscellaneous itemized deduction is allowed for the unrecovered cost on your (or your survivor's) final income tax return.

Lump-sum distributions

If you were born before 1936, you can elect to have a lump-sum distribution taxed at a special optional method called *ten-year averaging*. To qualify for this special method, the lump sum must be your entire balance in all your employer's pension plans, and it must be paid within a single tax year. The distribution must be paid because of one of the following reasons:

>> You die.

>> You leave the firm.

>> You're self-employed and become totally and permanently disabled.

TIP

Instead of electing the special ten-year averaging, a lump-sum distribution from your employer's pension plan can be rolled over to an IRA or to your new employer's retirement plan. If you don't need the immediate use of the money, a rollover probably is your best bet, because it allows you to continue deferring taxation of the money. (Letting your employer transfer the money on your behalf is also best.) You don't have to roll over the entire amount. The part that you don't roll over is subject to tax. Voluntary after-tax contributions that you made to the plan can now be rolled over, but we advise against doing so, because such contributions are tax-free to you when received and aren't subject to the 20 percent withholding tax that lump-sum distributions are subject to. A lump-sum distribution is eligible for capital gain or special averaging treatment if the participant was in the plan for at least five years. We discuss these options further in this section.

WARNING

You can't roll over a hardship distribution from your employer's 401(k) plan to an IRA. It's not allowed. If you try it, you'll be taxed on the distribution from your 401(k) plus will be liable for penalties under the excess contribution rules governing your IRA. You probably weren't looking for this result, were you?

If you have your employer make a direct rollover from the retirement plan to your IRA, tax doesn't have to be withheld. On the other hand, if you receive the lump-sum payment directly, tax must be withheld because the IRS doesn't trust you to complete the rollover in time. *Note:* Remember you have 60 days from the receipt of the money to roll it over into an IRA. This creates a problem, because in order to avoid paying tax on any of the rollover, you're required to put the full amount into the new account, not the full amount less the tax withheld. So, in order to escape owing a barrel of taxes, you need to cough up the amount of the tax that was withheld when you open the new account with the understanding that the withheld taxes will be refunded to you in the next year. Remember, insisting on a trustee-to-trustee transfer, which doesn't even need to be reported to the IRS, is easier, less financially burdensome, and much less stressful.

TIP

If you don't roll over your withdrawal within 60 days due to factors beyond your control, the IRS may waive the 60-day requirement if you apply for its approval of an extension to the 60-day limit. Here are some of the excuses the IRS may approve for an extension to complete a rollover: being hospitalized, foul-ups by the post office, disasters, or circumstances beyond your control.

A single tax year means exactly that if you want to elect the ten-year averaging method. If, for example, you received $10,000 in 2021 and the balance in 2022, you're out of luck.

TIP

If your former employer's retirement plan includes the company's stock (say you work for GE, for example), you may want to transfer the stock to your taxable brokerage account instead of an IRA rollover account. Why? When you take the stock, you pay taxes only on the value at the time you purchased it and not the value when you left the company. For example, you bought shares through your company's retirement account that cost $10,000; the shares are now worth $100,000. You pay tax on $10,000 and not on the current value. And if you're younger than 55, the 10 percent penalty also is computed on the $10,000 value (see the section "Tax on early distributions" later in this chapter). Only when you sell the shares are you taxed on the appreciation in value, and then you're taxed at capital gain rates that can be as low as 0 percent but no more than the new maximum 20 percent rate (plus, of course, net investment income tax of 3.8 percent for those whose income exceeds certain limits).

Capital gains treatment

If you reached the age of 50 before 1986, you can choose to treat a portion of the taxable part of the lump-sum distribution as a capital gain that is taxable at the 15 percent or 20 percent rates. This treatment applies to the portion that you receive for your participation in the plan before 1974. You can select this treatment only once, and you use Form 4972, Tax on Lump-Sum Distributions, to make this choice.

The tax on the balance of the lump-sum distribution is computed under the ten-year averaging method described in the next section. For most people, a tidy sum can be saved between the capital gain and averaging methods. Box 3 of Form 1099-R contains the capital gain amount.

Special averaging method

If you reached age 50 before 1986 (you were probably born before 1936, right?), you can elect the ten-year averaging method of the ordinary income portion of your lump-sum distribution. (This procedure also includes the capital gain portion of the distribution if you don't choose capital gain treatment for it.) To qualify, you must elect to use special averaging on all lump-sum distributions received in the tax year.

To use special averaging, you must have been a participant in the plan for at least five full tax years. You can make only one lifetime election to use this method. If you choose the special averaging method, use Form 4972 and figure your tax as if you received the distributions spread across ten years in ten equal amounts, one for each year in the calculation.

When you treat the distribution as though you received it over ten years, you must use 1986 tax rates. The instructions accompanying Form 4972 contain a 1986 tax-rate schedule. Ten-year averaging can save you a bundle.

You pay the tax on the lump sum in the year that you receive it, even though the tax on the distribution is computed as if you received one-tenth of the distribution in each of the ten years. After you pay the tax, the balance is yours, free and clear.

Form 1099-R

If you receive a total distribution from a retirement plan, you'll receive a Form 1099-R. If the distribution qualifies as a lump-sum distribution, box 3 shows the capital gain amount, and box 2a minus box 3 shows the ordinary income amount. Code A is entered in box 7 if the lump sum qualifies for the ten-year special averaging. If you don't receive a Form 1099-R, or if you have questions about it, contact your plan administrator.

PENSION DISTRIBUTIONS ON FORM 1099-R

Pension distributions are reported on Form 1099-R, which is the same one used to report IRA distributions. The difference between how the information on an IRA distribution is reported to you and how the distribution from your pension is reported is as follows:

Box 3: If the distribution is a lump sum and you were a participant in the plan before 1974, this amount qualifies for capital gain treatment.

Box 5: Your after-tax contributions are entered here.

Box 6: Securities in your employer's company that you received are listed here. The appreciation in value isn't taxed until the securities are sold. Only the actual cost of the shares is taxed when they're received. See the earlier section "Lump-sum distributions."

Box 7: This box informs you if you are receiving a normal retirement payment, a distribution that's subject to the 10 percent penalty because you're under 59½, whether the distribution isn't subject to the penalty, or if it's a direct rollover to an IRA, and so on. Here is a list of the codes that you will most likely encounter in box 7:

- Code 1: Early distribution, no known exception
- Code 2: Early distribution, exception to 10 percent penalty applies
- Code 3: Disability
- Code 4: Death
- Code 7: Normal distribution
- Code 8: Excess contributions and earnings, or excess deferrals, taxable in 2008
- Code 9: Cost of current life insurance protection
- Code A: May be eligible for ten-year averaging
- Code G: Direct rollover to an IRA or another retirement plan
- Code J: Early distribution from Roth IRA and no known exception to the 10 percent penalty applies
- Code N: Recharacterized IRA contribution made for 2008 and recharacterized in 2008 (see Chapter 7, line 32)
- Code P: Distribution of excess contributions plus earnings or excess deferrals taxable in 2007
- Code Q: Qualified distribution from a Roth IRA
- Code R: Recharacterized IRA contribution made in 2007 and recharacterized in 2008 (see Chapter 7, line 32)
- Code S: Early distribution from a SIMPLE IRA in first two years, no known exception to 10 percent penalty
- Code T: Roth IRA distribution, exception applies

Box 8: If you have an entry here, seek tax advice.

Box 9a: Your share of a distribution if there are several beneficiaries.

Tax on early distributions

Distributions that you receive from your employer's retirement plan before the age of 59½ are subject to a 10 percent penalty and are taxable. But here are some of the exceptions to the 10 percent penalty on employer retirement plans, in the order of how frequently the IRS sees these exceptions:

» Death.

» Distributions made after you stopped working (retirement or termination) during or after the calendar year you reach age 55.

» Distributions made to you (to the extent you have deductible medical expenses in excess of 7.5 percent of your adjusted gross income). You don't have to itemize your deductions for this exception to apply.

» Distributions made under a Qualified Domestic Relations Order (QDRO), which is a divorce decree or order that spells out in specific detail who is to be awarded the retirement benefit. (See "Transfers pursuant to divorce" on line 4a where we discuss IRA distributions.)

» Distributions (after separation from service) paid over your lifetime or the joint lives of you and your beneficiary.

» Distributions to correct excess amounts in the plan.

» Total and permanent disability.

You report the penalty you have to pay on Form 5329, Additional Taxes Attributable to Qualified Retirement Plans (Including IRAs) and Other Tax-Favored Accounts, if none of the exceptions apply. Attach the form to your return and carry over the 10 percent to Form 1040, Schedule 2, line 8.

WARNING

The penalty-free (but taxable) withdrawals allowed for first-time homebuyers and for paying college tuition don't apply to your employer's pension plan, Keoghs, SEPs, or 401(k)s — only to IRAs.

Minimum distributions

The same rule that applies to IRAs also applies to pension plans for failing to take a minimum distribution by April 1 of the year following the year you turned 72. So does the exception to the rule for tax year 2020, when RMDs were suspended.

The 72 rule doesn't apply if you're still employed. You can delay making withdrawals until you retire. This rule doesn't apply to IRAs or to someone who owns 5 percent or more of a business.

Disability income

If you retire on disability, your pension usually is taxable. The way the IRS figures it, pensions are taxable, so how you retire shouldn't make a difference. However, nonpension payments made because of the permanent loss of use of part of the body or because of permanent disfigurement are exempt from tax. Sounds like a distinction without a difference.

If you're 65 or older (or if you're younger than 65 and are retired because your disability is total and permanent and you receive disability income), you may be able to claim a credit for the elderly or the disabled. You compute the credit on Schedule R (see Chapter 16).

If you contributed to a plan that paid a disability pension, the part of the pension that you receive that is attributable to your payments isn't subject to tax. You report all your taxable disability on line 1 of your 1040 until you reach the *minimum retirement age* — that is, the age stated in your plan when you're entitled to a regular retirement annuity — and then on line 5a or 5b. You must use the Simplified Method or the General Rule to compute the part of a disability pension that isn't taxable because of your contribution.

Veteran's Administration disability benefits are tax-free. If you're a military retiree and receive disability from another source than the VA, don't include in your income the amount of those benefits that are equal to your VA benefits.

TIP

Military and government disability pensions that you receive as the result of an injury or sickness that occurred in a combat or extra hazardous area are exempt from tax. So are disability payments made to a government employee as a result of a terrorist attack outside the United States. Since (and because of the events of) September 11, 2001, this provision covers all terrorist attacks, not only those occurring outside the United States and not only for government employees or the military. See Publication 3920 *(Tax Relief for Victims of Terrorist Attacks)*.

Here is a quick reference list on sickness and injury benefits:

>> **Benefits from an accident or health insurance policy:** Not taxable if you paid the insurance premiums.

>> **Compensation for permanent loss, or loss of use of a part or function of your body, or for permanent disfigurement:** Not taxable if paid because of the injury. The payment must be figured without regard to any period of absence from work, because payments for lost wages are taxable.

>> **Compensatory damages:** Not taxable if received for injury or sickness.

>> **Disability benefits:** Not taxable if received for loss of income or earning capacity because of an injury covered by a no-fault automobile policy.

>> **Federal Employees' Compensation Act (FECA):** Not taxable if paid because of personal injury or sickness. However, payments received as a continuation of pay for up to 45 days while a claim is being decided and pay received for sick leave while a claim is being processed are taxable.

>> **Life insurance:** Death benefit paid to a beneficiary is exempt from tax.

>> **Reimbursements for medical care:** Not taxable; the reimbursement may reduce your medical expense deduction.

>> **Workers' compensation:** Not taxable if paid under a workers' compensation policy because of a work-related injury or illness.

Effective August 21, 1996, damages received for age, gender, or racial discrimination, and injury to your reputation and emotional distress not related to physical injuries or sickness aren't tax-exempt. Prior to this change, courts had reached differing results on this issue.

EARLY RETIREES, WATCH YOUR STEP

People who retire early but continue working part-time to supplement their Social Security income may be in for a nasty surprise when they sit down to complete their tax returns.

If you're between the ages of 62 and full retirement age (66 and 2 months if you were born in 1955, 66 years and 4 months if you were born in 1956), you lose out on $1 of Social Security benefits for every $2 you earn above $18,960 for 2021. (Remember, this is earned income only; unearned income, such as from investments or a pension, doesn't penalize your benefits.)

This loss of benefits is known as the Social Security giveback, though it seems like a takeback to us. (At full retirement age, you can earn as much as you like without forfeiting any of your benefits.) Every year the full retirement age increases by two months until it reaches age 67.

Not only do you have this giveback to contend with, but more of your Social Security is subject to tax. Married couples with incomes above $44,000 and singles who make more than $34,000 will pay tax on 85 percent of their Social Security income.

Clearly, if you're not careful, working a little extra to add to your income from Social Security income can end up costing you money. Suppose that you earned $2,000 above the year 2021 threshold of $18,960 and, bad luck, it pushed you from the 12 to the 22 percent tax bracket. First, you pay 7.65 percent Social Security and Medicare tax on the extra $2,000 of income, which works out to $153. Next, you have to pay income tax on the extra $2,000 you earned, and to make matters worse, that extra income subjected an additional $1,000 of your Social Security to tax. Then you'd have to give back $1,000 of your Social Security benefit. Your cost of making that extra two grand: $1,628!

Our advice to early retirees still younger than the full retirement age: After you reach the 2021 earnings level of $18,960, take a vacation until December 31. One other point: Workers who take early retirement (after age 62 but before your full retirement age) and then reach full retirement age in 2021 can earn up to $50,520 in the months before they reach full retirement age without forfeiting benefits. Additionally, you don't lose $1 for every $2 you earn above $50,520. It's $1 for every $3 you earn above $50,520. Think of it as a gift for reaching full retirement age in 2021.

Lines 6a and 6b: Social Security benefits

Politicians don't want to do away with Social Security; they just want to pay fewer benefits and to tax more of it. As a result, they have made retirement more complicated. Here's how to figure out what to plug in.

REMEMBER

Don't forget that if you're married and file a joint return for 2021, you and your spouse must combine your incomes and your benefits when figuring whether any of your combined benefits are taxable. Even if your spouse didn't receive any benefits, you must add your spouse's income to yours when figuring whether any of your benefits are taxable.

Form SSA-1099

Every person who receives Social Security benefits will receive a Form SSA-1099. If you receive benefits on more than one Social Security record, you may receive more than one Form SSA-1099. Your gross benefits are shown in box 3 of Form SSA-1099, and your repayments are shown in box 4. The amount in box 5 shows your net benefits for 2021 (box 3 – box 4). This is the amount you use to figure whether any of your benefits are taxable. If you misplaced Form SSA-1099, you can order a duplicate at the Social Security by either creating an online account at ssa.gov/myaccount/ or by phoning 800-325-0778.

How much is taxable?

In order to determine the taxable portion of your Social Security income, add one half of your Social Security income to all of your other income, including tax-exempt interest. You must also include the following: interest from qualified U.S. savings bonds, employer-provided adoption benefits, foreign earned income or housing, and income earned by bona fide residents of American Samoa or Puerto Rico. The base income worksheet we give you (see the next section) shows you how to compute this amount.

IRS Publication 17 gives you the worksheets you need to figure out what part, if any, of your Social Security benefits you need to include on line 6b of your Form 1040. We provide you an easier set of worksheets right here that give you the same result — just pencil your numbers in over ours.

Base Income Worksheet

For example, say you're married filing jointly and have interest and dividend income of $10,000, a $20,000 pension, and you received $16,000 from Social Security.

1.	Total income (1040, line 9) without Social Security	$30,000
2.	Social Security (box 5, SSA-1099)	$16,000
3.	50 percent of line 2	$8,000
4.	Tax-exempt interest income (1040, line 2b)	$0
5.	Foreign earned income and housing exclusion (Form 2555, lines 45 and 50)	$0
6.	Other income (Form 1040, Schedule 1, line 9)	$0
7.	Qualified U.S. Savings Bond interest (Form 8815, line 14)	$0
8.	Adoption benefits (Form 8839, line 31)	$0
9.	Certain income of bona fide residents of American Samoa (Form 4563, line 15)	$0 or Puerto Rico
10.	Total of lines 3, 4, 5, 6, 7, 8, and 9	$8,000
11.	Base income (add lines 1 and 10)	$38,000

Now use one of the following worksheets to figure the taxable portion of your Social Security benefits: If line 11 is more than $44,000 (if you're married and filing jointly) or $34,000 (if unmarried), you have to use Worksheet II.

Worksheet I

1.	Base income	$38,000
2.	Enter the appropriate amount below	
	Married filing jointly — $32,000	
	Married filing separately and living with spouse at any time during year — $0	
	All others — $25,000	$32,000
3.	Subtract line 2 from line 1	$6,000
4.	50 percent of line 3	$3,000
5.	Social Security (box 5, SSA-1099)	$16,000
6.	50 percent of line 5	$8,000
7.	Taxable Social Security — smaller of lines 4 and 6	$3,000

Enter the amount on line 5 ($16,000) on line 6a, Form 1040, and the amount on line 7 ($3,000) on line 6b, Form 1040.

Worksheet II

Example: Assume the same facts in the example on Worksheet I, except that your AGI is $36,000, your Social Security is $16,000, and your only adjustment to your base income worksheet above is $6,000 in tax-exempt interest.

1.	AGI without Social Security	$36,000
2.	Tax-exempt interest	$6,000
3.	50 percent of Social Security	$8,000
4.	Base income (add lines 1 through 3)	$50,000

Tier-one adjustment

5.	Enter the appropriate amount below	
	Married filing jointly — $32,000	
	Married filing separately and living with spouse at any time during year — $0	
	All others — $25,000	$32,000
6.	Subtract line 5 from line 4	$18,000
7.	50 percent of line 6	$9,000
8.	Enter the appropriate amount below	
	Married filing jointly — $6,000	
	Married filing separately and living with spouse at any time during year — $0	
	All others — $4,500	$6,000
9.	The smaller of lines 3, 7, and 8	$6,000

Tier-two adjustment

10.	Enter the appropriate amount below	
	Married filing jointly — $44,000	
	Married filing separately and living with spouse at any time during year — $0	
	All others — $34,000	$44,000
11.	Subtract line 10 from line 4	$6,000
12.	85 percent of line 11	$5,100

Taxable portion

13.	Add lines 9 ($6,000) and 12 ($5,100)	$11,100
14.	85 percent of box 5, SSA-1099 ($16,000)	$13,600
15.	Taxable Social Security (smaller of lines 13 and 14)	$11,100

You would enter the amount in box 5, SSA-1099 ($16,000), on line 6a of Form 1040 and $11,100 from 15 on line 6b, Form 1040.

Repayment of benefits

In some cases, your Form SSA-1099 will show that the total benefits you repaid (box 4) are more than the gross benefits you received (box 3). If this situation occurs, your net benefits in box 5 will be a negative figure, and none of your benefits will be taxable. If you receive more than one form, a negative figure in box 5 of one form is used to offset a positive figure in box 5 of another form. If you have any questions about this negative figure, contact your local Social Security Administration office.

Remember, if you and your spouse file a joint return and you both receive an SSA-1099, combine the 1099s to arrive at the total benefits for both of you. That way, even if one of your statements shows a negative amount in box 5, you'll be able to offset that against the other spouse's positive benefits.

Repayment of benefits received in an earlier year

If the sum of the amount shown in box 5 of each of your SSA-1099s is a negative figure, and all or part of this negative figure is for benefits you included in gross income in an earlier year, you can take an itemized deduction on Schedule A for the amount of the negative figure — or you can claim credit for the tax that was paid on this in a prior year, because you included it in your income. We explain how to make the computation for this claim of right in our discussion of unemployment insurance in Chapter 6.

WARNING

If you're married, living together, and filing separately, you'll get caught in a special trap and receive no exemption. If, on the other hand, you were married but lived apart for the entire year and filed separately, you are entitled to a $25,000 exemption amount, just like if you were single. Be careful, though — a Tax Court case held that living apart meant separate residences, not separate bedrooms. The long and short of all this is that 85 percent of married individuals' Social Security benefits end up being taxed when they file separately and didn't live apart the entire year.

LUMP-SUM SOCIAL SECURITY PAYMENTS

If you receive a lump-sum payment of Social Security benefits in 2021 that includes benefits for prior years, you have two choices. You can consider the entire payment as the amount of Social Security received in 2021 and compute the taxable portion by using Worksheet I or II. Or you can allocate the amount that you received for a prior year as being received in that year.

Doing it the latter way makes sense if your income was lower in a prior year. If that's the case, maybe none or perhaps less than 50 percent or 85 percent would have been taxable.

If you elect the second way of treating a lump sum that covers more than one year, you don't file an amended return for that year. Here's what you do. You compute the amount of the lump sum that would have been taxable had it been received in the prior year. You then add that amount to your income for the current year.

For example, suppose that you receive a lump-sum payment of $20,000 in 2021 that includes $10,000 of benefits for 2019. If you report the whole amount in 2021, 85 percent, or $17,000, is taxable. If you elect to treat the $10,000 for 2019 as being received for that year, you can save some dough. Why? Because, based on your 2019 income, only 50 percent, or $5,000, of the $10,000 lump-sum income attributed to that year would have to be added to your taxable income. By splitting the payment between the two years (including one where less of your Social Security benefit would have been taxed), you pay tax on only $13,500 ($5,000 for the 2019 benefit, and $8,500 for the 2021 benefit), instead of tax on $17,000 (85 percent of the entire $20,000 benefit). Isn't it better to have to report only $13,500 in 2021 rather than $17,000?

TAX CUT

If you're married and the income for one of you is only Social Security, it may make sense to file a separate federal income tax return from your spouse, who may have enough income to push a portion of your Social Security into the taxable zone if you're filing jointly. Remember, if you only have Social Security, and Social Security alone, you're going to be taxed on 85 percent of half of your benefit, which may well be less than the standard deduction that you're entitled to, making your Social Security essentially untaxed.

Line 7: Capital gain (or loss)

You have a capital gain when you sell stocks, bonds, mutual funds, ETFs, or investment property for a profit. When you sell an asset like your house for a profit, you have a gain that may be taxable (we cover the rules on the exclusion from tax on home sales in Chapter 14), but you have a nondeductible loss if you lose money on the sale of your house. Losses on other investments — such as stocks, bonds, and mutual funds — made outside of retirement accounts are generally deductible. Capital gains and losses get reported on Schedule D with the net result being reported here. If all you have are capital gain distributions from a mutual fund, you can skip Schedule D and enter your capital gain distribution(s) on line 7. If you fall into this category, don't forget to check that little box to the left of the amount you entered on line 7. See Chapter 14 for a more in-depth explanation of capital gains and losses and of Schedule D.

Line 8: Other income from Schedule 1, line 26

Line 8 of Form 1040 is a catchall for reporting income that doesn't fit the income categories listed on page one of Form 1040. Hey, even if you find some money, the IRS treats it as income! Just report all this miscellaneous income here. Don't forget to write a description of these earnings on the dotted line next to the amount.

NEW STUFF

As a result of the Tax Cuts and Jobs Act of 2017, the Form 1040 was substantially shortened, and three new Schedules were born: Schedules 1, 2, and 3. Schedule 1 covers two topics — all the other forms of income on which you might be taxed, and adjustments to income. The seven types of income that show up on the front of Form 1040 are only the beginning and the most popular forms of income; all the other types of income, like bartering, gambling, cancellation of debt, taxable state tax refunds, and jury duty pay, are all included on the first page of Schedule 1, which we'll go into in much greater depth in Chapter 6. But we didn't want to completely ignore them here, because you're going to need the total from Schedule 1, line 26, to put on Form 1040, line 8.

Here are some examples of stuff that will be carried over from Schedule 1, line 26.

Bartering

Bartering is the trading of your services for goods or other services. You usually must declare the fair market value of goods you receive. If you participate in a barter exchange, you may get a Form 1099-B — and the IRS gets a copy, too. For example, suppose that you're a carpenter with a child who needs braces; you agree to make cabinets in a dentist's office in exchange for your child's braces and treatment. Although no cash changed hands, you have to pay tax on what the dentist normally would charge, because that is your income from making the cabinets. The dentist makes out better. Because the cabinets are used in his business, he is entitled to a business deduction equal to the income he has to report. Even poor Jack of beanstalk fame had taxable income when he traded his cow for those beans.

WARNING

Not every Form 1099-B is for barter transactions. It's also used to report the sale of stocks and bonds (and other marketable securities) through a broker. Broker, barter — they're both Bs. In some convoluted way, it makes sense. Still, if you have a broker transaction, report it on Schedule D (check out Chapter 14).

Canceled debt

A canceled debt, or a debt paid for you by another person, is generally income to you and must be reported. For example, a discount offered by a financial institution for the prepaying of your mortgage is income from the cancellation of the debt. However, you have no income from the cancellation of a debt if the cancellation is a gift. For example, suppose you borrow $10,000 from a relative who tells you that you don't have to repay it. It's a gift! (And be sure to invite that relative to Thanksgiving dinner every year.) If you received a sweetheart deal on a loan, make sure that you read the rules on below-market interest rates for loans in Chapter 12.

Life insurance

The death benefit paid to the beneficiary of a life insurance contract is exempt from tax. It's also possible to receive the death benefit prior to death as advance, or accelerated, payments, provided that the insured is terminally ill and has been certified by a physician as being expected to die within 24 months of that certification. If the payments are made to someone who has been certified as chronically ill, that person may exclude from their income the larger of $380 per day or the actual long-term care expenses incurred.

The tax lingo for these advanced payments is *viatical settlements*. Aren't you glad you took Latin in high school? Report viatical payments and the portions exempt from tax in Section C of Form 8853, Archer MSAs and Long-Term Care Insurance Contracts.

Other stuff

Here are some more examples of things that you may be including in the total on line 8:

» **Alaska Permanent Fund distributions (dividends):** When you think of Alaska, you may picture open spaces, clean air, and plenty of snow. All true, but you also need to think of all that oil hiding underneath the tundra. And thanks to the oil, every year residents receive a small cash dividend, ranging in value from $500 to $2,000, depending on the year. Although normal dividends and distributions are reported on Form 1099-DIV, distributions from the Alaska Permanent Fund aren't; the state sends a notice of payment instead.

» **Fees that you snare:** Maybe you're a corporate director or a notary public, and you made some extra cash. Good job! You get to take a trip to Schedule 1.

» **Free tour:** The free tour you received from a travel agency or the group organizer is taxable at its fair market value. Bon voyage.

» **Gambling winnings:** Gambling winnings are taxable. But you can also deduct your gambling losses — as long as they don't exceed your winnings — as an itemized deduction on line 16 of Schedule A. We'll explain this further in Chapter 11.

» **Illegal income:** Al Capone found out about this too late. Remember, he spent time in Alcatraz for tax evasion, not for his health.

» **Jury duty:** The whopping $7 a day (more or less) that you received for jury duty goes here. If you must repay this amount to your employer because your employer continued to pay your salary while you served on the jury, you can deduct the repayment. You're going to do both of these on Schedule 1.

» **Prizes and awards:** If you get lucky and hit the lottery or win a prize in a contest, the winnings are taxable. Sorry!

However, some employee achievement awards may be nontaxable. These include noncash awards, such as a watch, golf clubs, or a TV, given in recognition for length of service or safety achievement. The tax-free limit is $400 if given from a nonqualified employer plan and $1,600 from a qualified plan. Check with your human resources department.

» **Qualified tuition program payments:** These programs more commonly are known as *Section 529 plans* in which you prepay a student's tuition or establish an account to pay their higher education expenses. To the extent that any earnings are distributed that aren't used to pay higher education expenses, the beneficiary, not the person who established the account, has to pay tax on those earnings. The earnings are reported on Form 1099-Q, box 2. Check out Chapter 26 for details about Section 529 plans as well as other options for saving for educational expenses. Taxable earnings on Coverdell Education Savings Accounts, if you have any, are reported on this line.

>> **Treasure trove:** Say you buy a used sofa at an auction for $500 and discover a diamond ring under one of the cushions when you get it home. Guess what — you owe the tax on the value of the ring. Unfair! Just think of it as your fellow citizens wanting to share in your good fortune. Forgive us if we confronted you with a moral dilemma on what you have to do.

>> **Whistle-blower fees:** It's true! No good deed ever goes unpunished. If you blow the whistle on a tax-evader and receive an award from the IRS for information you provided after December 19, 2006, the income you receive is taxable to you. Fortunately, you may deduct the attorneys' fees and court costs you incur as a result of being a good citizen up to the amount of the award as an adjustment to income rather than an itemized deduction.

TAX CUT

Frequent-flier miles that you earn on business trips but use for personal travel aren't taxable. One taxpayer stretched this rule too far. He had his travel agent bill the employer for first-class tickets. Next, he purchased coach tickets and used the frequent-flier miles to upgrade to first class. He had the travel agent refund the difference to his personal account. The IRS held that the refunds were taxable.

Deductions

You'll also carry to line 8 two types of deductions: a net operating loss and the foreign earned income and housing exclusion.

NET OPERATING LOSS (NOL)

This deduction to your income occurs when your business expenses in a prior year exceed your income for that year. We explain NOLs to you in full in Chapter 6.

FOREIGN EARNED INCOME AND HOUSING EXCLUSION

TAX CUT

In 2021, U.S. citizens and permanent residents working abroad are entitled to exclude up to $108,700 of their foreign salary or their self-employed income. (If you've ever considered working abroad, this exclusion may help you make up your mind.) The portion of their foreign housing costs above an annual threshold can also be deducted. The exclusion isn't automatic. You have to file Form 2555, Foreign Earned Income, to claim the exclusion and the housing deduction, and attach it to your return.

You have to jump through some hoops to qualify for the foreign earned income exclusion, but we're going to explain each and every one of those in Chapter 6. We'll also tell you what you need to know about the foreign housing exclusion and the foreign housing deduction there.

Line 9: Your total income

Whew! Are you ready to do the math? Don't be stubborn or proud; grab the calculator. Add lines 1 through 8 and put the final figure on line 9. Congratulations! This amount is your total income. Because you don't want to pay tax on this amount, we tell you what deductions and other adjustments to income you're entitled to in the chapters that follow, so you can get away with paying the least amount possible.

IN THIS CHAPTER

» Discovering there's more to income than just wages, interest and dividends

» Finding out how to calculate income

» Understanding the different types of income — active, passive, and capital gains

» Figuring out foreign earned income and what to do about it

» Calculating net operating losses and using them to reduce other years' taxes

Chapter **6**

Form 1040, Schedule 1, Part I: Additional Income

O h, imagine how easy it would be if all income we earned was taxed in the same way. We'd just add all our bits and pieces together, apply the tax rate or table, and presto! We'd be done.

But that's not the way of the U.S. income tax system and the rules that govern it. Instead, there's a myriad of different types of income. Many of them, we cover in Chapter 5, such as wages, income from retirement accounts, capital gains, interest, and dividends. The rest of them, we cover here in Chapter 6. Some of these types of income will seem obscure, and you may wonder why we bother touching on such esoteric topics, but trust us — even if you don't need to know about one of these topics this year, someone else will. And who knows when the beloved Alaska Permanent Fund Dividend may show up on your tax return someday?

So, in this chapter we take a whirl through Schedule 1, Other Income, which is where all the types of income that no longer belong on the front of Form 1040 now go to play.

Schedule 1, Part I, Line 1: Taxable Refunds, Credits, or Offsets

Line 1 of Schedule 1, Part I, deals with taxable refunds, credits, or offsets of state and local income taxes. If you itemized your deductions last year and deducted your state or local income tax, and if you either received a refund of a portion of that tax or applied a portion of what you paid last year to this year's tax liability, you have to declare that portion as income. When you think about it, adding back this amount that you deducted from your income last year to income this year is only fair.

If you didn't itemize your deductions last year and you received a refund, you're off the hook. Likewise, if you itemized but didn't receive any benefit from your deduction because of the $10,000 deduction limit on state and local taxes, this won't be considered taxable income to you. What benefit are we talking about? If your total tax liability wasn't reduced because of the deduction for taxes paid to your state and/or city, you didn't receive any benefit from the deduction.

TAX CUT

If you itemized your deductions but declined to deduct your state and local income tax, and deducted your state's sales tax instead, guess what? You're in the clear, and none of your state tax refund is includable in income. You don't need to even attempt the state and local income tax refund worksheet shown in Figure 6-1.

State and local tax refunds that you receive are reported on Form 1099-G, a form that your state department of revenue sends to you. If you chose to apply part or all of your 2020 state tax overpayment to your 2021 estimated state or local tax payments that you have to make (instead of having it refunded), the overpayment still is considered a refund even though a check wasn't sent to you. Box 2 of Form 1099-G has the amount of your refund.

TIP

Check to see what tax year your refund is for before you begin celebrating because you used the standard deduction in 2020. Sometimes (and we can't imagine why this happens), refunds are delayed for months, and even years, so the check you may have received recently may be for, say, tax year 2019. If so, you need to take a look back at those years before you decide to trash the Form 1099-G that's just arrived. The rule regarding whether you need to include these older refund amounts in income this year is based on whether or not you itemized in the year that's being refunded. If you itemized in 2019 and have just received your 2019 refund, you have to declare it as income.

But, like just about every tax rule, there is an exception. Even though you may itemize your deductions, only the part of your refund that represents the amount of your itemized deductions in excess of the standard deduction is taxable. That means you have to do some number crunching to make this computation. The following worksheet (see Table 6-1) gives you the answer. Suppose that your 2020 state refund was $1,900, you filed jointly, and your itemized deductions were $26,000.

SCHEDULE 1
(Form 1040)

Department of the Treasury
Internal Revenue Service

Additional Income and Adjustments to Income

▶ Attach to Form 1040, 1040-SR, or 1040-NR.
▶ Go to *www.irs.gov/Form1040* for instructions and the latest information.

OMB No. 1545-0074

2021

Attachment
Sequence No. **01**

Name(s) shown on Form 1040, 1040-SR, or 1040-NR

Your social security number

Part I   Additional Income

1	Taxable refunds, credits, or offsets of state and local income taxes	1
2a	Alimony received	2a
b	Date of original divorce or separation agreement (see instructions) ▶ _____	
3	Business income or (loss). Attach Schedule C	3
4	Other gains or (losses). Attach Form 4797	4
5	Rental real estate, royalties, partnerships, S corporations, trusts, etc. Attach Schedule E	5
6	Farm income or (loss). Attach Schedule F	6
7	Unemployment compensation	7
8	Other income:	
a	Net operating loss	8a ( )
b	Gambling income	8b
c	Cancellation of debt	8c
d	Foreign earned income exclusion from Form 2555	8d ( )
e	Taxable Health Savings Account distribution	8e
f	Alaska Permanent Fund dividends	8f
g	Jury duty pay	8g
h	Prizes and awards	8h
i	Activity not engaged in for profit income	8i
j	Stock options	8j
k	Income from the rental of personal property if you engaged in the rental for profit but were not in the business of renting such property	8k
l	Olympic and Paralympic medals and USOC prize money (see instructions)	8l
m	Section 951(a) inclusion (see instructions)	8m
n	Section 951A(a) inclusion (see instructions)	8n
o	Section 461(l) excess business loss adjustment	8o
p	Taxable distributions from an ABLE account (see instructions) .	8p
z	Other income. List type and amount ▶ _____	8z
9	Total other income. Add lines 8a through 8z	9
10	Combine lines 1 through 7 and 9. Enter here and on Form 1040, 1040-SR, or 1040-NR, line 8	10

FIGURE 6-1:
Schedule 1,
Part I,
Additional
Income.

For Paperwork Reduction Act Notice, see your tax return instructions.   Cat. No. 71479F   Schedule 1 (Form 1040) 2021

Source: Internal Revenue Service

Table 6-1   State and Local Income Tax Refund Worksheet

	Form Instructions		Example	Your Computation
1.	Enter the income tax refund from Form(s) 1099-G (or similar statement).	1.	$7,800	
2.	Is the amount of state and local income taxes, real estate taxes and personal property taxes paid in 2020 (2020 Schedule A, line 5d) more than the amount on your 2020 Schedule A, line 5e? If no, enter the amount on line 1 on line 3 and go to line 4. If yes, subtract the amount on 2020 Schedule A, line 5e from 2020 Schedule A, line 5d.	2.	$7,500	
3.	Is the amount on line 1 more than the amount on line 2? If no, none of your refund is taxable. If yes, subtract line 2 from line 1.	3.	$300	
4.	Enter total itemized deductions from 2020 Schedule A, line 17.	4.	$29,750	
5.	Enter the amount shown for the filing status claimed on your 2019 Form 1040 or 1040-SR: • Single or married filing separately - $12,400 • Married filing joint or qualifying widow(er) - $24,800 • Head of Household - $18,650	5.	$24,800	
6.	Add up the number of items that apply: a. You were born before 1/2/1956 b. Your spouse was born before 1/2/1956 c. You are blind d. Your spouse is blind Multiply the number of items you checked, and multiply by $1,700 for single or head of household, or by $1,350 for married filing joint or qualifying widow(er)	6.	$1,350	
7.	Add lines 5 and 6	7.	$26,150	
8.	Is the amount on line 7 less than the amount on line 4? If no, none of your refund is taxable. If yes, subtract line 7 from line 4.	8.	$3,600	
9.	Taxable part of your refund – enter the smaller of line 3 or line 8 here, and on Schedule 1, line 1.	9.	$300	

If state sales taxes were deducted in 2020 instead of income taxes, or if married filing separately, please refer to Schedule D instructions at www.irs.gov *or in Form 1040 instruction booklet for more information.*

Schedule 1, Part I, Lines 2a and 2b: Alimony Received (by You)

NEW STUFF

For divorce or separation agreements executed after December 31, 2018, the Tax Cuts and Jobs Act changed the rules, making new support payments nondeductible for the payer, and non-includable in income for the payee. If your divorce or separation agreement was executed prior to January 1, 2019, the old rules apply, which state that the payer gets to deduct alimony payments, and the recipient must include those payments as income.

If you're the recipient of alimony payments and your agreement predates the change, oh well — you get to include all alimony that you received in 2021 on line 2a. On line 2b, you're going to put the date of the divorce or separation agreement governing the payment of alimony to you, so you better go dig that out of your files.

If, on the other hand, you're receiving alimony, but your divorce came after that all important December 31, 2018 date, leave lines 2a and 2b blank. The alimony you receive is free and clear of all income taxes to you. Congratulations!

What, exactly, constitutes alimony? The alimony rules aren't simple —we offer a more detailed explanation of alimony in Chapter 7.

TIP

Here's an important tip about alimony and about separate maintenance payments and IRAs. These payments are considered income from employment that entitles you to set up and make deductible contributions to an IRA. Basically, if you receive taxable alimony, you can set up an IRA and deduct what you contribute to it — 100 percent of your alimony and employment income up to $6,000 (or $7,000 if you're age 50 or older) is deductible. However, your deduction may be reduced or eliminated if you're covered by a retirement plan through your work. See Chapter 22 for more on how to set up IRAs. Chapters 7 and 22 give the lowdown on IRAs, which come in deductible and nondeductible varieties, and Roth IRAs, which are always nondeductible.

Schedule 1, Part I, Line 3: Business Income (or Loss)

If you're self-employed, you must complete a Schedule C to report your business income and expenses. If you just receive an occasional fee and don't have any business expenses, you can report that fee on Schedule 1, Part I, line 8z as other income. And remember, if you're a statutory employee (a life insurance salesperson, agent, commission driver, or traveling salesperson, for example), report the wages shown in box 1 of your W-2 form on Schedule C along with your expenses. How do you know if you're a statutory employee? Simple: Box 13 of your W-2 will be checked. For a quick reminder on this statutory employee title, check out Chapter 5.

As a general rule, you're better off reporting your self-employment income on Schedule C, if you're eligible. Although more complicated than entering your income on line 8, you can deduct business-related expenses against your income on Schedule C, and that can lower your income and the tax that you have to pay.

The amount that you enter on line 12 is the result of figuring and jumbling that you do on Schedules C, which is a shorter version. Check out Chapter 13 to dive into that material.

Schedule 1, Part I, Line 4: Other Gains (or Losses)

You guessed it, grab another form — Form 4797, Sales of Business Property. Fill out that form and enter the final figure on Schedule 1, Part I, line 4. Use Form 4797 when you sell property that you've been depreciating (such as a two-family house that you've been renting out). We explain this form in Chapter 14.

Schedule 1, Part I, Line 5: Rental Real Estate, Partnerships, and More

This line is an important one for all you self-starters who are landlords, business owners, authors, taxpayers collecting royalties (like us!), and those people lucky enough to have someone set up a trust fund for them. Jump to Chapter 15 to find out more about this and good old Schedule E — the necessary form to wrestle with for this line.

And we do mean "wrestle." Some of the more complex ideas contained in the Internal Revenue Code show up here, as this is where active versus passive income is separated out. But have no fears — all is explained in Chapter 15.

Schedule 1, Part I, Line 6: Farm Income (or Loss)

What comes after E? You got it. If you have farm income or losses, go directly to Schedule F (see Chapter 13), fill it out, and fill in the final number on line 6. Schedule F is quite similar to Schedule C, but with obvious differences — it's unlikely that, even if you have an office dog and houseplants, you're going to need separate categories for livestock, fertilizer, and seeds on Schedule C. The same holds true for Schedule F, where you would be unlikely to find categories for office supplies and internet service.

Schedule 1, Part I, Line 7: Unemployment Compensation

Losing your job was bad enough. And now you receive another nasty surprise — the news that the unemployment compensation that you received is taxable. The government should have sent you a Form 1099-G (see Figure 6-2) to summarize these taxable benefits that you received. Unemployment compensation is fully taxable, and you enter it on line 7.

PAYER'S name, street address, city or town, state or province, country, ZIP or foreign postal code, and telephone no.		1 Unemployment compensation $	OMB No. 1545-0120 **20 21** Form **1099-G**	**Certain Government Payments**
		2 State or local income tax refunds, credits, or offsets $		
PAYER'S TIN	RECIPIENT'S TIN	3 Box 2 amount is for tax year	4 Federal income tax withheld $	**Copy B For Recipient**
RECIPIENT'S name		5 RTAA payments $	6 Taxable grants $	This is important tax information and is being furnished to the IRS. If you are required to file a return, a negligence penalty or other sanction may be imposed on you if this income is taxable and the IRS determines that it has not been reported.
Street address (including apt. no.)		7 Agriculture payments $	8 If checked, box 2 is trade or business income ▶ ☐	
City or town, state or province, country, and ZIP or foreign postal code		9 Market gain $		
Account number (see instructions)		10a State	10b State identification no.	11 State income tax withheld $ $

Form **1099-G**   (keep for your records)   www.irs.gov/Form1099G   Department of the Treasury - Internal Revenue Service

FIGURE 6-2: Form 1099-G shows unemployment compensation benefits received in box 1.

Source: Internal Revenue Service

You can elect to have tax withheld at the rate of 10 percent on your unemployment, so you won't be caught short next April. This is one offer most people are likely to refuse.

On occasion, you may be required to repay some of your unemployment benefits. Why? Because when you're collecting unemployment insurance, you have to be looking for a job. And if you aren't, the folks at the unemployment office may determine that you weren't entitled to all the benefits you received and that you owe some money back. If you gave back the benefits in the same year that you received them, no problem, just subtract what you returned from the total you received and enter that amount on line 7. You also need to enter "REPAID" and the amount that you repaid on the dotted line next to the amount column on line 7.

But if you returned money in 2021 that you paid tax on in 2020, things aren't as easy. Suppose that in 2020 you received and paid tax on $10,000 of unemployment benefits. Then during 2021 you had to repay $2,500, as determined by the unemployment office. The $2,500 you paid can be deducted on Schedule A (see Chapter 11).

If you repaid unemployment compensation (that was less than $3,000) in 2021 that you included in gross income in an earlier year, you may deduct the amount repaid with Form 1040, Schedule A (line 27). If the amount you repaid was more than $3,000, you can take either a deduction for the amount repaid as an itemized deduction or a credit against your tax for the amount of tax you originally paid by including this amount in your income in a prior year.

Schedule 1, Part I, Line 8: Other Income

NEW STUFF

Before the IRS came up with Schedule 1, Part I, line 8, the following items were scattered all over the income portion of Form 1040. The IRS has seen the confusion caused by lumping these all together, so in 2021, it now gives you a handy-dandy list so you don't lose your way or potentially forget to add something here. The following sections take a look at all the types of income included on line 8.

Line 8a: Net operating losses (NOLs)

For many people, the thought of having to deal with an NOL on their own is right outside their skill set and their comfort level. And no surprise — this isn't beginning tax stuff. However, most of the rules here are readily understandable if you pay attention. We're giving you all the rules to let you determine if you're able to do this by yourself, or if this may be the time to call in an expert.

NEW STUFF

The NOL deduction to your income occurs when your business expenses in a prior year exceed your income for that year. Beginning with any tax years ending after December 31, 2017, the new rules under the Tax Cuts and Jobs Act (TCJA) state that NOLs can only be carried forward, not back. That is unless, of course, you meet the exception of having an NOL in 2018, 2019, or 2020, for which the CARES Act included special treatment. If you had an NOL in any of those years, you are allowed to elect a special five-year carryback, meaning that, if you chose to use this exception, you'd have to amend those prior years' returns in order to use your loss. Chapter 20 deals with filing amended returns and how NOLs are carried back and forward. When you carry an NOL forward from a previous year, you enter it as a negative number (for example, <$10,000> on line 21).

And to make life a little more complicated, in taxable years beginning after December 31, 2020 (that's 2021, in normal speak), the deduction for a net operating loss is limited to 80 percent of the excess (if any) of taxable income, determined without regard to the deduction itself, to the Qualified Business Income Deduction (QBID), and to Section 250 (a deduction of 37.5 percent of foreign-derived intangible income of a domestic corporation plus 50 percent of the global intangible low-taxed income amount included in the gross income of a domestic corporation under Section 951A, and the amount treated as a dividend received by the corporation under Section 78 attributable to the amount attributable to global intangible low-taxed income under Section 951A.) If you're confused by all of that, no worries. So is almost everyone else.

SEEK ADVICE

You can probably wrap your head around most of what we've mentioned in the calculation in the prior paragraph, especially once you actually sit down and start plugging in numbers. But once you get into the woods of Section 250 and foreign-derived intangible income of a domestic corporation, plus all its associated gobbledygook, you may want to find a good accountant with experience in this area to give you a hand. What you save on your taxes may more than cover the cost of hiring someone to help.

NOLs are cumulative, so you add together any pre-2018 NOLs that carried to 2021 to the new formula and put this number on line 8a of Schedule 1.

And, because otherwise it wouldn't be the IRS, there are always exceptions to every rule. Here are the NOL exceptions:

>> All insurance companies (except life insurance) are allowed to carry back NOLs for 2 years, or carry them forward for 20 years, and they are not subject to the 80 percent limitation.

>> Farming losses are eligible to be carried back for two years, and carried forward indefinitely, subject to the 80 percent limitation.

Line 8b: Gambling income

If you're a casual gambler and you've had a lucky streak, congratulations! If you won the COVID-19 vaccine lottery and received one million dollars in winnings (yes, some states paid such amounts), excellent! But no streak of luck ever goes completely unpunished — your winnings represent income to you, and you're required to report them on line 8b of Schedule 1.

If you won enough money, you may receive a Form W2-G, Certain Gambling Winnings, by January 31, 2022. You may even have had some money withheld for taxes by whoever was running the game, and you'll find that number entered in box 4 of Form W-2G. The withholding rate for 2021 is 24 percent of the total amount won, not net of the cost of your wager, whether for backup withholding (you declined to give or gave incorrect information when you went to collect your winnings) or the size of the win created a withholding requirement. Okay, gambling winnings are taxable income, but what about gambling losses? Well, here's a bit of good news for you: Gambling losses are deductible, so long as they don't exceed your winnings, on Schedule A as an Other Itemized Deduction on line 16. You'll need to be able to prove that you lost what you said you lost, though, so hang onto every losing lottery ticket, keep count of your nickels and quarters at the slot machine, and maintain an account of all the wagers that you made at the track or at the poker table.

Line 8c: Cancellation of debt

Cancelled debt of $600 or more is reported to you on Form 1099-C, Cancellation of Debt.

NEW STUFF

Beginning with the mortgage crisis of 2007–2009, debt cancellation of mortgages on your principal residence became nontaxable under many circumstances. With COVID-19, some of those provisions have been extended, so if you started the process with your mortgage lender and have an agreement with them that was entered into in writing prior to January 1, 2021, even though the debt wasn't officially cancelled until after that date, you may exclude that cancellation of debt on your principal residence from your 2021 taxable income.

WARNING

If you receive notice of debt forgiveness because the bank foreclosed on real estate you own, be careful. The bank may issue you a 1099-C, Cancellation of Debt, showing the full amount of the outstanding mortgage in box 2, but may neglect to fill in box 7, the fair market value of the property. When a bank forecloses, only the difference between the debt forgiven and the fair market value of the property that secured that debt is income to you.

There is some relief for beleaguered homeowners who have lost their homes to foreclosure. When the bank forecloses on your home (as opposed to investment real estate), provided your mortgage was a nonrecourse loan, you realize no ordinary income. A nonrecourse loan is one where the lender can only repossess the property held as collateral for that loan (that is to say, your home), but can't come after you personally for additional money. You may have a capital gain, however, if the basis in your home is less than the amount of the debt forgiven. Of course, if you've lived in the house for at least two out of the last five years, $250,000 of the gain ($500,000 if you're married filing jointly) is tax-free to you. If your basis is greater than the amount of the loan, you have a nondeductible loss. Check out Chapter 14 for all the rules regarding the sale of your personal residence. If you're not sure if you have cancellation of debt income on your personal return, refer to the IRS questionnaire, www.irs.gov/help/ita/do-i-have-cancellation-of-debt-income-on-my-personal-residence, located on the IRS website.

If your debt is canceled as the result of bankruptcy or because you are insolvent, the cancellation of the debt negates your having to pay tax on the income. And you don't have to report it as income if your student loan is canceled because you agreed to certain conditions to obtain the loan — and then performed the required services.

TIP

In the murky waters of student loans, there is a whole raft of ways that qualified student loans can be forgiven with no income reportable by you. Among these are that you worked for a certain period of time in certain professions such as doctors, firefighters, members of the military, nurses, certain public service workers, and teachers. If you are currently working in one of these areas and still have outstanding student loans, check to see how to fill the requirements to have your loans forgiven.

Qualified student loans can also be forgiven without being taxed if you die or have a permanent and total disability.

If you are one of the unfortunate people whose school unexpectedly closed either prior to your obtaining a degree or certificate or shortly thereafter, your loans, both federal and private, whether owed by you or by your parents, may be forgiven under the Closed School or Defense to Repayment discharge process. If you are able to get your loans discharged under either of these provisions, you may exclude that forgiveness of debt from your gross income.

Line 8d: Foreign earned income and housing exclusion

To qualify for the $108,700 exclusion we describe in Chapter 5, you must either be a resident of a foreign country or be physically present in a foreign country. Earnings from employment by the U.S. government don't qualify, so if you're a staff member of a U.S. embassy or consulate, you're out of luck here.

To qualify as a resident, you must reside in a foreign country for an uninterrupted period that includes the entire year (January 1 to December 31). So, if you start working in London on March 31, 2021, you can't qualify for the exclusion under the entire-year rule, but you can possibly qualify under the physical presence test. Brief trips back to the United States don't disqualify you from being a resident of a foreign country.

Under the physical presence test, you must be in a foreign country for 330 days during a 12-month consecutive period. If you weren't physically present or a bona fide resident for the entire year, the $108,700 exclusion has to be reduced based on the number of days you were out of the country.

TECHNICAL
STUFF

To determine whether you meet the 330-day test, you may have to apply for an extension of time to file (Form 4868, Application for Automatic Extension of Time to File U.S. Individual Income Tax Return). Say you started to work in Paris on July 1, 2021 (great assignment!); you won't know until July 1, 2022, if you meet the 330-day test for the 12-month period of July 1, 2021 to July 1, 2022.

TIP

Say that you weren't in a foreign country for 330 days between July 1, 2021, and July 1, 2022. You can still claim a partial exemption for 2021 (half of $108,700) if you meet the bona fide residence test for 2022. If you meet this test, you're considered a bona fide resident since July 1, 2021. While you're waiting to qualify as a bona fide resident for 2022, so that you can claim the foreign earned income exclusion for 2021, you can put off filing your 2021 return until October 17, 2022.

You enter your foreign earnings from Form 2555, line 26, on Form 1040, Line 1. Then, you enter the amount you can exclude, plus your foreign housing deduction, as a negative number on Schedule 1, Line 8d. When you add up all the numbers on Schedule 1, you're going to carry the total over to Form 1040, line 8, Other Income.

WARNING

You may be wondering if you qualify for the foreign earned income exclusion if you live and work in Puerto Rico, the U.S. Virgin Islands, Guam, or American Samoa. Unfortunately, you don't. All U.S. territories and possessions are excluded. And for those of you who truly like the cold, so is Antarctica. We know you needed to know that.

Line 8e: Taxable Health Savings Account distribution

This one is easy: If you took a nonqualified distribution from your Health Savings Account, you need to include that in your total income. Schedule 1, line 8e is where you report this.

What qualifies as a nonqualified distribution? Any distribution amount that exceeds your unreimbursed qualified medical expenses in 2021 that were not included in a qualified rollover is considered a nonqualified distribution. Any questions?

Line 8f: Alaska Permanent Fund dividends

When you think of Alaska, we're sure you're thinking of everything but the Alaska Permanent Fund dividend, which is generated by income from the accumulated oil revenues that have been invested over the years by the State of Alaska. That is, unless you are a resident of Alaska and have become accustomed to receiving your annual check from the Alaska Permanent Fund. Every year, thanks to all that oil from under the tundra, residents receive a cash dividend from the fund, typically ranging in value from $500 to $2,000, depending on the year. Enter the amount you received in 2021 here, on line 8f.

Line 8g: Jury duty pay

We know you've just been dying to sit on a jury, and if you're reading this because you had the opportunity to do so in 2021, congratulations! Any pay you received from the court to be on that jury is included here, on line 8g. But wait — if you had to give your jury pay over to your employer because they continued to pay you while you were on that jury, go directly to Schedule 1, Line 24a, and enter the amount you paid to your employer there. You're only going to be taxed on jury duty pay if your employer didn't pay you during your stay on the jury.

Line 8h: Prizes and awards

Congratulations! 2021 was the year you won the Nobel Prize, the Pulitzer, and a MacArthur Genius Grant. Or maybe you won the local raffle and walked off with a brand-new washing machine. Whatever prizes you won or awards you earned, if they carried a monetary value, these represent income to you. You should enter the value of any prize or award here on line 8h. If the value of the award was $600 or greater, you should receive a Form 1099-MISC, showing an amount in box 3.

TECHNICAL STUFF

An award you receive because you've just passed your 25th anniversary with your employer or a prize you win because you surpassed all the other salespeople in your firm isn't included here. Instead, if the prize was paid to you by your employer, its value will be included on your W-2, and you'll include that income on line 1 of Form 1040. If you're a contractor winning a sales prize, the value of that prize will be included on Form 1099-NEC, in box 1 for non-employee compensation. Check out Chapter 13 to find out how to declare it.

Line 8i: Activity not engaged in for profit income

For all you hobbyists out there who sold a painting you created or charged someone $100 to alter their grandmother's wedding dress, if you're not in the business of doing this sort of work, and you do it for fun, the IRS considers it a hobby, not a business, and you're subject to special rules. Money you receive for selling something that you created as part of your hobby is included on line 8i of Schedule 1. You're entitled to deduct your costs up to the amount of income you are including, but those costs belong on Schedule A, and they're only useful to you if you itemize your deductions.

Line 8j: Stock options

Some of you may receive a portion of your employment compensation in the form of stock options. A stock option is a benefit your company grants you to buy stock in your employer's company at a discount or at a stated fixed price.

As you've probably figured out by now, if it's part of your wage package, it's going to be taxable to you. If you belong in this group, here's a quick rundown of the two most popular forms of stock options, and what you're supposed to do with them (on your tax return, of course):

>> **Incentive stock options:** There is no taxable income when the option is granted by your employer, and there probably won't be any income when you exercise the option (that's buying the shares at the price stated in the plan, to you and me), unless you are subject to the Alternative Minimum Tax, which we cover more fully in Chapter 8. The income you'll most typically report will be when you sell the shares you purchased, and those will be reported on Schedule D. Your employer will issue you Form 3921, Exercise of an Incentive Stock Option Under Section 422(b), which will tell you the values you need to report here, or more likely, on Schedule D.

- >> **Employee stock purchase plan:** If your employer has a plan that allows you to purchase company stock by exercising an option granted under an employee stock purchase plan, your employer will issue you Form 3922, Transfer of Stock Acquired Through an Employee Stock Purchase Plan under Section 423(c), which will report the dates and values you'll need to determine the correct amount of capital gain and ordinary income. Capital gain income will be reported on Schedule D, but any ordinary income will be reported here, on line 8j.

- >> **Nonstatutory stock options:** If your employer gives you this type of option, when and how you declare it as income will depend on whether it is actively traded on an established exchange so that its fair market value (FMV) can be readily determined, or if no fair market value can be determined at the time the option is granted. If you are able to establish the FMV of the option at the time of granting, then you're going to pick up the value of that option as part of your compensation in the year the option is granted. If it's not possible to determine the FMV of the option at the time of granting, you're going to hold off declaring the value of the option until you either exercise or transfer the option.

SEEK ADVICE

You've probably already determined that this is fairly complex stuff. When you're trying to complete your returns, if you're not sure whether now is the time to declare the income from your options, and where and how much you should declare, it probably makes sense to ask an expert. The Internal Revenue Code was not designed to be user friendly, and while we try our best, there are some elements of it that defy even us.

Line 8k: Income from the rental of personal property

Actually, the full description here is "Income from the rental of personal property if you engaged in the rental for profit but were not in the business of renting such property." The key here is "personal property," not real property, so we're not talking about renting your house out for a day or two. Instead, perhaps you have tools that are in demand, and you rent those out periodically as opposed to just lending them because if someone has to pay for the privilege of using them, maybe they'll actually return them. Whatever it is that you're renting, enter the income here on Line 8k.

REMEMBER

This is only for property that you rent on occasion, not for something that you're renting as part of a business. Rentals as part of a business belong on Schedule C.

Line 8l: Olympic and Paralympic medals and USOC prize money

We're delighted to know that, if this pertains to you, we're writing for Olympic and Paralympic athletes! If you fall into this category, in most cases, any prize money you won for winning (or coming in second or third) isn't taxable. That doesn't mean you don't have to declare it; you do. Put whatever the value of your win was here, on line 8l. So, that's $47,500 for each gold medal, $22,500 for every silver medal, and $15,000 for bronze.

Now, if you don't want to read ahead to Chapter 7, we'll tell you that, if your adjusted gross income doesn't exceed $1 million dollars in 2021 ($500,000 if you use the married filing separately status), you get to deduct the full amount of the prize on Schedule 1, Part II, line 24c.

If, because of your healthy endorsement contracts, you can't meet that income limitation, we're sorry. The full amount of your prize money is taxable to you.

Lines 8m and 8n: Section 951(a) inclusion and Section 951A(a) inclusion

SEEK
ADVICE

If you have any of these types of income (and when the only descriptions given are Internal Revenue Code sections, you know the IRS is serious), it's time to not only find a tax professional, but also a tax expert in these areas. For the purpose of trying to be as complete as possible, Section 951(a) and Section 951A(a) refer to U.S. individuals who are shareholders in controlled foreign corporations. We've taken courses on this but have to admit that it's not something we see every day.

Line 8o: Section 461(l) excess business loss adjustment

As for Section 461(l), this code section was enacted in 2017 as part of the Tax Cuts and Jobs Act (TCJA), and it limited the amount of net business loss an individual can take to $250,000 if filing single, or $500,000 if married filing jointly. Any excess loss is converted into a net operating loss, covered earlier in this chapter, which can then be used in a subsequent year to offset income.

TAX CUT

The CARES Act amended this provision, allowing a 100 percent deduction of excess business losses in 2018, 2019, and 2020. This provision expired as of December 31, 2020; however, if you were not aware of the change and you did have an excess business loss that exceeded the limits in the initial TCJA, you still have time to go back and amend your 2018 through 2020 returns.

Line 8p: Taxable distributions from an ABLE account

ABLE accounts were established through passage of the Stephen Beck Jr. Achieving a Better Life Experience Act of 2014 (the ABLE Act). Under the provisions of the ABLE Act, individuals with disabilities with an age of onset before age 26, and who are either receiving benefits under Social Security Disability (SSDI) or Supplemental Security Income (SSI), or those who meet the requirements and criteria Social Security sets out regarding functional limitations *and* have a letter of disability from a licensed physician, osteopath, dentist, and under certain circumstances, a podiatrist, optometrist, or chiropractor, are allowed to open so-called ABLE accounts.

ABLE accounts allow the disabled individual, plus family and friends, to put money in that account to cover disability-related expenses. ABLE account contributions aren't tax deductible at the time of the contribution, so when the money comes out, those contributions aren't ever taxed. It's the income earned on the contributions while the money is in the account that's in play here. If you take money from the account that isn't disability related, the income portion of the distribution is going to be taxed. Put that number on Schedule 1, line 8p.

Line 8z: Other income

Skipping right ahead to the end of the alphabet (honest, the IRS seems to have forgotten about q through y here, but we think they're saving those letters for future years' Schedule 1), here's where you're going to put every other type of income that hasn't been discussed either in Chapter 5 or in this Chapter 6.

The types of income that can be included here seem endless, probably because they are. If you have any of the following items, (and trust us, this list is not exhaustive), they belong here, on line 8z:

>> Bartering income, that is, goods or services received in exchange for goods or services provided. The value of what you received, less any expenses you may have incurred, is taxable income to you.

>> Dividends on whole-life policies that exceed the premiums paid.

>> Reimbursements for amounts you received for items you deducted in a prior year, such as medical expenses, home mortgage interest, or insurance proceeds from a casualty loss.

>> The taxable part of disaster relief payments.

>> Taxable distributions from a Coverdell education savings account (an ESA) or a qualified tuition program (QTP).

It may be easier to list items that you may think are income, but which aren't taxable under any circumstances. These include

>> Child support payments.

>> Hardest Hit Fund payments you received to help pay your mortgage.

>> Life insurance proceeds after the death of the covered individual. (Please note that certain employer-owned life insurance policy payments may be taxable.)

>> Monetary gifts and bequests. (Please note that, in the case of bequests, you may receive a Schedule K-1 from the estate listing a small amount of income and/or deductions that you are responsible to report. See Chapter 15 for more on this Schedule.)

>> Pay-for-Performance Success payments you received that reduced the principal balance of your home mortgage under the Home Affordable Modification Program.

TIP If you've received money or goods during 2021 and you're not sure how to categorize it or where it belongs on your tax return, the best place to look (other than this book) is the IRS website. Go to www.irs.gov, and plug your question into the search bar at the top. Chances are good you'll enjoy an afternoon of pleasurable reading.

Schedule 1, Part I, Line 9: Total Other Income

Okay, you know you can do this. Add up any amounts you have on lines 8a through 8z and enter the total here. If you're doing this on your computer, it has probably already done this for you. If you're doing it manually, add the numbers twice to make sure you get the same answer both times. Math mistakes are easy to avoid, and your life will be so much simpler if you just don't make them.

Schedule 1, Part I, Line 10: Combine Lines 1 through 7 and 9

More math, and we know how much you love math. Once again, if you're doing this on your computer with a software program, there's not really anything for you to do here. If you're doing this on paper, please add carefully and check your math. There is absolutely nothing worse than dealing with the stress of an IRS notice for an addition mistake.

Once you're sure you have your math correct, transfer your answer here back to Form 1040, line 8. Make sure you transfer whatever number is located here on line 10 carefully; transposition errors (where you swap two of the digits in a number, so you write 27 instead of 72) are easy to make.

If you're thinking to yourself that you're filing a different Form 1040 than the regular one, and you're not sure where to put your answer to this little math quiz, no worries. All of the Forms 1040 have the same line 8.

CHANGES TO IRA DISTRIBUTION RULES UNDER THE SECURE ACT OF 2019

TIP

The Setting Every Community Up for Retirement Enhancement ("SECURE") Act, which was signed into law in December 2019, significantly changes the rules for retirement distributions, especially in two specific situations: the date that you must begin taking your required minimum distributions, and what happens if you still have funds in your retirement accounts when you die.

Required minimum distributions under the SECURE Act must now begin in the year after the year in which you turn 72 (as opposed to 70½, under prior law). This allows you to postpone beginning to draw down your retirement accounts for another 18 months or so. The rules regarding the timing of your first distribution remain the same; you still must take that first distribution by April 1 of the year following the year your 72nd birthday occurs. And, if you don't take that first distribution until the following year, in that first year of distributions, you must take two distributions: the first for the year of your 72nd birthday, and then your ordinary distribution by December 31 of the current year. You'll use the market value of your account on December 31 of the year prior to your 72nd birthday to determine the amount you must take for that first distribution, and then the market value of your account on December 31 of the year of your 72nd birthday to calculate your RMD for the current year.

Here's how this all works: If you turned 72 during 2021, you can delay your first distribution until April 1, 2022. This first distribution will be based on the market value of your retirement accounts on December 31, 2020. Your regular 2022 distribution must be taken by December 31, 2022, and will be based on the market value of all your retirement accounts on December 31, 2021 (except for Roth accounts, which are excluded since they're not taxable to you).

If you turned 72 in 2020, you're in a special category. Because RMDs were not required in 2020 due to the stock market crash in March and April of 2020 (this was one provision in the CARES Act of 2020), you only need to take one distribution in 2021, by December 31.

As for what happens after you die, well, that's a question we're all curious about. But as regards your retirement accounts, the ability for your heirs to stretch the payments out over long periods of time has diminished. Now, the general rule is that you must completely deplete the accounts, including Roth accounts, within ten years after the death of the original owners.

Because nothing that Congress does is ever straightforward, there are exceptions to this general rule, and exceptions to the exceptions. We explain it all in Chapter 5. Look at the rules stated there and see where you fit in terms of your relationship to the decedent. There may be decisions you have to make, especially if you're the surviving spouse. Think carefully about how you want to distribute these accounts, as your decisions now may impact your tax returns for many years to come.

IN THIS CHAPTER

» Calculating your adjusted gross income

» Checking on health savings account deductions and moving expenses

» Finding deductions if you're self-employed

» Reporting alimony paid (that you deduct!)

» Keeping track of IRA deductions for you and your spouse

» Seeking student loan interest, tuition, and fees deductions

Chapter **7**

Form 1040, Schedule 1, Part II: Adjustments to Income Stuff

ongratulations! If you're reading this chapter, you've probably made it through the first part of your income tax return. If the amount on Form 1040, line 9, represents all your income, you may now think that all you have to do is figure your tax on that amount. But wait! All you've done so far is figure out your total income. Your taxable income will be much, much less. In this chapter, you can find out about the first set of deductions you can subtract from the total, the so-called adjustments to income.

Figuring Out Your Adjusted Gross Income (AGI)

In this section (see Figure 7-1), you're going to add your adjustments to income on Form 1040, Schedule 1, Part II, lines 11 through 25. Once you add these all up, you'll then subtract the total (which you'll place on Schedule 1, Part II, line 26) from your total income shown on your Form 1040 on line 9 and arrive at your adjusted gross income (AGI). Finally, you'll enter your AGI on line 11 of your Form 1040. Your AGI is an important number because it's used as the benchmark for calculating many allowable deductions — such as medical expenses — and the taxable amount of your Social Security income.

REMEMBER

You don't have to itemize your deductions on Schedule A to claim adjustments to income in this section. Everyone gets to make these adjustments.

Here's the line-by-line rundown of the adjustments you may be able to make. The headings refer to line numbers where you plug your data into your Schedule 1, Part II.

Line 11: Educator expenses

Teachers who spend their own money for items they supply for the classroom are entitled to deduct these expenses from their income. For 2021, you can deduct up to $250 of these expenses on line 11. Expenses that qualify include professional development course fees, books, supplies, computer software and equipment, and supplemental material used in the classroom. If you're married filing jointly and both of you are educators, you may deduct up to $500.

To claim this deduction, you must be an educator, or more precisely, a teacher, instructor, counselor, principal, or aide in a public or private elementary or secondary school who works a minimum of 900 hours during the school year. Educators who exclude U.S. savings bond interest from income that was used to pay college tuition (see Chapter 12) or payments from a 529 plan, or those who made withdrawals from a Coverdell Education Savings Account, can claim this deduction only if the amount they paid for classroom supplies exceeds the amount that is tax-free under these other education tax breaks. For example, if you excluded $750 of U.S. savings bond interest and have educator expenses of $500, you can't claim a deduction.

For expenses you incurred after March 12, 2020, any expenses you incurred for personal protective equipment or sanitation used in your classroom are also deductible. If you have over $250 of legitimate classroom expenses without face masks, hand sanitizer, and so on, use all your other expenses for line 11, and add these COVID-19- related expenses to your unreimbursed medical expenses for the year. If you haven't spent the full $250 for your classroom without COVID-19 prevention costs, put as many of those expenses here as you need, as they will save you more in taxes here than on Schedule A.

NEW STUFF

Since miscellaneous itemized deductions subject to 2 percent of adjusted gross income have been eliminated from the tax code, you are not allowed to take a deduction on Schedule A for the amount that you spent in your classroom on unreimbursed expenses in 2021.

Part II	Adjustments to Income		
11	Educator expenses	11	
12	Certain business expenses of reservists, performing artists, and fee-basis government officials. Attach Form 2106	12	
13	Health savings account deduction. Attach Form 8889	13	
14	Moving expenses for members of the Armed Forces. Attach Form 3903 . . .	14	
15	Deductible part of self-employment tax. Attach Schedule SE	15	
16	Self-employed SEP, SIMPLE, and qualified plans	16	
17	Self-employed health insurance deduction	17	
18	Penalty on early withdrawal of savings	18	
19a	Alimony paid	19a	
b	Recipient's SSN . . . . ▶		
c	Date of original divorce or separation agreement (see instructions) ▶		
20	IRA deduction	20	
21	Student loan interest deduction	21	
22	Reserved for future use	22	
23	Archer MSA deduction	23	
24	Other adjustments:		
a	Jury duty pay (see instructions)	24a	
b	Deductible expenses related to income reported on line 8k from the rental of personal property engaged in for profit . . .	24b	
c	Nontaxable amount of the value of Olympic and Paralympic medals and USOC prize money reported on line 8l	24c	
d	Reforestation amortization and expenses	24d	
e	Repayment of supplemental unemployment benefits under the Trade Act of 1974	24e	
f	Contributions to section 501(c)(18)(D) pension plans	24f	
g	Contributions by certain chaplains to section 403(b) plans . .	24g	
h	Attorney fees and court costs for actions involving certain unlawful discrimination claims (see instructions)	24h	
i	Attorney fees and court costs you paid in connection with an award from the IRS for information you provided that helped the IRS detect tax law violations	24i	
j	Housing deduction from Form 2555	24j	
k	Excess deductions of section 67(e) expenses from Schedule K-1 (Form 1041)	24k	
z	Other adjustments. List type and amount ▶ _____ _____	24z	
25	Total other adjustments. Add lines 24a through 24z	25	
26	Add lines 11 through 23 and 25. These are your **adjustments to income.** Enter here and on Form 1040 or 1040-SR, line 10, or Form 1040-NR, line 10a	26	

Schedule 1 (Form 1040) 2021

Source: Internal Revenue Service

FIGURE 7-1: Form 1040, Schedule 1, Part II may lower your taxes.

Line 12: Certain business expenses of certain types of workers

If you believe you fall into the category of an armed forces reservist, a performing artist, a fee-basis government official, or you're an employee with impairment-related work expenses, read up! You may be able to deduct certain business expenses from your total income. Before you can decide, though, you need to know if your job and your expenses qualify. Here's the info:

>> **Armed forces reservists** may deduct travel expenses if traveling more than 100 miles away from their home in connection with their service.

>> **Performing artists** may deduct all of their employee business expenses on line 12, provided that they meet all four requirements:

- During the tax year, you perform services in the performing arts as an employee of at least two employers.

- You earn at least $200 each from at least two employers.

- The business expenses you incur from your performing arts jobs are more than 10 percent of the amount you earn from all your performing arts jobs.

- Your AGI (see line 11 at the end of this chapter) isn't more than $16,000 before deducting these business expenses.

If you're married and either you or your spouse is a performing artist, you need to file a joint return in order to qualify for this deduction unless you lived apart from your spouse for the entire tax year. And, to make matters more interesting, although both you and your spouse must figure the first three requirements separately, the AGI for both of you together can't be more than $16,000. If you can't make any of these requirements, you lose the deduction.

>> **Government officials** paid on a fee basis may deduct all their employee business expenses on line 12 if they're employed by their state or local government and are paid in whole or in part on a fee basis ($5,000 to prepare a particular report, for example).

If you do qualify, you need to fill out Form 2106 before you fill in an amount on line 24 of your Form 1040.

>> **Employees with impairment-related work expenses** aren't included in the line 12 description (maybe the IRS was trying to save on ink?), but if you fall into this category and incur expenses that allow you to do your job, this is where you're going to deduct those costs.

Line 13: Health Savings Account deduction (Form 8889)

Health Savings Accounts (HSAs) may allow you to pay for unreimbursed medical expenses on a tax-free basis. You may establish an HSA if you're covered by a qualified high-deductible health plan with minimum annual deductibles of at least $1,400 for individuals and $2,800 for families, with maximum out-of-pocket annual expenses capped at $7,000 and 14,000, respectively. You may not open or fund one of these accounts if you have other general health insurance (separate dental, accident-only, vision, workers' comp, disability, or long-term care policies don't count against you here). You also can't be claimed as a dependent on someone else's return.

An HSA works similarly to an individual retirement account (IRA). In this case, your HSA is invested and allowed to grow income-tax-free until you need to access the money to pay for qualified medical expenses (medical insurance premiums are excluded). Payouts for qualified medical expenses are tax-free. Unlike Flexible Spending Accounts that may be offered by your employer, there's no "use it or lose it" feature here. Your money continues to grow from year to year until you need to use it. You may contribute a maximum of $3,600 for individuals and $7,200 for families each year. If you're age 55 or older, you may make an additional contribution of $1,000. After you enroll in Medicare at age 65, contributions are no longer allowed, although you may continue to take distributions.

If you previously funded an Archer Medical Savings Account (MSA), you're allowed to roll that account into an HSA without paying any tax or penalty. Just like any IRA rollover, though, the safest way to avoid paying any tax or penalty is through a trustee-to-trustee transfer.

If you funded an HSA in 2021 (or from January 1 to April 15, 2022) or rolled your existing Archer MSA over to an HSA, you need to complete Form 8889, Health Savings Accounts (HSAs). After you complete that form, take the number from line 11 of the Form 8889 and put it on line 13 of your Schedule 1, Part II.

SEEK ADVICE

The rules for these accounts are fairly intricate, and you really need to consult a pro before setting one up. With health insurance premiums continuing to climb, these accounts, and the high deductible policies that they supplement, have become more the rule than the exception.

Line 14: Moving expenses for members of the Armed Forces (Form 3903)

NEW STUFF

The deduction for moving expenses for most people vanished as a result of the Tax Cuts and Jobs Act; however, if you're an active-duty member of the military, you may still qualify for this tax deduction.

If you incur moving expenses because you relocated to either start or end your active-duty military service, or Uncle Sam has changed your posting from one location to another, you can deduct moving expenses for which you either haven't received an allowance or haven't been reimbursed. You may deduct any unreimbursed costs for yourself, your spouse, and your dependent children. If you have household employees, such as a nanny or housekeeper, you may not deduct the costs of their move.

The place to deduct moving expenses is Form 3903, Moving Expenses. You then enter the deductible amount on line 14. See Chapter 17 for more about filling out Form 3903. Don't forget to attach Form 3903 to your return.

Line 15: One-half of self-employment tax

One of the great drawbacks of being self-employed is that you get hit not only with income tax on your earnings but also with self-employment tax. This wonderful invention combines the 7.65 percent ordinary wage earners pay for combined Social Security and Medicare contributions with the employer's matching 7.65 percent. So, because self-employed people are both the employer and the employee, they get stuck with both halves of this tax, or a whopping 15.3 percent of all earnings from self-employment up to $142,800, and 2.9 percent on all earnings above that.

If you're subject to this additional tax (and you know who you are, because you've already filled out Schedule SE, Self-Employment Tax, which we cover in Chapter 17), line 15 provides some tax relief. You're allowed to deduct one half of your self-employment tax from your total income.

Line 16: Self-employed SEP, SIMPLE, and qualified plans

In case you were looking and you're self-employed, you've just found the place to deduct contributions to your HR10, 401(k), Keogh, SEP, or SIMPLE retirement accounts. These types of accounts allow you to make substantial pretax contributions toward your retirement savings.

Looking through your self-employed retirement plan options

A *SEP* is a combination IRA/profit-sharing plan and is available only for self-employed individuals and their employees (but not corporations). With a SEP (Simplified Employee Pension), you're allowed to stash up to 25 percent of your net income from self-employment, but not to exceed a $58,000 contribution. You can set up your plan and make this contribution for 2021 up to the day that you file your income tax return in 2022, including extensions. Only the amount that you contribute for yourself belongs on line 16; if you make contributions to your employees, they will be shown on either the business return for the company or on your Schedule C (see Chapter 13).

Employers with fewer than 100 employees can establish what's known as *SIMPLE* (Savings Incentive Match Plan for Employees) plans. SIMPLEs come in two forms: a SIMPLE IRA and a SIMPLE 401(k). A SIMPLE plan allows an employee to contribute up to $13,500 in pretax dollars with the employer matching a like amount — $16,500 if you turned 50 in 2021 or earlier. Unlike regular retirement plans, the nondiscrimination coverage rules don't apply, which means you don't have to include your employees in your retirement plan. See Chapter 22 for more about SIMPLE and other small-business retirement plan options.

As a self-employed person or the owner of an unincorporated business, you can also set up a qualified defined contribution plan using an *HR10 plan*. Your contributions to the plan are not only deductible, but also are exempt from tax until you start receiving benefits. But to make an HR10 contribution in 2022 that's deductible on your 2021 return, the plan had to be set up by December 31, 2021. With an HR10 plan, you can contribute up to the lesser of 100 percent of compensation or $58,000 in 2021. Plans can either be profit-sharing or defined contribution plans; in a profit-sharing plan, if there are no profits in any particular year, you're not required to fund the plan in that year, whereas in a qualified defined contribution plan, you are limited to the lesser of $58,000 or 25 percent of your net income from self-employment. HR10 plan holders are required to file Form 5500 annually for the plan.

Another option for highly compensated taxpayers (we're thinking doctors and lawyers, but maybe someday authors of tax books will qualify) is a defined benefit *Keogh Plan.* The maximum contribution you're allowed to make into a defined benefit plan (that's a plan where you're funding an account to provide you with a set benefit in retirement) in 2021 is $230,000. As with the HR10 plans, there is an annual Form 5500 filing requirement.

SEEK ADVICE

HR10 and Keogh plans are fairly sophisticated types of accounts, and the penalties for failing to set them up properly, deal with annual funding, and prepare the annual reporting are serious. Because these types of accounts require far more due diligence than either SEP or SIMPLE plans, you may want to check in with an attorney or accountant who specializes in ERISA (Employee Retirement Income Security Act of 1974) matters to make sure all your t's are crossed and your i's are dotted.

REMEMBER

Remember, if you have employees and want to contribute to a SEP, HR10, or Keogh plan for yourself, you can't ignore your employees. Check out Chapter 22 for the rules on contributions. If you and your spouse are the only ones covered by the plan, you don't have to file an annual information return with the IRS until the plan's assets exceed $250,000. If you're subject to the filing requirements, file Form 5500-EZ. If you have employees, use Form 5500. This form need not be filed for a SEP.

TIP

Another retirement plan possibility is called the *Solo (k)*, which is a cross between a 401(k) and a profit-sharing Keogh. What's unique about the Solo (k) retirement plan is that business owners without employees — consultants, independent contractors, lawyers and doctors in solo practices, and mom-and-pop shops — can put away significantly more than they can under a qualified defined contribution plan. Here's how it works. Say the earnings of your consulting business are $40,000. Under an HR10 or SEP-IRA, you can contribute and deduct $8,000 (25 percent of $40,000 after deducting the $8,000). With a Solo (k), you get to contribute the $8,000 plus the maximum 401(k) limit of $19,500 for a total contribution of $27,500, as long as the combination of the two contributions doesn't exceed $58,000. There's more! If you're older than 50, you can contribute an additional $6,500 to the 401(k) portion of the plan. This extra amount isn't subject to the overall $58,000 limit. So, if your income is $180,000 and you're older than 50, you can contribute $19,500 under the 401(k) arrangement, plus $6,500 because you're older than 50, and another $36,000 in normal profit-sharing contributions (25 percent of $180,000 after deducting the $36,000) for a total retirement deduction of $62,000. By comparison, if all you have is a SEP-IRA or HR10 plan, the most you can contribute is $36,000.

TIP

If you're both an employee and a sole proprietor, the most you can contribute to either your employer's 401(k) or the 401(k) feature of your Solo (k) is $19,500. Some taxpayers mistakenly believe they can contribute $19,500 to each 401(k). Don't make that mistake. However, if your employer contributes on your behalf to a profit-sharing plan, you can also contribute to the profit-sharing feature of your plan. However, if you're an owner where you're employed, the profit-sharing plan of your separate business won't be considered a separate plan, meaning that the most you can contribute to both plans is $58,000.

TIP

If you find this Solo (k) business intriguing, major investment companies such as the leading mutual fund companies and investment brokerage firms offer such plans. The website at www.401khelpcenter.com also features a calculator that instantly computes the maximum you can contribute. Just enter your age, earnings, and presto! Because the menu options at this site change so often, type in Solo (k) at the search button to go to the "Solo (k) menu."

Computing your maximum retirement deductions

We wish we could tell you that all you have to do to figure your deduction is to multiply your self-employment earnings by 25 percent. Why should the government make it that simple? You must follow two rules to arrive at the amount you are allowed to deduct:

>> **Rule 1:** You have to reduce your earnings by deducting one-half of your self-employment tax and your contribution to get the amount that you multiply the percentage by; say it's 25 percent.

>> **Rule 2:** The maximum amount of your earnings reduced by this adjustment that you multiply the 25 percent by can't exceed $290,000.

See Table 7-1 to determine your effective contribution rate based on the actual plan percentage that you choose to contribute.

Table 7-1   Keogh and SEP Conversion Table

Actual Plan Rate	Effective Rate That You Contribute
1%	.009901
2%	.019608
3%	.029126
4%	.038462
5%	.047619
6%	.056604
7%	.065421
8%	.074074
9%	.082569
10%	.090909
11%	.099099
12%	.107143
13%	.115044
14%	.122807
15%	.130435
16%	.137931
17%	.145299
18%	.152542
19%	.159664
20%	.166667
21%	.173554
22%	.180328
23%	.186992
24%	.193548
25%	.200000

TIP

With a Keogh *defined-benefit retirement plan*, the annual contribution isn't determined by a percentage of your earnings or by your employees' salaries. You select an annual pension benefit that you want to receive at retirement, say $75,000. Next, an insurance actuary determines — based on your age — how much you need to contribute to the pension every year to have a nest egg at retirement that's large enough to pay you $75,000 a year during retirement. If the actuary determines that you need to put away $95,000 a year to accomplish that goal, then you can ignore the 2021 maximum annual deduction limitation of $58,000. Sounds great, but all this red tape is extremely complicated and costly to administer. You can select a retirement benefit as high as $230,000. Because the amount that you can put away every year is based on your age, you can, as a general rule, put away more money under this type of plan at about age 50. That's because at that age, you have fewer years to put money away, so a greater annual contribution to the plan must be made.

WARNING

If you have a SEP or a profit-sharing plan, you can wait until you file your return in 2022 (including the extension period, which ends on October 17, 2022) to make your contribution to the plan and have it count toward 2021. On the other hand, if you have a defined-benefit or a regular pension plan (other than a SEP or profit-sharing plan), you must make your contribution by September 15, 2022, regardless of whether you have an extension of time to file until October 17, 2022. Dealing with the IRS rules is a virtual mine field to the unknowing.

Line 17: Self-employed health insurance deduction

If you're self-employed, you may deduct 100 percent of your health insurance premiums from your income, with one caveat: You may not deduct more than your net profit from your business.

A general partner (but not a limited partner), an independent contractor, or a shareholder in an S Corporation may also claim this deduction. The deduction is allowed for premiums paid for you, your spouse, and your dependents. A portion of your long-term-care premiums also qualifies for this deduction (see Chapter 11 for the maximum deductible amount).

Line 18: Penalty for early withdrawal of savings

If you withdraw funds from a savings account before maturity or redeem a certificate of deposit before it's due and you're charged a penalty, you can deduct it here, on Schedule 1, Part II, line 18. You don't have to itemize to claim this deduction. You can deduct the entire penalty, even when it exceeds the interest income reported on the Form 1099-INT that you received. The penalty amount, if any, is shown in box 2 of the 1099-INT or box 3 of 1099-OID, which your bank or brokerage will send you by January 31, 2022.

Lines 19a, b, and c: Alimony paid

The alimony you paid is deducted on line 19a; right below that, you have to enter your former spouse's Social Security number on line 19b, and to show the IRS that you're allowed to deduct the alimony payments you make, you need to put the date of your original divorce or separation agreement on line 19c. Because of the new rules eliminating this deduction for divorce or separation agreements dated after December 31, 2018, you'll want to be extra careful and make sure you add that all-important date. And please, don't forget to also fill in line 19b; failure to provide that Social Security number will cost you a $50 penalty, and your alimony deduction may be disallowed. If you paid alimony to more than one person, enter the total amount of alimony you paid on line 19z, and then list the amount, Social Security number, and date of original agreement for each recipient on a separate statement and attach it to your return.

NEW STUFF

If your original divorce or separation agreement is dated after December 31, 2018, you get no deduction for alimony paid, and your former spouse isn't required to include the alimony received as income on their Form 1040.

Before you can deduct it as an expense, you need to know what the government defines as alimony. The alimony rules aren't simple, so hang in there.

This is alimony

Payments count as alimony only if all the following conditions are met:

» Payments are required by the divorce decree or a separation decree.

» The alimony payer and the alimony recipient don't file a joint return with each other.

» The payment is in cash (including checks or money orders).

» The spouses who are separated or divorced aren't members of the same household.

» The payments aren't required after the death of the spouse who receives the alimony.

» The payment isn't designated as child support.

This isn't alimony

Payments don't count as alimony if any of the following conditions are true:

» The payment is a noncash property settlement.

» The payments are a spouse's part of community income.

» The payments are destined to keep up the payer's property.

» The payments aren't required as part of the separation or divorce settlement.

Rules and exceptions to alimony

Looks simple, you say? Sorry. The rules on alimony are one of the most complex areas of the law. The reason for this absurd complexity is that each party to a divorce is trying to achieve opposite goals. The payer usually wants to deduct every payment, and the recipient wants to pay as little tax as possible. To keep everyone honest, regulations breed regulations! The following additional information can help you plug in the right amount on Schedule 1, Part I, line 2a, for alimony received, or Schedule 1, Part II, line 19a for alimony paid:

» **Cash payments:** A cash payment must be made in cash. (Makes sense, doesn't it?) Therefore, property settlements don't qualify. The transfer of a home or business is considered a property settlement.

MEMBERS OF THE SAME HOUSEHOLD

You're members of the same household even if you and your spouse separate yourselves physically in your home (or in your tropical hut, just like Gilligan and the Skipper once did after they had a fight). However, payments made within one month of departure qualify as alimony. For example, suppose that on June 1, while you're still residing in the same residence with your spouse, you make a support payment. If you move out by July 1, this payment is deductible. Any payments made prior to June 1 don't qualify. A technical exception exists, however. If you're not legally separated under a decree of divorce or separate maintenance, a payment made under a written separation agreement or support decree can qualify as alimony even if you are members of the same household. Although this sounds like a distinction without a difference, in plain English this means that temporary payments until the separation or divorce is finalized can be deducted as alimony even if you continue to live in the same residence.

>> **Payments to a third party:** Payments to a third party qualify as alimony if they are used in place of alimony and are requested in writing by your former spouse. These payments can be for medical expenses, housing costs, taxes, tuition, and so on.

>> **Life insurance premiums:** Life insurance premiums on your life insurance qualify as deductible alimony if the payment is required by the divorce or separation agreement and your former spouse owns the policy.

>> **Mortgage payments:** Mortgage payments are alimony if you must make mortgage payments (principal and interest) on a home jointly owned with your former spouse — and the terms of the decree or agreement call for such payments. You can deduct half of the total of these payments as alimony. Your spouse reports this same half as income. If you itemize deductions and the home is your qualified residence, you can include the other half of the interest portion in figuring your deductible interest. If the home is your ex's residence, they can deduct half of the mortgage interest.

>> **Taxes and insurance:** Tax and insurance payments qualify as alimony if you must make them on a home that you hold as *tenants in common* — which means that your heirs, not the person you own the property with, get your share when you die. You can deduct half of the tax and insurance payments as alimony, and your ex-spouse reports this amount as income. If you and your ex-spouse itemize deductions, you each may deduct one-half of the real estate taxes. If the property is held as tenants by the entirety or as joint tenants (where the survivor gets it all), none of your payments for taxes and insurance qualify as alimony. If you itemize your deductions, you can deduct all of the real estate taxes.

>> **Minimum payment period:** For alimony agreements executed in 1985 and 1986, annual payments in excess of $10,000 had to continue for at least six years. For agreements made after 1986, no minimum payment period exists.

>> **Recapture:** To keep people from disguising large divorce settlements as alimony, a recapture provision was enacted for agreements executed after 1986. *Recapture* means that you have to report as income part of what you deducted during the first two years that you started paying alimony. The recapture rule applies if your average payments decline in the first three years by more than $15,000.

For example, suppose that in year one and year two, you paid and deducted $25,000 in alimony, but in year three, you paid only $5,000. You triggered the recapture rule, because your payment decreased by more than $15,000. See a tax expert. This area is one you don't want to fool around with. However, recapture doesn't apply if your spouse dies or remarries, or if your alimony payments are geared to a fixed percentage of your income and your income decreases.

>> **Payments after death:** Alimony payments must stop at your ex-spouse's death. If you must continue to make payments after your spouse's death — because of the legalese included in the agreement — none of the payments that you made before or after death qualify as alimony that you can deduct.

>> **Child support:** A required payment that's specifically designated as child support under your divorce decree isn't deductible as alimony. Even if a payment isn't specially designated as child support, part of it will be considered child support if the payment is to be reduced when your child reaches a specified age, dies, marries, leaves school, or becomes employed.

For example, suppose that you're required to pay your spouse $2,000 a month. However, when your child reaches age 21, your payment will be reduced to $1,250. Only $1,250 of your $2,000 monthly payment is considered alimony, and the remaining $750 is considered nondeductible child support.

For pre-1985 divorce decrees, combined spouse and child support payments that are reduced when the child comes of age are treated as alimony. The IRS deemed this deal too good (of course) and thus changed the rules for agreements executed after 1984.

>> **Payments to nonresident aliens:** Alimony paid to nonresident aliens is considered U.S. source income. As a result, you have to withhold 30 percent for tax and send it to the IRS, just like your employer does with the tax withheld from your salary. Find out whether the United States has a tax treaty with the country of your former spouse — under a number of tax treaties, alimony is exempt from withholding. See *IRS Publication 901 (U.S. Tax Treaties)* for some really interesting reading!

Normally when a property settlement is reached in a divorce, the transfer isn't taxable to either of the parties. However, there are exceptions (what a surprise!). For example, if you give shares of stock or stock options that you own to your former spouse, the transfer, depending on the type of option, may become a taxable event, as a qualified incentive stock option (not subject to taxation until it is exercised) will become a nonqualified stock option upon transfer, which is taxable immediately to your former spouse. This rule also applies to other assets. Chapter 14 contains the rules on stock options.

Line 20: Your and your spouse's IRA deduction

Saving for your eventual retirement is a good thing, which is why the tax laws are structured to give you all sorts of benefits if you do save for retirement. The IRA is one way that you may sock away $6,000 per year ($7,000 if you're age 50 or older in 2021) for your golden years.

Originally, IRAs came in plain vanilla. Basically, you were allowed to contribute $2,000 each year into an account and defer paying tax on both your yearly contributions and any money that you earned on your contributions. When you took distributions from your account after retirement, you paid the income tax on the full amount of your distribution at ordinary income rates. What can be easier?

This sort of account still exists, only now it's called a "traditional, fully deductible IRA." Other types of IRAs — essentially variations on a theme — have joined it. Now you may own a traditional deductible IRA, a traditional nondeductible IRA, or even a Roth IRA. Here's how they differ:

>> **Traditional deductible IRA:** You make contributions that you haven't paid tax on yet. When you begin taking money out at retirement, you'll be taxed on the full amount of your distributions.

>> **Traditional nondeductible IRA:** You make contributions into your IRA account with after-tax dollars or money you've already paid tax on. When you begin to take distributions, you're not taxed on the amounts you contributed, but only on the investment earnings — interest, dividends, and capital gains/appreciation — that have accumulated in your account.

>> **Roth IRA:** Just like the traditional nondeductible IRA, you make contributions into your Roth with after-tax dollars. You don't pay any income tax on distributions.

Because line 20 is concerned only with the deduction you can take for a contribution to a traditional IRA, we concentrate on the rules for the deductible IRA here. Even though you don't get a deduction for the nondeductible IRA and Roth IRA, for some people, these accounts can be useful retirement planning tools. You can find out more about all retirement plans in Chapter 22.

REMEMBER

You and your spouse (if you're married) are both entitled to contribute and deduct the maximum to your IRAs if you meet the compensation and age requirements that we introduce in this section. This means that, if you're married and able to take advantage of the maximum deduction in 2021, you can exclude up to $12,000 from your total income if you're both under 50, $14,000 if you've both reached that milestone birthday prior to January 1, 2022. These aren't small potatoes!

TIP

Putting real dollars into a real account is required to get the deduction, but you don't have to do it in 2021 to get a deduction on your 2021 Form 1040. Provided you've put the money into an account by April 18, 2022 (April 19, 2022, if you live in Massachusetts or Maine), you're entitled to take your 2021 IRA deduction.

Types of compensation needed to qualify for an IRA

WARNING

In order to make contributions to an IRA, you need to have taxable earned income from wages, commissions, tips, self-employment, nontaxable combat pay, or the receipt of alimony that is taxable to you. If you (or your spouse, if you aren't currently earning from these sources) don't have income from at least one of these, you can't make contributions, so you can't get the deduction. For many of you who received unemployment insurance during 2021, unemployment insurance is considered unearned income and is therefore not eligible to be used to determine whether you can contribute to an IRA. However, if you are married, and your spouse has enough income, you can contribute to a spousal IRA even though you may not have enough income to qualify on your own.

TECHNICAL STUFF

If you're self-employed, your self-employed earnings for the purpose of determining IRA contribution eligibility are reduced by amounts you contribute to another retirement plan (Keogh or SEP) and by the deduction you're taking for one-half of your self-employment tax. (For more on Keogh plans or SEPs, see Chapter 22.)

Contribution limits

If you have earned income, congratulations! You've passed the first hurdle. Now you need to figure out how much you can contribute.

For 2021 returns, the maximum you're allowed to contribute to your IRA is $6,000. If you have less than $6,000 of earned income, you may contribute up to 100 percent of your earned income. If you're 50 or older, you can contribute an additional $1,000 (provided you have at least $7,000 of earned income). As long as you turned 50 years old on or before January 1, 2022, you can take advantage of this extra $1,000 amount, which is more commonly referred to as a "catch-up contribution." See Chapter 2 for details.

TIP

Remember, the earlier in the year that you make your IRA contribution, the sooner it starts growing tax-free. For example, if you're turning 50 in December 2021, you don't need to wait until then to make your catch-up contribution. As long as you turn the magic number this year, you can make that contribution at any time during the year.

Age limits

NEW STUFF

Unlike driving a car, funding an IRA doesn't have a minimum age requirement. Beginning January 1, 2020, it no longer places a maximum age limit on contributions, either. Provided you have earned income, you're allowed to make those contributions.

Deductible IRA contributions

As a general rule, you can claim a deduction for the contribution that you're allowed to make to your IRA. That rule has only one qualification: If you or your spouse is covered by a retirement plan at work, your ability to claim a deduction may be reduced or eliminated. This restriction doesn't mean you can't make a $6,000 ($7,000 if you're 50 or older) nondeductible IRA or Roth IRA contribution.

Table 7-2 shows who may make a deductible contribution to a traditional IRA.

TECHNICAL STUFF

These limits and phaseouts refer to your *modified adjusted gross income,* or "modified AGI" for short. To figure your modified AGI, fill out the worksheet that we include in the sidebar "How to figure partial IRA deductions" later in this chapter.

Are you covered by your employer's plan?

If you're not sure whether you (or your spouse) are covered by a pension plan at work, check out box 13 of your W-2. If your employer has some sort of pension plan that you're eligible to participate in, the "Retirement Plan" box will be checked.

You're considered covered, or an active participant, even if you haven't earned the full right (known as *vesting*) to the benefits under your plan. If you switch employers during the year, and one of the employers has a plan and the other doesn't, you're considered covered.

You're also considered covered by a plan when you're both salaried and self-employed, provided that you have your own HR10, Keogh, SEP, or SIMPLE plan, and you aren't covered by a plan where you're employed. You're also considered covered by a plan if you're self-employed and have a HR10, Keogh, SEP, or SIMPLE plan.

Table 7-2   Who Can Make a Deductible Contribution?

Filing Status	Employer's Plan	Income Phaseouts/Limits (based on modified AGI)
Single **or** Head of Household	No	Fully deductible
	Yes	Up to $66,000, fully deductible; Between $66,000 and $75,999, partially deductible; $76,000 and over, no deduction
Married Filing Jointly **or** Qualifying Widow or Widower	Neither spouse	Fully deductible
	One spouse	Up to $198,000, fully deductible for spouse whose employer doesn't have a plan; between $198,000 and $207,999, partially deductible for spouse whose employer doesn't have a plan; $208,000 and over, no deduction
	Both spouses	Up to $105,000, fully deductible; Between $105,000 and $124,999, partially deductible; $125,000 and over, no deduction
Married Filing Separately	No	Fully deductible
	Yes	Up to $9,999, partially deductible; $10,000 and over, no deduction

If your employer offers you a retirement plan that you can contribute to, such as a 401(k) or 403(b), and you and your employer didn't add any money to your account and no forfeitures were allocated during the tax year, you're not considered covered during the year. Thus, you can make the maximum tax-deductible IRA contribution if your spouse also isn't covered by a pension plan. If you spouse is covered by a pension plan, you can still put away, and fully deduct, the $6,000 maximum, provided your joint income is less than $196,000.

Nondeductible IRA contributions (Form 8606)

Although your deduction for an IRA contribution may be reduced or eliminated because of the AGI modifications, you still can make nondeductible IRA contributions of up to $6,000, or 100 percent of your compensation, whichever is less, plus the $1,000 catch-up amount if you're 50 or older. The difference between your allowable deductible contribution, which is entered on line 20, and your total contributions made, if any, is your nondeductible contribution.

REMEMBER

Your total IRA contributions, including deductible, nondeductible, and Roth IRAs, can't exceed $6,000 (or $7,000 if you're 50 or older).

WARNING

You must report nondeductible contributions to the IRS on Form 8606, Nondeductible IRAs, even if you don't have to file a tax return for the year. If you're filing a Form 1040, you attach Form 8606 to your 1040. The penalty for not filing your Form 8606 is $50, and if your IRA contributions are more than the permissible amount, you must correct the overpayment; otherwise, you may be subject to a 6 percent penalty. The penalty is imposed annually until the excess amount is removed. You can also be penalized an additional $100 if you overstate the computation of your nondeductible contributions on Form 8606. We show you how to complete

Form 8606 in Chapter 17 and how to calculate your deductible IRA contribution in the sidebar in this chapter.

TIP

Say you discovered while preparing your 2021 return that you contributed too much in 2021. Three ways to avoid the penalty are as follows:

>> **Considering the excess 2021 contribution part of your 2022 IRA contribution.** This way works best. For example, if you contributed $1,000 too much in 2021 and you're entitled to contribute $6,000 for 2022, just change that excess $1,000 contribution for 2021 to a $1,000 contribution to 2022. Now you need to add only an additional $5,000 contribution later in 2022 to reach the maximum $6,000 contribution allowed for 2022. With this simple shift, no penalty will be assessed, and you still manage to contribute the full amounts for both 2021 and 2022.

>> **Withdrawing the excess amount by the due date (including extensions) for filing your return.** If you withdraw the excess and the earnings on the excess amount before April 15, 2022, no penalty. However, you'll owe tax on the earnings and, if you're younger than 59½, the earnings are subject to the 10 percent additional tax discussed in Chapter 6.

>> **Withdrawing the excess contribution and paying tax on it when it's too late to use either of the other two methods, even when you didn't claim a deduction for the excess amount.** Ouch!

TIP

If after filing your return, you discover that you should have deducted your IRA contribution instead of claiming it as a nondeductible contribution (or vice versa), you can amend your return by filing Form 1040X. You also have to amend Form 8606 and attach it to Form 1040X.

The Roth and other IRAs

Deductible IRAs, nondeductible IRAs, and rollover IRAs for lump sums of your former employer's retirement plan (check out Chapter 5 for more on lump-sum distributions) are only half the story. Be aware of other types of IRAs: MSAs, HSAs, Coverdell Education Savings Accounts (formerly known as Education IRAs), Medicare Plus Choice MSAs, and Roth IRAs. See Chapter 22 for more information about the Roth IRAs and Medicare Plus Choice MSAs. Chapter 26 covers the Coverdell Education Savings Account.

Converting traditional IRAs to Roth IRAs

Although funding your Roth IRA isn't a matter for your Form 1040 (which is why we cover it in Chapter 22), you may decide at some point to convert a traditional IRA into a Roth IRA. The conversion of a traditional IRA to a Roth works similarly to any rollover from one pension plan to another, and if you do it properly, you shouldn't have to pay the 10 percent early withdrawal penalty. (We discuss the merits and drawbacks of conversions in Chapter 22). In order to let the IRS know what you've done, you show your conversion on the back of Form 8606, Nondeductible IRAs.

NEW STUFF

If you converted from a traditional IRA to a Roth during 2021 but discover at the end of the year that you really didn't want to do that, you are no longer able to recharacterize that conversion, essentially having a "do-over." Recharacterizations were eliminated beginning on January 1, 2018.

HOW TO FIGURE PARTIAL IRA DEDUCTIONS

You get a partial deduction when your employer has a pension plan that you're eligible to participate in, and your modified AGI falls between $66,000 and $76,000 when you're single, or between $105,000 and $125,000 when you're married filing jointly or a qualifying widow or widower.

If your modified AGI is above the phase-out limits, you aren't entitled to any deduction.

Figure your partial IRA deductions by first determining your modified AGI, which is your AGI from line 11 on Form 1040 less the following deductions:

- The deductible part of your self-employment tax (Schedule 1, Part II, line 15)

- Your IRA deduction (Schedule 1, Part II, line 20)

- Student loan interest deduction (Schedule 1, Part II, line 21)

- Foreign earned income and housing deductions (this deduction applies only to taxpayers who live and work abroad) per Form 2555 (see Chapter 6)

- The exclusion for Series EE U.S. Savings Bond interest (shown on Form 8815), explained in Chapter 12

- The exclusion for adoption assistance (Form 8839) — see Chapter 10

If you didn't live with your spouse at any time during the year and you file a separate return, your filing status is considered single for this purpose.

1. Depending on your filing status, enter one of the following:

    $76,000 — single or head of household

    $125,000 — joint or qualifying widow or widower

    1._____

2. Enter your modified AGI.   2._____

3. Subtract line 2 from line 1.   3._____
4. Your IRA contribution.   4._____

    (See instruction A below.)

5. See instruction B and C below.   5._____

6. Your IRA deduction. Enter the smaller of 4 or 5.   6._____

7. Your nondeductible contribution Subtract 6 from 4.   7._____

If line 2 is larger than line 1, you aren't entitled to an IRA deduction — enter zero -0-.

A. Remember, your contribution can't exceed your compensation.

B. If line 3 is $10,000 or more, enter $6,000 (or $7,000 if you're 50 or older in 2021) on line 6 above. No further computations are required.

(continued)

(continued)

C. If line 3 is less than $10,000, multiply line 3 by 30 percent (0.30) or 35 percent (0.35) if you were 50 or older by the end of 2021. Round up or down to the nearest $10. If the amount that you arrive at is less than $200, enter $200. Don't ask why. These are the rules. Simply enter the amount you arrive at or the $200 minimum on line 5.

D. Line 6 is your IRA deduction; enter this amount on Schedule 1, Part II, line 20.

E. Your nondeductible IRA contribution is the difference between your maximum IRA contribution, which generally is $5,000, and the portion of the $5,000 you're entitled to deduct (computed on line 6 above). You must also enter this amount on line 1 of Form 8606, Nondeductible IRAs, where you keep track of all your nondeductible IRA contributions made through the years. For example, if only $500 of your $5,000 can be deducted, that is the amount you claim on Schedule 1, Part II, line 20. The $4,500 balance is entered on Form 8606, line 1.

If a pension doesn't cover you but does cover your spouse (or vice versa), enter $208,000 on line 1 of this worksheet, and then complete lines 2 through 7.

Your spouse's IRA deduction

Whether or not your spouse is earning wages, tips, commissions, alimony, or income from self-employment, or isn't employed outside the home, they are eligible to contribute to an IRA account. Add your spouse's deductible IRA contribution to yours and place the total deductible amount of both your and your spouse's IRA contributions on Schedule 1, Part II, line 20.

If your spouse isn't employed outside the home, you can set up a spousal IRA account and contribute up to $6,000 for your spouse ($7,000 if they're 50 or older) for a total IRA deduction of $12,000 ($14,000 if both of you are age 50 or older).

WARNING

You can't put the combined total contribution amount into one account and ignore the other spouse's account. You each need your own account, and only the maximum contribution per person can be put into either account.

A spouse who isn't working outside the home can set up a fully deductible IRA even if the other spouse is covered by a pension at work, provided the couple's income doesn't exceed $198,000. If their income is between $198,000 and $208,000, a partial deduction is allowed. At $208,000, the deduction is eliminated. See the phase-out worksheet earlier in this chapter to determine whether you qualify for a partial deduction. If this phaseout works against you, don't overlook a nondeductible IRA.

If your spouse is employed

If your spouse is employed during the year, you can each have IRAs and can each contribute up to the $6,000 or $7,000 limits, unless your taxable compensation (or your spouse's) is less than $6,000. Qualifying income ranges are the same as those we explain earlier in this chapter in the section "Types of compensation needed to qualify for an IRA." For example, Michael and Lisa file a joint return for 2021. Michael earned $28,000, and Lisa earned $1,800. Michael and Lisa can each contribute $6,000 to their respective IRAs for a total of $12,000. Even though Lisa earned less than $6,000, she is deemed to have earned Michael's $28,000 less his $6,000 IRA deduction, or $22,000, as the compensation she needs to qualify for her IRA.

If your spouse isn't employed

If your nonearning spouse decides to set up their own IRA, the most the two of you can contribute is 100 percent of your taxable compensation up to $12,000, or $14,000 if both of you are 50 or older. You can divide your IRA contributions between your IRA and your spouse's IRA any way you choose, but you can't contribute more than $6,000 or $7,000 to either IRA (depending on your age). For example, if your salary is $5,500, you can contribute $5,500 — that is, $3,000 for you and $2,500 for your spouse, $500 for you and $5,000 for your spouse, or $2,750 for you and $2,750 for your spouse — but no more than $5,500 total. If your salary is more than $12,000, the most you can contribute to your separate accounts is $6,000.

Contribution age-limits for you and your spouse

NEW STUFF

The days of no longer being able to fund your own or your spouse's IRAs after you each reached age 70½ are no more. So long as either you or your spouse are working and earning income, you are now allowed to continue contributing to your traditional IRA for as long as you have earned income. Of course, required minimum distributions do kick in when you turn age 72, but you may find it advantageous, if you're still working, to take that mandatory distribution out even while you continue to put money back into the account in the form of new contributions.

Line 21: Student loan interest deduction

While most types of personal interest are not deductible, you may deduct up to $2,500 of interest on a loan used to pay higher education and certain vocational school expenses (ask the vocational school whether it qualifies for this deduction if you have to borrow to pay the tab). You can claim this deduction as long as it takes to pay off the loan and as long as you're paying interest on it.

Whenever something seems too good to be true, there are usually caveats attached. In this case, they come in the form of income phase-outs. If you earn too much money (is there such a thing?), your deduction can be reduced, or even eliminated.

In 2021, for single filers, the deduction doesn't start to get eliminated until your income hits $70,000 and doesn't completely disappear until $85,000. For joint filers, the phaseout of the deduction starts at the $140,000 income level, with the deduction getting wiped out at $170,000. If you're filing using the married filing separately status, you're completely out of luck here; this deduction is not available to you.

TIP

The beauty of the student loan interest deduction is that you don't have to itemize your deductions to claim it. You can claim the standard deduction (see Chapter 11) and the student loan deduction. This deduction should be of great benefit to recent graduates.

To take this deduction, you must meet the following requirements:

>> You're not filing as married filing separately, and no one else can claim you as a dependent.

>> The loan must be incurred to pay the higher education expenses of you, your spouse, or anyone you claimed as a dependent when you took out the loan.

- >> The expenses must be paid within a reasonable amount of time after the loan is taken out. We wish we could tell you what's reasonable, but you know how it is: The IRS knows what's reasonable when it sees it. One way the IRS views as reasonable is when the loan proceeds are used within 60 days before the start or end of an academic semester to pay your allowable higher education expenses.

- >> You must be the person primarily responsible for the loan.

- >> The student must be a degree candidate carrying at least half the normal workload of a full-time student or be attributable to a period during which this requirement was met.

- >> The loan was taken out to pay higher education expenses for tuition, fees, room and board, books, supplies, and other necessary expenses, such as transportation.

- >> Loans from related family members don't qualify for the deduction.

- >> Revolving lines of credit don't qualify unless you agree that the line will be used only to pay for education expenses.

DISCOVER THE "BACK-DOOR" ROTH CONVERSION STRATEGY

With traditional nondeductible IRAs, you don't get the tax deduction up front, but when you start taking distributions, only the amount you put into the account comes back to you tax-free, while all the accumulated earnings are taxed at your highest marginal rate. So, if you put in $100,000 over the years into the account, but it's worth $1,000,000 when you begin taking your required minimum distributions, only 10 percent of your distribution ($100,000/$1,000,000 = 10 percent) will come back to you tax-free.

What if you had another option, one that didn't cost you anything upfront when you fund the account, but potentially saved you tax dollars on the distribution end? Such a strategy actually exists, and it can be a pretty sweet deal for taxpayers. If you are fortunate enough to earn more than the limits on deducting a traditional IRA, you can fund a nondeductible IRA, and then immediately convert that to a Roth IRA. Why add the additional step? Why not just contribute to a Roth IRA in the first place? Well, if you're earning more than is allowed for deducting your traditional IRA, you may also be earning more than is allowed to directly fund a Roth IRA. In 2021, if your adjusted gross income is greater than $140,000 if you're single or head of household, $208,000 if you're married filing joint, or $10,000 if you're married filing separately, you're not allowed to directly fund a Roth IRA.

But you can still indirectly fund it through the back door. As a result of the SECURE Act of 2019, income limits were removed from Roth conversions, as well as age limits being scuttled for contributions to all IRA accounts. So now, take that money that really didn't make much sense in a traditional IRA, fund the nontraditional IRA, and then convert it immediately to a Roth IRA.

A couple of the benefits of the back-door Roth conversion are

- 100 percent of all distributions to you during your lifetime will come to you tax-free.

- There are no required minimum distributions from a Roth IRA. If you don't need the money, it can continue compounding tax-free in your account and wait for your heirs to inherit it.

Students usually take out these loans because they can obtain lower interest rates, but their parents won't be able to claim the deduction, even if they make all the payments. That's because the parents didn't borrow the money. If the student is liable for the loan, the student can't claim the interest deduction when they can be claimed as a dependent on someone else's return. But in an interesting twist, if a nondependent student takes the loan but the parents make the payments, the student may be allowed to take the interest deduction on their return.

Institutions making education loans are required to issue Form 1098-E, Student Loan Interest Statement, listing the interest if the interest you paid during the year was at least $600. Your instruction booklet has a worksheet for 1040 filers to compute the phase-out amount and so do we.

Here's how the phaseout works:

Step	Single	Married
1. Income	$76,000	$155,000
2. Threshold amount	$70,000	$140,000
3. Subtract line 2 from line 1	$6,000	$20,000
4. Phase-out range	$15,000 ($85,000 – $70,000)	$30,000 ($170,000 – $140,000)
5. Divide line 3 by line 4	$6,000 ÷ $15,000	$15,000 ÷ $30,000
6. Result	40%	50%
7. Maximum deduction	$2,500	$2,500
8. Multiply line 7 by line 6	$1,000	$1,250
9. Allowable deduction (subtract line 8 from line 7)	$1,500	$1,250

You figure income for line 1 by adding the following items back to your AGI (line 11, Form 1040):

>> Student loan interest deduction (Schedule 1, Part II, line 21)

>> Foreign earned income and housing deductions (this applies only to taxpayers who live and work abroad) per Form 2555 (see Chapter 6)

>> Exclusion of income for bona fide residents of American Samoa and the exclusion of income from Puerto Rico

TIP

For all those students and former students who have taken advantage of low interest loan consolidations in the past couple of years, remember that you can deduct the interest on your refinanced loan as long as the loan was refinanced with another educational institution or tax-exempt organization.

REMEMBER

This deduction is only allowed for interest you actually paid during the tax year, not for interest that accrued on your loan during 2021. And, for most people who owe federal student loan money, no interest was actually paid in 2021 due to COVID-19 and the suspension of federal student loan payments. However, if you took your loans from a bank and they were not federally guaranteed, then the interest on those payments will qualify for this deduction.

Line 22: Reserved for future use

Sometimes it's best not to look a gift horse in the mouth. This line is blank, and you don't need to do anything with it.

Line 23: Archer MSA deduction

Why this isn't included in the HSA deduction on line 13, we'll never know, but if you still have one of these old accounts and you put money into your account during 2021, this is where that deduction goes.

Just to refresh your memory, the only people who can make Archer MSA contributions are tax-payers who had an active Archer MSA account prior to January 1, 2008, or who became an active Archer MSA participant for a tax year ending after December 31, 2007 because they are covered under a high-deductible health plan (HDHP) or an Archer MSA–participating employer. Try saying that three times fast.

If you do have an eligible account and you did put money into it in 2021, use Form 8853 to calculate your deduction and then carry that result to line 23, here. For your reference, if you are employed by someone who uses one of these HDHP plans, the minimum annual deductible for singles is $2,350, the maximum deductible is $3,550, and the maximum annual out-of-pocket expenses (other than for premiums) is $4,750. For a family, the minimum annual deductible is $4,750, maximum is $7,100, and maximum annual out-of-pocket expenses is $8,650.

Lines 24a - z: Other adjustments

Most of us will never use any of these categories, but here's a quick rundown of what you'll find here:

Jury pay returned to your employer

Serving on a jury is one of those obligations of citizenship that sounds good in theory but often doesn't seem so brilliant in reality. Not only are you pulled from your comfortable daily routine, but you often also pay a financial price for the privilege. Though many courts pay jurors a little something for their time or their expenses, that amount often doesn't begin to cover what that juror would earn at their regular job.

Some employers do continue to compensate their employees who've been called for jury duty. If you belong to this particular fraternity, count yourself lucky that your regular wages continue even when you're performing your civic duty. Some employers ask you to give them any money the court gives you for jury duty pay or incidental expenses. Pay up quickly and completely. Deduct the amounts of jury duty pay you reimburse your employer here, on line 24a. Remember, you included your jury duty pay on Schedule 1, Part I, line 8g.

Deductible expenses related to income reported on line 8k from the rental of personal property engaged in for profit

You may want to refer to Chapter 6 for what sort of income the IRS is referring to here, but line 24b is where you deduct any offsetting expenses in the production of that income.

One recent example that comes quickly to mind is the relatively new business of renting your personal vehicle as if you're one of the big car rental companies. With the disruptions in supply chains as a result of COVID-19, and the big car rental companies suffering from too few cars and too many renters as a result of selling off huge chunks of their fleets during the pandemic to keep cash flowing and debt service on those vehicles low, a new opportunity is presenting itself to rent your personal vehicle if you find you're not using it all of the time.

Line 24b is where you're going to deduct the expenses of those rentals.

Non-taxable amount of the value of Olympic and Paralympic medals and USOC prize money reported on line 8l

If you're a prize-winning athlete who doesn't have the big endorsement contracts and who comes well under the $1 million dollar limit on earnings from the Olympics, Paralympics, or USOC medals you've won, and you reported the income you did receive on line 8l; here's where you're going to deduct that same income.

TIP

You may be asking yourself why you even need to include the number on line 8l, and then deduct it here. Good question, and we can answer it easily: Any money that is reported to you by any entity should show up somewhere on your return, even if it's not taxable to you. When you fail to include it, the IRS assumes that you forgot the income, and they'll issue you a notice requiring you to pay some outrageous amount of tax on that forgotten income. It is far better to include it all, and then reduce the total amount of income by amounts that are tax-free than to receive a love letter from the IRS.

Reforestation amortization and expenses

Qualifying reforestation costs, for both the purpose of a deduction and of amortization, are the direct expenses incurred in establishing a stand of timber, whether by planting, seeding, or natural regeneration. Expenses for improvements of an already existing stand do not qualify for this deduction.

You are allowed to deduct outright $10,000 in the first year of the reforestation ($5,000 if married filing separately), and then amortize the remaining expenses over 84 months. All of these deductions will show up here, on line 24d.

Repayment of supplemental unemployment benefits under the Trade Act of 1974

If you had to repay some of your supplemental unemployment benefits to qualify for trade readjustment allowances under the Trade Act of 1974 in the same year as you received the benefits, enter the reduction here, on line 24e.

Contributions to section 501(c)(18)(D) pension plans

This type of retirement plan refers to a trust created prior to June 25, 1959, and confers tax-exempt status to these trusts, which are funded solely by member contributions. The funds inside these trusts can only be paid out as pension benefits, so many of the exceptions that apply to other types of retirement plans discussed in Chapter 6 and here, in Chapter 7, do not apply to these plans.

These plans were originally set up to allow unions to provide union members to fund pensions. If you are funding a pension through a union plan and your employer is not contributing anything at all to the plan, this is where you will put your 2021 contributions.

Contributions by certain chaplains to section 403(b) plans

If you are an ordained clergyperson (priest, minister, rabbi, imam, cantor, chaplain, and so on), line 24g is where you're going to put contributions into your Section 403(b) plan. Only your contributions go here — if your employer also contributes to the plan, their contributions into your retirement plan belong on their tax return, not yours.

Attorney fees and court costs for actions involving certain unlawful discrimination claims (see instructions)

Normally, in 2021, attorney's fees for pursuing a lawsuit are not deductible; however, there are two exceptions. The first one is located here, on line 24h of Schedule 1, Part II.

If you incurred attorney fees and/or court costs with regard to an unlawful employment discrimination claim, the Tax Court has determined that, since the only reason you're paying the fee is in order to obtain taxable compensation that was denied you due to the discriminatory practices of your employer, you can deduct the fee to the full extent of the award. So, if you were awarded $45,000, and you paid a one-third contingency fee to your attorney of $15,000, you get to deduct the full $15,000 attorney's fee here, on line 24h.

WARNING

If the combination of attorneys' fees and court costs exceeds the amount of compensation the court has awarded you, you're only allowed to deduct an amount that doesn't exceed the total amount of the award. In other words, you can't use the expenses of pursuing your claim to reduce other income on your return.

Attorney fees and court costs in connection with an award from the IRS for information that helped them find tax law violations

And here's the second exception to the rule that attorneys' fees aren't deductible. On line 24i, you can deduct your attorneys' fees and court costs incurred in any whistleblower activity as it pertains to tax law.

So, if you drop a dime on your ex-spouse, for example, because you know they're majorly cheating on their taxes, and you hire an attorney to represent you in this action, you may deduct the cost of that attorney from the amount of the whistleblower award. Once again, you may not deduct more than you received in payment.

Housing deduction from Form 2555

We don't know why the housing deduction from Form 2555, the Foreign Earned Income Exclusion, is included here and not on Schedule 1, Part I, line 8d. After all, it's just another number that you're pulling off the same form as the Foreign Earned Income Exclusion, and you can easily add them together. But it's our job to write this book, not to understand the deep, dark reasoning of the IRS.

If you qualify under either the bona fide residence test or the physical presence test (see Chapter 6), and your tax home is in a foreign country, you may qualify for this housing exclusion (if you're employed by someone other than yourself) or housing deduction (if you're self-employed). Housing expenses that are allowed to be deducted include reasonable amounts incurred or actually paid for housing in a foreign country for you and your family, if they are living with you. Housing costs cannot be for lavish or extravagant accommodations (no staying at the local Ritz, for example), and they don't include the cost of buying or furnishing a property. However, if you take a mortgage to purchase the property, the mortgage interest is a valid expense. So are the cost of utilities.

Your eligible housing expenses depend on where you're living and how many days in the current year you've lived there. For example, if you're living in Costa Rica, you can either deduct or exclude up to $37,800 in 2021 if you lived there for the full year, while if you're residing in Hong Kong, that amount increases to $114,300. The instructions to Form 2555 have the tables you'll need to determine the maximum amount you're eligible to either exclude or deduct. Figure 7-2 is the worksheet you'll need to complete before you can calculate your foreign housing exclusion or deduction.

FIGURE 7-2: Limit on housing expenses worksheet.

Source: Internal Revenue Service

Excess deductions of section 67(e) expenses from Schedule K-1 (Form 1041)

We know, it truly seems like we're in the weeds here, but this is an important deduction if you inherited some money in 2021. Estates and trusts are taxpayers, just like you are, but how their income and deductions are treated is a little different.

If you have received a payment from an estate or trust, you can expect to receive a Schedule K-1 from the executor or trustee, which will list out any number of items of income and deduction. And a major rule of trust and estate taxation is that any items of income and/or deduction maintain their character in the hands of the recipient. In plain English, this means that if the trust or estate earned interest and then gave you money, you're going to report interest. If they earned qualified dividends, that's what you'll be reporting, too, if you received a distribution during the current tax year.

In the final year of a trust or estate, though, there may not be enough income on the trust or estate return to fully fund the deductions that an estate or trust is entitled to. In this case, if you received a portion of the residue (the balance in the account when the estate or trust terminates), your K-1 may show that you have no income items to report at all, but that you do have excess deductions on termination. The number shown on Schedule K-1 (1041), box 11, Code A, is the same number you should put on Schedule 1, Part II, line 24k.

Other adjustments

As long as the Schedule 1, Part II, is, the IRS just didn't want to make it any longer. When you have more adjustments to income than lines to put them on, you can always add items to the form by making a notation in the open space to the left of line 24z. Put the total amount of additional adjustments on line 24z, and then add them to the ones you've already placed on lines 24a through 24k. The total of lines 24a through 24z then gets placed on line 25.

Once you've added up all the line 24 adjustments and put the total on line 25, you're now ready to add up the whole shebang. That total lands first on Schedule 1, Part II, line 26, and then carries over to Form 1040, line 10.

Form 1040, Line 11: Adjusted Gross Income

The next step is subtracting the amount on Form 1040, line 10, from Form 1040, line 9, and placing the result on Form 1040, line 11. You've arrived at your adjusted gross income (AGI).

Congratulations! You've finished with the income portion of your tax return, and the so-called "above-the-line deductions," otherwise known as adjustments to income. The rest of the return should be smooth sailing now, but keep in mind that this AGI number is critically important as you wind your way through the rest of your return. Many calculations that you'll need to do are going to peg off of your AGI, so you'll find that we are going to refer to it often as we move forward into future chapters.

IN THIS CHAPTER

» Calculating the Alternative Minimum Tax

» Dealing with the excess advance premium tax credit

» Paying back any overpayment of the child tax credit

» Figuring your self-employment tax

» Handling household employment taxes

» Understanding investment income and additional Medicare taxes

Chapter 8

Form 1040, Schedule 2: Additional Taxes

t's a common misconception that filing your 1040 every year is solely for the purpose of determining how much income tax you owe on your income for the prior year. In fact, the 1040 covers not only your annual income tax, but also a myriad of other taxes that you may be liable for. On Schedule 2 of Form 1040, you'll dive into those additional types of taxes, penalties, paybacks, alternative methods of calculating tax, and so on. We actually like to refer to this portion of your tax return as "so many taxes, so little time."

NEW STUFF

The creation of Schedules 1, 2, and 3 of Form 1040 was actually just a way to shorten the actual 1040 form itself. Most of these items contained on these three schedules used to show up on your 1040, but as a result of the Tax Cuts and Jobs Act of 2017, Form 1040 was given a complete new look. In 2018, they tried to shrink it down enough that it would fit on a postcard, but by 2019, the IRS had given up that idea as a wasted effort. In each year since then, the Form 1040 plus all three schedules have just become longer and longer.

With that said, this chapter takes a look at Schedule 2 of Form 1040 and helps you figure out all these additional taxes.

Schedule 2, Part I: Tax

Schedule 2, Part I, is pretty straightforward as it contains only two types of taxes: the Alternative Minimum Tax and the excess advance premium tax credit repayment. Strictly speaking, the latter isn't an additional tax at all; instead, it's a repayment of your health insurance premium subsidy if your subsidy based on your 2020 return was too large when calculated based on your 2021 income. Figure 8-1 shows you what you're going to see in Part I.

Line 1: Alternative Minimum Tax (Form 6251)

WARNING

Just when you thought you were getting this income tax system down (and it was safe to go back into the water), along comes the *Alternative Minimum Tax* (AMT), which is a parallel tax system with its own set of rules and regulations. It was created in 1969 to make higher-income taxpayers pay their fair share of the federal government's budget but wasn't updated to move with the times until recently, trapping more and more people in the AMT as each year passed. The Tax Cuts and Jobs Act of 2017 has made a fair attempt at removing most of the people who had been caught by the AMT by permanently adjusting the AMT exemption amounts significantly upwards and making them subject to annual inflation adjustments, thereby reducing the number of people caught by this unpopular tax (was there ever a popular tax?). Even though most people won't be stung by this tax in 2021, if your income is high enough, you're still required to do the math.

If you need to understand what the AMT is about, think about it as part of a multiverse or as a parallel universe. The universe we're most familiar with is the graduated income tax that most of us use to calculate what we owe. With the AMT, we're in more of a flat tax world. Unfortunately, you don't get to choose which universe you're going to be taxed in — under the rules set by Congress, you must figure both methods and then pay the higher tax.

The AMT is a flat tax, assessed at either 26 or 28 percent, depending on your income. It starts with your taxable income (line 15 of Form 1040), adds back your deductions (whether standard or itemized), subtracts out any taxable tax refunds, and then further adjusts for things like investment interest expense, depletion, net operating losses, interest from specified private activity bonds exempt from ordinary income tax, incentive stock options, depreciation of property placed into service after 1986 — there's a whole list of so-called preference items that are used here to arrive at your alternative minimum taxable income (AMTI).

You calculate AMT on Form 6251, Alternative Minimum Tax — Individuals. We'd love to say that completing Form 6251 is as easy as pie, but that analogy only works if it's an incredibly complex pie and you've never cooked before. Fortunately, most of the information you're going to need to complete the form is included in the tax documentation you receive from all the companies that are reporting to you, on Forms 1099, Schedules K-1, and even on your W-2s. However, you need to recognize that there is information buried on these forms that relates to Form 6251.

Here are some of the more common adjustments you'll need to make and where you'll find them in your tax information:

>> Adjustments from an estate or trust are located on Schedule K-1(1041), in box 12.

>> Adjustments from a partnership interest you own is found on Schedule K-1(1065), box 1.

>> Adjustments from an S Corp in which you own shares is on Schedule K-1(1120S), box 15.

>> Exercise of a qualifying incentive stock option is reported by your employer on Form 3921; exercise of a nonqualifying incentive stock option appears on your W-2, in box 12, Code V (Chapter 14 tells you more about these).

>> Interest from specified private activity bonds otherwise exempt from tax appears on either Form 1099-DIV (when you own mutual funds) or Form 1099-INT.

>> Investment interest expense shows up on either your 1099-INT, your 1099-DIV, or, if you have a brokerage account, it's listed in the consolidated tax statement you receive from them.

>> State income tax refunds are reported on Form 1099-G.

TIP

If you're using tax preparation software and you enter the information you receive carefully, making sure you're matching up the boxes and entering all the codes that you see, all the AMT preference items should carry correctly to Form 6251, and you won't actually have to do any math. Please be aware of these items, though, as forgetting to enter something or ignoring a piece of information because you don't understand it is a sure way to mess up your AMT calculation.

SEEK ADVICE

If you are unsure about whether you're preparing Form 6251 correctly, this is a good time to find your local tax professional and ask their advice. Many tax professionals applaud when people prepare their own returns and are willing to help out on some of the stickier items for a fee. Because your tax life doesn't tend to change much from one year to the next, if you ask someone to help this year, you can probably rely on that advice for next year as well, provided no one tampers big-time with the Internal Revenue Code in the meantime.

TAX CUT

Can you avoid the AMT? Defer those deductions and tax incentives that trigger the AMT or accelerate income, so your deductions will be within the AMT limits. Unfortunately, this maneuver requires checking your income and deductible expenses periodically throughout the year. Investing in a tax software program or a tax advisor may help ease the burden.

How do you know if you should be completing Form 6251? If you're using tax preparation software, no worries — it will do it for you. But if you're using the pencil-and-paper method, here are the AMT exemption and beginning phase-out amounts for 2021:

» **Married filing jointly and qualifying widow(er):** $114,600, begins to phase out at $1,047,200

» **Single or head of household:** $73,600, begins to phase out at $523,600

» **Married filing separately:** $73,600, begins to phase out at $523,600

After you've applied your exemption amount, the AMT is charged at a flat 26 percent on your total AMTI up to $199,900 for all taxpayers (except married people filing separately, who only get $99,950 each), and then 28 percent on any amounts exceeding $199,900 ($99,500 for MFS). Ouch!

Line 2: Excess advance premium tax repayment (Form 8962)

The Affordable Care Act of 2010 created a system of federal government–paid subsidies (also known as the Advance Premium Credit) to provide direct financial aid to individual health insurance subscribers.

THE AMT IN BRIEF

Here is a quick glance at how the AMT works for a couple filing jointly.

	Regular Tax	AMT
Adjusted gross income	$275,100	
Standard deduction	<$25,100>	
Taxable income	$250,000	$ 250,000
Standard deduction		$ 25,100
Estate AMT preference items		$ 50,000
Incentive stock options		$ 50,000
AMT exemption		<$114,600>
Taxable income	$250,000	$ 260,500
Tax	$ 48,042	$ 68,942

The unlucky taxpayer in this example had to cough up $68,942, or a flat 26 percent of the first $199,900 of his AMT income (or AMTI), and then 28 percent of the remaining $60,600. That's $20,900 more than what the tax worked out to be under the regular method, or almost half again as much. You pay the higher of your regular tax or AMT. For simplicity, we didn't take into account all the various deduction phase-out amounts. If your AMT is higher than your regular tax as computed in this example, the $20,900 difference gets entered here on Schedule 2, Part I, line 1.

The challenge with the subsidies is that they are initially calculated based on your prior year's income or your best estimate for the coming year, but the amount of a subsidy that you're actually entitled to is based on your actual income for the current year. If income for both years is roughly the same, no worries — any adjustment you calculate on Form 8962, Premium Tax Credit (PTC) will be minor. But if you've had a major change of income, either because you changed jobs, you received an inheritance, or you had good luck in the stock market, the amount of your payback can reduce your refund or even cause a balance due situation where there wouldn't have been one without the subsidy.

So, how does Form 8962 work? It compares your income and the size of your family against the federal poverty line (FPL) in your state. You're entitled to a subsidy if you earn less than 400 percent of the federal poverty line in your state in 2021. The amount of the subsidy depends on how close to that 400 percent FPL number you earned.

In 2021, the FPLs for the contiguous 48 states and Washington, D.C., were as follows:

>> $12,880 for individuals

>> $17,420 for a family of two

>> $21,960 for a family of three

>> $26,500 for a family of four

>> $31,040 for a family of five

>> $35,580 for a family of six

>> $40,120 for a family of seven

>> $44,660 for a family of eight

>> Add $4,540 for each additional person above eight

The numbers for Alaska and Hawaii are higher, with Alaska beginning at $16,090 for an individual and then adding $5,680 for each additional family member, and Hawaii starting at $14,820 and then adding $5,220 for each additional person.

If you've been obtaining health insurance through your state's marketplace, you should receive Form 1095-A from the marketplace, which tells you the following: who in your family was covered through the marketplace, the dates covered, the total cost of the coverage you selected for 2021, the monthly second-lowest-cost silver plan premium for your state, and the amount of the monthly advance payment of the premium tax credit. You're going to need all this information in order to correctly complete Form 8962.

Here's how to complete Form 8962, Part I:

>> **Line 1:** Put in the total number of people in your tax family. This includes yourself, your spouse (if you have one), and any dependents claimed on your 2021 return who are not eligible for other forms of minimum essential coverage (MEC) such as Medicare, Medicaid, Children's Health Insurance Plan (CHIP), Tricare, healthcare for Peace Corps volunteers, or healthcare for incarcerated people.

>> **Line 2a:** Enter your modified AGI, which is the amount from line 11 of Form 1040 plus the amounts of untaxed Social Security, tax-exempt interest and dividends, and any foreign earned income you've excluded.

>> **Line 2b:** Enter the modified AGI (same formula as used in Line 2a) for all of your dependents who are required, on the basis of their income, to file a tax return. Do not include the income for any of your dependents who are filing a tax return only in order to receive a refund of taxes withheld.

>> **Line 3:** Add together lines 2a and 2b. This is your household's income.

>> **Line 4:** This is where you enter the federal poverty line for a family of your size. To determine the size of your family, you may only count those members who are not eligible for MEC under another plan or through their employer.

>> **Line 5:** The IRS includes a worksheet for this line in their instructions, but the gist of it is that you multiply line 4 by 4 and compare that with the number on line 3. If the number on line 3 is greater than 4 times the number on line 4, on line 5, enter 401. If 4 times the number on line 4 is greater than the number on line 3, divide the amount on line 3 by the amount on line 4, and then multiply your result by 100. Enter only a whole number on line 5; leave off anything to the right of the decimal point.

>> **Line 7 (there is currently no line 6):** An applicable figure chart is included in the instructions for Form 8962, where you find your applicable figure by locating the number you've placed on line 5. Enter that number here on line 7.

>> **Line 8a:** Multiply line 3 by line 7 and enter the total here. This is the maximum annual amount you should be paying out of pocket for health insurance during 2021.

>> **Line 8b:** Divide line 8a by 12. Guess what — this is the maximum monthly amount you should have paid in 2021.

Form 8962, Part II, is where you reconcile what you actually paid versus what you should have paid. And this is where all that great information from Form 1095-A will go. You're basically going to copy and paste what you see on Form 1095-A into Part II of Form 8962, so unless you transpose numbers as you copy, you really can't go far wrong here.

TIP

If you had the same coverage for the full year, and the premium payment and the subsidy were the same every month, you're not required to fill out the monthly totals. Just fill out the annual totals that appear on the bottom of Form 1095-A in the Annual Calculation on line 11 of Part II.

Once you've finished with Form 8962, you'll know whether you're going to receive more of a credit than you already have (see Chapter 9), or if you have to repay some portion of the subsidy you've received over the course of the year.

If you have to repay a portion of the credit, you may not have to repay the full amount that you were overpaid. There are limitations, as shown in Table 8-1:

On line 29, put the lesser of line 27 (the excess of the advance payment) or line 28 (the repayment limitation amount). And you're done! Take the number on line 29 and put it on Schedule 2, Part I, line 2.

Table 8-1:   **Repayment Limitation for Premium Tax Credit**

IF Form 8962, line 5, is	THEN enter on line 28 . . .	
	Single filing status	**All other filing statuses**
Less than 200	$325	$650
At least 200 but less than 300	$800	$1,600
At least 300 but less than 400	$1,350	$2,700
400 or 401	Leave line 28 blank	Leave line 28 blank

Line 3: Add lines 1 and 2

Finally, enter the totals here, on line 3, as well as on Form 1040, line 17. And remember, all types of Form 1040 are line-numbered the same, so it's line 17 for everyone!

Schedule 2, Part II: Other Taxes

If your only employment income comes from a job with an employer, you might not have "other taxes" to account for but don't count on it! Over the years, in Congress's push for more and more tax "revenue," there are increasing numbers of other taxes (see Figure 8-2). Please peruse this section as some may apply to you, especially if you're self-employed or a higher income earner.

Part II	Other Taxes	
4	Self-employment tax. Attach Schedule SE	4
5	Social security and Medicare tax on unreported tip income. Attach Form 4137	5
6	Uncollected social security and Medicare tax on wages. Attach Form 8919	6
7	Total additional social security and Medicare tax. Add lines 5 and 6	7
8	Additional tax on IRAs or other tax-favored accounts. Attach Form 5329 if required	8
9	Household employment taxes. Attach Schedule H	9
10	Repayment of first-time homebuyer credit. Attach Form 5405 if required	10
11	Additional Medicare Tax. Attach Form 8959	11
12	Net investment income tax. Attach Form 8960	12
13	Uncollected social security and Medicare or RRTA tax on tips or group-term life insurance from Form W-2, box 12	13
14	Interest on tax due on installment income from the sale of certain residential lots and timeshares	14
15	Interest on the deferred tax on gain from certain installment sales with a sales price over $150,000	15
16	Recapture of low-income housing credit. Attach Form 8611	16

(continued on page 2)

For Paperwork Reduction Act Notice, see your tax return instructions.   Cat. No. 71478U   Schedule 2 (Form 1040) 2021

FIGURE 8-2: Form 1040, Schedule 2, Part II, includes all the additional varieties of tax you may be required to pay.

Source: Internal Revenue Service

Part II   **Other Taxes** *(continued)*

17	Other additional taxes:	
a	Recapture of other credits. List type, form number, and amount ▶ _____	**17a**
b	Recapture of federal mortgage subsidy. If you sold your home in 2021, see instructions	**17b**
c	Additional tax on HSA distributions. Attach Form 8889	**17c**
d	Additional tax on an HSA because you didn't remain an eligible individual. Attach Form 8889	**17d**
e	Additional tax on Archer MSA distributions. Attach Form 8853 .	**17e**
f	Additional tax on Medicare Advantage MSA distributions. Attach Form 8853	**17f**
g	Recapture of a charitable contribution deduction related to a fractional interest in tangible personal property	**17g**
h	Income you received from a nonqualified deferred compensation plan that fails to meet the requirements of section 409A . . .	**17h**
i	Compensation you received from a nonqualified deferred compensation plan described in section 457A	**17i**
j	Section 72(m)(5) excess benefits tax	**17j**
k	Golden parachute payments	**17k**
l	Tax on accumulation distribution of trusts	**17l**
m	Excise tax on insider stock compensation from an expatriated corporation	**17m**
n	Look-back interest under section 167(g) or 460(b) from Form 8697 or 8866	**17n**
o	Tax on non-effectively connected income for any part of the year you were a nonresident alien from Form 1040-NR	**17o**
p	Any interest from Form 8621, line 16f, relating to distributions from, and dispositions of, stock of a section 1291 fund	**17p**
q	Any interest from Form 8621, line 24	**17q**
z	Any other taxes. List type and amount ▶ _____	**17z**
18	Total additional taxes. Add lines 17a through 17z	**18**
19	Additional tax from Schedule 8812	**19**
20	Section 965 net tax liability installment from Form 965-A . . .	**20**
21	Add lines 4, 7 through 16, 18, and 19. These are your **total other taxes.** Enter here and on Form 1040 or 1040-SR, line 23, or Form 1040-NR, line 23b	**21**

Schedule 2 (Form 1040) 2021

FIGURE 8-2:
(Continued)

Line 4: Self-employment tax (Schedule SE)

If you earn income from being self-employed and from other sources, use Schedule SE to figure another tax that you owe — the Social Security tax and Medicare tax. The first $142,800 of your self-employment earnings are taxed at 12.4 percent (this is the Social Security tax part). There isn't any limit for the Medicare tax; it's 2.9 percent of your total self-employment earnings. For amounts of $142,800 or less, the combined rate is 15.3 percent (adding the two taxes together), and above $142,800, the rate is 2.9 percent. See Chapter 17 for information about filling out Schedule SE.

Line 5: Unreported Social Security and Medicare tax on unreported tip income

Line 5 is reserved only for workers who received a portion of their income from tips. If you belong to this category of workers, you'll need to complete Form 4137, Social Security and Medicare Tax on Unreported Tip Income, and place your answer here on line 5.

If you receive a portion of your compensation in the form of tips but didn't tell your employer exactly how much you received, Form 4137 walks you through how to calculate the difference between your total tips and those your employer has already reported on Form W-2, box 8 (see Chapter 6). Remember, if you reported all of your tips to your employer, those will be included on Form W-2, box 1, and you don't have to complete Form 4137.

If your employer wasn't able to collect from you all the Social Security and Medicare tax you owe on your reported tip income, box 12 of your W-2 will show that amount. Code A next to the amount in box 12 is for Social Security tax, and Code B next to the amount in box 12 is for Medicare Tax. Enter the amounts in box 12 on the dotted line to the left of line 5, Form 1040, and to the left of the amount, write "UT," which stands for uncollected tax on tips. Don't forget to include the total amount on the dotted line in the total on line 5.

Line 6: Uncollected social security and Medicare tax on wages (Form 8919)

If you believe you should have had Social Security and Medicare taxes withheld by your employer, fill out Form 8919, Uncollected Social Security and Medicare Tax on Wages, instead.

When you work in a job where your employer fails to deduct Social Security and Medicare taxes from your wages, make sure you file Form 8919. This form alerts the IRS that your employer should be withholding and isn't. Is it a good idea to "tell" on your employer in this way, or should you continue to fly under the IRS radar? Honesty is really the best policy for you here. By filing Form 8919, you make your necessary contributions into the Social Security and Medicare systems, which will benefit you down the road. And because you are stating quite clearly that you are employed by someone else, and not by yourself, you get yourself off the hook for the other half of the contribution, the additional half that the self-employed have to pay.

Line 7: Total additional Social Security and Medicare tax

Oh, if only all lines were so easy. Add up the numbers on lines 5 and 6 and enter your answer here on line 7.

Line 8: Additional tax on IRAs or other tax-favored accounts (Form 5329)

Try as hard as you may, a day may come when you can't follow the rules exactly regarding what you should, or shouldn't, be putting in or taking out of your IRA, Roth IRA, Coverdell Education Savings Account, Section 529 (qualified tuition program) plan, Archer MSA, or Health Savings Account. And that's okay. The IRS understands that the rules for all these are complex and that sometimes people make mistakes. To show how understanding the IRS is, it created Form 5329, Additional Taxes on Qualified Plans (including IRAs) and Other Tax-Favored Accounts, that covers these types of accounts and helps you to calculate the penalty you may owe for goofing. And, since they don't want you to feel badly, the word "penalty" is found nowhere on the form. Instead, they use the phrase "additional tax," as though that may make you feel better for having to pay more.

Form 5329 is divided into clearly labeled parts. You need to complete only the parts that apply to your situation. If additional taxes are assessed (and there's a good chance they will be because you're filling out this form in the first place), add up all the additional taxes that have been assessed, and place the total amount from all sections of Form 5329 on line 8 of Schedule 2. There is no place on Form 5329 for you to do this.

Line 9: Household employment taxes (Schedule H)

The provisions of the household employment tax, also known as the nanny tax, can save you a tidy sum and simplify the number and type of returns that you have to file. The law covers housekeepers, babysitters, and yard-care workers, as well as nannies.

The nanny tax is figured on Schedule H, and the amount you owe is entered on Schedule 2, line 9. If you didn't pay cash wages of $2,300 or more in 2021, or $1,000 or more in any calendar quarter of 2020 or 2021, or didn't withhold any federal income tax, you can skip this form. If you paid more than $2,300 in wages in 2021 but less than $1,000 in any calendar quarter of 2020 or 2021, you have to fill out only page 1 and enter the amount from line 8d of Schedule H onto Schedule 2, line 9. If you paid more than $1,000 in any quarter, you must fill out page 2 of the form and enter the amount from line 26 of Schedule H onto Schedule 2, line 9. See Chapter 17 for more about filling out Schedule H.

Line 10: Repayment of first-time homebuyer credit (Form 5405)

If you purchased your home for which you received a first-time homebuyer credit in 2008, and you sold that home in 2021 *or* you ceased using it as your principal residence, this line is for you. Take a look at Form 5405, Repayment of the First-Time Homebuyer Credit, because this is where you're going to have to figure out how much of that credit you may have to repay.

REMEMBER

Not every situation requires that the loan be repaid. If you belong to one of the groups shown on Form 5405, line 2, including being on qualified official extended duty, or are in the military and other uniformed services (including commissioned corps of the National Oceanic and Atmospheric Administration and the Public Health Service), are a foreign service member, or are an employee of the intelligence community, you get a pass on the repayment provisions of this credit.

Line 11: Additional Medicare Tax (Form 8959)

As a way to shore up the Medicare Trust Fund, additional taxes were first assessed for high-income individuals back in 2013, as a part of the Affordable Care Act. For those who earn more than $200,000 for individuals and heads of household, $250,000 for couples married filing jointly (and qualifying widow[er]s with a dependent child), and $125,000 for each partner in a couple that files as married filing separately, you will pay an additional 0.9 percent on wages and other earned income above those limits.

The same limits hold for those who are self-employed. If you fall into this category and your earnings from self-employment exceed the limits in the previous paragraph, you too get to pay an additional 0.9 percent on the excess above the limitation.

Finally, if you're receiving Railroad Retirement Act compensation, you also must pay the additional 0.9 percent on the excess over the limitations.

All of these additional taxes are calculated on Form 8959, Additional Medicare Tax, as is the reconciliation between the amounts you had withheld and the additional amounts you are being assessed. For many highly compensated individuals, their employers have already calculated and withheld the additional tax if compensation from that single job exceeded the limits. This additional amount of Medicare tax withheld shows up on your Form W-2, box 6, as an addition to the 1.45 percent that is withheld on 100 percent of all wages from that job. But for people who work multiple jobs and get to these limits only by combining wages from all their jobs, none of this additional tax will have been withheld.

Line 12: Net investment income tax (Form 8960)

Another tax increase from the Affordable Care Act, the net investment income tax (NIIT) was established to enable higher-income people, estates, and trusts who earned all or a large part of their income from interest, dividends, nonqualified annuities, passive interests in partnerships or S Corporations, rental real estate (except for rental real estate professionals), and capital gains to pay higher federal income taxes to the Medicare Trust Fund that was helping to fund the new insurance subsidies.

The NIIT is a flat 3.8 percent and is assessed if your income from all of those sources exceeds certain limits. Those limits are the same as those for the additional Medicare tax: more than $200,000 for individuals and heads of household, $250,000 for couples married filing jointly (and qualifying widow[er]s with a dependent child), and $125,000 for each partner in a couple that files as married filing separately. The NIIT is calculated only on investment income, so that the tax is charged on the lesser of your net investment income or the amount by which your modified adjusted gross income exceeds the income limits.

TIP

If the sale of your personal residence produces a capital gain that is excluded from income under the rules outlined in Chapter 14, it is also excluded from the NIIT. If the gain on the sale of your home exceeds the exclusion amount, and some of the gain is taxable, only the taxable portion is subject to the NIIT.

NIIT is calculated on Form 8960, Net Investment Income Tax — Individuals, Estates and Trusts, and the number you arrive at on Form 8960, line 17, is the same number you'll place on Schedule 2, line 12.

Line 13: Uncollected Social Security and Medicare or RRTA tax on tips. . .

If your W-2 contains amounts in box 12 using codes A, B, M, or N, add the amounts together (if you have more than one of those codes on your Form W-2) and put the total on Schedule 2, line 13.

Line 14: Interest on tax due on installment income from certain residential sales

This isn't a tax, but interest on tax you owe on installment sales from certain residential lots and timeshares. In case you were wondering, an *installment sale* is one in which you receive the proceeds from the buyer over a period of years instead of all at once, even though the total price of the property is set at the time the property is sold. So, if you owned a residential lot or a timeshare, and you sold it in 2020, for example, but only received one-third of the sales price in 2020, and then the second third in 2021, with the balance due in 2022, you're not going to pay the tax on any gain for installments two and three until you receive those payments. However, the amount of the gain has been established at the time of the initial sale. Any tax that's assessed on installments two and three in this example is being delayed by one or two years, and the IRS wants to make sure you understand that, since you're taking your time paying the total tax, you're also going to pay interest on the tax assessed on installments two and three. Line 14 of Schedule 2 is where you put the interest that has accrued.

Interest is charged at the IRS's current rate for underpayment of taxes, which was 3 percent for all of 2021 (it adjusts quarterly). This interest is considered to be personal interest and is therefore not deductible on Schedule A, even though you can potentially consider it as an investment interest expense. Oh well, the IRS has quite specifically said it is not deductible for individuals.

Line 15: Interest on the deferred tax on gain from certain installment sales

Why line 15 is different from line 14 is a mystery to us, since both deal with installment sales, but it seems that the IRS is not concerned with saving paper and ink. So, here's the deal with line 15: If you sell property with a sales price of over $150,000 *and* your total balance of non-dealer installment obligations arising during and outstanding at the end of the tax year is more than $5 million, you're required to pay interest on the deferred taxes, just the same as in line 14.

There are exceptions to this rule. Farm property, personal use property by an individual, personal property sold before 1989, and real property sold before 1988 are all excluded from this rule.

SEEK ADVICE

Installment sales are tricky; we'd be lying if we told you otherwise. While we certainly would never discourage anyone from attempting to acquire a new skill, you may want to have a professional review your work on this part of your return, just to make sure you're doing everything correctly.

Line 16: Recapture of low-income housing credit (Form 8611)

If you disposed of a building that qualified for the low-income housing credit in 2021, or your qualified basis in the property decreased in 2021 (perhaps because you started renting to people who weren't income qualified to participate in low-income housing), some of the accelerated credits you received in prior years may have to be recaptured. You're going to figure this credit recapture on Form 8611, Recapture of Low-Income Housing Credit. In order to prepare Form 8611, you're going to need copies of Form 8586, Low-Income Housing Credit, from prior years to determine the total credits you've received over the years you've owned the building.

After completing Form 8611, enter the amount shown on line 14 onto Schedule 2, line 16, and you're done.

Line 17: Other additional taxes

SEEK ADVICE

We could write another book about all the additional taxes shown on lines 17a through 17z. These include recaptures of other credits, mortgage subsidies, additional taxes on HSAs and MSAs, charitable deductions to which you're no longer entitled, and so on. The reality is that most of these items are extraordinarily case-specific, and all of them are probably things for which you should seek professional counsel if you suspect you fall into any of these categories.

If you do find yourself having to use one of these lines, add up all your line 17 amounts, and put the total on Schedule 2, line 18.

Line 19: Excess advance child tax credit repayment (Form 8812)

Significant changes have come to the child tax credit in 2021. In fact, some of the provisions are so new that, as we're writing this, the IRS is still working to fix the kinks. But rest assured, by the time filing season rolls around, they'll have something in place that will hopefully work for most people. Be aware that, whenever there's a major change like this, there are always unintended results that have to be fixed later. For right now, the IRS has added a completely redesigned Form 8812, Credits for Qualifying Children and Other Dependents, and has also added a new line to Schedule 2 to accommodate the changes.

NEW STUFF

In March 2021, the American Rescue Plan Act was enacted and signed into law. One of its actions was to increase the Child Tax Credit for 2021 from $2,000 per qualifying child age 16 and younger to $3,600 for children ages 5 and younger, and $3,000 for children ages 6 to 17. Also, in 2021, the full amount of the credit is refundable, which means that, even if you don't have any tax liability, you'll still receive the full value of the credit. In prior years, this credit has only been partially refundable, and you must have had earned income to access it.

In an additional change, and in order to get money out to lower-income families more quickly, beginning in July, 2021, if you qualified based on your 2020 income tax return, you probably started receiving either $250 or $300 per qualifying child per month, deposited directly into your bank account. For some people, though, while they may have been eligible for the credit if their 2021 tax and family situation was identical to 2020, things may have changed, whether through custody arrangements, changes in income, or children aging out of the credit. The amounts deposited into their bank accounts shouldn't have been because they weren't eligible for it, but the IRS didn't know. What a shock that there's something the IRS doesn't know about us.

Anyway, it is clear from the guidance coming from the IRS that they are going to be looking for those amounts that were paid in error to be returned to the government. The IRS will be issuing Letter 6419 to tell you how much you received in payments during 2021. Form 8812 is where you're going to figure out how much you received, how much you were entitled to receive, and how much you may have to repay.

On the current draft version of the 2021 Schedule 2, this repayment is shown on line 19.

TIP

One of the most common questions we're hearing concerns children of divorced parents. Many parents share joint custody and switch off the dependent status of their children from year to year. If this is your situation, then the person who claimed those dependent children on their 2020 returns (the "2020 parent") is not the same as the person claiming them in 2021 (the "2021 parent"); however, the 2020 parent may be receiving these advance payments on the basis of their 2020 return even though the 2021 parent is entitled to them. Some 2021 parents are insisting that the 2020 parent turn over that money to them now. And that makes sense in a non-bureaucratic world. But we don't live in that world, and when it comes time for tax returns to be filed, the 2020 parent who mistakenly received the payments is going to be required to repay in full, and the 2021 parent will get the full amount of the credit applied against their 2021 return. Any amounts over their actual tax liability will be refunded to them.

It may be better if all parties agree for the 2020 parent to opt out of any future payments for 2021, and then do the reconciliation for the amounts already received, and let the 2021 parent claim it on their 2021 tax return in 2022. Both parents should visit www.irs.gov/credits-deductions/advance-child-tax-credit-payments-in-2021, with the 2020 parent electing to opt out of future payments and the 2021 parent attempting to opt in.

Line 20: Section 965 net tax liability installment from Form 965-A

Finally, we come to the last individual item on Schedule 2. What is a Section 965 net tax liability installment? Section 965 of the Internal Revenue Code refers to amounts of income based on the accumulated post-1986 deferred foreign income of certain foreign corporations. If that's not making your head spin, we don't know what will.

SEEK ADVICE

No one has ever accused either of us of being cowardly, but this is an area where you should duck and run to your nearest foreign income/dual status/cross-border tax expert — either an accountant, enrolled agent, or attorney — to help you negotiate through Form 965-A, Individual Report of Net 965 Tax Liability. This form looks at your income for not only 2021, but also for the three prior years. In our experience, whenever the tax code refers to code sections instead of telling what they're looking for in plain English, it's because they don't really understand it, either.

Bringing Us to Line 21

We know you've had a wonderful time filling out Schedule 2 and all its accompanying forms and schedules. Now all that's left to do is add up lines 4, 7 through 16, 18, and 19 and put the total on line 21. From there, you're going to carry your line 21 number over to Form 1040, line 23 (on Form 1040-NR, it's line 23b). And you're done . . . with this part of your return. Bring on the credits (see Chapter 9).

Chapter **9**

Form 1040, Schedule 3: Adding Up Your Credits and Payments

I f people focused on their tax liability every year, there would likely be more stress associated with the size of that number. Fortunately, you've probably been making payments throughout the year (at least we hope so), and Congress has devised a world of refundable and nonrefundable tax credits to reward you for behaviors they want to encourage, such as saving for retirement, adopting a child, or sending an older child to college. We're entitled to credits for putting solar panels on our roof or a wind turbine in our field. We're even eligible for credits if our income is low, but we still go to that regular job. And, since all of these credits or payments will reduce the amount that we owe on our annual tax return, or even produce a refund, some folks are more focused on these numbers than on the amount of tax assessed on the income that they earned during the year. Conversely, we've seen other people who ignore valuable credits that they are eligible to claim.

Sorting through all the credits you're entitled to and making sure you've picked up all the payments you've made over the course of the year is a necessary step in completing your tax return. You don't want to miss any one of these credits, as the IRS isn't going to necessarily know that you're eligible for a credit unless you give them that information. They should have a record of all your payments, whether made through withholding from wages or quarterly estimated tax payments you've made throughout the year, but the credits you report or miss aren't something the IRS is able to match up against information reported to them on your behalf by your employer or by, say, a car dealer where you purchased your new electric car. You have to provide the IRS more specifics.

Schedule 3, Part I: Nonrefundable Credits

It's always good to start with a definition so that you know exactly what we're talking about. *Tax credits* reduce your tax bill, dollar for dollar. There are credits on both your federal return and your state return, if you have one, so while we focus on the federal side, don't ignore money that may be on the table from your state. *Deductions*, on the other hand, only reduce your taxable income. A $1,000 tax deduction reduces the tax for someone in the 24 percent federal income tax bracket by only $240. A $1,000 tax credit reduces that same person's federal income tax by $1,000.

A nonrefundable credit only works if you actually have a tax liability on Form 1040, line 18 (that's at the top of the second page of Form 1040, in case you were wondering). If there is a zero on line 18, then you have no tax liability, so you won't be eligible for any nonrefundable credits.

Figure 9-1 shows you what Schedule 3, Part I, looks like.

Line 1: Foreign tax credit (Form 1116)

You don't have to be a multinational corporation to pay foreign taxes. With more and more people investing in international mutual funds and exchange-traded funds, the Foreign Tax Credit is being used more than ever before to reduce investors' U.S. tax bills for their share of the foreign taxes paid by the fund.

Taxes paid to a foreign government on income earned in that country can be either claimed as a deduction on Schedule A (see Chapter 11) or calculated as a credit on Form 1116, Foreign Tax Credit, provided that you're required to include this income on your Form 1040. And trust us, you are required to include it on your Form 1040, as the United States taxes you on 100 percent of your worldwide income from all sources. If you're not itemizing your deductions, you absolutely should claim the foreign tax that you paid as a credit if you want to use it to reduce your tax.

Unfortunately, the computation of this credit is a killer — and even the IRS agrees. The instructions say that it should take you about 6½ hours to read the instructions, assemble the data, and fill in the form. And that's with all the instructions in English (by and large) and all the parts included! Even if you're using a computer tax program, completing Form 1116 is not for the faint of heart. But still, give it a whirl.

If using a computer isn't your thing, see a tax advisor. If you're filing your return on paper, attach Form 1116 to your return and bid it good riddance! You enter the credit you arrive at on Form 1116, line 24 on Schedule 3, line 1. Remember, you're entitled to either claim the credit or take the deduction; you can't do both on the same piece of income. You can, however, take both the credit and the deduction if you have enough foreign income that you can use some of that income for the credit and the rest of the income for the deduction.

SCHEDULE 3
(Form 1040)

Department of the Treasury
Internal Revenue Service

Additional Credits and Payments

▶ Attach to Form 1040, 1040-SR, or 1040-NR.
▶ Go to *www.irs.gov/Form1040* for instructions and the latest information.

OMB No. 1545-0074

2021

Attachment
Sequence No. **03**

Name(s) shown on Form 1040, 1040-SR, or 1040-NR | Your social security number

Part I	**Nonrefundable Credits**		
1	Foreign tax credit. Attach Form 1116 if required	**1**	
2	Credit for child and dependent care expenses from Form 2441, line 11. Attach Form 2441	**2**	
3	Education credits from Form 8863, line 19	**3**	
4	Retirement savings contributions credit. Attach Form 8880	**4**	
5	Residential energy credits. Attach Form 5695	**5**	
6	Other nonrefundable credits:		
a	General business credit. Attach Form 3800	**6a**	
b	Credit for prior year minimum tax. Attach Form 8801	**6b**	
c	Adoption credit. Attach Form 8839	**6c**	
d	Credit for the elderly or disabled. Attach Schedule R	**6d**	
e	Alternative motor vehicle credit. Attach Form 8910	**6e**	
f	Qualified plug-in motor vehicle credit. Attach Form 8936	**6f**	
g	Mortgage interest credit. Attach Form 8396	**6g**	
h	District of Columbia first-time homebuyer credit. Attach Form 8859	**6h**	
i	Qualified electric vehicle credit. Attach Form 8834	**6i**	
j	Alternative fuel vehicle refueling property credit. Attach Form 8911	**6j**	
k	Credit to holders of tax credit bonds. Attach Form 8912	**6k**	
l	Amount on Form 8978, line 14. See instructions	**6l**	
z	Other nonrefundable credits. List type and amount ▶ _____	**6z**	
7	Total other nonrefundable credits. Add lines 6a through 6z	**7**	
8	Add lines 1 through 5 and 7. Enter here and on Form 1040, 1040-SR, or 1040-NR, line 20	**8**	

FIGURE 9-1:
Form 1040,
Schedule 3,
Part I,
Nonrefundable
credits.

(continued on page 2)

For Paperwork Reduction Act Notice, see your tax return instructions.   Cat. No. 71480G   Schedule 3 (Form 1040) 2021

Source: Internal Revenue Service

As a general rule, taking the credit produces a larger savings. For more on foreign taxes, refer to Chapter 11. You can also use the foreign tax credit for foreign taxes paid on income earned overseas that exceeds the $108,700 exclusion and the housing allowance. (See Chapters 6 and 29 for more about this tax credit.)

TIP

You can ignore the fiendish Form 1116 if the foreign tax you paid is $300 or less ($600 for joint filers). Simply enter the foreign tax you paid on Schedule 3, Line 1 if your foreign tax is less than these amounts. This simplified method of claiming the credit is available if the only type of foreign income you had was from dividends, interest, rent, royalties, annuities, or the sale of an asset.

TIP

Line 2: Credit for child and dependent care expenses (Form 2441)

If you hire someone to take care of your children so that you can work for income (doing house-work and errands doesn't cut it), you're entitled to the credit that you figure on Form 2441, Child and Dependent Care Expenses. To be eligible, your child must be younger than 13 or a dependent of any age who is physically or mentally handicapped. See Chapter 16 for information on Form 2441.

NEW STUFF

In 2021, thanks to the American Rescue Plan Act of 2021, this credit has become much more valuable for some folks. The maximum credit for one child or other qualifying individual has increased to $4,000 for one person and $8,000 for two or more qualifying people, and amounts up to 50 percent of work-related care expenses are eligible. For the first time, there is an upper income limit on the credit, so taxpayers with adjusted gross income over $438,000 no longer qualify for the credit. Employers who provide childcare for their employees are allowed a tax credit for a percentage of their expenses. Finally, also new in 2021, this credit may be refundable to you if you don't have enough income tax liability to use the full credit against your liability. We discuss this more in Chapter 16.

TAX CUT

The cost of your babysitter, daycare, or after-school care counts toward this credit (but not after-school activities, such as dance, music, and sports); options like summer day camps (overnight camps don't make the grade) do, too. Remember, if you weren't sending your child to that camp in the summer, you'd need to hire a sitter or daycare instead.

Line 3: Education credits (Form 8863)

On this line you claim the *American Opportunity Credit* and the *Lifetime Learning Credit*. Remember that credits reduce your tax, dollar for dollar. You claim both credits on Form 8863, Education Credits (American Opportunity and Lifetime Learning Credits). Here are snapshots of how these credits work:

» **The American Opportunity Credit** provides a credit of $2,500 per student per year for up to four years of college. The credit is equal to 100 percent of the first $2,000 of tuition and fees required to be paid by the school you, your spouse, or dependent child is attending, plus the cost of required books, supplies, and materials, even if you don't purchase those from the school but from a third party (but not room or board) and 25 percent of the next $2,000 of those expenses. A student must carry at least one-half the normal course load. But if you earn too much, you aren't eligible. For married taxpayers (filing jointly only), the credit starts to phase out at $160,000 of income and is gone at $180,000. For unmarried individuals, the phase-out starts at $80,000 and is completely wiped out at $90,000. The credit isn't available for anyone convicted of a felony drug conviction. Also, if you don't have enough tax liability to use up the entire credit and reduce your taxes, 40 percent of the credit, up to $1,000, is refundable.

» **The Lifetime Learning Credit** is a 25 percent credit on up to $10,000 of tuition, fees, and required books, supplies, and other expenses (but not room and board). This credit is per family per year, not per student, as is the case with the American Opportunity Credit. Unlike the American Opportunity Credit, the Lifetime Learning Credit doesn't have a limit on the number of years you may claim it. That's why it's called Lifetime Learning (it's so fun when things mean what they say!). In 2021, thanks to the Consolidated Appropriations Act passed in December, 2020, the same income limits and family-member restrictions that apply to the American Opportunity Credit also apply to this credit. Unlike the American Opportunity Credit, a student doesn't have to carry at least one-half the normal course load. Any course to acquire or improve job skills qualifies, but not courses involving sports or hobbies.

You can claim the American Opportunity credit for one child and the Lifetime Learning credit for another, but you can't claim both credits for the same student in a given tax year.

TIP

Families with more than one child can use both credits in concert, but it requires careful planning. You need to make sure tuition payments are made in the correct tax year for the correct student. Remember, these credits are designed to help you offset the high cost of college and other post-secondary school tuitions.

Sometimes students drop classes before the final drop date, and they or their parents receive refunded tuition that affects the amount of either an American Opportunity Credit or Lifetime Learning Credit to which they were entitled. If you fall into this category, read on. If you receive a tuition refund in 2021 or 2022 before you file your 2021 federal income tax return, subtract your refund from the tuition you paid in 2021 when figuring the credit. If you receive a refund after you file your 2021 return, you have to increase your tax for 2022 by the amount of the credit that the refund gave rise to. For example, in 2021 you paid tuition expenses of $3,000 and claimed a 25 percent Lifetime Learning Credit of $750. In 2022, after you filed your 2021 return, you receive a $1,000 tuition refund. You have to increase your tax on the 2022 return by $250 ($1,000 ÷ 25 percent). You should enter the amount and the type of credit on Form 1040, Schedule 2, line 17a.

WARNING

The IRS can check to see whether you're entitled to either the American Opportunity or Lifetime Learning credit because educational institutions are required to issue Form 1098-T, Tuition Payments Statement, which lists the student's name, Social Security number, the amount of tuition paid, whether the student was enrolled for at least half the full-time workload, and whether the courses led to a graduate-level degree. Make sure to check the amount on Form 1098-T against amounts you know you paid, whether by check, by automatic withdrawal from your bank or brokerage account, or by credit card. University bursars often go on vacation before Christmas and don't return until after the New Year, so payments you make near the end of the year are often not posted until the following year. If this happens to you, try to get the school to correct its records; if it refuses, calculate your credit based on the amount you actually paid, not the amount the school reported to the IRS, and keep copies of the bills you paid (and how you paid them) with your tax records. In the unlikely event that the IRS ever questions you on this credit, you'll have your supporting documentation easily at hand, and the matter should end right there.

REMEMBER

The rules regarding which person among family members is eligible to claim the American Opportunity or Lifetime Learning credits have changed dramatically. This change applies to divorced parents where one parent claims the child as a dependent and the other parent foots the tuition bill, or where, because of income phase-out limits, a parent can't claim the credit. A way now exists for the student to claim the credit and shelter any income they may have. Say, for example, you're the custodial parent (see Chapter 4) and claim your child as a dependent, but your former spouse pays the tuition. You're considered to have made the payment and may claim an education credit. However, you can twist that stipulation in a number of ways that entitles that person who "is considered to have paid the tuition and related expenses" to claim an education credit. When the student pays the tuition and you claim the student as a dependent, you're still considered to have paid tuition. For example, when someone else, such as a grandparent, pays the tuition, the student is considered to have paid the tuition, which again entitles you to claim an education credit because tuition that's considered paid by the student is considered paid by you.

TIP

The American Opportunity and Lifetime Learning credits provide nifty tax-planning techniques because education credits attach to whoever claims the dependency exemption: the student or the parent. If you can't claim the credits because your income is above the limits ($180,000 when filing jointly or $90,000 for others), maybe you need to look more closely at the dependency rules. It is possible that your college-age child is now providing more than 50 percent of their own support. Because students are considered to have paid their own tuition even though parents may have actually paid it, the students can claim the credit whenever their parents don't claim them as a dependent.

The scenario in the previous paragraph is based on the student having income that's subject to tax. If the student doesn't have such an income, you may want to try this suggestion: Give the student an investment that has gone up in value followed by a quick sale of that investment. Doing so shifts both the income and the tax burden from you to the student so the student can apply either of the education credits against the tax, which makes more after-tax money available for the student to pay the tuition. Of course, you need to remember when making any gift that there may be gift tax consequences. By keeping your annual gifts to $15,000 or less per donee ($30,000 or less if you and your spouse are making gifts together), you won't need to file gift tax returns. What a relief!

NEW STUFF

Of course, no good tax-saving strategy ever goes unchallenged, so in this scenario, you may also have to deal with the so-called "kiddie tax," which applies to students under age 24 who provide less than one-half of their own support from earned income. So, depending on how much investment income that "child" has, the sale of that appreciated stock may well be taxed at the parents' capital gains tax rate (maximum of 15 percent plus 3.8 percent net investment income tax).

TIP

Don't forget that other tax provisions can help you with the cost of education, including deductible student loan interest (Schedule 1, Part II, line 21, Chapter 6), and Section 529 plans and Coverdell Education Savings Accounts, which have become more attractive — see Chapter 26.

Line 4: Retirement savings contribution credit (Form 8880)

The *Retirement Savings Contribution Credit* encourages joint filers with adjusted gross incomes of less than $66,000 (heads of household below $49,500 and single filers below $33,000) to save for retirement by enabling them to claim a credit against their tax for a percentage of up to the first $2,000 that they contribute to Roth or traditional IRAs, 401(k)s, or elective deferrals to their employer's retirement plan.

Now for the fine print: If money was taken out of one of these accounts between January 1, 2018, and the due date for filing your 2021 return, including any extension of time to file, you must reduce the maximum $2,000 amount that is subject to the credit by the amount that you withdrew. Whoo! Okay, take a deep breath. For example, say you took $1,500 out of your IRA in

2020. Even though you contributed the $6,000 maximum allowed in 2021 to an IRA, the maximum amount that you can compute the credit on is $500 ($2,000 − $1,500).

In order to claim this credit, you need to fill out yet another form, Form 8880, Credit for Qualified Retirement Savings Contributions. Chapter 16 tells you what you need to know to fill out this form correctly and gives you more pointers on the credit for qualified retirement savings contributions.

Line 5: Residential energy credits (Form 5695)

Form 5695, Residential Energy Credits, is where you figure out how much tax relief you'll get from energy improvements you've made to your home in 2021. These credits are incredibly popular, and every time someone replaces windows, doors, a furnace, or the like, we are presented with all the bills for the cost of the new property plus the cost of installation. Our kudos go to the manufacturers and sellers of energy improvement property for making sure buyers know that these credits exist.

Form 5695 divides into two parts, the first for the big-money improvements, such as solar panels and water heaters, wind turbines, geothermal heat pumps, and biomass fuel property. When you install these sorts of energy improvements in your home, the tax savings can be significant. In 2021, the credit is the lesser of 26 percent of the total cost of the improvement (including the cost of installation) or $1,000 multiplied by the kilowatt capacity of the new property. So, for example, if you pay $30,000 for some solar panels that will produce 10 kilowatts of energy, you'll multiply $30,000 by 26 percent and arrive at $7,800, which is less than multiplying 10 kilowatts by $1,000, or $10,000. Remember, it's the lesser of these two numbers; in almost every case, you're going to be using the cost of the system as opposed to the kilowatts produced.

The second page of Form 5695 gives you a credit for passively improving your home's energy efficiency by upgrading insulation, installing new energy-efficient windows and doors, or putting on a new energy-efficient roof. This part of the credit has a yearly limit of $500 and a maximum lifetime limit of $2,000 and is calculated by multiplying the cost of the improvement, including installation, by 10 percent.

REMEMBER

In both cases, the improvements must be made to either your principal residence or your vacation home, and just buying the improvements won't trigger the credits; they must be actually installed by the end of the year to be eligible for the credit in 2021. The improvements that you buy (leased property doesn't count) must be new, and the cost that you use to calculate the credit must be reduced by any incentives you receive at the time of the purchase, such as from your utility company.

Many of these improvements are also eligible for state tax credits, and here you can double dip. There is one caveat here, though, and that is that you must reduce the basis in the property by the amount of all incentives and tax credits you receive. So that same $30,000 installation of solar panels is automatically reduced by the amount of the federal tax credit of $7,800, giving you basis in this property of $22,200.

And one final note: While the residential energy credits are nonrefundable, any amount that you're unable to use on your 2021 return will carry over to 2022, provided that you remember to fill out Form 5695 in 2022.

Line 6: Other nonrefundable credits

If you're looking for where the credit belongs for the electric car that you purchased, or the child you adopted, or the credit for the elderly or disabled, you'll find all of these, and more, on line 6. Here's a quick rundown (we discuss many of these credits in more detail in Chapter 16):

>> **Line 6a: General business credit (Form 3800),** which includes a myriad of credits available to businesses, such as increasing research activities, disabled access, orphan drugs, new markets, employer-provided childcare, alternative motor vehicle, employee retention, work opportunity, and many, many more. You may want to seek advice on whether you qualify for any of these.

>> **Line 6b: Credit for prior year minimum tax (Form 8801),** for those who were caught by the AMT in 2020, but not in 2021. The calculations this form requires are quite complicated, and you may want to seek advice here, too, even if you did ace Calculus.

>> **Line 6c: Adoption credit (Form 8839)** if you adopted a child in 2021. We cover this more fully in Chapter 16.

>> **Line 6d: Credit for the elderly or disabled (Schedule R)** for lower-income elderly or disabled. You're entitled to claim this credit (which can amount to as much as $7,500) if you're married and both you and your spouse are 65 or older — or both of you are disabled and any age. For single taxpayers, the maximum credit is $5,000. Check out Chapter 16 for more on Schedule R.

>> **Line 6e: Alternative motor vehicle credit (Form 8910)** if you purchased a new hydrogen fuel cell vehicle with at least four wheels in 2021 (sorry folks, this is straight from the instructions — we don't make this stuff up). You must own the vehicle, not lease it (the lessor gets the credit when you lease the car), and you must have put it into service by December 31, 2021. This credit is good for both business and individual taxpayers, so if you've purchased this car to use in your business, you'll claim the business portion of the credit on Form 3800, but any individual-use piece will be calculated on Form 8910.

>> **Line 6f: Qualified plug-in motor vehicle credit (Form 8936)** if you bought what is popularly known as a plug-in electric, or plug-in hybrid electric, but is actually described by the IRS as a new four-wheel vehicle.

>> **Line 6g: Mortgage interest credit (Form 8396)** if a state or local government agency issued you a Mortgage Credit Certificate (MCC). These certificates are issued as part of state and local governmental programs that provide taxpayers with financing to help them purchase their principal residence. If you're issued an MCC, it entitles you to a tax credit equal to between 10 percent and 50 percent of the amount of the mortgage interest you paid. If the MCC has a rate that exceeds 20 percent, the maximum credit is limited to $2,000. Amounts of more than $2,000 can be carried over to future years but are subject to the $2,000 annual limit. You must reduce your home mortgage interest deduction on Schedule A by the amount of the credit. A good mortgage broker can assist you in qualifying for a state-sponsored mortgage loan so you can qualify for this credit. If you qualify for this credit, you need to fill out Form 8396 first before inserting the amount of the credit on line 53 and checking the appropriate box next to the line.

>> **Line 6h: District of Columbia first-time homebuyer credit (Form 8859).** If this describes you, put the amount of your remaining available credit on line 1 of Form 8859, Carryforward of the District of Columbia First-Time Homebuyer Credit, apply any income limitation you

may have on line 2, put the smaller amount on line 3, and then carry that over to line 6h of Schedule 3. Any leftover amount of credit is placed on Form 8859, line 4, and carried over to 2022.

» **Line 6i: Qualified electric vehicle credit (Form 8834).** This is another carryforward credit, for the purchase of qualified electric vehicles placed in service before 2007.

» **Line 6j: Alternative fuel vehicle refueling property credit (Form 8911).** If you install a pump for alternative fuels — which must consist of at least 85 percent of either ethanol; natural gas; compressed natural gas; liquefied natural gas; liquefied petroleum gas; hydrogen; or a mixture that contains either biodiesel, diesel, or kerosene; or an electricity power point specifically for your car — you're entitled to the lesser of 30 percent of the cost of installation, or $30,000, as a credit. Of course, you must reduce your basis in the property by the amount of the credit, and the credit is subject to recapture rules if the property no longer qualifies. While this is a potentially large credit, any unused portion is lost; there is no carryforward to next year.

» **Line 6k: Credit to holders of tax credit bonds (Form 8912),** for those of you who have invested in clean renewable energy bonds (CREB), new clean renewable energy bonds (NCREB), qualified energy conservation bonds (QECB), qualified zone academy bonds (QZAB), qualified school construction bonds (QSCB), or Build America bonds (BAB). In lieu of, or in addition to, interest paid on these bonds, you are also allowed an income tax credit. If you own any of these bonds, complete Form 8912, Credit to Holders of Tax Credit Bonds, and put the amount of your credit here on line 6k.

SEEK ADVICE

» **Line 6l: Partner's additional reporting year tax (Form 8978).** If you believe you're eligible for this credit, you should seek professional help in completing Form 8978, Partner's Additional Reporting Year Tax. This is a multi-year form that permits partners in a partnership to refigure their tax liabilities based on the imputed underpayment amounts pushed out to them by the partnership under Section 6226 of the Internal Revenue Code. If that description doesn't make your head spin, you're a much more adventurous soul than either of us. Only use this line if the answer you get on Form 8978 is negative; a positive result on this form means that you owe additional tax.

Line 6z: Other nonrefundable credits. We don't know what the IRS has in mind for this line, since they've been fairly comprehensive up until now, but if you discover a nonrefundable credit that we haven't covered that you're eligible to claim, this is where you put it.

Lines 7 and 8: It's time to add!

On Schedule 3, line 7, you're going to add all the numbers you've put in lines 6a through 6z, and on line 8, add together the numbers you have on lines 1 through 5 and line 7. Easy as pie! Once you've done the math for line 8, transfer that number right over to Form 1040, line 20. You've now finished all the nonrefundable credits.

Schedule 3, Part II: Other Payments and Refundable Credits

No question, Schedule 3, Part I, was interesting, but Part II is even more fun. This is where you're going to put all the payments (other than wage and pension withholdings) you've made throughout the year, plus the refundable credits that you're entitled to, which is kind of like the IRS making tax payments for you. Don't ignore this section; you might be surprised to find all the money that the IRS might be holding for you. Time to take a look at what's on this part of Schedule 3 (see Figure 9-2).

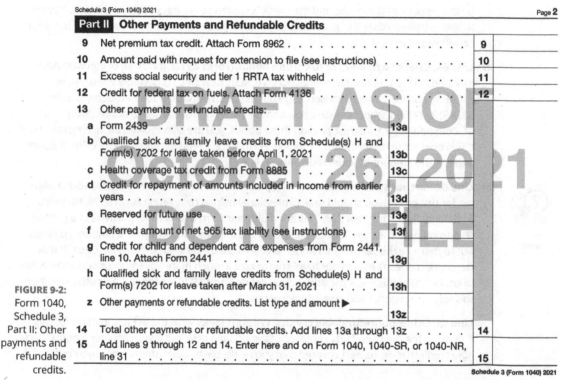

FIGURE 9-2:
Form 1040,
Schedule 3,
Part II: Other
payments and
refundable
credits.

Line 9: Net premium tax credit (Form 8962)

You may recall in Chapter 8, we talk about the excess advance premium tax credit repayment. That's where you repay money you received as a subsidy that you weren't eligible for based on your actual 2021 income. Well, that was for where you were overpaid; this is where you indicate that you were eligible for a subsidy you didn't receive. You use the same Form 8962, Premium Tax Credit (PTC), to calculate both the over- and under-payments. If you were underpaid, you'll end up with a number on line 26 of Form 8962. Put that answer here, on line 9.

Line 10: Amount paid with request for extension to file (Form 4868)

REMEMBER

If you requested a six-month extension of time by filing Form 4868, Application for Automatic Extension of Time to File U.S. Individual Income Tax Return, enter the amount that you paid when you requested the extension. (Unbelievably, despite the millions of taxpayers who file for extensions each year, the IRS still doesn't include this form in the Form 1040 instruction booklet.) It's really easy to file Form 4868. If you're using tax software, the form will fill itself out once you check the box for filing an extension, and then you can electronically file the extension form by itself. If you're still filing on paper, you'll need to put your full name and Social Security number on Form 4868 (and the same for your spouse, if you're married and filing jointly), the amount of your estimated total tax liability for 2021, the total amount of payments you've already made, whether through estimated tax payments or withholdings from your job or pension, the balance due, and finally, the amount you are paying with your extension request.

If you are a U.S. resident or green card holder *and* a bona fide resident of another country, or you meet the physical presence test, you have until June 15, 2022, to file either your Form 1040 or Form 4868. This will extend your return until October 17, 2022. Just make sure you check the box that says you are "out of the country" on April 18, 2022. Remember, though, that all taxes are due by the April 18, 2022, due date for the return.

If there is a balance due, please be sure to include a check with your extension request, make a payment through the EFTPS system with the IRS, or pay directly online at the IRS website at www.irs.gov/payments. The penalties for late payment are pesky and mostly unnecessary, and no one wants to get a bill from the IRS. Seeing that envelope stuck in between all the catalogs in your mail is just stress inducing, especially when you may have avoided it by including a check with your extension request back in April. Finally, if you're filing your extension request on paper, remember to always send it via Certified Mail by the due date. No return receipt is necessary; it's enough to be able to prove to the IRS that you mailed it timely — you don't need to be able to prove that they received it.

TIP

When you can't file on time, and you're not sure what your total tax liability will be for the year, but you typically make quarterly estimated tax payments, one way to insulate yourself from late payment penalties is to add the amount of your first quarter estimated tax payment for the current year to the extension payment for the prior, and then don't pay your first quarter of the current year's estimated tax. When you prepare your prior year's return, you'll have that additional cushion if there is income you didn't account for in your extension request. Any amount over and above that can then be applied to the current year. If you've completely underestimated your tax liability, and you need that entire cushion, plus an additional payment over and above what you paid in with the extension, you've still created a scenario where you can show the IRS that you paid in more than you thought you'd owe. In every situation where we've been assessed a penalty for late payment, we've had that underpayment penalty and interest waived because we paid the extra amount with our extension request instead of making a first quarter estimate. Remember, the penalty for late payment is much harsher than the penalty for underpaying your estimated taxes. Use that knowledge to your advantage.

Line 11: Excess Social Security and RRTA tax withheld

Line 11 applies only if you worked for two employers and your total wages were $142,800 or more. The maximum Social Security tax you're required to pay for 2021 is $8,855. So, if $9,000 was reported withheld on your W-2s, $145 is entered on line 11. Box 4 of your W-2s contains the amount of Social Security tax that was withheld from your salary. If you worked for only one employer and more than $8,855 was withheld, skip line 11; you have to get the excess back from your employer.

Line 12: Credit for Federal Tax Paid on Fuels (Form 4136)

This form is for claiming a refundable credit for the tax paid on gasoline and gasohol for off-highway use. Bulldozers, forklifts, generators, and compressors used in your business qualify for the credit. Fuel used in motorboats doesn't qualify. Tax paid on undyed kerosene used in home heaters also qualifies for the credit.

Line 13: Other payments or refundable credits

Here is yet another hodge-podge of credits and payments that have been lumped together under line 13, but are specified as follows:

>> **Line 13a, Form 2439, Notice to Shareholders of Undistributable Long-Term Capital Gain,** is used when you invest in a mutual fund where the company didn't distribute your share of the long-term capital gains that you were entitled to receive. Enter the amount from line 2 of this form on line 13a and attach a copy of the form to your 1040. See Chapter 14 for information on how to handle the capital gains retained by the fund.

>> **Line 13b, qualified sick and family leave credits from Schedule(s) H and Form(s) 7202 for leave taken before April 1, 2021,** is for those self-employed individuals who were unable to work between January 1 and March 31, 2021, due to COVID-19–related reasons. It provides a refundable tax credit equivalent to those COVID-19–related sick or family leave provisions for people who were employed by someone else.

>> **Line 13c, Health Coverage Tax Credit (Form 8885),** allows dislocated workers and uninsured retirees who are receiving pension benefits from the federal government's Pension Benefit Guarantee Corporations (PBGC) (and their eligible dependents) to claim a refundable credit equal to 72.5 percent of their health insurance expenses. This group of people is by no means small. In 2002, the PBGC took over the responsibility for paying the pensions of 95,000 retirees of Bethlehem Steel. Individuals can elect to forego the credit and instead have the government pick up the tab directly for 72.5 percent of their health insurance premiums.

To be eligible for the credit or the advance payment, you have to be receiving Trade Adjustments Assistance (TAA) allowances under the Trade Act or Alternative Trade Adjustments Assistance (ATAA) or be an uninsured retiree between 55 and 65 who is receiving pension benefits from the PBGC. TAA allowances are paid to workers who lost their jobs because of foreign trade. ATAA benefits are paid to displaced workers under the Trade Acts alternative program. The credit and the advance payment may very well become the prototype for all unemployed workers.

You can obtain TAA or ATAA allowances by submitting a request for determination of eligibility with the U.S. Department of Labor. A special hotline has been set up for the TAA and ATAA programs at 866-628-4282. The Health Coverage Tax Credit (HCTC) website is at www. irs.gov/credits-deductions/individuals/hctc.

The credit isn't available to individuals who are unemployed and paying health insurance premiums under COBRA unless they meet the eligibility requirements for receiving TAA, ATAA, or PBGC benefits. Coverage under a spouse's health insurance counts toward determining the credit. Individuals covered by Medicare aren't eligible.

» **Line 13d, Credit for repayment of amounts included in income from earlier years** is the line where you'll put taxes paid on income you declared in prior years that was repaid in 2021. So, for example, if you held a mortgage on a piece of real estate, and the borrower paid you your December mortgage payment, but the check didn't bounce until after you'd already filed your 2020 return, you'd be entitled to claim a credit here for the taxes you paid on the interest portion of that bounced payment.

» **Line 13f, Net section 965 inclusions** (there is no line 13e), is one of those complicated U.S. shareholders of foreign corporations deals that you're going to want to seek expert advice for.

» **Line 13g, Credit for child and dependent care expenses** (Form 2441, line 10) is used to pick up the refundable portion of your child and dependent care credit calculated earlier in this chapter, on line 2. You'll only use this line if you don't have enough tax liability to offset nonrefundable credits. For 2021, a portion of the child and dependent care credit can be refunded to you.

» **Line 13h, Qualified sick and family leave credits** from Schedule(s) H and Form(s) 7202 for leave taken after March 31, 2021. COVID-19 is the gift that keeps giving, at least in the world of tax credits. Look back at Line 13b — this same credit has now been extended through September 30, 2021, but as COVID-19 continues to plague the United States, it's reasonable to assume that the credit will continue to be extended until the worst of the pandemic is over. Watch this space!

» **Line 13z, Other payments or refundable credits.** Once again, we are at a loss to know what the IRS would like us to include here, since the other refundable credits, such as the Earned Income Tax Credit (EITC), the Child Tax Credit (CTC), the Additional Child Tax Credit (ACTC), tax withholdings, and estimated tax payments are not included here, but in the body of Form 1040 itself. We cover all these additional items in Chapter 10.

Lines 14 and 15: And even more math

Now you need to add up all the amounts you have on lines 13a through 13z and put the total on line 14. Line 15, not to be obvious, wants you to place the total of lines 9 through 12 and line 14. Transfer the total of all items, which you've now entered on line 15, also onto Form 1040, line 31. Hard to believe, but you're almost at the end of your tax return. Take a deep breath, and then go to Chapter 10 to figure out how to finish up your return.

Chapter **10**

Finishing Up the 1040

Y ou may feel that you've struggled through the income section of Form 1040 and Schedules 1, 2, and 3 (although we hope you haven't because you've had this book to help you along), but wait! There's more — you've now entered most of the necessary information, but you still need to finish up your return. Right now, you have all the ingredients for your tax return, but you haven't mixed them together. Relax and let us help you. We'll get you to the finish line, item by item, with your sanity intact.

Arriving at Taxable Income

You may be surprised to find out that this is going to be the simplest calculation you've ever made on a tax return. If you've already completed Schedules 1, 2, and 3, you're all set to plug the bottom line of each part of those schedules into your return to arrive first at adjusted gross income, and then, at taxable income. All you need to do is transfer the numbers on your schedules to the appropriate lines on Form 1040, do a little math, and Bob's your uncle, you'll be there with no problems. See Figure 10-1 for Form 1040, lines 10–15.

Form 1040, line 10: Adjustments to income

If you had any numbers on Schedule 1, Part II, you're going to place the total from line 26 of Schedule 1 onto Form 1040, line 10. This is the total of your so-called "above-the-line deductions" that you're not required to itemize on Schedule A and that every taxpayer who is eligible is entitled to take.

FIGURE 10-1:
Arriving at
taxable income
on Form 1040.

	10	Adjustments to income from Schedule 1, line 26		10	
• Married filing jointly or Qualifying widow(er), $25,100	11	Subtract line 10 from line 9. This is your **adjusted gross income** . . . . ▶		11	
	12a	**Standard deduction or itemized deductions** (from Schedule A) . .	12a		
• Head of household, $18,800	b	Charitable contributions if you take the standard deduction (see instructions)	12b		
	c	Add lines 12a and 12b		12c	
• If you checked any box under *Standard Deduction,* see instructions.	13	Qualified business income deduction from Form 8995 or Form 8995-A . . .		13	
	14	Add lines 12c and 13		14	
	15	**Taxable income.** Subtract line 14 from line 11. If zero or less, enter -0- . .		15	

For Disclosure, Privacy Act, and Paperwork Reduction Act Notice, see separate instructions.   Cat. No. 11320B   Form **1040** (2021)

Source: Internal Revenue Service

TIP

If you're preparing your return with paper and pencil, make sure to double check the numbers on Schedule 1, line 26, and Form 1040, line 10, to be certain they match. Transposition errors (switching around two digits in a number) are one of the most common errors the IRS comes across.

Form 1040, line 11: Arriving at adjusted gross income

We know, we're being pretty obvious here, but we did promise step-by-step instructions. The description of the line says it all — you're going to subtract any amount on Form 1040, line 10, from Form 1040, line 9, and place your answer on Form 1040, line 11. This brings you to that all-important number, adjusted gross income. We keep mentioning this number because it is very important in many of the calculations contained on your tax return, either in its unadulterated form, as it appears here on line 11, or as the basis for calculating modified adjusted gross income, which is used in things like your taxable Social Security calculation. If we could light up this line in neon, believe us, we would.

Form 1040, line 12a: Standard deduction or itemized deductions (Schedule A)

One of the biggest consequences of the Tax Cuts and Jobs Act of 2017 was the elimination of the personal and dependent exemptions and a substantial increase to the standard deduction. As a result, many more people now use the standard deduction as opposed to itemizing their deductions, as the standard deduction is, in most cases, larger than the amount of itemized deductions most people have. This is actually one of those rare cases of tax simplification.

How much is your standard deduction? That's an easy question to answer — it depends on your filing status, your age, and whether or not you're blind. Go back and look at the filing status you chose. The standard deduction amounts for non-blind people under age 65 that go on line 12a are as follows for the 2021 tax filing season:

>> **Single:** $12,550

>> **Head of household:** $18,800

>> **Married filing jointly:** $25,100

>> **Married filing singly:** $12,550

If you are filing a married filing singly return, your spouse must also choose that filing status, and both of you must choose to use either itemized deductions or the standard deduction. If you're not speaking with your spouse, you should know that the first return filed will determine whether the second return filed uses the standard deduction or itemizes. If you are in a situation where you are not communicating with your spouse but you're required to file as a married couple, you may want to make sure to file the first return so that you make the decision of itemizing or using the standard deduction.

If you're legally married but can qualify as head of household, you're treated as if you were unmarried, so you can claim the standard deduction even if your spouse chooses to itemize deductions. See Chapter 11 for the specifics.

If you've turned age 65 on or before January 1, 2022 (some senator's wife had a January 1 birthday, which is why it's not December 31, 2021), you're considered to have been 65 for all of the prior year, so you're eligible for an increased standard deduction. Likewise, if you're blind, you're also entitled to a larger standard deduction. And remember, if you have a spouse, and they are either age 65 or older by January 1, 2022, or blind, or both old and blind, you get an even larger standard deduction. Go back to the section on figuring your standard deduction in Chapter 4 to see how much more of a standard deduction you and your spouse can take.

Of course, if you're able to itemize your deductions and itemizing gives you a better result, check out Chapter 11 to see what's involved in completing Schedule A. It's really not that difficult, but as always, there are new twists in the itemizing game that you want to be aware of.

Form 1040, line 12b: Charitable contributions for non-itemizers

If you're better off using the standard deduction but you gave to charity, there's a bonus for you here, on line 12b. You're allowed to deduct up to $300 of charitable gifts ($600 if you're married filing jointly) in 2021 even if you use the standard deduction. The gifts must be to a recognized charity (no donor-advised funds or private charitable foundations), and they must have been made in cash (credit card, debit card, and checks all count as green stuff here).

Form 1040, line 12c: Add lines 12a and 12b

Like the line description says, add amounts that you have on line 12a (everyone should have a number here) and line 12b (only for people who are taking the standard deduction and who have given cash gifts in 2021 to charity) together, and put your result on line 12c. Every line should be this easy.

Form 1040, Line 13: Qualified business income deduction (Forms 8995 or 8995-A)

In an attempt to equalize the tax rates of entities that file as corporations with those rates applied to pass-through small businesses that are either sole proprietorships (Schedule C), S Corporations (Form 1120-S), or partnerships (Form 1065), the qualified business income deduction is a 20 percent reduction in the net profit from a qualifying business. This deduction is calculated on either Form 8995, Qualified Business Income Deduction Simplified Computation, or Form 8995-A, Qualified Business Income Deduction. While most people who are eligible to take this deduction are small business owners, the deduction is also available to shareholders of some dividend-paying corporations. If you receive a Form 1099-DIV that lists a number in box 5 for Section 199A dividends, put that box 5 number here.

SEEK ADVICE

Internal Revenue Code Section 199A is tricky stuff, and it has taken the experts a while to wrap their heads around it. The basic requirements are that the business producing this deduction must show a profit in the year for which you're taking the deduction, and the business must have either paid wages or have an investment in assets used by the company. If you have multiple businesses, and one has a loss but the others show profits, you must net the loss in 2021 against the 2021 profits. And if you have a loss from a prior year, that will carry forward to 2021 and reduce any 2021 profits. Finally, if you work in a business that the IRS deems as a highly compensated professional (a so-called SSTB, or specified service, trade, or business, where the principal asset is the owner's professional reputation), income limits may preclude you taking the deduction. As you can see, there's a lot going on here, and you may want to use tax preparation software or seek professional advice at least the first time you attempt to complete Form 8995 or Form 8995-A to make sure you're doing it correctly.

Form 1040, line 14: Add lines 12c and 13

Another easy one. Add the numbers on lines 12c and 13 and put your result on line 14.

Line 15: Taxable income

And now we arrive at the bottom of page 1 of Form 1040 and reach your taxable income. Subtract line 14 from line 11 and place your answer here. If you've had a really lousy year financially, and the number you arrive at is negative, sorry. Place a zero on line 15 and turn your paper over (or move to the next computer screen).

Calculating Your Tax Liability

You are getting so close to the finish line you should be able to smell it. Or, if you prefer, the light is shining brightly at the end of the tunnel. Whichever cliché you choose to use here, the meaning is the same. You're almost there, and there are just a few more steps to take to complete your return.

Figure 10-2 shows you all the component parts that comprise your tax liability. It doesn't matter whether you're using Form 1040-SR or Form 1040-NR, the line numbers are the same. So, with that said, it's time to take a look at the beginning of the end of your journey.

Form 1040, line 16: Tax

Now that you've arrived at your taxable income, you need to calculate your tax. The good news is that, if you're using a computer program to do your taxes, the program will calculate your taxes. The bad news is that, even if your computer calculates the tax, you need to double-check to make sure it has done the job correctly. This is especially true if you have any qualified dividends, long-term capital gains, you're including your child(ren)'s investment income on your return, or you've taken a lump-sum distribution from a retirement plan (provided you were born prior to 1936).

FIGURE 10-2:
Pulling
together all the
pieces of your
tax liability.

Form 1040 (2021)			Page **2**
16	**Tax** (see instructions). Check if any from Form(s): 1 ☐ 8814 2 ☐ 4972 3 ☐ _____		16
17	Amount from Schedule 2, line 3		17
18	Add lines 16 and 17		18
19	Nonrefundable child tax credit or credit for other dependents from Schedule 8812		19
20	Amount from Schedule 3, line 8		20
21	Add lines 19 and 20		21
22	Subtract line 21 from line 18. If zero or less, enter -0-		22
23	Other taxes, including self-employment tax, from Schedule 2, line 21		23
24	Add lines 22 and 23. This is your **total tax**	▶	24

Source: Internal Revenue Service

First, though, look at the basic tax calculation, because regardless of any wrinkles in your return, you're going to have to calculate this one, even if only for comparison's sake.

If your taxable income is $100,000 or less, you can use either the tax rate tables contained in the Form 1040 instructions, or you can use the tax rate schedules shown in Table 10-1. Either calculation should give you the same result, or at least within a few dollars. If, however, your taxable income is more than $100,000, you must use the tax rates for your filing status in the tax-rate schedules, shown in Table 10-1.

Here's how using the tax rate schedules works. Suppose that you're single and your taxable income (which includes no long-term capital gains or qualified dividends) is $118,800. Because your income is between $86,375 and $164,925, here's how to figure your tax:

		Tax
Taxable income	$118,800	$14,751
Less: Your starting tax bracket amount $86,375	($86,375)	
Balance	$32,425	
Tax bracket percentage for amount more than $86,375	× 24%	$7,782
Tax to be entered on line 16		$22,533

Remember, the IRS prefers that you use the whole-dollar method, where you round down for any pennies under 50 cents and round up to the next dollar for any pennies that are 50 cents or more. If you're working on a computer tax program, this will automatically happen, but if you're working with pen and paper, please make those adjustments. Putting in the pennies will just slow the processing of your return.

Capital gains and qualified dividends tax worksheet

If you had capital gains or qualified dividends last year, you know that thinking about making these calculations is worse than actually doing them. If you've never had capital gains or qualified dividends before, don't worry. Just follow the line-by-line instructions. This worksheet actually works!

Table 10-1 Tax Rate Schedules for 2021

Filing Status	Taxable Income	Tax Is
Married Filing Jointly, Surviving Spouse and Qualifying Widow(er)	Not more than $19,900	10 percent of taxable income
	Over $19,900 but not more than $81,050	$1,990 plus 12 percent of excess over $19,900
	Over $81,050 but not more than $172,750	$9,328 plus 22 percent of excess over $81,050
	Over $172,750 but not more than $329,850	$29,502 plus 24 percent of excess over $172,750
	Over $329,850 but not more than $418,850	$67,206 plus 32 percent of excess over $329,850
	Over 418,850 but not more than $628,300	$95,686 plus 35 percent of excess over $418,850
	Over $628,300	$168,993.50 plus 37 percent of the excess over $628,300
Heads of Household	Not more than $14,200	10 percent of taxable income
	Over $14,200 but not more than $54,200	$1,420 plus 12 percent of excess over $14,200
	Over $54,200 but not more than $86,350	$6,220 plus 22 percent of excess over $54,200
	Over $86,350 but not more than $164,900	$13,293 plus 24 percent of excess over $86,350
	Over $164,900 but not more than $209,400	$32,145 plus 32 percent of excess over $164,900
	Over $209,400 but not more than $523,600	$46,385 plus 35 percent of excess over $164,900
	More than $523,600	$156,355 plus 37 percent of excess over $523,600
Single	Not more than $9,950	10 percent of taxable income
	Over $9,950, but not more than $40,525	$995 plus 12 percent of excess over $9,950
	Over $40.525 but not more than $86,375	$4,664 plus 22 percent of excess over $40,525
	Over $86,375 but not more than $164,925	$14,751 plus 24 percent of excess over $86,375
	Over $164,925 but not more than $209,425	$33,603 plus 32 percent of excess over $164,925
	Over $209,425 but not more than $523,600	$47,843 plus 35 percent of excess over $209,425
	More than $523,600	$157,804.25 plus 37 percent of excess over $523,600
Married filing separately	Not more than $9,950	10 percent of taxable income
	Over $9,950, but not more than $40,525	$995 plus 12 percent of excess over $9,950
	Over $40,525 but not more than $86,375	$4,664 plus 22 percent of excess over $40,525
	Over $86,375 but not more than $164,925	$14,751 plus 24 percent of excess over $86,375
	Over $164,925 but not more than $209,425	$33,603 plus 32 percent of excess over $164,925
	Over $209,425 but not more than $314,150	$47,843 plus 35 percent of excess over $209,425
	More than $314,150	$84,496.75 plus 37 percent of excess over $314,150

WARNING

Qualified dividends and most long-term capital gains are taxed at rates less than your other forms of income. If you have numbers on lines 3a and/or 7 of your Form 1040, or if you have already completed Schedule D (see Chapter 14), you need to calculate your tax using the "Qualified Dividends and Capital Gain Worksheet" included in your Form 1040 instruction booklet. Otherwise, you're going to pay more tax than you should. The following is an overview of why these items may affect your total tax liability.

Qualified dividends and long-term capital gains

In 2021, qualified stock dividends, which we explain in Chapter 12, and long-term capital gains (check out Chapter 14) are taxed at the maximum rate of 20 percent. (Actually, higher income earners can face an additional 3.8 percent tax on investment earnings to help pay for Medicaid expansion under the Affordable Care Act.) If your taxable income is $40,400 or less if you're single or married filing singly, $80,800 or less if you're married filing jointly, or $54,100 if you're a head of household, then your qualified stock dividends and long-term capital gains this year are taxed at 0 percent. It just doesn't get much better than that!

Once your income goes above those limits, your tax rates also increase on these two forms of income, but never to the point where they exceed your ordinary income tax rate. So, for singles, as long as your taxable income remains at or below $445,850, you'll be taxed at 15 percent for these dividends and gains. For heads of household, that number goes to $473,750, and for couples filing jointly, the 15 percent bracket extends to amounts at or under $501,600.

If you have qualified stock dividends or long-term capital gains in excess of those amounts, they'll be taxed at a marginal rate of 20 percent.

REMEMBER

The additional 3.8 percent on net investment income to pay for the Affordable Care Act's Medicaid expansion applies to single taxpayers with at least $200,000 of adjusted gross income (AGI) and for married couples filing jointly with at least $250,000 of (AGI). See Chapter 8 for those details.

WARNING

Not every long-term capital gain is eligible for these preferential long-term rates. The maximum rate on the gain on the sale of collectibles is 28 percent. The rate for depreciable real estate is 25 percent on depreciation that's recaptured. If you find this capital gains stuff somewhat confusing, you're not alone. See Chapter 14 for an updated course on the capital gains rules, including what the heck *recapture of capital gain depreciation* is all about and what portion of the gain is taxed at 25 percent and what part is taxed at the lower maximum tax rates. We leave nothing out when it comes to these heady subjects.

We offer a worksheet in Table 10-2 that shows how you calculate your tax if you have qualified dividends or capital gains subject to these lower tax rates.

WARNING

If you sold your stamp collection or your baseball cards, if you've been enjoying great success on eBay and made profits on your sales, or if you've sold a piece of property that's subject to depreciation recapture (we explain it all in Chapter 14), you can't use the worksheet in Table 10-2. For you, because the IRS knows you're special, you get your very own special worksheet. And it looks grim. The print is tiny, and it has lots of lines. Don't panic. It's essentially the same as the Table 10-2 worksheet with some extra categories thrown in. If you can do the Table 10-2 worksheet, the "Schedule D Tax Worksheet" will be a piece of cake. And, of course, if you're doing your taxes with tax prep software, the software is going to calculate this worksheet for you, so long as you input your information correctly.

Table 10-2   Qualified Dividends and Capital Gain Tax Worksheet — Line 16

1.	Enter the amount from Form 1040, line 15.	1.	$125,000
2.	Enter the amount from Form 1040, line 3a.	2.	3,000
3.	Are you filing Schedule D? If so, enter the smaller of line 15 or 16 of Schedule D, but don't enter less than -0-. If not, enter the amount from Form 1040, line 7.	3.	12,000
4.	Add lines 2 and 3.	4.	15,000
5.	If you're claiming investment interest expense on Form 4952, enter the amount from line 4g of that form. Otherwise, enter -0-.	5.	0
6.	Subtract line 5 from line 4. If zero or less, enter -0-.	6.	15,000
7.	Subtract line 6 from line 1. If zero or less, enter -0-.	7.	110,000
8.	Enter the smaller of: The amount on line 1 or $40,400 if single or married filing separately, $80,800 if married filing jointly or qualifying widower, $54,100 if head of household.	8.	40,400
9.	Is the amount on line 7 equal to or more than the amount on line 8? If Yes, skip lines 9 through 11, go to line 12, and check the "No" box. If No, enter the amount from line 7.	9.	N/A
10.	Subtract line 9 from line 8.	10.	N/A
11.	Multiply line 10 by 5 percent.	11.	N/A
12.	Are the amounts on lines 6 and 10 the same? Yes. Skip lines 12 through 15; go to line 16. No. Enter the smaller of line 1 or line 6.	12.	15,000
13.	Enter the amount from line 10 (if line 10 is blank, enter -0-).	13.	0
14.	Subtract line 13 from line 12.	14.	15,000
15.	Multiply line 14 by 15 percent.	15.	2,250
16.	Figure the tax on line 7. Use the tax table or tax computation worksheet, whichever applies.	16.	20,421
17.	Add lines 11, 15, and 16.	17.	22,671
18.	Figure the tax on the amount on line 1. Use the tax table or tax computation worksheet, whichever applies.	18.	24,021
19.	Tax on all taxable income. Enter the smaller of line 17 or line 18. Also include this amount on Form 1040, line 16.	19.	22,671

Now that you've determined that you need to use the capital gain worksheet to calculate your tax, Table 10-2 shows you how to do it, using an example of a single taxpayer with $125,000 of taxable income, of which $3,000 comes from qualified dividends and $12,000 comes from long-term capital gains.

Wow! That taxpayer just saved a cool $1,350 ($24,021 calculated using tax tables — $22,671 using "Qualified Dividends and Capital Gain Tax Worksheet" = $1,350 tax savings) by spending a few minutes with this worksheet. If only all your endeavors were this lucrative!

The kiddie tax: Forms 8615 and 8814

Don't jump over to the next line quite yet. If you have children younger than 19, or younger than 24 if they're full-time students providing less than 50 percent of their own support who have investment income, you may need to complete some additional forms (see Chapter 17 for a discussion of Form 8615 and Form 8814). Form 8615 is used if your kid files their own return. Use Form 8814 if you qualify to report your kid's investment income on your return. The general rule: If your child is younger than 19, their investment income (interest, dividends, and so on) above $2,200 is taxed at your rate, not the child's.

Those tiny boxes on line 16: Forms 8814 and 4972

Form 8814, Parents' Election to Report Child's Interest and Dividends, is the form to use when you elect to report your kids' investment incomes on your own return instead of having the kids file their own returns. In order to use this option, your child's income must be less than $11,000 and can only come from dividends (including the Alaska Permanent Dividend), interest, and capital gains. See Chapter 17 for a detailed look at your choice.

Form 4972, Tax on Lump-Sum Distributions, however, is more common. If you decide to take all your money out of your employer's retirement plan in a lump sum, use this form to compute your tax under the ten-year averaging method if you're eligible. Using the averaging method can save you a bunch of dough. Refer to Chapter 8 for a complete discussion of this issue. You had to be born before 1936 to qualify.

Form 1040, line 17: Amount from Schedule 2, line 3

Remember back to Chapter 8, where you calculated the alternative minimum tax and the excess advance premium tax credit repayment? Well, this is where you're going to transfer the total of those two numbers from Schedule 2, Part I, line 3, to Form 1040, line 17. And that's all there is to this line.

Form 1040, line 18: Add lines 16 and 17

This couldn't be simpler. If you're doing your returns on paper, just add up the prior two lines and put the total here. If you're working on your computer, it's already done it for you, and there's really no need for you to check the math. We trust our computers to make this simple calculation accurately, and so should you.

Form 1040, line 19: Nonrefundable child tax credit or credit for other dependents

NEW STUFF

This number is calculated on Schedule 8812. The description on this line is somewhat misleading, as line 19 in 2021 is only for the $500 per qualifying dependent (but not qualifying child) that you're entitled to take to reduce your tax liability. As always, income limits apply here, and we explain how they work in Chapter 16.

Who is a qualifying dependent? A qualifying dependent is any person you support who meets the dependency requirements listed in Chapter 4 and is not your qualifying child. Remember, in 2021 (and currently only in 2021 — in 2022, the age is scheduled to return to children under age 17), qualifying children must be under age 18. And, in 2021, they are entitled to much larger credits than in the past: $3,600 for children under age 6, and $3,000 for children between the ages of 6 and 17.

Line 20: Amount from Schedule 3, line 8

We love lines like this. Pick up the number you entered on Form 1040, Schedule 3, line 8, and place it here.

Form 1040, line 21: Add lines 19 and 20

This line is almost as simple as the last one, but you do have to add the numbers together. Go wild, or let your computer do the math. Either way, you're getting closer and closer to the end of your return.

Form 1040, line 22: Subtract line 21 from line 18

We know — subtraction is tougher than addition, but do it anyway. It's always good to keep your basic math skills functional.

Form 1040, line 23: Other taxes, including self-employment tax

You've obviously done all the work, and now you're just transferring the number over from Schedule 2, line 21, to here, Form 1040, line 23. If you're working on your computer, it has already done this for you; if you're working on paper, be careful and double-check that the numbers match. You don't want to make a transposition error here.

Form 1040, line 24: Add lines 22 and 23. This is your total tax.

The line description says it all. This is the total amount of your 2021 federal tax liability. Now all that's left to do is add up all your payments and refundable credits to see if the IRS owes you money or, perish the thought, if it is you who owe the IRS.

Calculating Your Payments and Refundable Credits

This section of the return is where you finally, thankfully, get to tally up how much actual federal tax you paid during the year. See Figure 10-3 for how this plays out.

Form 1040, line 25: Federal income tax withheld

This year, the IRS has decided to list out where you had taxes withheld from rather than putting just a lump sum in line 25. So, for your reading pleasure, here's the rundown of where you should put your withholdings:

>> **Line 25a: Form(s) W-2:** If you had just one, put the amount in Box 2 here. Remember, use whole dollars. If you have more than one, add up box 2 from all your W-2s, and put the answer here.

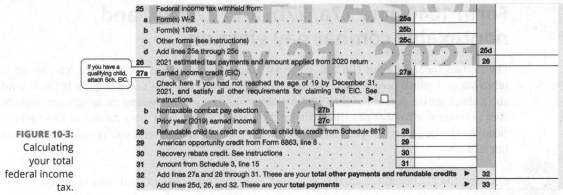

Source: Internal Revenue Service.

FIGURE 10-3:
Calculating your total federal income tax.

>> **Line 25b: Form(s) 1099:** This category includes everything in box 4 of the Form 1099 series, including Forms 1099-B, 1099-DIV, 1099-G, 1099-INT, 1099-R, 1099-NEC, and 1099-MISC. If you had income tax withheld on your Social Security income, be sure you include any amount in box 6 of Form 1099-SA.

>> **Line 25c: Other forms:** This is where you put taxes withheld on any Schedules K-1 you have, or Form(s) W-2G, or Form 1042 (if you're a foreign person and had tax withheld on U.S. source income). You should also put any additional Medicare tax you had withheld here.

Because these are sort of oddball scenarios, and because the IRS computers may not be picking up withheld taxes correctly from them, you should also attach the forms with your return. If you're filing on paper, you can staple a copy of the form showing the withheld amount to your return. If you're filing electronically, you can either attach a PDF copy of the source document to your return, or you can file Form 8453 on paper with the forms attached to that. Be sure, whenever mailing anything on paper to the IRS, that you send it Certified Mail, so you have proof that it was mailed timely. Add together any amounts you have on lines 25a, 25b, and 25c, and put the total on line 25d. You're finished with your withheld taxes.

Form 1040, line 26: 2021 estimated tax payments and amount from 2020 return

If you made estimated tax payments toward your 2021 tax, fill in the total amount of the payments here. If you applied last year's overpayment to this year's return, don't forget to enter that amount, too! The IRS isn't kind enough to send you a reminder; you have to keep track yourself.

Remember, the IRS doesn't want to wait until April 15, 2023, to collect your 2022 tax. So, if you expect to owe money come next April 15, you must file quarterly estimates if 90 percent of your tax isn't being withheld from your income and you'll owe more than $1,000.

Estimated tax payments are made on Form 1040-ES, Estimated Tax for Individuals. The form requires only your name, address, Social Security number, and the amount you're paying. For 2022 estimated payments, make sure that you use the 2022 1040-ES coupons. See Chapter 17 if you need help filling out Form 1040-ES.

Form 1040, line 27a, 27b, and 27c: EIC and nontaxable combat pay election

The Earned Income Credit (EIC) is a special credit for lower-income workers. The credit is refundable — which means that if it exceeds your tax or if you don't owe tax, the IRS will send you a check for the amount of the EIC. No matter whether you're making the election to include your non-taxable combat pay (line 27b) or the election to use your 2019 income as the basis to calculate the largest credit you can (line 27c), the amount of the credit you're claiming goes on line 27a.

TIP

Claiming the EIC doesn't disqualify you from receiving other federal and state benefits.

NEW STUFF

There have been numerous rule changes beginning in 2021 for the EIC, greatly widening the number of people who may be able to take advantage of it. And, if you qualify, the EIC can be substantial — as high as $6,728 for a married couple with three kids. To qualify for the credit, your AGI (Form 1040, line 11) or your earned income must be less than the following amounts:

>> $42,158 ($48,108 for married filing jointly) if you have one qualifying child

>> $47,915 ($53,865 for married filing jointly) if you have two qualifying children

>> $51,464 ($57,414 for married filing jointly) if you have three or more qualifying children

>> $21,430 ($27,380 for married filing jointly) if you don't have any children. If you're filing the EIC and you have no qualifying children, you must be at least 19 (24, if you are still a student), and you may not be claimed as a dependent by anyone else. Please note that the upper age limit, which used to be 65, has been eliminated beginning in 2021, so if you are still working and otherwise qualify, you can now claim the credit even if you have passed your 65th birthday.

The rules surrounding the EIC are pretty specific, and the IRS tends to look at these returns carefully. Just because the IRS reads these returns carefully doesn't mean you shouldn't claim this credit if you're entitled to it. It does mean that you need to carefully check out Chapter 16 though. All the rules are laid out for you there in plain English. We even show you how to calculate your EIC.

If you spent a portion of 2021 as a member of the military serving in a designated combat zone, you may elect to include all or a portion of your nontaxable combat pay when calculating the amount of your earned income for the purpose of calculating this credit. If you have very little earned income from other sources in 2021, you may find that using this election helps you get a bigger credit. To make the election, all you need to do is write in the amount of your nontaxable combat pay that you want to include in your EIC calculation on line 27b. Remember that this income is only being counted for the EIC calculation — you still don't have to pay income tax on it.

For 2021 tax returns, if your earned income in 2021 was too low to qualify for the credit, you may make an election to use your 2019 earned income to see if you qualify. To make this election, place your 2019 earned income on Form 1040, line 27c, and you're all set.

Form 1040, line 28: Refundable child tax credit or additional child tax credit

This credit is the refundable portion of the child tax credit that we explain on Form 1040, line 19, and in Chapter 16. To claim this additional credit, you have to file Form 8812, Additional Child Tax Credit.

Form 1040, line 29: American Opportunity Credit (Form 8863, line 8)

If you, your spouse, or your dependent is a qualifying student in the first four years of your post-secondary education, and you paid qualifying expenses such as tuition, fees, books, or supplies in order to obtain your education, you may be eligible for a refundable credit of up to $1,000. Complete Form 8863, Education Credits, and put the answer you arrive at on line 8 here, on Form 1040, line 29.

Form 1040, line 30: Recovery rebate credit

NEW STUFF

One economic recovery payment was made in 2021, beginning in late March. If you didn't receive it, or you didn't receive the full amount that you qualified for based on your 2021 income, claim it here as a refundable credit on your 2021 Form 1040. The full amount of the credit was $1,400 per taxpayer, taxpayer's spouse, and all qualifying dependents, not just qualifying children, as was the case with the two 2020 stimulus payments.

As usual with payments of this sort, there are income phase-outs here. This payment begins to phase out once your adjusted gross income (AGI) exceeds $75,000 for single filers, $112,500 for heads of household, and $150,000 for married filing jointly and qualifying widow(ers), and is completely gone once you reach $80,000 of AGI if single, $120,000 for heads of household, and $160,000 for married filing jointly taxpayers. You can't be claimed as someone else's dependent in 2021. You and all your dependents (except some military spouses) must have valid Social Security numbers to qualify for this stimulus.

The IRS should be issuing letters reporting the amount of stimulus you received during 2021. If you didn't receive the amount they say you did, review your bank records closely for any unidentified deposits, and then check with the IRS to see if the payment is uncashed.

Form 1040, line 31: Amount from Schedule 3, line 15

Copy the number you have, if any, from Schedule 3, line 15, to Form 1040, line 31, and double-check to make sure you've copied it correctly. Of course, if you're working with a computer program, this line is probably already filled in for you.

Form 1040, line 32: Total other payments and refundable credits

Add together any numbers you have on Form 1040, lines 27a and 28 through 31, and put the total here, on line 32.

Form 1040, line 33: Total payments

One more addition problem. Now you're going to add any amounts you see on lines 25d, 26, and 32. These are your total payments. You are so very close to the end now — just one more small calculation, and then some administrative nonsense, and you're done.

Refund or Amount You Owe

Okay, this is it. Now comes the moment you've worked so hard for. Do you get money back? Do you pay? Read on and find out.

Form 1040, line 34: The amount that you overpaid

If the amount of your total payments (line 33) is more than your total tax (line 24), subtract line 24 from line 33 (see Figure 10-4). The remainder is the amount you overpaid.

Form 1040, lines 35a, b, c, and d: Amount that you want refunded to you

TIP

You can speed up your refund by almost three weeks by having your refund electronically deposited directly to your bank or checking account. That way, you can ensure that your refund won't be lost or stolen. To do so, enter your *routing number* on line 35b. That's the nine-digit number at the bottom left in Figure 10-4. On line 35c, check the type of account: checking or savings. On line 35d, enter your account number. That's the number to the right of the routing number in Figure 10-4.

Deciding where to stash your cash when it comes back can be difficult, and too often, this windfall of overpaid taxes just ends up with the money that you use to pay your bills. Now, you no longer have to deposit your entire refund to one account but can instead choose up to three separate accounts, including your IRA, HSA, Archer MSA, or Coverdell ESA. If you're directing your refund to more than one account, fill out Form 8888, Direct Deposit of Refund, with your instructions.

WARNING

We know that accurate returns are the norm, but on occasion, the amount of your refund may be increased or decreased due to incorrect math, unpaid child or spousal support, federal and/or state taxes, or delinquent student loans. If your refund is decreased, the IRS will subtract any reduction first from the account shown on line 3 of Form 8888, then the one on line 2, and finally from the one listed on line 1. If your refund amount is increased, the additional amount will be tacked onto the last account listed. If you're using your tax refund to fully fund your IRA for 2021, make sure you don't list that account last; if you do, you may run the risk of making an excess contribution. If you're planning on using your refund to fund your 2021 IRA contribution, better make sure that you file your return well in advance of the April 18, 2022 (April 19, 2022, for Maine and Massachusetts residents), deadline. In order to constitute a valid 2021 IRA contribution, your bank must receive the cash prior to original filing deadline. Check out Chapter 7 for IRA contribution rules.

FIGURE 10-4:
The rest of the Form 1040. Fill it in and you're done.

Form 1040, line 36: Amount of line 34 you want applied to your 2022 estimated tax

Here you indicate what amount of your refund you want applied to your 2022 (next year's) estimated tax. After you make this selection and file your return, you can't change your mind and ask for it back. You have to claim it as a credit on your 2022 return.

Form 1040, line 37: The AMOUNT YOU OWE line

If your total tax (line 24) is larger than your total payments (line 33), subtract line 33 from line 24. This is the amount you owe.

There are numerous ways to pay the amount you owe. Here are some of the most popular, in the order in which we tend to use them:

>> **Enter your banking information directly into your tax software** and give the IRS the date you want to pay, provided it is not later than the payment deadline of April 18, 2022 (April 19, 2022, for Maine and Massachusetts residents). You can file your return earlier than the deadline and make the payment when it is convenient for you, so long as it is paid by the payment deadline.

- >> **Make an electronic payment** on the IRS website at www.irs.gov/payments.

- >> **Pay using the EFTPS system** (the Electronic Federal Tax Payment System).The EFTPS is a great system, but it does take a good two weeks to set up your account. So if you want to use this payment method and you haven't previously enrolled, you'll need to file Form 9783, Electronic Federal Tax Payment System Individual Enrollment or enroll online at www.irs.gov/payments/eftps-the-electronic-federal-tax-payment-system.

- >> **Pay using the IRS's mobile app, IRS2Go,** available for both Android and Apple devices.

- >> **Pay by personal or bank check, or by money order.** Please make sure that your name (and the name of your spouse, if filing jointly), your Social Security number, and the year and form you are paying for (in other words, 2021 Form 1040) appear on the face of the check. If you don't tell the IRS how to apply the payment, they'll use their best guess, which may not be in your favor.

- >> **Pay by credit card.** There are private companies that will accept credit or debit card payments for IRS debts, but additional fees do apply so we don't recommend this option. You can access the approved list of vendors at www.irs.gov/payments/pay-your-taxes-by-debit-or-credit-card.

- >> **Pay by cash.** We also don't recommend this method, as it is impossible for the IRS to track your payment if it goes astray. Plus, the IRS recommends that any cash payments be made 7 to 10 business days before they are due in order to be credited correctly. You're much better off using one of the other methods listed above instead.

Line 36: Estimated tax penalty (Form 2210)

If you owe more than $1,000 and haven't paid 90 percent of your tax liability in either quarterly estimates or in withholding, you'll be assessed an underestimating penalty. A number of exceptions either excuse or reduce this penalty. You calculate this penalty on Form 2210, Underpayment of Estimated Tax. See Chapter 20 on penalties to see whether one of the exceptions applies to you. Chapter 17 gives you all the facts on the 1040-ES, the estimated tax form, and the penalties that may apply if you don't fill it out. If you get socked for the penalty this year, take time to figure out the rules so it doesn't happen again next year.

WARNING

Remember, the IRS doesn't want to wait until April 18, 2022 (April 19, 2022, for Maine and Massachusetts residents), when you file your 2021 tax return, to collect your 2021 tax. You should have paid at least 90 percent of your tax by having tax withheld from your salary, pension, or IRA distributions — or by making estimated quarterly tax payments. If you don't calculate this penalty yourself, the IRS does and will bill you for it. You don't want the IRS to prepare this form, because the IRS will prepare it on the basis of your paying the maximum!

TIP

A good tax software program can breeze through this form to see whether you're eligible to have the penalty reduced or eliminated by one of the exceptions. The ability to calculate this form alone is worth the price of the software package.

Finishing Up

If you're filing on paper, sign your return. Attach your W-2s, W-2Gs, 1099s where federal tax was withheld, and all schedules. If you owe money, make sure you write your Social Security number on the front of the check along with the notation "2021 Form 1040-V." (Check out Figure 10-5.) You should also fill out Form 1040-V, Payment Voucher. Mail Form 1040-V and your check (but don't staple them to the return) with your Form 1040 (with all its attachments) to the IRS Service Center for the area in which you live. You can find the addresses in your instruction booklet or on the IRS website at www.irs.gov. Check out Chapter 4 for approved ways of filing.

Your Name + Your Spouse's Name
Address
Telephone Number

DATE: April 18, 2022

PAY TO THE ORDER OF United States Treasury

$ A,BCD.00

Alpha Beta Charley Delta Dollars and no cents ------------------------------------

2021 Form 1040-V
Social Security # 123-45-6789
FOR Balance Due

AUTHORIZED SIGNATURE (S)

Routing # (9 digits)   Account Number

FIGURE 10-5: A sample check.

If you're filing electronically, your signature is replaced with a five-digit (numbers only, and not all zeros), self-selected personal identification number. If you're filing a joint return, both of you need to have PINs. If you have a payment due, you can send it via the Post Office or through a private delivery service with Form 1040-V, arrange an electronic funds transfer (EFT), or pay by credit card. Because you no longer have to physically mail anything to the IRS, make sure that you keep a file with all of your tax information in a safe, and preferably fire-proof, place. You'll want to be able to produce these records should the IRS come calling.

3

Filling Out Schedules and Other Forms

Itemize your deductions on Schedule A.

Record your interest and dividend income on Schedule B.

Document your business revenue and expenses on Schedules C and F.

Track your capital gains and losses on Schedule D.

Summarize your supplemental income and losses on Schedule E.

Take other credits.

Complete other schedules and forms you must file.

IN THIS CHAPTER

» Taking standard deductions versus itemizing

» Getting compensated for medical and dental expenses

» Writing off taxes and interest you paid

» Considering gifts to charity and casualty and theft losses

» Perusing miscellaneous deductions

Chapter **11**

Itemized Deductions: Schedule A

You've now reached that point in preparing your return where you must decide whether to itemize your deductions or not. You've totaled your income and subtracted your allowable adjustments to income. To arrive at your taxable income, you either have to subtract your standard deduction and exemptions — or take the more difficult road and subtract your itemized deductions.

REMEMBER

If you choose to take your standard deduction, you get to subtract that amount of money from your adjusted gross income (AGI), *whether or not you actually paid anything close to that amount for deductible expenses.* But when you're itemizing your deductions, in most cases, you need to have actually paid the expenses you're claiming. You aren't allowed to claim expenses paid by someone else, and you can't include amounts that you promised to pay but haven't done so yet. You can, however, claim money that you've paid using borrowed money, such as charging a medical bill or making a charitable donation on a credit card, even if you haven't paid off that charge by December 31, 2021.

Claiming the Standard Deduction

Every taxpayer, regardless of filing status, is entitled to subtract a predetermined amount of money *(the standard deduction)* from their AGI and not pay income tax on it (see Figure 11-1). The amount of your standard deduction is based on your filing status and whether or not someone else may claim you as a dependent on their income tax return. For 2021, if you're younger than 65 and aren't blind, the standard deduction amounts are as follows:

>> Married filing jointly or a qualifying widow(er): $25,100

>> Head of household: $18,800

>> Single: $12,550

>> Married filing separately: $12,550

If you're married filing separately, you may claim the standard deduction only if your spouse also claims the standard deduction. If your spouse itemizes, you also must itemize. If you decide not to itemize your deductions, enter the standard deduction for your filing status on line 12a of Form 1040.

Older than 65 or blind

If you're 65 or older, you get to increase your standard deduction by $1,700 if you're single or a head of household, and by $1,350 if you're married filing jointly or a qualifying widow(er). If you're blind, you're entitled to an extra $1,700 if single and $1,350 if married. For example, if you're single, older than 65, and blind, the standard deduction of $12,550 increases by $3,400 for a total of $15,950.

If you don't want to do the math yourself, or you're not working on a computer, which will do the calculation for you if you've ticked the correct boxes and filled in your correct date of birth in the software, Table 11-1 does it for you. Check the appropriate boxes that appear under your name and address on Form 1040, and then find your standard deduction.

Additional charitable deduction for standard deduction filers

NEW STUFF

When the standard deduction was nearly doubled because of the Tax Cuts and Jobs Act, one concern was that charitable gifting might suffer as fewer folks would be itemizing their deductions, which included charitable deductions, on Schedule A. In response to this concern, a provision was added that allows those who use the standard deduction to take an additional deduction for charitable cash gifts up to $300 in 2021 for the taxpayer and, if married, for the taxpayer's spouse. So, in 2021, add up your charitable receipts, and put that total, not to exceed $300 if you're filing as single, head of household, or married filing separately, and $600 for those who are filing using the married filing joint status, on Form 1040, line 12b. Add this number to your regular standard deduction, and put the total on Form 1040, line 12c.

SCHEDULE A		Itemized Deductions	OMB No. 1545-0074

SCHEDULE A (Form 1040)

Department of the Treasury
Internal Revenue Service (99)

Itemized Deductions

▶ Go to *www.irs.gov/ScheduleA* for instructions and the latest information.
▶ Attach to Form 1040 or 1040-SR.
Caution: If you are claiming a net qualified disaster loss on Form 4684, see the instructions for line 16.

OMB No. 1545-0074

2021

Attachment
Sequence No. **07**

Name(s) shown on Form 1040 or 1040-SR

Your social security number

Medical and Dental Expenses

Caution: Do not include expenses reimbursed or paid by others.
1. Medical and dental expenses (see instructions) **1**
2. Enter amount from Form 1040 or 1040-SR, line 11 **2**
3. Multiply line 2 by 7.5% (0.075) **3**
4. Subtract line 3 from line 1. If line 3 is more than line 1, enter -0- **4**

Taxes You Paid

5. State and local taxes.
   a. State and local income taxes or general sales taxes. You may include either income taxes or general sales taxes on line 5a, but not both. If you elect to include general sales taxes instead of income taxes, check this box . . . . . . ▶ ☐ **5a**
   b. State and local real estate taxes (see instructions) **5b**
   c. State and local personal property taxes **5c**
   d. Add lines 5a through 5c **5d**
   e. Enter the smaller of line 5d or $10,000 ($5,000 if married filing separately) **5e**
6. Other taxes. List type and amount ▶ _____ **6**
7. Add lines 5e and 6 . . . . . . **7**

Interest You Paid

Caution: Your mortgage interest deduction may be limited (see instructions).

8. Home mortgage interest and points. If you didn't use all of your home mortgage loan(s) to buy, build, or improve your home, see instructions and check this box . . . . . . ▶ ☐
   a. Home mortgage interest and points reported to you on Form 1098. See instructions if limited **8a**
   b. Home mortgage interest not reported to you on Form 1098. See instructions if limited. If paid to the person from whom you bought the home, see instructions and show that person's name, identifying no., and address . . . . . .
      ▶ _____ **8b**
   c. Points not reported to you on Form 1098. See instructions for special rules **8c**
   d. Mortgage insurance premiums (see instructions) **8d**
   e. Add lines 8a through 8d **8e**
9. Investment interest. Attach Form 4952 if required. See instructions . **9**
10. Add lines 8e and 9 . . . . . . **10**

Gifts to Charity

Caution: If you made a gift and got a benefit for it, see instructions.

11. Gifts by cash or check. If you made any gift of $250 or more, see instructions **11**
12. Other than by cash or check. If you made any gift of $250 or more, see instructions. You **must** attach Form 8283 if over $500 . . . . **12**
13. Carryover from prior year **13**
14. Add lines 11 through 13 . . . . . . **14**

Casualty and Theft Losses

15. Casualty and theft loss(es) from a federally declared disaster (other than net qualified disaster losses). Attach Form 4684 and enter the amount from line 18 of that form. See instructions **15**

Other Itemized Deductions

16. Other—from list in instructions. List type and amount ▶ _____ **16**

Total Itemized Deductions

17. Add the amounts in the far right column for lines 4 through 16. Also, enter this amount on Form 1040 or 1040-SR, line 12a **17**
18. If you elect to itemize deductions even though they are less than your standard deduction, check this box . . . . . . ▶ ☐

For Paperwork Reduction Act Notice, see the Instructions for Forms 1040 and 1040-SR. Cat. No. 17145C Schedule A (Form 1040) 2021

FIGURE 11-1: Use Schedule A to determine the itemized deductions that you can claim.

Source: Internal Revenue Service

Table 11-1   Standard Deduction Chart for People Age 65 or Older or Blind

Check the appropriate boxes below and total. Then go to the chart.

You	65 or older	Blind
Your spouse, if claiming spouse's exemption	65 or older	Blind
Total number of boxes you checked	_____	

If Your Filing Status Is:	And the Total Number of Boxes You Checked Above Is:	Your Standard Deduction Is:
Single	1	$14,250
	2	$15,950
Married filing joint return or qualifying widow(er) with dependent child	1	$26.450
	2	$27,800
	3	$29,150
	4	$30,500
Married filing separate return	1	$13,900
	2	$15,250
Head of household	1	$20,500
	2	$22,200

Standard deduction for dependents

If you can claim your child or dependent on your own return or if someone else can claim that dependent on theirs, the dependent's standard deduction is limited to the greater of $1,100 or to the individual's 2021 earned income plus $350 for the year (whichever amount is larger — but not more than the regular standard deduction amount of $12,550). So, if you're helping your dependent child or an older household member that you claim as a dependent prepare their return, use the worksheet in Table 11-2 to compute their standard deduction. Remember, if your dependent is 65 or older or blind, they are still entitled to the extra $1,700 for each box checked if they're filing as single, or $1,350 if they are married (remember, a married person can only be your dependent if the only reason they are filing is to claim a refund; their tax return must show no tax liability). Whether you're preparing your own return (as a child being claimed on your parent's return, for example) or you're preparing a return for a dependent that you're claiming, you must complete this worksheet. Otherwise, use the regular standard deduction.

Earned income includes wages, salaries, tips, professional fees, and other compensation that you received for services performed. It also includes anything received as a scholarship that counts as income.

Table 11-2   Standard Deduction Worksheet for Dependents

If you are 65 or older or blind, check the boxes below. Then go to the worksheet.

You	65 or older	Blind	
Your spouse, if claiming spouse's exemption	65 or older	Blind	
Total number of boxes you checked	____		
1.	Enter your earned income. If none, go on to line 3.	1.	_____
	1a. Additional amount allowed in 2021	1a. $350	
	1b. Add lines 1 and 1a	1b.	_____
2.	Minimum amount	2.	$1,100
3.	Compare the amounts on lines 1b and 2. Enter the larger of the two amounts here.	3.	_____
4.	Enter on line 4 the amount shown below for your filing status.		
	Single, enter $12,550.		
	Married filing separate return, enter $12,550.		
	Married filing jointly or qualifying widow(er) with dependent child, enter $25,100.		
	Head of household enter $18,800.	4.	_____
5.	Standard deduction		
	5a.	Compare the amounts on lines 3 and 4.	
		Enter the smaller of the two amounts here.	
		If under 65 and not blind, stop here. This is your standard deduction; otherwise, go on to line 5b.	5a. _____
	5b.	If 65 or older or blind, multiply $1,700 by the total number of boxes you checked; if married or qualifying widow(er) with dependent child, use $1,350. Enter the result here.	5b. _____
	5c.	Add lines 5a and 5b. This is your standard deduction for 2021.	5c. _____

Locating Your Itemized Deductions

Some taxpayers simply compute their tax by using the standard deduction and don't even think about trying to complete Schedule A to calculate the amount of their itemized deductions. If you think there is a chance that the total of your deductible expenses exceeds the standard deduction, try completing Schedule A. You may be pleasantly surprised to find that all your deductions do add up to a larger total deduction.

Here's your itemized deduction shopping list:

>> Medical and dental expenses that exceed 7.5 percent of your AGI

>> State and local taxes you paid, not to exceed $10,000

>> Interest you paid

>> Gifts to charity

>> Casualty and theft losses from a federally declared disaster

>> Other miscellaneous itemized deductions. See the section on line 16 later in this chapter for an in-depth analysis of these types of deductions.

You claim these deductions on Form 1040 with Schedule A. You carry the total on line 17 over to Form 1040 (line 12a) where you subtract it from your adjusted gross income (AGI).

Separate returns and limits on deductions

If you're married and filing separately, you both must itemize your deductions if one of you itemizes deductions, or you both must use the standard deduction. One spouse can't use the standard deduction while the other itemizes.

If you're divorced or legally separated, though, you're now considered single for income tax purposes, and you may make the best choice for yourself without regard to what your former spouse is doing. However, if you opt to itemize, you may claim only those expenses for which you are personally liable. For example, if a residence is in your former spouse's name and you paid the property taxes and the mortgage interest, you can't deduct them. If you were required to pay them under the terms of your divorce or separation agreement, but the property (and therefore the liability) was in your former spouse's name, these expenses wouldn't qualify as itemized deductions, but they may constitute deductible alimony.

Generally, if your home is jointly owned and your divorce or separation agreement requires that you make the mortgage payments, one half of the payments can be deducted as alimony, but only if your original divorce or separation agreement was executed before the January 1, 2019, change that switched alimony paid from a deductible to a nondeductible item for the person making the payment. If you fall into this category, your former spouse reports one half of the payments as taxable alimony and is allowed to deduct one half of the mortgage interest if they itemize their deductions. You get to deduct one half of the mortgage interest paid if the home is your residence (which isn't very likely). Payments to a third party (a bank, for example) are treated as received and then paid by your ex. The general rule we just recited for mortgage payments also applies to real estate taxes, provided the title to the home isn't held as *tenants by the entirety* or in *joint tenancy*. We explain the meaning of these legal terms in the alimony section in Chapter 7 and in the sidebar "Separate returns and real estate taxes" later in this chapter. But if you hold title in this manner, here are the rules: None of the payments for real estate taxes are considered alimony payments, and you get to deduct all the real estate taxes.

Deciding who gets to deduct what when a couple divorces is almost as bad as dividing the property. The alimony rules in Chapter 7 explain who gets to claim various deductions. To dig into this further, take a look at IRS Publication 504 *(Divorced or Separated Individuals)*. If you live in a community property state, the rules we just recited are different, so you may want to take a look at IRS Publication 555 *(Federal Tax Information on Community Property)*.

If you and your spouse are separated but don't have a decree of divorce or separate maintenance, you may be able to itemize or use the standard deduction and file as either single or head of household. You can do this if you didn't live with your spouse during the last six months of 2021. And if you maintained a home for more than half of 2021 for you and a child that you are entitled to claim as a dependent, you can use the head of household filing status.

But if you change your mind

Oops! Suppose that you discover you should have itemized after you already filed. Or even worse, suppose that you went to all the trouble to itemize but shouldn't have done so. Just amend your return by filing **Form 1040X, Amended U.S. Individual Income Tax Return.** But if you're married and you filed separately, you can't change your mind unless both you and your spouse make the same change. And if either of you must pay additional tax as a result of the change, you both need to file a consent. Remember that if one of you itemizes, the other no longer qualifies for the standard deduction.

Lines 1–4: Medical and Dental Costs

WARNING

Your total medical and dental expenses (after what you were reimbursed by your health insurance policy and by pretax dollars from your Section 125 medical reimbursement account) must exceed 7.5 percent of your AGI (line 11 of your Form 1040). This detail knocks many people out of contention for this deduction. For example, if your AGI equals $30,000, you need to have at least $2,250 in medical and dental expenses. If you don't, you can cruise past these lines. (Because the threshold is so high, we hope, for your health's sake, that this is one deduction you *can't* take.)

You may deduct medical and dental expenses for you, your spouse, and your dependents. Because medical and dental deductions are claimed in the year in which they're paid, not the year in which the services were originally rendered, you may also be able to deduct the medical expenses of a person for whom you aren't claiming an exemption on your tax return for this year, but who was your dependent when the charges were incurred. You may also claim the medical expenses for a person who would be your dependent except for the fact that they have over $4,300 of income, they filed a joint return with their spouse, or you (or your spouse, if filing jointly) could be claimed as a dependent on someone else's return. If you're not sure whether you're eligible to deduct all the medical expenses you've paid this year, check out IRS Publication 502 *(Medical and Dental Expenses)* for more information.

ADOPTION AND MEDICAL EXPENSES

If you adopted a child, you can deduct the medical expenses you paid before the adoption if the child qualified as your dependent when the medical expenses were incurred or paid. If you have an agreement to pay an adoption agency or other persons for medical expenses they paid on behalf of the child, you can deduct the payment as a medical expense. But — bet you knew a *but* was coming — if you pay older medical expenses, which were incurred and paid before the adoption negotiations began, sorry, no deduction.

To claim the deduction, you fill in the amounts on lines 1 through 4 on Schedule A (see Figure 11-1). This rule means you can deduct the medical expenses you paid for your child, even though your ex-spouse is claiming the child. For the purposes of the medical deduction, the child is considered the dependent of both parents.

Medical and dental expense checklist

Medical and dental expenses consist of more than having a physical and filling the occasional cavity. The list of what qualifies is long and involved, but if you suspect you have something that may qualify, read on.

The following is a list of other items that are deductible, so remember to save all those bills:

>> Ambulance service.

>> Breast reconstruction surgery after a mastectomy.

>> Birth control pills.

>> Childbirth classes (but if your husband attends the classes as your coach, his portion of the fee isn't deductible).

>> Drugs and medicines prescribed by a doctor.

>> Electric wheelchairs (nonelectric ones as well) and electric carts such as the Rascal that you see advertised on TV, including their upkeep and operating cost, are deductible medical expenses. The cost of hand controls or special equipment for a car so a handicapped person can operate it may also be deducted.

>> Expenses in obtaining an egg donor.

>> Guide dog.

>> Hospital bills.

>> Laboratory fees and tests.

>> Laser eye surgery, including corrective procedures such as LASIK and radial keratectomy. This surgery is deductible because it corrects an eye problem even though a pair of glasses would, arguably, cost considerably less.

>> Legal abortion.

>> Medical equipment and supplies, crutches, bandages, and diagnosis devices such as blood sugar kits sold over the counter, even though over-the-counter medicines aren't deductible.

>> Medical equipment or modifications to your home for needed medical care.

>> Medical, hospital, and dental insurance premiums that you pay (but you can't deduct premiums paid by your employer, and you may not deduct premiums that you pay with pretax dollars); don't overlook premiums deducted from your paycheck. This includes a portion of your long-term health-care premiums (jump ahead to insurance premiums for the amounts).

>> Medical services (doctors, dentists, opticians, podiatrists, registered nurses, practical nurses, psychiatrists, and so on).

>> Oxygen equipment and oxygen.

>> Part of life-care fee paid to a retirement home designated for medical care.

>> Sexual dysfunction treatment.

>> Special school or home for a mentally or physically handicapped person.

>> Special items (artificial limbs, contact lenses, and so on).

>> Stop-smoking programs. The cost of prescription drugs to alleviate nicotine withdrawal also qualifies as a medical expense, but over-the-counter nicotine gum and patches don't. When will the IRS ever stop making these types of distinctions? A foolish question, we guess, because the IRS is in the business of splitting hairs.

>> Transportation for medical care.

>> Treatment at a drug or alcohol clinic.

>> Wages and Social Security tax paid for workers providing medical care.

>> Wages for nursing service.

>> Weight-loss programs rooted in a diagnosis of obesity or another disease. However, the restriction against deducting weight reduction costs for purely cosmetic reasons hasn't been lifted. That means you can't deduct the cost of going to Weight Watchers to lose a little weight so you'll look amazing at your 25th class reunion.

Just like alcohol or drug treatment addiction programs, where an individual often has to travel away from home to seek treatment, the limited $50-a-day deduction for lodging can be claimed for a stay at a weight-reduction clinic. Reduced-calorie diet foods aren't deductible. They are considered a substitute for a person's normal diet.

What about deducting health clubs? Here's the general rule: Health club costs are only considered a deductible medical expense when prescribed by a physician to aid in the treatment of a specific disease or ailment. Remember, though, that obesity is now classified as a disease. Ask your doctor for that all-important prescription and then keep it with all your other income tax documents.

NEW STUFF One can never say that Congress and the IRS are totally tone-deaf. In 2021, you're allowed to deduct the cost of COVID-19 prevention measures you've taken during the year, such as the purchase of masks, hand sanitizer, sanitizing wipes, and COVID-19 tests. The cost of all the toilet paper you bought and are hoarding, though? Sorry, that's not deductible.

WARNING

Be aware that many medical and dental expenses can't be deducted. Surprisingly, a number of expenses that you make to improve your health, which should reduce your medical expenses, aren't deductible. You can't deduct these things:

>> Diaper service

>> Funeral expenses

>> Health club or spa dues for activities and services that merely improve your general health

>> Household help (even if recommended by a doctor)

>> Life insurance premiums

>> Maternity clothes

>> Medical insurance included in a car insurance policy covering all persons injured in or by the car

>> Nursing care for a healthy baby

>> Over-the-counter medicines (except insulin); aspirin to relieve pain; toothpaste; toiletries; and cosmetics

>> Social activities (such as swimming or dancing lessons)

>> Surgery for purely cosmetic reasons (such as face-lifts, tummy tucks, and so on) — plastic surgery required as the result of an accident is deductible

>> Teeth whitening — to the IRS, it merely improves a person's attractiveness and doesn't serve to treat an ailment

>> Trips for general health improvement

SPECIAL CASES — WHO GETS THE DEDUCTION?

Sometimes, when two or more people support someone, special rules apply to determine who can claim the medical expenses that were paid.

One tricky case is that of divorced and separated parents. A divorced or separated parent can deduct the medical expenses they paid for a child's medical costs — even if the child's other parent is entitled to claim the child as a dependent.

For the purposes of claiming medical expenses, a child is considered the dependent of both parents if all the following conditions are met:

- The parents were legally separated or divorced or were married and living apart for the last six months of 2021.

- Both parents provided more than half the child's support in 2021.

- Either spouse had custody of the child for more than half of 2021.

Deductible travel costs

TAX CUT

The cost of traveling to your doctor or a medical facility for treatment is deductible. If you use your car, you can deduct a flat rate of 17 cents per mile for trips made in 2021. Or you can deduct your actual out-of-pocket expenses for gas, oil, and repairs. You can also deduct parking and tolls. You can't deduct depreciation, insurance, or general repairs.

Deductible travel costs to seek medical treatment aren't limited to just local auto and cab trips — a trip to see a specialist in another city also qualifies for the deduction. Unfortunately, though, transportation costs incurred when you're not going to and from a doctor's office or a hospital are a deduction the IRS likes to challenge (maybe because many taxpayers tried to deduct as a medical expense travel to a warm climate, claiming health reasons!). The cost of transportation to a mild climate to relieve a specific condition is deductible — but the airfare to Arizona, for example, for general health reasons isn't.

Trips to visit an institutionalized child have been allowed when a doctor prescribed the visits.

Travel expenses of a nurse or another person who has to accompany an individual to obtain medical care because the patient can't travel alone are deductible.

TAX CUT

In a victory for anyone with a chronic illness or who has a chronically ill child, the IRS now permits a deduction for the cost of a medical conference and the travel to get there. Now, if you need to go to a medical conference to find out about the latest treatment options, the cost of the conference and the travel to get there are deductible. Meals and lodging aren't.

Another complicated case is that of a *multiple-support agreement* in which two or more people together provide more than half of a person's total support — but no one on their own provides more than half. Such an agreement allows one and only one of the individuals to claim the exemption for the person (even without providing more than half the support). If you are the person entitled to claim the exemption under the agreement, you can deduct the medical expenses you pay. But any other taxpayers who also paid medical expenses can't deduct them.

Special medical expense situations

The deductibility of a medical expense depends on the nature of the services rendered and not on the qualifications, title, or experience of the person providing the service. This means that payments to an unlicensed medical provider are deductible if the provider renders medical care that isn't illegal.

When an expense is generally considered nonmedical, the burden falls on the taxpayer to prove that it meets the definition of a medical expense, which is especially true for expenses incurred for massages, yoga lessons, water filtration systems, and health centers.

Just like every other section of our tax laws, what qualifies as a medical deduction can get hopelessly complex. Here are a few examples:

>> You can't deduct marijuana used for medical purposes in violation of federal law, even though you obtained a prescription for it as required under state law.

>> You can deduct the cost of a wig purchased on the advice of a doctor to benefit the mental health of a patient who lost all hair as the result of a disease.

>> You can deduct vitamins only when prescribed by a doctor as part of a treatment for a specific ailment and not merely for nutritional needs.

>> Special foods that serve as supplements to a regular diet qualify as a medical expense only when prescribed by a doctor to treat a specific ailment. You can't deduct a special diet if it's part of the regular nutritional needs of a person. For instance, diabetics can't deduct the cost of food that doesn't contain sugar. Their sugarless diet merely acts as a substitute for the nutritional needs of a normal diet.

For people obtaining healthcare in other countries, you can deduct the out-of-pocket expenses you incur for medical care in that country so long as the exact procedure and/or drugs you use there are also available in the United States. You may not, however, bring those drugs into the United States unless they are preapproved by the Food & Drug Administration. Not only will that deduction be disallowed, but you'll probably have them confiscated in U.S. Customs as you come back, and you'll be put on a watch list for attempting to bring contraband into the United States.

Meals and lodging

TAX CUT

Your bill at a hospital or similar institution is fully deductible. That's the whole bill, including meals and lodging. You may be able to deduct as a medical expense the cost of lodging not provided in a hospital while you're away from your home if you meet all the following requirements:

>> The lodging is necessary for your medical care.

>> A doctor provides the medical care in a medical facility.

>> The lodging isn't extravagant.

>> No significant element of personal pleasure, recreation, or vacation is involved in the travel.

The amount that you can deduct as a medical expense for lodging can't exceed $50 a night for you and $50 a night for anyone accompanying you. Only meals that are part of a hospital bill are deductible.

Insurance premiums

Health insurance premiums that you pay that cover hospital, medical, and dental expenses; prescription drugs; and eyeglasses and the replacement of lost or damaged contact lenses are deductible as medical expenses provided that the money you use to pay those premiums is included in your AGI. So is the monthly Part B and Part D Medicare premium that gets deducted from your Social Security check. Based on your age, a limited portion of the premium for long-term healthcare also is deductible.

Here are the deductible amounts for long-term healthcare premiums:

Age	Deductible
40 or less	$310
More than 40, but not more than 50	$810
More than 50, but not more than 60	$1,630
More than 60, but not more than 70	$4,350
More than 70	$5,430

Reimbursements and damages

You must reduce your medical expenses by what you were reimbursed under your health insurance policy and from Medicare. Payments that you received for loss of earnings or damages for personal injury or sickness aren't considered reimbursement under a health insurance policy and don't have to be deducted from your medical expenses. If the total reimbursement you received during the year is the same as or more than your total medical expenses for the year, you can't claim a medical deduction.

If you are reimbursed in a later year for medical expenses you deducted in an earlier year, you must report as income the amount you received up to the amount you previously deducted as a medical expense. Your reimbursement isn't taxable if you didn't deduct the expense in the year you paid it because you took the standard deduction or because your medical expenses were less than 7.5 percent of your AGI.

If you receive an amount in settlement of a personal injury suit, the part that is for medical expenses deducted in an earlier year is taxable if your medical deduction in the earlier year reduced your income tax.

Special schooling

TAX CUT

You can deduct as a medical expense the cost of sending a mentally or physically handicapped child or dependent to a special school to help him or her overcome a handicap. The school must have a special program geared to the child's specific needs. The total costs, transportation, meals and lodging, and tuition qualify. The types of schools that qualify are ones that do the following things:

>> Teach Braille or lip reading

>> Help cure dyslexia

>> Treat and care for the mentally handicapped

>> Treat individuals with similar handicaps

Nursing home

TAX CUT

You can include in medical expenses the cost of medical care in a nursing home or home for the aged for yourself, your spouse, or your dependents. This deduction includes the cost of meals and lodging in the home if the main reason for being there is to get medical care. But you can't deduct nonmedical care expenses. For example, if a person enters a nursing home because they can't prepare meals or take care of personal needs, then that person can't take a deduction.

You can't deduct the cost of meals and lodging if the reason for being in the home is personal and nonmedical (such as taking up residence in a retirement home). You can, however, include as a deductible medical expense the part of the cost that is for medical or nursing care.

TIP

Nursing homes, rest homes, assisted-living facilities, and the like are all accustomed to breaking out their charges into medical and nonmedical amounts. If you're unsure how much of these payments to include on Schedule A, be sure to ask the facility's administrator or billing staff for some guidance.

If you, your spouse, or other dependent is in a nursing home or memory care facility not because of a general decline, but because medical care that cannot be provided by anyone other than skilled medical professionals is required, 100 percent of the cost of the nursing home, including the cost of the room and meals, is deductible. This is particularly important for those who suffer from a loss of cognitive ability, such as someone with Alzheimer's Disease, or any other form of dementia. The full cost of hospice care is also deductible.

Improvements to your home

TAX CUT

You can deduct as a medical expense the cost of installing equipment and making improvements to your home to help treat a disease or ailment. For example, you can deduct the cost of an air conditioner because you suffer from allergies or asthma. But if the equipment or improvement increases the value of your home, your deduction is limited to the cost of the equipment or improvement minus the increase in the value to your home.

Be prepared to have a battle when making a large improvement to your home for medical reasons. Unless you arrive at the audit in a wheelchair with tears streaming down your cheeks, don't expect an overly sympathetic IRS. On the other hand, deductions for swimming pools have been allowed as a form of therapy in treating a severe ailment or disease. But improvements that merely help improve someone's general health (such as a hot tub or workout room) aren't deductible.

The increase-in-value test for a home doesn't apply to handicapped persons. Modifying stairs and doorways; building ramps, railings, and support bars; and adapting a home to the special needs of the handicapped are allowed. Chairlifts, but not elevators, are also part of the no-increase-in-value category.

Figuring your medical and dental deduction

Your deductible medical and dental expenses equal the total expenses that you've paid minus what you were reimbursed by your insurance policy. The result is then reduced by 7.5 percent of your AGI.

For example, if your medical and dental expenses for the tax year were $4,500 and your health insurance company reimbursed $500 of that amount, you then have $4,000 of unreimbursed medical expenses. Enter $4,000 on line 1 of Schedule A. On line 2, you enter your AGI from Form 1040 (line 11). On line 3, you enter 7.5 percent of your AGI (if your AGI is $40,000; you would enter $3,000 — that's $40,000 × 0.075). Subtract this amount from the medical expenses reported on line 1 of Schedule A and stick the remainder ($1,000) on line 4.

Lines 5–7: Taxes You Paid

As a general rule, you may deduct only the following tax payments made during the tax year:

>> State and local income taxes

>> Local real estate taxes

>> State and local personal property taxes

>> Other taxes (such as foreign income taxes)

Federal income and Social Security taxes aren't deductible.

Line 5: State and local taxes

NEW STUFF

The Tax Cuts and Jobs Act of 2017, which was implemented in 2018, placed a limit of $10,000 on the state and local taxes you may deduct ($5,000 per spouse if you're using the married filing separately status and you're itemizing your deductions). For some people in higher tax states, this means that a portion of the taxes you pay to your state and town are no longer deductible. The taxes included in this category are

>> The greater of state and local income taxes or general sales taxes

>> Real estate taxes

>> Personal property taxes, such as a car or boat excise tax that is payable to your city or town

As this book goes to publication in late 2021, Congress has been considering legislation that increase the state and local tax (also known as SALT) deduction. It's unlikely that all such taxes will be allowed to be deductible as the benefit of that change would largely accrue to the highest income and most affluent taxpayers.

Line 5a: State and local income taxes or general sales taxes

This deduction consists of two elements: the amount of state and local taxes withheld from your salary (boxes 17 and 19 of your W-2) and what you paid in 2021 when you filed your 2020 state tax return. If you made estimated state and local income tax payments in 2021, they're also deductible. You can also deduct taxes relating to a prior year that you paid in 2021. For residents of California, New Jersey, or New York, mandatory payments you made to your state's disability fund are also deductible. So are the disability payments made to Rhode Island's temporary fund or Washington State's supplemental worker's compensation fund.

If you applied your 2020 refund on your state return as a payment toward your estimated 2021 state tax, that's also considered a deductible tax payment. However, if you deducted that amount on your 2020 income tax return, you may also have to report the amount as taxable income on Form 1040, Schedule 1, line 1. You are only required to report an amount on Schedule A, line 1, if you received a tax benefit from the deduction in 2020. If your 2020 state and local tax deduction maxed out at $10,000 in 2020, and you actually paid more than $10,000 in state and local taxes during 2020, the amount you'll have to claim on your 2021 Schedule A, line 1, will most likely be less than the amount of your actual 2020 overpayment, and you may find that none of your overpayment applied to 2021 is includable in your taxable 2021 income.

If you're deducting your state sales taxes, tick the box next to line 5a and then enter the total of your state and local tax payments on line 5a. You can choose to either add up the sales taxes you've paid throughout 2021 from every receipt you can locate, or you can elect to use the amount the IRS deems you to have paid, based on your income. While adding up all those tiny amounts from receipts may seem like an exercise from one of the circles of hell, it may be worth it if you made a major purchase in 2021, such as a new car or a boat.

Line 5b: State and local real estate taxes

TAX CUT

Some or a portion of real estate taxes you paid for your primary and secondary residences during 2021 may be deductible, but remember, you are limited by a maximum deduction for all state and local taxes of $10,000 in 2021. For some, the combination of state income and sales taxes plus real estate taxes will take you well over that limit, but it's still worth doing the math to make sure you're not missing even $1 of available deduction.

Calculating the total of your real estate taxes is easy! If you pay your tax check(s) directly to your city or town clerk or tax collector, just add up the total you paid in 2021 and insert that number on line 5b. If you escrowed your real estate taxes with your mortgage company, your mortgage company will send you an annual mortgage statement by January 31, 2022, that tells you how much the company paid to your city or town clerk or tax collector on your behalf. That's the number you put on line 5b.

Cooperative apartment

Tenants or stockholders of a cooperative housing corporation may include their share of the real estate taxes paid by the corporation in their state and local tax deduction. The corporation will furnish you with a statement at the end of the year, indicating the amount of real estate taxes you are deemed to have paid in 2021.

Special assessments

Water, sewer, and garbage pickup aren't deductible because they're considered nondeductible personal charges — and so are charges by a homeowners' association. Assessments by the local tax authorities to put in a new street, sewer system, or sidewalks aren't deductible. These types of assessments are added to the tax basis of your home. Either your annual mortgage statement from your bank or the tax collector's bill will indicate whether you're paying a special assessment or a real estate tax.

When you buy or sell real estate

When real estate is bought or sold, the buyer and the seller apportion the real estate taxes between them. This stuff is done at the closing when the buyer and seller are furnished a settlement statement. For example, suppose that you paid $1,000 in real estate taxes for the year on January 1. On June 30, you sell the property. At the time of the sale, your settlement statement should reflect a payment or credit from the buyer for the property taxes you already paid for the remainder of the year. This is how the buyer pays you for the taxes you've effectively paid on their behalf for the remainder of the year when the buyer will be in the home. Therefore, you can include only the taxes you paid ($1,000) minus what the buyer reimbursed you ($500). That means you only put $500 in real estate taxes for the year on line 5b of Schedule A.

TIP

You can find this information on your settlement statement and in box 5 of Form 1099-S, Proceeds from Real Estate Transactions. The 1099-S is normally issued to you when you sell your home. However, not all home sales have to be reported on 1099-S. See Chapter 14 for more about this issue.

TECHNICAL STUFF

If you, as the buyer of a property, pay back taxes (in other words, taxes that the property seller owed from the time they actually owned the home) at the closing or at a later date, you may not include them on line 5b. Instead, they are added to the cost of the property. The seller can deduct back taxes paid by the buyer from the sales price when computing the profit that is reported on Schedule D (Form 1040). See Chapter 14 for information about handling the sale of your home.

The downside of property tax refunds and rebates

REMEMBER

If you receive a refund or rebate in 2021 for real estate taxes you paid in 2021, you must reduce your number on line 5b by the amount refunded to you. For example, if you paid $2,000 in property taxes during the year and also received a $300 refund because of a reduction in your tax that was retroactively granted, you may claim only $1,700 as the amount on line 5b for real estate taxes.

If you received a refund or rebate in 2021 for real estate taxes that you took as an itemized deduction on Schedule A in any year prior to 2018, you must include the refund or rebate as income in the year you receive it. Enter this amount on your Form 1040, Schedule 1, Part I, line 8. In the unlikely event that your refund exceeds what you paid in taxes during the year, you need to include only the portion of the refund up to the amount of the deduction you took in the earlier year. For example, if you claimed a $500 deduction in 2020 and received a $600 rebate in 2021, only $500 of the rebate is taxable. If you didn't itemize your deductions in 2020, you don't have to report the refund as income in 2021.

If you received a refund or rebate for tax years 2019 or 2020, you'll have to calculate whether all or any portion of that refund or rebate is includable in income. Of course, if you took the standard deduction in the year in question, none of the refund is taxable income to you. But if you itemized in the affected year, you'll include 100 percent of the refund as taxable income if your state and local taxes paid in that year were $10,000 or less ($5,000 for married filing separately). If your state and local taxes paid were greater than $10,000, though, you'll have to figure how much to include in income, if anything at all. Chapter 6 shows you how to calculate the amount you need to include in income — just use Table 6-1 and replace all references to income taxes with real estate taxes instead.

Line 5c: Personal property taxes

TAX CUT

Personal property taxes, both state and local, are included in your state and local tax deduction calculation if the tax charged is based on the value of the personal property. Usually, you pay personal property taxes based on the value of your car and motorboat.

In most states, a registration fee is assessed on cars. These fees aren't deductible unless the fees are based on the car's value. The state agency that invoices you for this fee should state what portion, if any, of the fee is based on the car's value.

TIP

If you're paying business taxes, don't put them here; they belong on Schedule C. And if you pay sales tax on the purchase of equipment for business use, you can't deduct the sales tax separately; it's added to the cost of the asset, which is depreciated on Schedules C and E.

Line 5d: Add lines 5a through 5c

Do just as the line says and add together any numbers you have on those three lines. The result belongs here, on line 5d.

Line 5e: Enter the smaller of line 5d or $10,000 ($5,000 if married filing separately

This is where the limitation on state and local taxes is imposed, on line 5e. Look at the number you have on line 5d. If it is greater than $10,000, enter $10,000 on line 5e. If it is less than $10,000 ($5,000 if you're married filing separately), put the full amount on line 5d here on line 5e. The number on line 5e represents the amount of your state and local tax deduction.

Line 6: Other taxes (foreign income taxes)

TAX CUT

You can deduct foreign taxes you paid as an itemized deduction on Schedule A, or you can claim a credit for foreign taxes by filing Form 1116, Foreign Taxes. *Note:* If your foreign income wasn't subject to U.S. tax (because it was excluded under the $108,700 foreign earned income allowance), you can't claim a deduction or a credit for any foreign taxes paid on the income that you didn't pay U.S. tax on.

TIP

As a concession to taxpayers and in recognition of the truly incomprehensible nature of the Form 1116, the IRS allows taxpayers who have $600 or less of foreign tax paid if married filing jointly, or $300 or less for everyone else, to enter the full amount of their foreign tax paid on line 1 on Form 1040, Schedule 3, Part I. No Form 1116 is needed here.

In case you're asking yourself what foreign taxes have to do with you, the answer is that if you invested in a mutual fund that invests overseas, the fund may end up paying foreign taxes on some of your dividends. It seems more people are investing in these types of funds than ever before. If your mutual fund paid any foreign taxes, you'll find that information in box 6 of the Form 1099-DIV that you received.

You can either deduct the foreign tax you paid on this line of Schedule A or claim a credit on Form 1040, Schedule 3, Part I, line 1. A deduction reduces your taxable income. A credit reduces the actual tax you owe. So, if you're in the 24 percent tax bracket, claiming a deduction for $100 of foreign taxes will reduce your tax bill by $24. On the other hand, if you claim the $100 you paid as a foreign tax credit, you reduce your tax liability by $100, because credits are subtracted directly from the tax you owe.

Line 7: Add lines 5e and 6

Adding these two lines together gives you the total tax deduction you're allowed to take for taxes you've paid. Put the total here on line 7.

Lines 8–10: Interest You Paid

The IRS allows you to deduct interest on certain types of loans. According to the IRS, acceptable loans include some (but not all) mortgage loans and investment loans. Interest incurred for consumer debt, such as on credit cards and auto loans — so-called *personal interest* — isn't deductible. But private mortgage insurance is deductible in 2021 if you meet the income requirements. If you've paid interest as a result of your business, remember, business interest isn't deducted as an itemized deduction; it's deducted from your business income on Schedule C (see Chapter 13).

You can't deduct interest on taxes you owe. It's worth noting, however, that corporations can deduct interest on tax assessments. Doesn't it seem that everyone is allowed a special tax break but you?

Lines 8a through 8e: Home mortgage interest and points

TAX CUT

Most folks can generally deduct mortgage interest paid on any loan(s) taken to purchase their main home and a second or vacation home, provided the total of the loans initially taken don't exceed $750,000 ($375,000 if filing as married filing separately), and provided that the loans are secured using those properties as collateral. If the mortgage(s) you took in total on both your primary and secondary residences exceed that $750,000 amount, well, you're going to have to do some work to see how much your deduction will be limited. Knowing when you first borrowed the money and what you used that cash for is critical in calculating your mortgage interest deduction.

If you borrowed money prior to December 16, 2017, but after October 12, 1987, those amounts increase to $1 million ($500,000 for married couples filing separately). And, in the highly unlikely event that you took out a mortgage prior to October 13, 1987, and still have it today, your deduction is unlimited. You are also entitled to deduct the interest you pay on any loan you take to improve your primary or secondary residence provided that the starting amount of the new loan, when added to any other existing mortgage loans on your primary and secondary residences, doesn't exceed the limits of $750,000 ($375,000 MFS). It doesn't matter whether the loan on which you're paying interest is a mortgage, a second mortgage, a line of credit, or a home equity loan. The interest is deductible as long as your homes serve as collateral for the loan, and provided that the money lent to you is used solely for the purpose of either purchasing a home, refinancing an existing mortgage, or paying for improvements to that home.

NEW STUFF

The days of using your home as a piggy bank are over. You are no longer allowed to deduct the interest on a home equity line of credit that is used to pay for something other than your personal housing expense. So, while you are still allowed to dip into the equity in your home to consolidate your credit card debt or to finance an education, you're no longer allowed to deduct that interest on Schedule A.

Figure 11-2 shows how the interest paid on mortgages taken at various dates is treated. While we doubt there are too many mortgages remaining that originated prior to October 13, 1987, we're including that information here in case you happen to still have a very old mortgage on your home.

Where is the data?

If you paid mortgage interest of $600 or more during the year on any one mortgage, you will receive a Form 1098, Mortgage Interest Statement, from your mortgage lender, showing the total interest you paid during the year. Enter the amount from box 1 of Form 1098 on line 8a of your Schedule A. Enter mortgage interest not reported on a 1098 on line 8b. If you purchased a main home during 2021, add the amount shown on Form 1098, box 6, to the amount in Form 1098, box 1, and report the total on Schedule A, line 8a. If you paid points that weren't reported on Form 1098, you're going to put the amount of the points you paid on line 8c. If you paid less than $600 in mortgage interest to any lender, they are not required to give you Form 1098 at all. In that case, you should obtain that number from your lender, and put the interest on line 8b plus any points paid on a home purchase in 2021 on line 8c. The tax treatment of points paid when refinancing a mortgage is discussed later in this section.

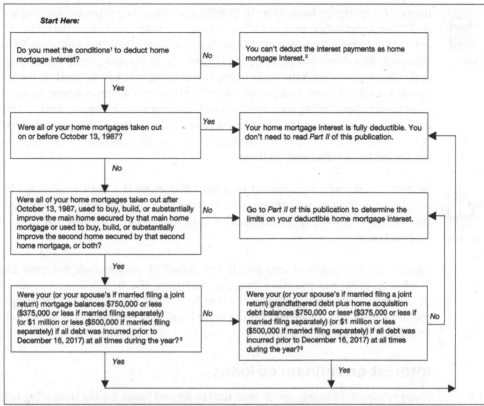

FIGURE 11-2: Use this decision tree to determine how much of your initial loan amounts you can use to determine your mortgage interest deduction.

Start Here:

Do you meet the conditions[1] to deduct home mortgage interest? — **No** → You can't deduct the interest payments as home mortgage interest.[2]

↓ **Yes**

Were all of your home mortgages taken out on or before October 13, 1987? — **Yes** → Your home mortgage interest is fully deductible. You don't need to read *Part II* of this publication.

↓ **No**

Were all of your home mortgages taken out after October 13, 1987, used to buy, build, or substantially improve the main home secured by that main home mortgage or used to buy, build, or substantially improve the second home secured by that second home mortgage, or both? — **No** → Go to *Part II* of this publication to determine the limits on your deductible home mortgage interest.

↓ **Yes**

Were your (or your spouse's if married filing a joint return) mortgage balances $750,000 or less ($375,000 or less if married filing separately) (or $1 million or less ($500,000 if married filing separately) if all debt was incurred prior to December 16, 2017) at all times during the year?[3] — **No** → Were your (or your spouse's if married filing a joint return) grandfathered debt plus home acquisition debt balances $750,000 or less[4] ($375,000 or less if married filing separately) (or $1 million or less ($500,000 if married filing separately) if all debt was incurred prior to December 16, 2017) at all times during the year?[3] — **No** →

↓ **Yes** ↓ **Yes**

[1] You must itemize deductions on Schedule A (Form 1040). The loan must be a secured debt on a qualified home. See *Part I, Home Mortgage Interest,* earlier.
[2] See Table 2 in *Part II* of this publication for where to deduct other types of interest payments.
[3] A taxpayer who enters into a written binding contract before December 15, 2017, to close on the purchase of a principal residence before January 1, 2018, and who purchases such residence before April 1, 2018, is considered to have incurred the home acquisition debt prior to December 16, 2017, and may use the 2017 threshold amounts of $1,000,000 ($500,000 for married filing separately).
[4] See *Part II* of this publication for more information about grandfathered debt and home acquisition debt.

Source: Internal Revenue Service

REMEMBER Even if you don't receive a Form 1098 from your lender, within the total loan limits discussed previously, every penny you pay in mortgage interest is deductible. Your lender should be able to provide you with an amortization schedule showing the interest and principal pieces of every payment you make over the life of the loan. Identify which of those payments you've made for 2021 and add up the interest portion of those payments to arrive at the amount of your deduction.

TIP You can deduct late payment charges as home mortgage interest. You find these charges on your annual mortgage statement.

If you can pay down your mortgage more quickly than required, don't assume that doing so is not in your best financial interests just because of the deductions allowed for it (see Chapter 25). If you are charged a prepayment penalty, you can deduct that as additional interest.

Limitations on deductions

In most cases, you'll be able to deduct all your home mortgage interest. Whether all of it is deductible depends on the date you took out the mortgage, the amount of the mortgage, and how the proceeds from the mortgage loan were used.

TAX CUT

Interest on mortgage loans of up to $1 million ($500,000 per person for couples filing as married filing separately) taken out after October 13, 1987, but before December 16, 2017, to buy, build, or improve a first or second home is deductible. Those numbers drop for mortgage loans taken out after December 15, 2017, to $750,000 ($375,000 per person for couples filing as married filing separately). Your main home is the home you live in most of the time. It can be a house, a condominium, a cooperative apartment, a mobile home, a boat, or similar property. It must provide basic living accommodations including sleeping space, toilet facilities, and cooking facilities. Your second or vacation home is similar property that you select to be your second home. These limits apply to the aggregate value of all mortgages when they were first taken, not the balances remaining on them.

WARNING

Interest on a home-improvement loan isn't deductible if it isn't a mortgage loan. The rule is simple: no mortgage, no interest deduction. So, if a relative lends you money to buy a home, any interest that you pay isn't deductible unless the relative secures that loan with a mortgage on your house.

Interest on mortgages of any size is tax deductible if you took out your mortgage before October 14, 1987, and you still retain that mortgage. If you've refinanced into a new mortgage since this magical date, you may be out of luck if you refinanced the mortgage for more than you owed prior to refinancing. On the other hand, you're probably saving a bundle because of reductions in your interest rate.

Interest on refinanced loans

If you refinanced a mortgage on your first or second home for the remaining balance of the old mortgage, you're safe, provided that the aggregate value of all mortgages on homes one and two at the time the loans were taken doesn't exceed the limits mentioned previously. If the interest on the old mortgage was fully deductible, the interest on the new mortgage is also fully deductible. To the extent of the remaining balance of the old mortgage, the new mortgage is considered a mortgage used to acquire, build, or improve a home.

But, if you refinanced your old mortgage for more than its remaining balance, the deductibility of the mortgage interest on the new loan depends on how you use the excess funds and the amount you refinanced. If the excess is used to improve, build, or buy a first or second home, and the excess plus all other mortgage loans is under $750,000 ($375,000 for couples filing married filing separately), the interest on the new loan is fully deductible.

Mixed-use mortgages

One mortgage can be both good fish and fowl, as the saying goes. If you take out a mortgage and only use a portion of those proceeds to purchase, build, or substantially improve a property, but you use the rest of the money to purchase a car or pay tuition for a student, for example, only the portion of the funds from the loan that are used toward the purchase, building, or improvement to your principal or secondary residence is deductible, and then only to the limits dictated by the date of the original loan. So, if you have a 40-year mortgage that you took in 1985, for example, your interest is unlimited, including the portion of the money you used to buy a car. But if that money was borrowed in 2018, the $750,000 loan limit applies ($375,000 if you're filing as married filing separately), and you have to exclude the interest you paid for the portion of the loan that went toward the car purchase from your total mortgage interest deduction, even though the entire loan is secured by using your home as collateral.

Points

TAX CUT

The term *points* is used to describe certain upfront charges that a borrower pays to obtain a mortgage. One point equals 1 percent of the loan amount financed. For example, if the loan is for $200,000, two points equal a $4,000 charge. You can deduct the amount you paid in points in 2021 if the loan was used to buy or build your main residence. The points you pay on a second home must be deducted over the term of the loan.

TIP

Points are sometimes referred to as *loan origination fees, processing fees, maximum loan charges,* or *premium charges.* Look for these charges on the settlement statement that the lender (by law) is required to provide you.

POINTS ON REFINANCING

WARNING

The points paid to refinance a mortgage on a main home aren't usually deductible in full in the year you pay them — even if the new mortgage is secured by your main home. However, if you use part of the refinanced mortgage to improve your main home and you pay the points instead of paying them from the proceeds of the new loan, you can deduct in full (in the year paid) the part of the points related to the improvement. But you must deduct the remainder of the points over the life of the loan. For example, suppose that the remaining balance of your mortgage is $100,000. You take out a new mortgage for $150,000 and use $25,000 for improvements to your home, $25,000 for personal purposes, and $100,000 to pay off the old loan. The points on the $25,000 used for improvements are deductible in 2021. The points on the $100,000 used to pay off the remaining $100,000 balance of the old mortgage have to be written off over the term of the new loan. The points on the $25,000 used for personal purposes can't be deducted. And remember, because this is a mixed-use mortgage, the interest on this part of the loan isn't deductible either.

TIP

Say that you refinanced your home three years ago and you're writing off the points you paid over the 25-year term of the mortgage. If you refinance your mortgage again in 2021, the points remaining to be written off on your old mortgage can be written off in full in 2021. Enter this amount on line 8c. The points on your new refinanced loan have to be deducted over the term of the new mortgage.

A penalty for paying off a mortgage early is deductible if the loan qualified for the mortgage interest deduction (the mortgage loan was used to buy, build, or improve your main home).

SELLER-PAID POINTS

TAX CUT

In times of troubled home-sales, desperate measures are sometimes required. So, if the seller pays the points that the buyer normally does, the buyer gets a double windfall. The buyer not only gets the seller to pay the points, but the buyer also gets to deduct them. The buyer must subtract seller-paid points from the tax basis of the home. And, although the seller paid the points, the seller can't deduct them; instead, that amount is deducted from the selling price.

So, if you're a buyer who had the seller pay the points on the purchase of your home but didn't deduct them, you can still do so by filing a Form 1040X, Amended Return. But you have to take this step before the three-year statute of limitations expires (see Chapter 20), or you can kiss any refund goodbye. When you file Form 1040X, write "Seller paid points" on the upper-right corner of the form if you are filing a paper return.

Qualified mortgage insurance premiums

Home buyers who buy a home with a mortgage exceeding 80 percent of the purchase price of the house generally are required by the mortgage lender to obtain *private mortgage insurance* (PMI). In 2021 you can deduct the PMI you paid on Schedule A. Of course, this deduction has restrictions: If your income is greater than $100,000 ($50,000 if you're married and filing separately), you must reduce your deduction by 10 percent for every $1,000 your income exceeds $100,000 (that's every $500 over $50,000 for married filing separately). You'll find the amount you paid for PMI on Form 1098, box 5. Place that amount on line 8d of Schedule A.

TIP

Just because your lender may require that you have PMI now doesn't mean that you need to keep it forever. When the principal amount on your loan drops below 80 percent of the value of your house, you can discontinue the insurance. Your lender will require proof, usually in the form of a valid real estate appraisal, which can be inconvenient to obtain, but well worth it; you'll recoup the cost of that appraisal in usually only two or three months. For more information, please consult *Mortgages For Dummies* by Eric Tyson and Ray Brown (Wiley).

Total deductible mortgage interest and points

Schedule A, line 8e, is the conclusion to your journey through the wonders of the mortgage interest deduction. Add up any amounts you have on lines 8a through 8d and place the total on line 8e.

Line 9: Investment interest

When you borrow against the value of securities held in a brokerage account, the interest paid on what is referred to as a margin loan is deductible. This deduction, however, can't exceed your total investment income. If it does, the excess is carried forward and deducted from next year's investment income — or carried over to future years until it can be deducted. You use Form 4952, Investment Interest, to compute the deduction and carry over the result to Schedule A (line 9).

REMEMBER

Investment income for the purpose of this deduction includes income from interest, nonqualified dividends (read more in Chapter 12), annuities, and royalties. It doesn't include income from rental real estate or from a *passive activity* (a passive activity — see Chapter 15 — is IRS jargon for a business deal or venture in which you are a silent partner). The following aren't usually considered investment income:

>> If you borrow money to buy or carry tax-exempt bonds, you can't deduct any interest on the loan as investment-interest expense. If 20 percent of your portfolio consists of tax-exempt bonds, 20 percent of your margin interest on your security account isn't deductible.

>> Although long-term capital gains and qualified dividends aren't usually considered investment income, you can choose to treat them as investment income in order to deduct the entire amount of the interest you paid on your margin account. There is a trade-off, however. You have to reduce the amount of your capital gains and qualified dividends that are eligible for the maximum long-term capital gain rate (0,15, or 20 percent, depending on your tax bracket) by the amount of your capital gains and/or qualified dividends you are treating as investment income. For example, suppose you have $2,000 of investment interest paid, $1,000 of investment income, and $10,000 of long-term capital gains and qualified

dividends. You may elect to deduct the full $2,000 of investment interest in 2021 if you treat $1,000 of your long-term capital gains and qualified dividends as investment income. Of course, this now means that you receive the preferential tax rate on long-term capital gains and qualified dividends on only $9,000, not $10,000.

>> Interest expense incurred in a passive activity such as rental real estate, a limited partnership, or an S Corporation isn't considered investment-interest expense unless it is separately stated as "investment interest" on the Schedule K-1 you receive. If your K-1 shows separately stated investment interest, fill out your Form 4952 and claim your deduction on line 9 of Schedule A. Any other type of interest expense shown on your K-1 may be deducted only from your passive-activity income.

TIP

Student loan interest isn't investment interest, although we think education is one of the best investments you can make. Even so, you can deduct up to $2,500 of student loan interest, and you don't even have to itemize your deductions. The deduction is claimed as an adjustment to your income along with the other adjustments we discuss in Chapter 7, in the section on Schedule 1, Part II, line 20.

Here's the fine print on student loan interest: Your modified adjusted gross income (MAGI) can't exceed $70,000 ($140,000 for joint filers); above these amounts, the deduction gets phased out. So, at the $85,000 income level if you're single, and the $170,000 income level if you're married, you can say "see ya" to this deduction.

Lines 11–14: Gifts to Charity

You can deduct your charitable contributions, but the amount of your deduction may be limited, and you must follow a number of strict rules. One good turn doesn't always deserve another!

After you understand the types of things you can and can't deduct, completing this section is a snap. Qualifying contributions that you make by cash and check are totaled and entered on line 11, and those made other than by cash and check (for example, you donate your old *Taxes For Dummies* books to charity when new editions come out) are entered on line 12.

If you make out a check at the end of the year and mail it by December 31, you can deduct your contribution even if the charity doesn't receive the check until January. If you charge a contribution on your credit card, you get to deduct it in the year you charged it — even if you don't pay off the charge until the following year.

REMEMBER

If you signed up for a program where a percentage of your credit card purchases is donated to charity, remember to deduct what the credit card company paid on your behalf.

Qualifying charities

You can deduct your contributions only if you make them to a qualified organization. To become a qualified organization, most organizations (other than churches) must apply to the IRS. To find out whether an organization qualifies, just ask the organization for its tax-exemption certificate.

DON'T OVERLOOK YOUR OUT-OF-POCKET EXPENDITURES

A commonly overlooked deductible charitable expense is your out-of-pocket expenses (money spent) incurred while doing volunteer work for a charity.

For example, you can deduct out-of-pocket expenses (such as gas and oil, but probably not rest-stop candy bars!) that are directly related to the use of your car in charitable work. You can't deduct anything like general repair or maintenance expenses, tires, insurance, depreciation, and so on. If you don't want to track and deduct your actual expenses, you can use a standard rate of 14 cents a mile to figure your contribution. You can deduct actual expenses for parking fees and tolls. If you must travel away from home to perform a real and substantial service, such as attending a convention for a qualified charitable organization, you can claim a deduction for your unreimbursed travel and transportation expenses, including meals and lodging. If you get a daily allowance (per diem) for travel expenses while providing services for a charitable organization, you must include as income the amount that is more than your travel expenses. Of course, you can deduct your travel expenses that are more than the allowance.

There's one restriction on these deductions: They're allowed only if there is no significant amount of personal pleasure derived from your travel. What is the limit the IRS sets on personal pleasure? Well, we can't find an IRS chart, but we can at least assure you that the IRS allows you to enjoy your trip without automatically disqualifying you from this deduction. The IRS doesn't mind if you decide to do some sightseeing, but you can't deduct expenses for your spouse or children who may accompany you. If you go to a church convention as a church member rather than as a representative of the church, you can't deduct your expenses.

You can deduct the cost and upkeep of uniforms that you must wear while doing volunteer work — as long as these uniforms are unsuitable for everyday use. A Boy or Girl Scout uniform, for example, wouldn't be the type of clothing you would wear just anywhere!

TIP

If for some reason you doubt that an organization qualifies, you can check IRS Publication 78 (*Cumulative List of Organizations*). Most libraries have Publication 78. You also can call the IRS toll-free tax help telephone number (800-829-3676) to request this publication. If you're internet-savvy, you can visit the IRS website at www.irs.gov and type Publication 78 in the window "Search for Forms and Publication." Click on Publication 78 and then "Search Now," where you can find out whether the charity is a qualified one. Nearly all the tax-exempt charities are listed. If that doesn't work, search www.guidestar.org.

Contributions that you make to the following charitable organizations are generally deductible:

>> Nonprofit schools

>> Organizations such as CARE, the Red Cross, the Salvation Army, Goodwill Industries, the Girl and Boy Scouts, and so on

>> Public park and recreational facilities

>> Religious organizations, including churches, synagogues, mosques, and so on. Keep track of how much money you're putting into the collection plate (and always pay by check or obtain a receipt, if you can). If your place of worship charges dues, the dues also fall into the charitable donation category.

>> War veterans' groups

>> Your federal, state, and local government — if your charitable contribution is only for public purposes

REMEMBER

Some people *tithe* (pay 10 percent of their income) to their place of worship and don't think twice about it. Remember, if you're tithing, make sure you retain proof (bank records, copies of cancelled checks, or receipts), then include your tithes and take the full amount of your deduction!

If it's your habit to put cash in the collection plate at church or give a cash donation when a charitable solicitor comes to your door, you may want to rethink this strategy if you're planning on claiming these contributions as a charitable donation. If you can't substantiate all of your contributions, you can't take them. What constitutes substantiation? For donations of $250 or more, you must have a receipt from the charity that shows the date and amount of the gift, and a statement of the value of any goods or services you received in exchange for your donation. For contributions under $250, your cancelled check (or a copy of it provided by the bank) works. So does a receipt from the charity or a credit card charge. It doesn't make any difference if you make donations in cash or in kind — you need the substantiation. So now, you may want to cultivate a new habit and put a check in the collection plate instead of cash.

Nonqualifying charities

Generally speaking, contributions or donations made to causes or organizations that just benefit the organization, as opposed to the greater society, aren't deductible. The following are examples of organizations or groups for which you can't deduct contributions:

>> Dues paid to country clubs, lodges, orders, and so on

>> Foreign charities (but you can deduct contributions to a U.S. charity that transfers funds to a foreign charity — if the U.S. charity controls the use of the funds). Contributions to charities in Canada, Israel, and Mexico are deductible if the charity meets the same tests that qualify U.S. organizations to receive deductible contributions.

>> Groups that lobby for law changes (such as changes to the tax code!)

The IRS doesn't want you to deduct contributions to organizations from which you may benefit — so include bingo and raffle tickets in this forbidden group.

>> Homeowners' associations

>> Individuals

Big surprise here! So, don't try to deduct what you gave to your brother-in-law, because he doesn't count in the eyes of the IRS! The contribution can be to a qualified organization that helps needy and worthy individuals — like your brother-in-law.

>> Labor unions

- » Lottery ticket costs (gee, we wonder why not?)

- » Members of the clergy who can spend the money as they want. If you want to give money to your clergyperson to use at their discretion, it's far better to send a check to the religious organization your clergyperson is affiliated with and ask that it be directed to that person's "discretionary fund."

- » Political groups or candidates running for public office

- » Social and sport clubs

- » Tuition to attend private or parochial schools, including supplemental schools at your place of worship or cultural center.

This list can go on and on — didn't you suspect that a list of nonqualifying charities would be longer than a list of qualifying ones? — but we think you get the idea. So, don't try to deduct the value of your blood donated at a blood bank, and don't even think about trying to deduct your contribution to your college fraternity or sorority!

Contributions of property

Generally, you can deduct the *fair market value* (FMV) of property given to a charity. FMV is the price at which property would change hands between a willing buyer and a willing seller. So, if you bought a painting for $2,000 that's worth $10,000 when you donate it to a museum, you can deduct $10,000.

THE RECORDS YOU NEED

If you want to take that charitable deduction, you need to be able to prove you made it. For cash contributions below $250, you can keep a canceled check, a bank record, a credit card receipt, or a receipt from the charity as proof that you gave the money.

For individual contributions of $250 or more, you need a receipt from the charity — otherwise, you could have your deduction tossed out in the event of an audit. The receipt should indicate either the amount of cash you contributed or a description (but not the value) of any property you donated. The receipt must also indicate the value of any gift or services you may have received, and you must have the receipt by the time you file your return. Remember, every donation is treated as a separate donation for applying the $250 threshold; if you give one charity two $150 checks, all that you need to substantiate those contributions are your records, not the charity's receipts.

If you contribute property worth more than $500, you have to attach Form 8283, Noncash Charitable Contributions. On the form, you list the name of the charity, the date of the gift, your cost, the appraised value, and how you arrived at the value. If the value of the property you contributed exceeds $5,000, you need a written appraisal from a qualified appraiser, who has to sign off on Part III in Section B of Form 8283. The charity has to complete and sign Part IV of the form. A written appraisal isn't needed for publicly traded stock or non-publicly traded stock worth $10,000 or less.

You can use the FMV only if — on the date of the contribution — the property would have produced a long-term capital gain or loss if it had been sold (property held more than one year). If you donate property you held for one year or less or you donate ordinary income property, your deduction is limited to your cost. *Ordinary income property* is inventory from a business, works of art created by the donor, manuscripts prepared by the donor, and capital assets held one year or less. Following are guidelines for deducting contributions of property:

>> **If you contribute property with a fair market value that is less than your cost or depreciated value:** Your deduction is limited to fair market value. You can't claim a deduction for the property's decline in value since you acquired it.

>> **If you have an asset that has declined in value:** Sell that asset to lock in the capital loss deduction (see Chapter 14) and donate the cash for an additional deduction.

For example, suppose that you paid $12,500 for shares of a mutual fund that invested in Russia that are now worth only $6,000. If you donate the shares, all you can claim is a $6,000 charitable deduction. By selling the shares and donating the cash, not only will you be entitled to a $6,000 charitable deduction, you also will have a $6,500 capital loss that you can deduct.

>> **If you have an asset that has appreciated substantially in value:** Give the asset to the charity rather than sell the asset, get stuck for the tax, and donate the cash you have left. If you donate the asset itself, you get to deduct the full value of the asset, thereby escaping the tax.

One exception to the FMV rule: If you donate artwork you've created, a patent, or other intellectual property (such as computer software, a copyright, trademark, trade secrets, or general know-how), your deduction is limited to the lesser of fair market value or your basis in the property (what it cost you).

And an exception to the exception of the FMV rule: If the property you've created or acquired through a gift from the artist is a musical work, you're entitled to value your donation using capital asset treatment (just like it was a gift of appreciated stock) instead of limiting the value of your donation to the lesser of fair market value or your basis in the property.

WARNING

You can't just tell the IRS you've donated property without documenting it, as well. If you've donated property worth $500 or less, just list the value on line 12; for values higher than $500 in the aggregate, you'll also have to complete Form 8283. For values more than $5,000, you may be required to obtain a written appraisal of the property. Depending on the type of property, you may have to attach a copy of that appraisal to your return. If you have donated property with a value in excess of $500, you may want to check out IRS Publication 561 (*Determining the Value of Donated Property*).

Used clothing and household goods

TAX CUT

Clean out those closets for next year so that you can save on your taxes! Hey, even Bill and Hillary Clinton took a deduction for this one! Used clothing and household goods usually have a fair market value that is much less than the original cost. For used clothing, you claim the price that buyers of used items pay in used-clothing stores. See IRS Publication 561 (*Determining the Value of Donated Property* — Household Goods section) for information on the value of items such as furniture and appliances and other items you want to donate.

You're no longer allowed to donate any old rag and claim a tax deduction. That old rag now needs to be in good or better condition. Who makes that determination? Most likely, you do, but you need to know that the IRS may challenge your assessment of your property. So, if you want to prove that the dress that you've donated was in good and saleable condition, you probably want to have some unassailable proof — a statement from the organization you donated to, or perhaps a photograph. The regulations also disallow any deduction for items of minimal value (so long, underwear and socks). Of course, there's an exception to this minimal value rule — if a single item has a value of $500 or more and is accompanied by a qualified appraisal, you may still claim the deduction.

TIP

What's used clothing or furniture worth? Many charities offer a free printed guide to estimated values. The Salvation Army Valuation Guide can be downloaded off the internet at www.satruck.org/Home/DonationValueGuide.

Cars, boats, and aircraft

Charities love when you donate one of these items to them. And we know that you loved that car or plane, and it holds great sentimental value to you, one that's hard to put a price on. Well, the IRS has arrived at a way to come up with an absolute value, and it doesn't involve looking up the book value in some pricing guide. Instead, you're limited to deducting the actual gross proceeds from the sale of that used vehicle, rather than a value you assign. How do you know how much to deduct? The charity must provide you with a written acknowledgment of the sales price within 30 days of the sale. What happens if you donate the car at the end of the year, and the charity doesn't have a chance to unload your old clunker before December 31? Just wait to file your tax return until they do. Even if the sale is transacted in the next tax year, your deduction is good for the year in which you transferred the title to the charity.

Of course, this rule does have a couple of exceptions (when aren't there exceptions?). You need to rely only on the actual sales price of the car, boat, or airplane if the sales price is more than $500, and, if the charity doesn't sell the vehicle, but instead uses it for a charitable purpose, you can go back to the old rules. Those rules, in case you're not current, say that you can assign a reasonable fair market value to that used car by consulting guides such as blue books that contain dealer sale or average prices for recent model years, or any other reasonable method. These guides also give estimates for adjusting values to take into account mileage and physical condition. The prices aren't official, however, and you can't consider a blue book as an appraisal of any specific donated property. But the guides are a good place to start.

If you're thinking of donating your old car, pick up IRS Publication 4303 (*A Donor's Guide to Vehicle Donations*) available by snail mail or on the web at onlinecardonation.org/pub4303.pdf, which can help guide you through this process.

Charitable deduction limits

The U.S. Congress, and by extension, the IRS, thinks that private contributions to charity are good. However, in 2021, some cash gifts are subject to limits. If you are itemizing in 2021 and you contributed cash, you may deduct up to 100 percent of your adjusted gross income if that money is given to a qualifying public charity. If, on the other hand, you contributed to a supporting organization, you started or continued to fund a donor-advised fund, or you donated to a private charitable foundation, the amount you can deduct is limited to either 30 percent (private charitable foundations and donor advised funds) or 60 percent (supporting organization) of your adjusted gross income (AGI). Non-cash gifts are subject to a 50 percent AGI limit.

CONTRIBUTIONS THAT ARE BOTH QUALIFIED AND NONQUALIFIED

If you receive a benefit from making a valid deductible contribution, you can deduct only the amount of your contribution that is more than the value of the benefit. For example, if you pay to attend a charity function such as a ball or banquet, you can deduct only the amount that is more than the fair market value of your ticket. You can also deduct unreimbursed expenses such as uniforms and actual automobile expenses or use a standard rate of 14 cents per mile. Just subtract the value of the benefit you received from your total payment. Ask the charity for a receipt that details the actual amount you contributed. Most charities are happy to provide this information. In fact, if the value of your contribution is $75 or more and that is partly for goods and services, the charity must give you a written statement informing you of the amount you can deduct. If you can't easily obtain a receipt, use an estimate based on something the IRS can't disagree with — common sense.

If the amount you donated in 2021 exceeds these limits, amounts that are disallowed in 2021 aren't lost; instead, they're carried forward for five years or until you're able to use the 2021 disallowed amount, whichever comes first. You can carryforward a contribution of qualified conservation property (you donated land to your town, for example, to preserve a wetlands) for 15 years.

All non-cash gifts are subject to income limits. A 30 percent AGI limit applies to gifts of capital gain property that has appreciated in value if you value your gift for charitable purposes on its appreciated value instead of its cost. Otherwise, the 50 percent limit applies. For example, you donate to a museum a painting worth $20,000 that you purchased for $10,000. Your AGI is $50,000. In this case, if you want to use the appreciated value, your deduction will be limited to $15,000, or 30 percent of your AGI of $50,000, and the balance of $5,000 will carry over to 2022. If you elect to use your purchase price, you may claim the entire deduction this year because $10,000 is less than 50 percent of your AGI.

REMEMBER

Contributions of capital property may be made only to a church or public charity, and you have to have owned that property for more than a year prior to making the gift. See Chapter 14 for the rules on how the one-year holding period is calculated.

IRA qualified charitable distribution (QCD)

While Congress has never made this provision permanent, gifting to charity directly from your IRA is a popular way to give substantial donations to charities while receiving positive tax benefits. In 2021, provided you are age 70½ or older, you can give up to a total of $100,000 in IRA assets directly to the charity or charities of your choice. As in everything, there are rules to be followed to make a valid IRA Qualified Charitable Distribution (QCD) in 2021:

>> You must be at least age 70½ to make a QCD.

>> You must direct your IRA trustee (usually a bank, mutual fund company, or investment advisor) to make the check payable to the charity.

>> The transfer must be made by December 31, 2021. If your QCD leaves your IRA trustee's hands after that date, you've lost the benefit of this strategy for 2021.

>> QCDs may only be made to qualifying public charities — no donor-advised funds or private charitable foundations qualify for this contribution.

>> QCDs may not exceed $100,000 in total, across all charities, in 2021.

If you make a QCD in 2021, you will receive Form 1099-R from your IRA provider by early February (it must be mailed no later than January 31, 2022). The full amount of the charitable gift will show in box 1, and you should enter this on Form 1040, line 4a. On Form 1040, line 4b, enter -0-, and next to that line, write in "QCD." If you're working on computer software, there should be a place in the software to indicate that this is a qualified charitable distribution.

If you're in a generous frame of mind and you meet the age requirements, making donations using this new provision can make a lot of sense. The following are among the reasons why making a direct IRA QCD may make sense:

>> Keeping this distribution out of your adjusted gross income may limit the amount of your Social Security income that is taxed.

>> If you itemize your deductions, keeping your AGI lower allows you to deduct more of your medical deductions, which are reduced by 7.5 percent of AGI.

REMEMBER

We've included QCDs in with itemized deductions, even though it isn't one. You are not including the amount of the distribution in income, and therefore, you're not entitled to take a deduction for it. Remember, though, that just because you've made this contribution directly from your IRA to qualified charities, you're not prohibited from giving other cash or non-cash donations, which can be deducted on Schedule A, if you're itemizing, or up to $300 ($600 if you're filing as married filing jointly) in addition to your standard deduction.

For the world's great humanitarians

If you have any charitable contributions from a prior year that you were unable to use and you haven't hit the 5-year deadline for carryforwards (15 years for qualified conservation property), line 13 is where you'll put amounts carried forward from your 2020 Schedule A.

Adding up all your deductible contributions

Add together any amounts you have on lines 11 through 13 of Schedule A and place your answer on line 14. This represents your total charitable contribution deduction for 2021.

Line 15: Casualty and Theft Losses (Form 4684)

We hope that you don't need to use this one. But if you do, and if you've come to view the IRS as heartless, this line may correct that impression. It's not — well, not completely. If you've suffered a casualty or theft loss from a federally declared disaster (other than net qualified disaster losses), you will find that the IRS can be somewhat charitable. Unfortunately, as is the case with any unusual deduction, you've got to jump through quite a few hoops to nail it down.

In 2021, only casualty and theft losses that arise due to a federally declared disaster are deductible. Unfortunately, there are an abundance of federally declared disasters, from hurricanes and tornados to wildfires and floods. If you're not sure if the recent storm that hit your area qualifies, there's a website for that: www.fema.gov/disaster/current. After you determine whether your loss is deductible, get a copy of Form 4684, Casualties and Thefts, on which you list each item that was stolen or destroyed. If your deduction ends up being more than your income — and it does happen — you may have what's known as a *net operating loss* (NOL). You can use this type of loss to lower your tax in an earlier or a later year. This rule is an exception (of course!) to the normal rule that you must be in business to have a net operating loss. See Chapter 20 for more details. Be aware that Form 4684 is used not only for personal income tax returns, but also for business returns such as Form 1120S and Form 1065. The only page of Form 4684 that you will be completing is page 1.

TIP

When a casualty loss occurs in a presidentially declared disaster area, a taxpayer has the choice of deducting the loss in the year that it occurred or in the preceding year. By electing to go the prior year route, you can obtain an immediate refund (usually within 60 days) instead of having to wait until the end of the year to receive the full benefit of the loss. Use Form 1040X to claim the loss in the prior year. You have up until the time you file (including extensions) for the year of the loss to make this decision. Remember, the earlier you make it, the quicker you will get your hands on the refund the loss entitled you to. This maneuver also makes sense if you were in a higher bracket in the prior year.

THE INSURANCE EFFECTS

You've got casualty insurance? Great. But there are a couple of things you need to watch out for. First, if you expect to be reimbursed by your insurer but haven't seen any cash by tax-filing time, you need to subtract an estimate of the expected reimbursement from your deductible loss. Second — and this sounds strange — you must reduce the amount of your loss by your insurance coverage even if you don't file a claim. Suppose that your loss is 100 percent covered by insurance, but you decide not to ask for a reimbursement for fear of losing your coverage. You can't claim a deduction for the loss. Only the amount of your loss that's above the insurance coverage would be deductible in that case.

If you're reimbursed by insurance and decide not to repair or replace your property, you could have a taxable gain on your hands. That's because the taxable gain is calculated by subtracting your cost from the insurance proceeds and not the property's fair market value. For example, imagine that your summer cottage, which costs $150,000 (the cost here refers to the cost of the building and excludes the land costs), burned to the ground. You get $190,000 in insurance money (the house's current FMV), giving you a fully taxable $40,000 gain.

To postpone the gain, you have to replace the property with a similar one, and it must be worth at least as much as the insurance money you received. If the new place is worth less than that, you must report the difference as a capital gain. In addition, you have to replace the property within two years. The two-year period begins on December 31 of the year you realize the gain. If your main home is located in a federally declared disaster area, you have four years, and you can generally get a one-year extension beyond that, if necessary.

Do you have a deductible loss?

TAX CUT

Strange as it may seem, the Tax Court has haggled extensively over what is and isn't a casualty. The phrase to remember is *sudden, unexpected, and unusual.* If property you own is damaged, destroyed, or lost as the result of a specific event that is sudden, unexpected, and unusual, you have a deductible casualty. Earthquakes, fires, floods, and storms meet this strict legal test.

But if you dropped a piece of the good china, if Rover chewed a hole in the sofa, if moths ate your entire wardrobe, or if termites gobbled up your brand-new backyard deck, you're doubly out of luck. You've suffered a nondeductible loss. These incidents don't meet the sudden-unexpected-unusual test.

Figuring the loss

Unfortunately, the amount of your deduction isn't going to equal the amount of your loss because the IRS makes you apply a deductible just as your auto insurer does. The IRS makes you reduce each individual loss by $100 ($500 for a qualified disaster loss) and your total losses by 10 percent of your AGI. So, if your AGI is $100,000 and you lost $11,000 when Hurricane Ida caved in your roof, your deduction is only $900. (That's $11,000 minus $100 minus 10 percent of your AGI, or $10,000.)

That stipulation effectively wipes out a deduction for plenty of people. For those whose losses are big enough to warrant a deduction, though, the fun is just beginning. That's because your deduction is limited to either the decrease in the fair market value of your property as a result of the casualty or the original cost of the property — whichever is lower.

Suppose that you bought a painting for $1,000 that was worth $100,000 when damaged by fire. Sorry. Your loss is limited to the $1,000 you paid for it. Now reverse it. You paid $100,000 for the painting, and thanks to the downturn in the market for black-velvet portraits of Elvis, it's worth only $1,000 right before it's destroyed. Your deductible loss is limited to $1,000. And you must apply this rule to each item before combining them to figure your total loss. (One exception is real estate. The entire property, including buildings, trees, and shrubs, is treated as one item.)

TAX CUT

The reduction rule ($100 plus 10 percent of your income) doesn't apply to property used in a business. It applies only to personal items. Neither is a business casualty limited to the value of the property at the time of the loss. Normally, the loss is what you paid less the depreciation to which you were entitled.

TIP

Because your loss is the difference between the fair market value of your property immediately before and after the casualty, an appraisal usually is the best way to calculate your loss. The only problem: The appraiser can't see your property before the casualty, and any photographs or records you may have had probably went up in smoke or floated away. Therefore, it makes sense to videotape both the outside of the property and its contents, including expensive jewelry, and keep the tape in a safe-deposit box, for example. You're not totally out of luck if you don't have before-and-after photos, though. A picture after the casualty and one showing the property after it was repaired comes in very handy when trying to prove the dollar value of your loss. See Chapter 3 for what to do in case all your tax records went up in smoke, for instance.

Normally, you can't deduct the cost of repairing your property because the cost of fixing something isn't really a measure of its deflated fair market value. As with nearly every IRS rule, however, this one has exceptions. You can use the cost of cleaning up or making a repair under the following conditions:

- >> The repairs are necessary to bring the property back to its condition before the casualty, and the cost of the repairs isn't excessive.

- >> The repairs take care of the damage only.

- >> The value of the property after the repairs isn't — because of the repairs — more than the value of the property before the casualty.

Another point is worth knowing: With leased property, such as a car, the amount of your loss is in fact the amount you must spend to repair it.

The IRS can, and usually does, extend the deadline for filing tax returns for up to one year in a presidentially declared disaster area. When the IRS declares a postponement to file and pay, it publicizes the postponement in your area and on its website. The postponement also delays the time for making contributions to IRAs. Neither interest nor penalties are charged during the postponement period.

TIP

If your casualty or theft loss exceeds your income, you may have a net operating loss (see Chapter 13). This NOL must be carried forward to future years and can be used to offset taxable income until the NOL is completely used up. There is no limit on the number of years it can carry forward, but it will expire at the taxpayer's death.

TIP

If you have a casualty loss from a disaster that occurred in a presidentially declared disaster area, you can choose to deduct the loss on your return in the year in which the casualty occurred or on an amended return for the preceding year. If you had more earnings in the prior year than in the current one (which is common because of lost earnings due to the disaster), you may gain more benefit from amending the prior return than taking the casualty loss on this year's. If you're not sure whether or not your disaster qualifies, the Federal Emergency Management Agency (FEMA) maintains a list of all the federal disaster zones for the year on its website (https://www.fema.gov/disaster/declarations).

Line 16: Other Itemized Deductions

Everybody likes to see a deduction that says something about "other." And this category used to be filled with such write-offs as tax prep fees, safe deposit box rentals, union dues, and investment advisory fees. But times change, and so does the tax code. These miscellaneous itemized deductions were ended when the standard deduction was greatly increased beginning in 2018.

TAX CUT

On the other hand, there are other miscellaneous itemized deductions which were never subject to the 2 percent of AGI limit. The following categories are 100 percent, Grade A, no-fat deductions!

>> **Estate tax on income you received as an heir:** Enter on line 16 of Schedule A. You can deduct the estate tax attributable to income you received from an estate that you paid tax on. For example, suppose that you received $10,000 from an IRA account when the owner died. You included this amount in your income. The owner's estate paid $2,000 of estate tax on the IRA. You can deduct the $2,000 on line 16. It's called an *IRD deduction*. That's IRS lingo for *income in respect of a decedent,* which means that because the IRA owner never paid income tax on the money in the IRA, guess what? You have to! But you get to deduct a portion of the estate tax paid on the value of that account.

>> **Gambling losses to the extent of gambling winnings:** Enter on line 16 of Schedule A. Remember, though, that you can only deduct up to the amount of your gambling winnings.

>> **Impairment-related work expenses:** These expenses are allowable business expenses of attendant care services at your place of work and expenses in connection with your place of work that are necessary for you to be able to work. See IRS Publication 907 *(Tax Highlights for Persons with Disabilities)* for more information.

    If you're an employee, enter your impairment-related work expenses on line 10 of Form 2106. This amount is also entered on line 16 of Schedule A.

>> **Repayment of income:** If you had to repay more than $3,000 of income that was included in your income in an earlier year, you may be able to deduct the amount you repaid or take a credit against your tax. This is known as a *claim of right.* However, if the repayment is less than $3,000, you must deduct it on line 16 of Schedule A.

>> **Unrecovered investment in a pension:** If a retiree contributed to the cost of a pension or annuity, a part of each payment received can be excluded from income as a tax-free return of the retiree's investment. If the retiree dies before the entire investment is returned tax-free, the unrecovered investment is allowed as a deduction on the retiree's final return.

>> **Work expenses for the disabled:** If you have a physical or mental disability that limits your being employed or that substantially limits one or more of your activities (such as performing manual tasks, walking, speaking, breathing, learning, and working), your impairment-related work expenses are deductible.

Line 17: Total Itemized Deductions

You've (thankfully) reached the end of Schedule A. Warm up that calculator again because you need to do some adding. Add the amounts on lines 4, 7, 10, 14, and 16, and place the total on line 17. If line 17 is greater than your standard deduction, carry that number over to Form 1040, line 12a, and double-check to make sure you've written the same number. We can't repeat too often that the number one cause of a tax notice is you copied a number incorrectly. Of course, if you're preparing your taxes using a computer program, you're good to go, as the computer has already filled in line 12a with the correct number.

REMEMBER If you're married filing separately, and your spouse has already filed their return, you're required to use the same method of deductions as your spouse. So, if they itemized, you must itemize; if they used the standard deduction, you have to use the standard deduction, too, even if it gives you a worse result than itemizing would.

Line 18: Check the Box

We love lines like this. If you're electing to itemize your deductions even though your itemized deductions are less than your standard deduction is, check the box next to line 18. And that's all that's required here.

WAIT, WHERE ARE MY MISCELLANEOUS ITEMIZED DEDUCTIONS SUBJECT TO 2 PERCENT OF AGI?

One of the casualties of the 2017 Tax Cuts and Jobs Act was to eliminate all of those miscellaneous itemized deductions subject to 2 percent of adjusted gross income. This was where all sorts of deductions were placed, such as union dues, trustee fees, investment advisory fees, safe deposit box fees, non-reimbursed employee business expenses, tax preparation fees, and even the cost of this book. Many of these deductions were tiny, and most people had difficulty reaching the 2 percent AGI threshold. And, as a sweetener for the loss of this deduction, we received a hugely increased standard deduction, which benefitted many taxpayers who formerly itemized.

There is a small number of people, though, who benefitted from this deduction. For those who can no longer deduct their investment advisory fees or trustee fees, well, there's not much that we can do or say to fix that.

If, on the other hand, you lost your non-reimbursed employee business expenses, we do have a suggestion for you. You should encourage your employer to set up an accountable plan, where you provide your employer with receipts and mileage logs to substantiate the costs you are incurring as you engage in your employer's business. In an accountable plan, you are reimbursed for actual expenses you incur without having to declare the reimbursement on your Form 1040. Especially in these days of remote work during the pandemic, many employers have set up accountable plans to help equip their employees' home offices with computers, printers, better internet service, and office supplies. If your employer has not yet offered this as an option, you should suggest it. After all, you shouldn't be spending your wages to provide the tools necessary to perform their business.

IN THIS CHAPTER

» Accounting for interest and
dividend income

» Deciphering the 1099-INT, 1099-DIV,
and 1099-OID

» Dealing with foreign accounts and
trusts

Chapter **12**

Interest and Dividend Income: Form 1040, Schedule B

Some have described real wealth as the ability to live off the income from your assets. Most people don't achieve that level of wealth, especially earlier in their working years, but for some people, their investment income has grown beyond being able to plop a number on the front of their Form 1040 or 1040A and say they're done. If you fall into the category of having more than $1,500 of interest or dividend income, Schedule B of the 1040 (which is located on the back side of Schedule A if you're filing on paper and have received a Form 1040 booklet from the IRS) is for you. And if you have a foreign bank account or are involved in a foreign trust, Schedule B has to be filed. Sorry!

TIP

Although you may not have sufficient interest and dividend income to file Schedule B, filling it out is still a good idea. It's a good worksheet and a terrific double-check to make sure that all the sources of interest and dividends you showed on last year's returns are accounted for on this year's.

What you need to complete Schedule B are those 1099s (1099-INT, 1099-DIV, and 1099-OID) that banks, corporations, brokerage firms, and mutual fund companies are required to send by January 31, 2022. Make sure that you have one of these forms for each and every nonretirement account that you owned during the tax year. If you're missing one, get on the horn to the responsible financial institution and request it. Check out Figure 12-1 for a visual of Schedule B.

SCHEDULE B
(Form 1040)

Department of the Treasury
Internal Revenue Service (99)

Interest and Ordinary Dividends

▶ Go to *www.irs.gov/ScheduleB* for instructions and the latest information.
▶ Attach to Form 1040 or 1040-SR.

OMB No. 1545-0074

2021

Attachment
Sequence No. **08**

Name(s) shown on return

Your social security number

Part I **Interest** (See instructions and the instructions for Forms 1040 and 1040-SR, line 2b.) **Note:** If you received a Form 1099-INT, Form 1099-OID, or substitute statement from a brokerage firm, list the firm's name as the payer and enter the total interest shown on that form.	**1** List name of payer. If any interest is from a seller-financed mortgage and the buyer used the property as a personal residence, see the instructions and list this interest first. Also, show that buyer's social security number and address ▶	**Amount**
		1
	2 Add the amounts on line 1	**2**
	3 Excludable interest on series EE and I U.S. savings bonds issued after 1989. Attach Form 8815	**3**
	4 Subtract line 3 from line 2. Enter the result here and on Form 1040 or 1040-SR, line 2b . . . . ▶	**4**

Note: If line 4 is over $1,500, you must complete Part III.

Part II **Ordinary Dividends** (See instructions and the instructions for Forms 1040 and 1040-SR, line 3b.) **Note:** If you received a Form 1099-DIV or substitute statement from a brokerage firm, list the firm's name as the payer and enter the ordinary dividends shown on that form.	**5** List name of payer ▶	**Amount**
		5
	6 Add the amounts on line 5. Enter the total here and on Form 1040 or 1040-SR, line 3b . . . . ▶	**6**

Note: If line 6 is over $1,500, you must complete Part III.

Part III **Foreign Accounts and Trusts** **Caution:** If required, failure to file FinCEN Form 114 may result in substantial penalties. See instructions.	You must complete this part if you **(a)** had over $1,500 of taxable interest or ordinary dividends; **(b)** had a foreign account; or **(c)** received a distribution from, or were a grantor of, or a transferor to, a foreign trust.	**Yes**	**No**
	7a At any time during 2021, did you have a financial interest in or signature authority over a financial account (such as a bank account, securities account, or brokerage account) located in a foreign country? See instructions		
	If "Yes," are you required to file FinCEN Form 114, Report of Foreign Bank and Financial Accounts (FBAR), to report that financial interest or signature authority? See FinCEN Form 114 and its instructions for filing requirements and exceptions to those requirements		
	b If you are required to file FinCEN Form 114, enter the name of the foreign country where the financial account is located ▶		
	8 During 2021, did you receive a distribution from, or were you the grantor of, or transfer to, a foreign trust? If "Yes," you may have to file Form 3520. See instructions		

For Paperwork Reduction Act Notice, see your tax return instructions.   Cat. No. 17146N   **Schedule B (Form 1040) 2021**

Source: Internal Revenue Service

FIGURE 12-1: Report your interest and dividend income on Schedule B.

⚠ **WARNING**

If you don't report all your interest or dividend income (or don't furnish the payer with your Social Security number), your future interest and dividend income is subject to backup withholding of 24 percent! To add insult to injury, about a year after filing your taxes, you'll receive a nasty notice called a *CP-2000* listing the interest and dividends that you didn't report. You'll end up owing interest and penalties in addition to the tax.

Although becoming ensnared in backup withholding is unpleasant, don't worry that the amounts withheld by financial institutions from your accounts and sent to the IRS are for naught. They simply represent a forced payment of your expected tax on your interest and dividends. You get "credit" for it on line 25b, "Federal income tax withheld from Form(s) 1099," on your Form 1040 (see Chapter 10 for more details).

Part I, Lines 1–4: Interest Income

In this first part of the schedule, you need to declare interest income that you earned during the tax year. Although this income can come from a variety of sources, as we tell you about in this chapter, most of it is reported by large, impersonal financial institutions that will send you a computer-generated Form 1099-INT, Interest Income, or Form 1099-OID, Original Issue Discount. Often, these banks and brokerages will send you something that looks different from what is shown in Figure 12-2, but no worries — what matters is that the line numbers on the form you have in front of you match up with the box numbers on the official form. Banks and brokerages are allowed to use substitute 1099s so as to consolidate all their information in one place, but the IRS must approve their format to make sure that all the information is reported correctly.

FIGURE 12-2: You receive Form 1099-INT from institutions that pay you taxable interest.

Source: Internal Revenue Service

Before you complete the lines on Schedule B, we want to explain how to read your 1099-INT and 1099-OID forms.

Understanding Forms 1099-INT and 1099-OID

You receive Form 1099-INT from the financial institution, such as a bank, that pays you interest. These forms aren't too difficult to read. The following are brief descriptions of little boxes and other stuff you find on your 1099-INT (see Figure 12-2).

WARNING

Don't assume that your 1099-INT forms are all correct. Big companies make mistakes, and they often cause taxpayers to pay more tax. Check your 1099-INT forms against the statements that you received throughout the year from the financial firm where you had the account paying the interest. If you receive an incorrect 1099-INT, ask the payer to issue a corrected one on the double! Form 1099-INT lists the telephone number of the person you need to contact in case it has to be revised.

One problem with filing too early is that you may receive a corrected 1099-INT, which means that you'll have to amend your return. And filing one return per year is more than enough for most people! While most of the corrected 1099-INTs are issued by mid-March of each year, it's not unheard of for corrected forms to continue to arrive well into September and even October. We wish we could give you definite dates that we know you'll have correct information by, but unfortunately, that's impossible, especially when Congress changes the rules after the fact. So, our advice is to do your best. If the numbers on the Form 1099-INT look reasonable, use them. Any changes on corrected forms are likely to be small, and many won't warrant filing an amended return.

Identifying the interest income on Forms 1099-INT and 1099-OID

The amount in box 1 and box 3 of the 1099-INT is the taxable interest that you have to report on line 1 of this schedule. But if you don't have more than $1,500 of total interest income for the tax year, you need not complete this part of Schedule B (you still have to complete Part II, "Dividend Income," if you had more than $1,500 in dividend income). If you don't have more than $1,500 in interest, skip Part I and enter the total of your interest income on line 2b of Form 1040. Don't concern yourself with the rest of the boxes on your 1099-INT right now. As we breeze through this chapter, we'll let you know what to do with them.

If you've purchased so-called *Original Issue Discount* or *Zero-Coupon* bonds, you'll receive a Form 1099-OID for each of these you own. The 1099-OID is similar to the 1099-INT; boxes 1, 2, and 8 show the interest you are being taxed on, even though you may not have seen any cash. Box 3 tells you about any early withdrawal penalty you may have paid because you sold before the bond matured, which you can deduct on Form 1040, Schedule 1, Part II, line 18. Box 4 shows any federal withholding on that interest, and box 8 gives you the amount of U.S. Treasury interest you've earned, which is taxable on your federal return but which you can exclude from your state income tax return. The information from Form 1099-OID is treated exactly like that from Form 1099-INT and is included on your tax return on Schedule B of Form 1040.

Dealing with market discounts and bond premiums

When most people purchase bonds, they are not buying this debt, whether corporate or governmental, when it is issued, but are buying it instead on the secondary market. What this means is that the bonds you purchase rarely are bought at exactly face value. When you purchase a bond for more than its face value, you've purchased it at a premium; when you buy it for less than its face value, you've acquired it at a discount.

These terms are important, because except in the case of very minor differences from face value, you are required to adjust the basis of that bond over the course of its remaining life to reflect either the discount or the premium that you bought it at. So, for example, if you purchase a $10,000 U.S. Treasury Bond that matures in three years at $10,300, you are required to reduce the basis of that bond by $100 per year for each of the three years remaining before maturity. Likewise, if you purchase that same bond for only $9,100, you must increase your basis by the prorated discount, so you're required to increase the basis by $300 per year for each year remaining.

Amortization (for bond premiums) and accretion (for bond discounts) amounts have not always been reported to the IRS by the investment company holding your securities, but the investment companies are now required to give this information to you, the taxpayer, as well as the IRS. You'll find bond premiums for ordinary bonds located on Form 1099-INT in box 11, and market discounts in box 10. For U.S. Treasury notes and bonds, the premiums can be found in box 12, and the premiums for tax-exempt bonds are in box 13. For original issue discount bonds, the acquisition premium is in box 6 of Form 1099-OID, while you'll find any market discounts in box 5.

The numbers that appear in the acquisition or discount boxes represent the adjustment you're required to make for the current year only. You'll either add (for discounts) or subtract (for premiums) from your total interest. Remember, you're required to maintain the character of the interest, so tax-exempt premiums and discounts are applied against tax-exempt interest, U.S. Treasury premiums and discounts go against U.S. Treasury interest, and premiums or discounts associated with corporate bonds are netted against your corporate bond interest. The best way to show this on your tax return is to list each item out separately, so that the IRS will be able to match up the interest as it appears on your 1099-INT or 1099-OID against your tax return, and also match up any premiums or discounts.

Completing lines 1–4

Now that you've located and understand Form 1099-INT and Form 1099-OID, you're ready to complete Part I of Schedule B.

Line 1: Taxable interest

Taxable interest includes interest you receive from bank accounts, interest income on loans you made to others, and interest income on loans from most other sources (anything except for municipal bond interest).

Taxable interest doesn't include interest on insurance dividends you leave on deposit with the Department of Veterans Affairs (for people who were in the armed services).

GIFTS FOR OPENING AN ACCOUNT

The value of that toaster you received is reported as interest on Form 1099-INT. Enjoy your toast! A gift valued at $10 or less for a deposit of less than $5,000 or $20 for a deposit of $5,000 or more isn't taxable, thanks to a kinder and gentler IRS.

INTEREST ON LIFE INSURANCE DIVIDENDS

This interest is taxable, but the dividends you receive aren't taxable until the total of all dividends received exceeds the total of all the premiums paid. Keep your annual dividend statements from your company in a file so that you can track that amount versus the premiums you paid.

INTEREST ON EE U.S. SAVINGS BONDS

If you don't have EE bonds, you may happily skip this line. (If you want to know about them, be sure to read Chapter 26.) Otherwise, you need to know that you have a choice regarding how and when to declare the interest you earn on them. You may report all the interest earned over the life of EE bonds when you cash them in. Or, you can choose to report the yearly interest in the year it is earned. Whatever method you choose, you must use the same method for all E, EE, and I bonds that you own.

If your child owns these bonds and has little or no other income, reporting the interest every year may make sense because the first $1,100 of interest is exempt from tax (see Chapter 26). Attach a statement to your child's return saying that you elect to report the interest annually. If the interest is under $1,100, you're going to have to file a return even if one isn't required, so that you can make this election for the initial year. After that, as long as the interest is under $1,100 (an amount that periodically is increased for inflation) and your child doesn't exceed earned income limits, you don't have to file.

Series E bonds stopped earning interest after 40 years; Series EE bonds stop earning interest after 30 years. (Series E were issued before 1980, and Series EE were issued after that.) You can avoid paying the tax on the accumulated interest at or before maturity by exchanging these bonds for HH bonds (see the next section, "U.S. H and HH bonds").

TIP

When the owner of an E or EE bond dies, the heir pays the tax when the bond is cashed in — unless the interest was reported on the decedent's final return. This choice makes sense if the bond's owner died at the beginning of the year and had little or no income (and was in a lower tax bracket than the heir).

For example, if the owner died on January 10 and filed a return reporting the accumulated EE bond interest of $4,000, no tax would be added because the decedent is entitled to a standard deduction of $12,550 (if single). On the other hand, if the heir reported the $4,000 of accumulated interest and was in the 24 percent tax bracket, they would pay $960 in tax.

TIP

Say you or the person you inherited a bond from had been reporting the interest on a savings bond annually and you redeem the bond. Guess what? You'll receive a 1099-INT for the entire amount of interest the bond earned through the years. Here's what to do so you don't pay tax on interest you don't have to. Report the entire amount of interest on line 1 of Schedule B and then enter, on the line below, the amount previously reported as a <negative number>. In the space for the name of the payer, write "U.S. Savings Bond Interest Previously Reported." This is how you subtract the interest on which you previously paid tax from the total interest you have to report.

A distribution of savings bonds from a qualified retirement account gets reported as a retirement distribution. The amount you report is the cost of the bond plus the interest up to the time of distribution. When you cash in the bond you will receive a 1099-DIV for all the interest earned through the years. No problem! Just follow the instructions in the preceding paragraph on how to deal with "U.S. Savings Bond Interest Previously Reported."

Here are the rules when you buy a savings bond with someone or in someone else's name. If you buy a bond in the name of another person who is the sole owner, the owner reports the interest. If you buy a bond jointly with your money, you report the interest. If each of you put up the dough, the interest is reported in proportion to what each of you paid. In a community property state, if the bond is community property and you file separately, generally, each spouse reports half the interest.

U.S. H AND HH BONDS

H and HH bonds were issued only in exchange for E and EE bonds. All Series H bonds have now matured and are no longer paying any interest; if you still have any Series H bonds, now would be a good time to redeem them. On Series HH bonds, interest is paid semiannually, and you receive a Form 1099-INT from the government showing the amount of interest you must report. H bonds have a 30-year maturity, and HH bonds have a 20-year maturity. (H bonds were issued before 1980, and HH bonds were issued after that time, but have not been issued since 2004.)

The amount of interest earned on the E or EE bonds that you exchanged is stated on the H or HH bonds. You report this amount when you cash in the H or HH bonds.

U.S. TREASURY BILLS

U.S. Treasury bills are short-term obligations of the U.S. government, issued at a discount. These bills mature in 1, 2, 3, 6, or 12 months. You report the interest in the year the bill matures, not when you purchase it.

For example, suppose that you purchase a $10,000, six-month T-bill for $9,700 in December 2021. You report the $300 of interest you earned when the bill matures in 2022. This maneuver is an excellent way to defer income to the next year.

Interest on U.S. Treasury bonds, notes, and bills is exempt from state tax.

TIP

I-BONDS

I-bonds are similar to EE bonds. The difference is that the interest that is paid at maturity (30 years) or when the bond is cashed in is linked to inflation. I-bonds are issued in denominations as low as $25 for electronic transactions, $50 for bonds issued on paper.

How do I-bonds stack up against regular inflation-indexed Treasury bonds? A regular inflation-indexed bond carries a fixed rate of interest, with the principal adjusted annually to keep up with inflation. Whereas I-bond holders don't pay tax until the bond is cashed in, holders of regular inflation-indexed bonds have to pay tax every year on the interest payment and the capital gains tax on the inflation-index increase in the value of the bond. Unlike I-bonds, regular inflation-indexed bonds can be purchased only in $1,000 denominations.

ZERO-COUPON BONDS

Zero-coupon bonds don't pay annual interest, but they are issued at a discount very similar to U.S. Savings Bonds. Each year, the bond increases in value equal to the amount of interest it is considered to have earned. In tax lingo, this is referred to as *original issue discount* (OID). Each year, the issuer or your broker will compute the amount of interest you have to report and send you a Form 1099-OID.

INTEREST ON BONDS BOUGHT OR SOLD

When you buy a bond between the interest payment dates, you pay the seller the interest that was earned up to the sale date.

For example, suppose that on April 30 you buy a bond that makes semiannual interest payments of $600 on June 30. You must pay the seller $400 for the interest earned up to April 30. You report the $600 in interest that you received for the bond on Schedule B. On the line below, subtract the $400 of interest you paid the seller, and to the left of the $400 amount, write "Accrued Interest Paid." Enter the $400 as a negative amount, <$400>. That's how you subtract the $400 of interest that you paid from the total interest reported.

JOINT RETURNS, MINORS, AND INTEREST STUFF

If your Social Security number is the one that's reported on the 1099-INT, the computers at the IRS check to see whether the interest from the 1099-INT is on your return. On a joint return, either your SSN or your spouse's number can be on the account because you're filing jointly.

But what about an account owned by you and someone other than your spouse (or if you're merely holding the money for someone else)? Suppose that only 50 percent of the $1,200 reported under your SSN is yours. Report the $1,200 on Schedule B, and on the line below, subtract the $600 belonging to the other person. In the space for the name of the payer, write "Nominee Distribution." Enter the $600 as a negative number, <$600>. This is how you subtract the $600 from the total that you must report, but that doesn't belong to you. The rules also require that you issue that person Form 1099-INT for their $600. What a pain!

When a minor has an account, make sure that the minor's Social Security number is on the account. If a minor has more than $1,100 in unearned income such as interest and dividends, the minor must file a return. If the minor is under the age of 19 (or under age 24 and a full-time student providing less than half of their own support), with interest and investment income exceeding $2,200, the excess is taxed at the parent's tax rate (find out more about the Kiddie Tax in Chapter 17).

Unfortunately, paying and receiving bond interest is sometimes not as easy as pie. The following list shows you how to account for a variety of situations where you need to make adjustments to the interest you receive (or pay):

>> **Sales and purchases between interest dates:** Say you sold a bond for $1,040, $25 of which represents interest on the bond that was earned but not yet paid. Here's how this plays out:

- In the year of the sale, $25 is reported as interest income. Next, you reduce the $1,040 you received by the $25 because the $25 is reported as interest income on Schedule B, but your proceeds for the sale of the bond are $1,015, which will be reported on Schedule D. Your selling price for computing your gain or loss is $1,015. If you paid $1,000 for the bond, you have a $15 gain. Chapter 14 shows you how to report the sale of a capital asset, in this case, a bond.

- When the buyer receives the next interest payment, they are entitled to reduce the payment by the $25 of interest they paid to you. Next, they make a reduction in their tax basis. They reduce the $1,040 by $25 and use $1,015 as their tax basis (cost) when they sell the bond to determine whether they have a profit or loss.

>> **Bond premiums and discounts:** Say you purchase a bond for $1,000 that pays 6 percent ($60) and matures in ten years at a $100 premium, for a total initial cost to you of $1,100. You can elect to deduct $10 ($100 ÷ 10 years) of the premium each year, so you have to pay tax on only $50. Enter $60 on line 1 of Schedule B. On the next line, enter <$10>, as a negative number. Next to this amount, write "ABP Adjustment," which stands for *amortized bond premium.* Here's a plain English definition of amortization: It's the $10 deduction you're entitled to. Additionally, every year you have to reduce the $1,100 you paid by the $10 you get to deduct. This is a current deduction that many investors fail to claim. If you don't make this election in the year of purchase, you treat the $100 as part of the cost of the bond in determining your profit or loss on its sale or maturity.

Reversing the earlier example, say you purchased a $1,000, 6 percent bond that matures in ten years at a $100 discount for $900. When the bond matures, you report the $100 as interest. Suppose you sell the bond for $950 after owning it for only five years; you don't have a capital gain of $50. Instead, you have interest income of $50. Adding a different twist to the example, you sell the bond after five years for $960. You report $50 as interest income ($10 × 5 years) and $10 as a capital gain. Instead of doing it this way, you can elect to report a portion of the $100 as interest income ratable over ten years at a rate of $10 a year. You make this election in the year of purchase by simply reporting the $10 as interest. If you make the election, every year you add the $10 to your tax basis of the bond. You may want to report the income annually because you have a lot of investment interest expense that can't be deducted because you don't have enough investment income to offset the interest expense (see investment interest in Chapter 11, line 9). This rule, which requires that part of the discount be reported as interest instead of capital gain, applies to bonds issued after July 19, 1984, regardless of when you bought them. For tax-exempt bonds, which we'll get to in a moment, this rule applies to bonds purchased after April 30, 1993, regardless of when the bond was issued.

TAX REFUNDS

Interest you receive on all tax refunds is taxable interest. You should include only the interest portion of your refund, whether it's federal, state, or local, on Schedule B (1040). Remember, a refund of federal taxes that you've paid isn't taxable. State and local tax refunds may be, depending on whether you received a tax benefit from their deduction on Schedule A in 2020. Look at Chapter 6 to see whether or not you have to declare your state income tax refund as income on your 2021 federal return.

TAX-EXEMPT BONDS (MUNICIPAL BONDS)

Tax-exempt interest (interest on city and state bonds) is reported to you on Form 1099-INT in box 8. You report this income on Form 1040, line 2a. Although this entry on line 2q isn't added to your taxable income, it is used to determine the amount of your Social Security that may be subject to tax, and if you are itemizing your deductions and have investment interest to report on Schedule A, line 9, you also may be required to allocate that investment interest expense between taxable and tax-exempt income.

Most states have a provision that tax-exempt bonds are exempt from state income tax only if the bonds are issued by that state. For example, a New York State resident pays state income tax on a tax-exempt bond issued by Ohio but doesn't pay state income tax on a tax-exempt bond issued by New York.

If you purchase a *municipal bond* at a discount — for example, a $1,000, 10-year, 6 percent bond for $900 — you have $100 of taxable interest at maturity. This isn't a misprint. The $100 is taxable. Say you sell the bond after five years for $960. You report $50 as interest and $10 as a capital gain. Here's the math on how this nasty bit of business is computed. Every year during the ten years until the bond matures, $10 of the discount is considered interest ($100 ÷ 10). This amounts to $50 during the five years you own the bond. The $50 is reported as interest and is added to the $900 you paid to figure your capital gain. All this probably comes as a surprise to you because you more than likely thought that 100 percent of the income on a municipal bond was tax-exempt. Just like a taxable bond, you can elect to report the discount annually. The interest the bond earns every year is tax-exempt, but not the discount you receive when either the bond matures or is sold.

Line 2: Total interest

Add all the amounts on line 1.

Line 3: U.S. Savings Bonds — education program

TAX CUT

One tax shelter that most people are unaware of is that Uncle Sam wants you to put money aside for the education of your children and provides you with a tax exemption to boot. All or part of the interest on certain Series EE or Series I U.S. savings bonds used to pay college tuition is exempt from tax under the following conditions:

>> The U.S. savings bonds were issued after December 31, 1989.

>> You're 24 years of age or older before the month in which you buy the bonds.

>> The total redemption proceeds — interest and principal — don't exceed the tuition and fees paid for the year. (Room and board aren't considered a part of tuition.) The tuition and fees paid have to be reduced by any nontaxable scholarships.

>> The tuition is for you, your spouse, or your dependents.

>> The exclusion isn't available if you're married filing separately.

>> The bond must be issued in either your name or in your name and your spouse's name as co-owners.

The amount of interest that can be excluded is reduced if your 2021 AGI meets the following requirements:

>> Unmarried taxpayers with an income of $83,200 or less are entitled to a full interest exclusion. Between incomes of $83,200 and $98,200, the exclusion is gradually phased out.

>> Married people filing jointly get a complete interest exclusion if their income is under $124,800 with a phase-out range between $124,800 and $154,800.

>> The preceding income limits are based on your AGI (Form 1040, line 11), adding back any student loan interest deduction (Form 1040, Schedule 1, Part II, line 21), foreign earned income and housing exclusion (Form 2555 or 2555-EZ), and the exclusion from income for employer-provided adoption assistance (Form 8839, line 20).

The amount of interest that you can exclude is computed on Form 8815, Exclusion of Interest from Series EE and I U.S. Savings Bonds Issued after 1989. The amount of excludable interest is entered on Schedule B, line 3, and the total interest is listed on line 1. For example, suppose you earned $500 of interest, all of which is excludable. You enter the $500 on lines 3 and 1.

WARNING

You can't redeem a bond and exclude the interest because you're paying higher education expenses and at the same time use those expenses to compute an American Opportunity Credit or Lifetime Learning credit, nor can you take tax-free distributions from either a Section 529 plan or a Coverdell Education Savings Account. Choose one; double dipping isn't allowed! Check out Chapter 26 for more on your higher education savings options. For all practical purposes, the amount of tax savings available from this particular tax strategy is far less than those you'll receive from any of the other tax strategies, such as available credits or using a Section 529 plan or a Coverdell Education Savings Account. You want to make certain you can't use any of those methods first before you see if you qualify for this one.

Interest-free loans

Some wise person once said that no good deed ever goes unpunished, and that is never truer than with interest-free loans. If you make an interest-free loan to someone, the IRS assumes the borrower paid you interest anyway. Welcome to the world of *imputed interest*, where the IRS *imputes* (states) what the minimum rate should be and then taxes you on it, whether you've actually charged it or not. In this strange new world, the borrower can deduct the interest they are considered to have paid if they use the money to make an investment that produces income, while you are required to report that same amount as income, despite the fact that no money has changed hands. For the applicable minimum rates, go to the IRS web page (www.irs.gov).

WARNING

To make this world even more interesting, there are gift tax consequences to this interest-free loan as well. The fact that interest should have been charged but wasn't creates a taxable gift of the interest amount. The person you lent the money to now not only gets the interest-free loan, but also a gift of the amount of interest that he should have paid to you. If it's a small loan, this information may be of little or no consequence to you — you pay the additional income tax and go merrily on your way. If, on the other hand, you've lent someone a large amount, to purchase a house or a business, perhaps, the annual interest you should be charging but aren't can be more than the annual exclusion amount of $15,000. Think before you get involved in interest-free loans — the tax consequences to you can be ferocious!

Rules for interest-free loans also apply to below-market-rate loans.

As with every other IRS rule, there are exceptions to this rule. Here they are:

>> Loans under $10,000 aren't subject to the rule.

>> For loans between $10,000 and $100,000, interest isn't imputed (that is, assumed to have been made) if the borrower's investment income for the year doesn't exceed $1,000. If the borrower's income exceeds $1,000, the imputed interest is limited to that amount of the person's investment income. Say you lend your son $50,000. If his investment income is under $1,000, no interest is imputed (considered to have been paid). If his investment income is $1,200, that's all the interest you have to report, even if you should have charged him $4,000.

>> Certain employee relocation loans to buy a new residence aren't subject to the interest-free loan rule that requires a minimum rate to be charged. See your company's employment benefits office or a tax advisor.

>> If the loan exceeds $100,000, you have to deal with the imputed interest rule in its full glory.

Interest-free or below-market-rate-of-interest loans usually occur when a family member taps you for money. In many cases, these types of loans end up not being repaid (see Chapter 14). If scaring someone off with the imputed interest rules doesn't work, try Shakespeare's "neither a borrower nor a lender be."

A lender reporting imputed interest or a borrower claiming an interest deduction must attach a statement to their return indicating how the interest was computed, the loan balance, the name of the borrower or lender, and the borrower's or lender's Social Security number. (If you're the borrower, it's the lender's number, and vice versa.) That should also frighten most would-be borrowers off. As a general rule, when the parties to a below-market-rate-of-interest loan don't make the imputed interest calculations, the IRS ends up drooling over doing it when an audit of either the borrower or the lender uncovers the loan.

Part II, Lines 5–6: Dividend Income

Well, we hope that you made a good bit of extra dough in Part I. Part II provides another opportunity to count your silver coins — er, we mean dividends. You find out about your dividends from another version of a 1099. Anyone who pays you a dividend is required to send you Form

1099-DIV, Dividends and Distributions (see Figure 12-3) by January 31, 2022. If your 1099-DIV is incorrect, get the payer to correct it; otherwise, you may pay tax on income you never earned. Getting an incorrect 1099 corrected isn't as much of a headache as it used to be; the telephone number of the person you need to contact is listed on the form.

☐ CORRECTED (if checked)

PAYER'S name, street address, city or town, state or province, country, ZIP or foreign postal code, and telephone no.		1a Total ordinary dividends $	OMB No. 1545-0110 20**21** Form **1099-DIV**	Dividends and Distributions
		1b Qualified dividends $		
		2a Total capital gain distr. $	2b Unrecap. Sec. 1250 gain $	**Copy B** **For Recipient**
PAYER'S TIN	RECIPIENT'S TIN	2c Section 1202 gain $	2d Collectibles (28%) gain $	
		2e Section 897 ordinary dividends $	2f Section 897 capital gain $	
RECIPIENT'S name		3 Nondividend distributions $	4 **Federal income tax withheld** $	This is important tax information and is being furnished to the IRS. If you are required to file a return, a negligence penalty or other sanction may be imposed on you if this income is taxable and the IRS determines that it has not been reported.
		5 Section 199A dividends $	6 Investment expenses $	
Street address (including apt. no.)		7 Foreign tax paid $	8 Foreign country or U.S. possession	
City or town, state or province, country, and ZIP or foreign postal code		9 Cash liquidation distributions $	10 Noncash liquidation distributions $	
	FATCA filing requirement ☐	11 Exempt-interest dividends $	12 Specified private activity bond interest dividends $	
Account number (see instructions)		13 State 14 State identification no.	15 State tax withheld $ ------- $	

Form **1099-DIV** (keep for your records) www.irs.gov/Form1099DIV Department of the Treasury - Internal Revenue Service

Source: Internal Revenue Service

FIGURE 12-3: Form 1099-DIV shows you the dividends you reaped in 2021.

To report the income from jointly owned stock, follow the rules explained for reporting interest on a joint bank account in the sidebar "Joint returns, minors, and interest stuff," earlier in this chapter.

WARNING

Watch out for corrected 1099s. If you file really early, you may need to file an amended return. (April 15 comes only once a year; it's best that way.)

Line 5: Name, payer, and amount

Schedule B, Part II, has a column for the payer's name and a column for the amount of the dividend you received. Enter the payer's name in the column that says to list the name of the payer. Enter the amount of the dividend you received in the column that says "amount." For each 1099-DIV you received, enter the name of the payer and the amount received.

Line 6: Total dividends

This is the easy part. Total all the dividends you listed on line 5 and enter that amount on line 3b of your 1040.

Your 1099-DIV: Decoding those boxes

Here's what all those boxes on your 1099–DIV mean:

>> **Box 1a: Total ordinary dividends.** Enter the total amount of your ordinary dividends on line 5. Make sure you list the payer's name to the left of the amount column.

If the total of your ordinary dividends doesn't exceed $1,500, skip Part II and enter the total on line 3b of Form 1040.

>> **Box 1b: Qualified dividends.** These dividends are eligible for either the 0, 15, or 20 percent rates, depending on the amount of your total income. Enter this amount on line 3a of Form 1040. The portion of your total dividends (line 3b) less your qualified dividends (line 3a) ends up getting taxed at whatever bracket your taxable income (Form 1040, line 15) places you in. Now that can't be simpler, can it?

>> **Boxes 2a–2f: Capital gain distributions.** Capital gains, although reported on Form 1099-DIV, aren't entered on Schedule B. Enter them on Schedule D.

- Box 2a has the total capital gain distributions. Enter this amount on Schedule D, line 13 — see Chapter 14. If the only amounts you have to report on Schedule D are capital gain distributions from box 2a because you have no other capital gains or losses and no amounts are entered in boxes 2b through 2f, you don't have to file Schedule D. Enter the amounts from box 2a on Form 1040, line 7, and check the box.

- Box 2b is for certain real estate capital gain dividends, those tricky unrecaptured Section 1250 gains. This is your opportunity to go directly to the "Unrecaptured Section 1250 Gain Worksheet" located in the Schedule D instructions of your 1040 Instruction Booklet. Follow this worksheet carefully to find out how much, if any, of this number lands on Line 19 of your Schedule D.

- Box 2c indicates the amount of a gain from a small business start-up and specialized small business investment companies; depending on when the stock was purchased, you may exclude 50, 75, or even 100 percent of these types of gains from tax. This is a highly technical area of the tax code; if you're not sure whether the stock you sold qualifies for this exclusion, or how much of the total gain on the sale you may exclude, consult a tax professional.

- Box 2d indicates the amount of the total gain in box 2a that gets taxed at 28 percent instead of the lower capital gain rate. This is the rate for the gain on the sale of collectibles (art, antiques, and so on). You get to do another worksheet (come on, they're fun!) found in the Schedule D instructions called "28% Rate Gain Worksheet" before putting any number on Line 18 of your Schedule D.

- Boxes 2e and 2f, Section 897 ordinary dividends and Section 897 capital gain, respectively, are only applicable if you are a foreign individual with a requirement to file a U.S. tax return. It does not apply to U.S. citizens or residents. Once again, this is a highly specialized area, and you may want to consult a tax professional.

To make sure you don't overpay the tax on capital gain distributions, go to Chapter 10, where we show you how to accurately calculate your income tax liability using the Schedule D worksheet.

WHEN IS A DIVIDEND *NOT* A DIVIDEND?

Stock dividends and splits

Stock dividends (not the cash variety) and splits aren't taxable. You now own more shares!

For example, suppose that you own 100 shares. If the stock is split two for one, you now own 200 shares. If you receive a 10 percent stock dividend, you now own 110 shares. Chapter 14 explains how you treat the shares that you received when they are sold.

Life insurance dividends

Life insurance dividends aren't taxable until the total dividends received exceed the total premiums paid.

Savings dividends

So-called dividends from savings and loans, credit unions, savings banks, and bond and money market funds have to be reported as interest.

>> **Box 3: Non-dividend distributions.** These used to be called "nontaxable distributions," and that is what they are: nontaxable. These non-dividend distributions aren't entered on your return, and you don't currently pay tax on them as dividends. What these distributions do is reduce the basis of your shares when figuring your gain or loss when the shares are sold. For example, suppose that you purchased shares in a company or a mutual fund for $10,000, and you received $500 in non-dividend distributions. Your basis for determining gain or loss when you sell the shares is now $9,500.

>> **Box 4: Federal tax withheld.** Report your federal tax withheld on Form 1040, line 25b.

>> **Box 5; Section 199A dividends.** Any amount in this box is included in Box 1a and passes through to you from a real estate investment trust (REIT) or registered investment company (RIC). It does not qualify for the qualified dividend rate but does qualify for a deduction of 20 percent of the amount in box 5 if other conditions are met. Check out Chapter 10 for help with filling out Form 8995 or Form 8995-A.

>> **Box 6: Investment expenses.** This box refers to shares you own in funds not available to the public, so it doesn't apply to most people. We have yet to see a 1099-DIV with an entry in this box! (But it must be there for a reason!) If this box applies to you, it means that you own shares in a non-publicly traded fund. You can deduct this expense as an itemized deduction on Schedule A, line 9 (see Chapter 11). Publicly traded funds don't pass investment expenses on to shareholders.

>> **Box 7: Foreign tax paid.** If you own shares in a company or fund that was required to pay tax in a foreign country, your share of the tax is recorded in box 7. You can claim this amount as a credit against your tax or as an itemized deduction. We discuss how to handle this in Chapter 11.

>> **Box 8: Foreign country or U.S. possession.** This one is easy. It states the country or U.S. possession where the tax was paid. You need this information when you fill out Form 1116, Foreign Tax Credit. See Chapter 16.

>> **Boxes 9 and 10: Cash and noncash liquidation distributions.** You report these amounts (cash and noncash) on Schedule D (Capital Gains and Losses). If you have entries in these two boxes, see a tax advisor. And check out Chapter 14 to find out more about Schedule D.

>> **Box 11: FATCA filing requirement.** This is a new item on the 2021 Form 1099-DIV, and payers (that's the company that is issuing you the 1099-DIV) are required to check this box in order to satisfy reporting requirements connected with Chapter 4 of the Internal Revenue Code. We haven't yet seen any versions of 2021 tax software, but there will likely be a box to check on your input form. If you find it, check the box; if you don't, well, we wouldn't worry too much about this one.

>> **Box 12: Exempt-interest dividends.** If you've invested during 2021 in any tax-exempt mutual funds, the dividends paid over the course of the year will be listed here. If you're using tax software, any amounts you put into this box on your input form will automatically carry to Form 1040, line 2a, tax-exempt interest. If you're preparing your return on paper, you want to be sure to add this amount to any tax-exempt interest reported to you on Form 1099-INT, and place the total on Form 1040, line 2a.

>> **Box 13: Specified private activity bond interest dividends.** If you own a tax-exempt mutual fund during 2021, chances are better than good that at least a portion of that fund will be invested in so-called "private activity bonds," which are bonds issued to fund joint public/private projects, such as a utility plant or a sports stadium. While the interest on these bonds is exempt from tax in the ordinary income tax world, if you're subject to the alternative minimum tax, the amount in Box 13 will be added back to income and will be taxed under the AMT. Fortunately, now that far fewer people are subject to the AMT since the passage of the Tax Cuts and Jobs Act of 2017, chances are good that you won't be taxed on this item.

Reduced tax rates on dividends

WARNING

The reduced 0, 15, and 20 percent maximum tax rates for qualified dividends don't apply to all dividends. What, exactly, is a qualified dividend?

Qualified dividends are those dividends paid by

>> U.S. corporations

>> A corporation incorporated in a U.S. possession

>> Foreign corporations traded on a U.S. stock exchange

>> A foreign corporation whose shares aren't traded on a U.S. market, from a country that has a comprehensive tax treaty with the United States that includes a program providing for the exchange of tax information. Because not many countries have such a comprehensive treaty with the United States, this will probably cause many investors in international funds to rethink whether it makes sense to continue to hold shares that don't entitle them to preferred tax treatment on their dividends.

Not only do you have to know where qualified dividends come from, but you also have to know what dividends aren't considered qualified and eligible for the reduced rates. These are dividends paid by

>> Banks on certificates of deposit

>> Bond funds

>> Credit unions

>> Farmers' cooperatives

>> Money market funds

>> Mutual insurance companies

>> Real estate investment trusts (REITs)

>> Savings banks and savings and loans

>> Tax-exempt corporations

Three other categories of dividends that aren't considered qualified are

>> Dividends paid on stock purchased with borrowed funds, if the dividend was included in investment income in claiming a deduction for investment interest (Chapter 11, line 9 provides a plain English explanation of what this is all about).

>> Payments in lieu of a dividend on a short sale (see Chapter 14).

>> Dividends on stock owned less than 60 days in the 121-day period surrounding the ex-dividend date, or the date the stock trades without the announced dividend, which is normally two days before the record day, the day when the company determines who is the record owner of the stock. You need to have owned the stock 60 days out of the 121-day period beginning 61 days before the ex-dividend day.

WARNING Qualified dividends that mutual funds receive (from stock holdings) and in turn distribute to you remain qualified and are eligible for the reduced rates. Because qualified dividends received by IRAs, 401(k)s, and retirement accounts are paid in a tax-free environment, you won't pay tax on these dividends as long as the stock is held in one of these accounts. As soon as you begin taking distributions, though, you don't get the reduced rate; all distributions from IRAs (unless you made after-tax contributions), 401(k)s, and other retirement accounts are treated as ordinary income, and receive no preferential income tax treatment. Sorry!

Part III, Lines 7–8: Foreign Accounts and Trusts

If you have a foreign bank or security account, you have to check "yes" on line 7a of Schedule B and enter the name of the foreign country. However, if the highest aggregate balance in all of your foreign accounts in 2021 was under $10,000, you can check "no." But if you had more than a total of $10,000 in foreign banks or security accounts during the year, then you have to file FinCEN Form 114, by the due date for your 2021 income tax return, as extended. On this form, you have to list where your account(s) are located, including the name of the bank, security firm, or brokerage firm; its address; and the account number. FinCEN Form 114 must be filed electronically; most income tax software packages have this form available, although you may have some trouble finding it. It will also need to be electronically transmitted separate from your income tax returns.

WARNING

Don't treat FinCEN Form 114 lightly. Although the penalties for failure to timely file any IRS form are monetary, the failure to file FinCEN Form 114 is a felony, punishable by a five-year prison term. If you need help or aren't sure what to do here, seek advice!

SEEK ADVICE

If you're unique enough to have to deal with line 8, it means that you have a foreign trust. You have to check "yes" and complete Form 3520, Annual Return to Report Transactions With Foreign Trusts and Receipt of Certain Foreign Gifts, or Form 926, Return by a U.S. Transferor of Property to a Foreign Corporation (the trustee completes Form 3520-A). Good luck! (These forms are complicated; seriously consider using a tax advisor.)

If you received a distribution from a foreign partnership or corporation in excess of $16,815 (this amount gets adjusted for inflation every year) that you have treated as a gift, you have to report it to the IRS. If you receive a gift or inheritance from a foreign individual or estate above $100,000, you also have to provide the IRS with the foreigner's name and address. Report this information on Form 3520. You also have to file Form 3520 if you're an owner of a foreign trust or if you received a distribution from one regardless of the amount. The penalty for not filing or for filing an incomplete or incorrect Form 3520 starts at $10,000 and heads up from there. Evidently, a lot of people were claiming that what they earned abroad was a gift or bequest. The amount you report to the IRS as a gift or inheritance isn't taxable. The IRS does, however, want to know about it. A distribution from a foreign trust, partnership, or corporation more than likely is taxable.

The due date for filing Form 3520 is April 18, 2022 (April 19, 2022, for residents of Maine and Massachusetts). Extending your Form 1040 automatically also extends Form 3520. File the form separately to: Internal Revenue Service Center, PO Box 409101, Ogden, UT 84409; do not attach it to your return. Form 3520 must be paper filed.

WARNING

Taxpayers with interest earned in Canadian Registered Retirement Savings Plans are probably unaware that they must file Form 3520. If you haven't been doing this, the good news is that the IRS has pardoned all those who haven't filed the form for all years before 2002. Starting with 2002, you either have to file Form 3520 or attach a statement to your return every year that you're claiming the benefit of Article XVIII (7) of the treaty, including the name of the savings plan's trustee, the account number, and the balance in the account at the beginning of the year. The amount in the plan isn't taxable until distributions are made.

Chapter **13**

Business Tax Schedules: C and F

R unning your own firm really can be the American dream. In fact, the only thing better than working for yourself is knowing how to keep more of what you earn. It's like giving yourself an immediate raise at tax time.

If you're self-employed, you must report your income and business expenses on Schedule C. If you are used to filing on Schedule C-EZ, that form was discontinued in 2019; going forward, Schedule C is your only choice for a business run as a sole proprietorship or a single-member LLC that has not made an election to be treated as an S corporation. You determine your profit, on which you pay tax, by subtracting your expenses from your income. (Farmers use Schedule F instead, but many of the same principles apply.)

REMEMBER

Married couples who operate a small business together no longer have to prepare and file an additional tax return to report their small-business activity, provided they file a joint return. You have the option of reporting your business income on a Schedule C for each of you, splitting the income and expenses of your business between both of you. Allocating the income between you allows each of you to receive credit for Social Security and Medicare tax contributions. Remember, this is an optional method; you can continue to prepare partnership returns for your business, if you prefer.

Schedule C

This schedule isn't as bad as it looks (see Figure 13-1). In this chapter, we take you through Parts I and II of Schedule C and give line-by-line instructions.

SCHEDULE C (Form 1040)

Department of the Treasury
Internal Revenue Service (99)

Profit or Loss From Business
(Sole Proprietorship)

▶ Go to *www.irs.gov/ScheduleC* for instructions and the latest information.
▶ **Attach to Form 1040, 1040-SR, 1040-NR, or 1041; partnerships must generally file Form 1065.**

OMB No. 1545-0074

2021

Attachment
Sequence No. **09**

Name of proprietor

Social security number (SSN)

A Principal business or profession, including product or service (see instructions)

B Enter code from instructions ▶

C Business name. If no separate business name, leave blank.

D Employer ID number (EIN) (see instr.)

E Business address (including suite or room no.) ▶
City, town or post office, state, and ZIP code

F Accounting method: (1) ☐ Cash (2) ☐ Accrual (3) ☐ Other (specify) ▶

G Did you "materially participate" in the operation of this business during 2021? If "No," see instructions for limit on losses ☐ Yes ☐ No

H If you started or acquired this business during 2021, check here ▶ ☐

I Did you make any payments in 2021 that would require you to file Form(s) 1099? See instructions ☐ Yes ☐ No

J If "Yes," did you or will you file required Form(s) 1099? ☐ Yes ☐ No

Part I Income

1	Gross receipts or sales. See instructions for line 1 and check the box if this income was reported to you on Form W-2 and the "Statutory employee" box on that form was checked ▶ ☐	1
2	Returns and allowances	2
3	Subtract line 2 from line 1	3
4	Cost of goods sold (from line 42)	4
5	**Gross profit.** Subtract line 4 from line 3	5
6	Other income, including federal and state gasoline or fuel tax credit or refund (see instructions)	6
7	**Gross income.** Add lines 5 and 6 ▶	7

Part II Expenses. Enter expenses for business use of your home **only** on line 30.

8	Advertising	8		18	Office expense (see instructions)	18
9	Car and truck expenses (see instructions)	9		19	Pension and profit-sharing plans	19
10	Commissions and fees	10		20	Rent or lease (see instructions):	
11	Contract labor (see instructions)	11		a	Vehicles, machinery, and equipment	20a
12	Depletion	12		b	Other business property	20b
13	Depreciation and section 179 expense deduction (not included in Part III) (see instructions)	13		21	Repairs and maintenance	21
				22	Supplies (not included in Part III)	22
				23	Taxes and licenses	23
				24	Travel and meals:	
14	Employee benefit programs (other than on line 19)	14		a	Travel	24a
15	Insurance (other than health)	15		b	Deductible meals (see instructions)	24b
16	Interest (see instructions):			25	Utilities	25
a	Mortgage (paid to banks, etc.)	16a		26	Wages (less employment credits)	26
b	Other	16b		27a	Other expenses (from line 48)	27a
17	Legal and professional services	17		b	Reserved for future use	27b

28	**Total expenses** before expenses for business use of home. Add lines 8 through 27a ▶	28	
29	Tentative profit or (loss). Subtract line 28 from line 7	29	
30	Expenses for business use of your home. Do not report these expenses elsewhere. Attach Form 8829 unless using the simplified method. See instructions.		
	Simplified method filers only: Enter the total square footage of (a) your home: _____ and (b) the part of your home used for business: _____. Use the Simplified Method Worksheet in the instructions to figure the amount to enter on line 30	30	
31	**Net profit or (loss).** Subtract line 30 from line 29.		
	• If a profit, enter on both **Schedule 1 (Form 1040), line 3,** and on **Schedule SE, line 2.** (If you checked the box on line 1, see instructions). Estates and trusts, enter on **Form 1041, line 3.**	31	
	• If a loss, you **must** go to line 32.		
32	If you have a loss, check the box that describes your investment in this activity. See instructions.		
	• If you checked 32a, enter the loss on both **Schedule 1 (Form 1040), line 3,** and on **Schedule SE, line 2.** (If you checked the box on line 1, see the line 31 instructions.) Estates and trusts, enter on **Form 1041, line 3.**	32a ☐ All investment is at risk.	
	• If you checked 32b, you **must** attach **Form 6198.** Your loss may be limited.	32b ☐ Some investment is not at risk.	

For Paperwork Reduction Act Notice, see the separate instructions.   Cat. No. 11334P   Schedule C (Form 1040) 2021

FIGURE 13-1: Schedule C, Page 1.

Source: Internal Revenue Service

Basic Information (A–E)

Lines A through D are pretty easy background stuff. Employer ID Numbers can now be obtained instantly by applying online at www.irs.gov/businesses; then click on "Employer ID Number (EIN)." You can also fax your information to 855-641-6935 if you're in one of the 50 states or the District of Columbia; 855-215-1627 if you have no legal residence, principal place of business, or principal office or agency in any state but you're still located in the United States; or 304-707-9471 if you're located outside the United States; or go the paper route by sending a completed Form SS-4, Application For Employer Identification Number, to the IRS at Internal Revenue Service, Attn: EIN Operation (EIN International Operation, if you're applying from outside the U.S.), Cincinnati, OH 45999. You can pick up your business code from the list located in the Schedule C section of your 2021 Form 1040 instruction booklet. On line E, simply fill in your business address.

Accounting Method Stuff (Boxes F–H)

The two methods to report income are *cash* and *accrual*. With the cash method, you report income when it's actually received, and you deduct expenses when they're actually paid. However, there is (of course) one exception to this rule: If you charge an expense on a credit card, you deduct this expense in the year charged, even if you pay the charge in a later year. (So, don't leave home without it!)

Does your business take in $25 million or less, and has it done so for each of the three preceding years, or since the start of the business if the business has not been in existence for at least three years? We knew that would get a smile out of you. If so, then you can use the cash method of accounting, but only if a bunch of restrictions don't apply. If you're in a purely service business, then you don't have to worry about these restrictions. You can use the cash method and skip the following paragraph.

If you're in the wholesale or retail trade, manufacturing, information services, or mining, then you can't use the cash method. However, this rule does have its exceptions: Even if you're in one of these businesses that disqualifies you from using the cash method, you still can use it if providing a service is the main thing you do. For example, you're a publisher (information services) whose main activity is the sale of advertising space. You can use the cash method even though information services isn't one of the businesses normally allowed to use the cash method. The reason? The sale of advertising space is considered a service. Similarly, businesses that manufacture or modify a product to a customer's specifications and design may use the cash method even though manufacturing isn't an eligible business.

TIP

A small business whose average annual income for the three prior tax years is $25 million or less may use the cash method regardless of its line of business. However, it can deduct the purchase of merchandise for resale only when it's sold and not when it's purchased, so read on.

Even though some people are permitted to use the cash method, if they use materials and supplies that aren't incidental to the services they perform, they face a hitch. Roofing contractors are an example. Even though they may use the cash method, they aren't allowed to deduct the cost of the materials they purchase until the later of either when it is used on the customer's job or when they pay for it. Say a contractor paid $5,000 for shingles in December 2021 but did not install them until January 2022. Sorry, it's a 2022 tax deduction, not a 2021 deduction. (The amount the contractor charges the customer is reported in the year it is received because the contractor is using the cash method.)

Say you must use the accrual method because you operate a clothing store; you report income in the year that sales are made — even when the sales are billed or collected in a later year. You deduct expenses in the year that they're incurred, even if those expenses aren't paid until a later year.

TIP

A hybrid method of accounting also exists. Even if you have to use the accrual method to report income and deduct merchandise sold, you nevertheless can use the cash method for the rest of your expenses: rent, telephone, wages, and so on. Doing so can make your bookkeeping less complicated.

TAX CUT

If you have the choice, the cash method of accounting gives you more control over how much profit your business sees from year to year. For example, if next year looks like a slower year for you, perhaps because you plan to take a sabbatical, you may elect to push income that you may realize this year into next year instead, when you may be in a lower tax bracket because you'll have less income. You legally can do this by not invoicing for work you've performed late in the current year until January. Instead of billing that work and being paid for it in December, for example, you can send those bills in January. Likewise, you can pay more of your expenses in December instead of waiting until January. Remember, if you're selling merchandise, you have to comply with the accrual method rules, unless your average income is $1 million or less. However, you can't deduct your merchandise purchases until you sell those goods. If you're providing a service, you can use the cash method.

This tax cut is the general rule, but it may not apply to everyone. For example, if you operate a business that receives large cash advances from customers before you undertake the work, you're better off using the accrual method. That way you don't have to report the cash advances until you actually do the work.

WARNING

"Did you 'materially participate' in the operation of the business?" is a trick question designed to limit losses that someone can deduct as a silent partner. If you put up the dough, but someone other than your spouse operated a business that lost money, then you can't deduct the loss. The reason? You didn't materially participate in the operation of the business, and (as a result) you're considered to be operating a tax shelter — see the tax shelter rules in Chapter 15. Seven criteria determine *material participation.* The IRS instructions for Schedule C list them all out in detail, but we'll give you the skinny version here. The basic criteria include whether you meet either the 500- and 100-hour rules regarding material participation, whether you were the only one who did the work, whether you can prove material participation for any of the three prior taxable years in a service business such as medicine, accounting, engineering, law, performing arts, or whether you participated on a regular, continuous, and substantial basis. Pass any one of the seven and you're okay.

If you're filing Schedule C to report a working interest in an oil or gas well, you automatically get to check the "Yes" box. Why? Ever heard of the oil and gas lobby?

Finally, to finish up the questions about your business, box H asks you to tick the box if you started or acquired this business in 2021.

Information Returns (Boxes I and J)

Box I asks if you made any payments that require you to file Form(s) 1099, and the final box, box J, asks if you actually issued these 1099s if they were required. Remember, the most common forms that may need to be filed are 1099-MISC and 1099-NEC (non-employee compensation), although there may be others. The rules state that payments to an attorney, medical services provider, any other vendor (for services received, but not for goods purchased), your landlord (all contained on Form 1099-MISC), or an independent contractor (Form 1099-NEC) who is not a corporation must be $600 or more in the aggregate during 2021 to require you to provide that person or company with the appropriate Form 1099, as well as give a copy of all Forms 1099 issued to the IRS. That number drops to $10 or more for things like the payment of royalties and substitute payments in lieu of dividends or interest (Form 1099-MISC). If you're paying out timber royalties more than $10, or you sold some real estate for $600 or more in the course of operating your business, you're going to file Form 1099-S, Proceeds from Real Estate Transactions. All Forms 1099 are required to be mailed or otherwise distributed to the recipients by January 31, 2022, although it is possible to request an extension of time to file these by filing Form 8809, Application for Extension of Time to File Information Returns, which will give you an additional 30 days to find the information, and complete and file the forms.

More information about the requirements for filing the various types of information returns and their due dates is available at www.irs.gov/businesses/small-businesses-self-employed/information-return-reporting.

Part I, Lines 1–7: Income

Time to tally. This section wants you to find some gross things: gross sales, gross profits, and gross income.

Line 1: Gross receipts or sales

If you operate a service business, enter the income from fees that you actually collected (because you're reporting income under the cash method). If clients have given you either Form 1099-MISC or Form 1099-NEC to report the payments that they made to you in 2021 to the IRS, add up the amounts in box 7. Remember, even if you didn't receive a Form 1099-MISC, you're still obligated to report all of the income you received. Likewise, if you received a Form 1099-K, Payment Card and Third-Party Network Transactions from your credit card company, or from PayPal, Square, or any of the other pieces of software that allow you to make electronic payments, you'll want to include those payments here, too.

TIP

Because one of the most common causes for a love note from the IRS is that what you've put on your return doesn't match what has been reported to the IRS by other organizations/people, it's wise to itemize the different 1099s you receive, either in a separate statement that you attach to your paper Form 1040, or by inputting each 1099 into the software you're using, if you're preparing your return on your computer. Different software programs do this differently, but the two most common systems are that the numbers you input into the 1099 interview form carry right over to the schedule where they apply (Schedules B, C, D, E, and F are the most common), or you have to enter the information in two places: once into the 1099 interview form inside the software, and then into the return itself, in this case, into Schedule C.

TIP

If you're filing this form because you're a statutory employee (see Chapter 6, the section about line 1), enter the amount from box 1 of your W-2 and check the box on this line. Also check the box next to line 1 if you and your spouse are only using Schedule C to report rental real estate income not subject to self-employment tax. If you've checked this box, you only need to enter your business expenses on lines 8 through 27, and you can ignore our instructions on line 31 about paying Social Security tax, because you've either already paid it (see lines 4 and 6 of your W-2), or this particular income isn't subject to it.

If you're required to use the accrual method, enter the total of all the sales that you billed to your customers on this line.

Line 2: Returns and allowances

If you had to return any fees, enter that amount here. If any customers returned merchandise, that amount also goes on this line, along with any discounts that those customers took.

Line 3: Subtraction quiz

All that you need to do on this line is subtract your returns and allowances (line 2) from your gross receipts and sales (line 1).

Line 4: Cost of goods sold

The IRS must think that you're an accountant; otherwise, it would simply tell you to subtract the amount you paid for merchandise that you sold from your sales to arrive at this figure. Businesses that don't sell products don't have to put an amount on this line.

But because you're not an accountant — thank heavens, you say? — you have to compute the cost of the merchandise that you sold in Part III (on the back of Schedule C). Part III is a ten-line schedule where you enter your beginning inventory, the merchandise that you purchased, the salary that you paid to your production workers (if you manufacture the product that you sell), and the cost of production supplies. You total all these expenses on line 40. From this total, you subtract your ending inventory to arrive, on line 42, at the cost of the goods that you sold. This amount goes back to line 4 (where you are right now!).

Remember, you may only deduct the cost of merchandise you sold during the year, not the cost of all the merchandise that you purchased. That's why you have to subtract your *ending inventory*, which is the stuff that you didn't sell. You get to deduct what's on hand when it's sold. You enter the amount of your ending inventory on line 41. Your ending inventory gets carried over to your 2022 return. So, don't forget to enter the amount from line 41, which becomes your inventory at the beginning of the year, on line 35 of your 2022 Schedule C.

TECHNICAL STUFF

The following example explains what this inventory business is all about. Say you own a retail furniture store. In 2021, you purchased two identical chairs, one for $1,200 and the other for $1,000. You sold only one chair (we hope business is better next year). Which one did you sell? The inventory method that you select determines that.

Under the *FIFO method* — First In, First Out — the first chair purchased is deemed the first one sold. If that's the $1,200 chair, then enter the cost of the $1,000 chair on line 41, because that's the one considered on hand at the end of the year. Under the *LIFO method* — Last In, First Out — the chair purchased last is deemed to be sold first. Under this method, the $1,000 chair is considered to be sold first, so enter $1,200 on line 41, because that's the cost of the chair that's considered the unsold one. Which method is better? In a period of rising costs, it's the LIFO method. FIFO is better when costs are declining.

Line 33 also requires you to select the method that you used to value your inventory. Three methods are available — cost (box a), lower of cost or market (box b), and other (box c). Skip box c because it's too complicated. Most people check box a because it's the easiest. Although using the lower of cost or market method can increase deductions if your inventory declines in value (you get to deduct the amount of the decline), it requires you to revalue your inventory every year.

WARNING

After you select a valuation method, you can change it only with permission from the IRS.

Line 5: Gross profit

Subtract line 4 from line 3.

Line 6: Other income

Just do what the schedule orders you to do — check out the Schedule C instructions of the 1040 booklet or find them online www.irs.gov in the Forms and Publications tab if you have any questions about other income. Some of the more common — and more obscure — examples of other income include the following:

>> Federal and state gasoline or fuel tax credit

>> Fee for allowing a company to paint an advertisement on the side of your building

>> Interest on accounts receivable

>> Scrap sales

TIP

Interest that your customers pay you when they're late paying their bills should be included here. But if you have an interest-bearing bank account for your business, you can put any interest that's earned inside that account to Schedule B (see Chapter 12) instead of Schedule C. Remember, once you get to the bottom of Schedule C, any profit that you're showing is going to be subject to self-employment taxes. Why should you pay an additional 15.3 percent tax on interest earned in your bank account?

Line 7: Gross income

This amount usually is the same as the amount on line 5. But if you had other items of income, such as a refund of a prior year's expense, enter that amount on line 6 and add it to the amount on line 5 to arrive at your gross income.

Part II, Lines 8–27b: Expenses

Take a breath and get ready for all those wonderful lines that are split into two columns — so they'd all fit on one page!

Line 8: Advertising

On this line, enter the cost of any advertising that your business does to promote itself — for example, online, radio, and newspaper ads, and any other promotional materials you purchase over the course of the year. Don't forget the little ads you take out in the affinity magazines for state troopers, police, firefighters, and other service agencies. If you're paying someone to advertise for you on the internet, include that here, too. Basically, anything that has your name and business information that's seen by any segment of the public is advertising. So, go ahead and take out an ad in your local high school's football program or annual yearbook, or buy pens, pocket protectors (does anyone wear these anymore?) or coffee mugs and t-shirts with your name and logo on them; just remember to deduct the cost here.

Line 9: Car and truck expenses

If you plan to make an entry on this line, be sure to answer questions 43 through 47b in Part IV on the other side of Schedule C, commonly referred to as page 2.

When you use your car for business, the expenses of operating your car are deductible. But remember that "using it for business" is the key phrase. You can compute this deduction by using either a flat rate per business mile (see the "Standard mileage rate" sidebar), or you can keep track of actual expenses (gas, oil, repairs, insurance, depreciation, and so on). Regardless of which method you use, you're supposed to keep a log or diary so that you can record the business purpose of your trips as well as the mileage ("Dear Diary . . ."). You also have to record the odometer reading at the beginning and end of the year. You need all this information to be able to divide your expenses into personal and business use. But here's a word of caution: Whether you use the flat rate or tabulate your actual expenses, proving that you use your car 100 percent for business is just about impossible. Unfortunately, there's always some personal use!

You don't have to write down the miles that you travel every time you get in and out of your car. Making entries in your diary on a weekly basis meets the IRS requirement that you keep a record of your car's business use near or at the time of its use.

No help from Uncle Sam with commuting expenses

Commuting expenses between your home and office aren't deductible. These expenses are considered personal commuting expenses, no matter how far your home is from your office or place of work. And making telephone calls from your car while commuting or having a business discussion with a business associate who accompanies you doesn't turn your ride into a deductible expense (besides, you should be watching the road). Using your car to display advertising material on your way to the office doesn't count as business use of your auto, either. Finally, the cost of parking at your place of business isn't deductible — but the cost of parking when you visit a customer or client is.

If you use your car to call on clients or customers and don't have a regular office to go to, the mileage between your home and the first customer that you call on — and the mileage between the location of the last customer that you call on and your home — is considered commuting. If your office is in your home, you can deduct all your auto expenses for calling on clients or customers. Use line 44 to split out your commuting from your business miles.

During these pandemic years, when many of us were working virtually from home, driving from home to a client, or running a business-related errand became business mileage because your office was in your home during any period when your physical office was closed due to COVID-19.

Second job

You can deduct the cost of getting from one job to the other if you hold more than one job. But transportation expenses going from your home to a part-time job on a day off from your main job aren't deductible. A meeting of an Armed Forces Reserve unit is considered travel to a second job, however; if it's held on the same day as your regular job, it's deductible.

Temporary job site

If you have a regular place of business and commute to a temporary work location, you can deduct the cost of the daily round trip between your home and the temporary job site.

If you don't have a regular place of work (but ordinarily work at different locations in the general area where you live), you can't deduct the daily round trip between your home and your temporary job site. But if you travel to a job site outside your general area, your daily transportation is deductible. Sounds like a distinction without a difference, right? But if this exception applies to you, don't look a gift horse in the mouth.

You can deduct the business portion of the following: depreciation, leasing and rental fees, garage rent, licenses, repairs, gas, oil, tires, insurance, parking, and tolls.

Self-employed individuals may deduct the business portion of car loan interest, but employees may not. Fines for traffic violations aren't deductible either — so slow down!

STANDARD MILEAGE RATE

Instead of figuring your actual expenses with those maddening depreciation computations, you can use a flat rate of 56 cents for every business mile you drove in 2021 if you're self-employed.

If you choose the flat-rate method, you can't claim any of your actual expenses, such as depreciation, gas, oil, insurance, and so on. If you want to use this method, you must choose it the first year that you start using your car for business. If you don't use the standard mileage rate in the first year, you can't use the standard mileage rate in a subsequent year. But if you use the standard mileage the first year, you can switch to deducting your actual expenses, but you probably won't want to after you take a look at the rules in the IRS Publication 463 *(Travel, Gift, and Car Expenses)*.

If you trade in your car, you can use the flat rate for both cars because you owned them at different times.

You can use the standard mileage rate whether you own or lease a vehicle.

In order to determine whether you made a taxable profit or loss when you sell your car, you must first reduce its tax basis by the amount of depreciation built into the flat rate. A table in IRS Publication 463 shows you how to make this computation.

TIP

Sales tax you pay when you purchase a car can't be deducted separately — it's added to the car's tax basis for the purposes of determining the amount of depreciation that you're entitled to claim. For the self-employed, deduct the business portion of your personal property tax on line 23 and the personal part on Schedule A.

Standard mileage rate or actual expenses?

You can deduct either the business portion of your actual expenses or use the standard mileage rate for your business miles (see the "Standard mileage rate" sidebar). The standard mileage method relieves you of the task of keeping track of your expenses. It only requires that you track your miles. Deducting your actual expense requires both.

Depreciation

TECHNICAL STUFF

Car depreciation rules are always tricky, and tax year 2021 is no exception. Still, if you feel you're going to have a better result using your actual car expenses instead of the standard per mile flat rate (see the "Standard mileage rate" sidebar in this chapter), you're going to have to figure them out. Look at the "Line 13: Depreciation" section, later in this chapter, to find out which method of depreciation you're supposed to use for your car for 2021. Strangely enough, even though it relates directly to your car and is one of the valid car and truck expenses, all of your auto depreciation gets lumped together on line 13 of Schedule C.

Leased autos

If you lease a car rather than buy it, you're probably asking yourself why we waited so long to discuss how leased autos are deducted. There are two reasons:

>> First, a special rule applies, which we explain later in this chapter at "Lines 20a or b: Rent or lease" (this is your lucky day!).

>> Secondly, lease payments for cars aren't deducted on line 9; they're deducted on line 20a. All your other car-related expenses, such as gasoline, oil changes, and insurance, are still deducted here on line 9.

Line 10: Commissions and fees

The fees that you paid to sell your merchandise or to bring in new clients (as in referral fees) go on this line.

REMEMBER

However, if you pay someone who isn't your employee more than $600 in a year, you have to file Form 1099-NEC with the IRS and send the person that you paid a copy of the form by January 31, 2022. IRS Publication 334 *(Tax Guide for Small Business)* explains how to comply with this requirement.

Line 11: Contract labor

This line is meant to clearly identify businesses using independent contractors. The IRS as well as most states are zeroing in on businesses that pay workers as independent contractors instead of as employees where the employer is obligated to withhold and pay Social Security and Medicare taxes and, most importantly, unemployment contributions, on their salaries. If someone works on your premises and under your control, that person is probably your employee, and the rules about withholding taxes and Social Security apply. IRS Publication 15-A *(Employer's Supplemental Tax Guide)* addresses the independent contractor issue in greater detail and gives many examples within certain industries that have historically classified workers as independent contractors even though they may actually be employees. Check your facts carefully before making the determination that someone performing services for you is an independent contractor; as the IRS and the states crack down on these designations, paying the back employment taxes and unemployment insurance contributions plus penalties and interest for multiple years can bring your business crashing down.

Line 12: Depletion

This line applies if your business deals with properties such as mines, oil and gas wells, timber, and exhaustible natural deposits. You can compute depletion two ways, and, of course, you want to use the one that produces the larger deduction. Unlike depreciation, which measures the useful life of property, *depletion* measures the actual reduction of a physical asset. To be on the safe side, take a look at IRS Publication 535 *(Business Expenses)*.

Line 13: Depreciation

Depreciation is the annual deduction that enables you to recover the cost of an investment in business equipment or in income-producing real estate that has a useful life of more than one year. Or, as an accountant friend of one of us explained (in a ten-words-or-less challenge), depreciation is "recovering an asset's value ratably over its useful economic life." The word "depreciation" is itself enough to send most readers to the next chapter, we know, but just think of depreciation as a way of reducing your tax! Now, are you more excited about depreciation possibilities? Unless you elect the special provision that allows you to deduct the first $1,050,000 of equipment or furniture used in your business (we explain this provision later in the chapter in "Section 179: The $1,050,000 depreciation deduction"), you have to write off your purchase of these assets over their respective useful lives — as established by the IRS (see Table 13-1). You can't depreciate land and works of art. (So, you can't depreciate your van Goghs!) See Chapter 23 for a discussion of the pros and cons of depreciating versus taking an outright deduction.

Table 13-1   Useful Life

Type of Property	Useful Life (Years)
Computers and similar equipment	5
Office machinery (typewriters, calculators, copiers)	5
Autos and light trucks	5
Office furniture (desks, files)	7
Appliances (stoves, refrigerators used in residential buildings)	5
Shrubbery	15
Residential buildings	27.5
Nonresidential buildings after 5/12/93	39
Nonresidential buildings before 5/12/93	31.5
Goodwill, customer lists, franchise costs, and covenants not to compete	15

NEW STUFF In addition to Section 179 depreciation, in 2021, there is also 100 percent bonus depreciation for all tangible personal property with a recovery period of 20 years or less. The property covered may be new or used, purchased or leased. Tangible personal property excludes real estate improvements or land purchases.

What is the difference between Section 179 depreciation and bonus depreciation? Section 179 depreciation is classified as an expense item rather than depreciation. In addition, Section 179 depreciation has a limit of $1,050,000 of new-to-you property in 2021; that limit begins to phase out once a business puts $2,620,000 of property into service in 2021 and is completely phased out at $3,670,000. You must make an election to use Section 179 depreciation; it's not automatically done for you. Finally, if you elect to use Section 179 depreciation but that election completely wipes out any taxable income you have and leaves you with a deficit, you'll have to carry forward any amounts greater than your taxable income to 2022 and beyond. Section 179 depreciation cannot be used to create a net operating loss (NOL).

Bonus depreciation, on the other hand, is automatic, unlimited, and treated as depreciation, not an expense. It's available on all qualifying property provided you haven't purchased your "used" vehicle from yourself in order to access the 100 percent depreciation. The use of bonus depreciation on your return can generate a net operating loss (NOL), reducing your taxable income to below zero, and creating a carryforward NOL to your 2022 return. If you don't want to use the bonus depreciation available to you, you may elect to opt out. That election is made on Form 4562.

TIP

For rental income reported on Schedule E, use Form 4562 for property that you started renting in 2021. For property that you started renting before 2021, you don't need to file Form 4562.

SEEK
ADVICE

We'd be lying if we said that calculating depreciation is quick and easy, although the ability to use either Section 179 or bonus depreciation does make life much simpler. But calculating multi-year depreciation isn't impossible. Still, you may have questions along the way or want to check with someone else after you've finished to make sure you've done it right. Consider asking a tax professional to double-check your depreciation calculations after you're done to make sure they're correct.

To file (or not to file) Form 4562

You compute your depreciation deduction for business property that you started using in 2021 on Form 4562, Depreciation and Amortization. Carry the amount of depreciation that you calculate on this form over to line 13 of Schedule C.

TAX CUT

The depreciation you normally can deduct every year is determined by an item's useful life. Based on that, you then take a percentage of the item's cost as a deduction.

If you are only depreciating property you started using prior to 2021, Form 4562 isn't required. On line 13 of Schedule C, just enter the amount to which you're entitled based on the useful life of the asset from the applicable schedule that we provide in this chapter. For example, if you want to depreciate an asset that has a five-year useful life, use Table 13-2. If you're depreciating cars, computers, or cellular phones, or other so-called listed property, however, you must use Form 4562, because you can depreciate only the business portion of those kinds of items.

IRS depreciation percentages

To calculate the amount of depreciation that you're entitled to claim, glance at the IRS depreciation tables (Tables 13-2 through 13-6). For business property other than real estate, you'll notice that each table has two categories: *half-year convention* and *mid-quarter convention*. Usually, you use the half-year convention, because the mid-quarter convention comes into play when the business assets you acquired and started using in the last three months of the year exceed 40 percent of all business assets that you placed in service during the year. Got that? Read on and follow the examples for both types of depreciation conventions.

WARNING

Residential real estate is depreciated over 27½ years. Nonresidential real estate, a factory or office building for example, placed in use after May 12, 1993, is depreciated over 39 years. If it was *placed in service* (that's the IRS term for when you started using it) after 1986 and before May 13, 1993, it's depreciated over 31½ years. You can get the depreciation rates for these two periods from IRS Publication 946 (*How To Depreciate Property*). For prior periods, you have to use the rates in IRS Publication 534 (*Depreciating Property Placed in Service before 1987*).

Table 13-2 MACRS (Modified Accelerated Cost Recovery System): 5-Year Property

Year	Half-Year Convention	First Quarter	Mid-Quarter Convention Second Quarter	Third Quarter	Fourth Quarter
1	20.00%	35.00%	25.00%	15.00%	5.00%
2	32.00	26.00	30.00	34.00	38.00
3	19.20	15.60	18.00	20.40	22.80
4	11.52	11.01	11.37	12.24	13.68
5	11.52	11.01	11.37	11.30	10.94
6	5.76	1.38	4.26	7.06	9.58

Table 13-3 MACRS: 7-Year Property

Year	Half-Year Convention	First Quarter	Mid-Quarter Convention Second Quarter	Third Quarter	Fourth Quarter
1	14.29%	25.00%	17.85%	10.71%	3.57%
2	24.49	21.43	23.47	25.51	27.55
3	17.49	15.31	16.76	18.22	19.68
4	12.49	10.93	11.97	13.02	14.06
5	8.93	8.75	8.87	9.30	10.04
6	8.92	8.74	8.87	8.85	8.73

Table 13-4 MACRS: 15-Year Property

Year	Half-Year Convention	First Quarter	Mid-Quarter Convention Second Quarter	Third Quarter	Fourth Quarter
1	5.00%	8.75%	6.25%	3.75%	1.25%
2	9.50	9.13	9.38	9.63	9.88
3	8.55	8.21	8.44	8.66	8.89
4	7.70	7.39	7.59	7.80	8.00
5	6.93	6.65	6.83	7.02	7.20
6	6.23	5.99	6.15	6.31	6.48

For example, say you purchased the building where you operate your business in March 2021 for $225,000. Because it's nonresidential property purchased after May 12, 1993, you have to depreciate it over 39 years. You make a reasonable determination that the land is worth $25,000, so you have a depreciable basis of $200,000. Next, you look up the rate in the 39-year column for March (2.033 percent). Your depreciation for 2021 is $4,066 ($200,000 × 2.033 percent). In later years, it is $5,128 ($200,000 × 2.564 percent).

REMEMBER

Real estate isn't eligible for the special $1,050,000 depreciation deduction.

Table 13-5 Residential Rental Property (27½-Year)

Month	Use the row of the month of the taxable year that the property was placed in service.					
	Year 1	Year 2	Year 3	Year 4	Year 5	Year 6
Jan	3.485%	3.636%	3.636%	3.636%	3.636%	3.636%
Feb	3.182	3.636	3.636	3.636	3.636	3.636
Mar	2.879	3.636	3.636	3.636	3.636	3.636
Apr	2.576	3.636	3.636	3.636	3.636	3.636
May	2.273	3.636	3.636	3.636	3.636	3.636
Jun	1.970	3.636	3.636	3.636	3.636	3.636
Jul	1.667	3.636	3.636	3.636	3.636	3.636
Aug	1.364	3.636	3.636	3.636	3.636	3.636
Sept	1.061	3.636	3.636	3.636	3.636	3.636
Oct	0.758	3.636	3.636	3.636	3.636	3.636
Nov	0.455	3.636	3.636	3.636	3.636	3.636
Dec	0.152	3.636	3.636	3.636	3.636	3.636

Table 13-6 Commercial Property (31½ Years and 39 Years)

Month	Use the row of the month of the taxable year that the property was placed in service.			
	(31½ Years)		(39 Years)	
	Year 1	Later Years	Year 1	Later Years
Jan	3.042%	3.175%	2.461%	2.564%
Feb	2.778	3.175	2.247	2.564
Mar	2.513	3.175	2.033	2.564
Apr	2.249	3.175	1.819	2.564
May	2.273	3.175	1.605	2.564
Jun	1.720	3.175	1.391	2.564
Jul	1.455	3.175	1.177	2.564
Aug	1.190	3.175	0.963	2.564
Sept	0.926	3.175	0.749	2.564
Oct	0.661	3.175	0.535	2.564
Nov	0.397	3.175	0.321	2.564
Dec	0.132	3.175	0.107	2.564

TIP

We love calculating depreciation schedules. Really! Fortunately, we're using computers to create and maintain our depreciation schedules, and carefully inputting all the property we purchased in 2021 to make sure we're making the elections we want to (electing into Section 179 or electing out of bonus depreciation). So long as we're entering the correct useful life for each depreciable item and selecting MACRS depreciation, the computer is then doing all the work for us. It's always good to check at least a few of the calculations to make sure they're calculated correctly, but it saves a lot of brainpower to let the computer expend most of the effort.

Additions or improvements to property

An addition or improvement that you make to your property is treated as a separate item for the purposes of depreciation — regardless of how you depreciate the original asset. For example, you own a house that you've rented since 1984 and fully depreciated over the next 19 years (you were allowed to use that short of a useful life back then). Then, in 2021, you added a new roof. The roof has to be depreciated over 27½ years and at the rate in the IRS depreciation tables for residential real estate. The depreciation tables reproduced in this chapter go up to only six years. For tables that go beyond six years, IRS Publication 946 *(How to Depreciate Property)* is available online at www.irs.gov/pub/irs-pdf/p946.pdf, or you can request a copy by snail mail.

Suppose that you're depreciating a computer that you purchased for $5,000 in 2021. First, you must look up its useful life (Table 13-1). According to the IRS, computers have a useful life of five years, so use the depreciation percentages for five-year property. Okay, easy enough so far.

Under the half-year convention for five-year property (Table 13-2), you find 20 percent as the amount. For 2021, you're entitled to a $1,000 depreciation deduction ($5,000 × 20 percent). In 2022, you'd multiply the $5,000 cost by 32 percent, for a deduction of $1,600. And then you'd use 19.20 percent, 11.52 percent, 11.52 percent, and 5.76 percent in each of the succeeding years. Of course, you only have to make these calculations if you choose not to use (or you've already maxed out) the special $1,050,000 depreciation you're allowed. Fun calculations, right? Based on the convention rules, the write-off period for stuff is one year longer than its useful life. That's because in the first year you're entitled to only a half-year's worth of depreciation. The half-year convention rule means that all assets are considered to have been purchased on July 1 — which entitles you to only half the normal amount of depreciation in the first year.

Half-year convention versus mid-quarter convention depreciation

As if trying to figure out what type of property you have isn't confusing enough, you also need to figure out the rules regarding how much depreciation you can take in the first year. Basically, the IRS makes an assumption that you'll purchase equal amounts of business property all through the year, putting some into service each month. Rather than have you track each and every purchase on your tax return, the IRS allows you to average it all together by using the half-year convention. The half-year convention considers that all property you purchased in 2021, regardless of the date it's actually purchased and put into service, was put into service on July 1.

For new tenants or lessors leasing office space in 2021, any leasehold improvements you make to the property will depreciate over 15 years, not 39. Keep in mind that, when the lease ends, you may deduct any part of the cost of the improvements that you haven't depreciated if you're a tenant. If you're the lessor, continue depreciating the improvements you made unless you remove them. If the tenant makes improvements, you won't recognize income unless the improvements are really intended as rent.

Not everyone purchases equal amounts of property throughout the year, though. Many people load their purchases into the last quarter of the year, when they have an idea of how much money they'll have to pay tax on if they don't sink some of it back into their business pronto. If you've purchased more than 40 percent of your total depreciable property in 2021 in the last quarter of 2021 (October through December), you must use the mid-quarter convention for each asset. These two designations mean that you have to keep track of when you purchased property and when you put it into service to depreciate it properly.

For example, say you bought a calculator for $500 on February 1, 2021, and a copier for $1,000 on October 1, 2021, and chose not to claim the special depreciation deduction. Under the half-year convention, you're entitled to a depreciation deduction of $300 ($1,500 × 20 percent). But because more than 40 percent of all your business property was bought and placed into service the last three months of the year, you have to switch to the mid-quarter convention for each asset. So, here's how you have to separately compute the depreciation for these two pieces of equipment.

Under the mid-quarter convention for five-year property (see Table 13-2), for an asset purchased in the first quarter, the depreciation rate is 35 percent. Therefore, you're entitled to a $175 depreciation deduction ($500 × 35 percent) for the calculator. For the copier, you have to use the 5 percent rate for property bought during the fourth quarter ($1,000 × 5 percent), which entitles you to a $50 deduction.

REMEMBER

The long and the short? By using the mid-quarter convention, you can claim only half the depreciation that you normally would. At this point, you're probably scratching the back of your head and wondering who thinks of these things. We must confess that we don't know either. Just play along.

TIP

You can save yourself the headache that this mid-quarter convention causes and get a larger deduction to boot by claiming up to *$1,050,000 of Section 179 depreciation*, which we point out in the next section.

Section 179: The $1,050,000 depreciation deduction

Instead of computing depreciation by using the standard depreciation tables, you can elect to deduct up to $1,050,000 of the cost of new and used business equipment that you purchased and started using in your business in 2021. Though this type of one-shot depreciation is available every year, the dollar limits change from year to year. Remember, in order to use this write-off, you must have actually spent up to $1,050,000 in 2021. This bonanza is known in IRS terms as *Section 179 depreciation*.

If you buy a few items, you can pick and choose which ones you want to write off completely and which ones you don't. If you want the largest possible deduction for all your listed property, allocate your $1,050,000 Section 179 depreciation first against property with the longest life, and work your way toward property with the shortest life. On the other hand, some property with a short-listed life has an even shorter actual life, such as computers. You may want to allocate Section 179 depreciation first to property that you know you won't own for the full depreciation term. After you've written off the cost for those items, you can then use the remainder to write off your longest-life property.

WARNING

If you're married filing separately, you can deduct only $525,000, unless you and your spouse agree upon how much Section 179 depreciation each of you is entitled to deduct.

If you buy equipment costing more than $2,620,000, the $1,050,000 that you're entitled to deduct is reduced dollar for dollar by the amount over $2,620,000. So, if the total cost is

$3,670,000 or more, you can kiss any part of your $1,050,000 write-off goodbye. Here's how this works: Say you purchased equipment costing $2,627,000. You have to reduce the maximum $1,050,000 you can write off by $7,000, leaving you with $1,043,000 of available Section 179 depreciation. The remaining balance of new equipment put in service in 2021 is $1,584,000, for which you can either use bonus depreciation to write off the full cost in 2021 if the property qualifies or elect to use standard depreciation rules for some or all of the remaining property.

The beauty of the $1,050,000 limit (besides the immediate deduction) is that it keeps you from having to wade through the depreciation tables to compute your depreciation. The second rule regarding the $1,050,000 expensing is that this deduction can't produce a loss from all your business activities. Suppose that your consulting income — after all other expenses — is $10,000, and you bought $24,000 worth of equipment. You can expense only $10,000. If you've elected Section 179 depreciation for the full amount, the $14,000 balance carries over to the next year when you can deduct it if you have enough consulting income after expenses. If you don't, it carries over until you do.

TIP

But there is a pleasant surprise. You can count all your earned income to determine whether you pass the no-loss test. So, in the preceding example, if you or your spouse had at least $14,000 in wages (in addition to your $10,000 consulting income), you can deduct the whole $24,000 of the equipment you purchased.

Listed property: Cars used 50 percent or more in your business

Listed property is an IRS term for autos, telephones, computers, boats, and airplanes — items that the IRS suspects you may use more for pleasure than for business. With listed property, you not only need to tell the IRS what you purchased and put into service in 2021, but also what percentage of the time you used that property for your trade or business. Although you still calculate depreciation using Tables 13-2 through 13-6, now you also need to multiply your potential total depreciation result by your amount of business use to get your actual depreciation amount.

The largest single item piece of listed property for most people is their car. The IRS considers cars to have a useful life of five years, which is the starting point to determine the amount of depreciation on the auto that you can deduct.

If the business use of your car is more than 50 percent of its total use, you compute your depreciation (under MACRS — Modified Accelerated Cost Recovery System) according to what is known as the half-year convention. The *half-year convention* means that assets, in the year of purchase, regardless of the month they were acquired, are considered to have been purchased on July 1, and you're therefore entitled to a half-year's depreciation. In subsequent years, you're entitled to a full-year's depreciation for that year provided that you continue to own the property for the full year.

REMEMBER

If you put that new car into service between October and December 2021 and if its value (added to whatever else you bought in that period) is greater than 40 percent of the value of the total property you put into service in 2021, you need to switch to the mid-quarter convention that we describe in the "Half-year convention versus mid-quarter convention depreciation" section earlier in this chapter.

Of course, Congress doesn't think you need to drive a Maserati in order to conduct business, so it subjects most cars, trucks, and vans to the so-called luxury car rules. Although the cost of what the IRS considers a "luxury car" fluctuates slightly from year to year, you're going to hit the depreciation limits pretty quickly, since your first-year depreciation (including bonus depreciation) can't exceed $18,200 for any car (including SUVs) with an unloaded gross vehicle weight of under 6,000 pounds, or truck or van with a gross loaded weight of less than 6,000 pounds in 2021. This regulation doesn't mean you're not allowed to spend more on a vehicle for your business; it only means that your annual depreciation will be limited if you do.

REMEMBER

But, to encourage you to spend more for a new car or truck in 2021, bonus depreciation is available if you purchase a car, truck, or van. So, even though the depreciation limits are generally low for passenger vehicles, in 2021 you can write off a much bigger chunk of that new-to-you car. Check out Table 13-7 to find the depreciation limits for your new chariot.

Table 13-7   Depreciation Deductions for New and Used Cars Subject to the Luxury Car Limits

	Limits for a Car		Limits for a Truck or Van	
	Without Bonus Depreciation	With Bonus Depreciation	Without Bonus Depreciation	With Bonus Depreciation
2021	$10,200	$18,200	$10,200	$18,200
2022	$16,400	$16,400	$16,400	$16,400
2023	$9,800	$9,800	$9,800	$9,800
2024–2026	$5,860	$5,860	$5,860	$5,860

REMEMBER

Cars are listed property with a five-year life, so the amounts in Table 13-7 represent the maximum amount of depreciation you may take. If your business usage is less than 100 percent, you only depreciate the business use of your car. If you didn't elect Section 179 depreciation, multiply the maximum depreciation deduction by your percentage of business use to determine the maximum amount of depreciation available to you in any given year.

TIP

Whether you elect to use Section 179 depreciation, bonus depreciation, or just use the standard 5-year depreciation table, your deduction is limited by not only the cost of the vehicle, but also by the percentage of business use. If usage is 50 percent or less, you're only going to get the ratable portion of regular depreciation — no Section 179 or bonus depreciation is available to you. Remember, Table 13-7 shows you the maximum depreciation available for passenger cars with an unloaded vehicle weight of less than 6,000 pounds, and trucks and vans with a gross loaded weight of less than 6,000 pounds.

REMEMBER

How do you calculate your new car's depreciation if you're using bonus depreciation for 2021? First, multiply the cost of the car by your business use percentage. If the car cost $36,000, and you use it 60 percent of the time for business, that means your starting point for depreciable basis is $21,600 ($36,000 × 60 percent). This is the amount of business use property you're dealing with. Remember, you're only allowed 60 percent of depreciation because your business use of the car is only 60 percent, but your total depreciation for this vehicle is capped at $18,200 in 2021. Since the capped amount is less than 60 percent of the cost of the car, your maximum depreciation deduction is $18,200. But since you only used the car 60 percent of the time for business, you're not entitled to the maximum amount of depreciation on that car. Multiply the $18,200 by 60 percent ($18,200 × 60 percent) to arrive at a total depreciation amount for 2021 of $10,920. This is your maximum depreciation on your new car in 2021, and the amount that you'll put on Form 4562. The amount of remaining depreciable basis in this car is $10,680 ($21,600 – $10,920), which you'll depreciate over the next five years if you own the car that long. If your business usage remains at 60 percent over the next five years, you'll take a depreciation deduction of $3,417.60 in year 2 ($10,680 × 32 percent), $2,050.56 in year 3 ($10,680 × 19.2 percent), $1,230.34 for years 4 and 5 ($10,680 × 11.52 percent), and $615.17 in year 6 ($10,680 × 5.76 percent).

On the other hand, you can elect to use Section 179 depreciation for your car, truck, or van instead of bonus and regular depreciation. Go back to the purchase price of $36,000 and business use of 60 percent, so the amount available for Section 179 is $21,600. Same as before. But your maximum Section 179 depreciation amount for a passenger vehicle that fails to meet the 6,000-pound weight restriction is also limited by the percentage you use it in business, so using the same circumstances as previously, the maximum you can deduct in year one is exactly the same as for bonus depreciation, and the following years also follow suit.

What's the difference between the two? You can create a net operating loss (NOL) by using bonus depreciation, but not with Section 179 depreciation, which is capped at no more than the total of your taxable income.

Finally, if you elect out of bonus depreciation and don't elect Section 179 depreciation, what happens then? You revert to the standard depreciation percentages shown on Table 13-2. Remember, you still have to limit your basis to the percentage of business use. The result of this strategy will be to give you a much smaller first-year depreciation deduction, but larger depreciation deductions for all following years because you're multiplying those Table 13-2 percentages on a much larger basis — $21,600 with standard depreciation versus $10,680 with either Section 179 or bonus depreciation.

If you leased that new car or truck rather than bought it outright, you're still subject to the luxury car rules, the weight rules, and the personal versus business allocation rules. The only things that change are the method of payment and the so-called "inclusion amount," which reduces the deductibility of your lease payments if your new car or truck comes under the 6,000-pound weight limits described before and costs over $51,000 in 2021. If you're preparing your return on paper, you can find the income inclusion rates for 2021 in IRS Rev. Proc. 2021-31, Table 3. If you're using a computer to help you prepare your return, make sure that you tick the box showing that this is a leased vehicle when you enter the information, and the computer should do all the heavy lifting.

Listed property: SUVs, vans, and heavier trucks

If the new car you bought to use for your business is one of the larger SUVs, a van, or a heavier truck, you may not be subject to the luxury car rules. What does this exemption from the luxury car rules mean to you? The limits on depreciation in Table 13-7 don't apply to you. You're allowed to follow the regular depreciation rules (including 100 percent bonus depreciation for the business use portion of the purchase price, provided that you're using that vehicle for more than 50 percent of the time in your business, and you're also allowed to use Section 179 depreciation described in the section "Section 179: The $1,050,000 depreciation deduction" earlier in this chapter.

Which SUVs and trucks qualify? An SUV or truck must rate as weighing at least 6,000 pounds unloaded to meet this requirement but cannot exceed 14,000 pounds unloaded. You can check out these figures with your local car dealer when you're researching your next SUV or truck purchase. If you're actually on a car lot and looking at vehicles, the gross weight unloaded and loaded is shown on the sticker inside the driver's side door.

WARNING

A heavy SUV must be built on a truck chassis to avoid the luxury car rules and get the benefit of the Section 179 deduction or unlimited bonus depreciation. Most heavy SUVs are built on a truck chassis, but a few are built on a car chassis. Again, ask your dealer about this before making your purchase. Furthermore, you can't claim an unlimited depreciation deduction (either Section 179 or bonus) on a heavy truck that has a cargo bed that is less than 6 feet long. The short-bed rule affects some big trucks with an extended cab. A heavy truck with a short bed is still exempt from the luxury car limits though. You just may not get Section 179 depreciation.

One exception to the 6,000-pound weight rule does exist (one always does!). If you've purchased a truck or van in 2021 that weighs less than 6,000 pounds, you may still be able to follow the regular depreciation rules if the truck or van is somehow modified so that it can be used only for your trade or business. The IRS is looking for modifications such as these:

>> Adding ladder racks and a tool chest on a truck or van

>> Having only a shelf-type seat in the front (with no seating in the back)

>> Including shelving in a van

>> Providing space for carrying merchandise and equipment

REMEMBER

If you use your SUV, van, or truck some of the time for personal use, you can't claim the Section 179 expense deduction or the depreciation deduction for the cost that is attributable to personal use. Here's how it works. Say you buy a big SUV for $70,000, and you use it 60 percent of the time for business. Of your $70,000 purchase price, only $42,000 ($70,000 × 60 percent) is available for expensing and depreciating. In 2021, you can expense the full $42,000 using Section 179 depreciation, or you can take 100 percent bonus depreciation of $42,000. Finally, you can elect to do neither, and just take ordinary depreciation as shown in Table 13-7, giving you an $8,400 depreciation deduction in 2021, $13,440 in year 2, $8,064 in year 3, $4,838.40 in years 4 and 5, and $2,419.20 in year 6. Or you can just look down at Table 13-10 later in this chapter.

Listed property: Cars used 50 percent or less for business

If the business use of your car is 50 percent or less, you must depreciate it using the MACRS *straight-line method* (see Table 13-8). Straight-line depreciation is relatively easy, right? Wrong . . . in this case. Remember, this calculation is for a car with a business use of less than 50 percent, so the IRS makes you reduce the amount of depreciation that you're allowed under the straight-line method by the percentage of personal use.

So, if you used your car for business 40 percent of the time, the maximum depreciation allowed by law in the first year is $4,080 ($10,200 × 40 percent).

Table 13-8 MACRS Straight-Line Method for Auto Depreciation Using the Half-Year Convention

Year	5-Year Property	Maximum Yearly Limit*
1	10%	$5,100
2	20%	$10,200
3	20%	$10,200
4	20%	$10,200
5	20%	$10,200
6	10%	$5,100

Remember that this amount is the maximum deduction if your car was used 100 percent for business.

In coming years, you calculate your depreciation deduction the same way. In years 2 through 5, you use a depreciation rate of 20 percent according to Table 13-8, and then 10 percent for year 6. Any depreciation that you can't claim in years 1 through 6 (because of the yearly maximum limits) is deducted in subsequent years at $5,100 a year, less your personal use, until your car is fully depreciated.

WARNING

You can't claim any bonus depreciation or Section 179 deduction on a car, truck, or SUV (or any other type of "listed" property) that is used 50 percent or more for personal purposes. If you claim the deduction in the year you buy the vehicle and in a later year your personal use increases to at least 50 percent, part of it can be added back to your income along with some of the depreciation you claimed.

All this auto depreciation stuff is almost enough to make you start using your feet to call on clients. But then, there's no depreciation allowance for shoes.

TIP

A tax software program can save you from all this mind-numbing number crunching. (See Chapter 2 for more information about selecting a tax software program.)

If you started depreciating your car prior to 2021, Table 13-9 shows you the maximum yearly depreciation limits for 2021.

Table 13-9 2021 Annual Depreciation Ceiling for Cars Put into Service Prior to 2021

Year	Depreciation Ceiling
2012	$5,760
2013	$5,760
2014	$5,760
2015	$5,760
2016	$5,760
2017	$5,760
2018	$5,760
2019	$9,700
2020	$16,100

Alternative fuel and hybrid vehicles

Hybrid (combination gasoline/electric) cars and electric cars follow the same depreciation rules as standard, gasoline-powered ones.

In addition to the depreciation you can claim, if you purchased either a hybrid electric, an all-electric, or some other alternative fuel vehicle this year, you may also qualify for the Alternative Motor Vehicle Credit (see Chapter 16). The government is encouraging you to save fuel and the environment; this credit can be as high as $7,500 for an electric car. You will need to split the credit between Form 3800, General Business Credits, and Form 8910, Alternative Motor Vehicle Credit, based on your business usage.

Remember, before figuring your annual depreciation deduction, you first need to subtract the total amount of your credit from the cost of the car. Any tax credits you receive due to the purchase of this car in 2021 reduces your basis by the amount of the credit.

Line 14: Employee benefit programs

Enter here the premiums you paid for your employees' accident, health, and group term life insurance coverage — but not those you paid for your own health insurance. See Chapter 7 to find out how to deduct 100 percent of your personal health insurance premiums.

Line 15: Insurance (other than health)

Enter on this line the premiums that you paid for business insurance, such as fire, theft, robbery, and general liability coverage on your business property.

Line 16a: Mortgage interest

If you own the building in which you operate your business, deduct any mortgage interest you paid on line 16a. If you're claiming a deduction for the business use of your home, the mortgage interest you paid is deducted on line 10 of Form 8829, Expenses for Business Use of Your Home. The amount of the deduction is stated on Form 1098, Mortgage Interest Statement, that you should receive in January 2022 from your bank.

Line 16b: Other interest

You can deduct interest on business loans here. If you took out a mortgage on your house and used the proceeds of the loan to finance your business, deduct the interest here — and not on Schedule A. If you borrowed money for your business from other sources, such as a bank or even your credit card, deduct the interest on those loans here as well.

You can't deduct the interest you paid on the taxes you owed on your personal tax returns. You can, however, deduct late interest paid on employment taxes (Social Security, Medicare, and withholding taxes) that you paid as an employer.

Line 17: Legal and professional services

On this line, enter any fees that you paid for tax advice, for preparing tax forms related to your business, and for legal fees regarding business matters. Professional services include fees for accounting and engineering work that you pay for. Garden variety consulting work gets entered on line 10, contract labor.

REMEMBER

If you pay someone more than $600 (your accountant, for example), you have to provide that person with Form 1099-MISC by January 31, 2022 — just like we told you to do with commissions and contract labor that you deducted on lines 10 and 11.

The IRS must love lawyers. You must report the aggregate of all payments made to your attorney — even for the reimbursement of expenses that you were billed — provided that they total $600 or more. Additionally, the exemption that allows you to not report payments made to corporations to the IRS on Form 1099 doesn't apply to lawyers. Know any good lawyer jokes? Finally, if you wrote a check to an attorney and a third party, perhaps in settlement of a lawsuit, you're required to give both the attorney and the third party a Form 1099-MISC for the full amount of the check, even if the attorney is only going to end up with a piece of the total pie.

Line 18: Office expense

Enter your costs for stationery, paper supplies, postage, printer toner, and other consumable items that you use in the operation of your office or business.

Line 19: Pension and profit-sharing plans

Enter only your contribution to your employees' Keogh, SIMPLE, or SEP account(s). As for your own Keogh or SEP, enter that amount on Form 1040, Schedule 1, Part II, line 16. See Chapter 8.

Employers with fewer than 100 employees may establish what's known as SIMPLE retirement plans. These plans have none of the mind-numbing rules to follow or forms to file that regular retirement plans have. A SIMPLE plan can also cover the owner(s) of a farm (see Chapter 22 for more about SIMPLE and other small business retirement plans).

Lines 20a and b: Rent or lease

If you rented or leased an auto, machinery, or equipment, enter the business portion of the rental payments on line 20a. But if you leased a car for more than 30 days, you may have to reduce your deduction by an amount called the inclusion amount if your leased car's value exceeded the following amounts (see Table 13-10) when you started leasing it.

WARNING

Whether you're entering your car lease payments here or on Form 2106, Employee Business Expenses, you aren't allowed to deduct the full amount of the lease payments on a new Bentley! In fact, you're not allowed to lease much of anything and claim the full amount of the lease payments. Just like there are luxury car rules for calculating depreciation, there are essentially luxury car rules for leased cars, as well (only the IRS refers to *inclusion amounts* for leased cars, or the amount by which your lease payments must be reduced, as opposed to luxury car rules). The inclusion amounts and luxury car rules do the same thing — they both effectively limit your deduction.

Table 13-10   Inclusion Amounts

Year Lease Began	Amount
2021	$51,000
2020	$50,000
2019	$50,000
2018	$50,000
2017	$19,000
2016	$19,000
2015	$19,000
2014	$19,000
2013	$19,000

You can find charts with the lease inclusion amounts for cars, SUVs, vans, light trucks, and electric cars in IRS Publication 463 *(Travel, Entertainment, Gift, and Car Expenses)*. These numbers are adjusted annually for inflation, so you do need to check every year. Fortunately, IRS Publication 463 is easy and cheap to obtain (it's free), either by calling 800-829-3676 or on the internet at www.irs.gov.

Even though you reduce your rental payments by the lease-inclusion amount, leasing may still provide you with a larger deduction than purchasing. But remember, lease payments that are payments toward the purchase price of a car aren't deductible. The IRS considers such leases a purchase contract, because you end up owning the jalopy at the end of the lease. If you have such an agreement, you must depreciate the car based on its value, and doing so sends you right back to the annual limit that you can claim for auto depreciation.

On line 20b, enter your office rent, for example.

Line 21: Repairs and maintenance

Enter the cost of routine repairs — such as the cost to repair your computer — on this line. But adding a new hard disk isn't a repair; that cost must be depreciated over five years unless it qualifies for the special election to write off the first $1,050,000 of business assets.

A *repair* (as opposed to an improvement) keeps your equipment or property in good operating condition. A repair that also prolongs the life of your equipment has to be depreciated, so make the most of the $1,050,000 deduction instead of depreciating the cost over its useful life.

If you're confused about what qualifies as a repair and what qualifies as an improvement, you're not alone. Through the years, the Tax Court has been clogged with cases dealing with repairs as current write-offs versus improvements that have to be depreciated. We suggest that you contact a tax advisor to evaluate your specific situation. The $1,050,000 immediate write-off should solve this problem.

Line 22: Supplies

If your company manufactures a product, you report factory supplies here. In other words, you deduct the cost of supplies that contribute to the operation of the equipment that you use in your office or business. For example, if you operate a retail store, you enter the cost of mannequins, trim, packaging, and other such items on this line. But supplies for anything you manufacture for sale correctly belong in cost of goods sold, on Schedule C, Part III, line 38.

Line 23: Taxes and licenses

On this line you deduct your business taxes, such as the employer's share of Social Security and Medicare taxes, and unemployment insurance contributions for your employees. Also enter the costs of permits and business licenses. Don't deduct the Social Security tax that you pay because you're self-employed here; instead, you can deduct half of this tax on Form 1040, Schedule 1, Part II, line 15 (see Chapter 7 for more on how this deduction works).

Lines 24a–b: Travel and meals

Probably no other group of expenses has created more paperwork than travel expenses. Taxpayers may spend more time on the documentation accounting for a business trip than they do planning for it. Unfortunately, this situation can't be changed. But at least we can help you deduct every possible expense in this area. So, we begin with the three basic rules regarding travel and entertainment expenses:

>> You have to be away from your business or home to deduct travel expenses. (Makes sense, doesn't it?)

>> You can deduct only 50 percent of your meal expenses.

>> You need to keep good records.

Travel expenses that are deductible include taxi, commuter bus, and limousine fare to and from the airport or station — and between your hotel and business meetings or job site. You can also deduct auto expenses, whether you use your own car or lease (see earlier in this chapter for more on car and truck expenses), and the cost of hotels, meals, telephone calls, and laundry while you're away. Don't forget tips and baggage handling. Finally, remember the obvious deductions on airplane, train, and bus fare between your tax home and business destination.

Your tax home and travel expenses

Yes, we said tax home. This is where the situation gets a little tricky because to be able to deduct travel expenses you must be traveling away from your tax home on business. You are traveling away from your tax home if the business purpose of your trip requires that you be away longer than an ordinary working day — and you need to sleep or rest so you can be ready for the next day's business or for your next shift, say if you're a railroad porter or a truck driver who rents a room between shifts at some point along the journey in order to rest up for your next shift.

Your tax home isn't where you or your family reside. Of course not. It's the entire city or general area in which you work or where your business is located. For example, suppose that you work in Manhattan but live in the suburbs. You decide to stay in Manhattan overnight because you have an early breakfast meeting the next morning. You aren't away from your tax home overnight; therefore, you can't deduct the cost of the hotel. The only meal expense you can deduct is 50 percent of the next morning's breakfast.

At this point, you probably want to know how far away from your tax home you have to be. Unfortunately, there isn't a mileage count. When it comes to determining whether you're away from home overnight, the IRS uses that famous U.S. Supreme Court definition: "I can't define it, but I know it when I see it."

Also, your tax home may not be near where you live. For example, if you move from job to job without a fixed base of operation, each place you work becomes your tax home. And travel expenses aren't deductible. And if you accept a temporary assignment that lasts for more than a year, you have moved your tax home to the place of the temporary assignment. Sorry, no deduction. Guess what? It gets worse. Say your assignment is expected to last more than a year but then it doesn't. That sort of assignment isn't considered a temporary assignment (one year or less) that makes your travel and living expenses deductible. It's considered a permanent assignment that doesn't allow you to deduct your travel expenses.

Trips that mix business with pleasure

TAX CUT

For travel within the United States, the transportation part of your travel expenses is fully deductible even if part of it is for pleasure. For example, perhaps the airfare and car services to and from the airport cost $700 for you to attend a business convention in Florida. You spend two days at the end of the convention playing poker with some old friends. Your transportation costs of $700 are fully deductible, but your meals and lodging for the two vacation days aren't.

Transportation costs for travel outside the United States have to be prorated based on the amount of time you spend on business and vacation. Suppose that you spend four out of eight days in London on business. You can deduct only 50 percent of your airfare and four days of lodging and meals. Any other travel costs (such as taxis and telephone calls while you were conducting business) are deductible.

But this general rule for transportation expenses on travel abroad doesn't apply if you meet any of the following conditions:

>> The trip lasts a week or less.

>> More than 75 percent of your time outside the United States was spent on business. (The days you start and end your trip are considered business days.)

>> You don't have substantial control in arranging the trip (for your employee[s]) who you send on a business trip who isn't related to you, and who isn't a managing executive of your company.

TAX CUT

Weekends, holidays, and other necessary standby days are counted as business days if they fall between business days. Great! But if these days follow your business activities and you remain at your business destination for personal reasons, they aren't business days.

For example, suppose that your tax home is in Kansas City. You travel to St. Louis where you have a business appointment on Friday and another business meeting on the following Monday. The days in between are considered tax-deductible business-expense days — you had a business activity on Friday and had another business activity on Monday. This case is true even if you use that time for sightseeing (going up in the Arch!) or other personal activities.

Trips primarily for personal reasons

If your trip was primarily for personal reasons (such as that vacation to the Grand Canyon), some of the trip may be deductible — you can deduct any expenses at your destination that are directly related to your business. For example, paying for internet at your hotel so you can check your work emails counts, as does the taxi to and from the one client meeting you went on because you happened to be in the area. But spending an hour on business does not turn a personal trip into a business trip to be deducted.

Convention expenses

You can deduct your convention-travel expenses if you can prove that your attendance benefits your work. A convention for investment, political, social, or other purposes that are unrelated to your business isn't deductible. Nonbusiness expenses (such as social or sightseeing costs) are personal expenses and aren't deductible. And you can't deduct the travel expenses for your family!

TECHNICAL STUFF Your selection as a delegate to a convention doesn't automatically entitle you to a deduction. You must prove that your attendance is connected to your business. For conventions held outside North America, you must establish that the convention can be held only at that site. For example, an international seminar on tofu research held in Japan would qualify if that seminar was unique.

You can deduct 100 percent of the money you spent on airfare, hotels, and other miscellaneous costs on line 24a. But be careful — money you spend on room service is limited to 50 percent, unless you work in the transportation industry. Because you can deduct only 50 percent of your meals and entertainment expenses, only enter the 50 percent you're allowed to deduct on line 24b.

If you're in the transportation industry and are subject to the Department of Transportation restrictions on the number of hours you can work, you're allowed to deduct 80 percent of your meals and entertainment, so deduct them here, on line 24b.

Standard meal and incidental allowance — or "my city costs more than your city"

TIP Instead of keeping records for your actual meal and incidental expenses (tips and cleaning), you may choose to deduct a flat amount using the high-low method. You don't need to keep receipts with this method, but you do have to establish that you were away from home on business. Using the high-low method, you receive a daily meal and incidental expense allowance of between $55 and $76, depending on where you traveled.

City-by-city per diem rates are listed in IRS Publication 1542. Employees and self-employed taxpayers can use the standard meals and incidental allowance; however, if you're self-employed, you must actually have a hotel receipt to deduct the cost of your hotel.

Taxpayers in the transportation industry (those involved in moving people and goods) can use a flat rate of $52 a day for travel within the continental United States and $58 for travel beyond the continental United States for meals and incidental expenses.

People in the transportation industry covered by the U.S. Department of Transportation work rules get to deduct 80 percent of their meal expenses instead of the normal 50 percent limit in 2008 and beyond. Airline pilots, flight crews, ground crews, interstate bus and truck drivers, railroad engineers, conductors, and train crews are eligible for this break.

Unfortunately, self-employed taxpayers can't use the flat per diem rates listed for hotel-and-meal expenses; only employees can. They can, however, choose to use the part of the rate that applies to meals and incidentals. If you are self-employed, you can compute your travel expense deduction based on $45 a day for meals and incidentals plus your hotel bills. If you're traveling in a high-cost area, it's $58 a day.

TECHNICAL STUFF

The per diem rates change every year on October 1. Why? The federal government is on a fiscal year that starts on October 1, and because the feds set the per diem travel rates, the IRS switched to the federal way of doing things. So now, two rates exist in a given tax year, one for the period January 1, 2021, through September 30, 2021, and another set for the period October 1, 2021, through December 31, 2021. Check your dates as you're adding up all your per diems for 2021; you don't want to lose out on any amount of an available deduction because you didn't take into consideration the change in rates as of October 1, 2021.

WARNING

You can't use the standard meal and hotel per diem allowances if you're traveling for medical, charitable, or moving-expense purposes. And, if you're employed by your brother, sister, half-brother, half-sister, ancestor, or lineal descendent, you have to collect receipts and substantiate your expenses. Finally, you can't use the standard allowance if your employer is a corporation in which you hold 10 percent or more ownership. So many details!

Line 25: Utilities

Can you imagine what this line is for? If you're thinking of electric and telephone bills, for example, you hit the nail on the head. However, if you're claiming a home office deduction (discussed in further detail later in this chapter), your utility costs associated with your home belong on Form 8829, Expenses for Business Use of Your Home, and not here.

Line 26: Wages

Enter here the wages that you paid your employees. However, make sure you deduct payments to independent contractors on line 11. Deduction of independent contractor expenses is a hot issue with the IRS. So, flip back to line 11.

Line 27: Other expenses

On the reverse side of Schedule C is Part V, a schedule where you list your expenses whose descriptions defy the neat categories of lines 8–26. Here you can enter dues, subscriptions to related business periodicals, messenger services, overnight express fees, and so on. If you have more than nine items in the other expense category, just add another Part V page but enter the grand total on line 48 of only one of the forms.

Line 28: Total expenses

Addition time — add lines 8–27. This amount is what it costs to operate your business.

Line 29: Tentative profit (loss)

Subtract line 28 from line 7. If line 28 is more than line 7, you have a loss, which you enter as a negative number. For example, show a $5,000 loss as <$5,000> (a negative number).

Line 30: Form 8829

Yes, you can deduct home office expenses. If you work out of your home, the rules for claiming a deduction for a home office are now more lenient. That's the good news. The bad news? You must use Form 8829, Expenses for Business Use of Your Home, to claim the deduction for the portion that you use for business. You can find detailed instructions for filling it out and other rules you must follow to nail down this deduction in Chapter 17. You can't take a loss because of the home office deduction. You can, however, carry over an excess deduction amount to another year's tax return.

REMEMBER

Because only a portion of your total mortgage interest and real estate taxes are deducted as part of your home office expenses, don't forget to deduct the balance of your total mortgage interest that you entered on line 10(b) of Form 8829, and the balance of your total real estate taxes from line 11(b) of this form. Your mortgage interest balance goes on line 8a or 8b of Schedule A; the real estate taxes balance goes on line 5b of Schedule A. These two amounts represent your mortgage interest and taxes related to the portion of the house you live in.

Line 31: Net profit (or loss)

After you arrive at your net profit or loss, copy it onto Form 1040, Schedule 1, Part I, line 3, and then on Schedule SE (line 2) so that you can compute the amount of Social Security tax that you have to pay. See Chapter 17 to find out how to complete Schedule SE.

Lines 32a and b: At-risk rules

Suppose that you borrow money to go into business. The *at-risk* rules limit the amount of business losses that you can deduct on borrowed money that you're personally not liable to repay. For example, you need $20,000 to go into business. You invest $10,000, and your rich uncle gives you $10,000. You lose the entire $20,000. You can deduct only the $10,000 that you personally invested in your business. See Chapter 15 for more details on the at-risk rules. Basically, if you're personally responsible for all the liabilities of your business, check box 32a. If you are, you can deduct all your losses. If you're not at risk for all the investment that was made in your business, check 32b. Guess what? You have to fill out Form 6198, At Risk Limitations. This form determines how much of your loss you're allowed to deduct.

SEEK ADVICE

If you aren't personally responsible, see a tax professional, because the rules in this area are anything but clear or simple.

Start-up expenses

Start-up expenses are the expenses incurred in getting into business before the business actually begins operating. The types of expenses usually incurred during this period are market studies, consulting and professional services, and travel in securing prospective suppliers, customers, and feasibility studies, as well as costs involved in the actual organization of your business. When and whether you can deduct these expenses depends on whether you start the business.

If your total start-up organizational costs don't exceed $50,000, you may elect to deduct $5,000 of business start-up and $5,000 of organizational costs on your 2021 Schedule C just by adding these items to line 27. The remaining costs must be amortized over 180 months, beginning with the month in which the business begins operating. The deduction is computed on Form 4562, Part VI, Depreciation and Amortization.

If you incur start-up costs, but don't go into business, you can deduct some of your start-up expenses in the year that your attempt to go into business failed. Which expenses qualify? The answer isn't all that clear. You can deduct your business start-up expenses but not investigatory expenses. What's the difference, you ask? Here's what the IRS says the difference is. *Investigatory expenses* are costs incurred in reviewing a prospective business prior to reaching a final decision to acquire or enter the business. *Start-up expenses* are costs incurred after you decide to go into business but prior to the time the business actually begins to operate. If you guessed that a lot of taxpayers end up in Tax Court as the result of how they decided to separate the two, you're right. Start-up expenses are deducted on Schedule C.

TIP

Start-up costs don't include deductible interest, taxes, or research and experimental costs. They do include any costs you paid or incurred to operate an existing active trade or business, and costs incurred before the day your active trade or business begins. Start-up costs include amounts paid for surveys of markets, products, labor supply, transportation facilities, advertisements for the opening of a business, salaries and wages for employees being trained and their instructors, travel and other necessary costs for securing prospective distributors, suppliers or customers, and salaries and fees for executives and consultants, or for similar professional services.

Operating Loss

Suppose that you start a business, and it produces an *operating loss*, where your costs — not just equipment, but rent, salaries, and other expenses — exceed your income. You may write off that loss against any other income that you and your spouse made that year. Pay attention, now, because the NOL rules are year and industry specific, which can make things confusing.

NEW STUFF

If the loss is greater than your combined income in the current year, you have what is known in IRS jargon as a *net operating loss* (NOL). If you have generated an NOL in 2021, you must carry forward that NOL for an indefinite number of years, until the loss is entirely used. And, since no IRS rule would be worth anything at all without exceptions, if you generate an NOL in 2021 as either a farmer or a non-life insurance agent, you're still allowed to carry the loss back 2 years before carrying it forward for 20 years. This is a change from prior practice where NOLs in tax years ending no later than December 31, 2017, were carried back for 2 years and then carried forward for 20 years, but with no limitation on how much can be deducted, up to and including 100 percent of taxable income in each impacted year. And then there are those tax years beginning January 1, 2018, and ending no later than December 31, 2020, where the NOL deduction must be carried back for up to five years before being carried forward indefinitely. For any year where the first option was to carry back to a prior year, you can elect to forgo the lookback period, but this election, once made, is irrevocable, so you can't change your mind.

REMEMBER

Keep in mind, however, that you can't operate a part-time business, for example, that continually loses money. This situation is known as a *hobby loss*. If you don't show a profit in at least three of every five consecutive years, you may have a fight — with the IRS — on your hands. You must show a profit in at least three of every five consecutive years, or the IRS can declare your business a hobby and disallow your losses. The IRS doesn't consider your enterprise a business when you have continuing losses. No business, no business deductions. Some taxpayers have challenged this rule in Tax Court and won. They were able to prove that they ran their enterprises like a business and anticipated making a profit but didn't. The three-out-of-five-year rule is more of a guideline than an actual rule and was established to keep the IRS off your back. If you meet this requirement, the IRS can't claim that the losses in the two other years can't be deducted because the business is a hobby. Not making a profit in three out of five years doesn't automatically make the venture a hobby, but it's a strong indication that it may be.

Schedule F: Profit or Loss from Farming

Schedule F, Profit or Loss from Farming, is the form that you use to report the income and expenses from selling crops or livestock. All types of farms and farming income are included here, including farms that produce livestock, dairy, poultry, fish, aquaculture products, bee products, fruit, or a truck farm (because produce isn't the only thing farmers raise and harvest). Even though Schedule F is titled "Profit or Loss from Farming," you use this form to tell the IRS what you took in from operating a plantation, ranch, nursery, orchard, or oyster bed. Schedule F isn't as bad as it looks. In fact, it's set up in exactly the same way as Schedule C, Profit or Loss from Business. Although a business is a business (and farming is certainly a business), the IRS clearly thought that there were enough tax items that were peculiar to farming that it deserved its own schedule.

In this section, we take you through the highlights of Schedule F (check out Figure 13-2).

TIP

Until 1986, all taxpayers could reduce their taxes by averaging their incomes over a number of years whenever their incomes suddenly shot up. In 1998, income averaging returned for farmers, but not other taxpayers. Now, if farmers' incomes suddenly shoot up, they can once again reduce their taxes by averaging their incomes over the past three years.

SCHEDULE F
(Form 1040)

Department of the Treasury
Internal Revenue Service (99)

Profit or Loss From Farming

▶ Attach to Form 1040, Form 1040-SR, Form 1040-NR, Form 1041, or Form 1065.
▶ Go to *www.irs.gov/ScheduleF* for instructions and the latest information.

OMB No. 1545-0074

2021

Attachment Sequence No. **14**

Name of proprietor

Social security number (SSN)

A Principal crop or activity

B Enter code from Part IV ▶

C Accounting method:
☐ Cash ☐ Accrual

D Employer ID number (EIN) (see instr.)

E Did you "materially participate" in the operation of this business during 2021? If "No," see instructions for limit on passive losses ☐ Yes ☐ No

F Did you make any payments in 2021 that would require you to file Form(s) 1099? See instructions ☐ Yes ☐ No

G If "Yes," did you or will you file required Form(s) 1099? ☐ Yes ☐ No

Part I Farm Income—Cash Method. Complete Parts I and II. (Accrual method. Complete Parts II and III, and Part I, line 9.)

1a	Sales of purchased livestock and other resale items (see instructions)	1a		
b	Cost or other basis of purchased livestock or other items reported on line 1a	1b		
c	Subtract line 1b from line 1a		1c	
2	Sales of livestock, produce, grains, and other products you raised		2	
3a	Cooperative distributions (Form(s) 1099-PATR) . 3a	3b Taxable amount	3b	
4a	Agricultural program payments (see instructions) . 4a	4b Taxable amount	4b	
5a	Commodity Credit Corporation (CCC) loans reported under election		5a	
b	CCC loans forfeited . 5b	5c Taxable amount	5c	
6	Crop insurance proceeds and federal crop disaster payments (see instructions):			
a	Amount received in 2021 . 6a	6b Taxable amount	6b	
c	If election to defer to 2022 is attached, check here ▶ ☐	6d Amount deferred from 2020	6d	
7	Custom hire (machine work) income		7	
8	Other income, including federal and state gasoline or fuel tax credit or refund (see instructions)		8	
9	**Gross income.** Add amounts in the right column (lines 1c, 2, 3b, 4b, 5a, 5c, 6b, 6d, 7, and 8). If you use the accrual method, enter the amount from Part III, line 50. See instructions ▶		9	

Part II Farm Expenses—Cash and Accrual Method. Do not include personal or living expenses. See instructions.

10	Car and truck expenses (see instructions). Also attach **Form 4562**	10		23	Pension and profit-sharing plans . .	23	
11	Chemicals	11		24	Rent or lease (see instructions):		
12	Conservation expenses (see instructions)	12		a	Vehicles, machinery, equipment . .	24a	
13	Custom hire (machine work) . . .	13		b	Other (land, animals, etc.)	24b	
14	Depreciation and section 179 expense (see instructions)	14		25	Repairs and maintenance	25	
				26	Seeds and plants	26	
15	Employee benefit programs other than on line 23	15		27	Storage and warehousing	27	
				28	Supplies	28	
16	Feed	16		29	Taxes	29	
17	Fertilizers and lime	17		30	Utilities	30	
18	Freight and trucking	18		31	Veterinary, breeding, and medicine .	31	
19	Gasoline, fuel, and oil	19		32	Other expenses (specify):		
20	Insurance (other than health) . .	20		a	_____	32a	
21	Interest (see instructions):			b	_____	32b	
a	Mortgage (paid to banks, etc.) . .	21a		c	_____	32c	
b	Other	21b		d	_____	32d	
				e	_____	32e	
22	Labor hired (less employment credits)	22		f	_____	32f	
33	**Total expenses.** Add lines 10 through 32f. If line 32f is negative, see instructions . . . . ▶					33	
34	**Net farm profit or (loss).** Subtract line 33 from line 9					34	
	If a profit, stop here and see instructions for where to report. If a loss, complete line 36.						
35	Reserved for future use.						
36	Check the box that describes your investment in this activity and see instructions for where to report your loss:						
a	☐ All investment is at risk. **b** ☐ Some investment is not at risk.						

For Paperwork Reduction Act Notice, see the separate instructions.

Cat. No. 11346H

Schedule F (Form 1040) 2021

FIGURE 13-2: Schedule F, Profit or Loss from Farming.

Source: Internal Revenue Service

When you get to line 44 of your Form 1040 — the line where you compute your tax — use Schedule J, Form 1040, Income Averaging for Farmers and Fishermen. Make sure that you attach this schedule to your return.

Before you even attempt to prepare your Schedule F, obtain a copy of IRS Publication 225 (*Farmer's Tax Guide*), either by calling 800-829-3676 or from the internet at www.irs.gov.

Figuring out Schedule F

Even though Schedule F is very similar to Schedule C, it does include some crucial differences between farms and other kinds of business. Here are some of the more important differences.

Line C: Accounting method

Most farmers use the *cash method* because it's the easier of the two methods. You total what you received and subtract what you paid. You don't need to figure out what you owe and who owes you. You don't need to determine your inventory at the end of the year (for crops or animals that you didn't sell). A slight exception to this rule also exists, however. If you bought live-stock or other items for resale, you must keep a separate record of the items that you didn't sell. These purchases can't be deducted until they're sold. And thanks to depreciation rules, farm structures and equipment can't be deducted in the year you paid for them. They have to be depreciated over their useful lives.

Under the *accrual method,* you report income in the year sales are made — even if the sales are billed or collected in a later year. You deduct expenses in the year in which the expenses are incurred, even if you don't pay these expenses until later.

Under both cash and accrual methods, you report all income and expenses for the calendar year ending December 31. You choose one of the two accounting methods in the year that you file your first Schedule F. After you select a method, you can't change an accounting method without IRS permission.

The cash method of accounting gives you more control over when your farm sees a profit from year to year. For example, if next year looks like a slower year for you, you may choose to shift more of your income into next year. Doing so will likely save you tax dollars, because you're more likely to be in a lower tax bracket that year (if it is, in fact, a less profitable year for you). You can legally shift your income by deferring sales or by delaying sending out bills until January (bills that you otherwise would have mailed in December, for example). Likewise, to lower your taxable income this year, you can pay more of your expenses in December instead of waiting until January.

TIP

Another reason for selecting the cash method of accounting is that you don't have to fill out lines 37 through 50 in Part III of Schedule F. That part is for accrual method folks. Isn't that reason enough?

If you're operating a farm and aiming to produce a tax deduction (commonly referred to as a *tax shelter*) rather than a profit, you're required to use the accrual method.

Part I: Farm Income — Cash Method

If you're able to use the cash method of accounting, you need to fill out Part I in order to arrive at your gross income. Unlike Schedule C, which is fairly unspecific about what to include and where to include it, Schedule F lists out each category of income. All you need to do is pop in the numbers and add them up on line 9.

REMEMBER

Cash basis means that you actually received payment in order for it to count as income in the current year. The fact that you sent an invoice for an item in 2021 doesn't mean you need to include it in your 2021 income; if your customer doesn't pay you until 2022, that income becomes next year's problem.

Part II: Farm Expenses — Cash and Accrual Method

Part II covers what you paid during 2021 for goods and services related to your farm, and every farmer filing a Schedule F has to fill out this part, whether you're a cash basis or accrual basis taxpayer.

Once again, most of the expenses are similar or even identical to those expenses you'll find on Schedule C; however, several do require additional explanation:

LINE 11: CHEMICALS

On line 11, enter the total amount you paid for pesticides and herbicides.

LINE 12: CONSERVATION EXPENSES

Want to see an angry farmer just before April 15? Just tell them that the $10,000 they spent to clear a pasture or cut diversion channels can't be deducted until they sell the land. Thankfully, though, these types of expenses are deductible if they're consistent with a government conservation program. But limits do exist. Conservation expenses can't exceed 25 percent of your total farming income. The 75 percent you can't deduct is carried over to 2022 and subject to that year's 25 percent limit. You can deduct the following conservation expenses:

>> Conditioning

>> Constructing diversion channels, drainage ditches, irrigation ditches, earthen dams, outlets, or ponds

>> Contour furrowing

>> Eradicating brush

>> Grading

>> Leveling

>> Planting windbreaks

>> Restoring soil fertility

>> Terracing

LINE 13: CUSTOM HIRE (MACHINE WORK) EXPENSES

If you paid someone to spray your crop, plow a field, or harvest a crop, enter the amount you paid here. Tax auditors are trained to investigate this deduction to find out whether you're deducting land-clearing expenses or paying someone to build structures that have to be depreciated.

Remember two things: Land-clearing can be deducted only as a conservation expense and is subject to the limit explained on line 12. And if you pay a custom hire $600 or more over the course of 2021, you have to file Form 1099-NEC with the IRS by February 28, 2022, if you're filing on paper, or March 31, 2022, if you're filing electronically; in either case, you must furnish a copy to the person you paid by January 31, 2022.

LINE 14: DEPRECIATION AND SECTION 179 EXPENSE DEDUCTION

Farmers are entitled to deduct the cost of their equipment over its useful economic life. And for most items, such as cars, farmers do it the same way as everyone else (see the explanation for Schedule C, line 13, earlier in this chapter). However, all farm property may not be depreciated in the same way as other business property. Although other businesses must depreciate using the *General Depreciation System* (GDS) (described on line 13, Schedule C, earlier in this chapter), farms may elect to use the *Alternate Depreciation System* (ADS).

What's the difference? Depreciation using GDS involves using uniform capitalization rules, whereas ADS depreciation doesn't. When the property involved is a computer or some other form of machinery that is productive from the time you put it into service, using uniform capitalization rules makes sense. When you're talking about fruit trees that take years and years before becoming truly productive, uniform capitalization isn't such a positive concept. Check out IRS Publication 225 *(Farmer's Tax Guide)* to find out more about your depreciation options.

NEW STUFF

Farmers may elect to completely depreciate up to $1,050,000 of 2021 purchases using Section 179 depreciation in 2021. The Section 179 depreciation deduction begins to phase out when total 2021 new purchases hit $2,620,000, and it's totally gone if you purchased $3,670,000 or more of property in 2021. In addition, 100 percent bonus depreciation is also available. Check out the section on depreciation earlier in this chapter, in the discussion for Schedule C, for more information on these two 2021 changes.

SEEK ADVICE

Choosing what method you need to use to depreciate your farm property is never easy, and after you make an election to use ADS depreciation, changing it is hard. Talking with a tax professional makes a great deal of sense. Make sure that you choose one who deals extensively with farmers. As the number of farmers continues to decrease, finding a professional with ample experience in this area is becoming increasingly difficult.

LINE 22: LABOR HIRED (LESS EMPLOYMENT CREDITS)

On line 22, enter the amount you paid in cash wages — that is, the total amount your employees earn before you withhold income, Social Security, and Medicare taxes. The cost of meals and lodging that you provide isn't considered wages, which means that employees don't pay tax on it. However, you're allowed to deduct those costs as a valid "other expense." On line 32, you can deduct the cost of food you buy for your employees.

Any cash allowance that you give employees to buy meals is considered part of their wages. Normally, you can deduct only 50 percent of the cost of meals. (See "Lines 24a–b: Travel and meals" earlier in this chapter for more information.)

TAX CUT

If you provide meals to employees for your convenience, the cost of those meals is not included in the employees' compensation, and you are allowed to deduct 50 percent of the cost from your farming income.

If you pay your employees *in-kind,* you can deduct (as a labor expense) the value of the goods they received. For example, suppose that you give an employee a horse worth $1,500 as payment for painting your barn. You can then deduct the $1,500 as a labor expense. However, remember that you must also report (as income) the $1,500 as if you sold the horse to your employee because bartering is a taxable event (and you need to fill out Form 1099-B to report the barter's value).

The wages you paid and the income tax and Social Security and Medicare taxes that you're required to withhold are reported to the government on Form 943, Employer's Annual Federal Tax Return for Agricultural Employees. You must file this form by January 31, 2022. All withheld taxes plus employer contributions must be paid by electronic funds transfer, either through your payroll provider or through the Electronic Federal Tax Payment System (EFTPS). If you withheld less than $2,500 for the year, you can pay what you owe when you file Form 943. But as soon as you withhold between $2,500 and $50,000 over the course of the year, you must turn over to the government what you withheld on a monthly schedule, by the 15th day of the following month. For payrolls that withhold over $50,000 over the course of the year, you're required to make your tax deposits on a semi-weekly schedule, where you make your tax deposit on the Friday following a payday that falls on Saturday–Tuesday, and deposit withheld taxes on the Wednesday following a Wednesday, Thursday, or Friday payroll. How do you know which deposit period to choose? Look back to your 2020 Form 943 and see what the total was on line 13. You'd think that if you're required to wire your withholding taxes in 2022, you'd have to do so because you withheld more than $50,000 in 2021 and not 2020. Guess what? You'd be wrong. If you operate more than a mom-and-pop family farm (that includes everyone who withholds $2,500 or more during the year), get your hands on IRS Publication 51 (*Circular A, Agricultural Employer's Tax Guide*), which explains everything about this subject in all its glorious detail.

The wages you pay to a child under the age of 18 aren't subject to Social Security and Medicare taxes. So, as long as the child's wages total less than $12,550 (the standard deduction for tax year 2021), the child doesn't have to pay any tax at all (as long as that $12,550 is the child's only source of income). And even better, you get to deduct the $12,550 as a labor expense. The only requirement is that the amount you pay for the child's services must be reasonable. For example, you can't claim that you paid your three-year-old $12,550 to clean out the barn. And because the standard deduction is tied to the rate of inflation, every year it goes up.

LINES 36A AND 36B: AT RISK

If you have a loss and are personally liable to pay back every dime that you borrowed to go into business, check line 36a. If not, check line 36b and checkout line 27 of Schedule C earlier in this chapter to find out more. The rules are complex regarding the deduction of losses when you have no economic risk.

Identifying tax issues specific to farmers

Unfortunately, you still have to cope with a few additional issues that we explain in the following sections.

Estimated taxes

The IRS doesn't want to wait until April 15 to collect what you owe. If two-thirds of your income was from farming in 2020 or 2021, you have to make an estimated income tax payment by January 18, 2022, for what you owe for 2021, or file your return (including your full tax payment) by March 1, 2022. If you don't make an estimated payment, you'll be charged a penalty equal to current market interest rates. The penalty is computed on Form 2210-F, Underpayment of Estimated Tax by Farmers and Fishermen.

The amount of your required estimated tax payment is 66⅔ percent of your 2021 actual tax or 100 percent of your 2020 tax, whichever is the smaller amount. For example, suppose that your 2021 tax is $10,000 and your 2020 tax was $1,000. Because your 2020 tax of $1,000 is smaller than $6,667 (⅔ of your 2022 tax of $10,000), you need to pay only $1,000 on January 18, 2022. The $9,000 balance can be paid when you file on April 15.

If you file your return by March 1, 2022, and pay what you owe, you can skip having to make the January 18 payment.

Even though you file your return by March 1, 2022, you have until April 18, 2022 (April 19, 2022, if you reside in either Maine or Massachusetts), to make and deduct your IRA contribution (see Line 16, Chapter 7). If two-thirds of your income in 2020 or 2021 wasn't from farming, then regular estimated tax rules apply. See Chapter 17.

If you're hearing about all this information for the first time — sorry. Mark your January 2023 calendar so you don't face it again when you file your 2022 return.

Operating at a loss

When operating any business, you must show a profit in at least three of every five consecutive years, or the IRS will term your business a hobby and disallow your losses, a situation known as hobby losses. If you're breeding, training, showing, or racing horses, however, you must make a profit in *two out of seven years* to keep the tax collector away. The IRS doesn't consider your enterprise a business if you have continuing losses — no business, no business deductions.

The three-out-of-five rule was established to keep the IRS happy. If you meet this standard, the IRS can't claim that the losses in the two other years can't be deducted because the business is a hobby. Not making a profit in three out of five years or two out of seven years doesn't automatically make the venture a hobby, but it is a strong indication that it may be.

However, if your farm does incur a net loss in 2021, you can write off that loss against any other income you and your spouse made that year. And there's more — if the loss is greater than your combined income in the current year, you can carry the loss back over each of the past five years and obtain a refund on the tax you paid at that time. If carrying it back still doesn't use up the loss, you can carry it forward to offset your income in the next 20 years. You can also choose not to carry the loss back and use it only in future years instead. See Chapter 20 for more information on amending a prior year's return and carrying losses back as well as forward.

Your Social Security tax

This tax is commonly referred to as the *self-employment tax*. Chapter 17 shows you how to compute this amount and take a deduction for half of what you pay in Social Security tax.

Farmers have an optional method for computing this tax. The computation is made in Part II of Schedule SE. Here's how it works. If your gross income (from line 9 on Schedule F) is $8,820 or less, or your net income (line 34) was less than $6,367, you can report two-thirds of your gross income as *your net farm income from self-employment*. Remember, you use this amount to compute your Social Security tax (not for figuring the amount on which you pay income tax). For example, suppose that your gross income was $1,800 and your net income (profit) was $500 — you can elect to report $1,200 (⅔ of $1,800) as your self-employment income, for the purpose of computing your Social Security tax. (However, you pay income tax on only the $500 of net income that you earned.) Why do all this?

>> You receive credit for Social Security coverage.

>> Your dependent childcare deduction and earned income credit increase with this method.

WARNING

According to the IRS, dividends from a farm cooperative are considered self-employment, and not investment income, which isn't subject to this tax. If you receive part of a crop from a tenant farmer, it's considered rental income, not subject to self-employment tax if you didn't materially participate in overseeing your tenant's activities.

Investment credits

The law allows an *investment credit*, which is similar to a direct payment of tax, for what you spent on reforestation or to rehabilitate historic structures and buildings placed in service before 1936. For reforestation, the law allows a credit for up to $10,000 of these expenditures. If you rehabilitate a historic structure, you can take an investment credit equal to 20 percent of your expenses. The *energy credit* equals 30 percent of what you spend installing solar or qualified fuel cell property or 10 percent of the cost of geothermal energy-producing equipment. These credits are computed on Form 3468, Investment Credit. Also check out the tax incentives for empowerment zones and other distressed communities in IRS Publication 954 *(Tax Incentives for Distressed Communities)*, and Form 8850, Work Opportunity and Welfare-to-Welfare Credits.

Fuel credits or refunds

You can claim a credit (against your current year's tax liability) or a refund where, provided the amount is for $750 or more, the IRS will cut you a quarterly check for the taxes you paid for the off-highway use of fuels on your farm. The credit is computed on Form 4136, Credit for Federal Tax Paid on Fuels. *Note:* The definition of *off-highway* use doesn't apply to pleasure boats.

You can also buy dyed diesel fuel tax-free for use on a farm. Ask the vendor for an exemption certificate. Fill it out, hand it back, and watch the price drop.

TIP

You can now claim a credit or refund for the excise tax on undyed kerosene or diesel fuel for home use.

Electric and clean fuel-burning vehicles

Don't overlook the Alternative Motor Vehicle Credit (refer to Chapter 16) if you purchased a new alternative fuel or hybrid vehicle in 2021. You claim this credit on Form 8910, Alternative Motor Vehicle Credit.

Sale of a farm or equipment

The sale of a farm or farm equipment gets tricky — you must consider many different factors, such as recapture of depreciation, credits, and basis (cost) adjustments to the property being sold. These types of sales are reported on Form 4797, Sales of Business Property. For more information on capital gains, see Chapter 14.

Cash-method farmers who use the installment method for reporting the sale of farm property don't have to take installment sales into account when determining whether they're subject to the Alternative Minimum Tax. See information in Chapter 8 if you're subject to this fiendish tax because you're claiming too many deductions.

SELF-EMPLOYMENT AND THE GIG ECONOMY

We'd be failing in our duty to fill you in on the ins and outs of the tax code if we didn't talk about the latest trend in employment: the gig economy. If you're driving an Uber or a Lyft, Door Dashing with the latest in COVID-19 healthy meals, or providing expert advice as a consultant, if the person paying you isn't paying wages, but rather a fee based on either hours worked, miles driven, or meals delivered, you're part of the gig economy, a world of flexible, temporary, or freelance jobs. Some folks are doing this sort of work in addition to a regular job, whereas other folks are only doing gig work, sometimes having two or three different gigs.

As with running a small business, as a gig worker, you're no longer just collecting a paycheck; you're also responsible for the business side of your business. You should track your expenses just as if you were a brick-and-mortar store. As we're fond of telling people, the reason most businesses fail is not because the person running the business is bad at what they do, but it is because they're terrible, and not very interested, in the business end of things.

The most important tool for success is to keep good records. They don't need to be fancy, and you don't need to run right out and get the best computer and the best bookkeeping software. Here are a few ideas for how to organize yourself, and your business:

- If you have a smartphone, there are many business recordkeeping apps. Put one on your phone to scan receipts and track mileage.

- If you're still working on paper, keep an envelope in your car, and one in your house, for all receipts as you receive them.

- Keep a notebook in your car to record all business miles, as well as whenever you buy gas. Make sure to record your starting mileage on January 1 of each year and your ending mileage on December 31.

- Many free business accounting programs are available on the internet. Try them out, decide on one, and then use it.

- If you have a separate space in your home that is used only to run your business, know that you're going to be taking a home office deduction on your tax returns, so make sure you keep all your utility bills, repair bills, mortgage interest statements, and the like. In fact, anything to do with your home can be used to calculate the deduction, so if you plant perennial flowers in your garden, have the house power washed, or repave your driveway, some portion of those expenses are going to come off your income tax return. Keep the receipts!

There is nothing worse than having income reported to the IRS but no substantiation of the deductions you're entitled to take to reduce that income to the amount you actually earned after expenses. Paying attention to the details of the running of your business will make preparing your tax returns a much easier task.

IN THIS CHAPTER

» Taking a look at Schedule D

» Seeing how Form 8949 fits in

» Finding your adjusted basis

» Looking at short-term and long-term capital gains and losses

» Dealing with the sale of your home, stock matters, and bad debts

» Discovering the tax implications of cryptocurrency

Chapter 14

Capital Gains and Losses: Schedule D and Form 8949

I f you sell something like a stock, bond, or mutual fund (or any other investment held outside of a tax-sheltered retirement account) for more than you paid for it, you've just received a capital gain, and you'll owe tax on that. Conversely, if you sell that asset for less than you paid for it, you've just generated a capital loss, which is tax deductible. Although it may seem unfair, a loss on the sale of your home, auto, jewelry, art, and furniture isn't deductible. That's a cruel reality regarding the sale of personal items.

Schedule D is the place where you plug in your profit or loss on the following examples:

» Your coin or stamp collection

» Your home (profit only, if you can't exclude all the gain)

» Household furnishings

» Jewelry and art

» Stocks and bonds

PROPERTY DEFINED

Definitions are the spice of life for IRS agents. Here's an important one.

When most people refer to property, they mean real estate. But when the IRS talks about property, it can be anything that you own, such as stocks, bonds, cars, boats, or computers. So, when you see the term property on a form, the government is talking about more than the actual old homestead. For example, a landlord's payment to a tenant to give up a rent-controlled apartment is considered the sale of property (in this case, not the apartment itself, but the right to stay in the apartment is the property that has been sold) subject to lower capital gain tax rates.

In this chapter, discover the wonderful world of capital gains. See what sorts of property qualify for preferential tax treatment when you sell them and what kinds don't. Figure out the rules surrounding the sale of your home (one of the last, truly great tax breaks out there), and find out the difference between a short-term sale and a short sale. Most of all, though, this chapter tells you what you need to know, and where to find all the information you need to successfully complete your Schedule D and Form 8849, which provides the back-up detail to Schedule D.

Claiming Capital Sales: Collectibles and Real Estate

The maximum capital gains rate on the sale of collectibles (art, antiques, stamp collections, memorabilia, and so on) is 28 percent.

SEEK ADVICE

One additional capital gains rate of 25 percent kicks in when you sell depreciable real estate. In that case, part of the profit — equal to the depreciation that you deducted through the years — is taxed at 25 percent, and the balance of the profit is taxed at the lower capital gains rate. Taxing all the depreciation at 25 percent relates only to real estate that you started to depreciate after 1986. If you started to depreciate it prior to 1987, part of the depreciation gets taxed at 25 percent and part at regular tax rates. Our advice: If you sell real estate that you started depreciating before 1987, see a tax pro.

Noting the Different Parts of Schedule D

After you determine that you have a capital sale you need to report, you need to figure out where to report it. The first page of Schedule D (see Figure 14-1) gives you two options: Part I, Short-term capital gains and losses (for property held one year or less), and Part II, Long-term capital gains and losses (for everything that you've owned for longer than one year). The length of time you owned the property determines whether you complete Part I or Part II. If you have a capital gain that is subject to the 25 percent or 28 percent rates, you must also use the worksheet in your instruction booklet. Finally, Part III summarizes all that you've done on Parts I and II of Schedule D plus the worksheets for 28 percent and 25 percent gains that you find in your instruction booklet.

SCHEDULE D
(Form 1040)

Department of the Treasury
Internal Revenue Service (99)

Capital Gains and Losses

▶ Attach to Form 1040, 1040-SR, or 1040-NR.
▶ Go to *www.irs.gov/ScheduleD* for instructions and the latest information.
▶ Use Form 8949 to list your transactions for lines 1b, 2, 3, 8b, 9, and 10.

OMB No. 1545-0074

2021

Attachment
Sequence No. **12**

Name(s) shown on return

Your social security number

Did you dispose of any investment(s) in a qualified opportunity fund during the tax year? ☐ Yes ☐ No
If "Yes," attach Form 8949 and see its instructions for additional requirements for reporting your gain or loss.

Part I — Short-Term Capital Gains and Losses—Generally Assets Held One Year or Less (see instructions)

See instructions for how to figure the amounts to enter on the lines below. This form may be easier to complete if you round off cents to whole dollars.	(d) Proceeds (sales price)	(e) Cost (or other basis)	(g) Adjustments to gain or loss from Form(s) 8949, Part I, line 2, column (g)	(h) Gain or (loss) Subtract column (e) from column (d) and combine the result with column (g)
1a Totals for all short-term transactions reported on Form 1099-B for which basis was reported to the IRS and for which you have no adjustments (see instructions). However, if you choose to report all these transactions on Form 8949, leave this line blank and go to line 1b .				
1b Totals for all transactions reported on Form(s) 8949 with **Box A** checked				
2 Totals for all transactions reported on Form(s) 8949 with **Box B** checked				
3 Totals for all transactions reported on Form(s) 8949 with **Box C** checked				

4 Short-term gain from Form 6252 and short-term gain or (loss) from Forms 4684, 6781, and 8824 . .	**4**	
5 Net short-term gain or (loss) from partnerships, S corporations, estates, and trusts from Schedule(s) K-1	**5**	
6 Short-term capital loss carryover. Enter the amount, if any, from line 8 of your **Capital Loss Carryover Worksheet** in the instructions	**6**	( )
7 **Net short-term capital gain or (loss).** Combine lines 1a through 6 in column (h). If you have any long-term capital gains or losses, go to Part II below. Otherwise, go to Part III on the back	**7**	

Part II — Long-Term Capital Gains and Losses—Generally Assets Held More Than One Year (see instructions)

See instructions for how to figure the amounts to enter on the lines below. This form may be easier to complete if you round off cents to whole dollars.	(d) Proceeds (sales price)	(e) Cost (or other basis)	(g) Adjustments to gain or loss from Form(s) 8949, Part II, line 2, column (g)	(h) Gain or (loss) Subtract column (e) from column (d) and combine the result with column (g)
8a Totals for all long-term transactions reported on Form 1099-B for which basis was reported to the IRS and for which you have no adjustments (see instructions). However, if you choose to report all these transactions on Form 8949, leave this line blank and go to line 8b .				
8b Totals for all transactions reported on Form(s) 8949 with **Box D** checked				
9 Totals for all transactions reported on Form(s) 8949 with **Box E** checked				
10 Totals for all transactions reported on Form(s) 8949 with **Box F** checked.				

11 Gain from Form 4797, Part I; long-term gain from Forms 2439 and 6252; and long-term gain or (loss) from Forms 4684, 6781, and 8824	**11**	
12 Net long-term gain or (loss) from partnerships, S corporations, estates, and trusts from Schedule(s) K-1	**12**	
13 Capital gain distributions. See the instructions	**13**	
14 Long-term capital loss carryover. Enter the amount, if any, from line 13 of your **Capital Loss Carryover Worksheet** in the instructions	**14**	( )
15 **Net long-term capital gain or (loss).** Combine lines 8a through 14 in column (h). Then, go to Part III on the back	**15**	

For Paperwork Reduction Act Notice, see your tax return instructions.   Cat. No. 11338H   Schedule D (Form 1040) 2021

FIGURE 14-1:
Schedule D,
Page 1.

Source: Internal Revenue Service

You list all your individual capital gains and losses on line 1 or 8. Line 1 is for short-term gains and losses, and line 8 is for long-term gains and losses.

WARNING

Accuracy counts when preparing your Schedule D. Be precise when figuring your holding period because there's a big difference between long-term and short-term capital gains tax rates. And make sure, because the IRS checks its records, that the total of line 3 and line 10 of Schedule D matches the total from all your Forms 1099-B, Proceeds from Broker and Barter Exchange Transactions.

Form 8949: Sales and other dispositions of capital assets

NEW STUFF

Over the years, the amount of information that gets reported to the IRS on your behalf and the details of that information that the IRS now requires you to submit made Schedule D unmanageable. Accordingly, rather than make Schedule D even more confusing than it now is, the IRS determined that they needed a separate form to list out all the separate transactions over the course of any given year. Welcome, Form 8949, Sales and other dispositions of capital assets, which is where you'll now list out all of your transactions, bringing only the totals from your Form(s) 8949 to Schedule D.

You may have as many as three Form(s) 8949 with your tax return. Once you've determined whether a sale is a long-term or short-term transaction, these are the additional categories you'll need to break your transactions into:

>> Transactions reported on Form (s) 1099-B showing basis was reported to the IRS (Box A);

>> Transactions reported on Form(s) 1099-B showing basis wasn't reported to the IRS (Box B); and

>> Transactions not reported to you on Form 1099-B (Box C).

You cannot mix and match these three categories on a single Form 1099-B; instead, you must check the appropriate box for each sort of transaction, and then list only those qualifying transactions on that part of Form 8949. Form 8949 lists short-term transactions on page 1 (see Figure 14-2), and long-term transactions on page 2.

TIP

If you're someone who is constantly trading stocks and bonds, and therefore has received pages and pages of Form 1099-B transactions from your broker, you may enter the aggregate total of all Box A (short-term) and Box D (long-term) transactions onto one line provided that the basis for all the transactions has been reported to the IRS, and you have no adjustments to basis to make to any of them. You must, however, enter all transactions belonging either in Boxes B or C (short-term) or E or F (long-term) individually on Form 8949.

Only after you have completed all the necessary Forms 8949 can you now begin to prepare Schedule D.

Here's how to enter the information into Form 8949: Suppose that you sold 100 shares of Wonder Widget stock for $4,000 on April 17, 2021. Because you paid $6,000 for the shares on April 16, 2020, you have a capital loss of $2,000. To figure out whether the loss is long term or short term, start counting on April 17. The 17th of each month starts the beginning of a new month. Because you sold the shares on April 17, 2021 — one day more than 12 months — the loss is long term, so you'll place this transaction in Part II of Form 8949. (Had you sold them on April 16 — exactly 12 months after buying them — the loss would have been short term, and your transaction would have been entered into Form 8949, Part I.) Here's how to show the IRS exactly what happened.

Form 8949

Department of the Treasury
Internal Revenue Service

Sales and Other Dispositions of Capital Assets

▶ Go to *www.irs.gov/Form8949* for instructions and the latest information.
▶ File with your Schedule D to list your transactions for lines 1b, 2, 3, 8b, 9, and 10 of Schedule D.

OMB No. 1545-0074

2021

Attachment
Sequence No. **12A**

Name(s) shown on return

Social security number or taxpayer identification number

Before you check Box A, B, or C below, see whether you received any Form(s) 1099-B or substitute statement(s) from your broker. A substitute statement will have the same information as Form 1099-B. Either will show whether your basis (usually your cost) was reported to the IRS by your broker and may even tell you which box to check.

Part I **Short-Term.** Transactions involving capital assets you held 1 year or less are generally short-term (see instructions). For long-term transactions, see page 2.

Note: You may aggregate all short-term transactions reported on Form(s) 1099-B showing basis was reported to the IRS and for which no adjustments or codes are required. Enter the totals directly on Schedule D, line 1a; you aren't required to report these transactions on Form 8949 (see instructions).

You *must* check Box A, B, or C below. Check only one box. If more than one box applies for your short-term transactions, complete a separate Form 8949, page 1, for each applicable box. If you have more short-term transactions than will fit on this page for one or more of the boxes, complete as many forms with the same box checked as you need.

☐ **(A)** Short-term transactions reported on Form(s) 1099-B showing basis was reported to the IRS (see **Note** above)
☐ **(B)** Short-term transactions reported on Form(s) 1099-B showing basis **wasn't** reported to the IRS
☐ **(C)** Short-term transactions not reported to you on Form 1099-B

1						Adjustment, if any, to gain or loss. If you enter an amount in column (g), enter a code in column (f). See the separate instructions.		
(a) Description of property (Example: 100 sh. XYZ Co.)	**(b)** Date acquired (Mo., day, yr.)	**(c)** Date sold or disposed of (Mo., day, yr.)	**(d)** Proceeds (sales price) (see instructions)	**(e)** Cost or other basis. See the **Note** below and see *Column (e)* in the separate instructions		**(f)** Code(s) from instructions	**(g)** Amount of adjustment	**(h)** Gain or (loss). Subtract column (e) from column (d) and combine the result with column (g)
2 Totals. Add the amounts in columns (d), (e), (g), and (h) (subtract negative amounts). Enter each total here and include on your Schedule D, **line 1b** (if **Box A** above is checked), **line 2** (if **Box B** above is checked), or **line 3** (if **Box C** above is checked) ▶								

FIGURE 14-2:
Form 8949,
Page 1.

Note: If you checked Box A above but the basis reported to the IRS was incorrect, enter in column (e) the basis as reported to the IRS, and enter an adjustment in column (g) to correct the basis. See *Column (g)* in the separate instructions for how to figure the amount of the adjustment.

For Paperwork Reduction Act Notice, see your tax return instructions.   Cat. No. 37768Z   Form **8949** (2021)

Source: Internal Revenue Service

Column (a) Description of the property	100 shares of Wonder Widget
Column (b) Date acquired	4-16-20
Column (c) Date sold	4-17-21
Column (d) Sales price	$4,000
Column (e) Cost or other basis	$6,000
Columns (f) and (g)	Leave blank
Column (h) Gain or <loss>	<$2,000>

If you need more lines than Form 8949 supplies, you can add continuation pages. If you're working on a computer, your program will automatically do this for you; if you're handwriting this out manually, start a new copy of Form 8949, tick the appropriate box, and continue entering your transactions.

What do you do with Columns (f) and (g)? If the basis that's been reported to the IRS by the broker isn't the basis you show, you're going to need to correct the basis information. There are codes that can be put into Column (f), from a list that's shown in the instructions for Form 8949. Find the letter code(s) that match your situation and enter that code into Column (f). If more than one code applies, enter all the applicable letters into Column (f) without any spaces between them. In Column (g), if the change involves a change in basis, you're going to enter the adjustment the IRS must make to arrive at the correct gain or loss. Once again, if you're doing this on paper, you need to work very carefully through this obstacle course; if you're preparing using a computer, you can just enter the codes into the tax program, and the program will make the adjustments and assign each transaction to the correct copy of Form 8949.

DETAILS FOR FIGURING SHORT TERM OR LONG TERM

In most cases, whether you've held a security or other asset for more than 12 months is obvious. Here are some details that may help in less-clear cases. For securities traded on an established securities market, you begin counting the days in your holding period the day after the trading date on which you bought the securities and stop on the trading date on which you sold them. For holding-period purposes, ignore the settlement date — this is the date when you actually pay the broker for a purchase or get paid from the broker for a sale.

For property that you received as a gift, you're considered to have purchased the property on the same day that the donor did — and not on the date of the gift — if you use the donor's tax basis as your basis. However, the holding period starts on the date of the gift if you sell it at a loss, and you're required to use the fair market value (FMV) of the property when it was given to you. Property inherited via someone's estate is treated as a sale of a long-term capital asset, even if you sold the shares or property the day after you received them, or the decedent bought them the day before they died. The more-than-12-months-rule is ignored.

When you purchase assets such as stocks or bonds by exercising an option, the holding period starts the day after the option is exercised — and not on the day that you received or purchased the option.

Calculating Your Adjusted Basis

Most of the columns on Form 8949 are fairly self-explanatory. The description of the property, the date sold, and the sales price can be lifted directly from Form 1099-B, Proceeds from Broker and Barter Exchange Transactions (in the case of marketable securities) or from your HUD settlement sheet if you've sold your house and have to report a taxable gain.

Column (e), your cost or other basis in the property, is where you tell the IRS how much money you have invested in this particular piece of property, either personally or because you received it as a gift, an inheritance, or as part of a divorce settlement. If you're working primarily with the sale of stocks and bonds, your broker should have your basis and will list it on Form 1099-B (or any substitute form they may use). But if you've sold something that your broker doesn't have that information for, or that has never touched the hands of your broker, here are some items to consider when calculating your adjusted tax basis.

What's the starting point?

Figure out when this particular property came into your possession and by what method. Remember, you didn't need to necessarily buy it — you may have inherited it, earned it, received it as a gift from Great-Aunt Sadie, or obtained it from your ex-spouse as part of the property settlement. Regardless of the method, it came in with a cost already attached to it.

Dealing with purchased property

If you purchased a security from a broker, you should have received a sales confirmation. The confirmation lists the number of shares, the stock's name, the price per share, the gross price for your total purchase, any commissions and fees that were charged when you bought, and the date you placed the trade. Keep that confirmation in a permanent file so you can access that information whenever you need it. For your home, you'll have received a HUD settlement sheet. And if you buy collectibles (artwork, baseball cards, and the like), keep your sales receipts.

Looking at property received via inheritance, gift, divorce, or for services

For inherited property, obtain from the estate's executor the property value on the date of the decedent's death, or if the executor elects, the alternate valuation date six months after date. Your acquisition date in the stock is the decedent's date of death. The following types of property have different requirements.

>> **Gifted property:** To figure the basis of property that you received as a gift, you must know the donor's basis at the time the gift was made, its fair market value (FMV) at the time the gift was made, and any gift tax that the donor paid.

- If the FMV at the time of the gift was more than the donor's basis, then your basis for figuring a gain or loss is the donor's basis.

- If the FMV at the time of the gift was less than the donor's basis, your basis for figuring a gain is the donor's basis, and your basis for figuring a loss is the FMV at the time of the gift.

>> **Property received for services:** The amount that you're required to include in your income becomes your basis. Suppose that for putting a deal together you receive 100 shares of stock valued at $10,000. Because you had to pay tax on the value of the shares, your tax basis for the 100 shares is $10,000.

>> **Property received in a divorce:** You use your spouse's basis. Generally, neither spouse is required to pay tax on property transferred as part of a divorce settlement.

Making adjustments to your basis

For many people, tracking their basis in property is like shooting at a moving target — the darned thing just won't stay put. Still, keeping track of your basis in property isn't impossible if you know what you're supposed to look at. The following list includes some of the more common basis adjustments:

>> **Dividend reinvestment plans:** Some people opt to increase their investment in a particular security or mutual fund by reinvesting their ordinary dividends, their capital gain distributions, or both. This is nothing more than using the cash dividends you would have received to purchase additional shares. Doing so adds not only shares to your holding, but also to the basis. For example, at the beginning of 2020, you owned 1,000 shares of XYZ Corp, with a basis of $20,000. XYZ Corp paid a $1 per share dividend during 2020, providing you a total dividend of $1,000, which you declared and paid tax on as dividend income in 2020. You reinvested the $1,000, buying shares at $20/share. At the end of 2020, you now had 1,050 shares of XYZ Corp, with a total basis of $21,000.

REMEMBER

Be careful when tracking the basis with dividend reinvestment plans; your holding period on each batch of new shares purchased is the dividend payment date, not the date of your original investment. If you sell those 1,050 shares at the beginning of 2021, the original 1,000 will have a long-term holding period (they were purchased prior to 2020), while the 50 shares purchased during 2020 through the dividend reinvestment program are a short-term asset. You'll have one entry on Form 8949, Part I, for the 50 short-term shares, and another one in Part II for the 1,000 long-term shares.

>> **Improvements and/or casualty losses to your home or rental property:** Increase your home's basis by the cost of any improvements you make plus the costs connected with purchasing the property — such as the fee that you paid the title company and your attorney. An added room, remodeled kitchen, or fancy landscaping all add to your basis. On the other hand, maintenance and repairs don't, so there's no basis adjustment for painting the house or repairing the plumbing. If you have a casualty loss, the total basis in your home is reduced by the portion of basis you assign to that part of the property. Say you purchase property including a house and a barn for $100,000, of which $10,000 belongs to the barn. If the barn blows down in a hurricane, you need to reduce your basis by that $10,000. If you own rental real estate or have a home office, depreciation and any casualty losses that you may have deducted (see Chapter 15 for more details) reduce your basis.

>> **Original Issue Discount, market discount, and bond premium adjustments:** When you buy a bond and pay a different amount for it than its face value, you've paid either a *premium* (more) or received a *discount* (less). The IRS requires that you make adjustments over the bond's life to make your tax basis in that bond equal the bond's face value on the date the bond matures. Sounds simple, doesn't it? In fact, every year that you own the bond, you're going to declare interest on your tax return that you haven't actually received (in

the case of a discounted bond) or subtract interest that you have received (in the case of a premium bond) and add or subtract those amounts to your basis on a year-by-year basis. Chapter 12 explains how this works in more detail. Just remember, every year you make an adjustment on Schedule B, you also need to carry that adjustment to your basis records to keep them up-to-date.

>> **Sale of partial holding:** You may decide to sell only part of what you own of stock ABC (many people do sell partial holdings). If you do, you need to either identify the shares that you're selling before the sale if you own multiple lots of that security that were purchased on multiple days or accept the IRS default determination that the first shares you buy are the first shares you sell (FIFO — First In, First Out method). Check out Chapter 24 to find out more about the tax benefits of selecting specific shares to sell rather than using FIFO. Chapter 24 also explains about the average cost method that's particularly useful when dealing with your mutual fund shares.

>> **Stock dividends, splits, and returns of capital:** If you receive additional stock as part of a nontaxable stock dividend or stock split, you must reduce the per-share basis (but not the total basis) of your original stock. You make this computation by dividing the cost of the stock by the total number of shares that you now have. You must, however, reduce your basis when you receive nontaxable cash distributions (that number in box 3 of Form 1099-DIV that no one seems to know what to do with), because this transaction is considered a return on your investment.

>> **Undistributed capital gains:** If your mutual fund had capital gains that it didn't distribute to its shareholders, you can increase your basis by that amount, which will reduce the amount of capital gains tax you'll owe when you eventually sell. We often see undistributed capital gains with technology and biotech funds. You'll be sent Form 2439, Notice to Shareholders of Undistributed Long-Term Capital Gains. You report your share of the undistributed gains and get a credit for the tax paid by the fund (Form 1040, Schedule 3, Part II, line 13a). Your tax basis in the fund is increased by the difference between the capital gain that was retained by the fund and the actual tax paid by the fund on your behalf.

TIP

Tracking basis is a long and often tedious process that many people opt not to do, but having accurate records is worth it in the end. Maintain a permanent file folder for receipts, confirmations, and any other important information. Keep your computer records up-to-date (if you use a computer to track your basis) so that you can prove your basis should the IRS ask.

Now that you know how and where to find the information that you need to tackle your 2021 Schedule D, you can confidently begin.

Part I, Lines 1–7: Short-Term Capital Gains and Losses

Lines 1 through 3 should be a breeze if you fine-tuned your form skills in the preceding Wonder Widget example. Now that you know how to split things out on Form 8949, you're just going to pick up the totals as follows:

>> Part I, Form 8949 with box A checked transfers to Schedule D, line 1a, but only if you have no adjustments to basis listed in Form 8949, columns (f) and (g).

» Part I, Form 8949 with box A checked transfers to Schedule D, line 1b, if you have adjusted your basis.

» Part I, Form 8949 with box B checked transfers to Schedule D, line 2.

» Part I, Form 8949 with box C checked transfers to Schedule D, line 3.

Line 4: Form 6252 short-term gain, and Forms 4684, 6781, and 8824 short-term gain or <loss>

All these form numbers! Because these forms rarely apply to most people, you may as well use them to play the lottery. Seriously, most people are going to deal with only Form 4684, Casualties and Theft, at some specific point in their lives. We cover this form in Chapter 11.

SEEK ADVICE

For those of you who are curious, Form 6252 is for installment sales, Form 8824 is for like-kind exchanges, and Form 6781 is for commodity straddles. You can find more on Form 6252 later in this chapter; if the other two forms apply to you, we suggest that you consult a tax advisor. Enter the short-term gains or losses from these forms on line 4 of Schedule D.

Line 5: Net short-term gain or <loss> from Schedules K-1: Partnerships, S Corps, and estates/trusts

Short-term gains or losses from a partnership, an S Corporation, an estate, or a trust are reported on a schedule called a K-1. On line 5, enter the short-term gain or loss as indicated on the K-1 (short-term gains and losses only; long-term gains and losses go to line 12).

Line 6: Short-term capital loss carry-over

If you had more short-term losses than you were able to use last year, you may carry over the amount you weren't able to use to this year's return. You need your 2020 Schedule D in order to complete the "Capital Loss Carryover Worksheet" contained in the Schedule D instructions. After you calculate your 2020 short-term loss carry-over on the worksheet, insert your result on line 6, Schedule D.

TIP

You never need to go back any farther than last year's return to find your capital loss carry-over. Even if that carry-over loss was due to a sale that happened many years ago, you've been carrying the loss forward from year to year on your Schedule D.

Line 7: Net short-term gain or <loss>

On line 7, combine lines 1 through 5 in column (h) and enter the total. If it's a loss, make sure you enter it as a negative number.

Part II, Lines 8–15: Long-Term Capital Gains and Losses

You want long-term capital gains because the government taxes them at lower rates and, in 2021, sometimes not at all.

Line 8: Columns (a), (b), (c), (d), (e), and (f)

As you did in Part I, you're going to carry over the numbers you've calculated on Form 8949 as follows:

>> Part II, Form 8949 with box D checked transfers to Schedule D, line 8a, but only if you have no adjustments to basis listed in Form 8949, columns (f) and (g).

>> Part II, Form 8949 with box D checked transfers to Schedule D, line 8b, if you have adjusted your basis.

>> Part II, Form 8949 with box E checked transfers to Schedule D, line 9.

>> Part II, Form 8949 with box F checked transfers to Schedule D, line 10.

TIP

When estates or heirs sell property that they inherited, they automatically get the long-term rate. If you're selling inherited property, put the date of death in as the acquisition date. If you're hand-writing the form, also place the word "inherited" either in the space for the acquisition date or next to it. If you're using computer software, check for a place in the interview form where you can code the acquisition as a sale of inherited property — the software will do the rest.

Line 11: Long-term gains and losses carried from other forms

Line 11 picks up all the gains and/or losses carried to Schedule D from the following forms:

>> Form 4797, Part I, Sales of Business Property (gain only)

>> Form 2439, Notice to Shareholder of Undistributed Long-Term Capital Gains (gain only)

>> Form 6252, Installment Sale Income (gain only)

>> Form 4684, Casualties and Thefts (gains or losses)

>> Form 6781, Gains and Losses from Section 1256 Contracts and Straddles

>> Form 8824, Like-Kind Exchanges (gain or loss)

Form 2439, Notice to Shareholders of Undistributed Long-Term Capital Gains

Mutual fund companies are required to distribute the income they earn to their shareholders each calendar year by January 31 of the following year. When they do, the mutual fund company shareholders (that's you and me) pay the tax on the income, and the company doesn't. Sometimes, though, long-term capital gains aren't paid to the shareholders, and the company then must pay the tax. When this happens, the company will issue Form 2439 to the shareholders, alerting them to the fact that there was additional long-term capital gain income that has already been taxed. When this happens, plug in the amount you see on line 1a of Form 2439 here, on line 11 of Schedule D. To be sure you don't pay taxes twice on this money (remember, the mutual fund company already has), fill in the amount of taxes paid shown on line 2 of Form 2439 on Form 1040, Schedule 3, Part II, line 13a.

Form 4797, Sales of Business Property

The odds of having to complete any of those other nasty forms thankfully are small. But just in case you sell a business property, such as a building or an office copier, and have to deal with Form 4797, here are some tips to help you get through that form.

TIP

First of all, you need to know that the reason for a separate form is that the tax treatment of this type of sale is extremely complex. So, what's new? The government believes that the maximum capital gains tax rates are too good of a deal — many taxpayers were claiming a depreciation deduction on business assets they owned, including real estate, and then having any gain when they sold the property taxed at the lower capital gains rate. Form 4797 changes all that, forcing you to recapture all the depreciation you've claimed, pay tax at your ordinary income tax rates for that amount (with the exception of real estate depreciation recapture — that rate is capped at 25 percent for post-1986 depreciation), and then, if there's any additional gain, you get to apply capital gains rates to those.

For the purposes of depreciation, business property is divided into two types:

>> Auto, business equipment, and machinery

>> Real estate

TECHNICAL STUFF

Here's how this depreciation recapture rule for real estate works. Say you sold a building for $400,000 that you originally paid $200,000 for. Through the years, you claimed depreciation of $100,000, which reduces your tax basis for figuring your profit to $100,000. You have a $300,000 profit — $400,000 minus your cost ($200,000) reduced by your depreciation ($100,000). Of the $300,000 profit, the $100,000, representing deductions that you took for depreciation, is taxed at 25 percent, and the $200,000 balance is taxed at 0, 15, or 20 percent, depending on what your tax bracket is without taking this gain into consideration. And, since capital gains of any sort have an unfortunate habit of pushing your income higher than you'd anticipated, let's not forget that you may also be liable for an additional 3.8 percent tax to pay for the Affordable Care Act, which applies to married couples who earn more than $250,000 of adjusted gross income (AGI) and single taxpayers with AGI above $200,000.

SEEK ADVICE

If you think *depreciation recapture* sounds complicated, you need to remember that this rule is for real estate that you started to depreciate after 1986. For depreciation claimed before 1987, part is taxed at the regular rate and part at 25 percent. Which part? See a tax professional.

For all other property, the recapture rules work like this: Suppose that you purchased machinery for $10,000 and that you used it in your business for three years before selling it for $12,000. In the three years that you owned it, you took depreciation deductions totaling $7,120. This step reduces your tax basis to $2,880 ($10,000 cost − $7,120 depreciation). Ordinarily, if you sold property with a basis of $2,880 for $12,000, you'd have a capital gain of $9,120. But because a portion of those proceeds represents depreciation you have to recapture, you have a capital gain of only $2,000; the remaining amount of gain of $7,120 equals the amount of depreciation you need to recapture and pay ordinary income tax rates on. When you sell property for more than your adjusted basis, but less than its original cost, all the gain represents recaptured depreciation and will be taxed at your ordinary income rates.

The depreciation recapture rules don't apply to business property sold at a loss. The loss is deductible from your income without limitation. The part of the profit that's recaptured and taxed at your regular tax rate is carried over from Form 4797 to Form 1040, Schedule 1, Part I, line 4. The long-term capital gain portion is carried over from Form 4797 to Schedule D (line 11). Use the long-term capital gain worksheet in Chapter 10 to make sure that you don't overpay.

SEEK ADVICE

This stuff may be more than you care to know about the sale of business property. But before you even contemplate the sale of business property, seek advice. If the amount involved is large, make sure that you get the best advice possible. See Chapter 2 for information about how to pick a good tax specialist.

Form 6252, Installment Sale Income

Here's the story on Form 6252, Installment Sale Income. Suppose that you sold a parcel of land for $60,000 in 2021. You paid $15,000 for it and will receive $10,000 in 2021 — and $10,000 a year for the next five years. You don't report the $45,000 profit that you made in 2021. You report a percentage of the profit as each installment is received.

You report the $10,000 that you receive every year on Form 6252, but you pay tax on only $7,500 of it, or 75 percent of what you received. (Your $45,000 profit is 75 percent of your $60,000 selling price.) The $2,500 that you don't pay tax on is the recovery of your cost. The $7,500 profit that you owe tax on is transferred to Schedule D.

You may elect out of the installment method and report the entire gain in the year of sale. You may want to go this way if you have a great deal of itemized deductions that would be wasted because they're more than your income or if you're in an Alternative Minimum Tax (AMT) situation. You may also elect out of the installment method if you think Congress may change the rules regarding installment sales in the middle of the installment period and give you less favorable treatment of the gain than you currently enjoy. See Chapter 10 for more about this tax.

TAX CUT

If you have more deductions than income, you'll waste those excess deductions unless you can come up with more income in a hurry. Here's where opting out (for tax purposes) of an installment sale agreement makes sense. Looking at the previous example, if you have $10,000 in salary income and personal exemptions and itemized deductions come to $55,000, you can report another $45,000 of income before you have to pay a dime in tax. So, reporting all the income from an installment sale in the year of the sale makes sense in this example.

TIP

If you're running a business, you can't use the installment method for sales of merchandise to customers. And you need to charge interest on the unpaid installments. If you charge an unrealistically low rate of interest on the sale, the IRS will impute a rate of interest equal to the Applicable Federal Rate (AFR) that it publishes monthly on its website. Say you make a sale of $100,000 that's due in one year and you don't charge the buyer interest when the AFR should have been 5 percent. The IRS will recast the sale as follows: $5,000 will be considered interest, taxed at ordinary income rates, and $95,000 will be considered the amount of the sale that qualifies as a capital gain with the associated lower tax rates.

Line 12: Net long-term gain or <loss> from different entities

Line 12 is similar to line 5. You report any long-term gains and losses, as indicated on Schedule K-1, from partnerships, S Corporations, estates, and trusts on line 12. We discuss these entities in Chapter 15.

Line 13: Capital gain distributions

Mutual fund distributions are reported on Form 1099-DIV, boxes 2a–2f. Capital gain distributions may also be earned by partnerships, S Corporations, and estates and trusts, and will be reported to you on Schedule K-1. Remember, you reported the long-term capital gains on line 12, but long-term capital gain distributions belong here, on line 13.

If your Form 1099-DIV shows numbers in boxes 2b–2e, these numbers are included in the total in box 2a, but they're not eligible for the 15 percent maximum capital gains tax. Copy the number in box 2a onto line 13 of Schedule D to help you reach your total capital gain result. The Schedule D instructions and worksheets can guide you in calculating the tax on each portion of gain, whether it's 0 or 15 percent maximum gain property, 25 percent gain property, or 28 percent gain property. Enjoy!

TIP

If all you have are capital gain distributions from mutual funds and no other capital gains or losses, you can skip Schedule D. If you qualify under this rule, tally all your capital gain distributions and enter the total on line 7 of Form 1040, which is titled "Capital gain or (loss)" and tick the box next to the line, indicating that Schedule D isn't required. See Chapter 10 to find out how to capture the information in box 2 from Form 1099-DIV, and to make certain you don't overpay your capital gains tax.

Line 14: Long-term capital loss carry-over

Enter your long-term capital losses that you weren't able to deduct in previous years because you didn't have enough capital gains in those years to offset them on this line. "Line 6: Short-term capital loss carry-over" explains how to handle carry-overs.

Line 15: Combine lines 8–14 in column (f)

Just follow the instructions. Add lines 8–14 in column (h). It can't be easier, and besides, you're almost finished. Remember, if you have a loss, enter it as a negative number.

Part III, Lines 16-22: Summary of Parts I and II

Hey, this part should be easy, right?

Line 16: Combine lines 7 and 15

If this line is a loss, skip lines 17 through 20 and move ahead to line 21. If it's a gain or your total short- and long-term gains net to zero, enter this number on your Form 1040, line 7.

Line 17: Comparing lines 15 and 16

If lines 15 (gross long-term capital gain) and 16 (combined long-term and short-term capital gain) are both gains, check the "Yes" box and go to line 18. If line 16 is a gain, but line 15 shows a loss, check the "No" box and go straight to line 22.

Line 18: 28 percent gains

If you were fortunate enough to sell your Honus Wagner baseball card (one sold at auction in 2016 for $6.6 million) and can now retire in comfort, you first need to pay capital gains tax on your collectible baseball card. This line is where you segregate the gains from the sales of collectibles from the rest of your capital gains. To figure out what number to put here, first fill out the "28% Rate Gain Worksheet" you can find with your Schedule D instructions and then enter the amount on line 7 of the worksheet here, on line 18.

TIP

Remember, if you're selling more than the occasional unwanted wedding gift on internet auction sites such as eBay, you're actually running a business, not realizing capital gains and losses, which is a good news–bad news scenario. The good news is you get to deduct all the expenses connected with that business; the bad news is that you now have to fill out Schedule C, and any income you have from this venture is subject to ordinary income tax rates as well as self-employment tax. Check out Chapter 13 to make sure you're not missing any of the deductions you're entitled to.

Line 19: 25 percent gains

If you're the recipient of a capital gain from the sale of depreciated real estate and need to recapture some or all of that depreciation, here's where you tell the IRS just how much that was. First, though, you're going to have to complete the "Unrecaptured Section 1250 Gain Worksheet" in your Schedule D instructions. The number you arrive at on line 18 of that worksheet belongs here, on Schedule D, line 19.

Line 20

If you don't have any numbers on lines 18 or 19, move to the head of the class. Complete your Form 1040 through line 15, and then calculate your tax using the "Qualified Dividends and Capital Gain Tax Worksheet" that's included in your instruction booklet. We also give you instructions on how to do this in Chapter 10. Put the answer to your tax calculation on line 16 of Form 1040.

If you have a number on either or both of lines 18 or 19, you get to complete the "Schedule D Tax Worksheet" located in your Schedule D instructions. It looks long, but it's really not so bad. All you're doing is calculating the tax on each category of income you have, and then adding them together. Be methodical; you'll do fine!

If you have numbers on lines 18 or 19, don't complete lines 21 or 22 of Part III. You're finished with Schedule D.

Line 21: Capital losses

If you've had an unfortunate year with your investments, you determine how much of that misfortune you can use to wipe out ordinary, taxable income this year on this line. For any filing status except married filing separately, if your loss on line 16 is less than $3,000, enter the amount of your loss here and on Form 1040, line 7. If it's greater than $3,000, enter $3,000 on line 21 and also on Form 1040, line 7. Remember, if you're married but filing separately from your spouse, you can claim losses up to only $1,500 — your spouse gets the same.

Line 22: Qualified dividends

Qualified dividends, which we discuss in Chapter 12, are taxed at a maximum rate of 20 percent, plus if you're higher income, you may also be liable for the additional 3.8 percent net investment income tax (NIIT), which we discuss in Chapter 8. If you have qualified dividends on line 3a of your 1040, check the "Yes" box and fill out the "Qualified Dividends and Capital Gain Tax Worksheet" that's located in your Form 1040 instruction booklet and also in Chapter 10. If you don't have any qualified dividends, go back and complete the rest of your Form 1040.

Using Schedule D for Home Sales

Selling your home may be one of the biggest financial decisions you make in your life. It may also provide you with one of the largest tax breaks that's available to the average Joe and Jane. Believe it or not, a married couple can exclude up to $500,000 of the profit they make on the sale of their home. A single person is entitled to a $250,000 exclusion from the capital gains tax.

Of course, nothing's that simple. You need to qualify. Here's how:

>> If you're married, you or your spouse must have owned the residence for at least two of the past five years, and both of you must have used it as your primary residence for two out of the past five years; a vacation home can't meet this test.

>> If you're single, you must have owned and used the residence as your primary residence for two of the past five years.

TIPS FOR THE NEWLY WIDOWED, MARRIED, OR DIVORCED

The ownership and use as a primary residence includes the period that a deceased spouse used and owned the residence.

The exclusion is available on an individual basis, which means that the $250,000 exclusion is available for the qualifying principal residence of each spouse for those who file jointly but live apart — not an uncommon arrangement these days. If you happen to marry someone who used the exclusion within the two-year period before your marriage, you're entitled to your $250,000 exclusion and vice versa.

If a residence is transferred in a divorce, the time period that the ex-spouse owned the residence is taken into account to determine whether the ownership-and-use tests have been met.

If you're a surviving spouse and owned your home jointly, your basis for the half-interest owned by your spouse is one-half of the fair market value (FMV) on your spouse's date of death. (Don't let the term "basis" throw you. For a quick, one-sentence explanation, check out "Calculating Your Adjusted Basis" earlier in this chapter.) The basis in your half-interest is one-half the tax basis of the house as computed in the next paragraph (usually the cost plus improvements).

For instance, if your home cost $200,000 and was worth $400,000 when your spouse died, your new basis is $300,000 (one-half of the $200,000 cost plus one-half of the $400,000 FMV).

In community property states, when a spouse dies, the FMV at the date of death becomes the tax basis of the entire house. So, in the previous example, the surviving spouse's tax basis is $400,000 (the FMV) and not $300,000.

How does the two-out-of-the-past-five-years rule work? The look-back starts on the date of the sale. For example, suppose that you sold your home on July 1, 2021. Between July 1, 2016, and July 1, 2021, you must have owned and used your home as your principal residence for any two years during this period. The periods don't have to be consecutive as long as they add up to two years.

Say you shuttle between two residences, one in New Jersey and one in Florida. The one that you use most of the time will ordinarily be considered your primary residence. Where it's a close call, the IRS looks at these factors to determine which residence is the primary one:

>> The taxpayer's place of employment

>> Where the taxpayer's family lives most of the time

>> The address listed on tax returns, driver's license, auto registration, and a voter registration card

>> The mailing address for bills and correspondence

>> The location of the taxpayer's religious institutions and recreational clubs they're a member of

>> Location of the taxpayer's bank

The $500,000/$250,000 exclusion replaces the old once-in-a-lifetime $125,000 exclusion that was available only to taxpayers older than 55. Age no longer matters. In addition to raising the exclusion limits, the new provision is more generous in another way: You may use it repeatedly, but not more often than every two years.

The two-year rule is waived for both singles and couples when they have to sell their homes within two years because a new job requires them to move (the new place of employment must be 50 miles farther from the old home than the old home was from the old workplace, they move for health reasons (it must be a specific illness and not just for general health), or they move for other unforeseen circumstances (more details in this section). The sale for health reasons must involve the health of:

>> The taxpayer, their spouse, or the co-owner

>> A member of the taxpayer's household

>> Members of the taxpayer's family — children, their descendents, brothers and sisters and their descendents and their children, parents, aunts, uncles, stepchildren, stepbrothers, stepsisters, stepparents, and in-laws, as well as descendents of the taxpayer's grandparents. I bet you thought this list would never end!

Here is the official IRS list of "unforeseen circumstances":

>> Becoming eligible for unemployment insurance

>> A change in employment that leaves you unable to pay your mortgage or basic living expenses

>> Damage to the residence resulting from a natural or man-made disaster or an act of war or terrorism

» Death

» Divorce or legal separation

» Multiple births resulting from the same pregnancy

For example, say you buy a house on August 1, 2020, for $350,000, and you sell it for $550,000 on August 1, 2021 (if we're going to make up a story, why not make it a good one?) because you're moving from New York to Los Angeles to start a new job. You're single. Because you owned the house for only 12 months of the required 24-month period, you're entitled to one-half of the $250,000 exclusion, or $125,000. That means that only $75,000 of your $200,000 profit is subject to tax.

WARNING

The $500,000/$250,000 exclusion may have given you the idea that, because of the increased exclusion amount, you no longer have to keep records of your purchases or improvements. Although this premise may be true for many people, it doesn't necessarily apply to everyone. Suppose that you're single and buy a house for $300,000. Because you don't know what you'll sell the house for in 20 years, you'd better hang on to the receipts for any improvements that you paid for. Suppose that you sell your house for $600,000 — a $300,000 profit — but you're entitled to only a $250,000 exclusion. Good records can help you reduce the profit even further.

TIP

The sale of vacant land adjacent to a principal residence qualifies for the $250,000/$500,000 exclusion if it's used as part of the principal residence. This qualification applies even if the land is sold separately, as long as the land sale occurs within the two-year period before or after the sale of the dwelling place. Say the land was sold in 2020, and the dwelling was sold in 2021. Because the adjacent land had to be reported on your 2020 return, you have to file an amended return for 2020 if the sale of the land and the dwelling are less than the exclusion. You're entitled to obtain a refund for the tax you paid on the land in 2020.

If your lender foreclosed on your principal residence in 2021, the cancelled mortgage debt is not considered as income to you (see Chapter 6 for more about debt cancellation). You will, however, need to include the disposition of your home through foreclosure on Form 8949 and Schedule D. Provided the property in question was your principal residence, and you meet all the other requirements listed previously, you are eligible for the $250,000/$500,000 exclusion. Be careful here, though — although the debt cancellation isn't a taxable event for you, if the amount of the cancelled debt exceeds the eventual sales price of the house, you may have a taxable gain as a result of the foreclosure. How you're going to report this transaction depends entirely on the price the bank receives when it sells the house. Here's how this works: Mr. Jones bought a house in 2000 for $200,000. His home appreciated in value, and he eventually refinanced his mortgage in 2017, taking out a $700,000 loan. Mr. Jones never made any mortgage payments, and the bank finally foreclosed in 2021; the bank then sold the house in 2021 for $500,000. The $200,000 difference between the outstanding mortgage and the sale price represents the amount of debt forgiven by the bank. Because of the current rules, this is not an item of ordinary income to Mr. Jones; however, since Mr. Jones's basis in the house was $200,000 before the debt was cancelled, his basis is now reduced by $200,000 and is therefore $0. Because Mr. Jones was single at the time of the sale, only $250,000 of the resulting $500,000 gain (sales price minus basis) was excluded. The remaining $250,000 gain is a taxable long-term capital gain to Mr. Jones in 2021. Had there been a Mrs. Jones who lived with Mr. Jones in their house for at least two out of the last five years, none of the $500,000 capital gain would have been taxed.

EXCEPTIONS FOR MILITARY MEMBERS

In order to not unduly burden members of the military, who often buy a house at one base only to be transferred to another before they qualify for the full exclusion amount, the Congress, through the Military Families Relief Act, has authorized the IRS to issue rules allowing you to suspend the five-year holding period under these circumstances. This act provides that if you buy a house in 2000 for $150,000, live there for three years, and then are transferred to other active military postings for the next five years, when you sell that house in 2008 for $400,000, you're still qualified to take the full $250,000 exclusion even though you weren't actually living there for two out of the last five years.

How do you know if you can suspend your holding period? If you're on qualified official extended duty at a posting at least 50 miles from your main home, or you're ordered to live in government quarters, you can. In addition, if you're ordered to active duty for a period of more than 90 days, or indefinitely, you also qualify.

Even better, the IRS has made this holding period suspension retroactive to the sale of your principal residence after May 6, 1997. If you sold a home after that date but paid capital gains tax on all or a portion of your gain because you were disqualified from taking the full exclusion under the old rules, you can amend your tax return and claim a refund using Form 1040X. Complete the form per its instructions and write across the top "Military Family Tax Relief Act." Remember, though, you can only claim a credit or refund within three years from the date you filed your original return, or two years from the date you paid the tax.

A couple of caveats are attached to this offer. First, you can't suspend your holding period for longer than ten years, and second, you can suspend the holding period on only one property at a time.

Computing your profit

Computing the profit on the sale of your home is simple.

From the sales price, subtract the following expenses in connection with the sale:

>> Advertising costs

>> Attorney fees

>> Real estate broker's commission

>> Title closing costs

From the sales price after the expenses of the sale, subtract the following (in this order):

>> Original cost of your castle

>> Improvements

>> Closing costs and attorney fees at the time of purchase

What constitutes an improvement? An *improvement* is anything that adds to your house's value or prolongs its life. Drapery rods, Venetian blinds, termite proofing, and shrubbery all fill the bill. If you own a condo or co-op, your cost basis also includes special assessments to improve the building, such as renovating the lobby or installing a new heating system. Co-op owners get an additional boost, because the part of their maintenance charges that goes to paying off the co-op's mortgage also is added to their cost.

REMEMBER

From your profit, subtract the exclusion that you're entitled to. If you're single, it's $250,000; for couples, it's $500,000. If this exclusion exceeds your profit, you can stop right there because there's nothing more to do. Regardless of whether you're required to pay any capital gains tax or you qualify for the exclusion, you should report the sale on Form 8949 and show the exclusion for the sale of your personal residence if you have been issued a Form 1099-S, Proceeds from Real Estate Transactions. All sales proceeds are reported to the IRS, and they're going to be looking for that sale on your tax return. They have no way of knowing that this is your personal residence, that you personally lived there for two out of the last five years, or what your basis in the house is. You need to let them know even if your profit doesn't exceed the exclusion amount.

WARNING

If you have a loss, it isn't deductible. Profits above the exclusion amounts are. We're sure that you've heard this before: "Heads, they win; tails, you lose."

TIP

You can find an excellent worksheet in the IRS Publication 523 (*Selling Your Home*) that can guide you through your profit computation. This publication also has a nifty list of examples of the types of improvements that increase the tax basis of a home. So don't overlook it.

Reporting a profit that exceeds the exclusion

TIP

You report the sale of your residence on Schedule D only if the profit exceeds the exclusion you're entitled to.

Normally, the purchaser (typically via the title company) reports the sale on Form 1099-S, Proceeds from Real Estate Transactions. If you're single and the sale is for $250,000 — or $500,000 or less for couples — and you meet the other requirements such as the two-year principal residence test, you can sign a certificate at the time of the sale so that a Form 1099-S doesn't have to be sent to the IRS.

Here's how you compute the profit on the sale of your home and report the profit on Form 8949 and Schedule D:

1. **Figure your tax basis.**

   Add your original cost, closing costs, and cost of improvements.

2. **Compute your net selling price.**

   That's your selling price less your selling and closing expenses.

3. **Subtract your tax basis from your net selling price.**

   For example, you sold your home for $610,000. Your closing costs were $10,000, and the original cost of your home plus improvements and closing costs when you purchased the house was $400,000.

Congratulations, you made a $200,000 profit ($610,000 – $10,000 – $400,000). If you're filing on paper, on Form 8949, show proceeds as $610,000, selling expenses as $10,000, and cost basis as $400,000. Instead of showing a $200,000 gain, in Column (h), show your gain/loss as $0. If that is the only entry on your Form 8949, carry the totals over to the correct line on Schedule D, once again reporting the gain as $0.

If your profit exceeds your exclusion, you have to report the profit on Form 8949, and then transfer it over to Schedule D. Here's how you do it. Report the entire gain on Form 8949 (most likely with either box E or F checked) filling out columns (a) through (h). Because you qualify for the exclusion, enter it on the line directly below the line where you reported the gain. Write Section 121 exclusion in column (a) and the amount of the exclusion in column (h) as a loss (in parentheses). For example, $250,000 is written as <$250,000> in column (h). If you're married, enter <$500,000>. Carry the total of all amounts in column (h) over to the correct line on Schedule D.

WARNING

If you used part of your home as an office or rented out your home, the exclusion doesn't apply to any depreciation that you claimed after May 6, 1997. For example, if you claimed $10,000 in depreciation after May 6, 1997, and you're entitled to a $500,000 exclusion and the gain on the sale of your home is $400,000, you can exclude only $390,000 of that gain. You owe tax on the $10,000 of depreciation claimed after May 6, 1997.

Following the home office and rental rules

Under the old rule, the IRS considered a taxpayer's home sale (where the home was partially used for business) the sale of two pieces of property — the portion used as the residence that qualified for the $250,000 or $500,000 exclusion, and the portion used for business that didn't. For example, if someone used 20 percent of their home for business and then sold the home at a $150,000 profit, $30,000 would be considered the sale of business property that had to be reported on Form 4797, Sales of Business Property, and would be taxed. The remaining $120,000 was considered the gain on the sale of a principal residence that was exempt from tax because it was less than the exclusion. At the end of 2002, the IRS had a change of heart!

Under the new rule, only the depreciation claimed after May 6, 1997, is taxable. The rest of the profit on the sale is eligible for the $250,000/$500,000 exclusion. You report the depreciation on Form 4797 and carry it over to line 11 of Schedule D. This profit is subject to the 25 percent maximum capital gains tax.

TIP

If under the old rule you paid tax on the part of the profit from the sale of your in-home office, file an amended return and get your money back (see Chapter 20 to find out how to file an amended return).

WARNING

If the portion of your home that's used for business is separate from the dwelling unit, the new rule doesn't apply, and you're considered to have sold two parcels: the business portion, which is taxable, and the residence, which is eligible for the exclusion. The clearest example: You have a townhouse with a finished basement that you convert into a separate unit and close off by removing the interior stairway that leads to the rest of the house.

Using Form 8949 and Schedule D for Other Stock Matters

You can use Schedule D to handle such issues as worthless securities, wash sales, small business stock, stock options, short sales, stock for services, and appreciated employer securities.

Worthless securities

Suppose that you felt certain that Company X was going to make a comeback, so you invested $15,000. But you were wrong. Not only has Company X failed to make this comeback, but its shares are also no longer even being quoted in the morning paper.

Great! So at least $15,000 is a write-off, right? No. The problem with this scenario is that you must be able to prove — with an identifiable event — that your investment is in fact completely worthless. Being partially worthless doesn't cut it. In one case, bondholders in a company canceled 30 percent of the face value of their bonds to keep the company afloat. But they can't deduct the portion of the debt they canceled because their investment hadn't become completely worthless. Likewise, the fact that the shares of a company are no longer being quoted doesn't make them worthless.

We wish that we could tell you that convincing the IRS that you're entitled to write off your $15,000 investment is as easy as losing it. It's not — and this is an area of the law that's more confusing than most. You may think that bankruptcy, going out of business, liquidation, the appointment of a receiver, or insolvency indicates that your investment no longer has any value. But these events only prove that the company is in financial trouble, not that its shareholders won't receive anything in liquidation. In order to claim a deduction for worthless securities, your investment must be completely worthless.

When is an investment worthless? As a general rule, you can say that an investment is worthless when a company is so hopelessly insolvent that it ceases doing business or it goes into receivership, leaving nothing for its stockholders. If you're not sure, one source worth checking is CCH, a Wolters Kluwer business (which also does the technical editing of this book). This outfit publishes an annual list of worthless securities as part of its "Capital Changes Reports." Most major brokerage firms and public libraries subscribe to this service, or you can reach the company directly at 800-TELL-CCH (800-835-5224).

If proving when unmarketable shares in a company actually became worthless is so difficult, why not lock in a loss by finding some accomplice — the broker who sold them to you, for example — to take the shares off your hands for a penny apiece? Nice try, but no go. A number of taxpayers have attempted to "structure sales" in this fashion, but both the IRS and the Tax Court have denied the losses because these sales weren't considered legitimate. Instead, the taxpayers were told to hang on to their investments and deduct them only when they became certifiably worthless. In other words, they were back to square one.

Securities that became worthless in a given tax year are considered to have become worthless on the last day of that year and reported in the short-term section of Form 8949. Make sure you include these transactions in the total you copy onto Part I of Schedule D. Enter your cost and zero (-0-) for the sales price because the investment is worthless. So, as you can see, Schedule D has a few other handy uses as well.

Wash sales

Suppose that you own a stock that has declined in value. You think that it will recover, but you want to deduct the money that you lost. If you sell the stock and buy back the shares within 30 days of the sale, you can't deduct the loss. This type of trade is called a *wash sale*. The loss can't be deducted in the year of the trade. The loss is deducted when you sell the new shares.

Here is an example of how the wash sale rule works. You paid $15,000 for a stock that has declined in value to $6,000. You sell it incurring a $9,000 loss. Then the stock starts to rebound, and you get that sense that it's going to stage a comeback. Two weeks later you buy the stock back for $7,000. You can't deduct your $9,000 loss, because you sold and repurchased shares of the same company within a 30-day period. Your $9,000 loss is added to the $7,000 you paid for the new shares. The cost you use to determine any gain or loss when the new shares are sold is now $16,000. When reporting this transaction, put a "W" into Form 8949, column (f), and the amount of the disallowed loss in column (g), reducing the amount of the loss in column (h).

Small business stock

You can deduct up to $50,000 ($100,000 if filing jointly) of a loss from the sale, or from worthless small business stock (more commonly called "Code Section 1244 stock"). A corporation qualifies as a "1244 corp." if at the time its stock is issued, the amount of equity in the corporation doesn't exceed $1 million. That means if you're married and sustained a $150,000 "1244 loss," you can deduct $100,000 from your income. The $100,000 loss is computed on Form 4797 on line 10, and then moves to Form 1040, Schedule 1, Part I, line 4, other gains or (losses). Amounts over the limit allowed for an ordinary loss go onto Form 8949 as follows: In column (a), enter "Capital portion of section 1244 stock loss"; columns (b) and (c) are acquisition and sales dates; in column (d) put the total amount of the proceeds, or if the stock has become worthless, put $0; in column (e), put your cost basis; in column (f) put the letter S; in column (g), put the smaller of your actual loss or $50,000 if you're single, $100,000 if you're married filing jointly; and in column (h), put the adjusted loss if you have had to adjust it. Remember, the loss here may be split into two pieces: the ordinary loss that shows up on Form 4797, and the capital loss that will appear on Form 8949 and Schedule D. The two loss amounts, when added together, should equal your total loss.

Stock options

Stock options, those opportunities to buy shares in a company in the future at a price that is set at the time the option is created, usually come in two varieties: *statutory options,* which have to meet certain IRS rules to qualify for special tax advantages, and *nonstatutory stock options,* which are also subject to special rules even though the tax savings aren't as great. Statutory stock options include incentive stock options and options under an employee stock purchase plan.

Incentive stock options (ISOs)

You aren't subject to tax when an incentive stock option is granted. You realize income or loss only when you sell the stock that you acquired by exercising the ISO.

You must exercise the option within ten years from the date that it was granted. The option price has to be at least equal to the value of the stock on the day that the option was granted. For example, you can't receive an option to buy shares for $10 a share when the shares are selling for $18 a share. In any one year, you can't receive an option to buy shares that are worth more than $100,000 on the date that the option was granted. If you go over $100,000, the excess isn't considered an ISO, so read on until you get to the section "Nonstatutory stock options."

When you sell stock that you acquired by exercising an ISO, you have a long-term capital gain if you held the shares for more than one year from the date when you exercised the option and more than two years after the ISO was granted. For example, say you exercise an option for $15,000. You later sell the shares for $25,000. You have a long-term capital gain of $10,000 if you meet the one- and two-year rules. If you don't meet these rules, the $10,000 gain is divided into two parts. The difference between the exercise price and the value on the day that you exercised the option is taxed as ordinary income. The difference between the value on the day that you exercised the option and the value on the day that you sold the stock is treated as a capital gain (either short- or long-term). In the previous example, if the shares were worth $20,000 on the day that you exercised the option, then $5,000 of the gain would be taxed as ordinary income, and $5,000 (the difference between the sales price, $25,000, and the $20,000 value on the day the option was exercised) is taxed as a long-term capital gain.

WARNING

Although the spread between the option price and the value on the day that you exercised the option isn't subject to tax for regular tax purposes, it is subject to the Alternative Minimum Tax (AMT). So, take a peek at the section about the AMT in Chapter 8, or better yet, speak to a good tax pro.

The holding period for determining long- or short-term capital gains on shares acquired by exercising a stock option starts on the day after you exercise the option. We explain the holding period rules earlier in this chapter, in the sidebar "Details for figuring short term or long term."

TIP

If an ISO is transferred, say in a divorce, it loses its special tax treatment. An ISO transferred at death doesn't.

Employee stock purchase plans

Employee stock purchase plans allow you to buy your company's stock at a discount. The discount isn't taxed until you sell the shares. If you hold the shares for more than two years after the option was granted and more than one year after you acquired the shares, the discount is taxed as ordinary income, and the difference between the value on the day that you acquired the shares is a capital gain (either short- or long-term). For example, you sold shares for $25,000 that you had purchased under an employee plan for $16,000. On the day that the options were granted, the shares were worth $18,000. Of the $9,000 gain, $2,000 ($18,000 − $16,000) is taxed at ordinary rates, and $7,000 ($25,000 − $18,000) is taxed as a capital gain, either short- or long-term.

If you sold the shares before the end of the two-year period, substitute the value of the shares on the day that you purchased them in place of the value when the option was granted to determine the ordinary income portion of the $9,000 gain. Suppose that the value of the shares on the day that you purchased them was $20,000. Of the gain, $4,000 ($20,000 – $16,000) is taxed as ordinary income, and the $5,000 balance ($25,000 – $20,000) is taxed as a capital gain. Is there a way around these maddening rules? Hold the shares for more than two years.

Nonstatutory stock options

Because nonqualified stock options don't have to meet any IRS rules, there are no restrictions on the amount of these types of options that may be granted. If a nonstatutory stock option doesn't have an ascertainable value when it's issued (which is usually the case for options that aren't traded on a stock exchange), no income is realized when you receive the option. When you exercise the option, you're taxed on the spread. For example, you exercise a $4,000 option to purchase stock trading at $10,000; you realize ordinary income of $6,000. Your tax basis for figuring a gain or loss when you sell the shares is $10,000. If the option has an ascertainable value, the value of the option is taxed as additional salary. For example, you receive an option to buy 100 shares that you can sell for $1,000 on the day that you receive the option. The bad news: You owe tax on the $1,000. The good news: When you exercise the shares, the $1,000 is added to the cost of the shares when determining whether you have a profit or loss when you sell the shares.

Unlike an ISO, a nonstatutory stock option can be transferred tax-free in a divorce.

REMEMBER

Options that have expired

Say you paid $1,500 in December 2020 to purchase an option to buy 1,000 shares of a stock for $60 a share that was good for 60 days, and you let the option expire in 2021 because you lost your bet when the stock never increased in value. You have a $1,500 short-term loss that you can deduct in 2021.

The reason we're warning you about this situation is because options that have expired aren't reported on the year-end tax statement that your broker is required by law to send. Only sales are reported, and consequently, many people tend to overlook this deduction. Don't be one of them.

WARNING

Short sales

Not many people get involved with short sales, but we thought you should know about them. When an investor believes a stock is going to tank and wants to take advantage of that fact, the investor "shorts" the stock by selling shares they don't own. How can you sell, you say, something that you don't own? You borrow the shares you sell from your broker. If you're right, and the stock goes down, you can buy the stock down the road for much less than you sold it for and replace the shares you borrowed from the broker. Doesn't everybody wish they had done this every time the market took a dive?

With a *short sale*, your gain or loss is reported when you buy the shares you have to return to the broker. Only, the normal rule (that you always use the trade date and not the settlement date) doesn't apply to short sales. If you made a profit, it's the trade date. If you have a loss, it's the settlement date. This rule is important at the end of the year. For example, say you make a short sale and then buy the shares you're going to return to the broker on December 31, 2021, but that purchase doesn't settle until January 4, 2022. If you made a profit, you report it in 2021. A loss, on the other hand, gets reported in 2022.

If, at the end of the year, you have an *open short position* (you hadn't returned the shares to the broker), your year-end tax statement (remember the IRS gets a copy of it) will probably report the short sale as a regular one. Report the sale on your return so that you and the IRS are in sync. By using the sales price as your cost, you obtain the net effect of showing a zero gain or loss on your Schedule D. That way you won't be reporting any actual income, and the IRS won't start up with you by claiming you failed to report all your sales. Report the sale when you buy the shares that you owe the broker.

WARNING

Short sales are considered short-term because with a short sale your holding period starts with the day you purchase the shares that you return to the broker, which usually is one day.

TIP

If your short position was open for more than 45 days, and your broker charged you for any dividends that you owed to the owner of the shares you borrowed, that charge gets deducted on line 9 of Schedule A as investment interest. See why good records are so important? If your broker charges you for short dividends on positions open for fewer than 46 days, you're going to add that dividend to your basis in the stock when you report the sale, which will either decrease your gain or increase your loss.

Stock for services

Stock for services is taxed as additional salary or fee income if you're an independent contractor. However, special rules apply as to when you have to report the income. If the stock is subject to restrictions, you report as income the value of the stock when the restrictions are lifted. For example, a restriction may be that you have to work for the company for three years; otherwise, you forfeit the shares.

TIP

Even if the shares are subject to restrictions, such as a substantial risk of forfeiture if you were to leave the company before ownership of the shares vests to you, you can elect to report the value of the shares as income in the year you receive them. This is known as a Section 83(b) election. Why would you want to do this? Say you receive shares in a start-up venture that have little value at the time you receive them. If you wait to report the value of the shares as income five years from now, when the restrictions are lifted and the shares are worth a great deal, you may be taxed at rates which currently are as high as 37 percent on the value at that time. On the other hand, if the shares currently are worth only a few thousand dollars, reporting the income now and paying a small amount of tax makes sense, because when you sell the shares after they've increased dramatically in value, the profit will be subject to the maximum 20 percent capital gain rate. An additional 3.8 percent tax applies to married couples who earn more than $250,000 of adjusted gross income (AGI) and single taxpayers with AGI above $200,000.

Remember, such a tactic is a gamble. If the company goes bust, you'll have paid tax on shares that ended up being worthless, but you will have a worthless stock deduction for the amount of income you paid tax on when you made the Section 83(b) election.

Appreciated employer securities

Many taxpayers overlook a special rule that applies when shares of the company where they work are distributed to them as part of a lump-sum distribution from a retirement plan. The value of the shares isn't subject to tax at the time you receive them. Only the cost of the shares when they were purchased is. For example, shares of your employer's stock that you bought through your employer's retirement plan for $50,000 now are worth $200,000. Only the $50,000 is subject to tax when you receive the shares. If you sell the shares the following year for $225,000, you have to report a $175,000 capital gain that year.

TIP

If you don't hold the shares for more than one year, part of the gain is taxed as a short-term sale. In the previous example, if you didn't hold the shares for more than a year after they were distributed, $25,000 of the gain is short-term, and $150,000 is long-term. The difference between the cost and the value on the day that they were distributed is treated as long-term ($200,000 − $50,000), and the difference between the sales price and the value on the date of distribution is short-term ($225,000 − $200,000).

Reporting Nonbusiness Bad Debts

Suppose that you lent your best friend $2,500 on New Year's Eve, and you haven't seen him since New Year's Day. All is not lost. You can deduct the $2,500. This news comes as a surprise to many people, because you can usually deduct losses only on investment and business trans-actions. But you must be able to prove that a valid debt existed, that the debt is worthless, and that you previously paid tax on the money that you lent.

» **What is worthless?** As with securities, there must be some identifiable event — such as bankruptcy, legal action, or the disappearance of the debtor — to prove that you can't col-lect what you're owed. You don't necessarily have to sue the debtor or even threaten to take legal action. This is one of the few instances where the IRS is on your side, not your lawyer's!

» **The right to sue:** To prove that you have a valid debt, you should be able to show that you have a right to sue. This situation creates a special problem with loans to family members. The IRS tends to view such loans as gifts. So, if you had your brother sign a promissory note and put up collateral when you lent him money, you may prevail if the IRS ever questions whether it was a valid debt. Yet, as you probably know, most dealings between family members are done a little more casually than that. See Chapter 12 for more on this painful subject.

» **Is the debt deductible?** Finally, to establish that a debt is deductible, you must have paid tax on what you lent. Suppose that you worked in a local bookstore in anticipation of being paid later. The bookstore went out of business, and you weren't paid. Sorry. Because you never received the bookstore income and didn't report it on your tax return, you're not entitled to a deduction if it's not paid.

You deduct nonbusiness bad debts on Form 8949, Part I, line 1, and then move it over to Schedule D as a short-term loss, regardless of how long the money was owed. If you don't have capital gains to offset the deduction, you can deduct up to $3,000 of the loss and carry over the balance to next year, just like with other investment losses. Additionally, you must attach a statement to your return explaining the nature of the debt, name of the debtor and any business or family relationship, date the debt became due, efforts made to collect the debt, and reason for determining that the debt is entirely worthless (only business debts can generate a deduction if they're partially worthless).

TIP

Don't confuse nonbusiness bad debts with business-related bad debts that can be deducted on your business tax returns. Refer to Chapter 13 for more on business-related bad debts.

Day traders

There are tax advantages to being considered a trader rather than a mere investor. Vast sums of money, however, have been lost day trading, and the tax impact has been significant (see Chapter 24 for more on investing and taxes). Most people are investors because they purchase securities they hold for a long time in anticipation the investment will appreciate in value and produce income (dividends). An investor reports gains and losses on Form 8949 and Schedule D. If losses exceed gains, an investor is limited to an annual deductible of $3,000 against ordinary income with unlimited time to offset the remaining loss in future years, first by using the loss to offset capital gains, and then by deducting the annual limit of $3,000 against ordinary income ($1,500 if you're married filing separately). Investment expenses, other than investment interest and short dividends, are not allowed, and neither is a home office deduction, no matter how much time investors spend analyzing their investments, because they're not carrying on a trade or business.

A *day trader,* on the other hand, typically tries to capture short-term swings in the market. A trader reports expenses on Schedule C and trading gains and losses on Schedule D. Traders can claim a home-office deduction because they're carrying on a trade or business. A trader can deduct all margin interest on Schedule C. Investors deduct theirs on Schedule A, provided it doesn't exceed their investment income. Gains aren't subject to self-employment tax, nor can a deduction for a contribution to an IRA or retirement plan based on the gain be claimed, because the gain isn't considered earned income. Traders are subject to the same $3,000 annual limit on trading losses that exceed gains. The wash sale rule also applies. To be a trader, your trading has to be, in IRS jargon, "sufficiently frequent and substantial." Like so many IRS definitions it falls under the heading of, "I can't define it, but I know it when I see it." The IRS tends to take the position that you can't be a trader if you have another regular job. They like to reserve trader status for people who trade on a full-time basis to the exclusion of other activities. This is plainly wrong. You can be a part-time trader. The New York Stock Exchange defines a trader as someone who buys and sells a stock in the same trading session at least four times a week.

Mark-to-market traders

A *mark-to-market trader* elects to treat any stocks held at the end of the trading day on December 31 as being sold on that day. Any of these deemed gains or losses are reported on the mark-to-market trader's return. For true day traders, this requirement shouldn't be of any consequence, because they typically don't own securities at the end of any day. A position trader, on the other hand, who has an open position on December 31, and who makes a mark-to-market election, loses the ability to use the year-end tax strategy of selling the losers and holding the winners. On the following January 1, a mark-to-market trader must adjust the tax bases of the securities deemed to have been sold. Gains that were reported because of the election are added to the basis of the securities held on December 31, and losses are subtracted from its basis.

A mark-to-market trader reports expenses on Schedule C and trading activity as ordinary gains and losses on Form 4797. The wash-sale rule doesn't apply to this type of trading. If net losses occur, all these losses can be used to offset other income; the $3,000 limit doesn't apply. If the losses produce a net operating loss (exceeding your other income), they can be carried back to a prior year to obtain a refund and then forwarded to future years. Trading gains aren't subject to self-employment tax, and no IRA or retirement deduction can be claimed.

WARNING

A true mark-to-market trader isn't the same as a day trader. All gains and losses received by a day trader are treated as short-term capital gains (so that you may deduct only a maximum of $3,000 of net loss against ordinary income), whereas the mark-to-market trader treats gain income as ordinary income.

TIP

That the gains are treated as ordinary income doesn't mean that mark-to-market traders can't have long-term capital gains taxed at the favorable lower rates. By holding investment securities in a separate account, a mark-to-market trader can still generate long-term capital gains.

It's too late to make the mark-to-market election for 2021. You have to make the election a year in advance. To be effective for 2022, you make the election on your 2021 tax return or on Form 4868 that is filed by April 18, 2022 (April 19, 2022, for Maine and Massachusetts residents). After you make the election, it applies to all future years unless you obtain IRS permission to change. Make the election by attaching the following signed statement to your return or extension request:

> I hereby elect to use the mark-to-market method of accounting under Section 475(f) of the Internal Revenue Code for my trade and business of trading securities. The first year for which this election is effective is the taxable year beginning January 1, 2022.
>
> _____ (Signed)
>
> (Your name and date)

Checking On Cryptocurrency

The IRS defines *cryptocurrency* as "a medium of exchange using cryptography to secure transactions, that is a digital asset using blockchain technology, that is bought and sold on exchanges, and that uses decentralized control instead of centralized electronic money and banking systems." Cryptocurrency has been hovering around the edges of traditional capital assets and currency for decades. Only in the past several years has it started to be accepted as a form of payment by some companies and institutions. More widely known cryptocurrencies have been attracting attention as an investment due to their increasing value over the past decade.

And, while in its early stages, there seemed to be no official way to track it, it therefore escaped most attempts to tax it. Now it is moving out of the shadows and is being accepted as a form of payment by some retailers as well as by some government agencies (the Ohio Department of Revenue comes to mind) and has even been touted as an alternative currency for the country of El Salvador. Congress and the IRS would like their piece of the pie.

Cryptocurrency is still difficult to track, and therefore the IRS is using a carrot/stick approach. Beginning in 2019, they started an effort to encourage you to voluntarily disclose any income you earn through cryptocurrency, whether you receive it as part of your wages or you invest in it as a capital asset. Should you fail to disclose your crypto transactions and the IRS finds out through other means that you have crypto income, the financial penalties for failing to disclose "voluntarily" are severe. There are accuracy-related penalties, civil fraud penalties, failure to file correct information return penalties, and failure to furnish correct payee statement penalties — and that's just on the civil side.

We strongly urge you to voluntarily comply with reporting your crypto transactions of whatever sort. Because cryptocurrencies don't pay dividends and interest, your transactions will be capital ones, which is why we've included them here in this chapter. If you buy cryptocurrencies as an investment, and then sell them, you're generating either a gain or a loss on the transaction, depending on your basis in the currency, exactly in the same manner as if you bought shares in ABC Corporation and then sold them. The holding periods for long-term and short-term gains and losses are the same as for garden variety stocks and bonds.

If you're wondering how to report these on your tax return, pretend that your crypto is a stock, and enter onto the correct section of Form 8949 the amount you sold, the name of the crypto you sold, your purchase date, your sales date, cost basis, proceeds, and your gain or loss. None of your sales will be reported on Form 1099-B, and neither will your basis, so for short-term sales, you'll tick box C on Form 8949, and for long-term sales, you'll check box F.

There is one major difference in the treatment of cryptocurrency versus ordinary property: At the death of the owner, the person inheriting the cryptocurrency doesn't receive a step-up in basis. Instead, the basis of inherited cryptocurrency is the same as the basis in the hands of the original owner.

Chapter 15

Supplemental Income and Loss: Schedule E

Don't let the words *supplemental income* throw you. That's just IRS-speak for the income you receive from rental property or royalties, or through partnerships, S Corporations (Corporations that don't pay tax; the owners report the Corporations' income or loss on their personal tax returns), trusts, and estates. To report your rental or royalty income, you use Schedule E, which is laid out in the form of a profit or loss statement (income and expenses). From your income, you subtract your expenses. The remainder is your net income, the income that you have to pay taxes on. If you have a loss, the rules get a little sticky as to whether you can deduct it. (Isn't that a surprise?) For partnerships, S Corporations, and trusts and estates, you're going to flip Schedule E onto page 2 and report ordinary income or loss and rental income or loss in Part II for partnerships and S Corporations, and in Part III for estates and trusts.

REMEMBER

Remember that if you're a self-employed taxpayer receiving royalties, such as a musician, you use Schedule C. The information in this chapter applies to people who receive royalties and aren't self-employed. For example, George Gershwin received royalties from *Porgy and Bess* and reported them on Schedule C. But he has passed away, and now his heirs receive royalties that must be reported on Schedule E.

TAX CUT

First-time authors get a break. They aren't subject to self-employment tax (Social Security tax on royalties), because being an author, at this point, isn't considered their regular line of work. Thanks to a Tax Court case, first-time authors don't become subject to self-employment tax until their particular book is revised or they start on a second one.

Part I: Income or Loss from Rental Real Estate and Royalties

If you receive rent or royalties, you should receive Form 1099-MISC. Box 1 is for rent, and box 2 is for royalties. (Even if you rent your summer home to the Queen of England, you report your rent and royalties separately.)

WARNING Just because you didn't receive a Form 1099-MISC from the tenants renting your summer house or the family who rents the other side of your two-family house doesn't mean you're off the hook and don't need to report that income. You're required to report all income, whether or not it is reported to the IRS on a Form 1099, on your income tax return. Check out Figure 15-1 for a look at Schedule E and how to report items discussed in the following sections.

Questions A and B

If you're running any sort of business, chances are good that you're paying other people to perform work for you. That person may be a painter, a plumber, your cleaner, or your attorney. It doesn't matter to whom you've paid the money — if they are not an incorporated business, and if the amounts paid are $600 or more for services performed, you need to give that person or business a 1099 and report that information to the IRS. Chapter 13 goes over the rules for this in detail, so take a look there to see how and when you should report.

WARNING Which brings us back to questions A and B at the top of the first page of Schedule E. If you made payments that require you to file Form 1099s, check the "Yes" box. And, if you've marked "Yes" in question A, you'd better be prepared to mark "Yes" in question B, asking if you have, or will, file the required Form(s) 1099. The penalty for failure to file an information return is $50 per return, and each failure (maybe you should have issued 10 or 20 of these?) costs you $50. The IRS will waive the penalty for reasonable cause, but the excuse of "I didn't know I had to do this" won't fly. Ignorance of the law is never a defense.

Line 1: Physical address and type of each property

On line 1a, enter the physical address. For example: 123 Main St., Albany, NY 12345. The line provides enough room for listing three properties. If you have more than three properties, enter the additional properties on another Schedule E, but use the total column on only one Schedule E to enter the total of all the properties. If you're preparing your returns on a computer, bring up a new interview sheet for each rental property or royalty you have; the computer will do all the rest, providing you with as many Schedule Es as your return requires. One thing to note, though, is that if you are declaring royalties, your computer software may still be looking for a physical address, even though you've entered "6" into line 1b, indicating that this is a royalty payment. In order to override the error message that can prevent your return from e-filing, make up something. You're earning royalties — you should be creative. We generally put "royalty income" into the physical address line, but then we write tax books — no one seems to want a creative accountant.

SCHEDULE E (Form 1040)	Supplemental Income and Loss	OMB No. 1545-0074
Department of the Treasury Internal Revenue Service (99)	(From rental real estate, royalties, partnerships, S corporations, estates, trusts, REMICs, etc.) ▶ Attach to Form 1040, 1040-SR, 1040-NR, or 1041. ▶ Go to *www.irs.gov/ScheduleE* for instructions and the latest information.	**2021** Attachment Sequence No. **13**

Name(s) shown on return | Your social security number

Part I   **Income or Loss From Rental Real Estate and Royalties**   **Note:** If you are in the business of renting personal property, use **Schedule C.** See instructions. If you are an individual, report farm rental income or loss from **Form 4835** on page 2, line 40.

A Did you make any payments in 2021 that would require you to file Form(s) 1099? See instructions   ☐ Yes ☐ No
B If "Yes," did you or will you file required Form(s) 1099?   ☐ Yes ☐ No

1a Physical address of each property (street, city, state, ZIP code)

A
B
C

1b Type of Property (from list below)	2 For each rental real estate property listed above, report the number of fair rental and personal use days. Check the **QJV** box only if you meet the requirements to file as a qualified joint venture. See instructions.		Fair Rental Days	Personal Use Days	QJV
A		A			☐
B		B			☐
C		C			☐

Type of Property:
1 Single Family Residence   3 Vacation/Short-Term Rental   5 Land   7 Self-Rental
2 Multi-Family Residence   4 Commercial   6 Royalties   8 Other (describe)

Income:	Properties:		A	B	C
3 Rents received	3				
4 Royalties received	4				
Expenses:					
5 Advertising	5				
6 Auto and travel (see instructions)	6				
7 Cleaning and maintenance	7				
8 Commissions	8				
9 Insurance	9				
10 Legal and other professional fees	10				
11 Management fees	11				
12 Mortgage interest paid to banks, etc. (see instructions)	12				
13 Other interest	13				
14 Repairs	14				
15 Supplies	15				
16 Taxes	16				
17 Utilities	17				
18 Depreciation expense or depletion	18				
19 Other (list) ▶	19				
20 Total expenses. Add lines 5 through 19	20				
21 Subtract line 20 from line 3 (rents) and/or 4 (royalties). If result is a (loss), see instructions to find out if you must file **Form 6198**	21				
22 Deductible rental real estate loss after limitation, if any, on **Form 8582** (see instructions)	22	(	)(	)(	)

23a Total of all amounts reported on line 3 for all rental properties		23a	
b Total of all amounts reported on line 4 for all royalty properties		23b	
c Total of all amounts reported on line 12 for all properties		23c	
d Total of all amounts reported on line 18 for all properties		23d	
e Total of all amounts reported on line 20 for all properties		23e	
24 **Income.** Add positive amounts shown on line 21. **Do not** include any losses		24	
25 **Losses.** Add royalty losses from line 21 and rental real estate losses from line 22. Enter total losses here		25	( )
26 **Total rental real estate and royalty income or (loss).** Combine lines 24 and 25. Enter the result here. If Parts II, III, IV, and line 40 on page 2 do not apply to you, also enter this amount on Schedule 1 (Form 1040), line 5. Otherwise, include this amount in the total on line 41 on page 2		26	

FIGURE 15-1: Schedule E, Page 1.

For Paperwork Reduction Act Notice, see the separate instructions.   Cat. No. 11344L   **Schedule E (Form 1040) 2021**

Source: Internal Revenue Service

Line 2: Vacation home questions

Here, you're asked whether you've personally used any of the listed rental properties, and for how long. For example, you may have rented out your beach home for July and August, but you used it in June and September. See the "Vacation homes" sidebar later in this chapter for information about vacation home expenses you can and can't deduct. In line 2, put the number of days the property was either rented or available for rental, and the number of days you, a co-owner, or a member of your family used the property if no rent was paid, or if rent was paid, if it was less than the fair market rental value. If you left the property unrented for a period of time while you made repairs to it, include those days as part of the rental period, even if you or family members were using the property while you were performing the repairs.

Lines 3–4: Income

Copy the amounts from box 1, rent, and box 2, royalties, of your 1099-MISC onto lines 3 (rent) and 4 (royalties) of Schedule E.

You may wonder whether some unusual cases of rent are counted as income. Rent paid in advance, for example, is counted as rent. If you sign a lease in December 2020 and collect January's rent of $1,000, this amount should have been included in 2020's rent income on this schedule, even though it applies to 2021's rent due. Security deposits that you must return aren't rental income. And if your tenant pays you to cancel the lease, the amount you receive is rent — it isn't considered a tax-free payment for damages. Although expenses paid by the tenant and applied against the rent are considered rental income, you're entitled to deduct those expenses. Finally, if you're a Good Samaritan and charge a relative or friend less than the fair rental value, your deductions for depreciation and maintenance expenses can't exceed the rent you collect.

Lines 5–19: Expenses

On these lines, you tabulate the amounts that you're allowed to deduct. Good bookkeepers to the head of the line. If you have good records, you can save a tidy sum. The expense lines apply to both royalties and rents.

WARNING If you rent out half of a two-family house and you occupy the other half, for example, you can deduct only 50 percent of your expenses, unless the expenses relate specifically to the rental unit. If it's a three-family unit and you occupy one of the units, you can deduct only 66 percent of the expenses. So, if you make repairs in your tenant's kitchen, you get to deduct the full amount, but you'll be able to deduct only a portion of roof repairs. Get the picture? But remember that the portion of your mortgage interest and property taxes that relates to the part you occupy gets deducted on Schedule A (see Chapter 11).

TIP If you're using a computer to prepare your return, the expense portion of Schedule E typically is separated out between direct expenses and indirect expenses. Direct expenses are for those items which only apply to the rental unit; indirect expenses are used for expenses incurred by the entire building if a portion of the building is used by you as opposed to being rented.

Line 5: Advertising

You're allowed to deduct the cost of ads, whether they're placed in your local newspaper or you're relying on the internet/websites to advertise your rental. The same goes if you had building signs made.

Line 6: Auto and travel

Travel to inspect your rental property is deductible. But if you live in Buffalo and go to Florida in January to inspect a vacation home that you rent out part of the time, be prepared for a battle with the IRS. Refer to the guidelines for deducting travel and auto expenses in Chapter 13.

Line 7: Cleaning and maintenance

You can deduct your costs for cleaning and maintenance, such as your monthly fee for the window washer and your payment to the guy who tunes up your furnace before the cold weather sets in.

Line 8: Commissions

You can deduct commissions paid to a real estate broker to find a tenant. The norm is 5 percent to 10 percent, although sometimes it's one-month's rent.

Line 9: Insurance

We hope that you carry insurance to protect against your building burning down, lawsuits, and other perils such as floods and earthquakes. You can deduct the cost of these policies. One tricky area to be aware of is if you pay for an insurance premium that covers more than one year. In that case, you deduct only the portion of the premium that applies to each year's Schedule E. For example, suppose that in 2021 you pay a $900 premium that covers a three-year period. You deduct $300 in 2021, another $300 in 2022, and the final $300 in 2023.

Line 10: Legal and other professional fees

Legal fees incurred in the purchase of the property must be added to the cost of the building and deducted as part of your depreciation deduction (coming later). Legal fees for preparing a lease are deductible. And if you're paying for tax preparation services, the portion of the fee attributable to this Schedule E is deductible. Look back at Chapter 13 about having to issue Form 1099-NEC to your tax preparer or attorney.

Line 11: Management fees

You can deduct the costs of managing the property — collecting the rent, seeing to all repairs, paying a management company (if you have one), and so on.

Line 12: Mortgage interest paid to banks (Form 1098)

This amount comes right off Form 1098, Mortgage Interest Statement, which you get from the bank that holds the mortgage. The bank sends you this statement by January 31, 2022. A copy goes to the IRS so it can check whether you're deducting the correct amount.

Line 13: Other interest

If the person from whom you purchased the property provided the financing and holds a mortgage on the property, the interest is entered here because this is where the interest that wasn't paid to financial institutions goes. All the fees you paid when you took out the mortgage are deducted over the duration of the loan. You also put the interest on a second mortgage here, as well as the interest on short-term installment loans for the purchase of appliances and other assets.

WARNING

Unlike with a personal residence, points and fees to obtain a mortgage on rental property aren't deductible in the year that you pay them. You must write off these amounts over the term of the loan and deduct them on this line. If you didn't receive a Form 1098, enter the interest you paid on this line.

Interest paid on an income tax bill can't be deducted. You can deduct interest on employment taxes that you were late in paying.

Line 14: Repairs

Repairs are deductible in full in the year in which you pay for them. Improvements are deducted over 27½ years for residential property and over either 31½ or 39 years, depending on when you acquired the building, for commercial or nonresidential property (refer to Chapter 13 to obtain the rate of depreciation that you can claim every year). A *repair* — such as fixing a leaky roof — keeps your property in good operating condition. It doesn't materially add to the value of the property or prolong its life. An *improvement,* such as adding an entire new roof, on the other hand, adds to the property's value or prolongs its life and thus is written off over its useful life.

Line 15: Supplies

You can deduct such things as cleaning supplies, light bulbs, and small items that you buy at a hardware store.

Line 16: Taxes

This line includes real estate taxes on the property. Additionally, if you employ a superintendent or a janitor, this line is where you enter the Social Security and unemployment taxes that you must pay. The bank holding the mortgage sends you an annual mortgage statement that gives you the tax information if your real estate taxes are being escrowed; otherwise, we know you kept good records and can easily go back to your files to find the paid real estate tax bills. The Social Security and unemployment taxes will be listed on your quarterly payroll tax return. Remember, water and sewer bills are not tax bills, even though they still get paid to your city or town. They are utility bills, and while they are deductible, you put them on line 17, not here.

Line 17: Utilities

Why don't you just go ahead and enter your electric, gas, fuel, water, sewer, and phone costs for your property here? We would.

Line 18: Depreciation expense or depletion

Tax law allows you to claim a yearly tax deduction for depreciation for rental real estate, but that's only for assets that you can actually use up, like the building, or a refrigerator. Land doesn't get used up — it just sits there. Not surprisingly, you can't depreciate land. You are therefore required to allocate some portion of your rental real estate to the land it sits on if your real estate is a stand-alone building. This doesn't apply if you've purchased a condo or co-op where you don't have deeded rights to the land itself but beware if you have a deeded parking spot in a condo parking lot (but not a condo parking garage, which would be depreciable). You will have to assign some portion of your acquisition cost to that parking space.

How can you determine the value of land versus the value of buildings on the land? A good place to start is your local city or town's list of all real estate parcels. Increasingly, an allocation is being made on each parcel between land and improvements (just another way of saying buildings). If your real estate bill or the town's listing sheet for your property differentiates between the two, you're all set. Otherwise, look at similar land purchases in your location to try to get some sense of a value. In many towns, the sales price of a house that is going to be torn down is a good place to start; that person who just bought the property had no interest in a 1950s ranch and wants to build a spec house on the property. They're only paying for the land and not the building.

You compute your depreciation deduction on Form 4562, Depreciation and Amortization, and you attach this form to your 1040 only if you first started to claim a deduction for a particular item in 2021. If you started claiming depreciation on an asset in an earlier year, the form isn't required. Compute the depreciation and enter the amount here. An annual depreciation rate schedule for residential real estate is available in Chapter 13. IRS Publication 946 *(How to Depreciate Property)* has the complete depreciation schedule for commercial real estate. Also check out Chapter 13 for an abridged schedule for commercial property, which must be depreciated over either 31½ or 39 years. We provide a detailed example there of exactly how depreciation is computed.

TIP

Even though an apartment building must be depreciated over 27½ years, furniture and appliances used in the building must be depreciated over only 7 years. Don't forget though, that even though you can't use Section 179 depreciation or bonus depreciation for the building, you may use it for furnishings. Check out Chapter 13 to see how Section 179 depreciation works and whether it makes sense for you to use it here.

We're pretty sure that most of you can probably pass an exam on depreciation by now, especially if you've read Chapter 13. But what about depletion? According to the IRS, depletion is the using up of natural resources extracted from a mineral property by mining, drilling, quarrying stone, or cutting timber. If you own an economic interest in mineral property or standing timber, you're entitled to take a deduction for depletion. And, if you've leased land so that someone else can extract minerals or timber from it, you, as the lessor, and the lessee split the depletion deduction. So, if you've leased some property so that oil and gas companies can frack for natural gas, you're not only entitled to the rents from the lease, but also a portion of the depletion deduction.

SEEK ADVICE

Considering the length of the Internal Revenue Code and the Regulations that go along with it, we can't possibly cram everything you need to know into one reasonably sized book. And depletion isn't an easy calculation. You should definitely be aware if you should be taking it, but you probably want to see someone with expertise in this area to make sure you're calculating it correctly.

Line 19: Other

This is one of those catchall lines for things whose descriptions don't fit on the preceding lines, such as gardening and permits. Your computer software may have additional categories other than the ones listed previously; one of ours lists out plumbers and plumbing supplies separately, for example. However, when we print returns with plumbers entered into the software, it just gives us a supplemental statement for line 19. Deductions that we like to put here are things like the yearly fee we pay to register our unit with the town it's located in, any inspection fees that are required to get a certificate of occupancy, and things along those lines that we just can't shoehorn into any of the other categories.

Lines 20–21: Calculating your income or loss per property

We know you love doing math problems, and here are some for you for each column (A, B, and C) on page 1 of Schedule E. If you have more than three rental or royalty properties, you'll have more than one Schedule E; make sure that you've added the columns for all your properties, not just the ones on your first Schedule E. Line 20 is straight math; lines 21 and 22 are a bit more complex, so read on.

Line 20: Total expenses

Add lines 5 through 19 and place the total on this line.

Line 21: Subtract line 20 from line 3 (rents) and/or 4 (royalties)

Easy as pie — for each column A, B, and C on however many Schedules E you have, subtract your total expenses (line 20) from either your rents received (line 3) or your royalties received (line 4). The total for each column gets listed on each column's line 21.

Here's where it becomes slightly more complicated. As Schedule E says, if the result is a loss, you may have to file Form 6198, At-Risk Limitations. This is where you're going to determine whether any portion of your loss is allowable under the passive activity rules in place for most real estate reported on Schedule E, or whether you're going to have to suspend those losses to a future year when you have enough passive income to offset your losses, or you sell the property and turn all those losses from passive to active.

What constitutes the basis for the at-risk limitations? Simply put, it's the money you personally stand to lose if this piece of real estate goes belly-up. Clearly, if you didn't put up all the money that makes up the basis in the property, your at-risk limitation is the amount of money you did pay toward this venture. But what many people don't know is that, if you have a non-recourse mortgage on the property, meaning your mortgage company can only take the property secured by the mortgage if they foreclose on you; they're not allowed to put their hand in your pocket if the amount of the debt they hold isn't covered by the sale of property. Check out Line 27: the at-risk and other tax shelter rules, later in this chapter for more information on at-risk limitations.

Line 22: Deductible rental real estate loss after limitation, if any, on Form 8582

You only need to complete this line if line 21 shows a loss. If line 21 is a positive number, move right along to line 23a. If your real estate property showed a loss for the year (on line 21), you may not actually be able to claim that entire loss on your tax return. If you didn't show a loss, skip ahead to the next line.

Line 22 is where you enter how much of the loss on line 21 can be deducted. Rental real estate is considered a passive activity, and you normally have to complete Form 8582, Passive Activity Loss Limitations, to determine the portion, if any, that you're allowed to deduct. However, if you meet all the following conditions, you're spared from Form 8582 (keep your fingers crossed):

>> Rental real estate is the only passive activity you're involved in. (Remember that passive activity is a business or investment where you act as a silent partner — you aren't actively involved.)

>> You actively participated in making management decisions or arranged for others to provide services, such as repairs.

>> Your rental real estate loss didn't exceed $25,000 — or $12,500 if you're married and filing separately.

>> You didn't have rental or passive activity losses that you couldn't deduct in a prior year.

>> If you're married and filing separately, you must have lived apart from your spouse for the entire year.

>> Your modified adjusted gross income (see the worksheet in the next section) is less than $100,000 (or $50,000 if you're married and filing separately).

>> You don't hold any interest in rental real estate as either a limited partner or as a beneficiary of an estate or trust.

If you meet all seven of these criteria, congratulations, you can skip the dreaded Form 8582 and write your deductible real estate loss right here on line 22.

SEEK ADVICE

If you have to fill out Form 8582 to compute your rental losses on Schedule E (line 22) because your modified adjusted gross income (AGI) is more than the limit (or you were involved in other passive activities), you have to be familiar with tax-shelter and other rules that allow you to deduct up to $25,000 of losses from rental real estate that you actively manage. If Form 8582 applies to you, oh taxpayer, you need a tax advisor! *Note:* You don't necessarily need professional tax help every year, but you do need to consult with an advisor in the year that you purchase the property to make sure you understand all the tax rules that you must obey. As long as nothing monumental changes in the future, you'll do perfectly fine on your own with just *Taxes 2023 For Dummies*. If we went into the tax-shelter rules in complete detail, we'd need a second volume to this book.

Worksheet to determine whether you need to file Form 8582

This little worksheet helps you compute your modified AGI so that you can determine whether it exceeds the limits that we just mentioned. If it does, off you go to Form 8582. Remember, enter every number here as a positive, even if it's a loss.

1. AGI from Form 1040 (line 11) $_____

2. Taxable portion of Social Security (line 6b of Form 1040) $_____

3. Subtract line 2 from line 1 $_____

4. Your IRA deductions (Form 1040, Schedule 1, Part II, line 20) $_____

5. Student loan interest (Form 1040, Schedule 1, Part II, line 21) $_____

6. One-half of self-employment tax (Form 1040, Schedule 1, Part II, line 15) $_____

7. Passive activity losses (line 3 of Form 8582) $_____

8. Interest from Series EE and I savings bonds used to pay education expenses (Form 8815) $_____

9. Exclusion for adoption assistance payments (Form 8839, line 30) $_____

10. Deduction allowed for foreign-derived intangible income and global intangible low-taxed income (Form 8993, lines 28 and 29) $_____

11. Add lines 4–10 $_____

12. Add line 11 to line 3; this equals your modified AGI $_____

The $25,000 special allowance

TIP

Here's why that $100,000 modified AGI figure is so important. You can deduct up to $25,000 of the losses you incurred in rental real estate if you actively participate in the management of the property and own at least 10 percent — which means that you have to make management decisions regarding the approval of new tenants and rental terms, approving expenditures, and other similar decisions. So, if you turn an apartment or home that you own over to a real estate agent to rent and manage, the $25,000 loss-deduction rule doesn't apply. You may be able to pull off this deduction, however, if you reserve the right to approve all expenditures and improvements that have to be made.

Now for the ever-present exception to the general rule: If your income exceeds $100,000, the $25,000 limit is reduced by 50 cents for every dollar of income you earn that's more than $100,000. When your income reaches $150,000, the $25,000 allowance is completely phased out. The loss that's phased out (the portion that you can't deduct in any year) doesn't just disappear. You carry it over and enter it on line 1c of Form 8582, Passive Activity Loss Limitations (this is IRS-speak for a tax shelter) to determine the amount of the carryover that's deductible in a future year. When you eventually sell the property, all your suspended losses for that property can be deducted in the year of the sale. We explain all this in greater detail in the section "The tax shelter rules" later in this chapter.

The $25,000 figure is reduced to $12,500 if you're married, filing separately, and living apart from your spouse for the entire year; the phase-out begins at $50,000 of your AGI (not $100,000) and is completely phased out at $75,000. If you lived with your spouse at any time during the year and you're filing separate returns, you can't use the $12,500 exception (half of $25,000). Please don't ask us about the reason for this one; it's way too complicated. On Form 8582, you compute the portion of the $25,000 allowance to which you're entitled.

TIP

Think twice before converting your personal residence you lived in to a rental property, because you may be forfeiting some or all of the $250,000 ($500,000 for couples) exclusion on your potential profit if you do. Because a residence must be your principal residence for two of the five years looking back from the date of the sale (see Chapter 12 for the rules on sales of a residence), after you've rented your former home for more than three years, you can kiss the exclusion goodbye.

The tax shelter rules

If you rent out your vacation home or part of a two-family house, you're operating a tax shelter — and you always thought that tax shelters were something that only movie stars and high-income athletes were involved with!

WARNING

In 1986, Congress decided to kill tax shelters and passed an anti-tax-shelter law. As a result, you can deduct a loss from a *passive activity* (that's what a tax shelter is now called in IRS jargon) only if you have income from another passive activity. If you don't, the loss is *disallowed* for the current year. Disallowed losses are suspended and carried over to future years. If you have *passive income* (that's income from a passive activity, such as a limited partnership or rental real estate) next year, you can deduct the loss. If you don't have passive income next year, you keep carrying over the loss until you do, or until you sell the property or your interest in the tax shelter.

For example, suppose that you have a rental loss of $5,000 in 2021 and no other passive income. You can't deduct any of the $5,000 loss in 2021 (but see "The $25,000 special allowance" earlier in this chapter). The loss is carried over to 2022. If in 2022 the property generates a $4,000 profit, you can deduct $4,000 of the suspended loss and carry over the $1,000 balance to 2023. If you sell the property in 2023, the $1,000 can be deducted — even if you don't have any passive income in 2023.

If you have two or more passive activities, you combine them to determine whether a loss in one can be used to offset a profit in another. For example, suppose that you own one building that you rent out at a $6,000 loss and another building that produces a $5,000 profit. You can use $5,000 of the $6,000 loss to offset the $5,000 profit from the second building, and the $1,000 balance is carried over to the next year.

If you have a passive activity loss, you compute the amount of the loss that can be deducted or that has to be carried over to future years on Form 8582, Passive Activity Loss Limitations. On this form, you combine your passive activity losses and income. If income exceeds losses, you have a deduction. If it doesn't, you have a suspended loss. Remember: If you sell the property, any suspended losses are deductible in the year of the sale.

WARNING

When isn't a loss a loss? When you have a sweetheart deal. In a recent Tax Court case, a taxpayer was denied a rental loss deduction because she gave her brother a big break on the rent. The court considered the days she rented to her brother as personal use. She therefore ran afoul of the 14 days or 10 percent of the days rented rule (see the "Vacation homes" sidebar in this chapter). And it doesn't end there: Any loss on a subsequent sale of the house isn't deductible. The low rent she charged shows she lacked a profit motive. No profit motive, no deductible loss.

VACATION HOMES

Determining the expenses you can deduct on a vacation home is no fun in the sun because you have to allocate the operating expenses based on how many days you rent your home and how many days you use it. What's deductible and what's not are based on the following three mind-numbing rules:

- **Rule 1:** If you rent your home for fewer than 15 days, you don't have to report the rent you collect, and none of the operating expenses are deductible. Your mortgage interest and real estate taxes still are deducted as itemized deductions.

- **Rule 2:** If you rent your home for 15 or more days and your personal use of your home is more than the greater of 14 days or 10 percent of the total days it's rented, then the property isn't considered rental property, and the expenses allocated to the rental period can't exceed the rental income. Expenses that are allocated to the rental period but can't be deducted are carried forward to future years. These expenses can be deducted to the extent of your future rental income or until you sell the property. If you have a profit on the rental of a vacation home, this rule doesn't apply. Tax shelter rules apply only to losses.

  In figuring the rental days, count only the days the home actually was rented. The days that you held the property out for rent but it wasn't rented don't count as rental days. After making this computation, you allocate your rental expenses based on the total number of days rented divided by the total number of rented days plus the days you used it. For example, suppose that your beach cottage was rented for 36 days and you used it for 36 days. In such a case, 50 percent of the operating expenses for the year would be allocated to the rental period, 36 days rented ÷ 72 days (36 rented and 36 personal days). Don't count any days that you worked full time to repair the property as personal days.

  The Tax Court is on your side when it comes to deducting mortgage interest and taxes, which don't have to be allocated under the preceding formula. You can allocate this stuff on a daily basis. So, in the example, only 10 percent (36 rental days ÷ 365) of your taxes and mortgage interest would have to be allocated to the rental period, leaving the other 90 percent to be deducted on Schedule A as an itemized deduction. This court decision means that a larger amount of your other rental expenses can be deducted from your rental income, and (better yet) you get to deduct 90 percent of your mortgage interest and taxes as an itemized deduction rather than just 50 percent.

- **Rule 3:** If the personal use of your residence doesn't exceed the greater of 14 days or 10 percent of the total days it's rented, then your vacation home is treated as rental property. If the total amount of your rental expenses exceeds your rental income, your loss is deductible if you have other passive income (or if the $25,000 special allowance permits). You still have to allocate the expenses of running the property between personal and rental days.

Have a nice vacation.

Lines 23–26: IRS math quiz

The IRS is looking for new and improved ways to slice and dice the numbers, so the rest of Schedule E, Part I, is simple math.

Lines 23a through 23e were created to fill a void that no one else thought was important. Still, if the IRS wants it, we must comply (and if you're doing this on your computer, you'll find that these numbers are already calculated for you). Here's what's required for line 23:

(a) Total of all rents received in 2021. If you only have one rental property, enter the number from line 3 here; if you have multiple rental properties, add all the line 3 amounts together and place the total here.

(b) Same as line 23a, except this time for royalties. Add all your royalty amounts on line 4 together and place the total here.

(c) The IRS wants to know about the mortgage interest you paid. Add all amounts on Schedule E, line 12, and put the total here.

(d) Add together all the depreciation amounts on Schedule E, line 18, and put the total here.

(e) Now they want your total expenses for all rental and royalty activities. Add all the amounts on line 20 for all your Schedule E rental and royalty activity and put the total here.

Once you've completed the line 23 math exercise, you're just going to ignore those questions, and results, and move to line 24, which would like you to enter all the positive amounts shown on Schedule E, line 21. On line 25, you're going to add together the allowable rental real estate losses on line 22 and the royalty losses on line 21. And finally, on line 26, you'll add together lines 24 and 25. Voilà! You're done with Schedule E, Part I.

Part II: Income or Loss from Partnerships and S Corporations

The average taxpayer finds page 2 of Schedule E the most daunting. You report income and losses from partnerships, S Corporations, estates, and trusts on that page. Instead of the nice, long, symmetrical columns of page 1, Schedule E's flip side looks as if it were designed to confuse rather than clarify (see Figure 15-2).

Partnerships and S Corporations are called *pass-through entities*. As that term implies, all the income and deductions of a partnership or an S corporation pass through to each partner or shareholder based on ownership percentage, with the income and deductions maintaining their character (interest remains interest, charitable deductions remain charitable deductions, and so on). Every year, each partner or shareholder receives a form called a Schedule K-1 that reflects the income, loss, or deduction that belongs on the return. Schedule K-1 is actually filed as part of the partnership (Schedule 1065-K-1) or S corporation's income tax returns (Schedule 1120S K-1), as well as a copy being sent to you.

Name(s) shown on return. Do not enter name and social security number if shown on other side.   Your social security number

Caution: The IRS compares amounts reported on your tax return with amounts shown on Schedule(s) K-1.

| Part II | Income or Loss From Partnerships and S Corporations — Note: If you report a loss, receive a distribution, dispose of stock, or receive a loan repayment from an S corporation, you **must** check the box in column **(e)** on line 28 and attach the required basis computation. If you report a loss from an at-risk activity for which **any** amount is **not** at risk, you **must** check the box in column **(f)** on line 28 and attach **Form 6198**. See instructions. |

27   Are you reporting any loss not allowed in a prior year due to the at-risk or basis limitations, a prior year unallowed loss from a passive activity (if that loss was not reported on Form 8582), or unreimbursed partnership expenses? If you answered "Yes," see instructions before completing this section . . . . ☐ **Yes**   ☐ **No**

28	(a) Name	(b) Enter P for partnership; S for S corporation	(c) Check if foreign partnership	(d) Employer identification number	(e) Check if basis computation is required	(f) Check if any amount is not at risk
A			☐		☐	☐
B			☐		☐	☐
C			☐		☐	☐
D			☐		☐	☐

	Passive Income and Loss			Nonpassive Income and Loss		
	(g) Passive loss allowed (attach **Form 8582** if required)	(h) Passive income from **Schedule K-1**		(i) Nonpassive loss allowed (see **Schedule K-1**)	(j) Section 179 expense deduction from **Form 4562**	(k) Nonpassive income from **Schedule K-1**
A						
B						
C						
D						

29a	Totals					
b	Totals					

30	Add columns (h) and (k) of line 29a.	30	
31	Add columns (g), (i), and (j) of line 29b.	31	( )
32	**Total partnership and S corporation income or (loss).** Combine lines 30 and 31	32	

| Part III | Income or Loss From Estates and Trusts |

33	(a) Name	(b) Employer identification number
A		
B		

	Passive Income and Loss		Nonpassive Income and Loss	
	(c) Passive deduction or loss allowed (attach **Form 8582** if required)	(d) Passive income from **Schedule K-1**	(e) Deduction or loss from **Schedule K-1**	(f) Other income from **Schedule K-1**
A				
B				

34a	Totals			
b	Totals			

35	Add columns (d) and (f) of line 34a	35	
36	Add columns (c) and (e) of line 34b	36	( )
37	**Total estate and trust income or (loss).** Combine lines 35 and 36	37	

| Part IV | Income or Loss From Real Estate Mortgage Investment Conduits (REMICs)—Residual Holder |

38	(a) Name	(b) Employer identification number	(c) Excess inclusion from **Schedules Q**, line 2c (see instructions)	(d) Taxable income (net loss) from **Schedules Q**, line 1b	(e) Income from **Schedules Q**, line 3b

39	Combine columns (d) and (e) only. Enter the result here and include in the total on line 41 below	39	

| Part V | Summary |

40	Net farm rental income or (loss) from **Form 4835**. Also, complete line 42 below	40	
41	**Total income or (loss).** Combine lines 26, 32, 37, 39, and 40. Enter the result here and on Schedule 1 (Form 1040), line 5 ▶	41	
42	**Reconciliation of farming and fishing income.** Enter your gross farming and fishing income reported on Form 4835, line 7; Schedule K-1 (Form 1065), box 14, code B; Schedule K-1 (Form 1120-S), box 17, code AD; and Schedule K-1 (Form 1041), box 14, code F. See instructions .	42	
43	**Reconciliation for real estate professionals.** If you were a real estate professional (see instructions), enter the net income or (loss) you reported anywhere on Form 1040, Form 1040-SR, or Form 1040-NR from all rental real estate activities in which you materially participated under the passive activity loss rules	43	

FIGURE 15-2: Schedule E, Page 2.

Schedule E (Form 1040) 2021

Source: Internal Revenue Service

Line 27: The at-risk and other tax shelter rules

You can hardly consider line 27 a simple yes or no question. Here you are asked whether you're reporting losses that weren't allowed in prior years because of at-risk or basis limitations, passive losses not reported on Form 8582, Passive Activity Loss Limitation (the name alone is enough to frighten most people), or unreimbursed partnership expenses. Just remember, passive losses are those losses in activities in which you didn't materially participate.

What this question is all about is that sometimes, when a tax shelter entity runs out of dough, partners are called upon to pay some of the expenses personally to keep the business afloat. When partners try to deduct these expenses, the IRS invariably claims they can't. The question on line 27 is an attempt to bring these expenses out in the open instead of burying them along with other deductions. However, a court case states that when an investor and a partner are essentially in the same type of business, any unreimbursed expenses that the investor pays on behalf of the partnership are deductible.

SEEK ADVICE

The purpose of the at-risk rules is to prevent investors from deducting losses in excess of what they actually stand to lose. This rule prevents you from investing $10,000 and deducting $30,000 when the partnership loses an additional $20,000 on money it borrowed that you weren't personally responsible for. The K-1 that you receive indicates what your risks are (see item F). At-risk rules are extremely complex and are an area where we recommend that you consult a tax advisor for help. But here's how they work — say you invest $30,000: $10,000 in cash and $20,000 in a *promissory note* that bears the language "without recourse against the maker (you)." Because you can't be forced to pay the $20,000, you're not at risk and, therefore, you can deduct losses only up to your $10,000 cash investment.

The basis limitation rule prevents you from limiting the amount you can lose when you make an investment and deduct more than that amount. Say you invest $25,000 . . . that's all you can deduct regardless of what your share of the entity's loss amounts to.

REMEMBER

Partnerships and S Corporations are not just investment opportunities; they are often the entity of choice for small companies that you may play an active role in. If you actively participate in the running of a business that has elected to be treated as a partnership or an S corporation, your interest is not passive, and neither is the income or loss you derive from it. Say, for example, you and a couple of your friends were working together to make and market an invention. The income or loss from that venture would be active in your hands. Should someone else give you money to further your research in exchange for a share of the profits, their interest would be passive, and the passive loss limitation rules would apply to them alone.

Lines 28–32: Name . . . and so on!

Now you have to deal not only with line numbers but also with letters! Here's what you enter in the following columns of line 28:

(a) Enter the name of the partnership or S corporation.

(b) Enter P for partnership or S for S corporation.

(c) Put a check here if it's a foreign partnership.

(d) Scribble in the tax identification number for the partnership or S corporation. (Hey, this line is pretty easy so far!)

(e) Place a check if basis computation is required. If you are the owner of S corporation stock and debt and you report a loss, receive a distribution, dispose of stock, or receive a loan repayment from an S corporation, you must tick the box and attach your basis calculation, which you can find on Form 7203, S Corporation Shareholder Stock and Debt Basis Limitations.

(f) This column is the easiest of all. Place a check mark here if you're not at risk for any of the liabilities of the entity.

Passive income and loss

If the *passive income amounts* (that's rent or ordinary income from a partnership or an S corporation, but not dividends, interest, or capital gains, which don't get entered here) on the Schedule K-1 are negative, and if you have enough positive passive income from all your partnerships and S Corporations to offset them, you enter the negative number in column (f). Because figuring these amounts out on the fly is tough, you need to go to Form 8582 first to compute what amount of loss is allowable before you fill out this part of Schedule E.

In column (g), enter the income from the passive activity. Refer to "The tax shelter rules," earlier in this chapter, for the definition of passive income and losses.

Nonpassive income and loss

Column (h) deals with nonpassive income and losses. If you're a working partner in a partnership or a working shareholder in an S corporation, line 1 of the K-1 shows the share of the loss you're entitled to deduct. Enter that amount here.

For column (i), the wonderful K-1 also shows the amount of the partnership or S corporation's special depreciation that you get to deduct — line 9 of the K-1 for partnerships and line 8 for S Corporations. Enter it here.

In column (j), enter the amount of income from Schedule K-1 — it's the amount on line 1.

Lines 29 through 32 are strictly addition. What a relief!

TECHNICAL STUFF

Where do you put all the other stuff, like interest, dividends, capital gains, charitable contributions, investment interest expense, and whatever else the partnership or the S corporation decides to report to you? Look at the instructions on the back of your Schedule K-1, which clearly show where to insert the information on each line into your tax return so that interest and dividends are put on Schedule B, charitable contributions on Schedule A, and so forth. Your Schedule K-1 should also arrive with pages of instructions. If what you're looking at on the front of the schedule isn't as clear as you want, look for the answers to your questions buried in the instructions' fine print.

Part III: Income or Loss from Estates and Trusts

In this part, you enter income or loss from an estate or trust of which you're a beneficiary. If you receive a Schedule K-1 from either an estate or the trust, it will indicate various types of income such as dividends, interest, and capital gains. Interest and dividends go on Schedule B (see Chapter 12), and capital gains go on Schedule D (see Chapter 14). The ordinary income or loss reported on the K-1 is what goes in this section of Schedule E. Maybe that's why the IRS gives only two lines to work with in this part of the form!

To start you off, in column (a), carefully enter the name of the estate or trust.

In column (b), enter the identification number for the trust or estate.

Which brings us right back to making a distinction between passive and active income in an estate or trust. It is very rare for a trust or estate to have active rental or ordinary income, but it is possible if the trust or estate is actively managing a business or a rental property. Go back and look at the active participation rules earlier in this chapter if you're not sure if any rental or ordinary income shown on your Schedule K-1 is active or passive. We won't say that active income never happens in an estate or trust, but it is relatively uncommon.

Passive income and loss

In column (c), you put the passive loss allowed from Form 8582.

In column (d), you enter passive income from the K-1s and Form 8582.

When calculating the amounts that are passive, remember that only ordinary income and rental income qualify here — all other forms of income shown on this Schedule K-1 are reported elsewhere on your return. Check the K-1 instructions carefully to see where to put all those other numbers.

Nonpassive income and loss

Columns (e) and (f) are mostly for show, because most heirs or beneficiaries don't participate in the management of the estate or trust, and so it is rare for an heir or beneficiary to have nonpassive income or loss.

Lines 34 through 37 are the simple part of this section. All it requires is simple addition.

Part IV: Income or Loss from Real Estate Mortgage Investment Conduits

If you've invested in a *Real Estate Mortgage Investment Conduit* (REMIC), which is a company that holds a pool of mortgages, you'll most likely receive interest on Form 1099-INT, Interest Income, or Form 1099-OID, Original Issue Discount. But if you received Form 1066, Schedule Q, from the REMIC, enter the amounts, names, and so on from that form on line 38. Add columns (d) and (e) and enter the total on line 39.

Part V: Summary

Unless you're a farmer and file Form 4835 (line 40) or a real estate professional (line 43), everything on Schedule E is pulled together on line 41. Do the math and transfer the amount to Form 1040, Schedule 1, Part I, line 5 and take a break. You deserve it.

If you rent out your farm, you report your rental income and expenses on Form 4835, Farm Rental Income and Expenses.

IN THIS CHAPTER

» Finding your way around the credit for child- and dependent-care expenses

» Understanding credit for the elderly and disabled

» Educating yourself about education and child tax credits

» Crediting certain contributions to retirement savings

» Profiting from the Residential Energy Credit and the Alternative Motor Vehicle Credit

» Adopting the adoption credit and calculating the earned income credit

Chapter **16**

Giving Credits Where Credits Are Due

To paraphrase Rudyard Kipling, a deduction is only a deduction, but a good tax credit can mean real cash in your pocket. Tax credits are a dollar-for-dollar reduction of tax, unlike deductions, which reduce only taxable income. The results to your personal bottom line as you wend your way toward the end of your Form 1040 may be spectacular.

Just like deductions, credits are designed to promote certain social policies, like raising children, adopting children, looking after those children, and educating them beyond high school. The credits may help you save for your retirement, become more energy efficient, or pay you back for taxes you've already paid, such as foreign taxes on income.

In order to qualify for these tax savings, you need to fill out yet another form (or forms, if you qualify for more than one of these credits). This chapter shows you how to maneuver your way through the most popular of these additional forms to give you the best (legal) result possible. A word of caution, though: There is a wide world of tax credits available. Just because we haven't spent any time on some of them doesn't mean they don't exist. We just don't have the space to look at each of them individually. Look through the credits available on Schedule 3 and the ones referenced in the Form 1040 instruction booklet. You'll find that, if you spent the year researching an orphan drug, there's a credit for that.

Child- and Dependent-Care Expenses: Form 2441 (1040)

If you hire someone to take care of your children so you can work, you're entitled to the credit that you figure on Form 2441 (1040).

For the purpose of taking this credit, you're not just limited to what you paid your babysitter. Nursery school, summer and vacation day camps, after-school programs, and daycare expenses also qualify for this credit. In order to be eligible to claim this credit, your child must be under the age of 13 or a dependent of any age who is physically or mentally handicapped. You're also entitled to the credit if your spouse is handicapped or is a full-time student and you incur expenses getting care for your kids so that you can work. Here are the ins and outs of the Child and Dependent Care Credit:

CREDITS: REFUNDABLE VERSUS NONREFUNDABLE

Just when you thought you had the difference down between a deduction and a credit, along comes another distinction: Some credits are refundable, while others aren't. What's the difference?

A *refundable credit* is one that you'll receive credit for and cash back in a refund, *even if you don't have enough tax showing on line 16 to offset it.* If you're eligible for refundable credits, you're going to check Box B at the top of Form 2441, and you may receive a larger tax refund than what you paid in withholdings during the year. To make refundable credits more interesting, in 2021 you'll find that there's a one-time recovery rebate credit, that the child and dependent care credit is refundable, and so is the entire amount of child tax credit.

A *nonrefundable credit,* on the other hand, can offset only taxes shown on line 16 of your 1040. If you don't have enough tax on those lines to use all, or even a part, of the credits to which you'd otherwise be entitled, tough! You're out of luck — better luck next year! Check Box A at the top of Form 2441, which lets the IRS know that you're only eligible for the nonrefundable credit.

- You can claim childcare expenses while you're working or looking for work, as long as you have some earned income. However, if you don't find a job and don't have any earned income, you can't claim the credit.

  What constitutes *earned income?* Wages, tips, strike benefits, disability pay reported as wages, voluntary salary deferrals such as for a 401(k) plan, meals and lodging furnished for the convenience of the employer (regardless of whether these fringe benefits are subject to tax), and earnings from being self-employed after deducting expenses — add all these up and that's what's called earned income. Want a shorter definition? What were you paid for working? But, because this is a tax book, we have to give you every last item.

- If you're married, you both must have a job or at least be looking for work. Looking for work assumes that you're planning on finding work; if you look for work all year but never find a job and have no earned income, you can't take the credit.

  You or your spouse are considered to be working and having earned income if either of you is a full-time student or unable to care for yourself. Only one of you may claim earned income in any month where both of you are either students or not able to care for yourselves.

- For your expenses to be considered work-related, they must help to enable you to work or look for work.

- Sleep-away camp doesn't qualify as a childcare expense.

- Payments to relatives count even if they live in your home, provided they're not your dependent. If the relative providing the care is your child, the child must be 19 by the end of the year and not your dependent for the payment to count as childcare expenses.

- Although fees paid for nursery school count as childcare expenses, after the child enters kindergarten, any tuition you pay must be allocated between the schooling expenses (if your child attends a private school) and the expenses incurred for childcare.

- Expenses incurred while you're out sick don't qualify. They weren't incurred for the purpose of enabling you to work. You incurred the expenses because you were sick and couldn't take care of your kids.

- Medical expenses incurred on behalf of a spouse or dependents who are unable to care for themselves count as work-related expenses. But you can't claim these expenses as both medical and work-related. You must claim one or the other. Claim medical expenses on Schedule A, Form 1040. (See Chapter 11.)

NEW STUFF

In 2021 only, the Child Care and Dependent Credit has been greatly expanded (due to the pandemic and government-mandated shutdowns) and is fully refundable to you, if filing singly or as head-of-household, or you and your spouse, if filing jointly, had a principal place of residence in the United States for more than half of 2021. The amount of qualifying expenses has risen from $3,000 per qualifying child to $8,000 per qualifying child for one child or disabled dependent, and $16,000 for two or more qualifying children or dependents. And the amount of the credit starts at 50 percent of qualifying expenses (an increase from 35 percent in the past) for families with income levels of $125,000 or less. Between $125,001 and $185,000, the credit reduces by 1 percent for every $2,000 over $125,000 until you reach $185,000. Between $185,001 and $438,000, the credit is a flat 20 percent. The credit vanishes once your income goes over $438,000. At the time this book goes to press in late 2021, it is unclear if this greater credit will be extended beyond 2021.

Parts I and II

To claim the Child and Dependent Care Credit, you can be single, a head of household, qualifying widow(er) with dependent child(ren), or married filing jointly. Generally, if you are filing as married filing separately, you're not allowed to take the credit at all. However, exceptions are made for a couple filing separately if they are legally separated, have lived apart for at least the last six months of the year, and the qualifying persons for the credit have resided with the spouse claiming the credit, who has provided more than 50 percent of that person's support.

Here's how to fill out Form 2441:

>> **Line 1:** Report the name, address, Social Security number, or Employer Identification Number (EIN) of the person or organization providing the care, and the amount that you paid to the provider. If you're paying your nanny or babysitter under the table (illegally), you can't claim this credit. However, if your annual payment to any one individual is less than $2,300, you're not liable for the payment of Social Security taxes for your childcare provider. See Chapter 17 for the nanny tax rules.

If you didn't receive dependent-care benefits from your employer, you need to complete only Part II in addition to line 1. If you did receive these benefits, you have to complete Part III on the back of the form to determine what part, if any, of the fees you paid you can use to calculate this credit. Employer-provided dependent-care benefits are noted in box 10 of your W-2.

>> **Line 2:** Enter the qualifying person's name (that's IRS jargon for your child), the child's Social Security number, and what it costs to care for the child so that you can work. Just because you're limited to a maximum of $16,000 of qualifying expenses if you have two or more qualifying persons doesn't mean those expenses need to be split evenly between your children. You can, for example, have one child with $12,000 of qualifying expenses, and another with only $4,000. The total for all qualifying children and other dependents, however, can't exceed $16,000.

>> **Line 3:** Enter the amounts from line 2, keeping in mind the $8,000 limit for one qualifying person and $16,000 limit for two or more. If you completed Part III, enter the amount from line 31.

>> **Line 4:** Enter your earned income.

>> **Line 5:** If you're married and filing jointly, enter your spouse's earned income. If your spouse doesn't have any income, you can't claim this credit; however, spouses who are either full-time students or unable to care for themselves are considered to have earned income even if they didn't receive any wages. In this exception, your spouse is deemed to have income of $250 per month if you have one qualifying child or dependent, and $500 per month if you have two or more qualifying children or dependents.

A second rule linked to this deemed-income business: Your credit is based on the lower of your spouse's income or your allowable childcare expenses. If this rule sounds more complex than most rules, here's how it works. Say your spouse was a full-time student for six months, and you have $3,000 in childcare expenses for caring for your 2-year-old daughter. Your spouse is deemed to have earned $1,500; six months times $250. Because this amount is lower than your actual expenses, it's the amount the credit is based on.

If you're not married and filing jointly, put the amount that you had on line 4 on line 5 as well.

>> **Line 6:** Enter the smaller of lines 3, 4, or 5.

>> **Line 7:** Enter your adjusted gross income (AGI) from line 11 of your 1040.

>> **Line 8:** Enter the percentage credit you're entitled to. If your income is $125,000 or less, enter 0.50 on line 8. If your income is over $438,000, leave line 8 blank, and enter 0 on line 9a. If your income is between $125,001 and $185,000, reduce the applicable percentage by 0.01 for every $2,000 of additional income. Finally, if your income is between $185,001 and $438,000, enter 0.20 on line 8.

How should you calculate the percentage you're allowed to claim if your income is between $125,001 and $185,000? Here's an example for a couple showing $165,000 on line 7: $165,000 – $125,000 = $40,000; $40,000 ÷ $2,000 = 20; 0.50 – 0.20 = 0.30. In this example, you'll multiply your qualifying expenses by 30 percent.

>> **Line 9a:** Multiply the amount on line 6 by the decimal amount on line 8.

>> **Line 9b:** If you paid 2020 expenses in 2021, complete Worksheet A in the instructions to see if any of your 2020 expenses are eligible qualifying expenses for 2021. The amount from line 13 of the worksheet goes here.

>> **Line 10:** Add together lines 9a and 9b. If you checked Box B at the top of Form 2441, this is your refundable credit for child- and dependent-care expenses. Enter this result on Form 1040, Schedule 3, line 13g. Box B tells the IRS that you qualify for the refundable credit

>> **Line 11:** If you checked Box A at the top of Form 2441, your credit is nonrefundable and limited by the amount of your tax. If you fall into this category, go to the Form 2441 instructions to find out how much of the credit shown on line 10 you'll receive.

TAX CUT

Many states also allow a credit for child- and dependent-care expenses. For example, New York bases its tax credit on the amount of the federal credit. Check with your state's tax office to find out what credit, if any, you can take.

Looking ahead, find out whether your employer offers you the ability to have money deducted from your paycheck — before taxes — into a dependent-care spending account. You may be able to use this account in the future and save even more tax dollars instead of taking this credit (you can't do both). But if you're likely to fall into the trap of the AMT, paying for dependent-care expenses with an employer-sponsored dependent-care spending account may be the only way you'll receive any tax relief.

Part III

If your employer has a daycare plan or provides daycare services under a qualified plan, the reimbursement paid to you or your care provider may not be completely tax-free. To determine whether any portion is taxable, you need to complete Part III of Form 2441. The amount your employer paid for daycare costs or the value of the daycare services that your employer provides is indicated in Box 10 of Form W-2. The amount that is excludable from tax is limited to the smallest of:

>> The amount in Box 10 Form W-2

>> The total of your child- and dependent-care expenses

>> Your earned income

>> Your spouse's earned income

>> $10,500 ($5,250 if married filing separately)

The portion of tax-free childcare benefits that you received reduces the amount of child- and dependent-care expenses eligible for the child-care credit.

NEW STUFF Because of the increased amount of the Child and Dependent Care Credit in 2021, even if you had the full amount of dependent care benefits paid by your employer, that only covers $10,500 in 2021. Remember, if you have two or more qualifying individuals for this credit, the maximum benefit is 50 percent of $16,000, so there can still be some money hanging out there, waiting for you to come and claim it. And, if you qualify for the refundable credit, even if you don't have enough tax to offset the full amount of the credit you're entitled to, you'll get a refund of any unused portion of the credit.

What's more, while you normally can't combine benefits across years, because of the pandemic, in 2021, you're able to carry over any unused amounts of employer benefits from your 2020 Form W-2 and apply them against 2021. You'll reduce your refundable credit because you'll have more employer benefits, but you won't have to pay income tax on the unused portion of 2020 benefits.

Credit for the Elderly or the Disabled: Schedule R (1040)

You're entitled to claim this credit (which may amount to as much as $7,500) if you're married and both you and your spouse are 65 or older — or both of you are disabled and any age. For single taxpayers, the maximum credit is $5,000. And, if you're married filing separately, and you lived apart from your spouse for all of 2021, the maximum credit is $3,750. If you lived with your spouse but you're filing separately, you're not eligible for the credit.

Giving a tax credit to the elderly and/or disabled sounds like a great idea, but some requirements may make most people ineligible for this credit. You have to reduce the amount of the income that's eligible for the credit by the nontaxable portion of your Social Security and other pension and disability benefits. Also, if your income is more than $17,500 if you're single (or $25,000 if you're married and both of you are eligible for this credit), you won't be eligible for any portion of this credit.

If ever there was an argument for automatically building cost-of-living increases into the tax code, this is it. The Credit for the Elderly or the Disabled hasn't moved with the times, and in almost every instance filling out these forms is an exercise in futility. While the potential credit is larger than it has been in the past, it's still only going to be available for very low-income taxpayers.

TIP

If you think you may be eligible for this credit, have the IRS figure it for you. Fill out page 1 of the form, which asks questions about your age, filing status, and whether you're disabled. Attach the form to your return, and on Form 1040, Schedule 3, Part I, line 6d, write "CFE" (an acronym for "credit for the elderly") on the dotted line. Remember: Always check the computation for a form that you asked the IRS to calculate to make sure that the IRS's computation is right. The IRS isn't infallible.

Don't be disappointed if you don't qualify for this credit. Almost no one does!

Education Credits (Form 8863)

If you think you're eligible for either the American Opportunity Credit or the Lifetime Learning Credit, you've come to the right place to find the answer. If you're not sure whether you, your spouse, or your dependent child qualifies, or which credit you qualify for, look at Chapter 9 for a host of useful information about these credits.

REMEMBER

Although you can't claim both credits for the same student, if you're the fortunate payer of more than one student's tuition bills, you may claim the American Opportunity Credit and the Lifetime Learning Credit for many different students in the same year, so long as you've paid qualifying tuition and fees for each of them. You may not transfer fees paid for one student to another student who may have attended a qualifying school, but who didn't pay enough in tuition and fees to qualify for the full amount of the credits.

Remember, the American Opportunity Credit is available to students in their first four years of post-secondary education leading to a degree or certificate, and the student must take at least one-half the normal amount of credits to be eligible, whereas the Lifetime Learning Credit is available for students who have either used up their American Opportunity Credit eligibility or who are in school less than half-time. The Lifetime Learning Credit is only available for post-secondary courses that lead to a degree or a certificate or that get or improve job skills. You may not take a credit for a course on the Japanese art of flower arranging unless you're already a florist or planning to become one.

Form 8863, Education Credits (American Opportunity and Lifetime Learning Credits) provides a reasonably systematic approach to breaking down what credits you're entitled to take for which students. It comes in three parts; you're going to begin at the end (Part III) and work your way back to Parts I (Refundable American Opportunity Credit) and II (Nonrefundable Education Credits).

Part III has you list your student's name, the educational institution they attended, and a series of questions, all of which can be answered by referring to Form 1098-T, Tuition Statement, provided by the school and available to you by January 31, 2022. You will need to complete Form 8863, Part III, for each eligible student. If you're preparing your return on a computer, the tax software will take care of this part for you.

TIP

If you do not receive Form 1098-T in the mail by early February, you should check the student portal at your student's school. Most schools have moved away from mailing paper forms and are now placing PDF (portable document format) copies of the 1098-T in a separate place in the student portal entitled "Tax Forms" or "Tax Information."

Once you've completed Form 8863 for all your eligible students, you're ready to move onto Part I, Refundable American Opportunity Credit and Part II, Nonrefundable Education Credits. You complete Part I first before moving to Part II.

The refundable American Opportunity Credit, the nonrefundable American Opportunity Credit, and the nonrefundable Lifetime Learning Credit are all subject to income phase-outs beginning at $80,000 for single filers ($160,000 for married filing jointly), and completely phasing out at $90,000 for single filers ($180,000 for married filing jointly). If your income falls below those limits, the full amount of the credit will be available to you provided you have enough qualifying expenses; if you're over those limits, don't even bother trying to prepare the form — you're not entitled to any of these credits.

Child Tax Credit and Credit for Other Dependents

NEW STUFF

In 2021, if you have qualifying children, the child tax credit knocks as much as $3,600 per child under age 6 as of December 31, 2021, from your federal income tax bill, or $3,000 for children between the ages of 6 and 18 during 2021. And this year, instead of only a portion of the credit being refundable, if you have no tax liability against which to offset the credit, the full amount of the credit may be refundable to you. Some of you have probably been receiving monthly payments since July 2021, which represent advance payments of a portion of the credit.

We start with the basics. The myriad of changes to the child tax credit are a result of the American Rescue Plan of 2021, which has substantially increased the size of the available credit and the income phase-out limitations, as well as making the credit refundable. This legislation was passed to help families due to government-mandated shutdowns during the pandemic.

The basic child tax credit is now $3,600 per child who is under age 6 at the end of 2021, and $3,000 for children who are ages 6–17. If you lived in the United States or Puerto Rico during at least half of 2021, you qualify for the refundable credit. Remember, a qualifying child is your child, either natural or adopted, stepchild, eligible foster child, sibling, stepsibling, half sibling, or a descendent of any one of them, provided that the child has not provided more than 50 percent of their own support in 2021. They must have lived with you for more than half of 2021 and must properly be claimed as your dependent. And, if the child is filing a joint tax return with their spouse, that return must show no tax liability and the purpose of filing must be to obtain a refund.

Now onto the advance payments some folks have been receiving since July 2021. If you receive all six payments in 2021, you will have received 50 percent of the total child tax credit the IRS thinks you're eligible for. The remaining 50 percent will be claimed on your 2021 Form 1040.

WARNING

As we say in Chapter 9, if you've had a significant increase in income in 2021, or you're divorced or legally separated and you and the other parent switch off the dependents in alternating years, you may have received advance payments that you're not entitled to. The IRS has strongly indicated that they're expecting these erroneous advance payments to be repaid come April, so be aware that there can be a substantial amount to repay if you claimed your children in 2020 but won't be claiming them in 2021.

Now for the phase-out amounts, which have also increased substantially. If your modified adjusted gross income exceeds $150,000 if you're married filing jointly, $112,500 if you're a head of household, or $75,000 if you're a single filer or married filing a separate return, your available credit will reduce in increments of $50 of credit for each $1,000 (or fraction thereof) of modified AGI until you reach $2,000 of available credit for all children, regardless of age. The $2,000 credit is further reduced once your modified AGI reaches $400,000 if you're filing as married filing jointly, and $200,000 for all other filing statuses. For this credit's calculation, your modified adjusted gross income is your AGI from Form 1040, line 11, plus any amount on line 45 or line 50 of Form 2555, Foreign Earned Income, and any amount excluded from gross income because it came from sources in either Puerto Rico or American Samoa.

In certain circumstances (children of divorced parents are one case that comes to mind), it's possible to claim this deduction for a child who isn't your dependent. To do so, though, you have to complete Form 8901, Information on Qualifying Children Who Are Not Dependents (Child Tax Credit Only). Not to worry — Form 8901 is as easy as pie to complete. It's just looking for your child's name, Social Security number, and relationship to you. What can be simpler?

For 2021, the child tax credit doesn't require that you have any earned income at all, so if you had zero wages or income from self-employment in 2021, you're still eligible for the refundable credit.

Form 8812, Credits for Qualifying Children and Other Dependents is where you'll calculate the amount of your child tax credit. It's also where you'll calculate your nonrefundable credit for other dependents, which has remained at $500 per qualifying person. Form 8812 calculates your modified adjusted gross income for you, and then separates out your dependents into children under age 6, children over age 6 but under age 18, and everyone else, assigning the appropriate credit to each of them. It also calculates any amounts you need to repay in Part III. If you're working on your computer, the computer is going to do all the work based on the information you've reported regarding your dependents; if you're preparing your return on paper, you'll have to do some math, but Form 8812 is fairly straightforward — just follow the line instructions, and you'll do fine.

AVAILABLE CREDITS IF YOU LIVE IN U.S. POSSESSIONS AND TERRITORIES

If you're a U.S. citizen but you live in Puerto Rico, you're entitled to the full amount of the 2021 child tax credit; however, you have not been receiving the advance payments. You will receive the full amount of your available credit as part of your 2021 income tax refund. The credit is also available to people living in American Samoa, the Commonwealth of the Northern Mariana Islands, Guam, and the U.S. Virgin Islands, but instead of applying for the credit from the IRS, you'll need to contact your local territory tax office for information regarding the credit, including whether any advance payments are available. Citizenship or residency status in the Federated States of Micronesia, the Republic of the Marshall Islands, or the Republic of Palau do not qualify for the credit unless you also have a main home in the 50 states or the District of Columbia.

Retirement Savings Contributions Credit (Form 8880)

If your AGI (line 11 of Form 1040) is $66,000 or less if married filing jointly, $49,500 or less if head of household, or $33,000 or less if single or married filing separately, and if you were able to make a contribution into a retirement plan, this credit was designed expressly for you. For people who qualify, this credit can be a whopping tax credit of up to $1,000 per person ($2,000 per married couple). In order to get the credit, you have to complete Form 8880, Credit for Qualified Retirement Savings Contributions.

Form 8880 is one of the better-designed IRS forms, and the directions are actually in understandable English. There's just one place that the IRS may have been clearer, so here's our best shot to make the instructions plainer:

> *Line 2 refers to elective deferrals to a 401(k) or other qualified employer plan, voluntary employee contributions, and 501(c)(18)(D) plan contributions for 2021.* The amounts that the IRS is looking for here are your contributions into your company's retirement plans or your contributions into your traditional or Roth IRA accounts. Only include on this line amounts that you put into your retirement accounts and not amounts your employer contributed.

REMEMBER

This credit is designed for full-time working people, not students working a part-time job, so three additional rules apply:

>> You have to be born before January 1, 2004.

>> You may not be someone else's dependent.

>> You may not be a student enrolled on a full-time basis during any five months of 2021, which means graduates of the class of June 2021 aren't eligible to claim this credit unless they went to school only part-time.

Residential Energy Credits (Form 5695)

In these days of higher fuel costs, Congress has tried to lessen the blow by providing a variety of credits for improving your home's energy efficiency. If your 2020 fuel bills pushed you to make changes to your home in 2021, you may qualify for some, or all, of these credits. Many of the smaller energy-saving changes, like adding insulation or replacing inefficient windows and doors, furnaces, and hot water heaters with more efficient counterparts, have an aggregate lifetime maximum credit of $500, although the maximum credits for individual components have smaller limits.

In addition to those smaller credits, you can receive larger credits for more far-reaching, and generally more costly, energy efficient improvements. In 2021, the property that qualifies for this credit includes

- 26 percent of the cost of purchasing and installing solar panels to produce electricity
- 26 percent of the cost of purchasing and installing qualified solar water heating in your home
- 26 percent of the cost of purchasing and installing qualified fuel cell property
- 26 percent of qualified small wind energy property costs
- 26 percent of qualified geothermal heat pump property costs
- 26 percent of qualified biomass fuel property costs

To qualify for these nonrefundable credits, your house must be in the United States, and the improvements must be new, must meet certain energy efficiency standards, and must reasonably be expected to stay in use for at least five years. If you've gone to town and turned your home into the ultimate in energy efficiency, you may find that you have more credits showing on Form 5695 than you can use this year. You can carry excess credits forward to 2022. There is no absolute limit on the size of this credit, nor are there any income phase-outs that may prevent you from taking these credits. The only limiting factor is that this credit is nonrefundable; therefore, you can't take a larger credit than the amount of tax shown on Form 1040, line 16.

REMEMBER

Don't forget, if you had credits that you couldn't use in 2020, even if they were for property that's no longer qualified in 2021, you can still use those credits in 2021. Enter your carry-forward credit from 2020 on line 12 of Form 5695 for 2021 to be sure you get the benefit for all those prior year improvements you made.

Adoption Credit (Form 8839)

If you adopted a child in 2021, if you began or completed adoption proceedings in 2021, or if you tried unsuccessfully to adopt a child in 2021, read on. Expenses that you incurred during the adoption process may be eligible for a tax credit. In order to be able to claim that credit on your Form 1040, you need to complete and attach Form 8839, Qualified Adoption Expenses.

Understanding the adoption credit and exclusion rules

The Adoption Credit has specific rules that include the following:

- If your AGI is $216,600 or less, you're entitled to the full credit. Between $216,660 and $256,660, the credit is phased out. At $256,660, it's gone. If you claimed a foreign income exclusion or housing deduction (Form 2555) because you're working abroad, because you're claiming an income exclusion from Puerto Rico, or because you're a resident of American Samoa (Form 4563), you have to adjust your income for the purpose of calculating your credit by adding these amounts to your AGI shown on line 11, Form 1040, when figuring whether your income is more than the income threshold.

>> The adopted child must be younger than 18 or physically or mentally incapable of self-care.

>> Adopting your spouse's child doesn't qualify, nor does a surrogate parenting arrangement.

>> Adoption expenses can't be paid with funds received from any federal, state, or local adoption program.

>> The credit is nonrefundable and can't exceed your tax liability (Form 1040, line 16) minus many of the credits claimed on Form 1040, Schedule 3. Check the instructions for Form 8839 for a complete list of the credits that must be subtracted from your tax before you can claim the adoption credit. Credits have an order of precedence, and certain nonrefundable credits, such as the foreign tax credit and the credit for child and dependent care are used first, with others, such as the adoption credit, being used later.

>> Any unused credit can be carried forward for five years until you use it up.

>> Married couples must file a joint return. However, if you're legally separated for the last six months of the year, you're eligible to file a separate return and claim the credit.

The types of expenses that qualify for the credits include adoption fees, court costs, attorney fees, traveling expenses (including meals and lodging), and other expenses directly related to adopting an eligible child.

In addition to the Adoption Credit, you may also exclude up to $14,400 from your income for adoption expenses paid by your employer under an adoption-assistance program. For example, you incur $28,800 in adoption expenses. You pay $14,400, and your employer pays $14,400 as part of an adoption-assistance program. You're entitled to a $14,400 credit for the expenses you paid, and you're not taxed on the $14,400 paid by your employer.

As a practical matter, owners or principal shareholders of a business aren't eligible to participate in an employer adoption-assistance program.

For a U.S. adoption, if you pay adoption expenses in any year prior to the year the adoption becomes final, the credit is taken in the year following the year the expenses are paid. If you pay adoption expenses in the year the adoption becomes final, you claim the credit in that year. If you pay adoption expenses in a year after the adoption becomes final, you claim the credit for those expenses in the year of payment.

For example, you incur $10,000 of adoption expenses in 2021 but pay $8,000 in 2021 and $2,000 in 2022 when the adoption is finalized. You have to wait until 2022 to claim the credit for the $8,000 of expenses, which is added to the $2,000 you paid in 2022. Had the adoption become final in 2021, you could claim the credit based on the $8,000 you paid in 2021. In this scenario, in 2022 you would base the credit on the $2,000 paid that year.

With a foreign adoption, you can't claim the credit or the exclusion until the adoption becomes final. Adoption expenses paid in an earlier year are considered paid in the year the adoption becomes final.

Regardless of the year paid, your adoption expenses or adoption exclusion can't exceed $14,440 for any child.

Figuring out Form 8839

You compute both the credit and the exclusion on Form 8839, Qualified Adoption Expenses. Enter the amount of the credit (line 16) on Form 1040, Schedule 3, line 6c. Carry forward any unused credit that you had in 2020 to your 2021 Form 8839 on line 13. The phase-out income limits don't apply to carryovers. The phase-out is applied only once in the year that generated the credit.

The amount of taxable employer-provided adoption expenses is computed in Part III of Form 8839. The taxable portion, if any, on line 29, gets reported on line 1 of Form 1040. Next to line 7, write "AB" for adoption benefit. How can you have a taxable benefit? Say your employer paid $7,000 in benefits, but you were entitled to exclude only $4,000 because your income exceeded $216,660. In that case, $3,000 of the benefit would be taxable.

TIP

You can claim the adoption credit for expenses on an unsuccessful adoption only if it is followed by a successful adoption. On line 1 of Form 8839 where the child's name goes, enter "See page 2." At the bottom of page 2 of Form 8839, indicate the name and address of the agency or attorney that assisted in the attempted adoption. Then complete the form as if the adoption had taken place, adding amounts from the unsuccessful adoption to the costs for the successful adoption. We know that this probably is painful, and we wish we knew what to say to ease that pain.

Motor Vehicle Credits (Form 8910 and Form 8936)

NEW STUFF

If you purchased an alternative motor vehicle, you may be entitled to a credit. What constitutes an alternative motor vehicle in 2021? That would be a new vehicle propelled by power derived from one or more cells that convert chemical energy directly into electricity by combining oxygen with hydrogen fuel, and that has four wheels. That description is taken directly from the horse's mouth, the instructions for Form 8910, Alternative Motor Vehicle Credit. To put it more plainly, we're talking about hydrogen fuel-cell cars, such as the Honda Clarity Fuel Cell, the Hyundai NEXO, and the Toyota Mirai. Use Form 8910 to figure this credit. The full amount of the credit is $8,000 — you may be eligible for state incentives as well — and the federal credit expires on December 31, 2021.

Since the United States doesn't yet have a multitude of hydrogen fueling stations, the alternative motor vehicle credit has a limited audience. The qualified plug-in electric drive motor vehicle credit, on the other hand, is available to many more people. This maximum $7,500 credit is available, in whole or in part, to purchases in 2021 of qualified two-wheel or four-wheel plug-in electric vehicles with a gross vehicle weight of less than 14,000 pounds. While credits are available for both two-wheel and four-wheel vehicles in 2021, only four-wheel vehicles will be eligible in 2022. And the credit is no longer available if you purchase a Tesla (credit expired for cars purchased after December 31, 2019) or a General Motors vehicle (credit expired for cars purchased after March 31, 2020), as both companies have sold more than 200,000 plug-in electric vehicles.

Not all vehicles qualify for the full $7,500 credit; the amount of the available credit for a specific car depends upon the relative fuel efficiency of that vehicle. An index to manufacturers, years and models, and total credit available can be found on the IRS website at www.irs.gov/businesses/irc-30d-new-qualified-plug-in-electric-drive-motor-vehicle-credit. You calculate your credit on Form 8936, Qualified Plug-In Electric Drive Motor Vehicle Credit.

For both credits, the vehicle must be new, not just new to you. And the credit is available for both business and personal use. The business portion of the credit calculated on Form 8910 and Form 8936 is transferred to Part III of Form 3800, General Business Credits, which then transfers to Form 1040, Schedule 3, Part I, line 6a. Your personal use portion of these credits is calculated on these forms, but then transferred directly to Form 1040, Schedule 3, Part I. We don't know why the business portion of these credits needs to make a pit stop on Form 3800 if both parts of each credit make their way eventually onto Schedule 3, but if that's how the IRS wants it, who are we to argue?

Earned Income Credit (EIC)

One of the largest of the refundable credits, the Earned Income Credit (EIC) has come to represent the link between making it and not making it financially in many households that live from paycheck to paycheck. Because receiving this credit may be so important to the health and well-being of your finances, take a moment to understand who it's designed to help, how it works, and how to prepare the tax forms correctly.

As its name suggests, the EIC is restricted to taxpayers with earned income. What the name doesn't tell you is that it's restricted to low-income taxpayers who earn the vast majority of their income from wages, tips, commissions, salaries, union strike benefits, disability benefits received before you reached your minimum retirement age, nontaxable combat pay, or net earnings from self-employment (for the purpose of this credit, net earnings from self-employment less one-half of your self-employment tax).

Even though you must have earned income in order to qualify for the credit, you must also meet the AGI guidelines. Table 16-1 shows you where the phase-outs begin and end, depending on your family's size.

Earned income doesn't include the following:

>> Alimony or child support

>> Interest and dividends

>> Pensions or annuities

>> Social Security benefits

>> Taxable scholarships or fellowships that weren't reported on your W-2

>> Unemployment insurance

>> Veterans' benefits

>> Welfare benefits

Table 16-1 Earned Income Credit Phase-Outs

Single or Head of Household	Married Filing Jointly and Qualified Widow(er)
With no qualifying children	**With no qualifying children**
Beginning phase-out amount: $8,800	Beginning phase-out amount: $17,600
Completely phased out: $21,430	Completely phased out: $27,380
With one qualifying child	**With one qualifying child**
Beginning phase-out amount: $19,550	Beginning phase-out amount: $25,500
Completely phased out: $42,158	Completely phased out: $48,108
With two qualifying children	**With two qualifying children**
Beginning phase-out amount: $19,550	Beginning phase-out amount: $25,550
Completely phased out: $47,915	Completely phased out: $53,865
With three or more qualifying children	**With three or more qualifying children**
Beginning phase-out amount: $19,550	Beginning phase-out amount: $25,550
Completely phased out: $51,464	Completely phased out: $57,414

Rules that everyone must follow include the following:

>> You need a valid Social Security number.

>> Your filing status can't be married filing separately.

>> You must be a U.S. citizen or resident alien for the entire year.

>> You can't file Form 2555 (see Chapter 6).

>> Your investment income must be $10,000 or less.

>> You must have earned income.

FIGURING THE EIC

If you meet all the requirements, figuring the EIC is easy. No math is required. The credit to which you're entitled usually is based on the lower of your earned income and adjusted gross income (AGI). If your earned income and AGI are the same, look up that amount for the corresponding income bracket in the Earned Income Credit Table and read across to the appropriate column: No qualifying child, one child, two children, or three children under your filing status, single or head of household, or married filing jointly. For example, your EIC is $3,618 if your earned income and AGI are $12,240, and you're filing as head of household with one qualifying child. If your earned income and AGI aren't the same, your EIC is based on the lower of these two figures. Attach Schedule EIC to your return and enter the credit on Form 1040, line 27(a).

If you don't want to risk putting the wrong number down on your Form 1040, you can take the easy way out and let the IRS figure your EIC. Complete and attach Form 1040 EIC to your return and write EIC to the right of Form 1040, line 27(a). Make sure that you complete all the other lines on your return.

In an effort to ease the burden on military families, you may elect to include the full amount of nontaxable combat pay you received in 2019 or 2020 (whichever gives you a better result) in calculating your earned income for the purpose of the EIC. It's important to calculate the credit both with and without your nontaxable combat pay in order to figure out which benefits you the most.

If you're thinking of electing to include your nontaxable combat pay, here's how this election works: Mark is married with one child. He was deployed in a combat zone for eleven months of 2021. He and his wife earned only $4,000 of taxable earned income for the year, while he earned $16,000 of nontaxable combat pay. If Mark and his wife calculate the EIC on the basis of $4,000 of earned income, their credit is only $1,369. If they elect to add Mark's $16,000 of combat pay (for a total of $20,000) for the purpose of calculating the credit, their credit is now $3,618. Remember, Mark's not electing to pay tax on his combat pay, but only to use it to give him and his family a bigger credit. All Mark and his wife need to do to make this election is to fill in the amount of nontaxable combat pay on line 27b of Form 1040.

Singles and couples with no children are entitled to take this credit if they meet the income requirements (plus you must have maintained a home in the United States for more than six months, file a joint return if married, not be a dependent of another, and be at least 19). If you're a former foster child who has aged out of the system or a qualified homeless young person, the minimum age for the earned income credit drops to 18; for certain students, the qualifying age is 24 if you have no children. However, the EIC is really focused on single- and two-parent families, and these people derive the greatest benefit. Not every family is equal in the eyes of the IRS, though. In order for your family to qualify as such, the child (or children) you're claiming as a qualifying child must pass all the uniform tests in Chapter 4. In addition, your qualifying child (or children) can't be another person's qualifying child. Similarly, you can't be the qualifying child of another person when you have a child who qualifies.

What do you do when your qualifying child can also be someone else's qualifying child? How do you choose who gets the qualifying kid and the larger EIC? You don't have to play "rock, paper, scissors." Instead, tiebreaking rules govern. If one of the taxpayers is the qualifying child's parent, the parent gets to claim the qualifying child. If neither taxpayer is the parent, the person with the highest AGI claims the child. Finally, if both parents seek to claim the credit but don't file jointly, the parent with whom the child resided longest during the year claims the child. If a tie still results, the qualifying child designation goes to the parent with the highest AGI.

To compute the credits, go to the EIC Table in your tax-instruction booklet. Based on your income and the number of qualifying children, read across for your earned income line to the amount of credit that you can claim.

WARNING If you don't list your dependent's Social Security number on the EIC form, you get no credit. If investment income exceeds $10,000 in 2021, you get no credit. Investment income includes capital gains, interest, dividends, and tax-exempt interest. Add them up (capital losses and rental losses aren't included) to see if you exceed the limit. Also, if you're married filing separately, you aren't entitled to the credit.

WARNING Anyone who fraudulently claims the EIC is ineligible to claim it for ten years. For those individuals who are reckless or intentionally disregard the rules, the penalty is two years. If you feel the IRS seems to be more interested in finding EIC infractions than any other kind of tax dodge, you may be right. The IRS is very concerned about rooting out fraudulent EIC claims and is examining returns with the EIC extremely closely. You may not be able to avoid the scrutiny if you file for the EIC, so make certain that your claim is a valid one.

IN THIS CHAPTER

» **Paying your estimated taxes**

» **Figuring out if you can deduct moving expenses (military members, you can!)**

» **Navigating nondeductible IRAs and the Kiddie Tax**

» **Checking on using your home for business expenses and seeking depreciation allowances**

» **Finding the forms for tax withholding, household employees, and the self-employed**

Chapter 17

Other Schedules and Forms to File

M ost taxpayers want to think that they need to fill out only the front and back of their 1040, and then they're done. Oh, if only life were so simple. The fact is that your life isn't, and you probably need to file a variety of other tax schedules and forms to accompany your 1040. These additional forms are tailored to specific tax situations, and trust us, there's something for everyone. This chapter discusses the more common forms and schedules.

Estimated Tax for Individuals (Form 1040-ES)

The U.S. tax system actually has a simple rule that most people never think about: It's a pay-as-you-owe system, not a pay-at-the-end-of-the-year one. That's why withholdings (having your taxes deducted from your paycheck and sent directly to the government) are great — what you don't see, you don't miss, and your tax payments are made for you. If you're self-employed or have taxable income, such as retirement benefits, that isn't subject to withholding, you need to be making quarterly estimated tax payments on Form 1040-ES.

WARNING

When you don't pay your taxes on your income as you earn it, you may get hit with penalties and interest when you do pay them, on or before April 15 of the following year.

You can avoid paying a penalty on tax underpayments if you follow these guidelines: You must pay in at least 90 percent of your current year's tax, either in withholdings or in estimated tax payments, as you earn your income, or you can use the Safe Harbor method.

Calculating your Safe Harbor estimated tax payments

If your income isn't constant or regular, you may choose to follow the so-called Safe Harbor rule and pay 100 percent of last year's tax on an equal and regular basis during this current tax year. This method is simpler than it sounds. If, for example, you have a $3,000 tax liability showing on your 2021 Form 1040, line 24, you may choose to either withhold $3,000 from your 2022 income or make four quarterly payments of $750 in 2022. Provided that you do one or the other, you won't owe any penalty for a 2022 tax underpayment, even if your 2022 tax liability is $15,000. Remember, though, you still do have to pay the balance of tax due by April 15, 2023 to avoid late payment penalties and interest.

Because the Safe Harbor rule is so easy, we never use anything else to calculate estimated taxes. The 90 percent rule is tricky to calculate, your amounts need to be adjusted every time during the year that your income rises or falls, and using it leads to a mountain of increased paperwork. Still, because it is one of the rules, we explain how to calculate your estimated taxes using the 90 percent rule in this section.

WARNING

If your 2022 adjusted gross income is more than $150,000, you have to make estimated tax payments equal to 110 percent of your 2021 tax to escape a 2022 underestimating penalty if your 2022 tax turns out to be substantially more than your 2021 tax. For example, if your 2021 tax is $100,000 (and your income is much higher), you need to make estimated tax payments of $110,000 ($100,000 × 110 percent) in order to qualify for Safe Harbor in 2022. Then, even if your tax in 2022 is $150,000, you won't have to pay any penalty or interest on the $40,000 balance due, despite the fact that your estimated tax payments were less than 90 percent of your tax. This rule doesn't apply to farmers or fishermen.

Completing and filing your Form 1040-ES

You need to accompany your estimated tax payments with Form 1040-ES (payment voucher), Estimated Tax for Individuals. This small form requires only your name, address, Social Security number, and the amount that you're paying. For 2022 estimated payments, make sure that you use the 2022 1040-ES. Write your checks to the "United States Treasury," making sure your name, Social Security number, and the words "2022 Form 1040-ES" are written on the face of the check, and then mail to the address listed in the Form 1040-ES booklet.

Alternatively, you can make your quarterly estimated payments through the IRS website (www.irs.gov/payments) if you create an account on their website. Please see Chapter 2 for the details. We actually recommend making your estimated tax payments electronically due to the ease of finding your estimates in the case something gets misapplied to the wrong period. We're hesitant to send anything to the IRS on paper that isn't absolutely required due to the pandemic staffing issues at the agency and the risk of mail being lost.

TIP

Quarterly estimated tax payments are due for the 2022 tax year on April 18 (April 19 if you're a resident of Maine or Massachusetts), June 15, and September 15, 2022, and January 17, 2023. If you file your completed 2022 tax return and pay any taxes due by January 31, 2023, you can choose not to pay your fourth quarter estimate (due January 17, 2023) without incurring any penalty.

If you're not sure how much you need to pay in estimates, Form 1040-ES (2022) also contains instructions and a worksheet to help you calculate your 2022 estimated tax payments. If you're using the Safe Harbor method to calculate your estimated tax requirements and you have nothing withheld from any source, you can skip the worksheet, take the number from line 24 of your 2021 Form 1040, divide it by 4, and drop that number into each of the vouchers. You're done! Now you just need to remember to pay your quarterly bills.

If, on the other hand, some, but not all, of your income has taxes withheld on it, or you want to only pay 90 percent of your 2022 tax liability upfront (maybe because your income in 2022 is going to be considerably less than it was in 2021), you're going to have to complete the worksheet that comes in the Form 1040-ES packet to calculate your estimated payment amounts.

The 2022 Estimated Tax Worksheet contained in the Form 1040-ES packet is a preview of your 2022 tax return, or what you think that tax return will show. On it you include your adjusted gross income (AGI), your deductions, whether you itemize or take the standard deduction, any credits you may be entitled to, and any additional taxes you may be subject to. The worksheet can help you calculate the minimum amount you must pay during 2022 in order to avoid paying penalties and interest at the end of the year.

REMEMBER

You're only estimating here. If your circumstances change and your income rises or falls, you can adjust any payments you haven't yet made. After you make a payment, though, you're stuck with it, and will need to wait until you file your income tax return for 2022 before you can claim a refund.

WARNING

Don't include your first estimated tax payment for 2022 with your 2021 Form 1040 if you're filing your tax return on paper; instead, we strongly urge you to make your estimated tax payments electronically. If you have no means to make an electronic payment and you must mail a check or money order, mail it separately to the address shown in the instructions for Form 1040-ES. The IRS routes different types of payments to different post office boxes to help eliminate confusion on their end, and a payment sent to the wrong address may be credited against the wrong year.

TIP

If you need an extension of time to file your 2021 Form 1040 and you ordinarily make estimated tax payments, you can skip making a separate first quarter estimated tax payment. Instead, you can add the amount of your first-quarter 2022 estimate to what you think you still owe on your 2021 tax return, and then pay that resulting balance due with your extension. Place the total of your projected 2021 tax liability and your first-quarter, 2022 estimate on line 4 of Form 4868, Application for Automatic Extension of Time to File U.S. Individual Tax Return, and pay the balance shown on line 6. If your 2021 projections are correct, apply the overpayment (which should equal what you would have paid with your first-quarter, 2022 Form 1040-ES) to your 2022 return. If your projections are off, though, and your 2021 tax liability is higher than you thought it would be, you've protected yourself from owing penalties and interest on the underpayment of your 2021 tax. Although you may owe a small penalty for underpaying your 2022 estimates, it will be minor in comparison to the penalty and interest you would owe on unpaid 2021 taxes that you're paying after April 18, 2022 (April 19, 2022, for residents of Maine and Massachusetts).

Moving Expenses (Form 3903)

With the across-the-board reduction in federal income tax rates and near doubling in the standard deduction that was implemented in 2018, some deductions bit the dust and for most taxpayers, that included the moving expense deduction. Active members of the Armed Forces may still claim such unreimbursed expenses for themselves, their spouse and their dependents as a federal income tax deduction if their move is necessitated by a military order and permanent change of station. Please note that some states still allow their residents to deduct moving expenses.

Eligibility for this federal income tax deduction for active-duty military members is subject to two mathematical tests. The first one: The distance between your new job location and your former home must be at least 50 miles more than the distance between your former home and your former job location. Allow us to run these specs by you one more time:

A. Miles from your old home to new workplace

B. Miles from your old home to old workplace

C. Subtract line B from line A.

If line C is at least 50 miles, you're entitled to a moving-expense deduction. For someone just entering the workforce, the new job must be at least 50 miles from their old residence.

The second test requires that you remain employed on a full-time basis at your new job location for at least 39 weeks during the 12-month period immediately following your arrival. In other words, you can't claim a deduction unless you pass the distance test and satisfy the employment-duration requirement.

Members of the United States military have one additional special case that allows them to deduct unreimbursed moving expenses and not have to meet the distance or employment requirements. When members of the military are making a permanent change in their military status — such as leaving the military or retiring — they can also claim moving expenses.

TIP

You can deduct moving expenses in either the year in which they're incurred or the year in which they're paid, which will most likely be the same year, because moving companies typically demand their money before they'll begin to unload the truck, and the move-it-yourself truck rental companies aren't going to let their trucks out of sight until they know they have your credit card information.

WARNING

Meals, temporary living expenses, and expenses incurred in the sale or lease of a residence aren't deductible. You may deduct only the cost of moving and storage of your household goods and personal effects from your former residence to your new one, plus travel and lodging costs for you and members of your household while traveling to your new residence. The cost of storing and insuring your household goods and personal effects can be deducted for any 30 consecutive days after the day your possessions were removed from your former home and before they are delivered to your new home. You can deduct lodging on the day of your arrival and lodging within the area of your former home within one day after you couldn't live in your former home because your furniture had been removed. Deductible moving expenses include connecting and disconnecting utilities, shipping an auto, and transporting household pets — so don't forget Fido. Meals are never deductible, even while traveling from one area to another.

Please remember: These are the federal rules. Some states allow a deduction for moving expenses — your state rules may or may not be similar to the federal rules.

The place to deduct moving expenses is Form 3903, Moving Expenses. If you haven't met the 39-week test by the time that you file your return, don't worry. You're still allowed to claim the deduction if you expect to meet the test. However, if it turns out that you fail the 39-week test, you must report the deduction as income on next year's tax return. No fun at all.

You've lucked out with Form 3903; it's only five lines to get through! Here's what you do:

>> **Line 1:** Enter the cost of transporting and storing your household and personal goods plus the other deductible moving expenses we discuss earlier in this section.

>> **Line 2:** Enter the travel and lodging expenses you're allowed for you and members of your household that you incurred in traveling from your old home to your new home, plus the one-day lodging expenses on the day of arrival and departure. Remember, you can claim only the costs for a single trip from your old residence to your new one. If you use your car, you can claim 16 cents a mile plus tolls and parking for 2021.

>> **Line 3:** Add lines 1 and 2 (your total moving expenses). All these expenses must be incurred within one year from the time you start to work at the new location. Expenses incurred beyond a year are deductible for reasons such as allowing a child to finish school.

>> **Line 4:** Enter the amount that your employer (the federal government) reimbursed you for your moving expenses. Here is where things can become confusing, and you can end up not deducting all that you're entitled to deduct or paying tax on part of the moving expenses for which you were reimbursed. When your employer reimburses you for moving expenses of the type that you may deduct if you had paid them directly, the reimbursement will be noted in box 12 of your Form W-2 with a code P next to it. If you didn't incur deductible moving expenses in excess of what you were reimbursed, you have nothing to deduct and need not file Form 3903.

If, on the other hand, the federal government gave you a specific amount, say $15,000, to cover your moving expenses, that amount will be reported in box 1 of your W-2 as taxable wages. Nothing will be entered in box 12 of your W-2. If that is the case, you can't be making a bigger mistake by believing that because you were reimbursed you have nothing to deduct. Because the $15,000 shows up as taxable wages, you're entitled to claim your deductible moving expenses. If you don't find out how the $15,000 was reported to the IRS, it's going to cost you dearly, because you'll pay more tax than you have to by not deducting the moving expenses to which you're entitled. Enter your deductible moving expenses on lines 1 and 2, and don't enter what you were reimbursed, because it's already been included in your taxable wages.

If the federal government reimbursed you for moving expenses of the type that you may have deducted if you had paid them directly and for moving expenses that you can't deduct, the reimbursement for the deductible expenses will be noted in box 12 of your Form W-2 with a code P. The nondeductible moving expenses included in the reimbursement are included in box 1 of your W-2 as taxable wages. Temporary living expenses paid by your employer are the type that can't be deducted if you had paid them. Sorry, you owe tax on this amount. If this situation occurred, enter all your deductible moving expenses on lines 1 and 2 of Form 3903 and what your employer reimbursed you as indicated in box 12 of your W-2 on line 4.

If the federal government didn't reimburse you, box 12 will have nothing in it, and nothing will be added to your taxable wages. Enter your deductible moving expenses on lines 1 and 2 and put a zero (-0-) on line 4 of Form 3903.

>> **Line 5:** Subtract line 4 from line 3. The result is the amount of your deductible 2021 moving expenses. Now enter this amount on your Form 1040, Schedule 1, Part II, line 14.

If line 3 is less than line 4, subtract line 3 from line 4 and include the amount on line 1, Form 1040, labeled "wages, etc." The reason? If you receive a reimbursement from the federal government that's larger than your deductible moving expenses, you have to pay tax on the difference and can't enter any amount on line 5 of Form 3903.

Nondeductible IRAs (Form 8606)

If you made contributions to a traditional nondeductible IRA in 2021; took distributions from a traditional, SEP, or SIMPLE IRA; converted from a traditional, SEP, or SIMPLE IRA to a Roth IRA, either in whole or in part; or took a distribution from your Roth IRA; you need to complete Form 8806, Nondeductible IRAs, and attach it to your return. This form is divided into three parts, and on this form is where you figure out what part, if any, of your distribution is taxable:

>> **Part I:** Nondeductible Contributions to Traditional IRAs and Distributions from Traditional, SEP, and SIMPLE IRAs

>> **Part II:** 2021 Conversions from Traditional, SEP, or SIMPLE IRAs to Roth IRAs

>> **Part III:** Distributions from Roth IRAs

Part I: Traditional IRAs

This section is important if you made or are making nondeductible contributions or if you're taking money out of a traditional IRA to which you've made nondeductible contributions. This form tells you how much money you have to pay tax on every time you withdraw money from your nondeductible IRA account.

>> **Line 1:** Enter your 2021 nondeductible IRA contribution, which would include the dough that you put in up until April 18, 2022 (April 19, 2022, for residents of Maine and Massachusetts). Enter your maximum $6,000 (or $7,000 if you're older than 50) contribution on this line if you meet either of the following criteria:

• You're contributing the $6,000 (or $7,000) maximum, you're covered by a pension plan where you work, and you earned more than $125,000 if married filing jointly, $76,000 if single or head of household, and $10,000 if married filing separate returns.

• You can't make any part of a Roth IRA contribution because your income exceeds $208,000 for couples or $140,000 if single.

If only a portion of your contribution qualifies for an IRA deduction or a Roth IRA and you elect to have the remaining balance treated as a nondeductible contribution, enter that amount here. For example, if you want to contribute $6,000, but because of the income phase-outs discussed in Chapter 7, you can deduct only $2,000 on Form 1040, Schedule 1, Part II, line 20, enter the remaining $4,000 on line 1 of Form 8606.

If you're able to deduct a portion of your contribution, refer to Chapter 7 for a worksheet that helps you calculate your deduction amount. Whatever amount is left is what you'll use on Form 8606.

>> **Line 2:** Now you need to look back at your Form 8606 from last year's return (or whenever you last made a nondeductible IRA contribution) and pick up the number from line 14. Remember, keeping track of how much money you've put into your nondeductible IRA is one good reason to always keep copies of your prior years' income tax returns.

>> **Line 3:** This part of the form is really easy. Add lines 1 and 2 and enter the total here.

If you didn't withdraw any money from this IRA, enter the amount from line 3 on line 14. Sign and date the form and attach it to your return. Nothing else is required.

If you withdrew any money from your nondeductible IRA, you have to tackle lines 4 through 13. They may look complicated, but they really aren't — just a lot of adding and subtracting, so get your calculator ready.

>> **Line 4:** If you made your nondeductible contribution for 2021 between January 1, 2022, and April 18, 2022 (April 19, 2022, if you reside in Maine or Massachusetts), you have to enter that amount again on this line. Why? To determine how much of your withdrawal is taxable, you must compare the total of all the nondeductible contributions that you made through December 31, 2021, with the value of your IRA on that date. You know the rules. Apples to apples!

>> **Line 5:** Subtract line 4 from line 3. This amount is the total of all your nondeductible contributions through December 31, 2021.

>> **Line 6:** Enter the value of all your IRAs on December 31, 2021.

>> **Line 7:** Enter what you withdrew in 2021. See the lengthy list of what not to include here.

>> **Line 8:** Enter the net amount you converted, if any, from a traditional IRA, including SEPs and SIMPLEs, into a Roth IRA. The IRS allows you to make this conversion if you pay the tax on the entire conversion in the year that you make it in exchange for not paying taxes on distributions when you take them.

>> **Line 9:** Add lines 6, 7, and 8. This amount is what your IRAs would've been worth on December 31, 2021, if you hadn't withdrawn any money.

>> **Line 10:** Get out your calculator. Divide the amount on line 5 by the amount on line 9 and enter it as a decimal on line 10. For example, if the total basis (your nondeductible contributions) of your IRAs is $10,000 (line 5) and the total value of your IRAs is $100,000 pre-distribution (line 9), divide $10,000 by $100,000 to get 0.1 (or 10 percent). Enter that number on line 10.

>> **Line 11:** On this line you begin to calculate the amount of tax you owe on your Roth conversion. Multiply the amount on line 8 by the decimal on line 10 to arrive at the portion of your conversion that won't be taxed because it represents your previously taxed contributions.

>> **Line 12:** Multiply line 7 (the amount that you withdrew in 2021) by line 10 to arrive at the amount of your distribution from a traditional, SEP, or SIMPLE IRA that isn't taxable (because you already paid the tax on your contribution amounts).

>> **Line 13:** Add lines 11 and 12. Line 13 is the nontaxable portion of what you withdrew.

>> **Line 14:** Subtract line 13 from line 3. The IRS refers to this amount as your tax basis, or the amount of money that is still sitting in your IRA after you've taken your distribution or made your conversion on which you've already paid tax. Remember, if you've paid income tax on it once, you don't have to pay tax on it again.

>> **Line 15a through c:** Subtract line 12 from line 7 and enter the difference here on line 15a. If you took out a portion of your nondeductible IRA to deal with a qualified disaster distribution in 2021, you'll pick up that amount from Forms 8915-D, line 23, and 8915-F, line 18. Enter any amounts on line 15b. Subtract any amount on line 15b from line 15a and enter the total on line 15c. The amount on line 15c represents taxable income to you in 2021.

Sign and date the form if you aren't attaching it to your return and hang on to it for dear life. If you ever need to prove to the IRS the amount of your nondeductible contributions, your Form 8606 from all the years in which you made contributions should be invaluable evidence.

WARNING

You must file Form 8606 to report nondeductible contributions even if you don't have to file a tax return for the year. If you file a Form 1040, there's a $50 penalty for not attaching your 8606 to it! Also, if your IRA contributions are more than permissible amounts, you may be subject to a 6 percent penalty, and you must withdraw the overpayment.

Part II: Conversions from traditional IRAs, SEPs, or SIMPLE IRAs to Roth IRAs

If you converted from a traditional, SEP, or SIMPLE IRA to a Roth IRA in 2021, you need to complete this section.

>> **Line 16:** Enter the amount you converted from your traditional (simple), SEP, or SIMPLE IRA to your Roth IRA. If you've already completed Part I of this form, just pick up the amount on line 8.

>> **Line 17:** Enter the amount from line 11 if you converted a nondeductible IRA.

>> **Line 18:** Subtract line 17 from 16 and carry it over to Form 1040, line 4b. This is the taxable amount of your Roth conversion.

Part III: Distributions from Roth IRAs

In this part, you compute the taxable portion, if any, on nonqualified distributions from your Roth IRA. For a quick review on how a Roth is taxed, check out Chapter 7. Remember, you have to keep money in a Roth for at least five years in order to have the entire withdrawal escape tax.

>> **Line 19:** Enter the amount you withdrew from your Roth IRA in 2021.

>> **Line 20:** Every rule has an exception, and this exception is the one for nonqualified Roth distributions. If you took a distribution so you could pay qualified first-time home-buyer expenses, such as your down payment, construction costs, mortgage points, or other closing costs, you don't have to pay the penalty on the nonqualified distribution. And, if you think that first-time home-buyer expenses are a thing of the past for you, think again: The IRS defines a first-time home buyer as anyone who hasn't held an ownership interest in a principal residence for at least two years prior to signing the contract on this home.

>> **Line 21:** Subtract line 20 from line 19. This amount represents the total of your nonqualified distribution.

>> **Line 22:** Enter the basis (what you contributed to your Roth) of what you withdrew. It sounds tough, but it's not. Here's how to compute Roth basis: Enter the total amount of all your Roth contributions on this line less any amounts you've withdrawn previously. For example, if you've contributed a total of $10,000 to your Roth since you started it in 2014, and in 2020, you withdrew $1,500, your basis in 2021 is $8,500 ($10,000 – $1,500).

>> **Line 23:** Subtract line 22 from 21. Enter zero (-0-) if line 22 is more than line 21.

>> **Line 24:** If you've made Roth conversions, enter your basis here. Calculate this number the same as you did for your Roth contribution basis in line 22.

>> **Line 25a–c:** Subtract line 24 from line 23. If line 24 is more than line 23, enter zero (-0-) and skip lines 25b and 25c. If you have a positive amount on line 25a, on line 25b, enter any amounts attributable to qualified disaster distributions made in 2021, the same as described for line 15b previously. Subtract line 25b from line 25a and place your answer on line 25c. This is the taxable amount of your Roth distribution. Carry this amount over to Form 1040, line 4b. If you're under age 59½, this amount may also be subject to a 10 percent penalty.

Forms 8615 and 8814, the Kiddie Tax

If you have children under age 18 who have investment income, you may need to complete Form 8615 or Form 8814. If your child reached age 19 in 2021, the kiddie tax doesn't apply unless they're a full-time student under age 24 who is providing 50 percent or less of their own support.

Form 8615 is the form that you use when your child files their own return; use Form 8814 when you elect to report your kid's investment income on your return. (See the sidebar "Why your 3-year-old may be in a high tax bracket" for more on making this election.)

Here's how the kiddie tax works. If a child has $3,000 in investment income, for example, the first $1,100 is exempt from tax. The next $1,100 is taxed at the child's tax rate. The remaining $800 is taxed at the parent's federal income tax rate.

WHY YOUR 3-YEAR-OLD MAY BE IN A HIGH TAX BRACKET

Once upon a time, if you were in the 70 percent tax bracket (rates were that high before 1981), it made sense to make a gift of investment property to your children, because the investment income the property produced would be taxed at the child's tax rate — which may have been as low as 11 percent. But that was back in the good old days (that is, if you think anything is nostalgic about 70 percent tax rates). This tax savings scheme ended in 1986. Nowadays, if a child is under the age of 19, or under age 24 if they're a full-time student providing 50 percent or less of their own support, all investment income higher than $2,200 is taxed at the parents' tax rate — which can be as high as 37 percent for 2021. The reason for the change is to remove the incentive for higher-income earners to transfer lots of money to their kids just to save tax dollars by benefiting from lower tax brackets.

Children whose investment income is more than $1,100 must file a federal income tax return. If they don't have any taxable investment income (you invested the money that their grand-parents gave them in tax-exempt bonds), they don't have to file a return until their earned income, such as income from a part-time job, exceeds $12,550. If your child wasn't 19 by the end of 2021 or was under age 24 and a full-time student providing 50 percent or less of their own support, here's how to compute the kiddie tax.

1. **Enter your Social Security number and taxable income on Form 8615.**

2. **Add the amount of your child's investment income that's in excess of $2,200 to your taxable income.**

3. **Recompute your tax.**

   The difference between the tax on your return and the recomputed figure is the kiddie tax.

   A good tax software program can save you all this math (see Chapter 2).

But if you don't have a tax software program and your child's investment income in excess of $2,200 is, say, $1,000, add the $1,000 to your taxable income. Now compute your tax on this amount. For example, if the tax on this amount is $9,250 and the tax on your return is $9,000, the $250 difference is the kiddie tax. Enter that amount plus whatever amount of tax has been calculated on the child's taxable income (the tax on the $1,100 that isn't exempt from tax, per the tax tables) on your child's return on Form 1040, line 16.

But there's more. (There always is.) If you and your spouse file separate returns, you enter the larger of either your or your spouse's taxable income on Form 8615. If you're separated or divorced, the parent who has custody of the child for the greater part of the year uses their tax-able income when completing Form 8615. But if you and your spouse live apart and qualify to file as unmarried (single or head of household), the custodial parent's taxable income is used on Form 8615.

And it gets worse (as it always seems to)! If you have two or more kids, you enter the total of all their investment income on Form 8615. The kiddie tax is computed and allocated among them. For example, suppose that your daughter's investment income in excess of $2,200 is $3,000, and your son's is $2,000; you enter $5,000 on each child's Form 8615. Then each child's share of the total kiddie tax is allocated. Your daughter's share is three-fifths of the tax, and your son's share is two-fifths.

TIP

By now you're looking for a way to avoid having to file a separate tax return because your child has $1 more than $1,100. Is there a way, you ask? Yes. If your child has investment income of only $11,000 or less and it's all from interest and dividends, you can report the income on your return by filing Form 8814. That's $11,000 for each child. But we don't recommend this course of action because the kiddie tax is higher on your return than it would be on the child's return, and your tax may also be higher. To find out more about the smartest ways to invest in your child's name, read Chapter 26. The $11,000 threshold is indexed for inflation.

Form 8829, Expenses for Business Use of Your Home

TAX CUT

Your home office no longer has to be the place where you meet customers or the principal place where you conduct business. You're entitled to claim a home office deduction if you have a dedicated space in your house that you use for your business, even if it's used only to conduct administrative or management activities of your business, provided you have no other office or other place of business where you can perform the same tasks. So, a person who brings work home is out of luck. So is the person who spreads out over the dining room table. So long as you eat there, that table isn't dedicated solely to the pursuit of your business. A carpenter who sets up his computer and desk in a corner of that dining room so that he can price jobs and bill his clients has a valid deduction, because that corner of his dining room is set aside solely for the administrative and management activities of his business.

The rule allowing taxpayers to claim a deduction for the portion of their home they use to perform administrative and management activities was designed to help doctors who perform their primary duties in hospitals, salespeople who spend most of their time calling on customers at their customers' offices, and house painters and other tradespeople who spend their time at job sites but use an office in their home to do all their paperwork. Use Form 8829, Expenses for Business Use of Your Home, to claim the deduction.

TAX CUT

If you use part of your residence for business, you can deduct the mortgage interest, real estate taxes, depreciation, insurance, utilities, and repairs related to that part of your house. Renters get to deduct their business portion of the rental expenses.

If you use a portion of your home to store inventory or samples, you're also entitled to deduct your home office expenses. Say that you sell cosmetics and use part of your study to store samples. You can deduct expenses related to the portion of your study used to store the cosmetics, even if you use the study for other purposes.

A home office deduction can't produce a loss. For example, suppose that your business income is $6,000. You have $5,000 in business expenses and home office expenses of $1,500 (of which $1,000 is for the portion of your mortgage interest and real estate tax allocated for the use of the office). First, you deduct the interest and taxes of $1,000, which leaves a balance of $5,000 for possible deductions. Then you deduct $5,000 of business expenses, which brings your business income to zero. You can't deduct the remaining $500 of your home office expenses, but you can carry it over to the next year. If you don't have sufficient income to deduct the $500 next year, you can carry it over again.

If you're a renter, filling out Form 8829 correctly means that you first determine your total rent — including insurance, cleaning, and utilities. Then you deduct the portion used for business. If you rent four rooms and one room is used for business, you're entitled to deduct 25 percent of the total. (If the rooms are the same size, you can use this method. If not, you have to figure out the percentage on a square-footage basis.)

For homeowners, you compute the total cost of maintaining your home, depreciation, mortgage interest, taxes, insurance, repairs, and so on. Don't forget to deduct the cost of your cleaning service if your office is cleaned in addition to the rest of the house. Then deduct the percentage used for business.

Considering the "simplified" home office deduction

Since 2013, taxpayers who qualify for claiming a home office deduction can do so with a "simplified" home office deduction. Here are the details of this newer option:

>> Your deduction is limited to $1,500 per year, which is based on a deduction of $5 per square foot for up to a 300-square-foot home office.

>> No depreciation deduction is allowed.

>> You can't deduct any other actual expenses related to your home. For example, you claim your mortgage interest and property tax deductions on Schedule A of Form 1040.

>> You can't carry forward a loss.

>> You may use either the simplified method or the regular method for any taxable year.

>> You choose a method by using that method on your timely filed, original federal income tax return for the taxable year.

>> After you choose a method for a taxable year, you can't later change to the other method for that same year.

>> If you use the simplified method for one year and use the regular method for any subsequent year, you must calculate the depreciation deduction for the subsequent year using the appropriate optional depreciation table. This is true regardless of whether you used an optional depreciation table for the first year the property was used in business.

Most taxpayers will be able to claim a larger home deduction through the regular method; you'll have to trudge through those calculations to see if that's the case.

Measuring your home office

Complete lines 1 through 7 on Form 8829 to find out how much of your home you used exclusively for your business.

>> **Line 1:** Enter the area, in square feet, of the part of your home that you used for business: for example, 300 square feet.

>> **Line 2:** Enter the total area, in square feet, of your home: for example, 1,500 square feet.

>> **Line 3:** To determine the percentage of your home that you used for business, divide line 1 by line 2 and enter the result as a percentage here. In the earlier example, you would enter 20 percent (300 ÷ 1,500). Keep this percentage handy; it's the percentage of the expenses for the whole house — such as interest, real estate taxes, depreciation, utility costs, and repairs — that you use on Form 8829 to determine your deduction.

>> **Line 7:** Unless you use your home as a daycare facility, you can skip lines 4 through 6 (which calculate the percentage of your home that you use for your daycare) and enter your deduction percentage from line 3 onto line 7. If you use your home to provide daycare services, multiply the result from line 6 by the number on line 3, and enter the result here.

Figuring your allowable home office deduction

Lines 8 through 36 (and beyond) on Form 8829 involve mega-computations, much more than our space allows. In this section, we take you through the basics that apply to most people. Take a peek at IRS Publication 587 *(Business Use of Your Home)* for additional information.

>> **Line 8:** Enter the amount from line 29 of your Schedule C (this amount is what you earned after expenses), plus any net gain or loss shown on Schedule D or Form 4797 that derives from your business. Your home office deduction can't exceed this amount.

>> **Lines 9 through 22, column (a):** Expenses that apply exclusively to your office go in this column. Repairs and maintenance, such as painting your office, are two such items.

>> **Lines 9 through 22, column (b):** Enter your expenses that apply to the entire house on these lines. The IRS refers to them as indirect expenses.

If you rent instead of owning your home, the rent that you paid goes on line 19, column (b).

>> **Lines 23 through 36:** It's number-crunching time — enough to make us wonder who came up with this form!

>> **Line 36:** This is your allowable deduction. Carry it over to line 30 on Schedule C.

REMEMBER

If you had more home office expenses than you could use last year, don't forget to add the amount you had left over from your tax year 2020 Form 8829, line 43 onto line 25 of your tax year 2021 Form 8829. The same goes for excess casualty losses from line 44 of your tax year 2020 Form 8829. Enter that amount on line 31.

Determining your home office's depreciation allowance

If you own your home, you also have to apply your home office deduction percentage (from line 7 of Form 8829) to your home's depreciation allowance. This section includes a line-by-line breakdown of the appropriate part on Form 8829.

Line 37: Your home's value

Here's where you compute your depreciation deduction. You get to write off the percentage of your home that you claim as a home office (in our earlier example, 20 percent) over either 31½ or 39 years, depending on when you set up your office. Residential property usually is written off over 27½ years, but because the office is used for business, it's considered business property and has a longer life.

On line 37, enter the smaller of what you paid for your home (including the original and closing costs, as well as any improvements you've made to the property) or its fair market value at the time you first started to use it for business. You don't have to make this comparison every year — only when you start claiming a home office deduction.

Line 38: Land not included

Because you can't depreciate land, you have to subtract the value of the land that your home sits on from the cost of your home so that you calculate the house's net cost. We discuss how to establish the basis of the land portion of your property in Chapter 15.

Line 39: Basis of building

Subtract line 38 from line 37. This amount is your home's basis after subtracting the value of the land that you can't depreciate.

Line 40: Business portion of your home

Multiply line 39 by your home office deduction percentage from line 7. In our continuing example, that's the 20 percent of the house used for business that you can write off.

Line 41: Depreciation percentage

If you set up your office before May 12, 1993, it's a 31½-year write-off. Use the depreciation table in IRS Publication 587 (*Business Use of Your Home*).

If you set up your office after May 12, 1993, the write-off is over 39 years. Use Table 17-1 to determine your depreciation percentage.

For example, if you set up your office in June 2016, you would enter 1.391 percent on line 40 of Form 8829 the first (partial) year. Every year thereafter, you'd use 2.564 percent.

Table 17-1   39-Year Depreciation Schedule for Business Use of Home (%)

Use the row for the month of the year you set up your office.		
Month	Year 1	Years 2–39
Jan	2.461	2.564
Feb	2.247	2.564
Mar	2.033	2.564
Apr	1.819	2.564
May	1.605	2.564
Jun	1.391	2.564
Jul	1.177	2.564
Aug	0.963	2.564
Sep	0.749	2.564
Oct	0.535	2.564
Nov	0.321	2.564
Dec	0.107	2.564

Line 42: Depreciation allowable

Multiply line 40 by line 41. This number is your depreciation deduction, based on the business use of your home. Enter this amount on lines 42 and 30 of this form.

WARNING

Many people avoid taking depreciation on their homes for a variety of reasons. Some may not understand how depreciation works. For others, the idea of trying to figure out their home's adjusted basis leaves them flustered. Yet others think that, if they depreciate now, they'll have a hard time calculating their gain or loss on the sale of that home down the road. What you may fail to realize is that the IRS deems that the value of your home has depreciated whether or not you deduct the depreciation to which you're entitled. When you go to sell that home, you're required to recapture that depreciation, even if you didn't actually take the deduction as part of your home office deductions on your tax return.

Deducting what's left

Remember that you can't take a loss because of the home office deduction. You can, however, carry over an excess deduction amount to another year's tax return.

On lines 43 and 44, compute the amount of your home office deduction that you can't deduct. You get to deduct it in future years, provided that you have enough income.

REMEMBER

On Schedule A, don't forget to deduct the balance (in our example, 80 percent) of your total mortgage interest that you entered on line 10(b) of Form 8829, and the balance of your total real estate taxes from line 11(b) of this form. Your mortgage interest balance goes on line 8 of Schedule A; the real estate tax balance goes on line 5 of Schedule A.

FALSELY CLAIMING TOO MANY EXEMPTIONS

If the IRS notifies your employer that your Form W-4 is invalid and that you're not entitled to claim exemption from all withholding (or claim as many exemptions as you show on that form) your employer must withhold taxes on your income according to instructions contained in an IRS notice called a *lock-in letter*, which states what marital status and the maximum number of exemptions you are allowed to claim. Your employer will furnish a copy of this notice to you within ten business days of receipt of the letter, and they're required to begin withholding at that level on the date specified in the lock-in letter. Your employer is required to continue withholding at this new level until either the IRS modifies its lock-in letter or you provide your employer with a new Form W-4 that provides for withholding at least at the level of the lock-in letter. If you give your employer a new Form W-4 that still claims more exemptions from withholding than the lock-in letter permits, or claims that you are exempt from withholding, your employer must disregard your new Form W-4 and continue withholding at the IRS's mandated level.

If you don't have reasonable basis for the number of exemptions that you claim, you'll be assessed a $500 penalty. Willfully supplying false or fraudulent information on Form W-4 is a criminal offense, costing you a fine of up to $1,000 or even a year in the pokey. A simple error or an honest mistake won't result in penalty. Phew!

Form W-4, Employee Withholding

If you owe a bundle to the IRS for 2021, chances are you aren't withholding enough tax from your salary. Unless you don't mind paying a lot on April 15, you need to adjust your withholding to avoid interest and penalties if you can't pay what you owe when it's due.

TIP

Relying on the worksheet on Form W-4 just once per year to accurately calculate the correct number of exemptions you should be claiming would be easy, but it's not that simple, especially if your situation changes during the (tax) year. If you get married, divorced, have the birth of a child (or two), adopt a child, or buy a home, those would be situations that warrant recalculating your W-4 withholding numbers. Ditto for changes on the job front such as increasing or decreasing your work time and income. Check out the IRS website, which has a nifty "Tax Withholding Estimator" (www.irs.gov/individuals/tax-withholding-estimator) that you can use at any time during the year to make sure you're having enough tax withheld from your paychecks. The estimator is easy to use and gives a reasonably accurate picture of how much you'll owe (or have refunded) next April 15.

Household Employment Taxes: Schedule H

If you have household workers (including housekeepers, babysitters, yard-care workers, and nannies) who earned more than $2,300 from you in 2021, you may be required to pay employment taxes for them (that's the employer's half of the Social Security and Medicare taxes, plus federal unemployment [FUTA] taxes). Please see Chapter 23 for help in making the determination. If your workers meet the employee test, fortunately, you don't need to figure out the ordinary employment tax forms, which need to be filed either monthly or quarterly; instead, if you qualify, you may use Schedule H to calculate what you owe.

Prior to the nanny tax, which began in 1994, household employers had to file quarterly reports and pay Social Security taxes if they paid household help more than $50 in a quarter. Now you don't have to withhold and pay Social Security taxes unless you pay a domestic worker more than $2,300 during the year.

Here are two important provisions of the nanny tax that you should be aware of:

>> You're not required to pay Social Security tax for domestic employees under the age of 21 (for any portion of the year), regardless of how much you pay them. The exemption doesn't apply if the principal occupation of the employee is household employment. So, you're off the hook for payroll taxes for your 12-year-old mother's helper, or the 16-year-old down the street who babysits occasionally.

>> You don't have to file quarterly payroll tax forms. Any Social Security, Medicare, or federal unemployment (FUTA) taxes, and income taxes that you choose to withhold can be paid when you file your return in April.

WARNING

If your withholding or estimated tax payments aren't enough to cover the Social Security, Medicare, and FUTA (we explain these taxes later in this section) taxes that you owe, a penalty will be assessed. So, make sure that you pay in enough.

Although the nanny tax simplifies your IRS filings, you still have to keep filing quarterly state unemployment tax returns, unless your state elects to conform to the IRS method of filing annually.

Schedule H looks more formidable than it really is. Here's the lowdown on what it's really about:

>> If you paid your household help less than $2,300 in 2021 and didn't withhold any income tax, you don't have to file this form.

>> If you paid any one household employee less than $2,300 during 2021, but you withheld federal income tax, you need to fill out only Part I beginning with line 7.

For example, suppose that you pay someone $60 a week. That's $780 a quarter and $3,120 for the year. You have to answer only questions A, B, and C on the form and fill out the eight lines in Part I. It's strictly simple math stuff. You have to multiply the $3,120 in cash wages that you paid by the 12.4 percent Social Security rate and the 2.9 percent Medicare tax rate. Add both of these taxes together on line 8a of Schedule H.

NEW STUFF

Whether you've been filing Schedule H for years or you're new to this form, you're going to have quite a shock when you see the 2021 version, especially lines 8a through 8n, which are confusing and tedious. We'd love to tell you to just ignore these and go on with your life as you've known it in the past. But we can't, especially if any of your employees were either diagnosed with COVID-19, had a family member diagnosed with COVID-19, or you paid any sort of health insurance coverage for your employees that had anything at all to do with COVID-19. You may want to seek the advice of a payroll specialist or tax advisor, or use a good tax software program to help you figure out all these refundable (lines 8e and 8f) and nonrefundable (lines 8b and 8c) credits. Before you do, though, pull together your pay records for 2021 as well as a list of when your employees were unable to work because of the pandemic — having your information all in one place will make the payroll specialist's work much easier.

If you had one or more household employees in 2021, and paid wages totaling $1,000 or more in any calendar quarter to all your household employees in either 2020 or 2021, you have to fill out Parts II and III of Schedule H. Not only do you owe Social Security and Medicare taxes, but you also have to pay federal unemployment tax, commonly known as FUTA. Of course, if you had no employees in 2021, but did in 2020, you're not required to fill out Schedule H at all.

By the time you work your way through all of Schedule H (especially if you're preparing this on paper as opposed to letting your computer do all the calculations) and arrive at a final value of household employment taxes to put on Form 1040, Schedule 2, line 9, and payroll refundable credits to put on Form 1040, Schedule 3, line 13b (for amounts on Schedule H, line 8e) and line 13h (for amounts on Schedule H, line 8f), you may want to reconsider hiring anyone at all for household help. But wait, there's more.

Don't forget that you also have to furnish your employee with a W-2 stating the amount that you paid, as well as the amount of Social Security, Medicare, and income tax that you withheld. Withholding income tax is optional on your part. One further chore: You have to file a copy of the W-2 and Form W-3 (if more than one W-2 is being filed) with the Social Security Administration in Wilkes-Barre, Pennsylvania, by January 31, 2022. You must also provide your employees with their W-2s by January 31, 2022.

Check with your state tax department to find out whether you have to register and pay state unemployment tax on a quarterly basis. Also check with your insurance broker to see whether your homeowner's insurance covers domestic employees or whether you need a separate workers' compensation policy. Don't play fast and loose in this area. If your nanny gets hurt or injured, you may have to pay a bundle if you don't have insurance coverage.

The immigration law requires you to verify that every new employee is eligible to work in the United States. You do this by completing Form I-9, Employment Eligibility Verification. You can get this form from the U.S. Citizenship and Immigration Service's website at www.uscis.gov. The form doesn't get filed. Hang onto it in case someone from the Immigration Service knocks on your door.

Schedule SE: Self-Employment Tax Form

If you earn part or all of your income from being self-employed, use Schedule SE to figure another tax that you owe — the Social Security tax and Medicare tax. The first $142,800 of your self-employment earnings is taxed at 12.4 percent (this is the Social Security tax part).

The Medicare tax doesn't have any limit; it's 2.9 percent of your total self-employment earnings. For amounts of $142,800 or less, the combined rate is 15.3 percent (adding the two taxes together), and for amounts above $142,800, the rate is 2.9 percent. If your self-employment earnings are under $400, you aren't subject to this tax.

Your self-employment earnings may be your earnings reported on the following:

>> Schedule C (line 31)

>> Schedule K-1, Form 1065 (box 14, code A) — if you're a partner in a firm

>> Schedule F (line 36), or Schedule K-1, box 14, code A (Form 1065) — if you're a farmer

>> Form 1040, Schedule 1, Part I (line 8z) — your self-employment income that you reported as miscellaneous income

TAX CUT

Remember, half of your self-employment tax is deductible. Complete Schedule SE and note the following: The amount on line 12 of Schedule SE is the amount of tax that you have to pay; you carry it over to Schedule 2 Form 1040 (line 4) and add it to your income tax that's due. Enter half of what you have to pay — the amount on line 13 of Schedule SE — on Schedule 1 Form 1040 (line 14).

4

Audits and Errors: Dealing with the IRS

Chapter **18**

Dreaded Envelopes: IRS Notices, Assessments, and Audits

I f you think that you received an IRS notice simply because you're unlucky, you may be mistaken. Winning the IRS notice lottery is easy, and you're hardly in exclusive company! Each year, the IRS issues millions of the following:

» Penalty notices

» Notices informing taxpayers that they didn't report all their income

» Notices to taxpayers stating that they failed to file a tax return

» Notices citing math or clerical errors

» Notices to taxpayers that they failed to pay what they owed

And every year, millions of beleaguered taxpayers contact the IRS back saying that the notices they received are either incorrect or unclear.

When you're dealing with the IRS, remember the three Ps — promptness, persistence, and patience! Don't become discouraged when matters move more slowly than you'd like, which has been especially true since March 2020 and the COVID-19 pandemic shutdowns and remote work.

One of the biggest headaches in dealing with the IRS is that the agency can be big and impersonal. Remember that although you may feel like the IRS is a huge, unfriendly bureaucracy, it's actually got some employees who may be able to help you, if you let them. "I shall overcome" should be your motto.

That's why the chapters in this part of the book (Part 4, if you're keeping track) provide you with suggested strategies and sample response letters developed from the decades of experience that have helped our clients deal with those daunting IRS notices. These strategies and letters work. When an IRS form can work better and faster than a letter, we include that form and suggest using it.

Understanding the IRS Notice Process

If you've never had a pen pal, you have one now. And you don't even have to write back — the letters just keep coming. However, disregard this pen pal at your peril; the IRS doesn't just get mad when you hide from it, it has the power to take your money.

Receiving your typical notice

There are seemingly zillions of points the IRS may decide to check on your return, and there seem to be just as many ways they can usher you into the twilight realm of notices, adjustments, and increasing assessments. Really, though, all of this paper follows a timeline, no matter what the name or number of the first letter you receive from the IRS.

Typically, when the IRS decides to check with you about your tax return, it sends you a first notice of adjustment, such as the CP-2000, Notice of Proposed Adjustment for Underpayment/Overpayment; the CP-13, We Changed Your Account; or a 30-day letter (notifying you of an audit's results). If you fail to respond to this first notice, if the IRS isn't satisfied with your reply, or if you fail to exercise your appeal rights, a Statutory Notice of Deficiency is issued. Remember that adjustments merely correcting a math or processing error — or assessing a penalty — don't require the issuance of a Statutory Notice unless the error results in you owing more tax. We get into what you should do when you receive a Statutory Notice in "Receiving a Statutory Notice of Deficiency," later in this chapter.

If you don't respond, the IRS then may make an assessment. That amount, plus penalties, is entered into the IRS service center's computers under your Social Security number. The service center then sends up to four notices (you can stop the notices at any time by paying the assessment). The first three come at approximately five-week intervals, covering a 15-week period. All three notices ask for payment within ten days. The fourth notice announces that things are about to hit the fan.

The first notice either informs you that there is a balance due (you filed but didn't pay what you owed), that there was a math error, or that an adjustment was made to your account (for example, you didn't make all the tax payments you claimed). It explains the reason(s) for the change plus any penalties that are being assessed. Unfortunately, interest is always charged when a balance is owed.

After you receive that first notice, you know that if you ignore it, the second will soon be winging its way to you. The second form is Form CP-503. It's marked, **"IMPORTANT immediate action is required."** It lists how much the IRS now thinks you owe and how much time you have to pay it.

And, if that doesn't get your attention, the third notice, **Form CP-504,** bears the legend **"Urgent! We intend to levy certain assets. Please respond NOW."** Now you'll find additional penalties and interest tacked on to your last balance, plus it gives you another deadline to pay the full amount owing or enter into a payment agreement.

The fourth notice is sent by certified mail 30 days after the third notice (the law requires that it be sent this way before the IRS can start seizing someone's property or wages). This notice bears the legend **Final Notice of Intent to Levy and Notice of Your Right to a Hearing.** This notice informs you that if payment isn't received within 30 days or you don't request a collection hearing within that period, the IRS has the right to seize your property and garnish your wages. (Remember, the IRS defines property as more than just your residence; it has its eye on your car, boat, personal property, other real estate, bank accounts, and investments, too.) Ouch! You can expect to receive this type of notice (letter) about 20 weeks after the first notice.

Don't think you can fob off the folks at the IRS. The IRS can and will use any and all means within its extensive arsenal to collect the tax it feels is due. If you ignore the IRS, don't expect the IRS just to go away. Instead, respond promptly and courteously. They aren't robots or monsters on the other end of the telephone, just IRS employees trying to do their jobs.

Now for some good news: You can now appeal a notice of intent to levy or a notice that a lien has been filed. When you do, the IRS must stop all collection activity while your appeal is pending. A separate notice is sent informing you of your appeal rights. For more information, see "Requesting a Collection Due Process Hearing" later in this chapter.

If you receive a Final Notice and can't pay what you owe, see Chapter 20 to review your options. If you haven't paid the balance or contacted the IRS to arrange payment within ten days after receiving a Final Notice, the contact section of the Automated Collection System (ACS) takes over, unless the IRS has what's known as *levy source information* — that is, the IRS knows where it can get your cash; it knows where to find your property or income. In that case, a Notice of Levy will be issued against your salary and bank accounts, for example. The contact section handles cases where the payment of tax can't be satisfied by levy. The ACS contacts you by telephone, and if it can't get you to pay, the ACS turns the case over to a revenue officer.

Deciphering a notice

Don't panic! If you're like most taxpayers, you'll look at the notice, see a dollar figure, and decide it's too painful to look at again. Do yourself a favor, take a peek at it again; the dollar figure may be a refund — but it isn't likely.

One critical bit of advice: The computers at the service centers won't tolerate being ignored. Maybe they hooked you by error, but there's no satisfying them until they reel you in, or until you convince the IRS that they've made an error. To do so, you must respond promptly to a notice. Otherwise, you severely prejudice your appeal rights and end up with no recourse but to pay the tax and forget the whole thing — or to pay the tax and then try to get your money back. The latter isn't as impossible as it sounds. We tell you how to get back what is rightfully yours in Chapter 19.

Every notice contains the following:

>> Date of the notice

>> Taxpayer identification number — your Social Security or Employer Identification number for businesses (make sure that it's yours)

>> The form number you filed — for example, 1040

>> Tax period — the year

>> A control number (evidently your name, address, and Social Security number aren't enough)

>> Penalties charged

>> Interest charged

>> Amount owed

>> Tax payments you made

Both you and the IRS can track any missing tax payment by a long series of numbers printed on the back of your check. The first 14 numbers make up the IRS's control or tracking number; the next nine are your Social Security number, followed by a four-letter abbreviation of your name. The next four numbers are the year the payment was applied (2012 means the year ending December 2020), and the last six digits record the date on which the payment was received.

More and more banks have stopped returning cancelled checks with their monthly statements; however, you can still retrieve a copy of both the front and back of your cancelled tax check from your bank when you need it, although you may have to pay a fee to do so. Don't let the fee deter you — pay up and get the information you need.

Unfortunately, not every notice provides all the information necessary to precisely determine what went wrong — IRS notices are famous for their lack of clarity. Our favorite is a client's notice that indicated that an error was made, an outstanding balance existed, not all the payments listed on the return were made, or a penalty was being assessed. The notice went on to promise that the IRS would send a separate notice (which, by the way, never came) stating which explanation applied.

All is not lost if you receive an IRS notice and, after careful inspection, you still don't understand it. Call the IRS at the telephone number indicated on the notice or at 800-829-1040 and request a Record of your Tax Account Information, which takes about seven to ten days to arrive. An even quicker way to get this is to create an account on the www.irs.gov website and access the information that way. This Record of your Tax Account Information lists every transaction posted to your account. With this additional information, you should be able to understand why you were sent the notice.

If the transcript of your tax account fails to clarify why you received the notice in the first place, write to the IRS and ask it to provide a better or more exact explanation. See Chapter 19 to find out more about getting a better explanation.

Assessing Assessment Notices

Assessment notices usually inform you of one of the following situations:

>> You weren't given credit for all the federal income tax payments that you claim you made.

>> You made a math error or used the wrong tax table or form.

>> You filed a return but neglected to pay what you owed.

>> You agreed to the results of a tax examination.

>> You owe a penalty.

General assessment notices — the CP series forms and other notices

The IRS uses one of the CP series forms to inform you that your refund is being reduced or eliminated. This may be the case if your refund is being applied to other taxes you owe, which will be announced on Form CP-49. Or it may be the result of one of the reasons from the list in the preceding section. The IRS also intercepts refunds to pay nontax governmental debts, such as defaults on student loans and nonpayment of child support. We discuss the IRS refund interception program in greater detail in Chapter 19.

In addition to the CP series notices, you may receive other correspondence from the IRS. If you've failed to pay your income taxes in the past, or you haven't given your correct Social Security number to your bank, brokerage, or any other institution, partnership, trust, or estate, or any other entity that is paying you income, the IRS may require these payers to withhold income tax from any payments they make to you. Likewise, if you're thinking to avoid with-holdings on your wages by some judicious fudging on your Form W-4, think again. Your employer is required to submit extreme withholding exemptions to the IRS, and it may ask you for clarification.

WARNING

The IRS also sends a general assessment notice to assess a penalty for filing or paying late, failing to make timely estimated tax payments, failing to report all your income, or overstating credits or deductions on your return. Watch out!

Income verification notice — Form CP-2501

The IRS will send you a Form CP-2501 when information on your federal income tax returns doesn't match information it's received about you from a third party on either a Form W-2 (wages and tips), a Form 1098 (mortgage interest), or a Form 1099 of any variety (which covers most other types of income). Don't believe that just because the notice is coming from the IRS that it's necessarily correct. As an example, here's what happened to one of the authors of this book: A 1099 for $820 was wrongly entered into the IRS's computer as $82,000. Based on that entry, the IRS issued a bill for additional tax, interest, and penalties totaling $50,000. One of our form letters in Chapter 19 corrected the error in a matter of weeks. No one is immune from such errors. Getting a notice from the IRS that you owe $50,000 doesn't exactly make your day, even if you happen to be a tax expert.

Income verification notices ask you to explain differences between the income and deductions you claimed on your return and the income and deductions reported to the IRS by banks, your employer, and brokerage firms. The IRS assumes that the information it collects from these third parties is correct and that you have made a mistake on your return.

Ignore an income verification request, and you'll receive a subsequent notice adjusting your account and billing you for penalties, interest, and additional tax. Often, the IRS doesn't bother sending an income verification notice; it simply assumes that the information about you in its computer is correct and sends Form CP-2000, Notice of Proposed Adjustment for Underpayment/Overpayment, which we discuss in "Receiving your typical notice" earlier in this chapter.

One of the quickest ways we know to become separated from your money is to ignore one of these nice little notices. If the notice you receive is wrong or unclear, you need to notify the IRS. To find out how to do this, see Chapter 19.

The IRS sends out millions of CP-2000 notices annually that lead to their collection of billions more yearly from taxpayers who didn't report all their income. If you fail to report all your income, you can expect to receive a CP-2501 or CP-2000 within 12 to 15 months after filing your return.

Request for tax return — Forms CP-515 and CP-518

Form CP-515, Request for your tax return, and CP-518, You didn't respond regarding your tax return, are reserved as the non-filers' first notice and then final notice of overdue returns. These notices are sent out to millions of people each year, asking why they didn't file a tax return.

The fact that the IRS expects you to file a return doesn't mean that you're actually required to. See Chapter 4 to verify whether your income falls below certain limits, which means you don't need to file a return. Still, if the IRS comes calling, looking for that return, you need to be able to answer.

Here are some of the reasons the IRS may be looking for a return from you when you don't feel you need to file one:

>> The income that the IRS says you didn't report is exempt from tax.

>> The income that the IRS says you failed to report isn't yours. For example, you opened a bank account for your child or for a relative, and you inadvertently gave the bank your own Social Security number.

>> The IRS counted the income twice. Perhaps you reported interest income on a schedule other than the proper one. Or your broker reported your total dividends to the IRS as having been paid by the broker, while you reported those dividends on your return according to the names of the corporations that paid them.

>> You reported income in the wrong year. Maybe someone paid you at the end of the year, but you didn't receive this income until the beginning of the next year — and you reported it in that year.

>> You made a payment to the IRS for which you weren't given credit.

If you think that the IRS's conclusions about your return are wrong, turn to Chapter 19 to find out how to respond to the various types of IRS notices.

We are proposing changes to your tax return — CP-2000

This form cuts right to the chase. It assumes the information that the government received regarding your income that doesn't appear on your return is correct. No questions are asked about whether this information is correct or not. The IRS assumes it's correct, and you're billed for additional tax and interest.

Backup withholding notice

As a trade-off for repeal of the short-lived mandatory withholding on interest and dividends, Congress enacted a system of *backup withholding* if you fail to furnish a payer of taxable income with your Social Security number. The IRS also notifies the payer that backup withholding should be started if you failed to report interest and dividend income on your tax return.

If the IRS determines that backup withholding is required, the payer is informed to withhold tax at the rate of 28 percent. What type of income most often gets hit for this type of withholding? Interest and dividends, payments of more than $600 per year to independent contractors, sales of stocks and bonds, and annual royalties in excess of $10 are usually targeted.

Backup withholding usually applies only to interest and dividend income. Other payments, however, are subject to withholding if you fail to provide the payer with your Social Security number. The IRS doesn't notify you that you're subject to backup withholding — it instead notifies the payer, who is required by law to notify you.

HARDSHIP, IRS STYLE

If backup withholding creates a hardship — that is, you need the dough to live on — you can request that it be stopped. IRS regulations state that undue hardship exists in several forms. For example, you're under hardship if backup withholding — when combined with other withholding and estimated tax payments — produces a substantial overpayment of tax. Or perhaps your ability to pay medical expenses may be affected. Maybe you rely upon interest and dividend income to meet basic living expenses, or you live on a modest fixed income. You're also a hardship case if you've filed a bankruptcy petition or if you're an innocent spouse who had no knowledge of your mate's failure to report all income. See Chapter 20 for more information on the latter topic.

Every October 15, the IRS makes a determination on whether backup withholding should be stopped, such as where there is no underreporting of interest and dividends, or the underreporting has been corrected. If the IRS decides in your favor, backup withholding stops on January 1 of the following year. The two exceptions to the January 1 rule: If the IRS determines that there was no underreporting or that you would suffer undue hardship, it notifies you and informs the payer either not to start backup withholding or to stop backup withholding within 45 days of its determination.

By notifying your local *Taxpayer Advocate* — the IRS problem-solving official (see Chapter 19) — you can stop backup withholding under certain circumstances:

>> You didn't underreport your income.

>> You did underreport — but you paid the tax, interest, and penalties on the unreported income.

>> The backup withholding will cause you undue hardship, and the underreporting probably won't happen again.

If you get hit with backup withholding, file all your returns for delinquent years, start reporting all your income, or pay what you owe. If you do this, the IRS will automatically stop backup withholding on January 1 if everything is in order by the preceding October 15.

Federal tax lien notice — Form 668(F)

A *statutory lien* automatically goes into effect when you neglect or refuse to pay the federal income tax the IRS demands. This type of lien attaches to all property that you own. A statutory lien is sometimes referred to as a secret lien because its validity doesn't depend on its being filed as a matter of public record. Statutory simply means that, under the law, the IRS has the right to do it. They don't have to prove that you failed to pay what you owe before they file a lien. Guilty unless proven innocent? Yup!

Because a statutory lien places the rights of only the IRS ahead of yours, the IRS will usually file a Notice of Lien so that it places itself first in line before your other creditors. (No cutting in line, please!) A federal tax lien covers all of a taxpayer's property, including real estate, cars, bank accounts, and personal property. These liens are filed in accordance with state law, usually with the county clerk, town hall, or court where the taxpayer lives.

WARNING

You should be aware that credit agencies routinely pick up liens that have been filed against you. After a credit agency has this information, your credit is marked as lousy. Even if paid, a lien stays on your credit history for seven years. But wait, it gets even better. If you're unable to pay the taxes you owe, the unpaid lien remains on your credit report for up to 15 years!

Although the law requires that the IRS release a lien within 30 days after it has been paid, the IRS doesn't always comply. Upon paying the tax, you can obtain a release of the lien by either contacting the revenue officer who filed the lien or by following the procedure in IRS Publication 1450 (*A Certificate of Release of Federal Tax Lien*).

Requesting a Collection Due Process Hearing

When the IRS files a Notice of Tax Lien or issues a Levy Notice, the law requires it to inform you of your right to a hearing before the IRS's Appeals Office, where you can protest the filing of the lien, the amount of tax the lien or levy is for, request an installment agreement, make an offer in compromise, or request innocent spouse relief. This is called a Collection Due Process Hearing. You'll receive Form 12153, Request for Collection Due Process Hearing, along with the lien or levy notice. You have 30 days from the date you receive the notice to make the request. The Taxpayer Bill of Rights (discussed in Chapter 20) tells you what to do when the IRS fails to release a lien. The IRS is liable for damages if it fails to release an erroneous lien or a lien that has been paid.

What you can't do at these hearings is re-argue the same issue that you addressed at a previous hearing. The law considers such actions a stalling tactic and allows no second chances when you're caught stalling. You can challenge the underlying amount of tax due only if you never received a Statutory Notice of Deficiency (explained in "Receiving a Statutory Notice of Deficiency" later in this chapter) or if you had no prior opportunity to dispute the tax liability.

If your appeal is rejected, you can appeal to the U.S. Tax Court. If, for some reason, the Tax Court lacks jurisdiction, you can appeal to a federal district court.

Property levy notice — Form 668-A(c)

A Notice of Levy is used to seize your property, and that includes your bank and brokerage accounts. You can kiss your money good-bye 30 days after this levy is served. A Notice of Levy usually isn't issued until after the IRS has exhausted all other possible collection procedures, however. The IRS makes an effort to contact you to try to arrange a payment schedule, and it usually sends at least four prior notices. Remember, you filed a tax return indicating where you work, where you bank, and where you have other assets!

Whenever the IRS issues a Levy Notice, you have the right to request a Collection Due Process Hearing. So, head back to that heading. You can't miss it; it's only a few paragraphs back.

You may be interested in knowing that some assets are exempt from levy:

>> A taxpayer's principal residence — if the amount of the levy doesn't exceed $5,000. When a levy exceeds this limit, the IRS can't grab a residence unless it has the written consent of a U.S. district court judge. Property used in a taxpayer's business can't be seized unless approved by a district director or an assistant district director (the head IRS official for your district), or if the collection of tax is in jeopardy.

>> 85 percent of unemployment benefits.

>> Tools and books of a taxpayer's trade, business, or profession up to a value of $4,290. (This amount is adjusted every year for inflation.)

>> Schoolbooks. (The IRS doesn't want you to stop studying!)

>> Court-ordered child-support payments.

>> Wearing apparel.

>> $8,570 worth of furniture and personal effects, livestock, and poultry. (This amount is adjusted annually for inflation.)

>> Undelivered mail.

>> 85 percent of worker's compensation and non-means–tested welfare payments.

>> Military service disability payments.

>> Certain AFDC (Aid to Families with Dependent Children), Social Security, state and local welfare payments, and Job Training Partnership Act payments.

>> Certain annuity and pension payments.

>> A minimum weekly exemption for wages, salaries, and other income (see "Wage levy notice — Form 668-W(c)" next in this chapter).

Wage levy notice — Form 668-W(c)

Form 668-W(c), Notice of Levy on Wages, Salary, and Other Income, is given to your employer (instead of you) and is used to take a portion of your wages to pay your outstanding tax liability. Whereas a Notice of Levy (see the preceding section) attaches only to property held by a third party (such as a bank) at the time the levy is issued, a wage levy is a continuing one — it applies to all wages, salaries, and commissions owed and to future wages, salaries, and commissions.

Continuous levies that apply to what you'll receive in the future not only cover your salary, but they also cover 15 percent of any unemployment, worker's compensation benefits, and non-means–tested welfare payments you're scheduled to receive. The meek won't inherit the world; the IRS will.

But part of every taxpayer's wages is exempt from levy. This exemption is determined by the taxpayer's filing status and number of dependents. For example, in 2021, a married taxpayer filing jointly with three claimed dependents would be entitled to a weekly exemption of $730.76.

These numbers are adjusted for inflation over the years. IRS Publication 1494 (*Table for Figuring Amount Exempt From Levy on Wages, Salary, and Other Income*) has the exemption amounts.

Handling Non-Assessment Notices

The IRS usually issues a non-assessment notice to inform you of one of the following situations:

>> You forgot to sign a return.

>> You failed to attach a W-2.

>> You omitted a form or schedule.

>> You didn't indicate filing status.

If you receive a non-assessment notice, simply write across it in bold lettering: "INFORMATION REQUESTED IS ATTACHED." Then attach the requested information to the notice and return it to the IRS in the envelope provided. After you provide the IRS with the requested information, the matter usually is closed — unless the information you submit conflicts with information previously reported on your return. If this situation occurs, the IRS will send a notice that assesses additional tax, interest, and possibly a penalty, or that instructs you to contact a particular person at the IRS.

A notice correcting a refund due to you (usually made on Form CP-49) shouldn't be viewed as a non-assessment notice. Just because a notice doesn't demand that you write a check, don't think that the IRS isn't billing you for something. Quite often, the IRS reduces a refund when it assesses additional tax or penalties.

Paying interest on additional tax

The IRS must send a notice of additional tax due within 36 months of the date when you file your return. If it doesn't send a notice before the 36 months are up, it can't charge interest after this 36-month period. Nor can the IRS resume charging interest until 21 days after it gets around to sending a notice.

This provision doesn't cover all notices, so here's what you should know about this 36-month rule:

>> Your return had to be filed on time — otherwise, you're not entitled to this suspension of interest.

>> The failure to file or to pay penalties isn't covered by this rule.

>> Additional tax due as the result of an audit isn't covered.

Receiving a delinquent tax return notice

WARNING

You should treat a delinquent tax return notice as seriously as it sounds. If your tax return is delinquent, you may be contacted by mail, by telephone, or in person. Remember that the IRS has the right to issue a summons commanding you to appear with your tax records and explain why you didn't file a tax return. Any taxpayer who receives a delinquent return notice should consider seeking the services of a qualified tax advisor (see Chapter 2).

Failure to file a required tax return or returns is a criminal violation of the Internal Revenue Code and can result in time in the big house. Usually, the IRS isn't terribly interested in prosecuting the small potatoes who don't owe a huge amount of tax, and saves its prosecutorial dollars for the big spuds who owe the farm. These cases make big headlines, serving as morality tales for everyone else who wonders what would happen if, just once, they "forgot" to file. Extra! Extra! Read all about it!

If you file late returns — even in response to an IRS inquiry — and don't owe a substantial amount of tax (what's considered substantial is known only to the IRS), the IRS probably will accept the return and assess a penalty for late payment and possibly fraud instead of trying to send you to prison (although they do have that option).

If you don't reply to a delinquent return notice, the IRS can take one of the following steps:

>> Refer the case to its Criminal Investigation Unit

>> Issue a summons to appear

>> Refer you to the Audit Division

>> Prepare a "substitute" return

If the IRS decides to prepare a substitute return for you, it will use the information that it has on you in its master file, using the married-filing-separately or filing-as-single tax table, and the standard deduction. Having the IRS prepare your return is the quickest way we know to become separated from your money. Although no fee is involved, you're likely to pay unnecessary tax. Remember, the IRS isn't interested in saving you money.

Why not beat the IRS to the punch? The IRS has an official policy of usually not prosecuting anyone who files a return prior to being contacted and makes arrangements to pay what is owed. Penalties and interest, however, will be assessed. This procedure is called a *voluntary disclosure.* The IRS wants customers back in the fold so badly that it lists voluntary disclosures in a prominent location on its website.

What You Must Know about Audits

On a list of real-life nightmares, most people would rank tax audits right up there with having a tooth pulled without local anesthetic. The primary trauma of an audit is that it makes many people feel like they're on trial and are being accused of a crime. Remain calm!

You may be audited for many reasons, and rarely because the IRS thinks you're a crook. You may receive that audit notice because some of the information on your return doesn't match up with information from third parties, because an IRS data entry operator added (or subtracted) a zero off a number on your return, or because your return deviates from average returns in your neighborhood or your income range. Finally, some returns are plucked at random, and searching for a reason will just make you crazy! About 15 percent of audited returns are left unchanged by the audit — that is, the taxpayers don't end up owing more money. In fact, if you're the lucky sort, you may be one of the rare individuals who actually get a refund because the audit finds a mistake in your favor! Unfortunately, it's more likely that you'll be one of the roughly 85 percent of audit survivors who end up owing more tax money, plus interest. How much hinges on how your audit goes.

Most people would agree that not knowing what to expect in a situation is what's most terrifying about it. This is even truer when dealing with the IRS. Here's what you need to know about audits:

>> **You needn't attend your audit.** An enrolled agent, CPA, or attorney can go in your place.

>> **If at any time during the audit you feel hopelessly confused or realize that you're in over your head, you can ask that the audit or interview be suspended until you can speak to a tax pro.** When you make this request, the IRS must stop asking questions and adjourn the meeting so you can seek help and advice.

>> **The burden of proof is on you.** You're considered to be guilty until proven innocent. Unfortunately, that's how our federal income tax system operates. However, if you and the IRS end up in court, the burden of proof switches to the IRS, provided you meet the IRS's substantiation and record-keeping requirements and present credible evidence. What all this means is that you can't just sit in court and say "Prove it" to the IRS.

>> **Although it's true that the percentage of people being audited is down in recent years, more people are likely to be audited in coming years as the government seeks to beef up tax collections.** The IRS's computers constantly compare the information received from employers, banks, and brokers with the information reported on people's returns. Because of these constant comparisons, millions of taxpayers each year are sent bills totaling billions of dollars.

>> **The IRS can only conduct a financial status audit if a routine examination reveals the likelihood of unreported income.** A financial status audit is conducted when the IRS has you complete Form 4822, Statement of Annual Estimated Personal and Family Expenses, so the IRS can determine how you lived on the income reported on your return.

Surviving the Four Types of Audits

During "normal times" (outside of the recent pandemic) four types of audits exist: office audits, field audits, correspondence audits, and random statistical audits, more commonly referred to as the audits from hell. With all four types of audits, maintaining good records is the key to survival. (Chapter 3 tells you what to do if you're audited and can't produce the needed evidence. If you haven't already taken out the trash and lost all your evidence, you can also refer to Chapter 3 for help filing and organizing the documents you may need.)

Office audits

An *office audit* takes place at an IRS office. The IRS informs a taxpayer that it's scheduling an office audit by sending Notice 904. The front of this notice lists the date, time, and place of the audit, and the back lists the items that the IRS wants to examine.

The audit date isn't chiseled in granite. If you can't gather the information necessary to substantiate the items the IRS is questioning, you can request a postponement. As a general rule, the IRS grants only two postponements unless you can demonstrate a compelling reason for an additional delay, such as an illness or the unavailability of certain tax records.

If you need more time but can't get an additional postponement, go to the audit with the records you have, put on your most confident face, and calmly inform the tax examiner that you need more time to secure the documents you need so that you can substantiate the remaining items the IRS is questioning. The tax examiner then prepares a list of the additional items the IRS needs to complete the audit, together with a mailing envelope so you can mail copies of the requested documents to the IRS.

REMEMBER

Never, ever, mail originals of any of your tax documentation to the IRS. If the additional documents don't lend themselves to easy explanation through correspondence, then schedule a second appointment to complete the audit.

Most office audits are concerned with employee business expenses; itemized deductions such as medical expenses, charitable contributions, tax and interest expense deductions, or miscellaneous itemized deductions; deductions for personal exemptions; and moving-expense deductions.

If the IRS is trying to verify your income, it may want to know about your lifestyle. How will the IRS find out about your lifestyle? You'll tell them, that's how. Auditors are trained to control the interview. They feign ignorance, use appropriate small talk, use "silence" and "humor" appropriately, and avoid overtly taking notes so as not to distract the taxpayer, and they pay attention to the taxpayer's nonverbal language. The IRS even has a form to flush out lifestyle information, Form 4822, Statement of Annual Estimated Personal and Family Expenses, which — thank heaven — the IRS can now only spring on you when a routine examination has established the likelihood of unreported income. The form asks all about your expenses, from groceries to insurance — anything you and your family would spend money for as consumers. We don't know what it is about this form, but when the IRS shoves it under someone's nose, many taxpayers can't resist the urge to respond, "I'll show them what it costs to live in this country."

REMEMBER

What most people are unaware of is that you're under no obligation to fill out this form. The law only requires you to fill out and file a tax return. Statistical research has revealed that the IRS can collect more tax by examining sources of income than by examining deductions. If you operate a small business or have rental income, be prepared to explain where every deposit into your bank account came from.

Field audits

Field audits are conducted at a taxpayer's place of business. These audits focus on business returns and complex individual returns. If you file Form 1040, Schedule C, you're a likely candidate for a field audit.

Again, be prepared to verify the source of every deposit into your bank account. Field agents are required to survey both your preceding and subsequent years' tax returns to determine whether similar items were treated in a consistent manner. If an audit results in a significant increase in tax, you are now suspect, and the tax examiner will audit your subsequent years' tax returns (which normally are only surveyed).

DECIDING WHERE YOUR AUDIT HAPPENS

Both field and office audits are conducted in the district where a return was filed. This practice may create a burden if you live in one district and are employed or have your business located in another. For example, if you work or your business is located in Manhattan and you live in Connecticut, you normally would be contacted by the examination branch in Connecticut. If your tax records are in Manhattan or you spend most of your time there, you can request that the examination be transferred to the Manhattan District.

Besides gaining the convenience of having the audit conducted where your records, your advisor, or your business is located, you also get a little more time to pull together your tax data.

To transfer an audit from one district to another, call the IRS auditor and tell that person why you want to transfer the audit to a different district. The transfer usually takes two to three months. The IRS also requires that you request the transfer in writing.

The following note will suffice when requesting that a tax examination be transferred from one IRS district to another:

[your address]

[date]

District Director

[address of district that issued exam notice]

Re: [your name and your Social Security number]

[exam year]

Dear District Director:

Because my tax records are located in [for example, Manhattan] and I spend most of my time there, I respectfully request that the audit you have scheduled be transferred to the [for example, Manhattan] District.

You may contact me during business hours at [telephone number]. Thank you in advance for your prompt attention to this request.

Very truly yours,

[your name]

Enclosed: Copy of exam notice

An office audit specifies what items will be examined from the very beginning of the process. Not so with a field audit — tax examiners have a great deal of discretion as to what items they review and to what depth they review the items. Count on having to verify your total income, travel and entertainment expenses, gifts, automobile expenses, commissions, payments to independent contractors, and any expenses that appear large in relation to the size of your business.

A tax examiner may examine each and every deduction or merely select a month or two of expenses and examine them on a sample basis. If they don't turn up any discrepancies, the examiner will accept the rest of the expenses for that category as correct.

Correspondence audits

Correspondence audits are exactly what the name suggests. The IRS conducts correspondence audits completely by mail and limits them to a few key areas of individual returns, such as itemized deductions, casualty or theft losses, employee business expenses, IRA and other retirement plan payments, dependency deductions, childcare and earned income credits, deductions for forfeited interest on early withdrawals from savings accounts, and exclusion from income of disability payments. Income items may also be examined by a correspondence audit.

If you're ever the proud subject of a correspondence audit, the IRS gives you a return envelope in which to submit your documents, canceled checks, bills, and statements to substantiate the items the IRS questions. Again, never send original documents — only copies. Retaining the originals is crucial in case you have to stare down further inquiries, or if the IRS (or the USPS) does the unthinkable and loses your documentation.

When it comes to substantiating any deduction, the burden of proof is on you. If what you must substantiate is complex or requires a detailed explanation, you can ask for an interview in which you can explain in person.

Random statistical audits

Although it's extremely unlikely, your return may be selected at random for an audit, just because the IRS can. These *random statistical audits* are used to gather information to determine pockets of tax cheating and errors. The IRS, however, never uses those words. It refers to failing to report income or inflating deductions as "noncompliance."

Under its research program, the IRS annually selects certain types of taxpayers' returns (waiters, taxi drivers, freelance writers, and so on) so it can measure the degree of tax compliance for particular industries, trades, or professions. On the basis of these audits, the IRS National Office determines which areas require stricter or greater enforcement efforts. Although being on the receiving end of one of these audit notices is never fun, in this environment of large federal budget deficits, the IRS is unlikely to suspend this current project.

If you are selected for a random statistical audit, the IRS may review your return in the following ways: computer checking, correspondence, and face-to-face. Everything is subject to verification, but in most cases, only certain lines will be checked. Be prepared, though, to provide your children's birth certificates to prove you're entitled to claim your kids as dependents. If something smells fishy or doesn't look right, you can count on being questioned in detail about the matter. The IRS looks under every rock, including matching up cash settlements you may have received in a personal injury lawsuit, for example.

Questioning Repetitive Audits

It's IRS policy not to examine an individual's tax return if the taxpayer has been examined for the same issue(s) in either of the two preceding years and the audit resulted in no (or only a small) tax change.

If you receive a notice of an audit questioning the same item(s) questioned in a previous audit, call the agent and inform him them that the IRS audited the same issue(s) in one of the two prior years with little or no change in tax. (And do note that the IRS has never bothered to define *little*. Changes of less than a few hundred dollars in tax, however, should meet this criterion.) The tax examiner will ask you to furnish proof. Mail the examiner a copy of the IRS notice that your prior return was accepted without change or mail the notice that adjusted your return.

If you can't document that the IRS is questioning items that it already questioned — with no change in tax — in one of the two preceding years, the lack of documentation doesn't mean that you can't get the current examination canceled. Just inform the examining agent by telephone about the prior year's tax examination. The tax examiner will postpone the audit and request a Record of your Tax Account Information from the two preceding years. If your tax account supports your contention, the IRS will cancel the audit.

Getting Ready for an Audit

Preparing for an audit is sort of like preparing for a test in school: The IRS informs you of which sections of your tax return the agency wants to examine so that you know what to "study." The first decision you face when you get an audit notice is whether to handle it yourself or to turn to a tax advisor to represent you. Hiring representation costs money but saves you time, stress, and possibly money.

If you normally prepare your own return and are comfortable with your understanding of the areas being audited, represent yourself. If the IRS is merely asking you to substantiate deductions, you'll probably do all right on your own. However, make sure you read "What You Must Know about Audits" earlier in this chapter.

What constitutes substantiation may at times involve a somewhat complicated interpretation of the law and its accompanying regulations. If the amount of tax money in question is small compared to the fee you'd pay a tax advisor to represent you, self-representation is probably the answer. However, if you're likely to turn into a babbling, intimidated fool and are unsure of how to present your situation, hire a tax advisor to represent you.

WHO CAN REPRESENT YOU IN AN AUDIT?

The IRS permits three types of individuals to fully represent taxpayers before the IRS: enrolled agents, certified public accountants, and attorneys. All three are bound by IRS rules of practice. (Tax preparers can still represent you at an audit but not in any appeals beyond that, but recent bills in Congress seem to support limiting unenrolled preparers from providing this service much longer.)

Enrolled agents (EAs) become enrolled to practice before the IRS by passing a two-day written examination administered by the IRS in which their knowledge of the tax code is tested. Alternatively, they must have at least five years of experience as an IRS tax auditor. Attorneys and certified public accountants are the other two groups permitted to represent taxpayers before the IRS. Many states have continuing education requirements for CPAs and attorneys. The IRS requires that EAs also meet continuing education requirements.

Probably the best way to find a qualified tax professional is to ask a relative or friend for a recommendation of someone whose level of service and performance they are more than satisfied with. To figure out which of these tax practitioners may be best suited to help you in an audit, be sure to read Chapter 2.

REMEMBER

Changing your mind regarding representation partway through the audit is okay. At any time during the examination — such as when you feel a dizzy sensation and before you throw up in the examiner's lap — the Taxpayer Bill of Rights allows you to request that the audit be suspended until you have time to consult with an enrolled agent, a certified public accountant, or an attorney. After you make this request, the IRS agent must stop asking questions or requesting documents until you're properly represented.

But if you do decide to handle the audit yourself, get your act together sooner rather than later. Don't wait until the night before to start gathering receipts and other documentation. You may discover, for example, that you can't find certain documents.

You need to document and be ready to speak with the auditor about the areas the audit notice said were being investigated. Organize the various documents and receipts in folders. You want to make it as easy as possible for the auditor to review your materials. Don't show up, dump shopping bags full of receipts and paperwork on the auditor's desk, and say, "Here it is — you figure it out."

Don't bring documentation for parts of your return that aren't being audited, either. Besides creating more work for yourself, you're required to discuss only those areas mentioned in the audit letter.

Whatever you do, don't ignore your audit request letter. The Internal Revenue Service is the ultimate bill-collection agency. And if you end up owing more money (the unhappy result of most audits), the sooner you pay, the less interest and penalties you'll owe.

Winning Your Audit

Two people with identical situations can walk into an audit and come out with very different results. The loser can end up owing much more in taxes and having the audit expanded to include other parts of the return. The winner can end up owing less tax money.

REMEMBER

Here's how to be a winner:

» **Treat the auditor as a human being.** Although this seems like obvious advice, your anger and resentment at being audited won't win you any points with your examiner. The examiner is just doing their job and knows you're busy and have other things to do. Ranting and raving in front of the auditor is likely to make them search extra hard for places where your return may be dicey. Treating the examiner with respect and courtesy will make the audit a much easier experience for everyone concerned.

» **Stick to the knitting.** You're there to discuss only the sections of your tax return in question. Don't volunteer other information unless you want the examiner to look at those areas as well.

» **Discuss and don't argue.** State your case. If the auditor wants to disallow a deduction or otherwise increase the tax you owe and you don't agree, state only once why you don't agree. If the auditor won't budge, don't get into a knockdown, drag-out confrontation. The auditor may not want to lose face and will only feel inclined to find additional tax money — that's the auditor's job. Remember that you can plead your case with several layers of people above your auditor. If that course fails and you still feel wronged, you can take your case to Tax Court.

» **Don't be intimidated.** Just because IRS auditors have the authority of the government behind them, that doesn't make them right or all-knowing. The audit is only round one. If you disagree with the results, you have the right to appeal.

» **Appeal the results of an audit, if necessary.** If you're dissatisfied with the results of an audit, refer to "Appealing the results of an audit" later in this chapter to figure out how to make an appeal.

» **Go to Tax Court.** If you receive a Statutory Notice of Deficiency (this notice comes after you have exhausted all your appeals within the IRS or if you don't respond to a notice that the IRS wants to audit your return), you have 90 days to appeal your case to the U.S. Tax Court. If you don't appeal, the IRS can enforce collection on the 91st day. Refer to "Receiving a Statutory Notice of Deficiency" at the end of this chapter for more information.

Understanding the Statute of Limitations on Audits

The IRS must make any assessment of tax, penalties, or interest within three years from the due date for filing a tax return. If the IRS grants you an extension of the filing deadline, the statute of limitations is extended to include the extension period. If the due date falls on a legal holiday or a Saturday or Sunday, the due date is postponed to the next business day.

YOUR STATE INCOME TAX RETURN AND THE IRS

The IRS and states have an agreement calling for the exchange of information about taxpayers. Under these agreements, individual states and the IRS notify each other about taxpayers who failed to file returns and when either a state or the IRS has adjusted a taxpayer's taxable income.

The tax laws of most states provide that if the IRS has adjusted your tax return, you must file an amended state income tax return with that state within 30 to 90 days of the IRS's adjustment. The amended state return must reflect the adjustments made by the IRS, and you must pay any additional tax plus interest. If an amended return isn't filed, your state's tax collector, upon receiving notice of the adjustments from the IRS, will send a demand for additional tax and interest and possibly a penalty for not notifying the state within the required time frame.

Here's how the statute of limitations works: The IRS must make an assessment regarding a 2021 tax return by April 15, 2025, three years from the April 15, 2022, due date. After the 2025 deadline, the IRS can make no demand for additional tax. If a return is filed after the due date, the three-year period starts on the date the return is filed. However, if you file your return on or before April 15, 2022, the three-year statute of limitations still expires on April 15, 2025.

If more than 25 percent of the income that you're required to report is omitted from your return, the statute of limitations extends to six years. No statute of limitations runs on a false or fraudulent return. Thus, if a false or fraudulent return was filed, there's no time limit on when the government can assess additional tax. The same goes for not filing a return; there's no time limit.

Extending the statute of limitations

If the statute of limitations is about to expire and you haven't resolved your problems with the IRS, you'll be asked to agree to extend the statute of limitations. If you don't agree, the IRS will immediately assess your tax based on the information it has.

The only way to stop the IRS from forcing you to pay the tax is to file a petition with the Tax Court within a 90-day period. Although IRS Publication 1035 (*Extending the Tax Assessment Period*) explains this process, our advice is to see a professional if you ever get into water this hot.

The statute of limitations on tax collection is . . .

Ten years — period. After ten years, the IRS can't collect a dime. The ten-year assessment period starts on the day the IRS receives your return or on April 15, whichever is later. For purposes of the statute of limitations, returns filed early are considered filed on April 15. However, if the government increases your tax or makes an adjustment, the ten years on the additional tax owed starts to run from the date of the additional assessment. The reason the IRS still can go after financier Marc Rich (the second most famous tax evader after Al Capone) after all these years for the hundreds of millions he owes is because the ten-year statute of limitations is suspended when a taxpayer (if you can call them that) is continuously out of the country for more than six months.

If the ten-year period is about to expire, the IRS usually attempts to extend the period by getting you to sign Form 900, Tax Collection Waiver. More often than not, the IRS will threaten to seize everything under the sun that you own unless you agree to sign. Here's when you absolutely need professional help — and not just any tax advisor, but someone who is an expert and specializes in these types of cases. Ask people that you trust for suggestions of people to contact.

Since January 1, 2000, the IRS is allowed an extension of the ten-year statute of limitations on collection only where it has issued a levy, entered into an installment, or instituted court action. Such suits, however, are rare.

If you have an installment agreement in force, the ten-year period isn't automatically extended until you pay off what you owe. The terms of the agreement at the time you and the IRS entered into it govern how long the government has to collect what you owe. If the agreement is silent as to the collection statute, it's ten years. So be careful what you sign when you request an installment agreement.

Appealing the results of an audit

The IRS issues Form 4549-A, Income Tax Examination Changes, and Form 1902-B, Report of Individual Tax Examination Changes, after an audit has been completed. Form 4549-A spells out any adjustments to income and expenses that have been made and any penalties and interest that are due.

These notices often are referred to as *30-day letters*. Within 30 days after receipt of an audit notice, you must agree to the adjustment, submit additional information explaining why an adjustment shouldn't be made, or request a hearing before the Appeals Division.

If you disagree with the proposed adjustment, and the amount of tax is more than $25,000, a written protest must be filed. IRS Publication 5 *(Your Appeal Rights and How To Prepare a Protest If You Don't Agree)* is extremely helpful in preparing a protest. Consider retaining a tax advisor when protesting large sums. This written protest is akin to a legal brief lawyers submit in outlining a case.

Appeals, you guessed it, are made to the Appeals Office, whose purpose is to settle disputes. The IRS agent who examined your return has no authority to take into account the time and expense to the IRS and the possibility that the IRS may lose in court. An appeals officer can. Approximately 90 percent of all cases referred to the Appeals Office are settled.

If the amount involved isn't more than $25,000, a formal written protest isn't required. A simple statement explaining the changes you don't agree with and why you feel your deduction should be allowed is all that is necessary.

The IRS also issues a 30-day letter if you fail to show up for an audit. In such an instance, the examining agent will review your return and make adjustments to both income and deductions that the agent deems warranted.

If you receive a 30-day letter because you failed to show — even if you missed the audit because you never received the original notice scheduling it — contact the agent at the number given on the letter and schedule an audit appointment. If you make a new appointment within 30 days, the examining agent or appointment clerk will place a hold on your adjusted return (that is, it won't be processed), pending the outcome of the rescheduled audit.

After completing the audit, the IRS issues a new notice of income tax changes that supersedes the preceding one. If you agree to the audit changes and sign off on them, you can pay what you owe at that time, or you can wait to be billed.

Receiving a Statutory Notice of Deficiency

Although a notice (such as one proposing income tax changes) informs a taxpayer that additional tax is due, the IRS can't legally enforce the collection of additional tax until a *Statutory Notice of Deficiency* — often referred to as a *90-day letter* — is sent to a taxpayer by certified mail at the taxpayer's last known address.

A Statutory Notice of Deficiency isn't required if additional tax is due because of a math error. Statutory Notices are generally required only if additional tax is due as the result of the IRS adjusting a taxpayer's income, deductions, or credits from what was originally reported on the tax return the taxpayer filed. Unless a petition is filed with the U.S. Tax Court in Washington, D.C., within 90 days of receipt of a Statutory Notice, the IRS can initiate collection action at the end of the 90-day period. If you file a petition with the Tax Court, all collection action is delayed until 60 days after the court renders its decision. If you live outside the United States, the 90-day period for filing a petition is extended to 150 days. The address of the Tax Court is included on the notice, but we give it to you here anyway, just in case:

> 400 Second Street, N.W.
>
> Washington, DC 20217

The notice will indicate when the 90-day period expires. If your petition gets lost in the mail or arrives late, you're out of luck. However, a certified mail, UPS, FedEx, or similar receipt showing that the petition was sent to the Tax Court within the 90-day period will save the day.

IN THIS CHAPTER

» **Demystifying IRS mistakes**

» **Responding to notices**

» **Mastering the generic response form**

» **Dealing with a nonresponsive IRS**

» **Finding a lost refund**

Chapter **19**

Fixing Mistakes the IRS Makes

lthough the IRS is reluctant to admit it, it does make mistakes. In fairness to the IRS, collecting taxes from more than 140 million individuals (not to mention all the returns from corporations, partnerships, trusts, estates, and other assorted entities) under an extraordinarily complex tax system is, to say the least, difficult. The number of errors can appear to be limitless, but most errors occur for simple reasons.

We wish we could explain why the IRS can't get it right the first time. We can't. But we can give you an idea of the number of mistakes made, the types of mistakes, and the action that you can take. We also can — and do! — offer tips to keep you away from the IRS paper trail.

The IRS processes more than a billion transactions a year. So, math wizard, what does an error rate of, say, 1 percent translate into? Ten million errors! That's a whole bunch of errors. In this chapter, we show you the types of mistakes the IRS is most likely to make, tell you how to respond effectively, help you find an advocate when you need one, and — last but not least — assist you in locating a refund that doesn't come when it should.

Seeing the Types of Mistakes the IRS Makes

The following is a long list of the types of flubs the IRS can make:

>> **Misapplied payments:** The IRS may not have posted tax payments that you made to your tax account (under your Social Security number). Payments are sometimes posted to the wrong year or type of tax. Perhaps the IRS didn't properly post overpayments from a preceding or subsequent year.

>> **Misunderstood date:** The IRS may claim that you didn't file or pay tax on time. Computers at a service center may not acknowledge that the due date for filing or paying fell on a legal holiday or on a Saturday or Sunday and may therefore blame you for filing late, when in fact you filed on the first business day following a legal holiday or a Saturday or Sunday. Or perhaps you had a valid extension of time to file, but the IRS said that you filed your tax return late.

>> **Wrong Social Security/ID number:** A data processing clerk may incorrectly input your Social Security number, or you may have been assigned two numbers. Because all data on a joint return is recorded under the Social Security number of the spouse whose name is listed first, any payments or credits that the other spouse made may not be posted under the first spouse's number. This situation frequently occurs when taxpayers file jointly for the first time or when a taxpayer files separately after having filed jointly in a prior year.

>> **Wrong income:** Income earned by another person may be inadvertently reported under your Social Security number. This often happens when a taxpayer opens a bank account for a child or another relative.

>> **Exempt income:** Money you earned on your IRA, SEP-IRA, pension account, or from municipal bond investments may be reported to the IRS as being taxable.

>> **Double-counted income:** Income earned from a taxpayer's business or profession may be recorded as income from wages — or vice versa — and the IRS moved the income to the line or schedule on the taxpayer's return where it correctly belongs. That's okay, but sometimes the IRS moves the income without removing it from the line or schedule where it first was incorrectly entered!

>> **Lost return:** The IRS or the U.S. Postal Service (or other approved private delivery service such as DHL, FedEx, or UPS) may have lost your return and payment, leaving you in the unenviable position of having to prove the timely filing of the return. Hopefully you made a copy and sent the original by an approved method, either certified mail from the post office, or an approved private delivery service!

>> **Partially corrected error:** The IRS may have corrected only one of the errors that were previously made. For example, an IRS error may be corrected, but the penalties and interest that were incorrectly charged may not have been removed.

>> **Data processing error:** A computer bug — or another unexplained phenomenon — may have caused a notice to be issued stating that a math error on your return was made where no error exists. Or someone may have failed to input all the data from the schedules attached to your return into the IRS computer.

Data processing errors are common with Form 2210, Underpayment of Estimated Tax by Individuals, Estates, and Trusts, where a taxpayer claims an exemption from the penalty for underestimating the amount of their required estimated tax payments. This type of error usually causes the IRS either to assess a penalty when it shouldn't or to issue a refund for the underestimating penalty that the taxpayer has paid.

>> **Incorrect 1099:** The IRS may receive an incorrect Form 1099 from a bank or brokerage firm — either the amount of income reported on the form is wrong or the income isn't yours. Even if the payer corrects it (and files the correction with the IRS), the correction may never make it into the IRS computer. Don't you just hate it when that happens?

Corresponding with the IRS: The Basics

TIP

There is elegance in simplicity when corresponding with the IRS. Keep to the point. No letter should be longer than one page (sorry, you can't email them). A half page gets even quicker results. Remember, the tax examiner reviewing your inquiry may have little experience in the area you're writing about. Such people are, however, extremely conscientious in performing their duties. You stand a better chance of achieving the results you want by making their jobs as easy as possible. Don't succumb to the temptation to go into a narrative on how unfair our tax system is or how you're paying more than your fair share. Save that stuff for your representative in Congress.

Your letter to the IRS should contain the following items — and nothing more:

>> Vital facts: your name, mailing address, Social Security number on the tax return, and the year of the disputed tax return

>> The control number from the notice, the type of tax, and a copy of the notice you received (refer to Chapter 16 to find out how to get your hands on this information)

>> The type of mistake the IRS made

>> The action you want the IRS to take

>> Copies of the documents necessary to prove your case — canceled checks, corrected Form 1099s, mailing receipts — but *never* the originals

Address your letter to the Adjustments/Correspondence (A/C) Branch at the service center that issued the notice. You should note the type of request you're making at the extreme top of the letter — REQUEST TO ADJUST FORM [form number]. Use the bar-coded envelope that was sent with the notice to mail your letter.

Include a simple thank-you and the telephone number where you can be reached in case the clerk at the IRS Service Center has any questions. Telephone contact between you and an IRS employee can take weeks off the Adjustments/Correspondence process. See Figure 19-1 for an example of a generic "Dear IRS" letter. This example addresses an adjustment to be made to Form CP-2000.

Request to Adjust Form CP-2000

[your address]
[date]

Adjustments/Correspondence Branch
Internal Revenue Service Center
[address]

Re: [your name, Social Security
number]
[tax year, DLN]

Dear IRS:

I have received your notice dated [date], in which you claim that I failed to report [$] of interest on my tax return.

Please be advised that your notice, a copy of which is enclosed, is incorrect. The interest that you claimed I earned was in fact earned on my daughter's bank account. Her Social Security number is [number], which should have been given to the bank, instead of mine, when the account was opened.

Please adjust your notice to reflect that no additional tax is due. Thank you for your prompt attention to this request. I can be reached at [phone number] should you require any additional information.

Very truly yours,
[your name]

FIGURE 19-1:
Here's how to compose a "Dear IRS" letter that gets right to the point.

Upon receipt of your letter, the A/C Branch is supposed to stop the computer from sending further notices until the matter is resolved, although you'll likely receive the next notice that was already in the pipeline. If your problem can't be resolved in seven days, you'll be sent a letter indicating when it can be resolved. If you receive a second notice, don't be alarmed. This delay isn't unusual. The IRS doesn't move all that fast. And delays greatly expanded as mail piled up during the COVID-19 pandemic shutdowns, but as we head into 2022, the IRS backlog is far more reasonable.

If 30 days go by and you haven't heard from the IRS or you receive a third notice, see the section "Getting Attention When the IRS Appears to Be Ignoring You" later in this chapter.

Sending a Simple Response to a Balance Due Notice

TIP

If you receive a balance-due notice for a tax that already has been paid, it's time to dig out the proof you kept that shows when and how much you paid. With proof in hand, it's a simple matter to write on the front of the notice:

"This balance has been paid. Enclosed is a copy of proof of payment of taxes that you have failed to credit to my account. Please remove all penalties and interest charges that were assessed."

If you paid by check, send a copy, front and back, of the cancelled check. For credit card payments, a copy of your credit card bill, with the date and amount of the payment to the IRS highlighted, should suffice. If the funds were transferred directly from your bank account through electronic funds transfer, send a highlighted copy of your bank statement that shows the amount taken from your account and the date. And, if you're enrolled in the Electronic Federal Tax Payment System (EFTPS), include a copy of the Electronic Funds Transfer (EFT) Acknowledgment and Number you received as a receipt.

Sending Generic Responses to Generic Notices

If you're like us, you probably dislike form letters with a passion. At times, however, you have no choice but to fight fire with fire. To simplify things, we've included an all-purpose generic response letter (see Figure 19-2).

Generic Response Letter
Request to adjust Form [number]
[your address]
[date]

Adjustments/Correspondence Branch
Internal Revenue Service Center
[address]

Re: [your name, Social Security
number]
[tax year, DLN, Form number]

Dear IRS:
I am in receipt of your notice dated [date] (copy enclosed). Please be advised that your notice is incorrect.

[Insert generic paragraph(s) we have provided pertaining to one of the issues to be corrected.]

I would appreciate your adjusting the notice that you sent me now that you have the information contained in this letter that was previously unknown to you.

I would also appreciate your abating any penalties and interest that were incorrectly assessed.

I thank you in advance for your prompt attention to this request. I can be reached at [number] should you have any questions.

Very truly yours,
[your name]

Enclosed: Notice [number]

You can use this letter simply by inserting any one of the following responses to frequent IRS errors. To keep it simple, we list the IRS error you want to address as the heading, and the response you can use appears beneath it, indented and between quotation marks. We also include some explanatory text without quotes.

REMEMBER

Just because we keep referring to canceled checks in these examples doesn't mean that you've paid your taxes by check. If you used one of the other approved payment methods, such as electronic funds transfer, credit card, or the Electronic Federal Tax Payment System, just fill in the appropriate method of payment and provide the necessary proof. (See the previous section for more on documentation of proof.)

Misapplied payments

"Enclosed is a copy of my canceled check, front and back, showing that the tax was paid."

Misunderstood due date

Here are several solutions to common problems with due dates.

Due date for filing or paying fell on Saturday, Sunday, or legal holiday

"Please be advised that your notice incorrectly penalizes me for filing/paying late. The due date for filing/paying fell on a [Saturday], and I made payment/filed on the next business day. Enclosed is a copy of my check dated [date], which is dated the date of the extended due date, as allowed by law. The serial number on the back of the check clearly indicates that the IRS negotiated my check on [date].

"Please correct your records to reflect that my return/payment was timely and remove all penalties and interest that were charged."

Valid extension of time to file

"Your notice incorrectly assesses a penalty for late filing. Enclosed is a copy of my extension that granted me an extension of time to file until [date]. I filed my return prior to the expiration of the extension on [date].

"Please correct your records by removing the penalties and interest that were incorrectly assessed."

TIP

Enclose a copy of any canceled check that may have accompanied the extension and refer to the check in the letter. If you have it, also enclose a copy of your certified mail or private delivery service receipt, clearly showing the postmark or other date it was mailed.

Late filing

If you mailed your return on time with a balance due that you didn't pay — and the IRS sent a notice demanding the balance plus an erroneous late-filing penalty — be prepared for lengthy correspondence with the IRS. If you mailed your return, but you don't have proof of timely mailing, you're out of luck. Many folks today file electronically and have proof of that, such as through a confirming email.

> "Your notice incorrectly assessed a late-filing penalty in the amount of [amount]. Please be advised that my return was timely filed on [date].

> "I am enclosing a copy of my electronic filing receipt (or certified mail receipt) that clearly shows this return was timely filed."

If you file on time and enter into an agreement to pay in installments, the late payment penalty gets reduced from 0.5 percent a month to 0.25 percent a month while you're making payments. See Chapter 20 if you can't pay on time. The total late payment penalty that can be charged can't exceed 25 percent of the tax owed.

Wrong income

> "The income on which you claim I owe additional tax per your notice isn't my income. The bank/broker/insurance company [or whatever] incorrectly reported the income that was earned on this account as belonging to me. This account, in fact, belongs to my [mother, for example], who reported it on her tax return for the year in question. Her Social Security number is [123-45-6789].

> "Enclosed, please find a copy of my [mother's] tax return and a statement from her stating that the balance in the account you are questioning belongs to her. I have instructed the bank to correct its records. Please correct yours so that my tax account reflects that no tax is owed."

Exempt income

We're constantly amazed when we review returns that clients prepared themselves. One thing that crops up all the time is how often they pay tax on income when they don't have to. Here are two prominent examples and the appropriate response when the IRS sends a bill for tax due on tax-exempt income.

Retirement account

> "The income on which you claim I owe additional tax is income earned from my [type of retirement] account and is exempt from tax. Enclosed is a copy of my year-end statement of that account. Please note that the number of this account is the same as the number that appears on your notice. Please correct your records so my tax account shows that no additional tax is owed your agency."

Municipal bonds

> "The income on which you claim I owe additional tax is tax-exempt municipal bond interest. Enclosed is a corrected statement from my broker/bank that clearly identifies that the amount of income reported on your notice is tax-exempt municipal bond interest. Please correct your records so my tax account shows that no tax is owed your agency."

Double-counted income

"The interest income you claim I failed to report on my tax return for the year in question was, in fact, reported on Schedule C of my return (copy enclosed). By adjusting Schedule B (Interest and Dividend Income) of my tax return without adjusting my Schedule C, you are requiring me to pay tax on the same item of income twice by double-counting it. Please correct your records so my tax account reflects that no tax is owed your agency."

Lost return

This is a tough one. But one secret the IRS closely guards is that it frequently loses or misplaces tax returns. The IRS even has a form letter when this happens. The letter requests that you send a duplicate. Unfortunately, when you do, you're likely to receive a follow-up notice saying that the IRS received the duplicate, but that it was filed late! When you file a duplicate return, always mark the top in bold lettering: "Duplicate — Original Filed (insert date)."

Refund return

"Enclosed is a copy of my return that your notice claimed was not filed. Please be advised that this return, which indicated a refund due, was filed on [date]."

If you have a filing receipt for the return, enclose a copy of it.

Balance due return

"Enclosed is a copy of the return that your notice (copy enclosed) dated [date] claimed was not filed. Please be advised that my return was mailed on [date]. However, as of this date, my check number [number] dated [date] that accompanied my tax return hasn't been returned to me by my bank.

"I call your attention to Estate of Wood, 92TC No.46 and Sorrentino, 171 FSupp2d 1150, cases in which the courts held that a timely mailed return is presumed to have been received by the IRS.

"I would appreciate your correcting your records to reflect that this return was timely filed. If you would be kind enough to send me a bill for the balance I owe without reference to any penalties, I will remit full payment on receipt of your bill."

TIP

If, in fact, you sent a payment for the balance due with your return that has now been lost, verify that your bank hasn't already charged your account before you authorize another payment. A cashed check or other debit supports your assertion that you timely filed the original return, and you don't want to pay the taxes twice. If your bank has cashed the check, then get a front-and-back copy and send it with your duplicate return. If your payment hasn't cleared, stop payment on it and send a fresh payment with the duplicate return. Including a copy of the stop-payment order is a good idea; remember that you're trying to establish that the original return was timely filed. The more proof you can provide, the likelier the IRS will see things your way.

Enclose any proof of mailing or other method of filing that you have.

Lost check

"Please be advised that my check, number [number], dated [date], was attached to my return that I filed on [date]. Because my bank still hasn't returned my check, I am placing a stop payment on it and have issued a new check for the same amount as the original check. I am enclosing a copy of my bank's stop-payment order. Kindly abate the interest that you charged on your notice. It would be unfair to charge me interest because your agency can't locate my check."

Tax assessed after statute of limitations

REMEMBER

By filing a Form 911, Request for Taxpayer Advocate Service Assistance (And Application for Taxpayer Assistance Order), or TAO, you put the IRS on notice that it may be liable for damages and costs up to $1 million resulting from its reckless and intentional behavior in dunning you. If the IRS's actions merely are negligent, you can collect damages and costs up to $100,000. TAOs are covered under the Taxpayer Bill of Rights, which we discuss in Chapter 20. This form is filed with the office of the IRS's Taxpayer Advocate in your area. You can get a copy of Form 911 by calling 800-829-3676, or you can fill out the form online at www.irs.gov. The downside of filing this form is that the statute of limitations is extended while this application is pending (see Chapter 18).

To cover all bases, write to the Adjustments/Correspondence Branch at the service center that issued the assessment.

"Please be advised that your assessment for additional tax, penalties, and interest was issued in violation of the statute of limitations. The time for making an additional assessment for the year in question expired on [date].

"Please remove this assessment from my tax account, along with any interest or penalties that were charged. The assessment you made is in direct violation of the law. An assessment must be made within three years after the return is filed. This assessment doesn't comply with that requirement."

Refer to Chapter 18 for more on the statute of limitations.

Partially corrected error

"Please make the following adjustment [insert] as requested in my original letter of [date] (copy enclosed) that your current notice [date] failed to adjust."

TIP

At this point, you may want to refer the matter to the local Taxpayer Advocate Office. (See "Getting Attention When the IRS Appears to Be Ignoring You," later in this chapter.)

Erroneous refund

Remember what your mother told you about keeping money that doesn't belong to you? She was right, of course — maybe because she had to deal with the IRS. As a practical matter, if you want to save yourself a great deal of time corresponding with the IRS, deposit the check, but don't spend the money (sorry). You ultimately will receive a bill for it. You may be asking, "Why not just return the check?" The problem with doing that is, if the IRS doesn't get its paperwork right, you won't have the money, but you will have a bill from the IRS demanding repayment.

You returned a refund check

"Enclosed is a refund check that was incorrectly issued to me."

If you choose to return the check, return it to the service center where you filed your return, not to the Treasury Department office that issued the check. Send this letter by certified mail and request a return receipt. This is one letter that you want to be able to prove that you sent and that they received.

You didn't return a refund check sent to you by mistake

"Your notice demanding interest on a refund sent to me in error is assessed in violation of the law. I discovered the error only when I received your notice demanding repayment. I call your attention to the fact that Section 6404(e)(2) of the Internal Revenue Code states that no interest may be charged if a taxpayer who receives an erroneous refund of $50,000 or less repays it when the IRS demands payment. Enclosed please find my check in the amount of the tax that was incorrectly refunded. Please correct your notice by removing the interest that you shouldn't have charged me."

If this approach doesn't work, contact the IRS Taxpayer Advocate in your area (see the section "Contacting the local Taxpayer Advocate" in this chapter).

Data-processing error

WARNING

A data-processing problem is probably the most difficult to cope with.

"Your notice incorrectly states that [choose appropriate problem(s)]:

(a) A mathematical error was made.

(b) I used the wrong tax table in computing my tax.

(c) I incorrectly claimed a credit.

"Please be advised that I rechecked my return and do not believe that any error was made. Enclosed is a copy of my return. Please review it and advise me exactly where you believe an error was made."

Incorrect 1099

Use (a) or (b) when appropriate.

(a) "Your notice incorrectly claims that I failed to report all the income I received from [name]."

(b) "Please be advised that the 1099 information that you received from [name] is incorrect."

"I have enclosed a copy of a corrected 1099 that [name] has reissued to me.

"I would appreciate your adjusting my tax account to reflect the information contained in the corrected 1099. When this is done, you will readily see that no additional tax is due."

TIP

Always try to get the 1099 corrected and send along a copy of the new one. Forms 1099 have to, by law, list the names, addresses, and telephone numbers of whom you can contact when the 1099 is wrong.

Wrong year

"The miscellaneous income your notice claims I failed to report for the year in question was not received until the following year and was reported on that year's return (copy enclosed). Additionally, I am enclosing a copy of my bank statement for the month in which this income was received. You will notice that this bank statement bears the following year's date."

Never received prior notices

"You don't have my correct address, which is probably why I never received your prior notices. Please send me copies of these notices so I can determine whether the most current notice that I have enclosed is correct. If it is, I will pay the amount I owe upon receipt of the prior notices I never received. If it is not correct, I will contact you."

To speed up the process, call the IRS at the number indicated on the notice and request a copy of the Record of your Tax Account Information. To obtain a copy of your tax account, flip to Chapter 3. This document reflects all postings made by the IRS for tax, interest, penalties, and payments. Also, send the IRS Form 8822, Change of Address.

Getting Attention When the IRS Appears to Be Ignoring You

At times, it seems that a black hole ravages every IRS service center, devouring loads of taxpayer correspondence. Naturally, the IRS won't respond right away in these cases. If you don't get a response, the IRS has a special office that handles these problems: the office of your local Taxpayer Advocate.

Getting to know your local Taxpayer Advocate

The local Taxpayer Advocate Office is the complaint department of the IRS. Every state has at least one local Taxpayer Advocate Office; in addition, each of the ten IRS service centers has one, too. An advocate's function is to resolve taxpayer problems that can't be resolved through normal channels.

The National Taxpayer Advocate, who is appointed by the Secretary of the Treasury, oversees all functions of the local Taxpayer Advocates and their employees. The national and local taxpayer advocates operate independently from the IRS and report directly to Congress. The purpose behind this independence is to provide taxpayers with a "customer-friendly" problem-solving office. Being independent of all other IRS offices enables the office of the local advocate to cut through red tape.

Local Taxpayer Advocates don't interpret tax law, give tax advice, or help in preparing tax returns. They resolve procedural, refund, notice, billing, and other problems that can't be fixed after one or more attempts by a taxpayer. A local advocate can abate penalties, trace missing tax payments, and credit them to a taxpayer's account. An advocate also can approve replacement refund checks for originals that were either lost or stolen, release a lien, and — of greatest importance — stop IRS collection action.

Meeting the criteria for a Taxpayer Advocate case

Under its Problem Resolution Program, caseworkers (called Associate and Senior Associate Advocates) working under the local Taxpayer Advocate are the folks who do the actual problem solving. They accept cases for a variety of reasons. The following types of cases are ones that you can cry on their shoulders about:

>> You call or write the IRS about a problem. After 30 days, you contact the IRS again, but the IRS still ignores you.

>> You file your return expecting a refund, but after 60 days, you're still waiting. You contact the IRS, but nothing happens.

>> You receive a letter from the IRS promising to respond to your particular inquiry by a certain date, but the IRS forgets about you.

>> You're suffering a hardship or are about to suffer one, such as the loss of your credit or livelihood.

Although an Associate Advocate can be helpful, keep in mind that they don't work for a charitable organization. They're experts at cutting through red tape. If the advocate won't take your case, they will refer it to the IRS office that should have handled it from the start.

IF THE ADVOCATE TAKES YOUR CASE

Taxpayer Advocate caseworkers are committed to resolving your problem in seven working days. If they can't, you'll be informed — usually by telephone — when you can expect the problem to be resolved. Most cases are closed in 30 days or less. If an advocate asks for certain information and it isn't sent, or you fail to contact the advocate to request additional time to comply, the case won't be held open indefinitely; after two weeks, it will be closed, in which case you must make a new Taxpayer Advocate contact. A caseworker closes a case by writing to the taxpayer and explaining what corrective action has been taken, if any. (If no corrective action can be taken, the advocate's letter offers an explanation.)

Contacting the local Taxpayer Advocate

Except in emergency cases, such as when a levy has been filed and the taxpayer owes no money, taxpayers should write to the advocate in the district where they reside. Your letter should contain the following:

>> A complete description of the problem

>> Copies of the fronts and backs of canceled checks (if applicable)

>> A signed copy of your tax return (if applicable)

>> Copies of all notices received from the IRS

>> Copies of previous letters written to the IRS regarding the problem

>> The number of phone calls you made to the IRS, whom you spoke with, the dates, and what was discussed

>> Any other documents or information that may help the advocate expedite the resolution of this problem

>> A telephone number where you can be reached during the day

In emergency situations, contact the Taxpayer Advocate by phone. The advocate can immediately take a variety of actions. For example, the advocate can issue a Taxpayer Assistance Order (TAO), if a notice of levy has been incorrectly issued. A TAO stops the original IRS action that the IRS never should have undertaken.

The Taxpayer Advocate toll-free phone number (877-777-4778) can direct you to the office of your local advocate, or you can find that information at www.irs.gov by plugging "Taxpayer Advocate" into the keyword search.

Finding Your Refund When It Doesn't Find You

If you didn't receive your refund, you may be one of the tens of thousands whose refund checks are returned annually to the IRS by the U.S. Postal Service. According to the IRS, these checks are undeliverable because of incorrect addresses or because the taxpayer moved and failed to leave a forwarding address. So if you move, make sure that you notify the IRS by filing Form 8822, Change of Address. That way, you'll be sure to get your refund.

The actual figures on how many taxpayers never receive their refund checks are substantially higher when you consider the refund checks that are either lost or stolen. There are also a number of other reasons why a taxpayer may not have received a refund. For example, the refund may have been used to offset another year's tax bill or to pay what was owed on a delinquent student loan or past-due child support.

If you have a bank account, consider having your refund deposited directly into that account, the information for which you provide on your Form 1040. And, although we appreciate the concept of not giving the IRS more information than it's strictly entitled to, this is one time where a little additional info can actually work to your advantage because you'll receive your refund much more quickly!

How to locate your refund

Yes, the IRS does have a lost-and-found department. You can find out the status of your refund by using the "Get Your Refund Status" system (www.irs.gov/refunds) or the IRS automated phone system (dial 800-829-4477 on a touch-tone phone and answer the automated questions).

Whether you use the phone or the IRS website to access this information, you'll have to give them some info: your Social Security number, your filing status, and the exact amount of your refund.

REMEMBER

You shouldn't start asking about your refund until at least four weeks after you filed your return. It takes about that much time for the IRS to process a tax return and input the information into its computers. Only after the IRS inputs the information on your return into its computer can you find out about the status of your refund.

If a mistake was made, the refund may have to be processed manually, which may take an additional four to six weeks. Whatever the reason for the delay, the "Where's My Refund" system informs you of the date your refund check was mailed or when it will be mailed.

If more than ten days to two weeks have elapsed since the date that a refund check was scheduled to be mailed and you still haven't received it, the check probably was lost or stolen. In situations like this, you can do one of three things:

>> Fill out Form 3911, Taxpayer Statement Regarding Refund, and send it to the service center where you filed. This one-page form asks whether you ever received the check, or whether you received it and lost it. Allow four to six weeks for processing.

>> Contact the office of your local Taxpayer Advocate. See "Contacting the local Taxpayer Advocate," earlier in this chapter, for more information.

>> Contact the IRS refund section at 800-829-1040. You'll have the opportunity to speak to an IRS employee instead of a machine.

Uncashed refund checks

You have to cash a refund check within 12 months. When your refund check isn't cashed within the required 12-month period, that doesn't mean you're not entitled to your refund. You are. A new refund check must be issued and the uncashed one returned to the IRS. This procedure can be accomplished by filing Form 3911, Taxpayer Statement Regarding Refund, with the service center where you filed your return. Across the top of the form, write:

"The enclosed refund check cannot be cashed; 12 months have passed since it was issued. Please issue a replacement check."

REMEMBER

You aren't entitled to additional interest on a replacement check because you failed to deposit or cash your refund. But you are entitled to interest if the IRS is late in issuing your refund. See the very next section.

Interest on refunds

TIP

If the IRS doesn't issue your refund within 45 days of filing your return, it must pay you interest which they should include in the refund check. So if you file by April 15 and you don't receive your refund by May 30, interest is due.

Refunds and estimated tax payments

If you requested that your refund be applied to next year's tax, you can't change your mind and subsequently request a refund. You can get your overpayment back only by taking credit for it on next year's tax return. No interest is paid on an overpayment of tax credited to next year's tax bill.

Joint refunds

SEEK ADVICE

When married couples divorce or separate, or when a dispute exists as to how much of the refund each is entitled to, Revenue Ruling 80-7 provides a formula for determining each spouse's share of the refund. Again, this is one of those times when consulting a tax advisor is a must. If the parties can't decide how to divide the refund, either spouse may request that the IRS issue a separate refund check by filing Form 1040X, Amended U.S. Individual Income Tax Return, and making the computation required by Revenue Ruling 80-7. The IRS will accept a joint 1040X with only one signature from a divorced or separated taxpayer requesting a separate refund check. The worksheet on the back of Form 8379, Injured Spouse Allocation, can guide you through the computation. Attach this form to your amended return. The refund belongs to the spouse whose income, deductions, and tax payments produced the refund. Filing jointly doesn't change who is entitled to the refund. Filing jointly only determines the amount of tax a couple has to pay.

Revenue Ruling 80-7 must be modified for taxpayers residing in community property states (Arizona, California, Idaho, Louisiana, Nevada, New Mexico, Texas, Washington, and Wisconsin).

Joint estimated payments

Where joint estimated payments have been made and a husband and wife file separate returns, the estimated payments may be divided in any manner the couple sees fit. However, if a couple can't agree on how estimated payments are to be divided, the payments will be divided in the same manner as joint refunds, as required by Revenue Ruling 80-7.

Deceased taxpayer

If a refund is due a deceased taxpayer, Form 1310, Statement of Person Claiming Refund Due a Deceased Taxpayer, must be attached to the return unless you're the surviving spouse filing a joint return. If the form isn't attached, the IRS will send back the return along with Form 1310. The refund is processed only after the IRS receives the completed Form 1310.

Statute of limitations

To get a refund, you must file a return within three years of its due date, including extensions of time to file (or within two years of the date tax was paid if that's later). After that time, you can kiss your refund goodbye. A return that's filed before the due date is considered to have been filed on the due date. For example, if the due date for filing a return is April 15, 2021, an amended return must be filed by April 15, 2022. After that date, no refund will be allowed.

If the April 15, 2021, filing date is extended to October 15, 2021, an amended return must be filed by October 15, 2022. Your acceptance of a refund doesn't bar a future claim for a refund if you subsequently discover that you made a mistake in computing the amended return and now realize that you're entitled to an even greater refund than you computed on your amended return.

REMEMBER

The statute of limitations is suspended when you become financially disabled, meaning that a disability has rendered you unable to manage your financial affairs. This change in the tax code was brought about by the case of a senile taxpayer who erroneously overpaid the IRS $7,000, and a timely (within three years) refund claim wasn't filed. Assuming that adequate proof of a medical disability can be provided, this taxpayer, under the new law, can still get his $7,000 back. How disabled does someone have to be? The disability or impairment must be expected to result in death or expected to last continuously for at least a 12-month period.

WARNING

This rule doesn't apply when a taxpayer's spouse, or another person such as a guardian, a conservator, or someone acting with a power of attorney, is authorized to act for the taxpayer on tax matters. In these cases, the normal three-year statute of limitations applies.

Protective claims

Sometimes you must file a tax return and pay tax even though you know the information on the return is incomplete and that you probably shouldn't owe any tax at all. And sometimes the resolution of these issues may take years, such as in a complex litigation. In those circumstances, you may file a so-called protective claim with your income tax return that will suspend the statute of limitations regarding refunds while the litigation is pending. If you feel that you fall into this category, use your big, black marker and write the words "Protective claim under Reg. Sec. 301.6402-2(a)" across the top of your original return, and make sure you file on time (as properly extended). Check with your attorney, accountant, or enrolled agent to make sure you qualify for this break, and to be certain you've complied with every hiccup in the regulation.

If your protective claim request is successful, you'll be able to file an amended return for the year in question and receive your refund (plus interest) even after the normal statute of limitations on refunds has expired.

Refund offset program

Yes, Virginia, if you or your spouse owes back taxes, a nontax federal debt (student loans, anyone?), or delinquent child support, the refund you thought you were getting may be history. The IRS will use the refund money first to offset back taxes. With what's left, the Treasury will try to recover delinquent student loan amounts and/or child support payments. What if you're filing jointly with your spouse, but only one of you owes this money? If the past due amounts clearly belong to only one of you, you may recover the portion of the refund that belongs to you. In this case, the nonobligated spouse must file Form 8379, Injured Spouse Allocation, to claim their share of the refund. Revenue Ruling 80-7 explains how to divide the refund. Every year, the IRS intercepts several million refunds as part of this program. Yes, Big Brother is watching and has long tentacles.

IN THIS CHAPTER

» **Fixing bad returns**

» **Making a deal with the IRS**

» **Abating penalties and interest**

» **Safeguarding yourself when filing jointly**

» **Understanding the Taxpayer Bill of Rights**

Chapter **20**

Fixing Your Own Mistakes

E veryone makes mistakes. To make them is human; typically, to admit that they're your fault isn't. Still, in most cases, when you've made a mistake on your tax return, the sooner you fix it, the happier and less poor you'll be. In some cases, you need to complete more paperwork; in others, you have to personally persuade an IRS employee. Regardless, here's our advice for how to do it now, do it right, and be done with it!

Amending a Return

Through the years, when taxpayers discovered that they failed to claim a deduction or credit in a prior year, they often asked whether they could claim that deduction on this year's return. They couldn't, and you can't, either.

TAX CUT

If you discover that you forgot to claim a deduction and the statute of limitations hasn't expired, you have to file an amended return. Similarly, if you discover that a deduction was improperly claimed, you must file an amended return and pay any additional tax plus interest.

If you forgot to claim a deduction in a prior year, you must file an amended return within three years from the date of filing your original return, or within two years from the time the tax was paid, whichever is later. Form 1040X, Amended U.S. Individual Income Tax Return, is used to correct a prior year's tax return.

Not surprisingly, more amended returns are filed when the flow of funds is going in a taxpayer's direction rather than in the government's. Although this discovery isn't a startling one, it has more to do with letting sleeping dogs lie than with people's honesty.

Suppose you filed your 2020 return on April 15, 2021. If you want to amend this return, you must do so by April 15, 2024. However, if you filed your return before April 15, 2021, the three-year statute of limitations still expires on April 15, 2024. If you had an extension of time to file until October 15, 2021, the three-year period starts to run from that date.

This three-year rule is suspended for anyone suffering from a serious disability that renders them unable to manage their financial affairs. We're not talking about an ingrown toenail type of disability, but truly incapacitating illness or disability that is expected to result in death or reasonably last for at least a year. This provision enables such taxpayers to recover tax that was erroneously overpaid in instances where the three-year statute of limitations would normally bar a refund. However, when a taxpayer's spouse or another person such as a guardian is authorized to act on the disabled taxpayer's behalf, this provision doesn't apply. The IRS believes that the person looking after the disabled person's financial affairs should be bound by the same three-year rule that everyone else has to follow.

In most cases, filing an amended return doesn't affect the penalty for underestimating your tax. For example, suppose that you were assessed a $1,000 penalty for underpayment of your estimated tax. Your amended return is for half the tax on your original return. The $1,000 underestimating penalty can't be reduced. This is one mistake that can't be amended.

Amended returns also are useful for changing how you reported an item on your original return. You can change your mind in the following situations:

>> You filed separately but now want to file jointly. It's important to note that you can't do this in reverse — you can't switch to filing separately if you originally filed jointly.

>> You want to change from itemizing your deductions to claiming the standard deduction, or vice versa.

>> You reported something incorrectly. This situation may occur if you claimed a deduction or an exemption of income to which you weren't entitled. An example may be when a non-custodial parent incorrectly claimed a child as a dependent on their return or claimed head of household filing status.

Some decisions to treat an item in a certain manner are irrevocable, such as using the straight-line depreciation method and taking a net operating loss forward instead of backward.

More expenses than income (net operating losses)

Net operating losses (NOLs) can no longer be carried back for two years. However, NOLs may now be carried forward indefinitely until they are used up. Previously the carry forward limit was 20 years. NOLs are limited each year to 80 percent of taxable income.

For tax years 2018 through 2020, the CARES Act allowed for a carryback of any NOL to each of the five taxable years preceding the taxable year in which the loss arises.

The tax benefit rule

Whenever you deduct an expense in one year and part or all of that expense is reimbursed in a subsequent year, you usually have to report the reimbursement as income. For example, suppose that you deducted $10,000 in medical expenses in 2020, and were reimbursed $3,000 by your insurance company in 2021. You have to report the $3,000 as income in 2021.

However, if the original deduction didn't result in a tax savings, you don't have to report the reimbursement. For example, you may receive a state tax refund for a year in which you claimed the standard deduction instead of itemizing your deductions — you don't have to report the refund.

Solving When You Can't Pay Your Taxes

"If you can't pay," goes the old saw, "you can owe." That's certainly the way the IRS looks at things. Every year, the IRS receives millions of returns from taxpayers who can't pay what they owe before the April 15 deadline, and that amounts to tens of billions of dollars of taxes due each year.

If you find yourself among the numerous Americans who can't pay all or any part of what they owe, you have four options:

>> You can pay it off in installments, which millions of taxpayers currently are doing.

>> You can put it off until you have more money.

>> You can try to convince the IRS to take less than the total that you owe. The IRS doesn't accept every offer that is made, but it is fairly pragmatic, and in recent years has reached agreements in about 25 percent of cases. From where the IRS sits, receiving some of what it's owed is better than receiving nothing. This acceptance rate is actually much higher when you consider that a third of the offers can't be processed because they don't contain all the information necessary to make them processible. The average settlement is around 13 percent of what is owed.

>> You can file for bankruptcy in the absolute worst-case scenario.

WARNING

Whatever you do, don't confuse filing with paying. More people get into hot water because they mistakenly believe that they need to put off filing until they can pay. If you're one of the approximately 2 million nonfilers that the IRS currently is looking for, file your return as soon as possible — even if you can pay only part of what you owe. Owing the IRS money is expensive, but owing money and tax returns is far worse! Although the interest rates the IRS charges are lower than what you'll get on your credit card (IRS rates in 2021 were 3 percent and are refigured periodically), interest compounds daily on the balance you owe, in addition to a late-payment penalty of half a percentage point per month. That kind of interest adds up quickly! If you haven't filed your tax return, though, the IRS tacks on additional nonfiling penalties of 5 percent per month, up to a maximum of 25 percent.

At first, the IRS comes after you through the mail. If you owe money, either from the findings of an audit or because you simply can't pay it all on April 15, you'll get four notices from the IRS at five-week intervals. If you don't pay everything you owe on April 15, the fourth and last letter arrives by certified mail around Labor Day. That's when things start to get ugly.

WARNING

In our experience, many taxpayers freeze when they receive one of these notices and then place the unopened envelope in a pile to be dealt with when the cows come home, or hell freezes over. Bad idea! Whether or not you've actually opened the envelope, you're still responsible to respond to the requests inside, even if to tell the IRS that you can't pay right now. If you fail to respond, your account is considered delinquent and is forwarded to the IRS Automated Collection System (ACS), which means you'll start getting telephone calls demanding payment — at home and, if the IRS can't reach you at home, at work, at your club, anywhere the IRS has a number for you. Although the IRS is trying to be a friendlier place, the collections are collections, and they want their money! If the ACS isn't successful in getting you to pay up, your account may be transferred to an IRS revenue officer who will contact you in person.

Because the IRS usually has what it refers to as *levy source information* about you in its files, it has the option to place a levy on your assets or salary, or to simply seize your property. IRS collection agents are especially fond of cars — used or new, they don't discriminate. Keep in mind that from the return you filed the IRS already knows where your income comes from and how much you make and has the right to get additional information about you from credit and governmental agencies, such as the Department of Motor Vehicles, passport agencies, and the U.S. Postal Service. It can make you pay in more ways than one. And every time you make a payment, the IRS makes a permanent record of your bank account.

TIP

To avoid that hassle, if there's any way that you can get the money together, send a partial payment when filing your return, a partial payment with the first, second, and third notices, and the balance (including interest and penalties) with the fourth notice.

REMEMBER

When the IRS sends a bill for less than $100,000, you have 21 interest-free days to pay it. When the amount you owe is more than $100,000, you have ten business days before you're charged interest.

The IRS must notify you of your right to protest a levy of your salary or property. You have 30 days from the date the IRS sends you a Levy Notice by certified mail to request what is known as a Collection Due Process Hearing. We explain how to request this type of hearing and what it's all about in Chapter 16.

Requesting an installment agreement

In some cases, people need more time to pay what they owe. If you need more time, you can request to pay in installments by attaching Form 9465, Installment Agreement Request, to your return or to any of the notices you receive. Then send it to the IRS Service Center where you file or to the center that issued the notice. You also can request an installment agreement by telephoning the IRS Taxpayer Services office at 800-829-1040.

TIP

If you owe less than $10,000 and can pay off what you owe in 36 months, the IRS is required by law to grant your request to pay in installments. However, some strings are attached. During the past five years, you had to have filed and paid your tax on time. Even if this rule knocks you out of contention, the IRS has a new policy that automatically grants installment agreements when the amount owed is less than $25,000 and can be paid off in 60 months. When you request an installment agreement, the IRS mails you an acceptance letter that tells you where to send the money. You won't have to provide a financial statement, and the IRS won't file a *federal tax lien,* which is no small matter, because a tax lien can affect your credit rating for seven years, even if you pay off your tax liability in a shorter period of time. There's a $105 charge for an installment agreement ($52 if you pay by electronic funds withdrawal) and a $45 charge for either changing an existing agreement or reinstating an agreement that's in default. If your income is below a certain level, you may qualify for a reduced fee of $43 to set up the installment agreement. Remember, if you set up one of these agreements, you're committed to filing all your returns and payments on time.

SEEK ADVICE

If you can't pay the full amount of your outstanding debt to the IRS, but can pay a substantial portion of it, you may be eligible to enter into a Partial Payment Installment Agreement (PPIA). In order to do so, you must provide complete and accurate financial information that the IRS will verify. This plan is subject to review every two years to see whether your financial situation has improved and whether you can make larger payments. It's possible that the IRS can terminate the plan entirely and the full balance would become due. If you're thinking that you may be a candidate for a PPIA, check with your local tax advisor, who can help walk you through the process.

WARNING

Be careful not to fall behind on your payments, or you may have to apply for an installment plan all over again. The IRS allows you to make payments using a variety of methods. Checks, money orders, electronic fund transfers, and credit cards (but no postage stamps, please, send it certified) are all acceptable forms of payment. You can use cash, but only if you pay in person at an IRS office (for safety and security reasons, we don't recommend this latter method!). If you want to be sure you don't fall behind on your payments, you can either pay by direct deposit (use Form 9465) or by payroll deduction (use Form 2159, available by calling the number on your notice or by visiting your local IRS office). If you can't make a payment, contact the IRS. You stand a good chance of being able to skip a payment if you have a plausible reason. Although the IRS isn't all that charitable, it reserves its wrath for taxpayers who ignore the agency.

Installments get trickier when you owe more than $25,000 or want to stretch your payments out for more than 60 months. You can either use Form 9465 or go straight to the IRS, either by mail, by phone, or even in person. (A representative, such as an enrolled agent, a CPA, or an attorney, can make this request on your behalf.) When you owe this higher amount, you'll need to file a financial statement listing your assets, liabilities, and monthly income and expenses, which is submitted on IRS Form 433-A, Collection Information Statement for Individuals. Use Form 433-A if you're self-employed. For a business, use Form 433-B.

After reviewing the information you've provided, the IRS will recommend one of the following courses of action or a combination of them. The IRS may tell you to

>> Make immediate payment by liquidating some of your assets

>> Obtain a cash advance from a credit line

>> Borrow against the equity in any assets you may have, such as your residence

>> Make an installment agreement

There is a fifth option: If there's just no way you can pay, the IRS will stop bothering you for the money. Yes, if you get the fifth option, the IRS will prepare Form 53, Report of Taxes Currently

Not Collectible, and you'll be off the hook — for a while. However, the IRS will contact you every 9 to 12 months for a new financial statement to find out whether your financial condition has changed. Remember, the IRS has ten years to collect what you owe before the statute of limitations on collections expires. Also keep in mind that just because the IRS isn't currently collecting from you, interest and penalties continue adding to your unpaid tax.

You can appeal any rejection of a request for an installment agreement to the IRS Appeals Office (see Chapter 16). Although the IRS doesn't have a specific form for this, you can try using Form 12153, Request for a Collection Due Process Hearing.

If you filed your return on time and enter into an installment agreement, the late-payment penalty gets reduced from 0.5 percent a month to 0.25 percent a month while you're making your payments. The total late-payment penalty that can be charged can't exceed 25 percent of the tax owed. On $10,000 of tax owed, this reduction amounts to a $25-per-month savings.

Making an offer

What if you think there's no way you'll ever be able to pay it all off? The IRS, believe it or not, often takes partial payment. First, you need to fill out **Form 656, Offer in Compromise**. This form is fairly involved and detailed to complete.

An Offer in Compromise is a matter of public record and, if accepted, may come with strings attached. You may have to agree that for a period of years, perhaps as many as five, you'll pay more than you offered in the event your financial condition improves. An aging Joe Louis had to accept such terms just in case he ever started earning millions again by going back into the boxing ring.

Who are candidates for Offers in Compromise? All types of taxpayers: senior citizens with few or no assets or in poor health, spendthrifts who earned large sums of money and squandered it, athletes and actors whose earning potential has diminished, casualties of downsizing, and people whose relatives are reluctant to leave them money because of their tax problems.

The Offer in Compromise is intended only for people deemed unable to pay their outstanding federal income tax bill. The IRS has a useful website tool called the "Offer in Compromise Pre-Qualifier" (irs.treasury.gov/oic_pre_qualifier), which can assist you in determining your possible eligibility and help you prepare a preliminary proposal.

Declaring bankruptcy

After many years of talking about it, Congress acted to make it more difficult to discharge your debts in bankruptcy. The result was the Bankruptcy Abuse Prevention and Consumer Protection Act of 2005, which applies a means test to determine whether or not you can completely wipe out your debts, or whether you'll have to enter into a five-year payment plan. What does this act mean to you? If things are really dire, you may still decide that declaring personal bankruptcy is the only way out; however, now you'll receive six months of credit counseling before you can apply. And, after you do file for bankruptcy, if you earn more than the median income for a family of your size in your locale, you may be required to repay a portion of your debts, including your unpaid taxes, over a five-year period. Although the provisions of this new law are definitely tougher than those provisions of the prior law, filing a bankruptcy petition still stops the IRS from garnishing your salary or seizing your property.

UNDERESTIMATING ESTIMATED TAXES

If you have income that isn't subject to withholding, the IRS doesn't want to wait until April 15 to be paid; it wants you to pay what you owe in quarterly estimates. The penalty kicks in when you owe $1,000 or more when you file your return, and you haven't made tax payments equal to 90 percent of your tax during the year or 100 percent of your prior year's tax liability.

The penalty for underestimating your tax may be abated because of a casualty, disaster, or another unusual circumstance. It also can be abated by filing Form 2210, Underpayment of Estimated Tax, if you meet one of the following conditions:

- You paid estimated 2021 taxes equal to 100 percent of your 2020 tax. If your 2020 income exceeded $150,000, however, you need to pay 110 percent of your 2020 tax to be certain you'll escape the penalty for 2021.

- You met the 90 percent tax payment of your 2021 tax liability requirement.

- You filed a return for the preceding year that showed no tax liability.

- You retired at age 62 or older, or became disabled, and your underpayment was due to reasonable cause.

If you operate a seasonal business or didn't earn your income evenly throughout the year, you may be able to reduce or eliminate the penalty by using the annualized income installment method. Not many taxpayers use it because of its complexity, but if you think it will save you money, IRS Publication 505 *(Tax Withholding and Estimated Tax)* explains how it works. For example, say you earned nothing for 11 months and then had income in the 12th month. You're required to make only one estimated payment instead of four.

To get the penalty waived, attach an explanation to Form 2210 along with any documentation that will prove you shouldn't be charged a penalty. See Chapter 10 for details about this fiendish penalty.

Of course, if your income falls below the median for a family of your size in your area, you can still file for a complete discharge of your debts, including unpaid income tax liabilities that are more than three years old. If you fall into this category, you're still required to have six months of credit counseling prior to visiting the bankruptcy court.

TIP

You can recover up to $1 million in damages if the IRS willfully violates the bankruptcy law's prohibition against seizing your salary or property.

Even if your tax liability isn't completely wiped out in bankruptcy court, as often happens, the IRS won't have as much power over you anymore. For example, you don't have to get IRS approval on an installment plan. If the bankruptcy court allows your repayment plan because the bankruptcy judge finds it fair and equitable, the IRS has to accept it.

TIP

Filing bankruptcy, in addition to being emotionally charged, has its pros and cons. Bankruptcy is a technical and difficult area of the law and one that you may not want to negotiate by yourself. If you find that you're contemplating filing for bankruptcy, you may want to use the services of a competent bankruptcy attorney. Your choice of an attorney is key; you can find a list of bankruptcy attorneys through Martindale-Hubbell, an attorney database available online at www.martindale.com/find-attorneys. *The New Bankruptcy* by Cara O'Neill (Nolo Press) and *How to File for Chapter 7 Bankruptcy* by Albin Renauer and Cara O'Neill (Nolo Press) are useful books that can help you figure out the right questions to ask in order to choose the best attorney.

REMEMBER

Filing for bankruptcy is a drastic step. Before heading down that road, be sure to analyze your overall financial situation, level of debt relative to your income, and your current spending. Eric's *Personal Finance For Dummies* (Wiley) can assist you with that analysis.

Planning ahead to avoid these problems

Making adequate provisions in the first place is your best defense against not being able to pay your tax bill on April 15. Routinely review your withholding allowances (Form W-4) to make sure that the proper amount of tax is being withheld from your salary. (See Chapter 17 if you need help determining how much to withhold.) If you're self-employed or have income that isn't subject to withholding, you need to make quarterly estimated payments using Form 1040-ES.

Abating a Penalty

Although the Internal Revenue Code contains more than 100 penalties, some are more common than others. The most common penalties include:

>> Accuracy errors (the IRS defines accuracy errors as either negligence or disregard of the rules)

>> Failure to file

>> Failure to pay

>> False Withholding Exemption Certificate (Form W-4)

>> Underestimating tax

TIP

Many taxpayers who receive a penalty notice believe that a penalty wouldn't have been charged unless it was correct, and they simply pay it. After all, penalties are asserted on official-looking documents. Never assume that any notice is correct. Thoroughly reading the notice is the primary requirement for making sure that you don't pay what you don't owe.

The IRS assesses tens of millions of penalties each year totaling tens of billions of dollars. And almost 50 percent of the penalties are abated or forgiven because taxpayers (or their representatives) questioned them and had either reasonable cause or because the penalty in question was improperly assessed. Taxpayers can look to several sources — the *Internal Revenue Manual*, court cases, IRS Rulings and Announcements, and regulations to the Internal Revenue Code — to determine whether they meet the definition of reasonable cause.

Unlike some taxes, penalties are never deductible. Because some penalties are additions to the tax you must pay, interest is computed on the total amount due — tax plus penalties.

The Internal Revenue Manual (IRM)

The *Internal Revenue Manual* is the IRS bible. It contains the rules that IRS employees must follow when applying the law (not that it helps you any when they don't). According to the manual, the following situations constitute reasonable cause for abating a penalty:

>> Your return was mailed on time but wasn't received until after the filing date, regardless of whether the envelope bears sufficient postage.

>> Your return was filed on time but was received by the wrong IRS office.

>> You relied upon erroneous information provided to you by an IRS officer or employee.

>> Your return was filed late because of the death or serious illness of the taxpayer or a close family member.

>> You were unavoidably away on the filing date.

>> Your place of business, residence, or business records were destroyed because of fire or other casualty. Victims of natural disasters, take note!

>> You applied to the IRS district director for proper tax forms prior to the filing deadline, but these forms weren't furnished in sufficient time.

>> You presented proof of having visited an IRS office before an IRS expiration date for filing returns to secure information on how to properly complete your return, but you weren't able to meet with an IRS representative.

>> You were unable, for reasons beyond your control, to obtain the records necessary to determine the amount of tax due, or, for reasons beyond your control, you weren't able to pay. For example, you can't get your money out of a bankrupt Savings & Loan to pay your taxes, or your account was attached by a lien or court order. Perhaps you earned money in a foreign country that you can't convert into dollars, or a person who was needed to cosign a check was ill or away.

>> Your tax advisor incorrectly advised you that you didn't need to file a return, even though you provided all the necessary and relevant documents, or the advisor prepared the return incorrectly.

Your ignorance of the law may be considered reasonable cause for a late return if other factors, such as a situation in which you are filing a return for the first time, support this contention. However, you must demonstrate that you exercised ordinary care and prudence.

Court cases that define reasonable cause

With the exception of fraud penalties, just about every penalty can be abated for what is known as reasonable cause. The IRS defines reasonable cause as follows: "If the taxpayer exercised ordinary business care and prudence and was nevertheless unable to file or pay within the pre-scribed time, then the delay is due to reasonable cause."

You're not the first person to think you have a reasonable excuse for why you shouldn't be charged a penalty. Many others have gone before you and fought until they got the result they were looking for. Here are some court cases that favored taxpayers. These legal precedents cre-ate guidelines that the IRS should follow. Be cautious, though, when using legal precedents to buttress your arguments to the IRS; your facts will almost never be identical to the facts in the case, and the IRS may just be itching to point out the differences to you.

Ignorance

The taxpayer's limited education and business experience, together with reliance on the advice of an attorney, caused his failure to file to be due to reasonable cause. C.R. Dexter, 306 F. Supp 415.

Litigation

The taxpayer's late filing was due to reasonable cause when litigation was necessary to deter-mine the taxability of income received. *F.P. Walker* (CA-9), 326 F. 2nd 261 (Nonacq).

Timely mailed and presumed received

The IRS requires taxpayers, if asked, to prove that they filed their returns on time. Now, in order to be able to provide the necessary proof, you should be sure to file your paper returns by the due date using certified mail or another approved method of filing. If you file electronically, be sure that you keep those receipts for documentation purposes.

Return executed but misplaced

Tax returns were signed and given to an employee whose duty was to mail the returns. Instead, the employee by error then placed the returns in a file together with copies of the returns of many other corporations. When the IRS sent a notice a year later, the error was discovered and the returns were filed at that time. *Bouvelt Realty*, 46 BTA 45.

Return misplaced by the IRS

The Commissioner failed to refute the taxpayer's evidence that the tax returns were timely filed but misplaced by the IRS. *J.J. Carlin*, 43 TCM (CCH) 22.

Mailing of return on time

The IRS asserted that a return due on the 15th hadn't been received for filing until the 17th. The corporate officer who had mailed the return had died, and because of the Commissioner's fail-ure to produce the envelope in which the return was mailed, it was held that no penalty should attach. *Capento Securities Corp.*, 47 BTA 691 (Nonacq) Aff'd CA-1.

Honest belief

The taxpayer's honest but mistaken belief that an extension of time to file allowed him to delay the filing of his tax return until he had sufficient funds to pay his tax constituted reasonable cause for the late filing of his tax return. *M.S. Alba*, DC, East.Dist.MO.No.80-764.

In another case, a taxpayer — while separated from her husband — attached her W-2 to a joint return that she gave back to her husband to file. The honest belief that the return was filed did not constitute willful neglect. *E. Barker*, 22 TCM 634.

Illness

The taxpayer's illness and hospitalization constituted reasonable cause for failure to file a tax return. *C. Freeman*, 40 TCM 1219, Dec. 37,236 (M).

Reliance on accountant

Where a corporate taxpayer selects a competent tax expert, supplies the expert with all necessary information, and asks the expert to prepare proper tax returns, the taxpayer has done all that ordinary business care and prudence can reasonably demand. *Haywood Lumber & Mining Co. v Comm.*, (CA-2) 178 F.2nd 769.REV'D CA-2.

Excuses that won't fly

The dog-ate-my-tax excuse won't work, nor will the following.

Delegation of authority

In a landmark case, the Supreme Court held that the reliance on an attorney as to the filing date of a return didn't constitute reasonable cause. *R.W. Boyle*, SCT. 105 S. Ct. 687. The Supreme Court held in this case that a qualified tax advisor's incorrect advice as to whether a tax return should be filed constitutes reasonable cause, but that the tax advisor's mistaken advice as to the correct date a return must be filed does not.

But subsequent to *U.S. v Boyle*, a disabled taxpayer's reliance on an attorney to timely file a return was considered reasonable cause. *C. Brown v U.S.*, 57 AFTR 2d (M.D. Tenn. 1985).

Incarceration

The Tax Court rejected a taxpayer's claim that incarceration constituted reasonable cause. *R. Llorente*, 74 TC 260.

IRS rulings and announcements

Some taxpayers are amazed when they discover that the IRS, rather than Congress, creates most of the tax rules that they must follow. That's because most tax laws include the following language: "in accordance with rules and regulations to be promulgated by the Secretary of the Treasury" — meaning that the Treasury Department makes and enforces the rules. Therefore, you must pay special attention to IRS rulings and announcements — there's a whole lot of promulgating going on.

Partnership returns — Rev. Proc. 84-35

If a partnership is composed of ten or fewer partners and each of the partners reports their share of the partnership's income and deductions, the partnership won't be charged a penalty for either not filing or filing late.

Erroneous advice given by IRS employees over the telephone

According to IRS Information Release IR-88-75, incorrect advice given over the telephone by an IRS employee may constitute reasonable cause. The only problem with this provision is how you prove that you called the IRS and received erroneous advice. The IRS will consider that a taxpayer received incorrect advice over the telephone if a taxpayer provides the following information:

>> Whether the taxpayer tried to find the answer to the question in IRS forms, instructions, or publications.

>> The questions asked, and the specific facts given to the IRS employee.

>> The answer the taxpayer received.

>> The IRS employee's name and ID number. Yes, every employee has one.

>> The date and time of the call.

If you're reading this provision for the first time, it's probably too late. But the next time you call the IRS for advice, make sure that you document this information in your notes from the call.

Erroneous written advice by IRS

Both the tax and the penalty attributable to the incorrect written advice can be abated. You can do this by filing Form 843, Claim for Refund and Request for Abatement, and checking box 5a that says, "*A penalty or addition to tax was the result of erroneous written advice from the IRS.*"

IRS criteria for determining reasonable cause

This IRS ruling spells out the criteria for reasonable cause. Here they are:

>> Do the taxpayer's reasons address the penalty that was assessed?

>> Does the length of time between the event that caused the late filing and the actual filing negate the fact that the taxpayer attempted to correct the situation in a timely fashion?

>> Does the continued operation of a business after the event that caused the taxpayer's non-compliance negate the taxpayer's excuse?

>> Should the event that caused the taxpayer's noncompliance or increased liability have been reasonably anticipated?

>> Was the penalty the result of carelessness, or does the taxpayer appear to have made an honest mistake?

>> Has the taxpayer provided sufficient detail (dates, relationships) to determine whether they exercised ordinary business care and prudence? Is a non-liable individual being blamed for the taxpayer's noncompliance? What is the nature of the relationship between the taxpayer and this individual? Is the individual an employee of the taxpayer or an independent third party, such as an accountant or a lawyer?

>> Has the taxpayer documented all pertinent facts?

>> Does the taxpayer have a history of being assessed the same penalty?

>> Does the amount of the penalty justify closer scrutiny of the case?

>> Can the taxpayer have requested an extension or filed an amended return?

Critical to getting the IRS to accept your reasons for late filing or paying is the time frame between the event that was clearly beyond your control and the date of your ultimate compliance with your obligation to file or pay. What the IRS considers to be an acceptable amount of time between these two events is based on the facts and circumstances in each case. Figure 20-1 shows a reasonable cause sample letter.

Sample Reasonable Cause Letter

Request to abate penalty
[your name and address]
[today's date]

Adjustments/Correspondence Branch
Internal Revenue Service Center
[address]

Re: [your name]
[Social Security number]
[tax year]

Dear IRS:

I am in receipt of your notice of [date] in which you asserted a late filing and payment penalty in the amount of [penalty $] plus interest on this amount of [interest $].

Please be advised that my late filing and payment were due to reasonable cause and, according to tax law, should be abated.

On [date], I was ill with [illness]. I was hospitalized and didn't recover sufficiently until [date]. When I was well enough to assemble the data necessary to file a return and pay what was owed, I immediately did so. Enclosed is a letter from my physician confirming the nature of my illness and the length of my recovery, as well as the hospital bill.

Regulation 301.6651-1(c) provides that:

"If a taxpayer exercised ordinary business care and prudence and was nevertheless either unable to file the return or pay within the prescribed time, the delay is due to reasonable cause."

Thank you in advance for your prompt attention to this request. If you require further clarification of any point, I can be reached at [number].

Very truly yours,

[your name]

Enclosed: Form CP-22A (Statement of Change to Your Account)
              Letter from physician and hospital

FIGURE 20-1:
A sample reasonable cause letter.

Penalty appeals

If the Adjustments/Correspondence Branch (see Chapter 19) rejects your request to have a penalty abated, you may appeal. Every service center has a penalty appeals unit. The A/C Branch notice informing taxpayers that their request was rejected will also inform them of their appeal rights and how to exercise them.

Payment of the penalty isn't a prerequisite to requesting an appeal. No official IRS form exists for requesting this type of appeal. Although some appeals within the IRS need not be in writing, this one must. Your original letter requesting an abatement can be used with one simple modification: Your opening sentence should state that you are requesting an appeal from a tax examiner's determination (which you are enclosing) that you failed to establish reasonable cause.

WARNING

Some IRS offices require that the tax and interest be paid before they will consider a penalty abatement. No specific law requires this; the IRS is famous for making up its own rules. Still, because you're not disputing the taxes owed here, and the interest is statutory (which means the IRS can't abate it), paying upfront may demonstrate to the agent that you're acting in good faith and may lead the agent to consider your request more favorably. Any interest you've paid on a penalty that is eventually abated will be refunded to you.

You may want to include any additional reasons that constitute reasonable cause, or any proof, such as:

>> Your passport showing that you were out of the country

>> Medical records stating that you were ill

>> A statement from a third party who saw you mail the return on time

>> A police or insurance report showing that the loss of your records was caused by a theft or other casualty

These documents, whenever available, need to be sent with the original abatement request. Hold nothing back!

At times, for inexplicable reasons, tax examiners take the position that a taxpayer should have quickly estimated their income and filed a return based on this estimate. In such instances, you should point out that the event that took place was the reasonable cause that prevented you from preparing an estimate.

TIP

The IRS has a policy that no collection action will be taken while a penalty appeal is pending — unless, that is, the case already was assigned to a collection officer who determined that the appeal was requested solely to postpone or delay payment. Whenever you're being bugged for the penalty, contact the office of your local Taxpayer Advocate to get the IRS Collection Division off your back. A Taxpayer Advocate has authority to do this. (See Chapter 19 for a Tax Advocate's duties.)

Be patient when requesting an abatement of a large penalty or when appealing a penalty abatement decision. The process isn't speedy.

Abating Interest

Whereas the IRS has the power to abate a penalty for reasonable cause, it doesn't have — as a general rule — the authority to abate interest. But like every IRS rule, there are some limited exceptions when interest can be abated.

When interest is incorrectly charged

If interest was assessed after the expiration of the statute of limitations or was assessed illegally, then it's probably correct to assume that the underlying tax also was incorrectly assessed. If this is the case, the interest, as well as the tax, can be abated.

Interest and tax that were incorrectly or illegally assessed may be abated in one of two ways. You can use Form 911, Request for Taxpayer Advocate Service Assistance, or you can write to the Adjustments/Correspondence Branch at the service center (or district office) that issued the notice. Figure 20-2 shows a sample letter with two possible reasons.

Sample Letter
[your name and address]
[today's date]

Internal Revenue Service Center
[address]

Re: [your name]
[Social Security number]
[tax year]

Dear IRS:

I respectfully request that you abate the tax assessment in the amount of [amount] that your agency made by error pursuant to the enclosed notice.

Reason (1): Section 6404(e) specifically allows for the abatement of tax that was assessed as the result of an IRS mathematical or clerical error.

Reason (2): Your assessment was made after the three-year statute of limitations had expired. Such assessments are prohibited by law.

I may be reached by telephone during the day at [number] should you require any further information.

Very truly yours,

[your name]

Enclosed: Copy of notice

FIGURE 20-2:
A sample letter to abate interest.

TIP

You can collect damages when the IRS willfully or negligently collects tax that isn't owed.

Erroneous refunds

The IRS is required to abate interest on a demand for repayment of a refund that was issued in error. For this rule to apply, the refund must be less than $50,000, and the taxpayer must in no way be responsible for causing the refund. On an erroneous refund, the IRS can charge interest only from the point in time when it demanded repayment and not for the period prior to the taxpayer being asked to repay it.

For example, suppose that you should have received a $100 refund, but instead, you received a $1,000 refund. No interest can be charged on the $900 for the period of time you held the money. If interest is assessed on the $900, filing Form 843, Claim for Refund and Request for Abatement, will get back the interest that you paid.

IRS delays

The Tax Reform Act of 1986 gives the IRS the authority to abate interest on any tax deficiency when an IRS official fails to perform a ministerial act and instead moves at a snail's pace in handling routine matters. (In this case, a *ministerial act* has nothing to do with performing the prescribed rituals of your favorite religious institution; the IRS official must act appropriately and in a timely manner to perform the prescribed rituals of your "favorite" government agency.) The IRS has the right to abate interest, but it isn't compelled to do so. When the failure to perform a ministerial act has occurred, interest is required to be abated from the time when the IRS first contacted you, not from the due date of your tax return, which normally is the case.

Here's how the IRS decided whether interest can be abated in the following cases:

>> You moved from one state to another. Your return was selected for audit. You request the audit to be transferred to your new location; the transfer is approved, but the IRS delays in transferring your case. Interest can be abated.

>> An audit reveals that additional tax is due. You and the IRS have agreed on the amount of additional tax due, but the IRS delays in sending you a bill. Interest can be abated.

>> You deducted a loss from a tax shelter that is being audited. The audit of the shelter takes a long time to complete. Interest can be abated.

>> The agent auditing your return is assigned to a training course, and, during the training course, your audit is neither worked on nor reassigned to a different agent. Interest can be abated.

Form 843, Claim for Refund and Request for Abatement, is used to abate interest in situations where the IRS has caused a delay. Check box 5a ("Interest was assessed as a result of IRS errors or delays").

Although delays by the IRS caused by loss of records, transfer of personnel, extended illness, leave, or training now are causes for abating interest, be forewarned that getting interest abated on an IRS delay nevertheless is a tough nut to crack. The IRS has the authority but, again, isn't compelled to abate interest when managerial acts cause delay.

When the IRS doesn't send a bill

When you sign off on the results of a tax examination or notice of proposed adjustments to your return, the IRS must send you a bill for payment within 30 days. If it doesn't, the agency can't charge interest until a bill is sent. Use Form 843 to abate any interest charges after the 30-day period.

When the IRS sends a bill

If the amount that you owe is less than $100,000, you have 21 interest-free days to pay it. If the amount you owe is more than $100,000, you have ten business days before you're charged interest.

The 36-month rule

The IRS must send a notice of additional tax due within 36 months of filing your return. If it doesn't, it has to stop charging interest after 36 months and until 21 days after it sends a notice. (Chapter 18 explains how this rule works.)

Not all IRS notices are covered by this provision. For example, audit notices aren't. See Chapter 18 for the ins and outs of how this provision works.

Protecting Yourself with Innocent Spouse Relief

Innocent spouse relief, like the Tooth Fairy and the Loch Ness Monster, used to belong to the category of whimsy, possible in some far-fetched way, but never actually experienced. Fortunately for many members of either troubled marriages or marriages where spouses keep their financial dealings separate and private, *innocent spouse relief* (including separation of liability and equitable relief) is now a useful area of tax law instead of a fantasy that exists on the books but not in reality. The IRS explains it in great detail in IRS Publication 971 (*Innocent Spouse Relief*), which is available by mail or through the IRS website, www.irs.gov.

Essentially, an *innocent spouse* is one who signs a joint tax return on which there is an understatement of tax while not knowing whether the information contained on the return is correct. Signing a joint return ordinarily makes you jointly or severally liable for all the tax due on that return, even if it's your spouse's income. (See Chapter 4 for the specific details about filing a joint return.) That means that if your spouse is a deadbeat and doesn't pay any tax owed, you may end up paying more than your fair share of the tax, or maybe all of it. However, a so-called innocent spouse may be able to convince the IRS that they knew nothing about the underreported income or overreported deductions and/or credits that created this additional tax.

If you live in a one of the community property states (Arizona, California, Idaho, Louisiana, Nevada, New Mexico, Texas, Washington, or Wisconsin), even if you filed married filing separately, you may be liable for a portion of your spouse's understatement of tax; however, innocent spouse rules will work for you, too. You just need to apply them a little differently by separating out what is your liability from what belongs to your spouse (or ex-spouse). Publication 971 can help you with all the flowcharts and worksheets you may possibly desire.

If you receive a bill from the IRS for additional tax and you had no knowledge of the extra income excluded and/or the extra deductions and credits claimed, you may be entitled to relief. In the innocent spouse rules, three forms of relief are available:

>> Innocent spouse relief

>> Relief by separation of liability

>> Equitable relief

Determining if you're eligible

If you've just received a notice or bill from the IRS referring to income or deductions you know nothing about, you may qualify as an innocent spouse. In order for the IRS to consider your request (which you're going to file on Form 8857, aptly named Request for Innocent Spouse Relief), you need to meet all of the following conditions:

>> You filed a joint return that has an understatement of tax due to erroneous items of your spouse or former spouse.

>> At the time that you signed the joint return, you didn't know and had no reason to know that the tax shown on the return was understated.

>> Taking into consideration the facts and circumstances, holding you responsible for the underpayment of tax is unfair.

For example, your spouse plays the horses on the side, and one day wins $10,000 at the racetrack. Your spouse never tells you about the money and spends it without your knowledge. When the time comes to complete your joint tax return, your spouse figures that what you don't know won't hurt you and leaves the $10,000 off the return. The IRS, on the other hand, knows about the $10,000 winnings because the racetrack has reported the information, and comes looking for the income tax due on the $10,000. In this case, you're clearly an innocent spouse, and provided you file your Form 8857, you won't be liable for the additional tax on the $10,000. You're still on the line for any other tax shown on the return that you know about.

You really have to be unaware of something your spouse did in order to obtain any type of innocent spouse relief. Being told that money that you're receiving isn't taxable still constitutes knowledge, because you know about the money. And, if you and your spouse are transferring assets back and forth between yourselves or a third party in the hopes of hiding taxable income from the IRS, that's fraud, and that's not allowed.

If, on the other hand, the IRS is hounding you for back taxes and you really think innocent spouse relief may apply, give it a try. You can't be penalized for applying, and who knows, you may just be successful!

Receiving relief by separation of liability

The IRS may separate any additional tax liability between you and your spouse (so-called *separation of liability*) if you are no longer married to, are widowed, or are legally separated from the spouse with whom you filed a joint return, or you weren't a member of the same household as an estranged spouse during any point of the 12-month period preceding the filing of Form 8857.

The IRS is fussy when determining whether or not you're living in the same household as your estranged spouse. In order for you to qualify on that point, you really must be living apart, in separate houses or apartments, and not just as a trial or for convenience. For example, couples who live in different cities because of job reasons but who are together for all other purposes don't qualify. Neither will your living in an RV parked in your spouse's driveway.

Once again, just as in traditional innocent spouse relief, you must have no knowledge of the erroneous items. If you even had an inkling that your spouse was cheating on your joint taxes, you both are liable for the additional tax even if you received no benefit.

Under what circumstances can the IRS say you aren't responsible for all or part of any unpaid tax? Your spouse runs off in the middle of the night with all your dough and jewelry. Suppose that the IRS then discovers an additional $20,000 of income, $5,000 of which the IRS proves you had knowledge of. You and your spouse are responsible for the tax on the $5,000 that you knew about. Your spouse is solely responsible for the tax on the remaining $15,000.

Obtaining equitable relief

If you aren't eligible for either innocent spouse relief or separation of liability relief, you may still qualify for relief under the IRS's guidelines for equitable relief. *Equitable relief* is different from either traditional innocent spouse relief or separation of liability because the IRS will, given the right set of circumstances, give you partial or full relief not only for a tax understatement, but also for a tax underpayment (where you signed a return, but the taxes showing weren't paid).

In addition, the requirements for equitable relief are specific, and you must meet them all. They are as follows:

>> You and your spouse or ex didn't transfer assets between yourselves as part of a fraudulent scheme.

>> Your spouse or ex-spouse didn't transfer property to you with the intention of avoiding tax.

>> You didn't file or fail to file your return with the intention of committing fraud.

>> You didn't pay the tax.

>> You can establish that, given all the facts, holding you liable for either the understatement or underpayment of the tax would be unfair.

>> The relief that you seek must be attributable to your present or ex-spouse unless you live in a community property state; the item is in your name, but you can prove it's not really yours; you didn't know that money you intended for tax payments was misappropriated by your spouse (or ex); or you can establish that you were a victim of abuse before signing the return and that you signed the return under duress.

Additional innocent spouse rules

You must elect innocent spouse relief within two years from the day the IRS begins to enforce collection, either by a garnishment or Notice of Intent to Levy, or a lawsuit by the IRS against you. For example, if the IRS sends you a Notice of Intent to Levy, you have two years from that date to file Form 8857. If all you receive is a notice demanding payment, no time limits are placed on when you can no longer request innocent spouse relief.

Relief is available under this provision for all taxes, no matter how old. You can apply for relief even if you were denied innocent spouse relief under the old law.

No collection activity may be undertaken while your application for relief is pending. And if relief is denied, you can appeal to the U.S. Tax Court. You have 90 days after the notice of denial to make your appeal.

Now for the bad news: The IRS must notify your ex and give them the opportunity to object to what you're doing.

When a married couple separates, the IRS should be informed of each spouse's new address so that all notices received by one spouse are received by the other. You can take care of this by filing Form 8822, Change of Address.

The Taxpayer Bill of Rights enables you to ask what the IRS is doing to get your ex-spouse to pay and how much they have paid. Because of possible hostility toward an ex-spouse, the IRS won't reveal the ex-spouse's home or business address.

Injured spouse relief

Wrapping your mind around the intricacies of the innocent spouse rules isn't enough; now you also need to contend with the injured spouse rules. Fortunately, these are much simpler than those for innocent spouses.

Essentially, the *injured spouse rules* address the inequity of having tax payments you made go toward the unpaid debts of your spouse. Say, for example, your spouse has unpaid child support payments. Your joint tax return indicates a refund, primarily because you, who earned wages, paid in more than was ultimately due. But the government snags that refund and uses it to pay the back child support (or spousal support or prior year's federal or state tax liabilities). Fair? No way — you're an injured spouse!

To claim injured spouse relief, you must have filed a joint return, received income, made tax payments (either through withholdings or by quarterly estimated tax payments), and reported all that income and those payments on the joint return. Then the IRS must have used the overpayment shown on the return to pay the past-due amounts of your spouse. File Form 8379, Injured Spouse Allocation, to claim your share of the overpayment.

INCREASED TAXPAYER RIGHTS IN A NUTSHELL

In 1998, the IRS received quite a bit of negative press after congressional hearings revealed the abuse taxpayers were routinely being subjected to. It made great headlines, "IRS horror stories." After hearing from individual taxpayers who thought they'd been put through the wringer by the tough guys down at IRS Central, Congress decided to come to the rescue and give taxpayers more protection and rights. We have to chuckle a bit at all this — after all, Congress was the organization that created all these ambiguous and cumbersome tax laws in the first place.

More than a decade later, the IRS is patting its own back for its kinder, gentler profile. Here are the major provisions that supposedly benefit taxpayers. We say supposedly because the actual benefit often is far, far less than meets the eye:

- **Burden of proof falls (more) on the IRS.** Unlike the criminal justice system, which operates under the premise that when charged with a crime, you're presumed innocent until proven guilty, the U.S. tax system has operated under the reverse, perverse presumption that you're guilty until proven innocent. However, to benefit from being presumed innocent until the IRS proves otherwise, your tax disagreement must actually land in court, and you must meet other requirements, including having good records and having been cooperative and compliant to that point.

- **Taxpayers have new protections regarding collections.** In recent years, the IRS got itself into trouble with the way it handled certain tax collections. In some cases, taxpayers experienced unjustified and confrontational seizure of property and other assets, even for small amounts of tax owed. Now, for example, the IRS needs a court order to sell someone's home and a higher level of approval within the IRS to seize someone's business.

- **Innocent spouse rules are enhanced.** As we discuss in this chapter, married couples heading toward divorce don't always cooperate about money and taxes. The tax bill passed in 1998 beefs up a spouse's ability to file separately while still married to avoid being held responsible for the other spouse's tax negligence. Although this option may sound attractive, we fear that it will increase total costs for both spouses, especially if you factor in the costs of a divorce lawyer wrangling over tax liabilities.

- **Advice given by tax advisors to taxpayers is confidential.** With legal matters, what a client tells their attorney is largely confidential. With tax issues, that same standard of confidentiality hasn't been applied to what a taxpayer tells their preparer or advisor. Taxpayers can now consult with tax advisors in the same confidential and privileged manner as they do with lawyers. Remember, however, that information disclosed in preparation of a tax return isn't covered by this rule!

The Taxpayer Bill of Rights: In the Beginning

This great republic was founded on the principle that taxation without representation is tyranny. But if you've ever had a run-in with the IRS, you know that taxation with representation isn't so hot, either. To feed its insatiable appetite for spending, Congress has given the IRS almost unlimited authority to collect taxes — an authority that, sadly, can be abused in all sorts of horrible ways.

In response to congressional hearings and a flurry of taxpayer horror stories in 1998, Congress enacted the so-called *Taxpayer Bill of Rights.*

Now, whenever you get a notice of any kind from the IRS, you get a two-page summary of the taxpayer bill, entitled "Your Rights as a Taxpayer." This remarkably readable document explains how to appeal an IRS decision, suggests where you can get free information, and assures you that you're entitled to "courtesy and consideration" from IRS employees. Reading it, you almost get the impression that the IRS is a friendly place that wants only what's best for you. Use your common sense here — remember, at the end of the day, the IRS is trying to get money that you're trying to hang onto. You and the IRS are still adversaries; the Taxpayer Bill of Rights just makes you more civilized adversaries!

The Taxpayer Bill of Rights has been through a few incarnations. The original Taxpayer Bill of Rights contained two significant points:

>> At any time during an audit or interview, you may ask to speak with an enrolled agent, attorney, or CPA. Whenever that happens, the IRS must stop what it's doing and let you do so.

>> The IRS may not take money or property from you on the same day that you comply with a summons. In other words, the IRS can't demand that you appear and then seize your car when you get to its office — something that used to happen a lot.

Despite those important rights, the original Taxpayer Bill of Rights left much to be desired. In too many cases, it allowed the IRS itself to interpret your rights. It's like having the same person as prosecutor, judge, jury, and executioner.

The Taxpayer Bill of Rights: Parts 2 and 3

Our complaint with the original Taxpayer Bill of Rights was that it didn't have teeth. Now it does. But not a full set. And, unlike in the Rocky movies, the Taxpayer Bill of Rights Part 2 that became law on July 30, 1996, and Part 3, which came about when the IRS was overhauled in 1998, don't see to it that the underdog always wins. Here's what the improved Taxpayer Bill of Rights does for you:

>> Abates the penalty for failing to deposit payroll taxes for first-time filers of employment tax returns.

>> Enables you to file a joint return after a separate return has been filed without having to pay the full joint tax.

>> Allows the return of levied property, including your salary, if you have an installment agreement to pay what you owe, and it would be a hardship (you can't pay your bills) not to return it. Under the old rules, once the IRS glommed your dough, it couldn't return it.

>> Requires that 1099s have the name, address, and telephone number of whom to contact in case the reported amount is incorrect and needs investigating.

- Shifts the burden to the IRS to prove that its position was substantially justified when you prevail in a suit with the IRS. If the IRS position wasn't substantially justified, you can collect for legal fees and court costs from the IRS. Under the old rule, *you* had to prove that the IRS's position wasn't substantially justified.

- Requires that the IRS, upon a taxpayer's request, make every reasonable effort to contact private creditors when a Notice of a Tax Lien has been withdrawn.

The bill also includes the following helpful provisions:

- If a few people, namely the owners or officers of a business, are personally responsible for payment of taxes that were withheld from their employees' salaries and one of these individuals pays more than their share, that person can sue to recover that amount from the others. The IRS now is obliged to tell what each person paid and what the IRS is doing to collect what is owed from the others. Because the IRS usually goes after the owner from whom it will have the least difficulty in collecting the entire amount that business owes, that poor soul now has the right to know what the other partners have paid so they can make the negligent partners pay their share of what the individual who overpaid was forced to pay.

- The IRS must notify taxpayers if it receives a payment that can't be applied against what is owed, instead of merely depositing the check and holding it in limbo.

- If you owe the IRS, the IRS must send you at least an annual bill so you know where you stand. The statement must include a detailed computation of the interest charged.

- For taxes that you and an ex-spouse jointly owe, you can ask the IRS what it's doing to get your ex-spouse to pay the tax, and you have the right to be told how much has been paid. Because of possible hostility toward an ex-spouse, the IRS, however, won't reveal the ex-spouse's home or business addresses.

- The innocent spouse rules have been made more lenient in a number of ways. Relief can also be obtained on an apportioned basis.

- If the IRS doesn't send a notice adjusting a taxpayer's return within 36 months, it must stop charging interest after 36 months and until 21 days after a notice is sent. See Chapter 18, because not all IRS notices are covered under this rule.

- You can collect up to $1 million in damages if the IRS acts with reckless or intentional disregard of the rules in collecting tax. If the IRS is merely negligent, the limit is $100,000. The IRS has the authority — but, again, isn't compelled — to abate interest because of delays on its part. Delays caused by loss of records, transfer of personnel, extended illness, leave, or training programs now are causes for abating interest.

- If someone issues you a fraudulent 1099, you can sue for damages of up to $5,000.

- Proof under the "timely mailing is timely filing" rule requires that a document or return had to be sent by either certified or registered mail. Using FedEx, DHL, or UPS now is equivalent to sending a return or document by certified or registered mail.

  A mailing receipt that you receive from the post office other than for certified or registered mail isn't considered valid proof of meeting the "timely mailing is timely filing" rule.

- Financial status audits to scrutinize a taxpayer's lifestyle are allowed only when a routine examination has established a likelihood of unreported income. See Chapter 18.

>> Taxpayers have a 30-day period to appeal a lien or levy. See Chapter 18.

>> The rejection of an Offer in Compromise or a request for an installment agreement can be appealed.

>> While an Offer in Compromise or a request for an installment agreement is pending or on appeal, the IRS can't levy against a taxpayer.

>> Your residence can't be seized unless authorized in writing by a U.S. district court judge. Business assets can't be seized unless authorized by a district or assistant district director.

>> The law shifts the burden of proof from the taxpayer to the IRS in court proceedings.

5

Year-Round Tax Planning

Chapter **21**

Tax-Wise Personal Finance Decisions

Managing your personal finances involves much more than simply investing money. It includes making all the pieces of your financial life fit together. And, just like designing a vacation itinerary, managing your personal finances means developing a strategy to make the best use of your limited dollars and being prepared to deal with some adversity and changes to the landscape.

Including Taxes in Your Financial Planning

Taxes are a large and vital piece of your financial puzzle. The following list shows some of the ways that tax issues are involved in making sound financial decisions throughout the year:

» **Spending:** The more you spend, the more taxes you'll pay for taxed purchases and for being less able to take advantage of the many benefits in the tax code that require you to have money to invest in the first place. For example, contrary to the hucksters on late-night infomercials, you need money to purchase real estate, which offers many tax benefits (see Chapter 25). And because taxes are probably your largest or second biggest expenditure, a budget that overlooks tax-reduction strategies is likely doomed to fail. Unless you have wealthy, benevolent relatives, you may be stuck with a lifetime of working if you can't save money.

>> **Retirement accounts:** Taking advantage of retirement accounts can mean tens, perhaps even hundreds of thousands more dollars in your pocket come retirement time. Who says there are no free lunches? Check out Chapter 22.

>> **Investing:** Merely choosing investments that generate healthy rates of return isn't enough. What matters is not what you make but what you keep — after paying taxes. Understand and capitalize on the many tax breaks available to investors in stocks, bonds, mutual funds, real estate, and your own business. See Chapter 23 for the details.

>> **Protecting your assets:** Some of your insurance decisions also affect the taxes you pay. You'd think that after a lifetime of tax payments, your heirs would be left alone when you pass on to the great beyond — wishful thinking. Estate planning can significantly reduce the taxes to be siphoned off from your estate. Peruse Chapter 27 to find out more about estate planning.

Taxes infiltrate many areas of your personal finances. Some people make important financial decisions without considering taxes (and other important variables). Conversely, in an obsession to minimize or avoid taxes, other people make decisions that are counterproductive to achieving their long-term personal and financial goals. Although this chapter shows you that taxes are an important component to factor into your major financial decisions, taxes should not drive or dictate the decisions you make.

Taxing Mistakes

Even if some parts of the tax system are hopelessly and unreasonably complicated, there's no reason why you can't learn from the mistakes of others to save yourself some money. With this goal in mind, this section details common tax blunders that people make when it comes to managing their money.

Seeking advice after a major decision

Too many people come across information and hire help after making a decision, even though seeking preventive help ahead of time generally is wiser and less costly. Before making any major financial decisions, educate yourself. This book can help answer many of your questions.

If you're going to hire a tax advisor to give advice, do so before making your decision(s). Read Chapters 2 and 31 for tips about finding a good tax advisor. The wrong move when selling a piece of real estate or taking money from a retirement account can cost you thousands of dollars in taxes!

TIP

Failing to withhold enough taxes

If you're self-employed or earn significant taxable income from investments outside retirement accounts, you need to be making estimated quarterly tax payments. Likewise, if, during the year, you sell an investment at a profit, you may need to make a (higher) quarterly tax payment.

WARNING

Not having a human resources department to withhold taxes from their pay as they earn it, some self-employed people dig themselves into a perpetual tax hole by failing to submit estimated quarterly tax payments. They get behind in their tax payments during their first year of self-employment and thereafter are always playing catch-up. Don't be a "should've" victim. People often don't discover that they "should've" paid more taxes during the year until after they complete their returns in the spring — or get penalty notices from the IRS and their states. Then they have to come up with sizable sums all at once.

To make quarterly tax payments, complete IRS Form 1040-ES, Estimated Tax for Individuals. This form and accompanying instructions explain how to calculate quarterly tax payments — the IRS even sends you payment coupons and envelopes in which to mail your checks. We walk you through the essentials of completing this form in Chapter 17.

TIP

Although we — and the IRS — want you to keep your taxes current during the year, we don't want you to overpay. Some people have too much tax withheld during the year, and this overpayment can go on year after year. Although it may feel good to get a sizable refund check every spring, why should you loan your money to the government interest-free? When you work for an employer, you can complete a new W-4 to adjust your withholding. Turn the completed W-4 in to your employer. When you're self-employed, complete Form 1040-ES. (See Chapter 17 for instructions on completing your W-4.)

If you know that you'd otherwise spend the extra tax money that you're currently sending to the IRS, then this forced-savings strategy may have some value. But you can find other, better ways to make yourself save. You can set up all sorts of investments, such as mutual funds (see Chapter 24), to be funded by automatic contributions from your paychecks (or from a bank or investment account). Of course, if you happen to prefer to loan the IRS money — interest-free — go right ahead!

Overlooking legitimate deductions

Some taxpayers miss out on perfectly legal tax deductions because they just don't know about them. Ignorance is not bliss when it comes to your income taxes . . . it's costly. If you aren't going to take the time to discover the legitimate deductions available to you (you bought this book, so why not read the relevant parts of it?), spring for the cost of a competent tax advisor at least once.

Fearing an audit, some taxpayers (and even some tax preparers) avoid taking deductions that they have every right to take. Unless you have something to hide, such behavior is foolish and costly. Remember that a certain number of returns are randomly audited every year, so even when you don't take every deduction to which you're legally entitled, you may nevertheless get audited! And how bad is an audit, really? If you read Chapter 18, you can find out how to deal with your audit like a pro. An hour or so with the IRS is not as bad as you may think. It may be worth the risk of claiming all the tax breaks to which you're entitled, especially when you consider the amounts you can save through the years.

Passing up retirement accounts

All the tax deductions and tax deferrals that come with accounts such as 401(k)s, 403(b)s, SEP-IRAs, and IRAs were put in the tax code to encourage you to save for retirement. So why not take advantage of the benefits?

You probably have your reasons or excuses, but most excuses for missing out on this strategy just don't make good financial sense. People often underfund retirement accounts because they spend too much and because retirement seems so far away. Many people also mistakenly believe that retirement account money is totally inaccessible until they're old enough to qualify for senior discounts. See Chapter 22 to find out all about retirement accounts and why you should probably fund them.

Ignoring tax considerations when investing

Suppose that you want to unload some stock so that you can buy a new car. You sell an investment at a significant profit and feel good about your financial genius. But, come tax time, you may feel differently.

REMEMBER

Don't forget to consider the taxes due on profits from the sale of investments (except those in retirement accounts) when making decisions about what you sell and when you sell it. Your tax situation also needs to factor in what you invest outside retirement accounts. When you're in a relatively high tax bracket, you probably don't want investments that pay much in taxable distributions such as taxable interest, which only add to your tax burden. See Chapter 24 for details on the tax considerations of investing and which investments are tax-friendly for your situation.

Not buying a home

In the long run, owning a home should cost you less than renting. And because mortgage interest and property taxes are deductible, the government, in effect, subsidizes the cost of home ownership.

Even if the government didn't help you with tax benefits when buying and owning a home, you'd still be better off owning over your adult life. If you instead rented, all your housing expenses are exposed to inflation, unless you have a great rent-controlled deal. So owning your own abode makes good financial and tax sense. And don't let the lack of money for a down payment stand in your way — methods exist for buying real estate with little upfront money. See Chapter 25 to find out about real estate and taxes.

Allowing your political views to distort your decision making

Some folks have strong political orientations. I'm sure you have your reasons why you believe and advocate what you do, and we're not here to talk you out of that. But we will tell you that we've seen plenty of people make poor financial decisions, especially with investments, because their political concerns get in the way.

Consider some recent examples. In late 2008, President Barack Obama was elected and his being a pretty liberal guy freaked out some conservatives, especially because the Democrats then controlled the Presidency and the House and Senate. Pundits, especially those of the conservative persuasion, warned that the economy, already in tough shape when he took office, was going to be in tatters for years to come as Obama would raise taxes and investments would do poorly. While economic growth wasn't rapid, the economy performed pretty well in 2009 and the following years, and stock prices bounced back nicely, as they generally do after a major bear market.

In late 2016, President Donald Trump was elected and his being an outspoken, inexperienced politician who espoused conservative policies freaked out some liberals, especially with Republicans in control of the House, Senate, and Presidency. Prognosticators, especially on the left politically, opined that Trump would cause the economy and stock market to crash and burn as his reckless tax-cutting policies would explode the deficit and cause myriad other problems. That didn't happen as economic growth accelerated, and stock prices did quite well. And while the COVID-19 pandemic and mandated government economic shutdowns upset things for some months in early 2020, the economy and stock prices quickly bounced back.

TIP

There's a simple moral to the stories here. To be a successful investor and make sound financial decisions, try to leave your political beliefs out of it and be unemotional. Extreme changes rarely occur even when one party–rule occurs for a couple of years in Washington, D.C. It's often soon replaced by divided government, which leads to more incremental change and eventually a switch in power back to the current out-of-power party.

Ignoring the financial aid (tax) system

WARNING

The college financial aid system in this country assumes that the money you save outside tax-sheltered retirement accounts is available to pay educational expenses. As a result, families who save money outside instead of inside retirement accounts may qualify for far less "financial aid" than they otherwise would. Financial aid is actually a misnomer because what colleges and universities are doing is charging a different price to different families after analyzing their finances. So, when a college appears to be giving you money, what they're actually doing is reducing their inflated prices to a more reasonable level.

If you're affluent and have done a good job saving and investing money, colleges are generally going to charge you more. So in addition to normal income taxes, an extra financial aid "tax" is effectively exacted. Be sure to read Chapter 26, which covers the best ways to save and invest for educational costs.

Neglecting the timing of events you can control

The amount of tax you pay on certain transactions can vary, depending on the timing of events. If you're nearing retirement, for example, you may soon be in a lower tax bracket. To the extent possible, you should consider delaying and avoid claiming investment income until your overall income level drops, and you need to take as many deductions or losses as you can now while your income still is high. Following are two tax-reducing strategies — income shifting and bunching or shifting deductions — that you may be able to put to good use when you can control the timing of either your income or deductions.

Shifting income

TAX CUT

Suppose that your employer tells you in late December that you're eligible for a bonus. You find out that you have the option of receiving your bonus in either December or January (ask your payroll and benefits department if this is an option). Looking ahead, if you're pretty certain that you're going to be in a higher tax bracket next year, request to receive your bonus in December. (See Chapter 1 to find out about your tax bracket.)

Or suppose that you run your own business and operate on a cash accounting basis and think that you'll be in a lower tax bracket next year. Perhaps business has slowed of late or you plan to take time off to be with a newborn or take an extended trip. You can send out some invoices later in the year so that your customers won't pay you until January, which falls in the next tax year.

Bunching or shifting deductions

When the total of your itemized deductions on Schedule A (see Chapter 11) is lower than the standard deduction, you need to take the standard deduction. This itemized deduction total is worth checking each year, because you may have more deductions in some years than others, and you may occasionally be able to itemize.

When you can control the timing of payment of particular expenses that are eligible for itemizing, you can shift or bunch more of them into select years when you're more likely to have enough deductions to take advantage of itemizing. Suppose that because you don't have many itemized deductions this year, you use the standard deduction. Late in the year, however, you feel certain that you'll itemize next year, because you plan to buy a home and will therefore be able to claim significant mortgage interest and some property tax deductions. It makes sense, then, to shift and bunch as many deductible expenses as possible into next year. For example, if you're getting ready to make a tax-deductible donation of old clothes and household goods to charity, wait until January to do so.

In any tax year that you're sure you won't have enough deductions to be able to itemize, shift as many itemizable expenses as you can into the next tax year. If you don't know what types of expenses you can itemize, be sure to peruse Chapter 11.

WARNING

Be careful when using your credit card to pay expenses. These expenses must be recognized for tax purposes in the year in which the charge was made on the card and not when you actually pay the credit card bill.

Not using tax advisors effectively

If your financial situation is complicated, going it alone and relying only on the IRS instructions to figure your taxes usually is a mistake. Many people find the IRS publications tedious and not geared toward highlighting opportunities for tax reductions.

Instead, you can start by reading the relevant sections of this book. You can figure out taxes for yourself, or you can hire a tax advisor to figure them out for you. Doing nothing isn't an advisable option!

TIP

When you're overwhelmed by the complexity of particular financial decisions, get advice from tax and financial advisors who sell their time and nothing else. Protect yourself by checking references and clarifying what advice, analysis, and recommendations the advisor will provide for the fee charged. If your tax situation is complicated, you'll probably more than recoup a preparer's fee, as long as you take the time to hire a good advisor. (See Chapter 2 for tips on hiring help.)

TIP

Remember that using a tax advisor is most beneficial when you face new tax questions or problems. If your tax situation remains complicated, or if you know that you'd do a worse job on your own, by all means keep using a tax preparer. But don't pay a big fee year after year to a tax advisor who simply plugs your numbers into the tax forms. If your situation is unchanging or isn't that complicated, consider hiring and paying someone to figure out your taxes one time. After that, go ahead and try completing your own tax return.

Comprehending the Causes of Bad Tax Decisions

When bad things happen, it's usually for a variety of reasons. And so it is with making financial blunders that cause you to pay more tax dollars. The following sections describe some common culprits that may be keeping you from making tax-wise financial maneuvers and what you can do about them.

"Financial planners" and brokers' advice

Wanting to hire a financial advisor to help you make better financial decisions is a logical inclination, especially if you're a time-starved person. But when you pick a poor planner or someone who isn't a financial planner but rather a salesperson in disguise, watch out!

WARNING

Unfortunately, many people calling themselves financial planners, financial consultants, or financial advisors actually work on commission, which creates enormous conflicts of interest with providing unbiased and objective financial advice. Brokers and commission-based financial planners (who are also therefore brokers) structure their advice around selling you investment and other financial products that provide them with commissions. As a result, they tend to take a narrow view of your finances and frequently ignore the tax and other consequences of financial moves. Or they may pitch the supposed tax benefits of an investment they're eager to sell you as a reason for you to buy it. It may provide a tax benefit for someone, but not necessarily for you in your specific situation.

The few planners who work on a fee basis primarily provide money-management services and typically charge about 1 percent per year of the money they manage. Fee-based planners have their own conflicts of interest, because all things being equal, they want you to hire them to manage your money. Therefore, they can't objectively help you decide whether you should pay off your mortgage and other debts, invest in real estate or a small business, or invest more in your employer's retirement plan. In short, they have a bias against financial strategies that take your investment money out of their hands.

WARNING

Be especially leery of planners, brokers, and money-managing planners who lobby you to sell investments that you've held for a while and that show a profit. If you sell these investments, you may have a hefty tax burden. (See Chapter 24 for more insight on how to make these important investing decisions.)

Advertising

Another reason you may make tax missteps in managing your personal finances is advertising. Although reputable financial firms with terrific products advertise, the firms that spend the most on advertising often are the ones with inferior offerings. Being bombarded with ads whenever you listened to the radio, watched television, or read magazines and newspapers was bad enough, but now email boxes, websites, and social media platforms are stuffed full of spam and promos too.

WARNING

Responding to ads usually is a bad financial move, regardless of whether the product being pitched is good, bad, or so-so, because the company placing the ad typically is trying to motivate you to buy a specific product. The company doesn't care about your financial alternatives, whether its product fits with your tax situation, and so on. Many ads try to catch your attention with the supposed tax savings that their products generate.

Advice from websites and publications

You read an article that recommends some investments. Tired of not taking charge and making financial decisions, you get on the phone, call an investment company, and — before you know it — you've invested. You feel a sense of relief and accomplishment — you've done something.

Come tax time, you get all these confusing statements detailing dividends and capital gains that you must report on your tax return. Now you see that these investment strategies generate all sorts of taxable distributions that add to your tax burden. And you may be saddled with additional tax forms to complete by April 15. You wish you had known.

WARNING

Articles on websites, in magazines, newspapers, newsletters, and so forth can help you stay informed, but they also can cause you to make ill-advised financial moves that overlook tax consequences. Article writers have limited time and space and often don't consider the big picture or ways their advice can be misunderstood or misused. Even worse is that too many writers don't know the tax consequences of what they're writing about.

Overspending

Far too many tax guides go on and on and on, talking about this tax break and that tax break. The problem is that to take advantage of many of the best tax breaks, you need to have money to invest. When you spend all that you earn, you miss out on many terrific tax benefits that we tell you about in this book. And the more you spend, the more taxes you pay, both on your income and on the purchases you make (through sales taxes).

Just like losing weight, spending less sounds good, but most people have a hard time budgeting their finances and spending less than they earn. Perhaps you already know where the fat is in your spending. If you don't, figuring out where all your monthly income is going is a real eye-opener. The task takes some detective work — looking through your credit card statements and your checkbook register to track your purchases and categorize your spending.

Financial illiteracy

Lack of personal finance education is at the root of most money blunders. You may not understand the tax system and how to manage your finances because you were never taught how to manage them growing up or in high school or college.

Financial illiteracy is a widespread problem not just among the poor and undereducated. Most people don't plan ahead and educate themselves with their financial goals in mind. People react — or, worse, do nothing at all. You may dream, for example, about retiring and never having to work again. Or perhaps you hope that someday you can own a house or even a vacation home in the country or by the shore.

You need to understand how to plan your finances so you can accomplish your financial goals. You also need to understand how the tax system works and how to navigate within it to work toward your objectives.

If you need more help with important personal financial issues, pick up a copy of the latest edition of Eric's *Personal Finance For Dummies* (Wiley).

Chapter **22**

Trimming Taxes with Retirement Accounts

S aving and investing through retirement accounts is one of the simplest yet most powerful methods to reduce your tax burden. Understanding the myriad account options and
rules isn't simple, but we do our best at explaining them in this chapter.

Unfortunately, most people can't take advantage of these plans because they spend too much
of what they make. So not only do they have less savings, but they also pay higher income
taxes — a double whammy. And don't forget, the more you spend, the more sales tax you pay
on purchases. To be able to best take advantage of the tax savings that come with retirement
savings plans, you should spend less than you earn. Only then can you afford to contribute to
these plans.

Identifying Retirement Account Benefits

Retirement may seem like the distant future to young folks. It's often not until middle age
that warning bells start stimulating thoughts about what money they'll live on in their golden
years. The single biggest mistake people at all income levels make with retirement accounts is
not taking advantage of them. When you're in your 20s and 30s (and for some individuals in
their 40s and 50s), spending and living for today and postponing saving for the future seems a
whole lot more fun than saving for retirement. But assuming that you don't want to work your
entire life, the sooner you start saving, the less painful it is each year, because your contributions have more years to grow.

RETIREMENT ACCOUNT PENALTIES FOR EARLY WITHDRAWALS

One objection that some people have to contributing to retirement accounts is the early withdrawal penalties. Specifically, if you withdraw funds from retirement accounts before age 59½, you not only have to pay income taxes on withdrawals, but you also pay early withdrawal penalties — 10 percent in federal plus applicable state charges. (There's a 25 percent penalty for withdrawing from a SIMPLE plan within the first two years, which decreases to 10 percent thereafter.)

The penalties are in place for good reason — to discourage people from raiding retirement accounts. Remember, retirement accounts exist for just that reason — saving toward retirement. If you can easily tap these accounts without penalties, the money would be less likely to be there when you need it during retirement.

If you have an emergency, such as catastrophic medical expenses or a disability, you may be able to take early withdrawals from retirement accounts without penalty. You may withdraw funds from particular retirement accounts free of penalties (and, in some cases, even free of current income taxes) for educational expenses or a home purchase. We spell out the specifics in the "Penalty-free IRA withdrawals" section later in this chapter.

What if you just run out of money because you lose your job? Although you can't bypass the penalties because of such circumstances, if you're earning so little income that you need to tap your retirement account, you'll surely be in a low tax bracket. So even though you pay some penalties to withdraw retirement account money, the lower income taxes that you pay upon withdrawal — as compared to the taxes that you would have incurred when you earned the money originally — should make up for most or all of the penalty.

Know also that if you get in a financial pinch while you're still employed, some company retirement plans allow you to borrow against a portion of your cash balance. Just be sure that you can repay such a loan — otherwise, your "loan" becomes a withdrawal and triggers income taxes and penalties.

Another strategy to meet a short-term financial emergency is to withdraw money from your IRA and return it within 60 days to avoid paying penalties. We don't generally recommend this maneuver because of the taxes and potential penalties invoked if you don't make the 60-day deadline.

In the event that your only "borrowing" option right now is a credit card with a high interest rate, you should save three to six months' worth of living expenses in an accessible account before funding a retirement account to tide you over in case you lose your income. Money market mutual funds and bank savings accounts are useful vehicles for this purpose.

You may be interested in knowing that if good fortune comes your way and you accumulate enough funds to retire "early," you have a simple way around the pre-age-59½ early withdrawal penalties. Suppose that at age 55 you retire and want to start living off some of the money you've stashed in retirement accounts. No problem. The U.S. tax laws allow you to start withdrawing money from your retirement accounts free of those nasty early withdrawal penalties. To qualify for this favorable treatment, you must commit to withdrawals for at least five continuous years, and the amount of the withdrawals must be at least the minimum required based on your life expectancy.

Each decade that you delay contributing approximately doubles the percentage of your earnings that you need to save to meet your goals. For example, if saving 5 percent per year in your early 20s gets you to your retirement goal, waiting until your 30s may mean socking away 10 percent; waiting until your 40s, 20 percent . . . it gets ugly beyond that!

So, the longer you wait, the more you'll have to save and, therefore, the less that will be left over for spending. As a result, you may not meet your goal, and your golden years may be more restrictive than you hoped.

We use this simple lesson to emphasize the importance of considering now the benefits you achieve by saving and investing in some type of retirement account.

Contributions are (generally) tax-deductible

Spend money today and you may get some instant gratification. Put some of that same money into a retirement account, and you may yawn with excitement and then get a headache figuring where to invest it!

Retirement accounts really should be called tax-reduction accounts. If they were, people may be more eager to contribute to them, especially during their younger years. For many people, avoiding higher taxes is the motivating force that gets them to open the account and start the contributions.

TAX CUT

If you're a moderate-income earner, you probably pay about 25 to 30 percent in federal and state income taxes on your last dollars of income (see Chapter 1 to identify your tax bracket). Thus, with most of the retirement accounts described in this chapter, for every $1,000 you contribute to them, you save yourself about $250 to $300 in taxes in the year that you make the contribution. Contribute five times as much, or $5,000, and whack $1,250 to $1,500 off your tax bill! Thanks to tax bills passed in the early 2000s, the contribution limits on retirement accounts have greatly increased since then and will continue to rise with inflation in the years ahead (the details are later in this chapter).

Check with your employer's benefits department because some organizations match a portion of employee contributions. Be sure to partake of this free matching money by contributing to your retirement accounts.

Special tax credit for lower-income earners

In addition to the upfront tax break you get from contributing to many retirement accounts, lower-income earners may receive tax credits worth up to 50 percent on the first $2,000 of retirement account contributions. Like employer-matching contributions, this tax credit amounts to free money (in this case from the government), so you should take advantage!

As you can see in Table 22-1, this retirement account contribution tax credit phases out quickly for higher-income earners, and no such credit is available to single taxpayers with adjusted gross incomes (AGIs) above $33,000, heads of household with AGIs above $49,500, and to married couples filing jointly with AGIs above $66,000. (*Note:* This credit isn't available to taxpayers who are claimed as dependents on someone else's tax return or who are under the age of 18 or full-time students.)

Table 22-1   2021 Tax Credit for the First $2,000 in Retirement Plan Contributions

Single Taxpayers AGI	Head of Household AGI	Married Couples Filing Jointly AGI	Tax Credit
$0 to $19,750	$0 to $29,625	$0 to $39,500	50%
$19,750 to $21,500	$29,625 to $32,250	$39,500 to $43,000	20%
$21,500 to $33,000	$32,250 to $49,500	$43,000 to $66,000	10%

Tax-deferred compounding of investment earnings

After money is placed in a retirement account, any interest, dividends, and appreciation add to the amount in the account without being taxed. You get to defer taxes on all the accumulating gains and profits until you withdraw the money, presumably in retirement. Thus, more money is working for you over a longer period of time.

Your retirement tax rate need not be less than your tax rate during your working years for you to come out ahead by contributing to retirement accounts. In fact, because you defer paying tax and have more money compounding over more years, you can end up with more money in retirement by saving inside a retirement account, even if your retirement tax rate is higher than it is now.

I NEED HOW MUCH FOR RETIREMENT?

On average, most people need about 70 percent to 80 percent of their pre-retirement income to maintain their standard of living throughout their retirement. For example, if your household earns $60,000 per year before retirement, you'll likely need $42,000 to $48,000 (70 percent to 80 percent of $60,000) per year during retirement to live the way that you're accustomed to living.

Remember that 70 percent to 80 percent is just an average. You may need more or less. If you currently save little or none of your annual income, expect to have a large mortgage payment or growing rent in retirement, or anticipate wanting to travel or do other expensive things in retirement, you may need 90 percent or perhaps even 100 percent of your current income to maintain your standard of living in retirement.

On the other hand, if you now save a high percentage of your earnings, are a high-income earner, expect to own your home free of debt by retirement, and anticipate leading a modest lifestyle in retirement, you may be able to make do with, say, 60 percent of your current income.

If you've never thought about what your retirement goals are, looked into what you can expect from Social Security (stop laughing), or calculated how much you should be saving for retirement, now's the time to do it. The latest edition of *Personal Finance For Dummies,* written by Eric Tyson (Wiley), goes through all the necessary details and even tells you how to come up with more to invest and do it wisely.

The tax rate on *long-term capital gains* — investments held more than one year — and stock dividends (see Chapter 24) is significantly lower than the rate on ordinary income. Watch out though — the current rates may increase, at least for some higher-income taxpayers. So, keep an eye on Washington and subsequent editions of this book to keep absolutely up-to-date.

And remember this: You may get an added bonus from deferring taxes on your retirement account assets if you're in a lower tax bracket when you withdraw the money. You may well be in a lower tax bracket in retirement because most people have less income when they're not working.

Note: When you're near retirement and already have money in a tax-sheltered type of retirement account (for example, at your employer), by all means continue to keep it in a tax-favored account if you leave. You can accomplish this goal by rolling the money over into an IRA account. If your employer offers good investment options in a retirement plan and allows you to leave your money in the plan after your departure, consider that option, too.

Don't go overboard

Over the years, we've seen some clients "over" contribute to retirement accounts. We don't literally mean that these well-intentioned souls broke the contribution limit rules in a given tax year. We're talking about unusual situations where people have contributed more to their retirement accounts than what makes good financial and tax sense.

For example, it may not make sense for a taxpayer who is temporarily in a very low tax bracket (or owing no tax at all) to contribute to retirement accounts, especially those offering an upfront tax break. (Roth accounts are an exception because their tax breaks are ongoing and at withdrawal, not upfront.) Ditto the person who has a large estate already and has piles inside retirement accounts that can get walloped by estate and income taxes upon their passing. Few people, of course, have this perhaps enviable "problem."

When in doubt, and if you have reason to believe you should scale back on retirement account contributions, consult with a competent financial/tax advisor who works for an hourly fee and doesn't sell products or manage money. Please see the latest edition of Eric's *Personal Finance For Dummies* (Wiley) for more details.

Naming the Types of Retirement Accounts

When you earn employment income (or receive alimony), you have the option of putting money away in a retirement account that compounds without taxation until you withdraw the money. In most cases, your contributions are tax-deductible. The following sections discuss "IRS-approved" retirement accounts and explain how to determine whether you're eligible for them and some other nitpicky but important rules.

WHY SO MANY DIFFERENT TYPES OF RETIREMENT ACCOUNTS?

The different types of retirement plans — 401(k)s, 403(b)s, SEP-IRAs, regular IRAs, Roth IRAs, 401(k)s, and SIMPLE — and the unique tax laws governing each are enough to drive taxpayers and some tax preparers wacky. The complexity of the different rules is another reason that some folks don't bother with these accounts.

As with the other complicated parts of our tax laws, retirement account regulations have accumulated over the years. Just like the stuff that you toss into your spare closet, attic, basement, or garage, the regulations just keep piling up. No one really wants to deal with the mess.

Our neighbors to the north in Canada have a retirement account system that we can learn from. In Canada, they have but one account — it's called the Registered Retirement Savings Plan (RRSP). Everyone with employment income can establish this account and contribute up to 18 percent, or up to a maximum annual total contribution of $27,830 — simple, equitable, and easy to understand. Why don't we do it? Go talk to the boneheads in Congress who brought us this supposedly "simple, equitable, and easy" tax system you're reading about!

Employer-sponsored plans

You should be thankful that your employer values your future enough to offer these benefits and grateful that your employer has gone to the trouble of doing the legwork of setting up the plan, and in most cases, selecting investment options. If you were self-employed, you'd have to hassle with establishing your own plan and choosing investment options. All you have to do with an employer plan is save enough to invest and allocate your contributions among the (generally few) investments offered.

401(k) plans

For-profit companies generally offer 401(k) plans. The silly name comes from the section of the tax code that establishes and regulates these plans. A 401(k) generally allows you to save up to $19,500 for tax year 2021. Your employer's plan may have lower contribution limits, though, if employees don't save enough in the company's 401(k) plan. Your contributions to a 401(k) generally are excluded from your reported income and thus are free from federal and, in some cases, state income taxes, but not from Social Security and Medicare taxes (and from some other state employment taxes).

Older workers — those at least age 50 — are able to put away even more: up to $6,500 more per year than their younger counterparts. The annual contribution limit on 401(k) plans and the additional amounts allowed for older workers rises, in $500 increments, with inflation.

Some employers don't allow you to start contributing to their 401(k) plan until you've worked for them for a full year. Others allow you to start contributing right away. Some employers also match a portion of your contributions. They may, for example, match half of your first 6 percent of contributions (so in addition to saving a lot of taxes, you get a free bonus from the company). Check with your company's benefits department for your plan's details.

Smaller companies (those with fewer than 100 employees) can consider offering 401(k) plans, too. In the past, it was prohibitively expensive for smaller companies to administer a 401(k) plan. If your company is interested in this option, contact a mutual fund or discount brokerage organization, such as T. Rowe Price, Vanguard, Schwab, or Fidelity (see Chapter 24). In some cases, your employer may need to work with a separate plan administrator in addition to one of these investment firms.

403(b) plans

Many nonprofit organizations offer 403(b) plans to their employees. As with a 401(k), your contributions to these plans generally are federal and state tax-deductible. 403(b) plans often are referred to as tax-sheltered annuities, the name for insurance-company investments that satisfy the requirements for 403(b) plans. For the benefit of 403(b) retirement-plan participants, no-load (commission-free) mutual funds also can be used in 403(b) plans.

Nonprofit employees generally are allowed to contribute up to 20 percent or $19,500 of their salaries, whichever is less. Employees who have 15 or more years of service may be allowed to contribute beyond the $19,500 limit. Ask your company's benefits department or the investment provider for the 403(b) plan (or your tax advisor) about eligibility requirements and details about your personal contribution limit.

As with 401(k) plans, the contribution limit for workers age 50 and older in 2021 is $26,000. The annual contribution limit on 403(b) plans and the additional amounts allowed for older workers rises, in $500 increments, with inflation.

TIP

If you work for a nonprofit or public-sector organization that doesn't offer this benefit, make a fuss and insist on it. Nonprofit organizations have no excuse not to offer 403(b) plans to their employees. Unlike 401(k) plans, 403(b) plans have virtually no out-of-pocket setup expenses or ongoing accounting fees. The only requirement is that the organization must deduct the appropriate contribution from employees' paychecks and send the money to the investment company handling the 403(b) plan. If your employer doesn't know where to look for good 403(b) investment options, send them to Vanguard (877-859-5756), Fidelity (800-548-2363), or T. Rowe Price (800-492-7670), all of which offer solid mutual funds and 403(b) plans.

AFTER-TAX 401(K) AND 403(B) CONTRIBUTIONS

Some employer-based retirement plans allow for "Roth" after-tax contributions to both 401(k) and 403(b) plans. Like Roth IRA contributions, Roth 401(k) and Roth 403(b) contributions not only grow tax-deferred but also allow for tax-free withdrawal of investment earnings.

Generally speaking, you still will likely be better off making pretax retirement plan contributions before considering after-tax (Roth) contributions. Most people are best served taking the sure tax break than waiting many years for an unspecified tax break. However, you may consider these accounts if you're currently in a very low tax bracket or you're an older worker who already has a large amount saved in traditional pre-tax accounts. Please see our discussion in the section "To Roth or not to Roth?" later in this chapter for further information.

SIMPLE plans

Employers in small businesses have yet another retirement plan option, known as the SIMPLE-IRA. SIMPLE stands for Savings Incentive Match Plans for Employees. Relative to 401(k) plans, SIMPLE plans make it somewhat easier for employers to reduce their costs, thanks to easier reporting requirements and fewer administrative hassles. (However, employers may escape the nondiscrimination testing requirements — one of the more tedious aspects of maintaining a 401(k) plan — by adhering to the matching and contribution rules of a SIMPLE plan, as described later in this section.)

The contribution limit for SIMPLE plans is $13,500 for tax year 2021 for younger workers ($16,500 for those age 50 and older). Annual contribution limits increase in increments of $500 with inflation.

Employers must make small contributions on behalf of employees. Employers can either match, dollar for dollar, the first 3 percent the employee contributes or contribute 2 percent of pay for everyone whose wages exceed $5,000. Interestingly, if the employer chooses the first option, the employer has an incentive not to educate employees about the value of contributing to the plan because the more employees contribute, the more it costs the employer. And, unlike a 401(k) plan, greater employee contributions don't enable higher-paid employees to contribute more.

Self-employed plans

Although setting up a self-employed plan means some work for you, you can select and design a plan that meets your needs. You can actually do a better job than many companies do; often, the people establishing a retirement plan don't do enough homework, or they let some salesperson sweet-talk them into high-expense (for the employees, that is) investments. Your trouble will be rewarded — self-employment retirement plans generally enable you to sock away more money on a tax-deductible basis than most employers' plans do.

WARNING

If you have employees, you're required to make contributions comparable to the company owners' (as a percentage of salary) on their behalf under these plans. Some part-time employees (those working fewer than 500 to 1,000 hours per year) and newer employees (less than a few years of service) may be excluded. Not all small-business owners know about this requirement — or they choose to ignore it, and they set up plans for themselves but fail to cover their employees. The danger is that the IRS and state tax authorities may, in the event of an audit, hit you with big penalties and disqualify your prior contributions if you have neglected to make contributions for eligible employees. Because self-employed people and small businesses get their taxes audited at a relatively high rate, messing up in this area is dangerous. The IRS has a program to audit small pension plans.

TIP

Don't avoid setting up a retirement savings plan for your business just because you have employees, and you don't want to make contributions on their behalf. In the long run, you can build the contributions you make for your employees into their total compensation package — which includes salary and other benefits like health insurance. Making retirement contributions need not increase your personnel costs.

NEW STUFF

The SECURE (Setting Every Community Up for Retirement Enhancement) ACT of 2019 provides for up to $5,000 in tax credits for eligible small-business owners when starting a retirement plan. This credit applies to new 401(k), profit sharing, SEP, and SIMPLE plans for small employers with up to 100 employees.

To get the most from your contributions as an employer, consider the following:

>> Educate your employees about the value of retirement savings plans. You want them to understand how to save for the future and to value and appreciate your investment.

>> If you have more than 20 or so employees, consider offering a 401(k) or SIMPLE plan, which allows employees to contribute money from their paychecks.

SEP-IRAs

Simplified Employee Pension Individual Retirement Account (SEP-IRA) plans require little paperwork to set up. Each year, you decide the amount you want to contribute to your SEP-IRA; no minimums exist. Your contributions to a SEP-IRA are deducted from your taxable income, saving you big-time on federal and usually state taxes. As with other retirement plans, your money compounds without taxation until withdrawal.

SEP-IRAs allow you to sock away about 20 percent of your self-employment income (business revenue minus expenses), up to a maximum of $58,000 for tax year 2021.

Self-employed/i401(k) plans

Another alternative is the "Self-employed" or "Individual 401(k)" plan, which offers traditional contribution and Roth (after-tax contribution) features. This plan type is only for sole proprietors (and their working spouses in the business) and partnerships with no eligible employees.

The pre-tax contribution limits are the same as a SEP-IRA. The after-tax limits are the same as the employee 401(k) limits — up to $19,500 except those age 50 or older can make "catch-up" contributions of up to $6,500 more.

Defined-benefit plans

These plans are for people who are able and willing to put away more than the SEP-IRA contribution limit of $58,000 per year. Of course, only a small percentage of people can afford to do so. Consistently high-income earners who want to save more than $58,000 per year in a retirement account should consider these plans.

SEEK ADVICE

If you're interested in defined-benefit plans, you need to hire an actuary to calculate how much you can contribute to such a plan.

Individual Retirement Accounts (IRAs)

A final retirement account option is an Individual Retirement Account (IRA). Because your IRA contributions may not be tax-deductible, contributing to an IRA generally makes sense only after you've exhausted contributing to other retirement accounts, such as the employer- and self-employed–based plans discussed earlier, which allow for tax-deductible contributions. The following sections discuss your IRA options.

"Regular" IRAs

The annual contribution limit for IRAs (both regular and the newer Roth IRAs, see "Nondeductible IRA contributions") is $6,000. People age 50 and older may contribute even more — an extra $1,000 per year for a total of $7,000.

Your contributions to a regular IRA may or may not be tax-deductible. For tax year 2021, if you're single and your adjusted gross income (AGI) is $66,000 or less for the year, you can deduct your IRA contribution in full. If you're married and file your taxes jointly, you're entitled to a full IRA deduction if your AGI is $105,000 per year or less. *Note:* These AGI limits will increase in future tax years (more details in a moment).

If you make more than these amounts, you can take a full IRA deduction if and only if you (or your spouse) aren't an *active participant* in any retirement plan. The only way to know for certain whether you're an active participant is to look at your W-2 form, that small (4-x-8½-inch) document your employer sends you early in the year to file with your tax returns. An *X* mark in a little box in section 13 on the W-2 form indicates that you're an active participant in an employer retirement plan.

UNDERSTANDING MANDATORY DISTRIBUTION RULES

If you're self-employed or retired from a company, the year you turn 72, you have to make some important decisions about how the money will come out of your regular IRA. (This policy isn't applicable to Roth IRAs.) The first choice: whether you receive yearly distributions based on your life expectancy or based on the joint life expectancies of you and your beneficiary. If your aim is to take out as little as possible, you'll want to use a joint life expectancy. That choice will stretch out the distributions over a longer period.

Next, you have to decide how you want your life expectancy to be calculated.

Sometimes, tax law changes actually make things simpler. You'll be happy to know that changes over the years to IRS regulations make required minimum distribution calculations easier.

Under the prior laws, retirees had several confusing methods for calculating their mandated retirement account withdrawal amounts. With the new regulations, seniors can generally take their retirement account balances and divide that by a number from an IRS life expectancy table. Investment companies typically can provide you with this number as well.

Another benefit of these new rules is that the newer tables generally produce lower required distributions and, therefore, a greater ability to preserve the account tax-free than was possible under the old regulations.

TECHNICAL STUFF

In some cases, you may see that the box is checked on your W-2 form indicating your active participation in a retirement plan when you haven't contributed any of your paycheck into a retirement plan. How can this be? Well, employers offer additional retirement plans outside those you contribute to from your paycheck. You're considered an active participant in a defined benefit plan (such as a traditional pension plan) as long as you're eligible to participate in the plan, even if you didn't make a required contribution, didn't perform the minimum service needed to accrue a benefit for the year, or never actively said you wanted to participate in the plan.

For tax year 2021, if you're a single-income earner with an AGI above $66,000 but below $76,000, or married filing jointly with an AGI above $105,000 but below $125,000, you're eligible for a partial IRA deduction, even if you're an active participant. If you're married filing a separate return from your spouse, your ability to deduct your IRA contribution disappears at $10,000 of AGI. The size of the IRA deduction that you may claim depends on where you fall in the income range. For example, a single-income earner at $71,000 is entitled to half of the full IRA deduction because their income falls halfway between $66,000 and $76,000.

Nondeductible IRA contributions

You can contribute to an IRA even if you can't deduct a portion or all of an IRA contribution because you're already covered by another retirement plan and you're a higher-income earner.

An IRA contribution that isn't tax-deductible is called, not surprisingly, a nondeductible IRA contribution. (We've never accused the IRS of being creative.) To make a nondeductible contribution, you have to have employment income during the year equal to at least the amount of your IRA contribution.

The benefit of this type of contribution is that the money can still compound and grow without taxation. For a person who plans to leave contributions in the IRA for a long time (a decade or more), this tax-deferred compounding may make nondeductible contributions worthwhile. However, before you consider making a nondeductible IRA contribution, be sure to read about the newer Roth IRAs (in the next section) that may offer better benefits for your situation.

If you end up making a nondeductible IRA contribution, you may wonder how the IRS will know not to tax you again on those portions of IRA withdrawals (because you've already paid income tax on the nondeductible contribution) in retirement. Surprise, surprise, you must fill out another form, Form 8606, which you file each year with your tax return to track these non-deductible contributions. We show you how to complete this form in Chapter 17. If you haven't filed your 2021 tax form yet, you may still make your IRA contribution.

Roth IRAs

For years, some taxpayers and tax advisors (and book authors and financial counselors) have complained about the rules and regulations on regular IRAs. The income limits that allowed for taking an IRA deduction were set too low. And many people who can't take a tax deduction on a contribution were unmotivated to make a nondeductible contribution, because earnings on the contribution still would be taxed upon withdrawal. (Granted, the tax-deferred compounding of earnings is worth something — especially to younger people — but that's a more complicated benefit to understand and value.)

So, rather than addressing these concerns by changing regular IRAs, Congress decided to make things even more complicated by introducing another whole IRA known as the Roth IRA, named after the Senate Finance Committee chairman who championed these new accounts. (Perhaps if congressional representatives couldn't name accounts after themselves, we may someday have real tax reform!)

UNDERSTANDING THE ROTH IRA

The Roth IRA allows for up to a $6,000 annual contribution for couples with AGIs under $198,000 and for single taxpayers with AGIs under $125,000. (Those individuals age 50 and older may contribute $7,000.) The $5,000 limit is reduced for married taxpayers with AGIs above $198,000 ($125,000 if single) and is eliminated for couples with AGIs above $208,000 ($140,000 for singles).

Although this newer IRA doesn't offer a tax deduction on funds contributed to it, it nevertheless offers benefits not provided by regular IRAs and some other retirement accounts. The distinguishing feature of the Roth IRA is that the earnings on your contributions aren't taxed upon withdrawal as long as you're at least age 59½ and have held the account for at least five years.

An exception to the age 59½ rule is made for first-time homebuyers, who can withdraw up to $10,000 income-tax-free from a Roth IRA (in existence for at least five years) to apply to the purchase of a principal residence.

Another attractive feature of the Roth IRA: For those not needing to draw on all their retirement accounts in the earlier years of retirement, the Roth IRA, unlike a standard IRA, doesn't require distributions after the account holder passes age 72.

TO ROTH OR NOT TO ROTH?

Before you go running out to contribute to a Roth IRA, keep in mind that the lack of taxation on withdrawn earnings is in no way guaranteed for the future — a future Congress can take that benefit away. If the government is running large deficits in future years, taxing Roth IRA withdrawals, especially for the more affluent, would increase tax revenue. (On the other hand, retired voters vote, and members of the Congress that tap the short-term benefit of taxing too many of these accounts may face a voter backlash.)

TIP

Consider contributing to a Roth IRA if you've exhausted your ability to contribute to tax-deductible retirement accounts and you aren't allowed a tax deduction for a regular IRA contribution because your AGI exceeds the regular IRA deductibility thresholds. If you find yourself in the fortunate situation that your high income disallows you from funding a Roth IRA, that would be a good reason to contribute to a nondeductible regular IRA (after having maxed out your contributions to other tax-deductible retirement accounts). In that case, if your nondeductible IRA contribution is the only money you have in IRA accounts, consider converting that money into your Roth IRA. Under current tax law (which can change in the future), you are allowed to do this.

Sorry, but you can't contribute $6,000 in the same tax year to both a regular IRA and a Roth IRA; the sum of your standard and Roth IRA contributions may not exceed $6,000 in a given year ($7,000 if you're over age 50).

Penalty-free IRA withdrawals

TAX CUT

Except for a few situations having mostly to do with emergencies, such as a major illness and unemployment, tapping into an IRA account before age 59½ (called an *early withdrawal*) triggers a hefty 10 percent federal income tax penalty (in addition to whatever penalties your state charges). You're allowed to make a penalty-free early withdrawal from your IRA for some specific expenses. First-time homebuyers — defined as not having owned a home in the past two years — may withdraw up to $10,000. Amounts also may be withdrawn for *qualified higher education costs* (college expenses for a family member such as a child, spouse, the IRA holder, or grandchildren).

NEW STUFF

You can also withdraw up to $5,000 per parent penalty-free from your retirement plan for a "qualified birth or adoption distribution" for the birth or adoption of a child. This new provision waives the normal 10 percent early withdrawal penalty and allows you to repay the withdrawn money as a rollover contribution.

Early withdrawals from regular IRA accounts still are subject to regular income tax in the year of withdrawal. Withdrawals from a Roth IRA (discussed in the "Understanding the Roth IRA" section) can be both penalty-free and federal income tax-free as long as the Roth IRA account is at least five years old.

Roth IRA accounts also are exempt from the normal retirement account requirement to begin taking minimum distributions at age 72 if you aren't working.

Annuities

Annuities, like IRAs, allow your capital to grow and compound without taxation. You defer taxes until withdrawal. Annuities carry the same penalties for withdrawal prior to age 59½ as IRAs do. However, unlike all other retirement accounts except a Roth IRA, you aren't forced to begin withdrawals at age 72; you may leave the money in an annuity to compound tax deferred for as many years as you desire.

And, unlike an IRA that has an annual contribution limit, you can deposit as much as you want in any year into an annuity — even $1 million if you have it! As with a so-called nondeductible IRA, you get no upfront tax deduction for your contributions. Thus, consider an annuity only after fully exhausting your other retirement account options.

What exactly is an annuity? Well, *annuities* are peculiar investment products — contracts, actually — that insurance companies back. If you, the annuity holder (investor), die during the so-called accumulation phase (that is, prior to receiving payments from the annuity), your designated beneficiary is guaranteed to receive the amount of your original investment.

TIP

Annuities carry higher fees than IRAs (which reduce your investment returns) because of the insurance that comes with them, so you should first make the maximum contribution that you can to an IRA, even if it isn't tax-deductible. Generally speaking, you should exhaust contributing to Roth accounts as they are superior because investment earnings aren't taxed upon withdrawal. Also, consider annuities only if you plan to leave the money in the annuity for 15 years or more. The reasons are twofold. First, it typically takes that long for the tax-deferred compounding of your annuity investment to make up for the annuity's relatively higher expenses. Second, upon withdrawal, the earnings on an annuity are taxed at ordinary income tax rates, which are higher than the more favorable long-term capital gains and stock dividend tax rates. If you don't expect to keep your money invested for 15 to 20-plus years to make up for the annuities' higher ongoing fees and taxes on the back end, you should simply invest your money in tax-friendly investments in nonretirement accounts (see Chapter 24).

Taxing Retirement Account Decisions

In addition to knowing about the different types of retirement accounts available and the importance of using them, we know from our work with counseling clients that you're going to have other problems and questions. This section presents the sticky issues that you may be struggling with, along with our recommendations.

Transferring existing retirement accounts

With employer-maintained retirement plans, such as 401(k)s, you usually have limited investment options. Unless you are the employer or can convince the employer to change, you're stuck with what is offered. If your employer offers four mutual funds from the Lotsa Fees and Lousy Performance Fund Company, for example, you can't transfer this money to another investment company.

After you leave your employer, however, you generally have the option of leaving your money in the employer's plan or transferring it to an IRA at an investment company of your choice. The process of moving this money from an employer plan to investments of your choice is called a *rollover*. And you thought you weren't going to be reading anything fun today!

WARNING

When you roll money over from an employer-based retirement plan, don't take personal possession of the money. If your employer gives the money to you, the employer must withhold 20 percent of it for taxes. This situation creates a tax nightmare for you because you must then jump through more hoops when you file your return. You also should know that you need to come up with the extra 20 percent when you do the rollover, because you won't get the 20 percent back that your employer withheld in taxes until you file your tax return. If you can't come up with the 20 percent, you have to pay income tax and maybe even excise taxes on this money as a distribution. Yuck!

We understand that some employers don't want the possible risk of issuing checks to myriad investment firms or advisors, especially smaller ones that they've never heard of. As a result, some employers will always issue a retirement plan check to you, mail it to your address on record, and include the investment company information you provide to them on the check. This is considered a direct rollover and as such, the employer won't withhold the 20 percent federal tax.

After you leave the company, you can move your money held in 401(k)s and many 403(b) plans (also known as tax-sheltered annuities) to nearly any major investment firm you please. Moving the money is pretty simple. If you can fill out a couple of short forms on the investment firm website or call their 800 number to request forms to be sent to you and send them back in a postage-paid envelope, you can transfer an account. The investment firm to which you're transferring your account does the rest. Here's the lowdown on how to transfer retirement accounts without upsetting Uncle Sam or any other tax collector:

1. **Decide to which investment firm you want to move the account.**

    When investing in stocks and bonds, mutual funds are a great way to go. They offer diversification and professional management, and they're low-cost. (For more information on mutual funds, see *Mutual Funds For Dummies* by Eric Tyson [Wiley].)

2. **Visit the website or call the toll-free number of the firm you're transferring the money to and ask for an account application and asset transfer form for the type of account you're transferring — for example, SEP-IRA, Keogh, IRA, or 403(b).**

    The reason for allowing the new investment company to do the transfer for you is that the tax authorities impose huge penalties if you do a transfer incorrectly. Allowing the company to which you're transferring the money to do the transfer for you is far easier and safer. If the company screws up (good investment firms don't), the company is liable.

3. **Complete and mail back the account application and asset transfer forms to your new investment company.**

    Completing this paperwork for your new investment firm opens your new account and authorizes the transfer. If you have questions or problems, the firm(s) to which you're transferring your account has armies of capable employees waiting to help you. Remember, these firms know that you're transferring your money to them, so they normally roll out the red carpet.

Transferring your existing assets typically takes a month to complete. If the transfer isn't completed within a month, get in touch with your new investment firm to determine the problem.

If your old company isn't cooperating, a call to a manager there may help to get the ball rolling. The unfortunate reality is that too many investment firms will cheerfully set up a new account to accept your money on a moment's notice, but they will drag their feet, sometimes for months, when it comes time to relinquish your money. If you need to light a fire under their behinds, tell a manager at the old firm that you're sending letters to the National Association of Securities Dealers (NASD) and the Securities and Exchange Commission (SEC) if they don't complete your transfer within the next week.

Taking money out of retirement accounts

Someday, hopefully not until you retire, you'll need or want to start withdrawing and enjoying the money that you socked away in your retirement accounts. Some people, particularly those who are thrifty and good at saving money (also known, by some, as cheapskates and tightwads), have a hard time doing this.

You saved and invested money in your retirement accounts to use at a future date. Perhaps you're in a pinch for cash and the retirement account looks as tempting as a catered buffet meal after a day of fasting. Whatever the reason, here's what you need to consider before taking the money out of your retirement accounts.

When should you start withdrawing from retirement accounts?

Some people start withdrawing funds from retirement accounts when they retire. This option may or may not be the best financial decision for you. Generally speaking, you're better off postponing drawing on retirement accounts until you need the money. The longer the money resides inside the retirement account, the longer it can compound and grow, tax-deferred. But don't wait if postponing means that you must scrimp and cut corners — especially if you have the money to use and enjoy.

REMEMBER

Suppose that you retire at age 60 and, in addition to money inside your retirement accounts, you have a bunch available outside. If you can, you're better off living off the money outside retirement accounts before you start tapping the retirement account money.

If you aren't wealthy and have saved most of the money earmarked for your retirement inside retirement accounts, odds are you'll need and want to start drawing on your retirement account soon after you retire. By all means, do so. But have you figured out how long your nest egg will last and how much you can afford to withdraw? Most folks haven't. Take the time to figure how much of your money you can afford to draw on per year, even if you think that you have enough.

Few people are wealthy enough to consider simply living off the investment income and never touching the principal, although more than a few people live like paupers so that they can do just that. Many good savers have a hard time spending and enjoying their money in retirement. If you know how much you can safely use, you may be able to loosen the purse strings.

WARNING

One danger of leaving your money to compound inside your retirement accounts for a long time after you're retired is that the IRS will require you to start making withdrawals the year you reach age 72. It's possible that because of your delay in taking the money out — and the fact that it will have more time to compound and grow — you may need to withdraw a hefty chunk per year. This procedure can push you into higher tax brackets in those years that you're forced to make larger withdrawals.

TAX CUT

This forced distribution no longer applies to people who are working for a company, and also doesn't apply to money held in the newer Roth IRAs (see "Roth IRAs" earlier in this chapter). Self-employed individuals still have to take the distribution.

If you want to plan how to withdraw money from your retirement accounts so that you meet your needs and minimize your taxes, consider hiring a tax advisor to help. If you have a great deal of money in retirement accounts and have the luxury of not needing the money until you're well into retirement, tax planning will likely be worth your time and money.

TIP

If you've reached the magic age of 72 and are required to take an IRA distribution but you don't need that additional income and you really don't want to pay any additional tax, you can now direct that your minimum distribution amount (or more if you're feeling generous) be paid directly to a qualified charity of your choice. The distribution qualifies as your annual required distribution, but the payment to charity excludes it from your adjusted gross income or your taxable income.

Naming beneficiaries

With any type of retirement account, you're supposed to name beneficiaries who will receive the assets in the account when you die. You usually name primary beneficiaries — your first choices for receiving the money — and secondary beneficiaries, who receive the money in the event that the primary beneficiaries also are deceased when you pass away.

The designations aren't cast in stone; you can change them whenever and as often as you desire by changing them on the investment's firm's website or by sending written notice to the investment company or employer holding your retirement account. Note that many plans require spousal consent to the naming of a beneficiary if other than the spouse.

Do the best you can in naming beneficiaries. You should know that you can designate charities as beneficiaries.

NEW STUFF

Inherited retirement accounts must now be tapped and emptied through distributions generally within ten years. In the past, when folks inherited a retirement account, the inheritor could stretch their distributions and associated tax payments out over their own life expectancy. For retirement accounts now inherited from original owners who have passed away in 2020 or later years, most beneficiaries must complete withdrawals from the account within ten years of the death of the account holder. There are some exceptions to this ten-year rule for retirement accounts left to a surviving spouse, a minor child, a disabled or chronically ill beneficiary, and beneficiaries who are less than ten years younger than the original retirement account owner. Consult a qualified tax advisor for more details.

Perplexing pension decisions

As discussed earlier in the chapter, if you've worked for a larger company for a number of years, you may have earned what is known as a pension benefit. This term simply means that upon attaining a particular age, usually 55 to 65, you can start to receive a monthly check from the employer(s) you worked for. With many pension plans today, you earn (vest) a benefit after you have completed five years of full-time work.

Make sure to keep track of the employer(s) where you have earned pension benefits as you move to new jobs and locations. Mail address changes to your previous employers' benefits departments. If they lose track of you and you forget that you've earned a benefit, you may be out a great deal of money.

WHAT AGE TO START?

With some plans, you may be able to start drawing your pension as early as 50 years of age — as long as you've worked enough years somewhere. The majority of plans, however, won't give you payments until age 55 or 60. Some plans even make you wait until age 65.

If you don't have a choice as to what age you want to start drawing benefits, that situation surely simplifies things for you. Before you become perplexed and overwhelmed if you do have options, remember one simple thing: Smart actuaries have created the choices available to you. Actuaries are the kinds of people who score 800s (a perfect score, in case you forgot) on their math SATs. These folks work, eat, breathe, and sleep numbers.

The choices you confront show you that the younger you elect to start drawing benefits, the less you are paid. Conversely, the longer you can wait to access your pension, the more you should receive per month. That said, here are some pointers:

>> Some pensions stop offering higher benefits after you reach a certain age — make sure that you don't delay starting your benefits until after you've reached this plateau. Otherwise, make your decision as to what age to start drawing benefits based on when you need the money and/or can afford to retire. Run the numbers or hire a competent tax or financial advisor.

>> If you're still working and earning a healthy income, think twice before starting pension benefits — these benefits are likely to be taxed at a much higher rate. You're probably going to be in a lower income tax bracket after you stop working.

>> If you know that you're in poor health and won't live long, consider drawing your pension sooner.

Attempting to calculate which age option will lead to your getting more money isn't worth your time. So many assumptions, such as the rate of inflation and the number of years you'll live, are beyond your ability to predict accurately. The actuaries have done their homework on these issues, and that's why the numbers vary the way they do.

WHAT ABOUT TAKING A LUMP SUM?

With some employer plans, you have the option of receiving a lump sum amount at your retirement date in place of receiving payments monthly over your retirement years. This lump sum can usually be rolled over into your personal IRA, so you don't get whacked with a slug of taxes at the time the lump sum comes your way.

So, should you take the lump sum or the monthly pension payments? The answer depends upon a number of factors and considerations. The attraction of a lump sum is that you have possession of the money and know exactly how much you are getting upfront. But you then have the responsibility of managing that money over time and making it last, presuming you need it for your retirement.

Here are some key issues to consider:

>> Do you have the knowledge and temperament to manage a lump sum? If not, then that would argue for the monthly pension.

>> Do you need this money for your monthly retirement spending needs or would you rather invest this money for the future benefit of your heirs? The pension is best suited for using the money yourself monthly via pension payments, whereas investing the lump sum may make more sense if you're investing the money for the future benefit of your heirs.

>> What's your current health and family longevity history? Of course, there are unknowns here, but if you have a relatively long life expectancy, the surety of the ongoing pension may have some value.

WHICH PAYMENT OPTION FOR YOU MARRIED FOLKS?

Besides deciding at what age you'll elect to start receiving benefits, you may have other choices if you're married, such as how much money you'll receive when you begin your pension benefit versus how much your spouse will receive if you pass away.

Before we dig into these choices, remember that actuaries are smart — don't make your selection based on age differences between you and your spouse. For example, if you're married to someone much younger, you may be tempted to choose the pension option that maximizes the amount your spouse receives upon your death because you're likely to predecease your spouse. However, each person's pension options already reflect the age differences between spouses, so don't waste your time with this line of thinking. Remember those smart actuaries.

Although the actuaries know your age and your spouse's age, they don't know or care about your ability and desire to accept financial risk. Pension options differ from one another in how much money you can receive now versus how much your spouse is guaranteed to receive in the event that you die first. As with many things in life, there are trade-offs. If you want to ensure that your spouse continues to receive a relatively high pension in the event of your passing, you must be willing to accept a smaller pension payment when you start drawing the pension.

The actuaries also don't know about your current health. All things being equal, if you're in poor health because of a chronic medical problem when you choose your pension option, lean toward that which provides your spouse with more.

The following are some of the typical options, which are ranked in order of providing the most to the fewest dollars at the beginning of retirement. The first choices, which provide more cash in hand sooner, are the riskiest from the standpoint of surviving spouses. The latter choices, which offer less cash in hand today, are the least risky for surviving spouses:

>> **Single Life Option:** This option pays benefits only as long as the pensioner (the person who earned the pension benefit) is alive. The survivor receives nothing. The single life option offers the highest monthly benefits but is also the riskiest option. For example, the pensioner receives $1,500 per month for as long as they're alive. The spouse receives nothing after the pensioner's death. Consider this option only if you have sufficient assets for your spouse to live on in the event of your dying early in retirement.

>> **Ten Years' Certain Option:** This option pays benefits for at least ten years, even if the pensioner passes away within the first ten years of drawing the pension. The pensioner continues receiving benefits for as long as they live, even if they live more than ten years. For example, a pensioner receives $1,400 per month for at least ten years until their death. The spouse then receives nothing.

>> **50 Percent Joint and Survivor Option:** With this option, the survivor receives 50 percent of the pensioner's benefit after their death. For example, a pensioner receives $1,350 per month. Upon the pensioner's death, their spouse receives a reduced benefit of $675 per month.

>> **Two-Thirds Joint and Survivor Option:** With this option, the survivor receives 66 percent of the pensioner's benefit after their death. For example, a pensioner receives $1,310 per month. Upon the pensioner's death, their spouse receives a reduced benefit of $865 per month.

>> **75 Percent Joint and Survivor Option:** With this option, the survivor receives 75 percent of the pensioner's benefit after their death. For example, a pensioner receives $1,275 per month. Upon the pensioner's death, the spouse receives a reduced benefit of $956 per month.

>> **100 Percent Joint and Survivor Option:** With this option, the survivor receives 100 percent of the pensioner's benefit after their death. For example, a pensioner receives $1,200 per month. Upon the pensioner's death, the spouse continues to receive $1,200 per month.

Choosing the best pension option for you and your spouse isn't unlike selecting investments. What's best for your situation depends on your overall financial circumstances and desire, comfort, and ability to accept risk. The Single Life Option is the riskiest and should be used only by couples who don't really need the pension — it's frosting on the financial cake — and are willing to gamble to maximize benefits today. If the surviving spouse is very much dependent on the pension, select one of the survivor options that leaves a high benefit amount after the pensioner's death.

WARNING

Beware of insurance salespeople and "financial planners" (who also sell life insurance and are therefore brokers and not advisors) who advocate that you purchase life insurance and take the Single Life Option. They argue that this option enables you to maximize your pension income and protect the surviving spouse with a life insurance death benefit if the pensioner dies. Sounds good, but the life insurance expense outweighs the potential benefits. Choose one of the survivor pension options that effectively provides life insurance protection for your survivor. This method is a far more cost-effective way to "buy" life insurance.

Chapter **23**

Small-Business Tax Planning

Whether you are your entire company or you have many employees, running a business can be one of the most frustrating, exhilarating, rewarding — and financially punishing — endeavors of your adult life. Many Americans fantasize about being their own boss. Tales of entrepreneurs becoming multimillionaires and multibillionaires focus our attention on the financial rewards without teaching us about the business and personal costs associated with being in charge.

The biggest challenges business owners face are the personal and emotional ones. It's sad to say, but these challenges rarely get discussed among all the glory tales of rags to riches. Major health problems, divorces, the loss of friends, and even suicides have been attributed to the passions of business owners consumed with winning or overwhelmed by their failures. Although careers and business success are important, if you really think about it, at best these things need be no higher than fourth on your overall priority list. Your health, family, and best friends can't be replaced — but a job or business can.

Business owners know the good and the bad. Consider the countless activities that your company has to do well to survive and succeed in the rough-and-tumble business world. You need to develop products and services that the marketplace will purchase. You have to price your wares properly and promote them. And your business will always face competitors who continually change the landscape.

With money flowing into and out of your coffers, you need to document your income and expenses. Otherwise, preparing your business's tax returns will be a frustrating endeavor. Being audited under these circumstances can produce big problems. And, unlike working for a corporation, owning a small business makes you responsible for ensuring that the right amount of tax is withheld and paid on both the state and federal levels.

This chapter can help you to make tax-wise decisions that will boost your business profits and yet comply with myriad tax regulations that annoy many entrepreneurs like you.

Organizing Your Business Accounting

If you're thinking about starting a business or you're already in the thick of one, you need to keep a proper accounting of your income and expenses. If you don't, you'll have a lot more stress and headaches when it comes time to file the necessary tax forms for your business.

Besides helping you over the annual tax-filing hurdle, you want accurate records so that you can track your business's financial health and performance during the year. How are your profits running compared with last year? Can you afford to hire new employees? Analyzing your monthly or quarterly business financial statements can help you answer these important business questions.

WARNING

Here's a final reason to keep good records: The IRS may audit you, and if that happens, you'll be asked that dreaded question: "Can you prove it?" Small-business owners who file Schedule C, Profit or Loss From Business, with their tax returns are audited at a much higher rate than other taxpayers. And businesses that do most of their business using cash are almost always eventually audited. Although that dubious honor may seem like an unfair burden to business owners, the IRS targets small businesses because more than a few small-business owners break the tax rules, and many areas exist where small-business owners can mess up.

The following sections cover the key tax-organizing things that small-business owners need to keep in mind.

Leave an "audit" trail

It doesn't matter whether you use file folders, software (see Chapter 2), or good old-fashioned paper and pencil to track your receipts and other important financial information. What does matter is that you keep records of expenses and income.

You'll probably lose or misplace some of those little pieces of paper that you need to document your expenses. Thus, one big advantage of charging expenses on a credit card or writing a check is that these transactions leave a paper trail, which makes it easier to total your expenses come tax time and deal with being audited when you need to prove your expenses.

Just remember to be careful when you use a credit card, because you may buy more things than you can really afford. Then you're stuck with a lot of debt to pay off. On the other hand (as many small-business owners know), finding lenders when you need money is difficult. Borrowing on a low-interest-rate credit card can be an easy way for you to borrow money without shamelessly begging a banker for a loan.

TIP

Likewise, leave a trail with your revenue. Depositing all your receipts in one account helps you when tax time comes or if you're ever audited.

Separate business from personal finances

One of the IRS's biggest concerns is that as a small-business owner, you'll try to minimize your business profits (and therefore taxes) by hiding business income and inflating your business expenses. Uncle Sam thus looks suspiciously at business owners who use personal checking and credit card accounts for business transactions. You may be tempted to use your personal account this way (because opening separate accounts is a hassle — not because you're dishonest).

Take the time to open separate accounts. Doing so not only makes the feds happy, it also makes your accounting easier.

WARNING

Please don't make the mistake of thinking that paying for an expense through your business account proves to the IRS that it was a legitimate business expense. If they find that the expense was truly for personal purposes, the IRS then will dig deep into your business's financial records to see what other shenanigans are going on.

REAL VERSUS BOGUS BUSINESSES AND HOBBY LOSS RULES

This chapter is about how small-business owners can make tax-wise decisions while running their businesses. It's not about how to start up a sideline business for the primary purpose of generating tax deductions.

Unfortunately, some self-anointed financial gurus claim that you can slash or even completely eliminate your tax bill by setting up a sideline business. They say that you can sell your services while doing something you enjoy. The problem, they argue, is that — as a regular wage earner who receives a paycheck from an employer — you can't write off many of your other (that is, personal) expenses. These hucksters usually promise to show you the secrets of tax reduction if you shell out far too many bucks for their audiotapes and notebooks of inside information.

"Start a small business for fun, profit, and huge tax deductions," one financial book trumpets, adding that, "The tax benefits alone are worth starting a small business." A seminar company that offers a course on "How to Write a Book on Anything in 2 Weeks . . . or Less!" (we must be doing something wrong) also offers a tax course entitled "How to Have Zero Taxes Deducted from Your Paycheck." This tax seminar tells you how to solve your tax problems: "If you have a sideline business, or would like to start one, you're eligible to have little or no taxes taken from your pay." Gee, sounds good. Where do we sign up?

Suppose that you're interested in photography. You like to take pictures when you go on vacation. These supposed tax experts tell you to set up a photography business and start deducting all your photography-related expenses: airfare, film, utility bills, rent for your "home darkroom," and restaurant meals with potential clients (that is, your friends). Before you know it, you've wiped out most of your taxes.

(continued)

(continued)

Sounds too good to be true, right? It is. Your business spending must be for the legitimate purpose of generating an income. According to the IRS, a sideline activity that generates a loss year in and year out isn't a business but a hobby.

Specifically, an activity is considered a hobby if it shows a loss for at least three of the past five tax years. (Horse racing, breeding, and so on are considered hobbies if they show losses in at least five or more of the past seven tax years.) Certainly, some businesses lose money. But a real business can't afford to do so year after year and still remain in business. Who likes losing money unless the losses are really just a tax deduction front for a hobby?

When the hobby loss rules indicate that you're engaging in a hobby, the IRS will disallow your claiming of the activity's expenses and the losses. To challenge this ruling, you must convince the IRS that you are seriously attempting to make a profit and run a legitimate business. The IRS will want to see that you're actively marketing your services, building your skills, and accounting for income and expenses. The IRS also will want to see that you aren't having too much fun! When you're deriving too much pleasure from an activity, in the eyes of the IRS, the activity must not be a real business.

What's the bottom line? You need to operate a legitimate business for the purpose of generating income and profits — not tax deductions. If you're thinking that it's worth the risk of taking tax losses for your hobby, year after year, because you won't get caught unless you're audited, better think again. The IRS audits an extraordinarily large number of small businesses that show regular losses.

Keep current on income and payroll taxes

When you're self-employed, you're responsible for the accurate and timely filing of all your income taxes. Without an employer and a payroll department to handle the paperwork for withholding taxes on a regular schedule, you need to make estimated tax payments on a quarterly basis.

When you have employees, you also need to withhold taxes on their incomes from each paycheck they receive. And you must make timely payments to the IRS and the appropriate state authorities. In addition to federal and state income taxes, you must withhold and send in Social Security and any other state or locally mandated payroll taxes and annually issue W-2s for each employee and 1099-MISCs for each independent contractor paid $600 or more. Got a headache yet?

REMEMBER

For paying taxes on your own self-employment income, you can obtain Form 1040ES, Estimated Tax for Individuals. This form comes complete with an estimated tax worksheet and the four payment coupons to send in with your quarterly tax payments. It's amazing how user-friendly government people can be when they want your money! The form itself has some quirks and challenges, but you'll be happy to know that we explain how to complete Form 1040ES in Chapter 17.

TIP

To discover all the amazing rules and regulations of withholding and submitting taxes from employees' paychecks, ask the IRS for Form 941. Once a year, you also need to complete Form 940 for unemployment insurance payments to the feds. Also, check to see if your state has its own annual or quarterly unemployment insurance reporting requirements. And, unless you're lucky enough to live in a state with no income taxes, don't forget to get your state's estimated income tax package.

If your business has a part-time or seasonal employee and the additional burden of filing Form 941 quarterly, the IRS has made the paperwork a tad easier for you. You may be able to file Form 944, Employer's Annual Federal Tax Return, if your tax withholding on behalf of employees doesn't exceed $1,000 for the year (which translates to about $4,000 in wages). If you qualify, you need to file only once each year. If you think you may qualify, call the IRS at 800-829-0115 or visit its website at www.irs.gov. If you do qualify, the IRS will send you something in writing.

SHIFTING INCOME AND EXPENSES

Many small-business owners elect to keep their business accounting on what's called a cash basis. This choice doesn't imply that all business customers literally pay in cash for goods and services or that the business owners pay for all expenses with cash. *Cash basis accounting* simply means that, for tax purposes, you recognize and report income in the year it was received and expenses in the year they were paid.

By operating on a cash basis, you can exert more control over the amount of profit (income minus expenses) that your business reports for tax purposes from year to year. If your income fluctuates from year to year, you can lower your tax burden by doing a little legal shifting of income and expenses.

Suppose that you recently started a business. Assume that you have little, but growing, revenue and somewhat high start-up expenses. Looking ahead to the next tax year, you can already tell that you'll be making more money and will likely be in a much higher tax bracket (see Chapter 1 for the personal income tax brackets and later in this chapter for corporate tax brackets). Thus, you can likely reduce your tax bill by paying more of your expenses in the next year. Of course, you don't want to upset any of your business's suppliers. However, some of your bills can be paid after the start of the next tax year (January 1) rather than in late December of the preceding year (presuming that your business's tax year is on a normal calendar year basis). *Note:* Credit card expenses are recognized as of the date you make the charges, not when you pay the bill.

Likewise, you can exert some control over when your customers pay you. If you expect to make less money next year, simply don't invoice customers in December of this year. Wait until January so that you receive more of your income next year. Be careful with this revenue-shifting game. You don't want to run short of cash and miss a payroll! Similarly, if a customer mails you a check in December, IRS laws don't allow you to hold the check until January and count the revenue then. After you receive the payment, it's supposed to be recognized for tax purposes as revenue.

One final point about who can and who can't do this revenue and expense two-step. Sole proprietorships, partnerships, S Corporations, and personal service corporations (which we discuss later in the chapter) generally can shift revenue and expenses. On the other hand, C Corporations and partnerships that have C Corporations as partners may not use the cash accounting method if they have annual receipts of more than $5 million per year.

TIP

Falling behind in paying taxes ruins some small businesses. When you hire employees, for example, you're particularly vulnerable to tax land mines. If you aren't going to keep current on taxes for yourself and your employees, hire a payroll company or tax advisor who can help you to jump through the necessary tax hoops. (Refer to Chapter 2 for advice on selecting a tax advisor.) Payroll companies and tax advisors are there for a reason, so use them selectively. They take care of all the tax filings for you, and if they mess up, they pay the penalties. Check with a tax advisor you trust for the names of reputable payroll companies in your area.

Minimizing Your Small-Business Taxes

Every small business has to spend money to make money. Most businesses need things like phone service, paper, computers and printers, software, and a whole bunch of other things you probably never thought you'd be purchasing.

But don't spend money on business stuff just for the sake of generating tax deductions. In some cases, business owners we know buy all sorts of new equipment and other gadgets at year's end for their business so that they can reduce their taxes. Although we endorse reinvesting profits in your business and making your company more efficient and successful, keep in mind that spending too much can lead to lower profits. Remember that nothing is wrong with paying taxes. In fact, it's a sign of profits — business success!

What follows is an overview of what you can do and what not to do to be a tax-wise spender for your business.

Business tax reform – The Tax Cuts and Jobs Act

For many years, corporations in the U.S. faced a much higher corporate income tax rate than did companies based in most overseas economies. As a result, increasing numbers of U.S. companies had chosen to expand more overseas rather than in the United States and to be headquartered outside of the United States, which wasn't good for the long-term health of the U.S. economy and labor market.

NEW STUFF

The Tax Cuts and Jobs Act was passed by Congress in late 2017 and took effect with tax year 2018. It was the most significant tax reform package passed since the Tax Reform Act of 1986.

At 35 percent, the U.S. had had one of the highest corporate income tax rates in the world before 2018. The Tax Cuts and Jobs Act slashed the corporate income tax rate to 21 percent, which represented a 40 percent reduction.

The corporate tax rules and deductions were simplified, including the elimination of the corporate alternative minimum tax, and some loopholes closed. We also moved to a "territorial" tax structure whereby U.S. companies would no longer pay a penalty to bring their overseas profits back home. The immediate impact of this change was to enable U.S. corporations to bring back to the United States more than $2 trillion being kept overseas to avoid excessive taxation.

The vast majority of small businesses are not operated as traditional so-called C-corps (more on those in a moment). Most small business owners operate as sole proprietorships (filing Schedule C), LLCs, partnerships, or S-corporations. In those cases, the business owner's profits from the business generally flow or pass through to the owner's personal income tax return, and that income is taxed at personal income tax rates.

Just as the corporate income tax rate was reduced by the Tax Cuts and Jobs Act legislation, so too were the individual income tax rates. Most of the tax bracket rates were reduced by several percentage points (see Chapter 1). This, of course, is excellent news for the vast majority of U.S. small business owners who operate their businesses as pass-through entities (for example, sole proprietorships, LLCs, partnerships, and S-corps).

You will note that at higher levels of income, the individual income tax rates begin to exceed the 21 percent corporate tax rate. Seeing this will help you to better understand the next point as to why pass-through entities are being granted a special tax deduction on their profits.

Twenty percent deduction for pass-through entities

In redesigning the tax code, Congress rightfully realized that the many small businesses that operate as so-called pass-through entities would be subjected to higher federal individual income tax rates compared with the newer 21 percent corporate income tax rate. Pass-through entities are small business entities such as sole proprietorships, LLCs, partnerships, and S-corporations and are so named because the profits of the business pass through to the owners and their personal income tax returns.

NEW STUFF

To address the concern that individual business owners who operated their business as a pass-through entity may end up paying a higher tax rate than the 21 percent rate levied on C-corporations, Congress provided a 20 percent deduction for those businesses. So, for example, if your sole proprietorship netted you $70,000 in 2021 as a single taxpayer, that would push you into the 22 percent federal income tax bracket. But you get to deduct 20 percent of that $70,000 of income (or $14,000), so you would only owe federal income tax on the remaining $56,000 ($70,000 − $14,000).

Another way to look at this is that the small business owner would only pay taxes on 80 percent of their profits and would be in the 22 percent federal income tax bracket. This deduction effectively reduces the 22 percent tax bracket to 17.6 percent.

This is a major change, which not surprisingly has made small business owners exceedingly optimistic about being able to grow their businesses. In fact, in a survey of small business owners conducted by the nonprofit National Federation of Independent Business just after the Tax Cut & Jobs Act bill was passed and signed into law, a record percentage of those surveyed (covering the survey's 45-year history) expressed optimism about it being a good time to expand their businesses.

This 20 percent pass-through deduction gets phased out for service business owners (for example, lawyers, doctors, real estate agents, consultants, and so on) at single taxpayer incomes above $157,500 (up to $207,500) and for married couples filing jointly with incomes over $315,000 (up to $415,000). For other types of businesses above these income thresholds, this deduction may be limited, so consult with your tax advisor.

Depreciation versus deduction

When you buy equipment such as computers, office furniture, business vehicles (that weigh over 6,000 pounds) and so on, each of these items is supposed to be depreciated over a number of years. Depreciation simply means that each year, you get to claim as a tax deduction a portion of the original cost of purchasing an item until you depreciate the entire cost of the purchase. Depreciation mirrors the declining value of equipment as it ages.

For example, suppose that you spend $3,000 on computer equipment. According to the IRS, computer equipment is to be depreciated over five years. Thus, each year you can take a $600 deduction for depreciation of this computer if you elect straight-line depreciation (which we define in Chapter 13).

NEW STUFF

Through so-called section 179 rules, small businesses have historically been able to immediately deduct the cost of equipment, subject to annual limits, they purchase for use in their business. But the 2017 tax bill expanded these limits beginning with tax year 2018.

For tax year 2021, more businesses can immediately deduct up to $1,050,000 in such equipment expense annually (up to the limit of their annual business income). And, this deduction can also now be used for purchases on used equipment. These provisions, which don't apply to real estate businesses, remain in effect through 2022 and then gradually phase out until 2027, when the prior depreciation schedules are supposed to kick back in.

TIP

Wanting to expense the full amount of equipment immediately is tempting, but that isn't always the best thing to do. In the early years of your business, for example, your profits may be low. Therefore, because you won't be in a high tax bracket, the value of your deductions is limited. Looking ahead — when you have reason to be optimistic about your future profits — you may actually save tax dollars by choosing to depreciate your purchases. By delaying some of your tax write-offs until future years (when you expect to be in a higher tax bracket because of greater profits), you save more in taxes.

Car costs

If you use your car for business, you can claim a deduction. The mistake that some business owners (and many other people) make is to buy an expensive car. This purchase causes two problems. First, the car may be a waste of money that may be better spent elsewhere in the business. Second, the IRS limits how large an annual auto expense you can claim for depreciation (see Chapter 13 for details about business deductions for cars). The limits were, however, increased notably in 2018 (we get to that in a moment).

The IRS gives you a choice of how to account for business automobile expenses. You can either expense a standard mileage charge (56 cents per mile for 2021) or keep track of the actual operating expenses (such as gas, insurance, repairs, and so on), plus take depreciation costs.

With expensive cars, the mileage expense method will probably shortchange your deduction amounts for auto usage. Now you have another reason not to spend so much on a car! When you buy a reasonably priced car, you won't need to go through the headache of tracking your actual auto expenses (in addition to not wasting money), because the mileage expense method probably will lead to a larger deduction. Tracking mileage and using the mileage expense method is so much easier.

NEW STUFF

The Tax Cut and Jobs Act bill that took effect in 2018 included a major increase in the maximum amount of auto depreciation that can be claimed. The annual amounts of auto depreciation have more than tripled. For tax year 2021, the annual maximum amounts that can be claimed are

Year 1: $10,200 without bonus depreciation ($18,200 with bonus depreciation)

Year 2: $16,400

Year 3: $9,800

Years 4 to 6: $5,860

These annual limits, which more than tripled in 2018 with the new tax laws, will increase with inflation for cars in future years.

WARNING

Auto dealers often push automobile leasing. For the auto dealers and salespeople in the showrooms, leases have the marketing appeal of offering buyers a monthly payment that's often lower than an auto loan payment — without the perceived noose around your neck of a large car loan. Don't be fooled. If you do your homework and hunt for a good deal on a car, buying with cash is usually the best way to go. Borrowing with an auto loan or leasing is much more expensive (with leasing generally being the highest cost) and tempts car buyers to spend more than they can afford.

Travel, meal, and entertainment expenses

The IRS clamps down on writing off travel, meal, and entertainment expenses because some business owners and employees abuse this deduction, trying to write off nonbusiness expenses. Some books, seminars, and unscrupulous tax preparers have effectively encouraged this abuse. So, be honest — not only because it's the right thing to do, but also because the IRS looks long and hard at expenses claimed in these areas. Travel must be for a legitimate business purpose. If you take a week off to go to Bermuda, spend one day at a business convention, and then spend the rest of the time sightseeing, you may have a great time — but only a portion of your trip expenses may be deductible.

TAX CUT

One exception exists: If you extend a business trip to stay over a Saturday to qualify for a lower airfare — and you save money in total travel costs by extending your stay — you can claim the other extra costs incurred to stay over through Sunday. If your spouse or friend tags along, their costs most definitely are not deductible.

Only 50 percent of your business expenses for meals and entertainment are deductible. In addition, the IRS doesn't allow any deductions for club dues (such as health, business, airport, or social clubs), entertainment facilities (such as executive boxes at sports stadiums), apartments, and so on. Please see Chapter 13 for details.

NEW STUFF

The tax reform bill of 2017 eliminated the entertainment expense deduction for businesses. Under prior tax law, 50 percent of those expenses were deductible when a business, for example, entertained customers and even employees at sporting events, fitness clubs, and restaurants.

The new rules do include some exceptions. On-site cafeterias at a company's offices and meals provided to employees as well as business meals associated with travel are 50 percent deductible. Meals provided to prospective customers as part of a seminar presentation are still fully deductible.

To help the ailing restaurant industry that got hit hard due to the government-mandated economic shutdowns, for tax years 2021 and 2022, eligible business meals provided by restaurants are 100 percent deductible, subject to the considerations identified in preexisting IRS regulations. Such deductible purchases must be made from restaurants and for meals available for "immediate consumption." Meals purchased from food providers such as a grocery store that sells primarily prepackaged foods or beverages not requiring immediate consumption don't qualify. Meals provided by on-site company cafeterias also do not count.

Home alone or outside office space?

When you have a truly small business, you may have a choice between setting up an office in your home or getting outside office space. You may be surprised to hear us say that the financial and tax sides of the home office decision actually aren't important — certainly not nearly as important as some business owners make them out to be. Why? First, the cost of office space you rent or purchase outside your home is an expense that you can deduct on your business tax return. If you own your home, you already get to claim the mortgage interest and property taxes as deductions on your personal tax return. So don't set up a home office thinking that you'll get all sorts of extra tax breaks. You'll qualify for some minor ones (such as deductions for utilities, repairs, and insurance) for the portion of your home devoted to business. Please see Chapter 17 for details.

The one extra home-based office deduction that you can take if you're a homeowner is depreciation. (See Chapter 25 to find out more about the other tips to avoid paying taxes on the profits from the sale of your home.)

Try as best you can to make your decision about your office space based on the needs of your business and your customers, along with your personal preferences. If you're a writer and you don't need fancy office space to meet with or impress anyone, working at home may be just fine. If you operate a retail or service business that benefits sufficiently from customers to come to you, getting outside office space is probably the best choice for all involved — and may be legally required. Check with governing authorities in your town, city, and county to find out what regulations exist for home-based businesses in your area.

Independent contractors versus employees

If you want to give yourself a migraine, read the tax laws applying to the classification of people that a business hires as either employees or independent contractors. When a business hires an employee, the business is required to withhold federal and state taxes and then send those taxes to the appropriate taxing authorities. The government likes the employee arrangement better because independent contractors (as a group) tend to pay less in taxes by underreporting their incomes. Contractors are also entitled to take more business deductions than are allowed for regular employees.

When a business hires independent contractors to perform work, the contractors are responsible for paying all their own taxes. However, business owners now are required to file Form 1099-MISC with the IRS and some state tax agencies. On Form 1099-MISC, you report the amount of money paid to contractors who receive $600 or more from the business. This form enables the IRS to keep better tabs on contractors who may not be reporting all their incomes.

Unless a company offers benefits to an employee (insurance, retirement savings plans, and so on), a person should prefer to be an independent contractor. Contractors have more leeway to deduct business expenses, including the deduction for a home office. Contractors can also tax-shelter a healthy percentage of their employment income in a self-employed retirement savings plan, such as a SEP-IRA (see Chapter 22 for details on retirement accounts).

However, one additional expense for contractors is their obligation to pay the full share of Social Security taxes (although they can then take half of these Social Security taxes as a tax deduction on their returns). An employer, by contrast, would pay half the Social Security and Medicare taxes on the employee's behalf.

So how do you, as the business owner, decide whether a worker is to be classified as a contractor or as an employee? Some cases are hard to determine, but the IRS has a set of guidelines to make most cases pretty clear-cut.

>> The classic example of an independent contractor is a professional service provider, such as legal, tax, and financial advisors. These people are considered contractors because they generally train themselves and, when hired, figure out how they can accomplish the job without much direction or instruction from the employer. Contractors usually perform work for a number of other companies and people, and they typically hire any others they need to work with them.

>> On the other hand, employees usually work for one employer and have set hours of work. For example, a full-time secretary hired by a business would be considered an employee because they take instructions from the employer regarding when, where, and how to do the assigned work. Another indication of employee status is whether the secretary's presence at the work site is important for completing the assigned work.

What do you do if your situation falls between these two types, and you're perplexed about whether the person you're hiring is a contractor or an employee? Ask a tax advisor or contact the IRS for the handy-dandy Form SS-8, Determination of Worker Status for Purposes of Federal Employment Taxes and Income Tax Withholding. Complete the form, mail it in, and let the IRS make the call for you. That way, the IRS can't blame you — although you may rightfully feel that you're letting the fox guard the henhouse!

Insurance and other benefits

A variety of insurance and related benefits are tax-deductible to corporations for all employees. These benefits include the following:

>> Health insurance

>> Disability insurance

>> Term life insurance (up to $50,000 in benefits per employee)

>> Dependent-care plans (up to $5,000 per employee, temporarily increased to $10,500 for 2021, may be put away on a tax-deductible basis for childcare and/or care for elderly parents)

>> Flexible spending or cafeteria plans, which allow employees to pick and choose the benefits on which to spend their benefit dollars

For businesses that are not incorporated, the business owner(s) can't deduct the cost of the preceding insurance plans for themselves — but they can deduct these costs for employees.

TAX CUT

Self-employed people can deduct 100 percent of their health insurance costs for themselves and their covered family members. You may do this for months when you were not eligible for employer-subsidized health insurance coverage.

Retirement plans

Retirement plans are a terrific way for business owners and their employees to tax-shelter a healthy portion of their earnings. If you don't have employees, regularly contributing to one of these plans is usually a no-brainer. When you have employees, the decision is a bit more complicated but often a great idea. Self-employed people may contribute to Simplified Employee Pension Individual Retirement Accounts (SEP-IRAs), self-employed/individual 401(k)s, or SIMPLE plans. Small businesses with a number of employees also should consider 401(k) plans.

Tax law changes in recent decades greatly increased the amount of money that both small employers and employees can sock away in retirement plans. A recent tax credit also helps small employers recoup some of the costs of establishing and maintaining a retirement plan. We discuss all these plans and the impact of the tax rules in detail in Chapter 22.

Know your interest deduction and net operating loss limitations

NEW STUFF

Effective in 2018, companies with annual gross receipts of at least $25 million on average over the prior three years are limited in their deduction of interest from business debt. Net interest costs are capped at 30 percent of the business's earnings before interest, taxes, depreciation, and amortization (EBITDA). Farmers and most real estate companies are exempt.

Then, effective in 2022, this provision actually gets more restrictive and would thus affect even more businesses. At that point, the 30 percent limit will apply to earnings before interest and taxes.

There are also revised rules for using net operating losses (NOLs). Net operating losses (NOLs) can no longer be carried back for two years. However, NOLs may now be carried forward indefinitely until they are used up. Previously, the carry forward limit was 20 years.

NOLs are limited each year to 80 percent of taxable income.

Deciding to Incorporate or Not to Incorporate

Starting a business is hard enough. Between mustering up the courage and swinging it financially, many business owners meet their match trying to decide what should be a reasonably straightforward issue: whether to incorporate. Just about every book that addresses the subject (and just about every lawyer or accountant who advises business owners) steers clear of giving definitive answers.

In some instances, the decision to incorporate is complicated, but in most cases, it need not be a difficult choice. Taxes may be important to the decision but aren't the only consideration. (Eric Tyson and Jim Schell's *Small Business For Dummies*, published by Wiley, offers additional information.) This section presents an overview of the critical issues to consider.

Liability protection

The chief reason to consider incorporating your small business is for purposes of liability protection. Attorneys speak of the protection of the *corporate veil.* Don't confuse this veil with insurance (or with the veil a bride normally wears on her wedding day). You don't get any insurance when you incorporate — or when you get married! You may need or want to buy liability insurance instead of (or in addition to) incorporating. Liability protection doesn't insulate your company from being sued, either.

When you incorporate, the protection of the corporate veil provides you with the separation or division of your business assets and liabilities from your personal finances. Why would you want to do that? Suppose that your business is doing well and you take out a bank loan to expand. The next year, however, the government enacts a regulatory change that makes your services or product obsolete. Before you know it, your business is losing money, and you're forced to close up shop. If you can't repay the bank loan because of your business failure, the bank shouldn't be able to go after your personal assets if you're incorporated, right?

LIABILITY INSURANCE — A GOOD ALTERNATIVE (IF YOU QUALIFY)

Before you incorporate, ask yourself (and others in your line of business or advisors who work with businesses like yours) what actions can cause you to be sued. Then see whether you can purchase insurance to protect against these potential liabilities. Insurance is superior to incorporation because it pays claims.

Suppose that you perform professional services but make a major mistake that costs someone a lot of money — or worse. Even if you're incorporated, if someone successfully sues you, your company may have to cough up the dough. This situation not only costs a great deal of money but also can sink your business. Only insurance can cover such financially destructive claims.

You can also be sued if someone slips and breaks a bone or two. To cover these types of claims, you can purchase a property or premises liability policy from an insurer.

Accountants, doctors, and a number of other professionals can buy liability insurance. A good place to start searching for liability insurance is through the associations that exist for your profession. Even if you aren't a current member, check out the associations anyway — you may be able to access any insurance they provide without membership, or you can join the association long enough to get signed up. Incorporating, however, doesn't necessarily preclude insuring yourself. Both incorporating and covering yourself with liability insurance may make sense in your case.

Unfortunately, many small-business owners who need money find that bankers ask for personal guarantees, which negate part of the liability protection that comes with incorporation. Additionally, if you play financial games with your company (such as shifting money out of the company in preparation for defaulting on a loan), a bank may legally be able to go after your personal assets. So, you must adhere to a host of ground rules and protocols to prove to the IRS that you're running a bona fide company. For example, you need to keep corporate records and hold an annual meeting — even if it's just with yourself!

A business can be sued if it mistreats an employee or if its product or service causes harm to a customer. But the owner's personal assets should be protected when the business is incorporated and meets the other tests for being a legitimate business.

REMEMBER

Before you call a lawyer or your state government offices to figure out how to incorporate, you need to know that incorporating takes time and costs money. So if incorporating doesn't offer enough benefits to outweigh the hassles and costs, don't do it. Likewise, if the only benefits of incorporating can be better accomplished through some other means (such as purchasing insurance), save your money and time and don't incorporate.

Corporate taxes

Corporations are taxed as entities separate from their individual owners. If your business isn't incorporated, all the profits from your business are taxed on your personal tax return in the year that those profits are earned. But some corporate-like entities, like the increasingly popular LLC, allow owners to pass through their profits to the individual owner's tax return (more on this in a moment).

NEW STUFF

The Tax Cut and Jobs Act that took affect in 2018 lowered the corporate income tax rate to a more reasonable and globally competitive 21 percent. It had previously been 35 percent, which placed it among the highest globally.

A tax-related reason not to incorporate (especially in the early days of a business) is that you can't immediately claim the losses for an incorporated business on your personal tax return. You have to wait until you can offset your losses against profits. Because most businesses produce little revenue in their early years and have all sorts of start-up expenditures, losses are common.

Because corporations are legal entities distinct from their owners, corporations offer other features and benefits that a proprietorship or partnership doesn't. For example, corporations can have shareholders who own a piece or percentage of the company. These shares can be sold or transferred to other owners, subject to any restrictions in the shareholders' agreement.

Corporations also offer continuity of life, which simply means that corporations can continue to exist despite the death of an owner — or the owner's transfer of their share (stock) in the company.

Don't incorporate for ego purposes. If you want to incorporate to impress friends, family, or business contacts, you need to know that few people would be impressed or even know that you're incorporated. Besides, if you operate as a sole proprietor, you can choose to operate under a different business name ("doing business as" or *d.b.a.*) without the cost — or the headache — of incorporating.

Another possible tax advantage for a corporation is that corporations can pay — on a tax-deductible basis — for employee benefits such as health insurance, disability, and up to $50,000 of term life insurance. The owner usually is treated as an employee for benefits purposes. (Refer to the "Insurance and other benefits" section earlier in this chapter for details.) Sole proprietorships and other unincorporated businesses usually can take only tax deductions for these benefit expenses for employees. Benefit expenses for owners who work in the business aren't deductible, except for pension contributions and health insurance, which you can deduct on the front of Form 1040.

Limited liability companies (LLCs)

Just in the past generation, a new type of corporation has appeared. *Limited liability companies* (LLCs) offer business owners benefits similar to those of S Corporations (discussed next) but are even better in some cases. Like an S Corporation, an LLC offers liability protection for the owners. LLCs also pass the business's profits through to the owners' personal income tax returns.

Limited liability companies have fewer restrictions regarding shareholders. For example, LLCs have no limits on the number of shareholders. The shareholders in an LLC can be foreigners, and corporations and partnerships also can be shareholders.

REMEMBER

Compared with S Corporations, the only additional restriction LLCs carry is that sole proprietors and professionals can't always form LLCs (although some states allow this). All states now permit the formation of LLCs, but most state laws require you to have at least two partners for an LLC to be taxed as a partnership and not be a professional firm. (The IRS has stated that one-owner LLCs will be treated as sole proprietorships and must file Schedule C for tax purposes unless the owner elects to file as a corporation on Form 8832.)

S Corporations

Subchapter S Corporations, so named for that part of the tax code that establishes them, offer some business owners the best of both worlds. You get the liability protection that comes with being incorporated, and the business profit or loss passes through to the owner's personal tax returns. So if the business shows a loss in some years, the owner may claim those losses in the current year of the loss on the tax returns. If you plan to take all the profits out of the company, an S Corporation may make sense for you.

The IRS allows most — but not all — small businesses to be S Corporations. To be an S Corporation in the eyes of the almighty IRS, a company must meet all the following requirements:

>> Be a U.S. company

>> Have just one class of stock

>> Have no more than 100 shareholders (who are all U.S. residents or citizens and aren't partnerships, other corporations, or, with certain exceptions, trusts)

TAX CUT

So long as you are paying yourself a reasonable salary, an S Corporation structure may save you money on taxes. Extra profits can be paid out at year-end as a dividend, which can save you on Social Security taxes. You should consider all the additional costs of being an S Corporation, especially at the state level, and additional tax filing costs. Consult a qualified tax advisor for more information and details.

Where to get advice

If you're totally confused about whether to incorporate because your business is undergoing major financial changes, getting competent professional help is worth the money. The hard part is knowing where to turn, because it's a challenge to find one advisor who can put all the pieces of the puzzle together. And be aware that you may get wrong or biased advice.

Attorneys who specialize in advising small businesses can help explain the legal issues. Tax advisors who do a lot of work with business owners can help explain the tax considerations. If you find that you need two or more advisors to help make the decision, it may help for all of you to get together for a meeting — which may save you time and money.

TIP

If you've weighed the pros and cons of incorporating and you're still on the fence, our advice is to keep it simple. Don't incorporate. Remember that after you incorporate, it takes time and money to unincorporate. Start off as a sole proprietorship and then take it from there. An LLC would be a sensible possible next step. Wait until the benefits of incorporating for your particular case outweigh the costs and drawbacks of incorporating.

Investing in Someone Else's Business

Putting money into your own business (or someone else's) can be a high-risk but potentially high-return investment. The best options are those you understand well. If you hear about a promising business opportunity from someone you know and trust, do your research and make your best judgment. The business may well be a terrific investment. But keep in mind that people are always willing to take more risk with other people's money than with their own — and that many well-intentioned people fail at their businesses.

Before investing in a project, ask to see a copy of the business plan. Talk to others (who aren't involved with the investment!) about the idea and take their comments and concerns into account. But don't forget that many a wise person has rained on the parade of what turned out to be a terrific business idea.

WARNING

Avoid limited partnerships and other small-company investments pitched by brokers, financial planners, and the like. They want you to buy limited partnerships because they earn hefty commissions from the sales. If you want a convenient way to invest in businesses and earn tax breaks, buy some stock mutual funds inside a retirement account.

Buying or Selling a Business

SEEK ADVICE

When you're buying or selling an existing business, consider getting the help and advice of competent tax and legal advisors. As a buyer, good advisors can help you inspect the company you're buying and look for red flags in the financial statements. Advisors can also help structure the purchase to protect the business you're buying — and to gain maximum tax benefits. When you're a seller, your advisors can help you prepare your business for maximum sale value and minimize taxes from the sale price.

If your business is worth a lot, make sure to read Chapter 27 on estate planning, because hefty taxes may be owed upon your death if you don't structure things properly. Your heirs may be forced to sell your business to pay estate taxes!

For more information about successfully starting, buying, selling, and running a small business, check out the latest edition of *Small Business For Dummies* by Eric Tyson and Jim Schell (Wiley).

IN THIS CHAPTER

» **Understanding tax-friendly investment strategies**

» **Comprehending the tax ramifications of reinvesting and dollar-cost averaging**

» **Knowing which tax-favored investments are best**

» **Deciding what investments to sell when and how**

» **Understanding special tax issues with mutual funds and stock options**

Chapter **24**

Your Investments and Taxes

When you have money to invest, or you're considering selling investments that you hold outside a retirement account, taxes should be an important factor in your decisions. But tax considerations alone should not dictate how and where you invest your money and when you sell. You also need to weigh issues such as your desire (and the necessity) to take risks, your personal likes and dislikes, and the number of years you plan to hold on to the investment.

Note: This chapter focuses on tax issues relating to investments in mutual funds, exchange-traded funds, stocks, bonds, and other securities. Other chapters in this part of the book cover tax matters for investing in real estate or small businesses, investing for your children's future, and protecting your assets from estate taxes.

Tax-Reducing Investment Techniques

For investments that you hold inside *tax-sheltered* retirement accounts such as IRAs and 401(k) plans (see Chapter 22), you don't need to worry about taxes. This money isn't generally taxed until you actually withdraw funds from the retirement account. Thus, you should never invest money that's inside retirement accounts in other tax-favored investments, such as tax-free money market funds and tax-free bonds (discussed later in this chapter).

WARNING

You're far more likely to make tax-related mistakes investing *outside* of retirement accounts. Consider the many types of distributions produced by nonretirement account investments that are subject to taxation:

>> **Interest:** Bank accounts, for example, pay you interest that is fully taxable, generally at both the federal and state levels. Bonds (IOUs) issued by corporations also pay interest that is fully taxable. Bonds issued by the federal government, which are known as *Treasury bonds,* pay interest that is federally taxable.

>> **Dividends:** Many companies distribute some of their profits to shareholders of stock (shares of company ownership) as dividends. Lower tax rates apply to stock dividends than ordinary income (see Table 24-1).

>> **Capital gains:** The profit from the sale of an investment at a price higher than the purchase price is known as a *capital gain.* Capital gains generally are federally and state taxable. Lower tax rates apply to capital gains for investments held for the long term (see Table 24-1 and the next section).

Table 24-1   **Federal Tax Rate (2021) on Stock Dividends and Long-Term Capital Gains**

2021 Tax Rate	Single Taxpayers	Married Couples Filing Jointly
0%	Up to $40,400	Up to $80,800
15%	$40,401 to $445,850	$80,801 to $501,600
20%	$445,851 or more	$501,601 or more

Ordinary income tax brackets top out at 37 percent versus the top rate of 20 percent on stock dividends and long-term capital gains. Obamacare added a 3.8 percent additional tax on investment income on top of the percentages shown in Table 24-1 for higher-income earners (single taxpayers with adjusted gross incomes over $200,000 and married couples filing jointly with adjusted gross incomes over $250,000). So the top tax rate on stock dividends and long-term capital gains is actually 23.8 percent.

The following sections detail specific strategies for minimizing your taxes and maximizing your after-tax returns — that is, the return you actually get to keep after payment of required taxes.

Buy and hold for "long-term" capital gains

A *long-term* capital gain, which is the *profit* (sales proceeds minus purchase price) on an investment (such as a stock, bond, or mutual fund) that you own for more than 12 months, is taxed on a different tax-rate schedule. *Short-term* capital gains (securities held for one year or less) are taxed at your ordinary income tax rate.

The maximum federal tax rate on long-term capital gains is currently 20 percent for holding periods of more than 12 months. For investors with an adjusted gross income below $40,400 for singles and $80,800 for married couples filing jointly in tax year 2021, the long-term capital gains tax is 0 percent for assets held more than 12 months.

When investing outside retirement accounts, investors who frequently trade their investments (or who invest in mutual funds that do the same) should seriously reconsider these strategies and holdings. With longer-term capital gains being taxed at lower tax rates, trading that produces short-term gains (from investments held 12 months or less), which are taxed at higher ordinary income tax rates, penalizes higher bracket investors the most. The sane strategy of buying and holding not only minimizes your taxes but also reduces trading costs and the likelihood of being whipsawed by fluctuating investment values.

Why, you may wonder, is there a set of capital gains' tax rates that are different from (lower than) the regular income tax rates presented in Chapter 1? In addition to the possibility that our government wants to make our tax lives more difficult, some logic lies behind the lower long-term capital gains tax rates. Some argue that this lower tax encourages investment for long-term growth. However, others complain that it's a tax break that primarily benefits the affluent.

When you buy and hold stocks and stock mutual funds outside retirement accounts, you can take advantage of two major tax breaks. As we discuss in this section, appreciation on investments held more than 12 months and then sold is taxed at the low capital gains tax rate. Stock dividends (not on real estate investment trusts) are also taxed at these same low tax rates.

Pay off high-interest debt

Many folks have credit card or other consumer debt, such as auto loans costing 8 percent, 9 percent, 10 percent, or more per year in interest. Paying off this debt with your savings is like putting your money in an investment with a guaranteed tax-free return that's equal to the interest rate you were paying on the debt. For example, if you have credit-card debt outstanding at a 15 percent interest rate, paying off that loan is the same as putting your money to work in an investment with a guaranteed 15 percent annual return. Because the interest on consumer debt isn't tax-deductible, you actually need to earn more than 15 percent on your other investments to net 15 percent after paying taxes.

REMEMBER

Still not convinced that paying off consumer debt is a great "investment"? Consider this: Banks and other lenders charge higher rates of interest for consumer debt than for debt on investments (such as real estate and businesses). Debt for investments is generally available at lower rates of interest and is tax-deductible. Consumer debt is hazardous to your long-term financial health (because you're borrowing against your future earnings), and it's more expensive.

In addition to ridding yourself of consumer debt, paying off your mortgage quicker may make sense, too. This financial move *isn't always* the best one because the interest rate on mortgage debt is lower than that on consumer debt and is usually tax-deductible (see Chapter 25).

Fund your retirement accounts

TAX CUT

Take advantage of opportunities to direct your employment earnings into retirement accounts. If you work for a company that offers a retirement savings plan such as a 401(k) or 403(b) plan, try to fund it at the highest level that you can manage. When you earn self-employment income, look into SEP-IRAs and self-employed/i401(k)s. See Chapter 22 for all the details on retirement accounts.

You get three possible tax bonuses by investing more of your money in retirement accounts.

>> Your contributions to most of these retirement accounts come out of your pay before taxes are figured, which reduces your current tax burden. The after-tax Roth accounts offer tax-free retirement withdrawals, but you don't get a tax break on the contributions.

>> Some employers provide matching contributions, which is free money to you.

>> The earnings on the investments inside the retirement accounts compound without taxation until withdrawal. Funding retirement accounts makes particular sense if you can allow the money to compound over many years (at least 10 years, preferably 15 to 20 years or more).

If you need to save money outside retirement accounts for short-term purposes such as buying a car or a home, by all means, don't do all your saving inside sometimes-difficult and costly-to-access retirement accounts. But if you accumulate money outside retirement accounts with no particular purpose in mind (other than that you like seeing the burgeoning balances), why not get some tax breaks by contributing to retirement accounts? Because your investments can produce taxable distributions, investing money outside retirement accounts requires greater thought and consideration, which is another reason to shelter more of your money in retirement accounts.

Use tax-free money market and bond funds

A common mistake many people make is not choosing a tax-appropriate investment given their tax bracket. Here are some guidelines for choosing the best type of investment based on your federal tax bracket:

>> **32 percent or higher federal tax bracket:** If you're in one of these high brackets, you should actively seek to avoid investments that produce taxable income. For tax year 2021, the 33 percent federal bracket started at $164,926 for singles, $164,901 for heads of household, and $329,851 for married couples filing jointly.

>> **22 or 24 percent federal tax bracket:** If you invest outside retirement accounts, in most cases, you should be as well or slightly better off in investments that don't produce taxable income. This may not be the case, however, if you're in tax-free money market and bond funds whose yields are depressed because of a combination of low interest rates and too-high operating expenses.

>> **10 or 12 percent federal tax bracket:** Investments that produce taxable income are generally just fine. You'll generally end up with less if you purchase investments that produce tax-free income, because these investments yield less than comparable taxable ones even after factoring in the taxes you pay on those taxable investments.

When you're investing your money, it isn't the return that your investment earns that matters; what matters is the return you actually get to keep after paying taxes. The following material and sections describe some of the best investment choices you can make to reduce your overall tax burden and maximize your after-tax return.

If you're in a high enough tax bracket (federal 32 percent or higher), you may come out ahead with tax-free investments. Tax-free investments yield less than comparable investments that produce taxable earnings. But the earnings from tax-free investments can end up being greater than what you're left with from taxable investments after paying required federal and state taxes.

Tax-free money market funds, offered by mutual fund companies, can be a better alternative to bank savings accounts that pay interest (which is subject to taxation) during periods of normal interest rates. The best money market funds pay higher yields and give you check-writing privileges. If you're in a high tax bracket, you can select a tax-free money market fund, which pays dividends that are free from federal and sometimes from state tax. You can't get this feature with bank savings accounts.

Unlike bank savings accounts, the FDIC (Federal Deposit Insurance Corporation) doesn't insure money market mutual funds. For all intents and purposes, though, money market funds and bank accounts have equivalent safety. Don't allow the lack of FDIC insurance to concern you, because fund companies haven't failed. And in those rare instances when a money fund's investments have lost value, the parent company has infused capital to ensure no loss of principal on the investor's part.

Just as you can invest in a tax-free money market fund, so too can you invest in tax-free bonds via a tax-free bond mutual fund. These funds are suitable for higher-tax-bracket investors who want an investment that pays a better return than a money market fund without the risk of the stock market. Bond funds are intended as longer-term investments (although they offer daily liquidity, they do fluctuate in value).

As a starting point, examine the tax-free money market funds and bond funds offered by Vanguard (800-662-7447; www.vanguard.com). Vanguard has low management fees and highly competitive yields. They also offer increasing numbers of exchange-traded funds which may offer you even lower costs and higher yields.

Invest in tax-friendly stock funds

When selecting investments, people often mistakenly focus on past rates of return. We all know that the past is no guarantee for the future. But an even worse mistake is choosing an investment with a reportedly high rate of return without considering tax consequences. Numerous mutual funds and exchange-traded funds (ETFs) effectively reduce their shareholders' returns because of their tendency to produce more taxable distributions (dividends and capital gains).

Historically, however, many mutual fund and ETF investors and publications haven't compared the tax-friendliness of similar mutual funds. Just as you need to avoid investing in funds with high sales commissions, high annual operating expenses, and poor relative performance, you also should avoid tax-unfriendly funds when investing outside of retirement accounts.

When comparing two similar funds, most people prefer a fund that averages returns of 14 percent per year instead of a fund earning 12 percent. But what if the 14 percent-per-year fund causes you to pay a lot more in taxes? What if, after factoring in taxes, the 14-percent-per-year fund nets just 9 percent, while the 12-percent-per-year fund nets an effective 10 percent return? In that case, you'd be unwise to choose a fund solely on the basis of the higher reported rate of return.

Greater fund distributions = more taxes!

All stock fund managers buy and sell stocks during the course of a year. Whenever a fund manager sells securities, any gain from those securities must be distributed, by year's end, to the fund shareholders. Securities sold at a loss can offset those liquidated at a profit. When a fund manager has a tendency to cash in more winners than losers, significant capital gains distributions can result.

TAX CUT

Choosing mutual funds and ETFs that minimize capital gains distributions, especially short-term capital gains distributions that are taxed at the higher ordinary income tax rates rather than the tax-favored long-term capital gains rates we discuss earlier in this chapter, can help investors defer and minimize taxes on their profits. By allowing their capital to continue compounding, as it would in an IRA or other retirement account, fund shareholders receive a higher total return. (You can find the historic capital gains distribution information on a fund by examining its prospectus.)

Long-term investors benefit the most from choosing funds that minimize capital gains distributions. The more years that appreciation can compound in a fund without being taxed, the greater the value to the fund investor. When you invest in stock funds inside retirement accounts, you need not worry about capital gains distributions.

In addition to capital gains distributions, mutual funds and ETFs produce dividends that are subject to normal income tax rates (except in the case of qualified stock dividends, which are taxed at the same low rates applied to long-term capital gains). Again, all things being equal, nonretirement account investors in high tax brackets should avoid funds that tend to pay a lot of dividends (from bonds and money market funds). Hold such funds inside of tax-sheltered retirement accounts.

Timing of fund purchases affects tax bill

TAX CUT

Investors who purchase mutual funds and ETFs outside tax-sheltered retirement accounts also need to consider the time of year they purchase shares in funds, so they can minimize the tax bite. Specifically, investors should try to purchase funds after rather than just before the fund makes the following types of distributions:

>> **Capital gains distributions:** December is the most common month in which funds make capital gains distributions. If making purchases late in the year, investors should find out whether and when the fund may make a significant capital gains distribution. Often, the

unaware investor buys a fund just prior to a distribution, only to see the value of the fund decline. But the investor must still pay income tax on the distribution. The December payout is generally larger when a fund has had a particularly good performance year and when the fund manager has done more trading that year.

>> **Dividend distributions:** Some stock funds that pay reasonably high dividends (perhaps because they also hold bonds) tend to pay out dividends quarterly — typically on a March, June, September, and December cycle. Try to avoid buying shares of these funds just before they pay. Make purchases early in each calendar quarter (early in the months of January, April, July, and October). Remember that the share price of the fund is reduced by the amount of the dividend, and the dividend is taxable.

Don't get too concerned about when funds make distributions, because you can miss out on bigger profits by being so focused on avoiding a little bit of tax. If you want to be sure of the dates when a particular fund makes distributions, that information is generally posted on their website, or you can call the specific fund you have in mind.

Understanding the tax virtues of index funds

TIP

Fund managers of actively managed portfolios, in their attempts to increase their shareholders' returns, buy and sell individual securities more frequently. However, this trading increases the chances of a fund needing to make significant capital gains distributions.

Index funds, by contrast, are funds that invest in a relatively fixed portfolio of securities. They don't attempt to beat the market averages or indexes. Rather, they invest in the securities to mirror or match the performance of an underlying index, such as the S&P 500 index of 500 mostly larger company, U.S. stocks.

Although index funds can't beat the market, they have the following advantages over actively managed funds:

>> Because index funds trade much less often than actively managed funds, index fund investors benefit from lower brokerage fees.

>> Because significant ongoing research need not be conducted to identify companies in which to invest, index funds can be run with far lower operating expenses. All factors being equal, lower brokerage and operating costs translate into higher shareholder returns.

>> Because index funds trade less often, they tend to produce lower capital gains distributions. For funds held outside of tax-sheltered retirement accounts, this reduced trading effectively increases an investor's total rate of return. Thus, index mutual funds are tax-friendlier.

The Vanguard Group (800-662-7447; www.vanguard.com), headquartered in Valley Forge, Pennsylvania, is the largest mutual fund provider of index funds. Vanguard also offers some of the best exchange-traded funds, which are index funds that trade during the trading day on the major stock exchanges. Exchange-traded funds may offer an even lower-cost way for some investors to buy and hold a broad market index for the longer term.

Tax-Favored Investments to Avoid

WARNING

Investment and insurance brokers and "financial planners" (who sell products, work on commission, and are therefore salespeople) love to pitch investment products that supposedly save you on your taxes. Salespeople generally don't examine your entire financial situation. Therefore, the salesperson may sell you an inappropriate or lousy investment that pays (the salesperson!) hefty commissions. The following sections discuss the main investments these commission-driven folks try to sell you — along with the reasons why you shouldn't buy them.

Limited partnerships

Avoid limited partnerships (LPs) sold through brokers and financial planners. They are fundamentally inferior investment vehicles. That's not to say that no one has ever made money on one, but they are burdened with high sales commissions and ongoing management fees that deplete your investment. You can do better elsewhere.

Limited partnerships invest in real estate and a variety of businesses. They pitch that you can get in on the ground floor of a new investment opportunity and make big money. They also usually tell you that while your investment is growing at 20 percent or more per year, you get handsome dividends of 8 percent or so each year. Sound too good to be true? It is.

Many of the yields on LPs have turned out to be bogus. In some cases, partnerships have propped up their yields by paying back investors' original investment (principal) — without clearly telling them, of course. The other LP hook is the supposed tax benefit. The few loopholes that did exist in the tax code for LPs have largely been closed. (Amazingly, some investment salespeople hoodwink investors into putting their retirement account money — which is already tax-sheltered — into LPs!) The other problems with LPs overwhelm any small tax advantage, anyway.

The investment salesperson who sells you this type of investment stands to earn a commission of up to 10 percent or more — so only 90 cents, or less, of your dollar actually gets invested. Each year, LPs typically siphon off another few percentage points for management fees and other expenses. Most partnerships have little or no incentive to control costs. In fact, the pressure is to charge more in fees to enrich the managing partners.

Unlike with a mutual fund or ETF (which you can sell if it isn't performing), with LPs you can't vote with your dollars. If the partnership is poorly run and expensive, you're stuck. LPs are *illiquid*. You can't get your money out until the partnership is liquidated, typically seven to ten years after you buy in.

REMEMBER

The only thing limited about a limited partnership is its ability to make you money. If you want to buy investments that earn profits and have growth potential, stick with stocks (preferably using mutual funds), real estate, or your own business. For income as opposed to longer-term growth potential, invest in bonds.

REINVESTING AND DOLLAR-COST AVERAGING TAX ISSUES

When you make small purchases in a particular nonretirement account investment over time, you increase your accounting complexity and tax-filing headaches. For example, if you buy shares in a mutual fund, you'll be asked if you want the dividends and capital gains paid out to you as cash or reinvested into buying more shares in the fund. Most investment brokers enable you to reinvest dividends on individual stock holdings.

If you're retired or need to live off your investment income, receiving cash payments probably works best. If you don't need the money, reinvesting dividends allows your money to continue compounding and growing in the investment. Although reinvesting complicates your tax situation, because you're buying shares at different times at different prices, the benefits should outweigh the hassles. (But please take note: You still must pay current taxes on reinvested distributions in nonretirement accounts.)

Another investing approach is dollar-cost averaging, which can also cause tax headaches when you sell investments held outside of retirement accounts. *Dollar-cost averaging* simply means that you're investing your money in equal chunks on a regular basis, such as once a month. For example, if you have $60,000 to invest, you can choose to invest $2,000 per month until it's all invested, which takes a few years. The money that awaits future investment isn't lying fallow. You keep it in a money-market-type account, where it earns a bit of interest while it waits its turn.

The attraction of dollar-cost averaging is that it enables you to ease a large chunk of money into riskier investments instead of jumping in all at once. The possible benefit is that if the price of the investment drops after some of your initial purchases, you can buy more later at a lower price. If you had put all your money at once into an investment and then the value dropped like a stone, you'd kick yourself for not waiting.

The flip side of dollar-cost averaging is that if your investment of choice appreciates in value, you may wish that you had invested your money faster. Another possible drawback of dollar-cost averaging is that you may get cold feet as you continue to invest money in an investment that's dropping in value. People who are attracted to dollar-cost averaging out of fear of buying before a price drop can become scared to continue boarding what may look like a sinking ship.

Dollar-cost averaging is most valuable when the money you want to invest represents a large portion of your total assets and you can stick to a schedule. It's best to make your contributions automatic so that you're less likely to be frightened off should prices begin falling after you start investing. If you aren't investing a lot of money, or the amount is a small portion of your total holdings, don't bother with dollar-cost averaging.

When you buy an investment via dollar-cost averaging or dividend reinvestment at many different times and prices, accounting is muddied as you sell portions of the investment. Which shares are you selling: the ones you bought at a higher price or the ones you bought at a lower price?

For record-keeping purposes, most mutual fund and investment companies, for example, provide year-end summary statements that show all transactions throughout the year. Be sure to keep these statements or know how to access them online. For purchases made in recent years and in the future, fund companies should also be able to tell you what your average cost per share is when you need to sell your shares.

Cash-value life insurance

WARNING

Life insurance that combines life insurance protection with an account that has a cash value is usually known as *universal, whole,* or *variable life.* Life insurance should not be used as an investment, especially if you haven't reached the maximum allowable limit for contributing money to retirement accounts. Agents love to sell cash-value life insurance for the high commissions.

The cash-value portion of such policies grows without taxation until withdrawn. However, if you want tax-deferred retirement savings, you should first take advantage of retirement savings plans, such as 401(k)s, 403(b)s, SEP-IRAs, and so on, which give you an immediate tax deduction for your current contributions. These accounts also allow your investments to grow and compound without taxation until withdrawal.

Money paid into a cash-value life insurance policy gives you no upfront tax breaks. When you've exhausted contributing to tax-deductible retirement accounts, you may find that a non-deductible IRA, Roth IRA, and other employer-based Roth accounts can provide tax-deferred compounding of your investment dollars. Roth retirement accounts allow for tax-free compounding and tax-free withdrawal of investment earnings, something that cash-value life policies don't do. See Chapter 22 for the details on retirement accounts.

The only real financial advantage cash-value life insurance offers is that, with proper planning, the proceeds paid to your beneficiaries can be free of federal estate taxes. You need to have a fairly substantial estate at the time of your death to benefit from this feature. And numerous other, more cost-effective methods exist to minimize your estate taxes (see Chapter 27 for more details on estate planning).

Analyzing Annuities

Annuities are a peculiar type of insurance and investment product — sort of a savings-type account with slightly higher yields that are backed by insurance companies.

WARNING

Insurance agents and financial planners working on commission happily sell annuities to many people with money to invest. The problem is annuities are suitable investments for relatively few people. If annuities do make sense for you, you can buy no-load (commission-free) annuities by bypassing salespeople and dealing directly with mutual fund companies.

The major selling hook of annuities is the supposed tax savings. "Why pay taxes each year on your investment earnings?" the agent or financial planner will ask. As in other types of retirement accounts, money that's placed in an annuity compounds without taxation until withdrawal. However, unlike most other types of retirement accounts (discussed in Chapter 22) — 401(k)s, 403(b)s, SEP-IRAs, and so on — your contributions to an annuity give no upfront tax deductions. And, unlike Roth retirement accounts, you get no tax break upon withdrawal of your investment earnings from an annuity. The only annuity income tax benefit, as with cash-value life insurance, is that the earnings compound without taxation until withdrawal. Thus, it makes sense to consider contributing to an annuity only after you fully fund your tax-deductible and Roth retirement accounts.

TIP

Because annuities carry higher annual expenses due to the insurance that comes with them, they generally make sense only if you have many years to allow the money to compound. So annuities are not appropriate if you're already in or near retirement. Also, the lower tax rate on long-term capital gains and stock dividends (which we discuss earlier in this chapter) makes investing money in annuities relatively less attractive than simply investing in tax-friendly nonretirement account holdings. All earnings on an annuity are taxed upon withdrawal at ordinary income tax rates, whereas with a nonretirement account investment, much of your profits can be deferred into lower-taxed long-term capital gains and lower-taxed stock dividends.

Selling Decisions

After you've owned a stock, bond, mutual fund, or ETF for a while, you may want to contemplate selling some or all of it. Taxes should factor into the decision when you consider selling investments that you hold outside tax-sheltered retirement accounts. For investments held inside retirement accounts, taxes aren't an issue because the accounts are sheltered from taxation (unless you're withdrawing funds from the accounts — see Chapter 22 for the details). In most cases, you need not waste your money or precious free time consulting a tax advisor. In the sections that follow, we outline issues for you to consider in your selling decisions.

Selling selected shares

Before we get into the specific types of investment decisions you're likely to confront, we must deal with a rather unpleasant but important issue: accounting methods for security sales. Although this stuff gets a little complicated, with some minimal advance planning, you can acquire sound methods to reduce your tax burden. If you sell all the shares of a security that you own, you can ignore this issue. Only if you sell a portion of your shares of a security should you consider *specifying* which shares you're selling.

Suppose that you own 200 shares of stock in Intergalactic Computer Software, and you plan to sell 100 shares. You bought 100 of these shares ten years ago at $50 per share, and then another 100 shares two years ago for $100 per share. Today, the stock is worth $150 per share. What a savvy investor you are!

So, which 100 shares should you sell? The IRS gives you a choice, from a tax-accounting standpoint. You can identify the specific shares that you sell. In the case of Intergalactic, you can opt to sell the last or most recent 100 shares you bought, which would minimize your tax bill — because these shares were purchased at a higher price. At the time you want to sell the shares through your brokerage account, identify the shares you want to sell by noting the original date of purchase and/or the cost of those shares. So in the case of your Intergalactic stock holdings, simply tell your broker that you want to sell the 100 shares that you bought two years ago (give the date) at $100 per share. (The broker should include this information on the confirmation you receive for the sale.) Please note that if these shares had been bought within the past year and you had a gain, you may not want to sell those shares, because the profit wouldn't be taxed at the lower long-term capital gains tax rate discussed earlier in this chapter.

The other method of determining which shares you're selling is the method the IRS forces you to use if you don't specify before the sale which shares are to be sold — the *first-in-first-out*

(FIFO) method. FIFO isn't a dog with a funny name; it's an accounting term that means that the first shares you bought (*first in*) are the first shares that you sold (*first out*). Not surprisingly, because most stocks appreciate over time, the FIFO method leads to paying more tax sooner. In the case of Intergalactic, FIFO means that the first 100 shares that you bought (ten years ago at the bargain-basement price of $50 per share) are the first 100 shares sold.

Although you'll save taxes today if you specify that you're selling the shares you bought most recently (at a higher price), don't forget (and the IRS won't let you) that when you finally sell the other shares (bought long ago at a low price), you'll then owe taxes on the larger profit you realize from those shares. The longer you hold these shares, the greater the likelihood that their value will rise, realizing a larger profit for you (although you end up paying more taxes). Of course, the risk always exists that Congress will raise tax rates in the future or that your particular tax rate will rise. If you sell some of your investments, keep your life simple by considering selling all your shares of a specific security. That way, you don't have to hassle with all this accounting nonsense for tax purposes.

REMEMBER

To be able to choose, or specify, which shares you're selling, you must select them before you sell. If you don't, the IRS says that you must use the FIFO method. You may wonder how the IRS knows whether you specified which shares before you sold them. The IRS doesn't know. But if you're audited, the IRS will ask for proof.

Selling securities with (large) capital gains

Capital gains tax applies when you sell a security at a higher price than you paid for it. As we explain earlier in this chapter, the long-term capital gains rate is lower than the tax rate you pay on ordinary income (such as from employment earnings or interest on bank savings accounts). Odds are, the longer you hold securities such as stocks, the greater the capital gains you'll accrue, because stocks tend to appreciate over time.

Suppose that your parents bought you 1,000 shares of XYZ company stock ten years ago, when it was selling for $10 a share. Today, it's selling for $20 per share; but you also vaguely recall that the stock split two-for-one a few years ago, so now you own 2,000 shares. Thus, if you sell XYZ stock for $40,000 today, you'd have a capital gain of $30,000 on which to pay taxes. So why would anyone want to sell?

The answer depends on your situation. For example, if you need the money for some other purpose — buying a home, starting a small business, taking some time off to travel — and the stock is your only source of funds, go for it. If you can't do what you want to do without selling, don't let the taxes stand in the way. Even if you pay state and federal taxes totaling some 20 to 25 percent of the profit, you'll have lots left over. Before you sell, however, do some rough figuring to make sure that you have enough to accomplish what you want.

What if you hold a number of stocks? To diversify and meet your other financial goals, all you need to do is prioritize. One approach is to give preference to selling your largest holdings (total market value) that have the smallest capital gains. If some of your securities have profits and some have losses, sell some of each to offset the profits with the losses. (Gains and losses on securities held one year or less are taxed at your ordinary income tax rates — see Chapter 14 for more details.)

Don't expect to obtain objective, disinterested, tax-wise advice regarding what to do with your current investments from a stockbroker or from most financial planners. If they earn commissions on the products they sell, their bias will be to tell you to sell. Even though some financial planners don't get commissions, they can charge fees on what they manage. When you seek objective help with these "sell versus hold" decisions, turn to a competent tax or financial advisor who works on an hourly basis.

Selling securities at a loss

Perhaps you own some losers in your portfolio. If you want to raise cash for some particular reason, you may consider selling some securities at a loss. Don't hold on to an investment just because its value now is less than what you paid for it. Waiting until its value rises to what you originally paid is a natural, but silly, human desire. Selling a loser now frees up your money for better investments. Losses can also be used to offset gains (investments sold at a profit) — just remember that long-term losses will offset long-term gains first. Only after you've completely exhausted your long-term gains can you use them against short-term gains, which are taxed at a higher rate.

Both short-term and long-term losses can be deducted against ordinary income, subject to limitations. If you want to sell securities at a loss, be advised that you can't claim more than $3,000 ($1,500 if you're married but filing separately) in short-term or long-term losses on your federal tax return in a given tax year. If you sell securities with losses totaling more than $3,000 in a year, the losses must be carried over to future tax years. This situation not only creates more tax paperwork, but also delays realizing the value of deducting a tax loss. So try not to have net losses (losses plus gains) exceeding $3,000 in a year.

Some tax advisors advocate doing *year-end tax-loss selling.* The logic goes that if you hold a security at a loss, you should sell it, take the tax write-off, and then buy it (or something similar) back. Sounds good in theory, but when you eventually sell the shares that you bought again at the lower price, you'll owe tax on the increased price anyway. (When you sell other stocks during the year at a profit, tax-loss selling to offset these taxable gains makes more sense.) But many people who sell an investment that has declined in value don't want to buy the same investment again. This reluctance can cause other investment blunders. For example, suppose you had the misfortune to buy some stocks back in 2007. In the next couple of years, your stocks plummeted about 50 percent or more. It wasn't because of your poor stock-picking ability. You simply got caught in the U.S. stock market downdraft during the financial crisis that hit hard in 2008. You'd make a bad situation worse by panicking and selling at reduced price levels just to take a tax loss. If anything, under such circumstances consider doing the opposite — take advantage of the sale and buy more!

If you do decide to sell for tax-loss purposes, be careful of the so-called *wash sale* rules. The IRS doesn't allow deduction of a loss for a security that you sell if you buy that same security back within 30 days. As long as you wait 31 or more days, you'll have no problem. When you're selling a mutual fund, you can easily sidestep this rule simply by purchasing a fund similar to the one you're selling.

When you own a security that has ceased trading and appears worthless (or even if you've made a loan that hasn't been repaid — even if to a friend), you can probably deduct this loss.

See Chapter 14 for more information on what situations are deductible and how to claim these losses on your annual tax return.

Mutual funds and the average cost method

In the United States, you never have a shortage of choices — so why shouldn't it be the same with accounting methods? When you sell shares in a mutual fund, the IRS allows you an additional method — *the average cost method* — for determining your profit or loss for tax purposes. (This information doesn't apply to money market funds, which don't fluctuate in value.)

If you bought fund shares in chunks over time and/or reinvested the fund distributions (such as from dividends) into more shares of the fund, tracking and figuring what shares you're selling can be a real headache. So the IRS allows you to take an average cost for all the shares you bought over time.

Be aware that after you elect the average cost method, you can't change to another method for accounting for the sale of the remaining shares. If you plan to sell only some of your fund shares, and it would be advantageous for you to specify that you're selling the newer shares first, choose that method (as we describe in the "Selling selected shares" section earlier in this chapter).

Stock options and taxes

Some companies grant particular employees *stock options*. If you're the proud holder of this type of option, congratulations! You're either an important employee or work for a company that believes in sharing the success of its growth with its employees.

If you have *statutory stock options*, sometimes known as *incentive stock options*, you face a number of important decisions that can have significant tax consequences. Basically, stock options grant you the right to buy shares of stock from your employer at a predetermined price. For example, suppose that you take a job with a large discount retailer and the company tells you that, after December 31, 2016, you may "exercise the right" to purchase 1,000 shares of its stock at $50 per share.

In the years ahead, you and other store employees help the company to continue growing and expanding. Suppose the company's stock price eventually rises to $75 per share in the next year. Thus, because your options enable you to buy company stock for $50 per share, and it's now at $75 per share, you have a profit on paper of $25,000 (1,000 shares × $25 profit per share)!

To realize this profit, you must first exercise your option (your company benefits department can tell you how). After you are the proud owner of the shares, you can sell them if you want to. However — and this is a big *however* — if you sell the shares within a year of having exercised the options, or within two years after the grant of the option (whichever is later), you will owe ordinary income tax on the profit. If you hold the shares for the required period of time, then you will pay the lowest possible long-term capital gains tax. (You may also be subject to the Alternative Minimum Tax, or AMT — see Chapter 8 to find out more about this tax.)

When you're a high-income earner, holding on to your exercised stock options for more than 12 months so that you qualify for the favorable capital gains tax treatment is normally to your advantage. The risk in waiting to sell is that your profits shrink as and if the stock price drops.

Nonstatutory stock options are a bit different. Unlike incentive stock options, nonstatutory stock options aren't given special tax treatment. With nonstatutory stock options, you must pay tax on the options either when you receive them (if you can determine their fair market value) or when you exercise them. You must also pay income tax on the difference between the fair market value of the stock at the time you exercise the option minus the value of the option on which you pay tax. After you exercise the option, the decision on when to sell (and the tax consequences) is the same as for incentive stock options. If you don't know which type of option your employer offers, ask the benefits department.

WARNING

If you aren't a high-income earner and waiting to sell offers no tax advantage, selling your shares as the shares become exercisable is usually prudent. When the stock market plunged in the early 2000s, and then again in 2007–2009, a number of employees, especially in high-tech companies, got clobbered with taxes on nonstatutory stock options on stock they'd held onto that then plummeted in value. So the employees ended up being out a lot of dough in taxes and in some cases holding worthless or near worthless stock. We should also note that having too much of your wealth tied up in the stock of your employer is risky. Remember that your job is already on the line if the company's success wanes.

Selling securities whose costs are unknown

When you sell a security or a fund that you've owned for a long time (or that your parents gave you), you may not know the security's original cost (also known as its *cost basis*). If you can only find the original account statement that shows the original purchase price and amount . . .

If you can't find that original statement, start by calling the firm through which you purchased the investment. Whether it's a brokerage firm or fund company, it should be able to provide you with copies of old account statements. You may have to pay a small fee for this service. Also, investment firms (particularly fund companies) are required now to track and report cost basis information on investments that you sell through them. This requirement took effect for stocks in 2011; for mutual funds in 2012; and for bonds, options, and commodities in 2014. See Chapter 3 for more ideas on what to do when original records aren't available.

IN THIS CHAPTER

» **Dealing with home ownership and home-buying tax breaks**

» **Making decisions about mortgages taxes**

» **Knowing strategies for keeping the IRS at bay when selling your house**

» **Finding tax considerations when investing in real estate**

Chapter **25**

Real Estate and Taxes

Tax benefits are a significant reason why many people, especially people in the real estate business — such as real estate agents, bankers, mortgage brokers, and others in the lending business — advocate property ownership.

Buying a home or investing in real estate can provide financial and psychological rewards. And tax breaks can help reduce the cost of owning real estate. On the other hand, purchasing and maintaining property can be time-consuming, emotionally draining, and financially painful.

Surveying Real Estate Tax Breaks

Just as contributing money to retirement accounts (see Chapter 22) yields tax breaks, so does buying a home and investing in other real estate. The U.S. income tax system favors home and other real estate ownership because of the widely held belief that owners take better care of their property when they have a financial stake in its future value. Arguing with this logic is difficult if you have visited almost any government-subsidized tenement.

All the powerful real estate lobbies also contribute to the addition and retention of real estate tax benefits in our tax code. Builders, contractors, real estate agents, the banking industry, and many other real estate–related sectors have an enormous financial stake in the American hunger to own and improve properties.

You should understand the tax aspects of owning a home and investing in other real estate so that you can make the most of these tax-reduction opportunities. Making wise real estate decisions also requires that you know how to fit real estate into your overall financial picture. After all, you have limited income and other options on which to spend your money.

WARNING

Don't make the mistake of depending on those individuals involved in the typical real estate deal to help you see the bigger picture. Remember that these folks make their livings off your decision to buy real estate, and the more you spend, the more they generally make.

Before we get to detailing real estate tax breaks, we kindly ask you to remember two important caveats to gaining these property tax advantages:

>> You have to spend money on real estate — acquiring property, paying the mortgage and property taxes over the years, and improving the property while you own it — to even be eligible for the tax breaks. As we discuss in this chapter, if you purchase a high-priced home or make the wrong financial moves, you may not be able to claim some of the real estate tax benefits available.

>> The price of real estate in the United States reflects the fact that buyers and sellers know about the tax deductions. This is a major reason why so many people are willing to pay sums with many zeroes for a piece of the American Dream. Other countries that don't offer tax breaks for home ownership, such as Canada, have comparatively lower prices because buyers can't afford to pay higher prices when they can't bank on a tax deduction to help subsidize the cost.

The following sections offer an overview of the tax goodies available to U.S. homeowners. The benefits are similar to, but different from, the tax benefits for rental or income property owners, which we discuss later in this chapter.

Mortgage interest and property tax write-offs

When you buy a home, you can claim two big ongoing expenses of home ownership as tax deductions on Schedule A of Form 1040. These expenses are your property taxes and the interest on your mortgage.

You're allowed to claim mortgage-interest deductions on a primary residence (where you actually live) and on a second home for mortgage debt totaling $750,000. For mortgages taken out before December 16, 2017, you can take mortgage interest deductions on up to $1 million ($500,000 if married filing separately) of mortgage debt.

Property taxes on your home when combined with other deductible state income tax payments are deductible on Schedule A up to $10,000 per year. This deduction is typically referred to as the SALT (state and local tax) deduction. At the time this book goes to press in late 2021, Congress has been considering raising this deduction limit and perhaps eliminating the deduction cap altogether as it was prior to 2018. We don't think there's much chance for complete elimination of the cap as the tax benefits of doing that would largely accrue to the wealthiest and highest income taxpayers. Far more likely but by no means certain, is the possibility that the SALT limit may be raised to say $20,000 or $25,000 per year from the current $10,000.

Home ownership capital gains exclusion

Normally, when you make an investment in a stock or business, for example, and you later sell it for a profit (also known as a *capital gain*), you owe tax on the profit. Some real estate, however, receives special treatment in this regard.

The tax laws pertaining to the sale of a primary residence allow for a significant amount of profit to be excluded from taxation: up to $250,000 for single taxpayers and up to $500,000 for married couples filing jointly. Moreover, to take advantage of this tax break — unlike under the old house-sale rules — house sellers need not be over a particular age or buy a replacement residence of equal or greater value to the one just sold. In the five years leading up to the home sale, you would need to have lived in the home for at least two of those years.

When calculating your profit upon sale of your home, your "cost basis" for your home includes the price you originally paid to buy it plus improvements you've made over time. See the section, "Tracking your home expenditures," later in this chapter.

DEALING WITH "EXCESS" HOUSING PROFITS

Although the house-sale capital gains tax laws benefit many people, the rules do have a negative twist. If you live in an area with relatively inexpensive real estate, you may find this difficult to believe: Some longer-term homeowners, especially in the higher-cost sections of the country, may have profits in excess of the law's limits ($250,000 for singles and $500,000 for married couples filing jointly).

For those in that admittedly enviable position, the tax laws offer no escape hatch. At the time of sale, single homeowners with accumulated profits (which also include those profits rolled over, under the old tax laws, from previous sales) greater than $250,000 and couples with profits greater than $500,000 must pay capital gains tax on the excess.

When they start to bump up against the maximum amounts that can be shielded from capital gains taxation, long-term homeowners and those buying expensive homes may want to consider selling and moving, even if it's within the same neighborhood.

Those whose homes have appreciated well in excess of the limits may want to consider, if possible, holding their homes until their deaths, at which point, under current tax laws, the IRS wipes the capital gains slate clean (see Chapter 27). Please also be aware that increasing numbers of taxpayers are finding themselves subject to the dreaded Alternative Minimum Tax (AMT) for many reasons, including the realization of larger capital gains.

Also keep in mind that thanks to inflation, increasing numbers of house sellers over time will find their profits to be in excess of the $250K/$500K limits because those thresholds are fixed and aren't scheduled to increase with inflation. Thus, in the years ahead, increasing numbers of homeowners will be affected by the limits. That's why you should heed our advice to keep receipts for all of your home improvements, which allow you to increase your home's cost basis for tax purposes and thus reduce your potentially taxable capital gain. See the section "Tracking your home expenditures" later in this chapter.

So, if you're longing to move to a less-costly housing market, you're largely free of tax constraints to do so. This tax break also benefits empty nesters and others nearing or in retirement who want to buy a less-costly home and free up some of their home equity to use toward retirement.

House losses aren't deductible

Some homeowners have discovered firsthand that real estate prices go down as well as up. If it's time for you to sell your house and move on, you may be disappointed to discover that you can't deduct the loss if your house sells for less than what you paid for it. If you lose money investing in the stock market, on the other hand, those losses are usually deductible (see Chapter 24). Although you may think it's unfair that home ownership losses aren't tax-deductible, remember that you're already getting many tax perks from your home — the mortgage interest and property tax deductions. And the substantial capital gains tax exclusion when you sell your home.

Converting rental property to save on taxes

If you want to sell appreciated rental property, the house-sale rules may benefit you as well. How? By moving into a rental property that you own and making it your primary residence for at least two years, you can shield the profits from the sale of the property from taxation. (Obviously, this strategy is feasible only for certain types of properties that you would be willing or able to live in. Also, it doesn't apply to depreciation taken after May 7, 1997 — see Chapter 14.)

WARNING

When you move from your house, rent it out for a period of time, and then sell it, the IRS may consider that you have converted your home from a primary residence to a rental property. Thus, you may lose the privilege of excluding tax on the profit from the sale. The only exception: You actively tried to sell the house after you moved and only rented it temporarily to help defray the costs of keeping it until you sold it.

Home office deductions

When you run your business out of your home, you may be able to take additional tax deductions beyond the mortgage interest and property taxes that you may claim as a homeowner. Check out Chapter 23 for a more in-depth discussion of this issue.

Purchasing Your Humble Home

Financially speaking, you really shouldn't buy your own place unless you anticipate being there for at least three years, and preferably five years or more. Many expenses accompany buying and selling a property, such as the cost of getting a mortgage (points, application and credit report fees, and appraisal fees), inspection expenses, moving costs, real estate agents' commissions, and title insurance. And remember, most of these expenses are not tax-deductible (at best, some of them can be added to your home's tax basis as we explain in the section "Tracking your home expenditures" later in this chapter). To cover these transaction costs plus the additional costs of ownership, a property needs to appreciate a fair amount before you can be as well off financially as if you had continued renting. A property needs to appreciate about 15 percent just to offset these expenses, even factoring in the tax benefits that homeowners enjoy.

If you need or want to move in a couple of years, counting on that kind of appreciation is risky. If you're lucky (that is, if you happen to buy before a significant rise in housing prices), you may get it. Otherwise, you'll probably lose money on the deal.

Some people are willing to buy a home even when they don't expect to live in it for long because they plan on turning it into a rental when it's time to move on. Holding rental property can be a good long-term investment, but don't underestimate the responsibilities that come with rental property.

Exploring the tax savings in home ownership

To quickly estimate your monthly tax savings from home ownership, try this simple shortcut: Multiply your marginal federal tax rate (refer to Chapter 1) by the total monthly amount of your property taxes and mortgage. (Technically, not all your mortgage payment is tax-deductible; only the portion of the mortgage payment that goes to interest is tax-deductible. However, in the early years of your mortgage, the portion that goes toward interest is nearly all of the payment. On the other hand, your property taxes will probably rise over time, and you can also earn state tax benefits from your deductible mortgage interest and property taxes.)

KEEP TRACK OF YOUR TAX BRACKET

When you first consider purchasing a home or purchasing a more expensive home, it usually pays to plan ahead and push as many so-called itemizable deductions as you can into the tax year in which you expect to buy your home.

For example, suppose that this year you're using the standard deduction because you don't have many itemized deductions. You decide late in the year that you expect to buy a home next year and therefore will have mortgage interest and property taxes to write off and you'll probably be able to itemize the next year. It makes sense, then, to collect as many deductible expenses as possible and shift them into next year. For example, if the solicitations surrounding the December holidays prompt you to contribute money to charities, you can wait until January to donate. Take a look at the deductible items on Schedule A (see Chapter 11) to determine what else you may want to postpone paying.

Also, be aware that your income tax bracket may change from year to year. Thus, when possible, you can choose to pay more or less of some itemizable expenses in one year versus another. Suppose that you receive your monthly mortgage bill in the middle of the month and it's not due until early the following month. If for some reason you expect to be in a lower tax bracket next year — perhaps you're going to take a sabbatical and will earn less income — you may choose to pay your December mortgage bill before the current year ends. In this case, the mortgage interest deduction has greater value to you in the current year because you're in a higher tax bracket. (Conversely, if you expected to be in a higher tax bracket next year, you should wait to pay your December mortgage bill in early January, so you get more of your mortgage interest deduction next tax year.)

Be sure to read Chapter 1, which explains how to figure your current and future expected tax bracket for planning purposes to minimize your taxes.

To figure out more precisely how home ownership may affect your tax situation, try plugging some reasonable numbers into your tax return to guesstimate how your taxes may change. You can also speak with a tax advisor.

TIP

When you buy a home, make sure to refigure how much you're paying in income taxes, because your mortgage interest and property tax deductions should help lower your income tax bills (federal and state). Many homebuyers skip this step and end up getting a big tax refund when they file their tax returns. Although getting money back from the IRS and state may feel good, it means that, at a minimum, you made an interest-free loan to the government. In the worst case, the reduced cash flow during the year may cause you to accumulate debt or miss out on contributing to tax-deductible retirement accounts. If you work for an employer, ask your payroll/benefits department for Form W-4 (see Chapter 17 for information about how to fill out this form). If you're self-employed, you can complete a worksheet that comes with Form 1040-ES (see Chapter 17).

Deciding how much to spend on a home

When you fall in love with a home and buy it without looking at your monthly expenditures and long-term goals, you may end up with a home that dictates much of your future spending. Real estate agents and mortgage lenders are more than happy to tell you the maximum that you're qualified to borrow. They want your business, and the more money you spend, the more they make. But that doesn't mean that you should borrow the maximum.

Typical is the advice of this real estate broker who writes about real estate:

> "The first step is to find out what price you can afford to buy. The easiest way to do this is to make an appointment with a loan agent or a mortgage broker."

Easy, yes. But doing so probably won't get you the right or best answer. Like real estate agents, mortgage brokers tell you the maximum loan you can qualify for. This amount isn't necessarily what you can "afford." Just ask one of the many folks who overextended and ended up with their home in foreclosure during the late 2000s real estate slump. Remember, mortgage and loan agents get a commission based on the size of your loan. Taking into consideration your other financial goals and needs, such as saving for retirement, isn't part of their job description (nor generally their expertise).

In addition to analyzing your retirement planning, questions you should ask yourself before buying a home may include how much you spend (and want to continue spending) on fun stuff, such as travel and entertainment. If you want to continue your current lifestyle (and the expenditures inherent in it), be honest with yourself about how much you can really afford to spend as a homeowner.

WARNING

Often, first-time homebuyers are apt to run into financial trouble because they don't know their spending needs and priorities and don't know how to budget for them. Buying a home can be a wise decision, but it also can be a huge burden. Some people don't decrease their spending as much as they should, based on the large amount of debt they incur in buying a home. In fact, some homeowners spend even more on all sorts of gadgets and furnishings for their homes. Many people prop up their spending habits with credit. For this reason, a surprisingly large percentage of people — some studies say about half — who borrow additional money against their home equity use the funds to pay other debts.

Don't let your home control your financial future. Before you buy property or agree to a particular mortgage, take stock of your overall financial health, especially in terms of retirement planning if you hope to retire by your mid-60s.

Tracking your home expenditures

Although it may be a bit of a hassle, documenting and tracking money spent improving your property is in your best financial interests. For tax purposes, you can add the cost of these improvements to your original purchase price for the home. So, when you sell the property someday, you get to reduce your profit, for tax purposes, accordingly.

Keep in mind that under the current tax laws, most people won't owe capital gains tax from the sale of a house. Single people can make a $250,000 profit, and married couples filing jointly can realize $500,000 in profit without paying tax on the proceeds of the sale. However, you still need to track your home improvement expenditures because it's impossible to know while you're living in your home if your future sale, which may be many years off, can trigger capital gains tax. Who knows how much real estate will appreciate in the interim or what changes can happen to the tax laws?

As we discuss later in this chapter, when you sell your house, you may need to report to the IRS, on Schedule D, Capital Gains and Losses, the selling price of the house, the original cost of the house, and how much you spent improving it. Therefore, we strongly advise setting up a simple file folder, perhaps labeled "Home Improvements," into which you deposit receipts for your expenditures.

The challenging part for most people is simply keeping the receipts organized in one place. Another task is correctly distinguishing between spending on *improvements*, which the IRS allows you to add to your cost of the home, and spending for *maintenance and repairs*, which you can't add to the original purchase price of the home.

REMEMBER

Improvements include expenses such as installing an alarm system, adding or remodeling a room, planting new trees and shrubs in your yard, installing a new fence, replacing your roof, and purchasing new appliances. These improvements increase the value of your home and lengthen its life. Maintenance and repairs include expenses such as hiring a plumber to fix a leaky pipe, repainting, repairing a door so that it closes properly, replacing a broken window pane, and replacing missing roof shingles.

It's interesting to note that if you hire a contractor to do home improvements, the IRS allows you to effectively add the cost of the contractor's time (the labor charges) into the overall improvements that reduce your home's profit for tax purposes. On the other hand, if you elect to do the work yourself, you gain no tax benefit for your sweat. You can't add a cost for the value of your time — the IRS assumes that your time isn't worth anything. You work for free! Now you have another reason for hiring someone to do the work for you.

Also, don't forget to toss into your receipt folder the *settlement statement*, which you should have received in the blizzard of paperwork you signed when you bought your home. Don't lose this valuable piece of paper, which itemizes many of the expenses associated with the purchase of your home. You can add many of these expenses to the original cost of the home and reduce your taxable profit when it comes time to sell. You also want to keep proof of other expenditures that the settlement statement may not document, such as inspection fees that you paid when buying your home.

Per the IRS, the following are some of the settlement fees and closing costs that you can add to the original basis (purchase price) of your home.

>> Abstract fees (abstract of title fees)

>> Charges for installing utility services

>> Legal fees (including fees for the title search and preparation of the sales contract and deed)

>> Recording fees

>> Surveys

>> Transfer or stamp taxes

>> Owner's title insurance

>> Any amount the seller owes that you agree to pay, such as back taxes or interest

>> Recording or mortgage fees, cost for improvements or repairs, and sales commissions

Reporting revenue if you sometimes rent

The IRS allows you to rent your home or a room in your home for up to 14 days each year without having to declare the rental income and pay income taxes on it. Renting your home or a portion thereof for more than 14 days requires that you report the income when you file your annual tax return. You can declare real estate rental income by filing Schedule E. (Refer to Chapter 15 for more information.)

Making Tax-Wise Mortgage Decisions

The largest expense of property ownership is almost always the monthly mortgage payment. In the earlier years of a mortgage, the bulk of the mortgage payment covers interest that generally is tax-deductible subject to IRS limits. In this section, we discuss how to factor taxes and your financial circumstances into making intelligent mortgage decisions.

15-year or 30-year mortgage?

Unfortunately, you have thousands of mortgage options to choose from. Fixed-rate and adjustable-rate mortgages come with all sorts of bells and whistles. The number of permutations is mind-numbing.

From a tax perspective, one of the most important mortgage selection issues is whether to take a 15-year or 30-year mortgage. To afford the monthly payments, most homebuyers need to spread the loan payments over a longer period of time, and a 30-year mortgage is the only option. A 15-year mortgage requires higher monthly payments because you pay it off more quickly.

Even if you can afford these higher payments, taking the 15-year option may not be wise. The money for making extra payments doesn't come out of thin air. You may have better uses for your excess funds. What you're really asking, if you're considering whether you should take a 30-year or a 15-year mortgage, is whether you should pay off your mortgage slowly or quickly. The answer isn't as simple as some people think.

First, think about alternative uses for the extra money you're throwing into the mortgage payments. What's best for you depends on your overall financial situation and what else you can do with the money. When you elect the slow, 30-year mortgage payoff approach and you end up blowing the extra money on a new car, for example, you're better off paying down the mortgage more quickly. In that case, take the 15-year version. (If you want to buy a car in the future, saving in a money market fund so that you don't need to take out a high-cost car loan makes sound financial sense.)

But suppose that you aren't so frivolous with your extra money, and instead, you take the extra $100 or $200 per month and contribute it to a retirement account. That step may make financial sense. Why? Because additions to 401(k)s, 403(b)s, SEP-IRAs, and other types of retirement accounts are typically tax-deductible (see Chapter 22).

REMEMBER

When you dump that $200 into a retirement account, you get to subtract it from the income on which you pay taxes. If you're paying 30 percent in federal and state income taxes, you shave $60 (that's $200 multiplied by 30 percent) off your tax bill. (You're going to pay taxes when you withdraw the money from the retirement account someday, but in the meantime, the money that would have gone to taxes is growing on your behalf.) You get no tax benefits from that $200 when added to your mortgage payment when you elect a faster payoff mortgage (15-year mortgage).

With kids, you have an even greater reason to fund your retirement accounts before you consider paying down your mortgage faster. Under current rules for determining financial aid for college expenses, money in your retirement accounts isn't counted as an asset (see Chapter 26) that you must use toward college costs.

If you're uncomfortable investing and would otherwise leave the extra money sitting in a money market fund or savings account — or worse, if you would spend it — you're better off paying down the mortgage. Take the 15-year approach. If the investments in your retirement account plummet in value, the impact of the tax-deferred compounding of your capital may be negated. Paying off your mortgage quicker, on the other hand, is just like investing your money in a sure thing — but with a modest rate of return.

In most cases, you get to deduct your mortgage interest on your tax return. So if you're paying 4 percent interest, it really may cost you only around 3 percent after you factor in the tax benefits. If you think that you can do better by investing elsewhere, go for it. Remember, though, that you owe income tax from profits on your investments held outside retirement accounts. You aren't going to get decent investment returns unless you're willing to take risks. Investments such as stocks and real estate have generated better returns over the long haul. These investments carry risks, though, and aren't guaranteed to produce any return.

When you don't have a burning investment option, paying down your mortgage as your cash flow allows is usually wiser. If you have extra cash and have contributed the maximum allowed for retirement accounts, you may want to invest in real estate or perhaps a business. You have to decide if it's worth the extra risk in making a particular investment rather than paying down your mortgage.

As we've stated for many years now, we were concerned with the increasing promotion and popularity in the past of interest-only and other low down payment mortgages. Not only do such loans carry higher interest rates and other costs (such as private mortgage insurance), but consumers may also be in for some rude surprises. For example, interest-only loans lure people with their relatively low initial payments. However, years into the mortgage, the payment leaps higher as you begin to finally work at paying down the principal. For more information regarding mortgage options and decisions, pick up a copy of *Mortgages For Dummies* by Eric Tyson and Robert Griswold (Wiley).

How large a down payment?

What if you're in the enviable and fortunate position of having so much money that you can afford to put down more than a 20 percent down payment (which generally is the amount needed to qualify for better mortgage terms, including not having to take out private mortgage insurance)? Perhaps you're one of those wise people who doesn't want to get stretched too thin financially, and you're buying a less expensive home than you can afford. How much should you put down?

Some people, particularly those in the real estate business (and even some tax and financial advisors), say that you should take as large a mortgage as you can for the tax deductions — that is, don't make a larger down payment than you have to. This is silly reasoning. Remember that you have to pay out money in interest charges to get the tax deductions.

Again, what makes sense for you depends on your alternative uses for the money. When you're considering other investment opportunities, determine whether you can reasonably expect to earn a higher rate of return than the interest rate you'll pay on the mortgage.

In the past century, stock market and real estate investors have enjoyed average annual returns of around 8 to 9 percent per year (just remember, the past doesn't guarantee the future). So if you borrow mortgage money at around 4 to 5 percent today, you should come out ahead by investing in these areas. Besides possibly generating a higher rate of return, other real estate and stock investing can help you diversify your investments.

Of course, you have no guarantee that you can earn 8 to 9 percent each year. And don't forget that all investments come with risks. The advantage of putting more money down for a home and borrowing less is that paying down a mortgage is essentially a risk-free investment (as long as you have emergency money you can tap).

If you prefer to limit the down payment to 20 percent and invest more elsewhere, that's fine. Just don't keep the extra money (beyond an emergency reserve) under the mattress, in a savings account, or in bonds that provide returns lower than the mortgage is costing you.

Refinancing decisions and taxes

When your mortgage has a higher rate of interest than loans currently available, you may save money by refinancing. Because refinancing requires money and time, you need to crunch a few numbers and factor in taxes to determine whether refinancing makes sense for you. Ask your mortgage lender or broker how soon you can recoup the refinancing costs, such as appraisal expenses, loan fees and points, title insurance, and so on.

For example, if completing the refinance costs you $2,000 and reduces your monthly payment by $100, the lender or broker typically says that you can save back the refinance costs in 20 months. This estimate isn't accurate, however, because you lose some tax write-offs when your mortgage interest rate and payments are reduced. You can't simply look at the reduced amount of your monthly payment (mortgage lenders like to look at that reduction, however, because lowering your payments makes refinancing more attractive).

To get a better estimate without spending hours crunching numbers, take your marginal tax rate as specified in Chapter 1 (for example, 24 percent) and reduce your monthly payment savings on the refinance by this amount. For example, if your monthly payment drops by $100, you really save only around $76 a month after factoring in the lost tax benefits. So you recoup the refinance costs in 26 months ($2,000 of refinance costs divided by $76) — not 20 months.

If you can recover the costs of the refinance within a few years or less, go for it. If it takes longer, refinancing may still make sense if you anticipate keeping the property and mortgage that long. If you estimate that you need more than five to seven years to break even, refinancing probably is too risky to justify the costs and hassles.

When you refinance, don't forget to adjust the amount of tax you pay during the year. See the section "Exploring the tax savings in home ownership," earlier in this chapter, for more information on how to change your tax withholding.

Besides getting a lower interest-rate loan, another reason people refinance is to pull out cash from the house for some other purpose. This strategy can make good financial sense, because under most circumstances, mortgage interest is tax-deductible. If you're starting a business or buying other real estate, you can usually borrow against your home at a lower cost than on a business or rental property loan. (If you're a high-income earner and have a mortgage of more than $750,000 or considering one, you may lose some of the tax deductibility of your home mortgage interest deductions — read the explanation in the section earlier in this chapter, "Mortgage interest and property tax write-offs")

If you've run up high-interest consumer debt, you may be able to refinance your mortgage and pull out extra cash to pay off your credit cards, auto loans, or other costly credit lines, thus saving yourself money. You usually can borrow at a lower interest rate for a mortgage and get a tax deduction as a bonus, which lowers the effective borrowing cost further. Interest on consumer debt, such as auto loans and credit cards, isn't tax-deductible.

WARNING

Borrowing against the equity in your home can be addictive and may contribute to poor spending habits. An appreciating home creates the illusion that excess spending isn't really costing you. Remember that debt is debt, and you have to repay all borrowed money. In the long run, you wind up with greater mortgage debt, and paying it off takes a bigger bite out of your monthly income. Refinancing and establishing home-equity lines also costs you more in loan application fees and other charges (points, appraisals, credit reports, and so on).

Selling Your House

As we discuss earlier in this chapter, homeowners can realize large profits (capital gains) when selling their house. Schedule D, Capital Gains and Losses, is filed only when gains exceed the $250,000/$500,000 threshold. You file Schedule D with Form 1040 from the same tax year in which you sell your house.

Form 1099-S must be filed to report the sale or exchange of real estate unless the sale price is $250,000 or less ($500,000 or less for married couples) and all the sellers provide written certification that the full gain on the sale is excludable from the sellers' gross income. Neither you nor the IRS receives Form 1099-S from the firm handling the sale of your house unless the gross sale price exceeds $500,000 for married couples or $250,000 for an unmarried seller.

The following sections discuss the tax issues affecting house sales.

Not wanting to sell at a loss

Many homeowners are tempted to hold on to their properties when they need to move if the real estate market is soft or the property has a lower value than when they bought it, especially because the loss isn't tax-deductible. We don't recommend this strategy.

You may reason that in a few years, the real estate storm clouds will clear and you can sell your property at a higher price. Here are three risks associated with this way of thinking:

>> You can't know what's going to happen to property prices in the next few years. They may rebound, but they also can stay the same or drop even further. A property generally needs to appreciate at least a few percentage points each year just to make up for all the costs of holding and maintaining it. So you're losing more money each year that you hold the property and it doesn't appreciate at least a few percentage points in value.

>> If you haven't been a landlord, don't underestimate the hassle and headaches associated with the job. Being a long-distance landlord is even more of a challenge. You can always hire someone to manage your property, but that approach creates costs, too — usually about 6 to 10 percent of the monthly rental income.

>> After you convert your home into a rental property, you need to pay capital gains tax on your profit when you sell (the only exception is if you temporarily rent your home while you're still actively trying to sell it). This tax wipes out much of the advantage of having held on to the property until prices recovered. If your desire is to become a long-term rental property owner, you can, under current tax laws, do a tax-free exchange into another rental property after you sell (we discuss this topic in the section, "Rollover of capital gains on rental or business real estate" later in this chapter).

We understand that selling a house that hasn't made you any money isn't much fun. But too many homeowners make a bad situation worse by holding on to their homes for the wrong reasons after they move. No one wants to believe that they're losing money. But remember, the money is already lost. Many people who hold on rub salt into their real estate wounds. If and when the value of the property you're waiting to sell finally increases, odds are that other properties you'd next buy also will have increased. Unless you have sufficient money for the down payment to buy your next home, or you want to keep such a property as a long-term investment, holding on to a home you move from usually isn't wise.

Converting a home into rental property

One advantage to keeping your current home as an investment property after you move is that you already own it. Locating and buying a property takes time and money. Also, you know what you have with your current home. When you go out and purchase a different property to rent, you're starting from scratch.

One of the tax benefits of rental real estate is the depreciation deduction. As your property ages, the IRS allows you to write off or deduct from your rental income for the "wearing out" of the building. Although this deduction helps reduce your income taxes, be aware that you may not be able to deduct as much for depreciation expenses when you convert your home to rental property as you can on a rental bought separately. If your home has appreciated since you bought it, the IRS forces you to use your original (lower) purchase price for purposes of calculating depreciation. To make tax matters worse, if your home has declined in value since you originally purchased it, you must use this lower value, at the time you convert the property, for purposes of depreciation.

Don't consider converting your home into a rental when you move unless this decision really is a long-term proposition. As we discuss in the preceding section, selling rental property has tax consequences.

If the idea of keeping the home you move from as a long-term investment appeals to you, take stock of your overall financial situation before you make the final call. Can you afford to purchase your next home given the money that's still tied up in the home you're considering keeping as a rental? Can you afford to contribute to tax-deductible retirement plans, or will the burden of carrying two properties use up too much of your cash flow? Will your overall investments be well-diversified, or will you have too much of your money tied up in real estate (perhaps in one area of the country)?

House sales, taxes, and divorce

A divorce complicates many personal and financial issues. Real estate is no different. In the past, if ownership of a home that had appreciated in value were transferred between spouses because of a divorce, capital gains tax was owed. This is no longer one of the additional costs of divorce. Transfers of property between spouses aren't taxed if the transfers are made within one year of divorce (and both spouses are U.S. residents or citizens).

If you're selling your house because of a divorce, when you sell the house can have significant tax ramifications. If you agree to sell the house in the divorce settlement, each of you can make up to $250,000 in profit before any tax is levied.

Investing in Real Estate

For most people, the only real estate they own or consider owning is the home in which they live. If that's all you desire, we aren't going to push you into the business of investing in and managing rental property. It's a great deal of work, and other investments are certainly available, such as mutual funds (that own stocks), that are far more convenient and just as profitable.

But some people just have that itch to own something tangible. Real estate is, well, real, after all. You can fix it up, take pictures of it, and drive your friends by it!

Deciding whether real estate investing is for you

Whether you should invest in real estate versus other investments, such as stocks, bonds, mutual funds, and exchange-traded funds, depends on many factors. The first and most important question to ask yourself is whether you're cut out to handle the responsibilities that come with being a landlord. Real estate is a time-intensive investment — it isn't for couch potatoes. Investing in stocks can be time-intensive as well, but it doesn't have to be if you use professionally managed mutual funds. Conversely, you can hire a property manager with real estate experience to reduce your workload. But the time required to own and oversee rental property can still be significant.

An often-overlooked drawback to investing in real estate is that you earn no tax benefits while you're accumulating your down payment. Rental property also is usually a cash drain in the early years of ownership. Retirement accounts, on the other hand, such as 401(k)s, 403(b)s, SEP-IRAs, and so on (see Chapter 22), give you immediate tax deductions as you contribute money to them. Although real estate offers many tax deductions, as we discuss earlier in the chapter, the cost of real estate reflects the expected tax breaks. So don't invest in real estate because of the tax deductions.

A final consideration with regard to whether real estate investing is for you: Do you have a solid understanding of real estate and how to improve its value?

Enjoying rental property tax breaks

When you purchase property and rent it out, you're essentially running a business. You take in revenue — namely rent from your tenants — and incur expenses from the property. You hope that, over time, your revenue exceeds your expenses so that your real estate investment produces a profit (cash flow, in real estate lingo) for all the money and time you've sunk into it. You also hope that the market value of your investment property appreciates over time. The IRS helps you make a buck or two through a number of tax benefits. The major benefits follow.

GOOD VERSUS BAD REAL ESTATE INVESTMENTS

You can invest in real estate in a number of ways. The traditional and best method is to purchase property in an area that you've researched and are familiar with. Single-family homes and multi-unit buildings generally work best for most investors. Make sure that you do your "due diligence." Have the property professionally inspected and secure adequate insurance coverage.

If you want a stake in real estate but don't want the responsibilities and hassles that come with being a landlord, consider *real estate investment trusts* (REITs). REITs offer the benefits of property ownership without the headaches of being a landlord. REITs are a collection of real estate properties, such as shopping centers, apartments, and other rental buildings. REITs trade as securities on the major stock exchanges and can be bought through mutual funds such as Fidelity Real Estate Investment, T. Rowe Price Real Estate, and Vanguard Real Estate Index Fund.

Be careful, though; some real estate investments rarely make sense because they're near-certain money losers. Many investors get sucked into these lousy investments because of the supposed high expected returns and tax breaks. Limited partnerships, for example, which are sold through stockbrokers and financial planners who work on commission, are burdened by high sales commissions, ongoing management fees, and illiquidity (see Chapter 24).

Time-shares are another nearly certain money loser. With a time-share, you buy a week or two of ownership, or usage, of a particular unit, usually a condominium in a resort location. If you pay $8,000 for a week (in addition to ongoing maintenance fees), you're paying the equivalent of more than $400,000 for the whole unit year-round, but a comparable unit may sell for only $150,000. That extra markup pays the salespeople's commissions, administrative expenses, and profits for the time-share development company.

Operating-expense write-offs

In addition to the deductions allowed for mortgage interest and property taxes, just as on a home in which you live, you can deduct on your tax return a variety of other expenses for rental property. Almost all these deductions come from money that you spend on the property, such as money for insurance, maintenance, repairs, and so on.

But one expense — depreciation — doesn't involve your spending money. Depreciation is an accounting deduction that the IRS allows you to take for the overall wear and tear on your building. The idea behind this deduction is that, over time, your building will deteriorate and need upgrading, rebuilding, and so on. The IRS tables now say that for residential property, you can depreciate over 27½ years, and for nonresidential property, 39 years. Only the portion of a property's value that is attributable to the building(s) — and not the land — can be depreciated.

For example, suppose that you bought a residential rental property for $300,000, and the land is deemed to be worth $100,000. Thus the building is worth $200,000. If you can depreciate your $200,000 building over 27½ years, that works out to a $7,272 annual depreciation deduction.

If your rental property shows a loss for the year (when you figure your property's income and expenses), you may be able to deduct this loss on your tax return. If your adjusted gross income (AGI) is less than $100,000 and you actively participate in managing the property, you're allowed to deduct your losses on operating rental real estate — up to $25,000 per year. Limited partnerships and properties in which you own less than 10 percent are excluded. (See Chapter 15 for details.)

To deduct a loss on your tax return, you must *actively participate* in the management of the property. This rule doesn't necessarily mean that you perform the day-to-day management of the property. In fact, you can hire a property manager and still actively participate by doing such simple things as approving the terms of the lease contracts, tenants, and expenditures for maintenance and improvements on the building.

If you make more than $100,000 per year, you start to lose these write-offs. At an income of $150,000 or more, you can't deduct rental real estate losses from your other income. People in the real estate business (for example, agents and developers) who work more than 750 hours per year in the industry may not be subject to these rules. (Refer to Chapter 15 for more information.)

You start to lose the deductibility of rental property losses above the $100,000 limit, whether you're single or married filing jointly. You can carry the loss forward to future tax years and take the loss then, if eligible. This policy is a bit unfair to couples, because it's easier for them to break $100,000 with two incomes than for a single person with one income. Sorry — this is yet another part of the marriage tax penalties!

TAX CREDITS FOR LOW-INCOME HOUSING AND OLD BUILDINGS

The IRS grants you special tax credits when you invest in low-income housing or particularly old commercial buildings. The credits represent a direct reduction in your tax bill because you're spending to rehabilitate and improve these properties. The IRS wants to encourage investors to invest in and fix up old or rundown buildings that likely would continue to deteriorate otherwise.

The amounts of the credits range from as little as 10 percent of the expenditures to as much as 90 percent, depending on the property type. The IRS has strict rules governing what types of properties qualify. Tax credits may be earned for rehabilitating nonresidential buildings built in 1935 or before. "Certified historic structures," both residential and nonresidential, also qualify for tax credits. See IRS instructions for Form 3468 to find out more about these credits.

Included in the Tax Cuts and Job Act of 2017 was a new package of "Opportunity Zones" tax benefits. These tax perks are available for qualified investments in more than 8,000 of the United States' most rural and financially distressed areas. Visit www.irs.gov/credits-deductions/businesses/opportunity-zones to learn more.

Rollover of capital gains on rental or business real estate

Suppose that you purchase a rental property and nurture it over the years. You find good tenants and keep the building repaired and looking sharp. You may just find that all that work pays off — the property may someday be worth much more than you originally paid for it.

However, if you simply sell the property, you owe taxes on your gain or profit. Even worse is the way the government defines your gain. If you bought the property for $100,000 and sell it for $150,000, you not only owe tax on that difference, but you also owe tax on an additional amount, depending on the property's depreciation. The amount of depreciation that you deducted on your tax returns reduces the original $100,000 purchase price, making the taxable difference that much larger. For example, if you deducted $25,000 for depreciation over the years that you owned the property, you owe tax on the difference between the sale price of $150,000 and $75,000 ($100,000 purchase price minus $25,000 depreciation).

All this tax may just motivate you to hold on to your property. But you can avoid paying tax on your profit when you sell a rental property by "exchanging" it for a similar or *like-kind* property, thereby rolling over your gain. (You may not receive the proceeds — they must go into an escrow account.) The rules, however, are different for rolling over profits (called *1031 exchanges*, for the section of the tax code that allows them) from the sale of rental property than the old rules for a primary residence.

Under current tax laws, the IRS continues to take a broad definition of what like-kind property is. For example, you can exchange undeveloped land for a multiunit rental building.

SEEK ADVICE

The rules for properly doing a 1031 exchange are complex. Third parties are usually involved. Make sure that you find an attorney and/or tax advisor who is an expert at these transactions to ensure that you do it right.

Real estate corporations

When you invest in and manage real estate with at least one other partner, you can set up a company through which you own the property. The main reason you may want to consider this setup is liability protection. A corporation can reduce the chances of lenders or tenants suing you.

Read the discussion in Chapter 23 about incorporating, the different entities under which you may do business, and the pros and cons of each. For a crash course on rental property investing, pick up the most recent edition of *Real Estate Investing For Dummies* by Eric Tyson and Robert Griswold (Wiley).

Chapter **26**

Children and Taxes

Raising children involves many decisions and trade-offs. New parents are sometimes surprised at the financial and tax consequences of having kids. We include this chapter so that you can spend more time enjoying the first smile, first step, first word, and first high-five, and save on your taxes.

Bringing Up Baby

Although kids can cost a bunch of money, the expenses, or the thousands of diaper changes during the infant years, rarely deter people from wanting a family. And for good reason — kids are wonderful, at least most of the time. They're the future. (If you don't have kids, who do you think is going to fund your Social Security and Medicare benefits during your retirement years?)

Raising a family can be the financial equivalent of doing a triathlon. It can stretch and break the budgets of even those who consider themselves financially well off and on top of things. Taxes are an important factor in a number of kid-related issues. This chapter includes our take on some of the important tax issues that you may confront before conception and during the many years you're raising a child.

Getting Junior a Social Security number

TAX CUT

In order to claim tax benefits relating to your newborn, you need to get them a Social Security number. You also need a Social Security number for your child whenever you want to establish investment accounts in the child's name (although you may not want to after you understand the drawbacks of doing so, which we discuss later in this chapter).

The IRS requires a Social Security number because people were inventing children — you know, telling the IRS they'd just had twins when the closest they actually came to becoming parents was babysitting their best friend's kid one evening!

If you need Form SS-5, Application for a Social Security Card, simply contact the Social Security Administration (800-772-1213; www.ssa.gov) and ask to have one mailed to you or you can print it out yourself at www.ssa.gov/forms/ss-5.pdf.

Childcare tax goodies

In addition to the extra personal deduction that you can take with each new child and the tax savings that come with that deduction, you also need to be aware of the tax perks (for childcare and related expenditures) that may save you thousands of dollars.

Dependent-care tax credit

TAX CUT

When you hire childcare assistance for your youngster(s), you may be able to claim a tax credit on your annual return (which you claim on Form 2441). To be eligible for this credit, you (and your spouse, if you're married) must work at least part time, unless you're a full-time student or you're disabled. Your kid(s) must be younger than the age of 13 or physically or mentally disabled.

Because a credit is a dollar-for-dollar reduction in the taxes you owe, it can save you hundreds of tax dollars every year. And not only do you count childcare expenses toward calculation of the tax credit, but you may also be able to count the cost of a housekeeper, or even a cook, if the expense benefits your kids. As the name of this credit suggests, expenses can be for taking care of dependents broadly, not just for your children under age 13. Caring for a physically or mentally ill spouse or others, such as an elderly parent, for at least half of the year, counts too.

For 2021, the dependent-care tax credit is a maximum of $4,000 for one qualifying person with an $8,000 limit for two or more qualifying persons, and the credit is now refundable for those not owing enough federal income tax to get the full amount of it. This is based upon having up to $8,000 in qualifying expenses for one dependent and up to $16,000 for two or more.

The income threshold at which the credit begins to be reduced increases to $125,000 of adjusted gross income (AGI) and phases out completely at $438,000 of AGI. The portion of qualifying employment-related expenses for which credits can be claimed is 50 percent.

As we discuss later in this section, tax and other considerations influence your desire as a parent to work outside the home. Working at least part-time makes you eligible for this tax credit. If you choose to be a full-time mom or dad, unfortunately, you aren't eligible for the dependent-care tax credit.

If your employer offers a dependent-care assistance plan (discussed in the following section), you may be able to reduce your taxes by taking advantage of that benefit rather than the dependent-care tax credit. Your tax credit is reduced or eliminated whenever you use your employer's dependent-care plan spending account. To find out more about how to claim this credit on your annual tax return, see Chapter 16.

Dependent-care spending accounts

Increasing numbers of employers offer flexible benefit or spending plans that enable you to choose from among a number of different benefits, such as health, life, and disability insurance; vacation days; and dependent-care expenses.

You can put away money from your paycheck to pay for childcare expenses on a pretax basis. Doing so saves you from paying federal, state, and even Social Security taxes on that money. These flexible benefits plans allow you to put away up to $10,500 for 2021 or $5,250 if you're married filing separately. However, the exact amount that you can put away depends on the specifics of your employer's plan. Unlike in the past, unused amounts in 2021 can be rolled over into 2022.

WARNING Dependent-care spending accounts historically have been a use-it-or-lose-it benefit. If you don't spend the money for childcare expenses during the current tax year, the IRS forces you to forfeit all the unused money at the end of the year. So, be careful not to go overboard by contributing more than you're certain to use.

As we mention in the preceding section, participating in your employer's dependent-care assistance plan reduces your tax credit. You can't do both.

You can also use the dependent-care tax credit and spending accounts that we discuss in this section to pay for the costs of taking care of other dependents, such as an ill or elderly parent. Please see Chapter 16 and your employer's employee benefits manual for more information.

Child tax credit

In 2018, the maximum Child Tax Credit was doubled to $2,000 from $1,000 previously thanks to the 2017 Tax Cuts and Jobs Act. Also, the refundable portion of the credit was bumped up to $1,400 and will increase over time with inflation.

NEW STUFF

The American Rescue Plan Act increased the Child Tax Credit for 2021 only to $3,000 for children under age 6 and $3,600 for children ages 6 to 17. These higher credit amounts expire after 2021 and revert to the levels set by the Tax Cuts and Jobs Act for 2022. See Chapter 16 for more information about how to claim this credit.

Adoption tax credit

Recent tax law changes have substantially increased the tax credits to parents who adopt children.

For 2021, the adoption tax credit is for up to $14,440 in qualifying expenses and increases annually with inflation. This credit phases out between the modified adjusted gross income limits of $216,600 to $256,660 in 2021. To claim the credit, you file Form 8839, Qualified Adoption Expenses. Please see Chapter 16 for all the details.

Costs and benefits of a second income

One of the most challenging decisions that new parents face is whether to work full time, part time, or not at all. We mean work at a paying job, that is — parenting is the lowest-paid but potentially most rewarding job there is. The need or desire to take paid work is obvious — doing so brings more money home.

In addition to less sleep at night and frequent diaper changes, children mean increased spending. Although you may have less time to shop for yourself, causing your personal spending to decrease, you're likely to spend more on housing, insurance, food, childcare, clothing, and education. And don't forget the host of not-so-incidental incidentals. Toys, art classes, sports, field trips, musical instruments, and the like can rack up big bills, especially if you don't control what you spend on them.

You may rightfully feel that working full time prohibits you from playing as active a role in raising your children as you want. As you consider the additional expenses of raising children, you may also need to factor in a decrease in income.

TIP

Financially speaking, taxes can have a big impact on the value or benefit of working full time, especially for two-income couples. Remember that the tax brackets are set up so that the last dollars of earnings are taxed at a higher rate (refer to Chapter 1).

Deciding whether to work full time by counting the salary that your employer quotes you as the total value of that second income leaves you open to making a potentially big personal and financial mistake. Of course, people enjoy other benefits from working besides income. Be sure, however, to examine taxes and other expenses on that second income to ensure that you're making your financial decision to work based on complete and accurate information.

Navigating Education Tax Breaks and Pitfalls

What, you may ask, do taxes have to do with educational expenses? How you invest to pay for educating your children can have an enormous impact on your family's taxes, your children's ability to qualify for financial aid, and your overall financial well-being.

The (hidden) financial aid tax system

The financial aid system (to which parents apply so that their children are eligible for college scholarships, grants, and loans) treats assets differently when held outside rather than inside retirement accounts. Under the current financial aid system, the value of your retirement plans is *not* considered an asset. Thus, the more of your money you stash in retirement accounts, the greater your chances of qualifying for financial aid and the more money you're generally eligible for.

WARNING

Most new parents don't place their savings in retirement accounts. Many non-wealthy parents make the error of saving and investing money in a separate account for their child (perhaps even in the child's name) or through some other financial product, such as a life insurance policy. Doing so is a mistake because these products are taxed at a much higher level than other savings strategies.

Most important, parents should save and invest in retirement accounts that offer tax benefits. Contributions to a 401(k), 403(b), SEP-IRA, and other retirement accounts (see Chapter 22) usually produce an upfront tax deduction. An additional and substantial benefit is that after the money is placed in these accounts, it grows and compounds without being taxed until you withdraw it.

Therefore, forgoing contributions to your retirement savings plans so you can save money in a taxable account for Junior's college fund doesn't make sense. When you do, you pay higher taxes both on your current income and on the interest and growth of this money. In addition to paying higher taxes, money that you save *outside* retirement accounts, including money in the child's name, is counted as an asset and leads colleges to charge you higher prices (in other words, reduces your child's eligibility for "financial aid"). Thus, you're expected to contribute more (pay higher prices) for your child's educational expenses.

Note: As we discuss later in the chapter, if you're affluent enough that you expect to pay for your kid's entire educational costs, investing through custodial accounts, Education Savings Accounts, and Section 529 college savings plans can save on taxes.

College cost tax deductions

Student loan interest of up to $2,500 annually is deductible on your tax return as an adjustment to income. Thus, anyone who meets the income limitations can claim this deduction as it's not on the list of itemized deductions on Schedule A.

To qualify for this full deduction, your modified adjusted gross income (MAGI) can be up to $70,000 for single taxpayers (and phases out up to $85,000) and for married couples filing jointly, you get a full deduction for up to $140,000 MAGI (it phases out up to $170,000).

Hope and Lifetime Learning Credits are discussed later in this chapter.

Section 529 plans — state tuition plans

Section 529 plans (named after Internal Revenue Code section 529) come in two basic varieties: prepaid tuition plans and savings plans.

>> In a *prepaid tuition plan,* you buy tuition credits at today's cost, and those credits are used when your qualifying student actually attends college. You forsake all future investment returns on this money in exchange for paying college costs today. Also, you may be quite limited in which schools your child may attend to use the payments.

>> A *529 savings plan* works more like a traditional investment account, investing your education contributions and allowing them to grow, tax-free, until you need that money to pay for qualified post-secondary educational expenses.

A parent or grandparent can put more than $300,000 into one of these plans for each child. You can put up to $75,000 into a child's college savings account immediately, and that counts for the next five years' worth of $15,000 tax-free gifts (actually, a couple can immediately contribute $120,000 per child) allowed under current gifting laws (see Chapter 27). Money contributed to the account isn't considered part of the donor's taxable estate (although if the donor dies before five years are up after gifting $75,000, a prorated amount of the gift is charged back to the donor's estate).

Section 529 plan investment earnings can be withdrawn tax-free (that's right — completely free of taxation) as long as the withdrawn funds are used to pay for qualifying higher educational costs. In addition to paying college costs (tuition, room and board, or other related expenses), you can use the money in Section 529 plans to pay for graduate school and for the enrollment and attendance expenses of special-needs students.

Some states provide tax benefits on contributions to their state-sanctioned plans, whereas other states induce you to invest at home by taxing profits from out-of-state plans.

Unlike contributing money to a custodial account with which a child may do as they please when they reach the age of either 18 or 21 (it varies by state), these state tuition plans must be used for higher education expenses. Many plans even allow you to change the beneficiary or take the money back if you change your mind. (If you do withdraw the money, however, you owe tax on the withdrawn earnings, plus a penalty — typically 10 percent.)

A big potential drawback — especially for families hoping for some financial aid — is that college financial aid offices treat assets in these plans as parent's nonretirement assets, which, as discussed earlier in the chapter, can greatly diminish financial aid eligibility.

Another potential drawback is that you have limited choices and control over how the money in state tuition plans is invested. The investment provider(s) for each state plan generally decides how to invest the money over time within given investment options. In most plans, the more years your child is away from college, the more aggressive the investment mix is. As your child approaches college age, the investment mix is tilted more to conservative investments. Most state plans have somewhat high investment management fees, and some plans don't allow transfers to other plans.

Please also be aware that a future Congress can change the tax laws affecting these plans and diminish the tax breaks or increase the penalties for nonqualified withdrawals.

Clearly, there are pros and cons to Section 529 plans. They generally make the most sense for affluent parents (or grandparents) of children who don't expect to qualify for financial aid. Remember, the income accumulated in these plans remains untaxed, provided it's used to pay for qualified educational expenses.

Do a lot of research and homework before investing in any plan. Check out the investment track record, allocations, and fees for each plan, as well as restrictions on transferring to other plans or changing beneficiaries. These plans are relatively new, and the market for them is changing quickly, so take your time before committing to one of them.

Education Savings Accounts

You can establish an Education Savings Account (ESA; sometimes referred to as a "Coverdell ESA") for each child and make contributions of up to $2,000 per child per year until the child reaches age 18. Contributions to an ESA, which can be made up until the due date of the income tax return, aren't tax-deductible. However, ESA investment earnings can compound and be withdrawn free of tax as long as the funds are used to pay for college costs. In the year of withdrawal, the Hope Scholarship and Lifetime Learning Credits may not be claimed for the student, unless you elect to pay income tax on the earnings portion of your withdrawal — see the next section for more about these credits.

Because of their similarities to Section 529 Plan accounts and the fact that they have much lower contribution limits, some financial institutions no longer offer these accounts.

ESA balances can be used for pre-college educational costs (in other words, for schooling costs up through and including grade 12). Eligible educational expenses for primary and secondary students include tuition, fees, books, supplies, computers and other equipment, tutoring, uniforms, extended-day programs, transportation, internet access, and so on, while qualified expenses for college students include only tuition, fees, room, and board, required books and supplies, and special-needs services. (College room and board expenses qualify only if the student carries at least one-half the normal workload.) Contributions to the accounts of special-needs children are permitted past the age of 18, and balances can continue in those accounts past the age of 30.

WARNING

There are pros and cons to contributing to an ESA, so don't rush out to contribute to these until you've done your homework. Be aware that college financial aid officers treat these accounts as a parent asset, which reduces aid awards. Contributions to or withdrawals from an ESA can also adversely affect your ability to claim other educational tax benefits (Hope and Lifetime Learning credits) and to qualify for the tax benefits on these accounts.

If you're a high-income earner, you may not be eligible to contribute to an ESA. The full $2,000 per child contribution to an ESA may be made only by couples with AGIs less than $190,000 and single taxpayers with AGIs less than $95,000. The $2,000 limit is reduced for married taxpayers with AGIs of more than $190,000 ($95,000 if single) and eliminated if the AGI is more than $220,000 ($110,000 for singles).

TIP

If you earn more than these thresholds and want your kids to have ESAs, there's a loophole. Simply have someone else who isn't earning more than the threshold amounts, such as a grandparent, make the ESA contribution on your behalf.

Here are some other ESA rules and regulations that you need to be aware of:

>> The tax-free exclusion of the earnings isn't available on a distribution from the ESA in the same year you claim a Hope Scholarship or Lifetime Earning Credit.

>> Contributions to the account must be made before the child reaches 18 unless the child is considered special needs, which is defined as "an individual who, because of a physical, mental, or emotional condition (including learning disability), requires additional time to complete his or her education."

>> The money in the account can't be used to invest in a life insurance policy.

>> When the beneficiary reaches age 30, any balance must be distributed to the beneficiary, and that person must include any earnings in their income (unless the account holder is considered special needs). However, prior to reaching 30, the beneficiary may transfer or roll over the balance to another beneficiary who is a member of their family. The distribution must be made within 30 days of the beneficiary's 30th birthday, or within 30 days of their death.

>> Any part of a distribution that must be included in income because it wasn't used to pay college expenses is subject to a 10 percent penalty, unless the distribution is paid as a result of death or disability, or the amount distributed would have been used for educational expenses except for the fact that your student received a scholarship or some other sort of award.

American Opportunity and Lifetime Learning Credits

TAX CUT

Tax credits assist some parents with the often-high costs of education. We say some because the credits are phased out for higher-income earners. These credits phase out for single tax filers with AGIs between $80,000 and $90,000 and married couples filing jointly with AGIs between $160,000 and $180,000. These phase-out ranges annually increase with inflation.

The first of the two credits — the American Opportunity tax credit — allows up to a $2,500 annual tax credit toward tuition and fees in each of the first four years of higher education. This credit is composed of 100 percent of the first $2,000 of qualified educational expenses you pay for an eligible student and 25 percent of the next $2,000 in qualified educational expenses. Up to 40 percent of this credit ($1,000 per year) is refundable if you don't owe federal income tax.

The second credit — the Lifetime Learning Credit — allows a credit for up to 20 percent of $10,000 in tuition and fee expenses (worth $2,000) per taxpayer. The Lifetime Learning Credit can be used toward undergraduate and graduate education and toward coursework that upgrades job skills.

If you, as a taxpayer, claim either of these credits in a tax year for a particular student, you aren't eligible to withdraw money without taxation from an ESA or a Section 529 plan account for that same student, nor can you take the tuition and fees tax deduction. Also, you can't take the Hope Scholarship Credit in the same year that you use the Lifetime Learning Credit for the same student; if you have more than one student who qualifies, though, you may be able to take the Hope credit for one, and the Lifetime Learning Credit for the other(s).

Minimizing your taxes and paying for college

Socking money away into your tax-sheltered retirement accounts helps you reduce your tax burden and may help your children qualify for more financial aid. However, accessing retirement accounts before age 59½ incurs tax penalties.

TIP

So how do you pay for your children's educational costs? There isn't one correct answer, because the decision depends on your overall financial situation. Here are some ideas that can help you meet expected educational expenses and minimize your taxes:

>> **Don't try to do it all yourself.** Unless you're affluent, don't even try to pay for the full cost of a college education for your children. Few people can afford it. You and your children will, in all likelihood, have to borrow some money.

>> **Consider the increasing numbers of faster and lower-cost alternatives to college.** College isn't the right choice for everyone. For starters, the high price can make a traditional four-year college education prohibitively expensive for many families. Also, college simply isn't the only pathway to a rewarding career. Not only are there plenty of well-paying jobs that don't require a four-year degree, but lower-cost alternatives to the four-year degree are also growing fast. It pays to investigate the alternatives and consider all of your child's options before making an informed choice. You can potentially save lots of money and find a great fit that's better for your child and your personal finances.

Some of the programs available today have been around for generations while others are new and emerging. These include last-mile programs/"boot camps," apprenticeships, staffing firms, vocational and trade Schools, and college cooperative educational experiences.

>> **Apply for aid, regardless of your financial circumstances.** A number of loan programs, such as Unsubsidized Stafford Loans and Parent Loans for Undergraduate Students (PLUS), are available even if your family isn't deemed financially needy. Only Subsidized Stafford Loans, on which the federal government pays the interest that accumulates while the student is still in school, are limited to those students deemed financially needy.

In addition to loans, a number of grant programs are available through schools, the government, and independent sources. Specific colleges and other private organizations (including employers, banks, credit unions, and community groups) also offer grants and scholarships. Some of these have nothing to do with financial need.

>> **Save in your name, not in your children's.** If you've exhausted your retirement account contributions, saving money that you're earmarking to pay for college is okay. Just do it in your name. If your children's grandparents want to make a gift of money to them for college expenses, keep the money in your name; otherwise, have the grandparents keep the money until the kids are ready to enter college.

>> **Get your kids to work.** Your child can work and save money to pay for college costs during junior high, high school, and college. In fact, if your child qualifies for financial aid, they're expected to contribute a certain amount to their educational costs from money earned from jobs held during the school year or summer breaks and from their own savings. Besides giving the student a stake in their own future, this training encourages sound personal financial management down the road.

>> **Borrow against your home equity.** If you're a homeowner, you can borrow against the equity (market value less the outstanding mortgage loan) in your property. Doing so is usually wise because you can borrow against your home at a reasonable interest rate, and the interest is generally tax-deductible. (See Chapter 25 for information about tax-deductibility rules.) Be careful to borrow an amount you can afford to repay and that won't cause you to default on your loan and lose your home. *Mortgages For Dummies,* which Eric Tyson co-wrote with Ray Brown (Wiley), can help you with such borrowing decisions.

>> **Borrow against your company retirement plans.** Many retirement savings plans, such as 401(k)s, allow borrowing. Just make sure that you're able to pay back the money. Otherwise, you'll owe big taxes for a premature distribution.

REMEMBER

The growing "alternatives" trend to costly four-year colleges is good for you, the consumer. Competition for your time and dollars is slowly spurring some positive changes at colleges and universities, as it should. Colleges should earn your business and not get it by default. Traditional colleges and universities are not the only pathways to success. Keep an open mind about the alternatives available to your child because they too can lead to career satisfaction and a bright future. For more information, please see Eric's book, *Paying For College For Dummies* (Wiley).

DOUBLE-WHAT BONDS?

Among the many forms of bonds (debt) that our fine government issues are Series EE ("double E") and Series I bonds, the interest on which is exempt from state and local taxes. These are one of the many classes of Treasury bonds issued by that national organization with a penchant for borrowing money. You may hear about these bonds as a suggested investment for children's college expenses.

EE bonds purchased after 1989 and all I bonds have a unique tax twist if you use the proceeds to pay for educational tuition and fees. (Room and board and other education-related costs aren't covered.) The interest earned on the bonds is fully exempt from federal taxation (interest on the Treasury bonds is already state tax–free) as long as two other requirements are met:

- The purchaser of the bond must be at least 24 years of age.
- At the time the bonds are redeemed to pay for educational tuition and fees, the holder of the bond may not have a modified AGI in excess of $98,200 if single or $154,800 if married and filing a joint return. (For single filers with a modified AGI between $83,200 and $98,200 and married couples between $124,800 and $154,800, a partial interest–tax exemption applies.)

Even if you're somehow able to know years in advance what your income will be when your toddler has grown into a college-bound 18-year-old, you've gotta file yet another tax form, Form 8815, to claim the exclusion of the interest of EEs and Is from federal taxation. And don't forget that not a year goes by without Congress messing with the federal tax laws. So the income requirements for the tax exemptions can change.

The interest rate for EE bonds, for example, bought from May 2021 through October 2021 was an annual rate of 0.10 percent. Regardless of the rate, at 20 years your EE bond will be worth twice what you pay for it. If you keep the bond that long, a one-time adjustment is made to fulfill this guarantee. The recent interest rate for I bonds was 3.54 percent.

Regardless of how you use the EE and I bond proceeds, you may defer taxation of the interest on them until you cash them, or you may choose to pay tax on each year's interest in the year it's earned. If you're planning on using these bonds to pay qualified higher education expenses, make sure you don't pay the tax on a yearly basis — after you've paid the tax, you can't get a refund even if you do eventually use these bonds to pay for Junior's college tuition.

We generally don't recommend these complicated bonds. They are testimony to the absurdly complex tax code and government rules. You're better off investing in mutual funds that offer some growth potential. But if we haven't dissuaded you, make sure that you buy these bonds from the Federal Reserve Bank in your area and hold them in an account with the Federal Reserve, or you can purchase them online at www.treasurydirect.gov. Doing so ensures that you'll always get a statement on your account and won't lose track of the bonds when you're no longer being paid interest!

Being Aware of Taxes on Your Kids' Investments

Parents of all different financial means need to be aware of the financial aid implications of putting money into an account bearing a child's name. Read the section "Navigating Education Tax Breaks and Pitfalls" earlier in this chapter before investing money in your children's names.

Taxes for kids under 18 and dependent college students

For tax year 2021, if a child is under 18 (or 24 if a full-time student), the so-called kiddie tax applies: The first $1,100 of *unearned income* (income from interest and dividends on investments) that a child earns isn't taxed at all. It's tax-free! In contrast, *earned income* is considered income earned from work. Refer to Chapter 17 to find out when you need to file a tax return for your child.

The next $1,100 of unearned income for this age set is taxed at the child's tax rate. Everything higher than $2,200 is taxed at the parents' income tax rate. The system is set up in this fashion to discourage parents from transferring a lot of assets into their children's names, hoping to pay lower taxes.

WARNING

Because the first $2,200 of unearned income for the child is taxed at such a low rate, some parents are tempted to transfer money into the child's name to save on income taxes. Quite a number of financial books and advisors recommend this strategy. Consider this passage referring to transferring money to your children, from a tax book written by a large accounting firm: "Take advantage of these rules. It still makes sense to shift some income-producing assets to younger children."

This is potentially very wrong from plenty of parents! As we discuss in "The (hidden) financial aid tax system" earlier in this chapter, this shortsighted desire to save a little in taxes today can lead to your losing out on significant financial aid later. And what about your limited discretionary income? You don't want to put money in your child's name if it means that you aren't fully taking advantage of your retirement accounts.

Consider putting money into an account bearing your child's name only if

>> You expect to pay for the full cost of a college education and won't apply for or use any financial aid, including loans that aren't based on financial need.

>> You're comfortable with the notion that your child will have legal access to the money at age 18 or 21 (depending on the state in which you live) if the money is in a custodial account in the child's name. At that age, the money is legally your child's, and they can blow it on something other than a college education.

After all the caveats and warnings, if you're still thinking about putting money into an account bearing your child's name, consider buying tax-friendly investments that won't generate more than $2,200 annually in unearned income. (See Chapter 24 for tax-friendly investment ideas.)

You also can buy investments in your name and then transfer them to your child when they are an adult. (Each parent is limited to giving $15,000 to each child per year before they have to start worrying about preparing and filing a gift tax return.) That way, if the investment declines in value, you can take the tax loss; if the investment turns a profit, you can save on your taxes by transferring the investment to your grown child. This strategy won't work to save on income taxes if your kid enjoys early career success and is in a higher tax bracket than you are!

Tax-wise and not-so-wise investments for educational funds

You hear many sales pitches for "tax-wise" investments to use for college savings. Most aren't worthy of your consideration. Here's our take on the best, the mediocre, and the worst.

Mutual funds and exchange-traded funds are ideal

Mutual funds, which offer investors of all financial means instant diversification and low-cost access to the nation's best money managers, and their close cousin, exchange-traded funds, are ideal investments when you're saving money for educational expenses. See Chapter 24 for a discussion of the tax-wise ways to invest in funds.

Think twice about Treasury bonds

Many tax and financial books recommend investing college funds in Treasury bonds issued by the federal government. We aren't enthusiastic about some of these (see the sidebar "Double-what bonds?"). Zero-coupon Treasuries are particular tax headaches. They are sold at a discount of their value at maturity instead of paying you interest each year. Guess what? You still have to report the effective interest you're earning each year on your tax return. And just to give you a headache or pad your tax preparer's bill, you or your preparer have to calculate this implicit interest. Yuck!

Don't bother with cash-value life insurance

WARNING

Life insurance policies that have cash values are some of the most oversold investments to fund college costs. The usual pitch is this: Because you need life insurance to protect your family, why not buy a policy that you can borrow against to pay for college? Makes sense, doesn't it? Insurance agents also emphasize that the cash value in the policy is growing without taxation over time. Although this part of their sales pitch is true, you have better alternatives.

The reason you shouldn't buy a cash-value life insurance policy is that, as we discuss earlier in this chapter, you're better off contributing to retirement accounts. These investments give you an immediate tax deduction that you don't receive when you save through life insurance. Because life insurance that comes with a cash value is more expensive, parents are more likely to make a second mistake — not buying enough life insurance coverage. When you need life insurance, you're better off buying lower-cost term life insurance.

Make sure your money grows

An investment that fails to keep you ahead of inflation, such as a savings or money market account, is another poor investment for college expenses. The interest on these accounts is also taxable, which doesn't make sense for many working parents. You need your money to grow so you can afford educational costs down the road.

Chapter **27**

Estate Planning

Among the dreariest of tax and financial topics is the issue of what happens to your money when you die. Depending on how your finances are structured and when you pass on, you (actually, your estate) may get stuck paying estate taxes when you die. These taxes may be assessed at the federal level but also by some states. (Other states levy an inheritance tax.)

Unfortunately, you can't predict when the grim reaper will pay a visit. That doesn't mean, however, that we all need to participate in complicated estate planning. On the contrary, if your assets are modest, a few simple moves may be all you need.

Estate planning takes time and money, which are precious commodities for most people. Whether spending your time and money on estate planning is worthwhile depends on your personal and financial circumstances, both now and in the near future.

Figuring Whether You May Owe Estate Taxes

With all the warnings about the enormous estate taxes that you may owe upon your death, you may think that owing estate taxes is a common problem. It isn't, but that hasn't stopped some insurance agents, attorneys, and estate-planning "specialists" from using scare tactics to attract prospective clients, often by luring them to free estate-planning seminars. What better way to find people with money to invest! Very few folks are subject to federal estate taxes, at least given the current rules. Some states, however, have far lower thresholds at which their estate tax or inheritance tax kicks in. And, we must remind you that any and all of these rules can change in the future. Recent decades clearly show that the rules will keep changing and evolving.

Consider what quirky rules Congress had in place back in 2010 when your estate could be worth billions of dollars and be passed on to your heirs without any estate tax. In that year and that year alone, the estate tax vanished! However, in the next year — 2011 — the allowable amount that could be passed on free of estate tax reverted back to $1 million (today's limits, which we'll get to shortly, are much higher). Does that sound ridiculous or what?

Understanding the federal estate tax exemption and rate

In tax year 2021, upon death, an individual can pass $11.7 million to beneficiaries without paying federal estate taxes. On the other hand, a couple, if they have their assets, wills, and trusts properly structured, can pass $23.4 million to beneficiaries without paying federal estate taxes. (See "Establishing a bypass trust" later in this chapter for more info.) Because most people still are trying to accumulate enough money to retire or take a trip around the world someday, most folks typically don't have this problem and have this much money around when they die.

Under current tax law, if your estate totals more than $11.7 million at your death, you may owe federal estate taxes. The top federal estate tax rate for 2021 is a hefty 40 percent.

As this book goes to press in late 2021, Congress, which is controlled by the Democrats, has been considering a dramatic lowering of the federal estate limits as well as other related tax increases. We can't and don't want to predict future tax laws, but it appears unlikely that we will see major tax law changes given the ultra-thin majorities that the Democrats hold in Congress. Ultimately, what happens with future changes in the estate tax laws will be driven by the composition of Congress and which party holds the presidency. We discuss a variety of estate tax–reduction strategies later in this chapter, but first we talk about estate and inheritance taxes at the state level and then discuss how the IRS figures your taxable estate.

State estate and inheritance taxes

States also can levy additional *estate* (levied on the estate) and *inheritance* (charged to the recipient) taxes. With the elimination in 2005 of the provision that allowed states to share in federal estate taxes collected, more states imposed their own estate or inheritance tax, or chose to calculate the tax due to the state on the basis of the share of federal estate taxes they would have received under prior federal law.

While the federal estate tax threshold impacts very few people currently, far more people get hit at the state level by state estate and inheritance taxes. A dozen states and the District of Columbia levy estate taxes while six impose inheritance taxes. Maryland holds a unique distinction as it is the only state to impose both an estate and inheritance tax. See Figure 27-1 for a map of state estate and inheritance taxes.

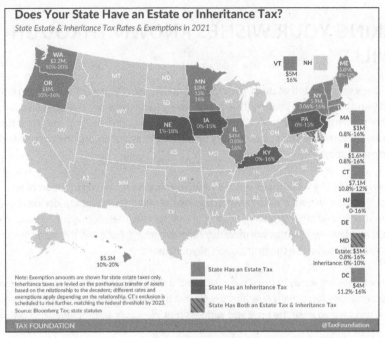

Does Your State Have an Estate or Inheritance Tax?
State Estate & Inheritance Tax Rates & Exemptions in 2021

WA
$2.2M,
10%–20%

OR
$1M
10%–16%

MN
$3M,
13%–
16%

NE
1%–18%

IA
0%–15%

IL
$4M
0.8%–
16%

KY
0%–16%

VT
$5M
16%

NH

ME
5.8M,
8%–12%

NY
5.9M,
3.06%–16%

PA
0%–15%

MA
$1M
0.8%–16%

RI
$1.6M
0.8%–16%

CT
$7.1M
10.8%–12%

NJ
0–16%

DE

MD
Estate: $5M
0.8%–16%
Inheritance: 0%–10%

DC
$4M
11.2%–16%

$5.5M
10%–20%

Note: Exemption amounts are shown for state estate taxes only. Inheritance taxes are levied on the posthumous transfer of assets based on the relationship to the decedent; different rates and exemptions apply depending on the relationship. CT's exclusion is scheduled to rise further, matching the federal threshold by 2023.
Source: Bloomberg Tax; state statutes

State Has an Estate Tax

State Has an Inheritance Tax

State Has Both an Estate Tax & Inheritance Tax

TAX FOUNDATION   @TaxFoundation

FIGURE 27-1:
State estate
and inheritance
taxes.

Source: Tax Foundation.org; `https://taxfoundation.org/`
`state-estate-tax-state-inheritance-tax-2021/`

As you can see from the map, many of the states with their own estate taxes have those taxes kick in at far lower levels of net worth than does the federal estate tax. For example, Massachusetts and Oregon have exemption levels of just $1 million. And some of the state estate tax rates are quite high — the District of Columbia's rate is 16 percent, while Hawaii and Washington state have a 20 percent rate.

Determining your taxable federal estate

Unless you already possess great wealth or die prematurely, whether your assets face estate taxes depends on the amount of your assets that you use up during your retirement. How much of your assets you use up depends on how your assets grow over time and how rapidly you spend money.

To calculate the value of your estate upon your death, the IRS totals up your assets and subtracts your liabilities. Assets include your personal property, home and other real estate, savings and investments (such as bank accounts, stocks, bonds, and mutual funds held inside and outside of retirement accounts), and life insurance death benefits (unless properly placed in a trust, as we describe later in this chapter). Your liabilities include any outstanding loans (such as a mortgage), bills owed at the time of your death, legal and other expenses to handle your estate, and funeral expenses.

MAKING YOUR WISHES KNOWN THROUGH A WILL

Wills — legal documents that detail your instructions for what you want done with your personal property and assets upon your death — won't save you on taxes or on probate. Wills are, however, an estate-planning basic that most people should have but don't. Most of the world doesn't bother with wills, because laws and customs divvy up a person's estate among the spouse and children or other close relatives.

The main benefit of a will is that it ensures that your wishes for the distribution of your assets are fulfilled. If you die without a will (known in legalese as *intestate*), your state decides how to distribute your money and other property, according to state law. Therefore, your friends, more-distant relatives, and favorite charities will probably receive nothing. For a fee, the state appoints an administrator to supervise the distribution of your assets.

If you have little in the way of personal assets and don't really care who gets your possessions and other assets (state law usually specifies the closest blood relatives), you can forget about creating a will. You can save yourself the time and sadness that inevitably accompanies this task.

When you have minor (dependent) children, a will is necessary to name a guardian for them. In the event that you and your spouse both die without a will, the state (courts and social service agencies) decides who raises your children. Therefore, even if you can't decide at this time who would raise your children, you at least need to appoint a trusted guardian who can decide for you.

Living wills, medical powers of attorney, and durable powers of attorney are useful additions to a standard will. A *living will* tells your doctor what, if any, life-support measures you would accept. A *medical power of attorney* grants authority to someone you trust to make decisions with a physician regarding your medical options when you aren't able. A *durable power of attorney* gives someone else the authority to act for you in other legal transactions if you're away or incapacitated, including signing your tax returns. These additional documents usually are prepared when a will is drawn up.

If you're married at the time of your death, all assets that you leave to your spouse are excluded from estate taxes, thanks to the unlimited marital deduction (which we discuss later in this chapter). The IRS also deducts any charitable contributions or bequests that you dictate in your will from your assets before calculating your taxable estate.

Reducing Expected Estate Taxes

WARNING

You have your work cut out for you as you try to educate yourself about estate planning. You can find many attorneys and non-attorneys selling estate-planning services, and you can encounter many insurance agents hawking life insurance. All are pleased to sell you their services.

The good news is that most people don't need to do complicated estate planning with high-cost attorneys. We give you the straight scoop on what, if anything, you need to be concerned with now and at other junctures in your life, and we tell you the conflicts of interest that these "experts" have in rendering advice.

Thanks to all the changes in the tax laws and the thousands of attorneys and tax advisors working to find new ways around paying estate taxes, a dizzying array of strategies exist to reduce estate taxes — including taking up residence in a foreign country! We start with the simpler stuff and work toward the more complex.

Giving it away

Nothing is wrong with making, saving, and investing money. But someday, you have to look in the mirror and ask, "For what purpose?" You can easily rationalize hoarding money — you never know how long you'll live or what medical expenses you may incur. Besides, your kids still are paying off their student loans and don't seem to know a mutual fund from an emergency fund. (Not that you'd want to be judgmental of your kids or anything!)

Upon your passing, your money has to go somewhere. By directing some of your money to people and organizations now, you can pass on far more now because you'll be saving the portion that would have gone to estate and inheritance taxes, both at the state and federal levels. Plus, while you're alive, you can experience the satisfaction of seeing the good that your money can do.

How much can you give?

TAX CUT

Current tax law allows you to give up to $15,000 per individual each year to as many people — such as your children, grandchildren, or best friends — as you desire without any gift tax consequences or tax forms required. If you're married, your spouse can do the same. The benefit of giving is that it removes the money from your estate and therefore reduces your estate taxes. Even better is the fact that all future appreciation and income on the gifted money also is removed from your estate, because the money now belongs to the gift recipient. (The current annual tax-free gifting limit of $15,000 per recipient will increase in future years with inflation.)

You can use gifting to remove a substantial portion of your assets from your estate over time. Suppose that you have three children. You and your spouse each can give each of your children $15,000 per year for a total gift of $75,000 per year. If your kids are married, you can make additional $15,000 gifts to their spouses for another $75,000 per year. You also can gift an unlimited amount to pay for current educational tuition costs and medical expenses. Just be sure to make the payment directly to the institution charging the fees.

SEEK ADVICE

Yet another tax — the *generation-skipping transfer tax* — can be assessed on a gift above the $15,000 annual limit per recipient. This tax applies if the gift giver is a grandparent making a gift to a grandchild (and the grandparent's son or daughter is still alive) or in the case of a gift made to an unrelated individual who is more than 37½ years younger. Seek the advice of a qualified tax advisor if this tax may apply.

What should you give?

TIP

You have options in terms of what money or assets you give to others. Start with cash or assets that haven't appreciated since you purchased them. If you want to transfer an asset that has lost value, consider selling it first; then you can claim the tax loss on your tax return and transfer the cash.

Rather than giving away assets that have appreciated greatly in value, consider holding onto them. If you hold such assets until your death, your heirs receive what is called a stepped-up basis. That is, the IRS assumes that the effective price your heirs "paid" for an asset is the value on your date of death — which wipes out the capital gains tax that otherwise is owed when selling an asset that has appreciated in value. (Donating appreciated assets to your favorite charity can make sense because you get the tax deduction for the appreciated value and avoid realizing the taxable capital gain.)

Please note that at the time this book is going to press in late 2021, Congress has been considering legislation that would eliminate the stepped-up basis for more affluent people. We don't see the chances of this passing as likely, but you should stay tuned.

MAKING GIFTS GREATER THAN $15,000 PER YEAR

You can make gifts of greater than $15,000 per year to an individual; however, you have to prepare and file Form 709, United States Gift (and Generation-Skipping Transfer) Tax Return. Chances are good that you won't have to pay any tax on the transfer, but when giving gifts that large, the IRS does want to have a record.

You're allowed to make gifts larger than $15,000 per year to pay for another person's tuition or medical expenses without filing a Form 709. If you decide you want to pay your beloved niece's tuition to her pricey private college (how nice of you), just make sure that you write the check directly to the school. Please be aware, however, of the impact that such payments will have on the price (and therefore "financial aid") that that college will provide that student. Likewise, in the case of paying someone else's medical expenses, send your check directly to the medical care provider or institution.

If you make a large gift of cash or property to charity, and you otherwise aren't required to file Form 709, you don't need to report this gift, even if its value is in excess of $15,000, provided that you gave up all interest in the property you transferred. Don't forget to include your gift on Schedule A of your Form 1040 — even though the property you're gifting may not be part of this year's income, you're still entitled to an income tax deduction. Check out Chapter 11 for all the rules.

Gifts to political organizations aren't really gifts at all. If you're so inclined and make large payments to political organizations, you don't trigger a requirement to file a Form 709, even if your gift is greater than $15,000. What a deal!

A more complicated way to give money to your heirs without giving them absolute control over the money is to set up a Crummey Trust (named after the first man to gain approval to use this type of trust). Although the beneficiary has a short window of time (a month or two) to withdraw money that's contributed to the trust, you can verbally make clear to the beneficiary that, in your opinion, leaving the money in the trust is in their best interest. You also can specify in the trust document itself that the trust money be used for particular purposes, such as tuition. Some of the other trusts we discuss later in the "Setting up trusts" section may meet your needs if you want more control over the money you intend to pass to your heirs.

Leaving all your assets to your spouse

Tax laws wouldn't be tax laws without exceptions and loopholes. Here's another one: If you're married at the time of your death, any and all assets that you leave to your spouse are exempt from estate taxes normally due upon your death. In fact, you may leave an unlimited amount of money to your spouse, hence the name *unlimited marital deduction*. Assets that count are those willed to your spouse or for which your spouse is named as beneficiary (such as retirement accounts).

WARNING

Although leaving all your assets to your spouse is a tempting estate-planning strategy for married couples, this "short-term" strategy can backfire. The surviving spouse may end up with an estate tax problem, especially at the state level, upon their death because they will have all the couple's assets. (See the following section for a legal way around this issue, appropriately called a bypass trust.) You face three other less likely but potential problems:

>> You and your spouse may die simultaneously.

>> The unlimited marital deduction isn't allowed if your spouse isn't a U.S. citizen.

>> Some states don't allow the unlimited marital deduction, so be sure to find out about the situation in your state.

Establishing a bypass trust

A potential estate tax problem is created upon the death of a spouse if all the deceased's assets pass to the surviving spouse. When the surviving spouse dies, $11.7 million (for tax year 2021) can be passed on free of federal estate taxes.

TAX CUT

If you have substantial assets, both you and your spouse can take advantage of the $11.7 million estate tax–free rule and pass to your heirs a total of $23.4 million estate tax–free. Each of you can, through instructions in your will, direct assets to be placed into a *bypass trust* (also known as credit shelter or exemption equivalent). Please keep in mind that even if you don't have this kind of money, you may well live in a state with a much lower estate tax threshold so you may benefit from a similar trust at that level.

Upon the first death, assets belonging to the deceased spouse equal in value to the amount that can be passed tax-free (the exemption amount) go into a trust. The surviving spouse and/or other heirs still can use the income earned from those assets and even some of the principal. Depending on how the trust is written, they may be able to withdraw a small percentage of the value of the trust or up to a particular dollar amount, whichever is greater, each year. They also can draw additional principal if they need it for educational, health, or living expenses. Ultimately, the assets in the bypass trust pass to the designated beneficiaries (usually, but not limited to, children).

TIP

For a bypass trust to work, you likely will need to rework how you hold ownership of your assets (for example, jointly or individually). You may need to individually title your assets so that each spouse holds some portion of the total assets and so that each can take full advantage of the estate tax–free limit for your state and at the federal level if your net worth is substantial enough. Our attorney friends tell us that you need to be careful when setting up a bypass trust so that it's funded up to the full amount of the current federal tax–free exemption amount. The reason: The surviving spouse may otherwise end up with less than what would've been desired. Be sure to read the section "Getting advice and help," later in this chapter, for how to obtain good legal and tax advice.

Buying cash-value life insurance

Two major types of life insurance exist. Most people who need life insurance — and who have someone dependent on their income — should buy *term life insurance,* which is pure life insurance: You pay an annual premium for which you receive a predetermined amount of life insurance protection. If the insured person passes away, the beneficiaries collect; otherwise, the premium is gone but the insured is grateful! In this way, term life insurance is similar to auto or homeowner's insurance.

The other kind of life insurance, called *cash-value life insurance,* is probably one of the most oversold financial products in the history of Western civilization. With cash-value policies (whole, universal, variable, and so on), your premiums not only pay for life insurance, but some of your dollars also are credited to an account that grows in value over time, assuming that you keep paying your premiums. On the surface, a cash-value life policy sounds potentially attractive.

When bought and placed in an irrevocable life insurance trust (which we discuss later in this chapter), life insurance, it's true, receives special treatment with regard to estate taxes. Specifically, the death benefit or proceeds paid on the policy upon your death can pass to your designated heirs free of estate taxes. (Some states, however, don't allow this.)

People who sell cash-value insurance — that is, insurance salespeople and other life insurance brokers masquerading as estate-planning specialists and financial planners — too often advocate life insurance as the best, and only, way to reduce estate taxes. But the other methods we discuss in this chapter are superior in most cases.

BUYING CASH-VALUE LIFE INSURANCE FOR THE WRONG REASONS

Some insurance salespeople aggressively push cash-value policies because of the high commissions (50 percent to 100 percent of the first year's premium paid by you) that insurance companies pay their agents. These policies are expensive ways to purchase life insurance.

Because of their high cost (about eight times the cost of the same amount of term life insurance), you're more likely to buy less life insurance coverage than you need, which, unfortunately, is the sad result of the insurance industry pushing this stuff. The vast majority of life insurance buyers need more protection than they can afford to buy in cash-value coverage.

Agents know which buttons to push to get you interested in buying the wrong kind of life insurance. Insurance agents show you all sorts of projections implying that after the first 10 or 20 years of paying your premiums, you won't need to pay more premiums to keep the life insurance in force. The only reason you may be able to stop paying premiums is that you've poured too much extra money into the policy in the early years of payment. Remember that cash-value life insurance costs eight times as much as term.

Insurance agents also argue that your cash value grows tax-deferred. But if you want tax-deferred retirement savings, you first need to take advantage of retirement savings plans such as 401(k)s, 403(b)s, SEP-IRAs, and so on. These plans, which have substantial contribution limits, give you an immediate tax deduction for your current contributions in addition to growth without taxation until withdrawal. Money paid into a cash-value life policy gives you no upfront tax breaks. When you've exhausted the tax-deductible plans, then Roth IRA and Roth company-based plans can provide tax-deferred compounding of your investment dollars, plus Roth accounts offer the added bonus of tax-free retirement withdrawals. There are also other accounts that provide tax-deferred compounding that are superior to cash value life insurance (see Chapter 24).

Life insurance tends to be a mediocre investment anyway. The insurance company quotes you an interest rate for the first year only. After that, the rate is at the company's discretion. If you don't like the future interest rates, you can be penalized for quitting the policy. Would you invest your money in a bank account that quoted an interest rate for the first year only and then penalized you for moving your money in the next seven to ten years?

WARNING Insurance companies aren't stupid. In fact, they're quite smart. If you purchase a cash-value life insurance policy that provides a death benefit of, say, $1 million, you have to pay substantial insurance premiums, although far less than $1 million. Is that a good deal for you? No, because the insurance company invests your premium dollars and earns a return the same way as you otherwise would have, had you invested the money instead of using it to buy the life insurance.

Through the years, between the premiums you pay on your life policy and the returns the insurance company earns investing your premiums, the insurance company is able to come up with more than $1 million. Otherwise, how can it afford to pay out a death benefit of $1 million on your policy?

TIP

Using life insurance as an estate-planning tool may be beneficial if your estate includes assets that you don't want to subject to a forced sale to pay estate taxes (either at the state or federal level) after you die. For example, small-business owners whose businesses are worth millions may want to consider cash-value life insurance under special circumstances. If your estate will lack the other necessary assets to pay expected estate taxes and you don't want your beneficiaries to be forced to sell the business, you can buy life insurance to pay expected estate taxes.

For advice on whether life insurance is an appropriate estate-planning strategy for you, don't expect to get objective information from anyone who sells life insurance. Please see the section "Getting advice and help" later in this chapter.

Setting up trusts

If estate planning hasn't already given you a headache, understanding the different types of trusts can. A *trust* is a legal device used to pass to someone else the management responsibility and, ultimately, the ownership of some of your assets. We discuss some trusts, such as bypass, Crummey, and life insurance trusts, earlier in this chapter; in this section, we talk about other trusts you may hear about when planning your estate.

Living trusts

A *living trust* effectively transfers assets into a trust. When you use a *revocable living trust*, you control those assets and can revoke the trust whenever you desire. The advantage of a living trust is that upon your death, assets can pass directly to your beneficiaries without going through probate, the legal process for administering and implementing the directions in a will.

Living trusts keep your assets out of probate but, in and of themselves, do nothing to help you deal with estate taxes. Living trusts can contain bypass trusts and other estate tax–saving provisions.

Property and assets that are owned by *joint tenants with a right of survivorship* (owned by two or more individuals, with the deceased owner's share passing upon death to the surviving owner[s]) or inside retirement accounts — such as IRAs or 401(k)s — and have designated beneficiaries generally pass to heirs without going through probate.

Many states also allow a special type of revocable trust for bank accounts called a *Totten trust*, sometimes also referred to as a payable-on-death or POD account, which also insulates the bank accounts from probate. Such trusts are established for the benefit of another person, and the money in the trust is paid to that beneficiary upon the account holder's death.

ESTATE PLANNING FROM THE GRAVE

It goes without saying that not everyone does the right type of estate planning before passing on. Some people die before their time, and others just can't seem to get around to the planning part, even when they're in failing health.

Although further planning after you're dead and gone is impossible, your heirs may legally take steps that can, in some cases, dramatically reduce estate taxes. Some legal folks call these steps postmortem planning. Here's an example of how it works.

Suppose that Peter Procrastinator never got around to planning for the distribution of his substantial estate. When he died, all of his estate was to go to his wife. No dummy, his wife hired legal help so that she can disclaim, or reject, part of Peter's big estate. Why would she do that? Simple, so that part of the estate can immediately go to their children. If she hadn't disclaimed, Peter would have missed out on his state's estate tax exclusion. By disclaiming, she possibly saved her heirs substantially on estate taxes.

The person doing the disclaiming, in this case, Peter's wife, may not direct to whom the disclaimed assets will go. Peter's will or other legal documents specify who is second in line. Disclaimers are also irrevocable, must be made in writing, and are subject to other IRS rules and regulations. A knowledgeable executor and attorney can help you with disclaiming.

Probate can be a lengthy, expensive hassle for your heirs. Attorney probate fees may approach 5 percent to 7 percent of the estate's value. In addition, the details of your assets become public record because of probate. Properly drafted and funded, a living trust can save on probate fees and maintain your financial privacy. This trust is also useful in naming someone to administer your affairs in the event you become incapacitated.

TIP

You can't escape the undertaker or the lawyers. Setting up a trust and transferring property in and out costs money and time. Thus, living trusts are likely to be of greatest value to people who are age 60 and older, are single, and own assets worth more than $100,000 that must pass through probate (including real estate, nonretirement accounts, and businesses). Small estates are often less expensive to probate in some states than the cost and hassle of setting up a living trust. (The key is to maintain an *independent administration*, which is when the probate court trusts the executor to make most of the decisions without the court's supervision.)

Charitable trusts

If you're feeling philanthropic, charitable trusts may be for you. With a *charitable remainder trust*, you or your designated beneficiary receives income from assets that you donate to a charity.

At the time you fund a charitable remainder trust, you'll also be entitled to a current charitable deduction on Schedule A, calculated on a complicated formula that includes reference to life expectancies and the present value of the gift. Although not inexpensive to set up or to administer, a charitable remainder trust makes especially good sense in cases where a person holds an asset that they want to donate that has greatly appreciated in value. By not selling the asset before the donation, a hefty tax on the profit is avoided.

In a *charitable lead trust,* the roles of the charity and beneficiaries are reversed. The charity receives the income from the assets for a set number of years or until you pass away, at which point the assets pass to your beneficiary. You get a current income tax deduction for the value of the expected payments to the charity.

Getting advice and help

The number of people who happily will charge you a fee for or sell you some legal advice or insurance far exceeds the number actually qualified to render objective estate-planning advice. Attorneys, accountants, financial planners, estate-planning specialists, investment companies, insurance agents, and even some nonprofit agencies stand ready to help you figure out how to dispense your wealth.

Most of these people and organizations have conflicts of interest and lack the knowledge necessary to do sound estate planning for you. Attorneys are biased toward drafting legal documents and devices that are more complicated than may be needed. Insurance agents and financial planners who work on commission try to sell cash-value life insurance. Investment firms and banks encourage you to establish a trust account that requires them to manage the assets in the future. Although the cost of free estate-planning seminars is tempting, you get what you pay for — or worse.

Start the process of planning your estate by first looking at the big picture. Talk to your family members about your financial situation. Many people never take this basic but critical step. Your heirs likely have no idea what you're considering or what you're worried about. Conversely, how can you develop a solid action plan without understanding your heirs' needs and concerns? Be careful not to use money to control or manipulate other family members.

For professional advice, you need someone who can look objectively at the big picture. Attorneys and tax advisors who specialize in estate planning are a good starting point. Ask the people you're thinking of hiring whether they sell life insurance or manage money. If they do, they can't possibly be objective and likely aren't sufficiently educated about estate planning, given their focus.

For preparation of wills and living trusts, check out the high-quality software programs on the market. Legal software may save you from the often-difficult task of finding a competent and affordable attorney. Preparing documents with software also can save you money.

Using legal software is generally preferable to using fill-in-the-blank documents. Software has the built-in virtues of directing and limiting your choices and keeping you from making common mistakes. Quality software also incorporates the knowledge and insights of the legal eagles who developed the software. As for the legality of documents that you create with software, remember that you and your witnesses properly signing the document, such as a will, make it legal and valid. An attorney preparing a document isn't what makes it legal. If your situation isn't unusual, legal software may work well for you.

For will and living trust preparation, check out *WillMaker and Trust* by Nolo Press. In addition to enabling you to prepare wills (in every state except Louisiana), this software can help you create a living will, medical power of attorney, and a living trust. Living trusts are fairly standard legal documents that serve to keep property out of probate in the event of your death (remember that they don't address the issue of estate taxes). The software package advises you to seek professional guidance for your situation, if necessary.

SEEK ADVICE

If you want to do more reading on estate planning, pick up a copy of *Plan Your Estate* by attorney Denis Clifford (Nolo Press). When you have a large estate that may be subject to estate taxes, consulting an attorney or tax advisor who specializes in estate planning may be worth your time and money. Get smarter first and figure out the lingo before you seek and pay for advice.

6

The Part of Tens

Reduce your chances of being audited.

Take advantage of often overlooked tax reduction opportunities.

Know the tax benefits available to members of the military.

Use these interview questions when searching for a tax advisor.

Chapter **28**

Ten Tips for Reducing Your Chances of Being Audited

I f you've never been audited, you probably fall into one of these categories: You're still young, you haven't made gobs of money, or you're just plain lucky. The fact is that many taxpayers are audited at some point or two during their adult lives. It's just a matter of time and probability.

You can take some common-sense steps (honesty being the star of the show) to reduce your chances of having to face an audit. So here are our top tips for lessening your chances of being audited and avoiding all the time and associated costs of an audit.

Double-Check Your Return for Accuracy

Review your own return before you send it in. If the IRS finds mistakes through its increasingly sophisticated computer-checking, you're more likely to be audited. They figure that if they find obvious errors, some not-so-obvious ones lurk beneath the surface.

Have you included all your income? Think about the different accounts you had during the tax year. Do you have interest and dividend statements for all your accounts? Finding these statements is easier if you've been keeping your financial records in one place. Recognize that increasing numbers of firms send out such documents electronically so you may need to search old emails or visit their websites. Check your W-2s and 1099s against your tax form to make sure that you wrote the numbers down correctly.

Don't forget to check your math. Have you added, subtracted, multiplied, and divided correctly? Are your Social Security number and address correct on the return? Did you sign and date your return?

Such infractions won't, on their own, trigger an audit. In some cases, the IRS simply sends you a letter requesting your signature or the additional tax you owe (if the math mistake isn't too fishy or too big). In some rare instances, the IRS even sends a refund if the mistake it uncovers is in the taxpayer's favor — really! Regardless of how the IRS handles the mistake, it can be a headache for you to clear up, and, more important, it can cost you extra money.

Declare All Your Income

When you prepare your return, you may be tempted to shave off a little of that consulting income you received. Who will miss it, right? The IRS, that's who.

Thanks largely to computer cross-checking, the IRS has many ways of finding unreported income. Be particularly careful if you're self-employed; anyone who pays you more than $600 in a year is required to file a Form 1099, which basically tells the IRS how much you received.

WARNING

When you knowingly hide income, you face substantial penalties and, depending on the amount, criminal prosecution. That wouldn't be a picnic, especially if you can't afford to hire a good defense attorney.

Don't Itemize

People who itemize their deductions on Schedule A are far more likely to be audited because they have more opportunity and temptation to cheat. By all means, if you can legally claim more total deductions by using Schedule A than you can with the standard deduction (this deduction stuff is all spelled out in Chapter 11), we say "itemize, itemize, itemize." Just don't try to artificially inflate your deductions.

On the other hand, if it's basically a toss-up between Schedule A and your standard deduction, taking the standard deduction is safer, and the IRS can't challenge it.

Earn Less Money

At first glance, earning less money may seem like an odd suggestion, but there really are costs associated with affluence. One of the costs of a high income — besides higher taxes — is a significant increase in the probability of being audited. Your chance of being audited is less than 1 in 200 if your income is less than $50,000 but more than doubles if your income is more than $100,000. You see, besides being subjected to lower income tax rates, there are additional advantages to earning less!

WARNING

If you manage to pile up a lot of assets and don't enjoy them in retirement, your estate tax return — your final tax return — is at great risk of being audited. Do you think a 1 in 20 or 1 in 100 chance is bad in the audit lottery? Uncle Sam audits about 1 in 7 estate tax returns. The IRS collects an average of more than $100,000 for each estate tax return it audits! So enjoy your money while you're alive or pass it along to your heirs in the here and now — otherwise, your heirs may have trouble getting it in the there and later!

Don't Cheat and Put Down Your Protest Sign

Over time, through audits, the folks at the IRS discover common ways that some taxpayers cheat. That then leads them to conduct more audits of taxpayers who appear to potentially be doing similar things. Cheaters beware!

The IRS also offers rewards for informants. If you're brazen enough to cheat and the IRS doesn't catch you, you may not be home-free yet. Someone else may turn you in. So be honest — not only because it's the right thing to do but also because you'll probably sleep better at night knowing that you aren't breaking the law.

WARNING

Tax protesters, take note. The IRS may flag returns that are accompanied by protest notes. Threats are bad, too — even if they're meant in fun (humor isn't rife at the IRS, we suspect). The commandment to follow is this: Thou shalt not draw attention to thyself. The protest issue is interesting. During congressional hearings, tax protesters stand up and tell members of Congress that the income tax is unconstitutional. They say they have proof. If we can get our hands on the proof, we'll include it in the next edition of this book. In the meantime, pay your taxes and resist the temptation to send along a cranky letter with your tax returns and payments. To read the IRS's "The Truth About Frivolous Tax Arguments," point your web browser to www. irs.gov/privacy-disclosure/the-truth-about-frivolous-tax-arguments-introduction or www.irs.gov/pub/taxpros/frivolous_truth_march_2018.pdf for 73 action-packed pages, including legal citations.

Stay Away from Back-Street Refund Mills

Although this advice doesn't apply to the majority of tax-preparation firms, unfortunately, some firms out there fabricate deductions. Run away — as fast as you can — from tax preparers who tell you, after winking, that they have creative ways to reduce your tax bill, or those who base their fees on how many tax dollars they can save you.

The IRS is actively going after fly-by-night preparers, who promise you the moon and the stars but may end up landing you in the muck. When the IRS audits a preparer, they look at many of the returns the preparer has worked on and filed for taxpayers. If it finds problems in how that preparer runs their business, you can expect the IRS to also look more closely at all the returns that preparer prepared.

Also beware of any preparer who promises you a refund without first thoroughly reviewing your situation. Please refer to Chapter 2 and Chapter 31 for how to find a top-quality tax preparer.

Be Careful with Hobby Losses

Some people who have full-time jobs also have sideline businesses or hobbies with which they try to make a few bucks. But be careful if you report the avocation as showing a loss year after year on your tax forms. Filers of Schedule C, Profit or Loss from Business, are at greatest risk for audits.

Here's an example. You like to paint surreal pictures, and you even sold one in 2016 for $350. But since then, you haven't sold any paintings (the surreal market has faded). Nevertheless, you continue to write off your cost for canvas and paint. The IRS will take a close look at that record, and you may be a candidate for an audit.

Don't Be a Nonfiler

The IRS has a special project with a mission to go after the millions of nonfilers. Lest you think that the IRS does things in small ways, the IRS assigned hundreds of agents to this project. Again, when you get caught — which is just a matter of time — in addition to owing back taxes, interest, and big penalties, you may also face criminal prosecution and end up serving time in the slammer. So keep a clear conscience, continue to enjoy your freedom, and file your tax returns. And remember, better late than never!

Don't Cut Corners if You're Self-Employed

People who are self-employed have more opportunities to make mistakes on their taxes — or to creatively take deductions — than company-payroll wage earners. As a business owner, you're responsible for self-reporting not only your income but also your expenses. You have to be even more honest when dealing with the tax authorities, because the likelihood of being audited is higher than average.

Don't disguise employees as independent contractors. This maneuver is covered by another IRS project. Remember the old barb: You can't put a sign around the neck of a cow that says, "This is a horse." You don't have a horse — you have a cow with a sign around its neck. Just because you call someone an independent contractor doesn't mean that person isn't your employee. If you aren't sure about the relationship, refer to Chapter 23.

Nothing is wrong with being self-employed. But resist the temptation to cheat because you're far more likely to be scrutinized and caught as a self-employed worker.

Carry a Rabbit's Foot

Try as you may to be an obedient taxpayer, you can be audited simply because of bad luck. Every year, the IRS audits some taxpayers at random. Although such an undertaking may seem like a colossal waste of time to a tax neophyte like yourself, this effort provides the IRS with valuable information about the areas of tax returns where people make the most mistakes — and about the areas where people cheat!

So, if you do get an audit notice, don't assume that you did anything wrong. However, be prepared for your audit — see Part 4 of this book.

Chapter 29

Ten Overlooked Opportunities to Trim Your Taxes

This chapter presents the more commonly overlooked opportunities to reduce individual income taxes. The income tax you pay is based on your taxable income minus your deductions. We start first with overlooked ways to minimize your taxable income. Then we move on to often-ignored deductions. We don't want you to be like all those people who miss out on perfectly legal tax-reduction strategies simply because they don't know what they don't know.

Make Your Savings Work for You

Out of apathy or lack of knowledge of better options, far too many people keep extra cash dozing away in their bank accounts. Yes, the bank has a vault and sometimes-friendly tellers who may greet you by name if you bank locally, but banks also characteristically pay relatively low rates of interest. Keeping your household checking account at a bank is fine, but even with such transaction accounts you've got other options today with investment firms' cash management accounts, but you're generally throwing away some interest if you keep your extra savings money in most banks.

During periods of more normal interest rates, the better money market mutual funds often pay substantially greater interest than bank savings accounts and offer equivalent safety. And if you're in a high tax bracket, money market funds come in tax-free flavors. Please see Chapter 24 to find out more about tax-friendly investments.

Getting a slightly higher interest rate on your cash balances is a step in the right direction but hardly the golden ticket you're looking for! In our experience, often times folks accumulating excess cash don't know where else they can and should invest for better returns. They sense correctly that higher-return investments fluctuate far more in value, especially over the short-term, but they may be overlooking the risk of their cash balances not keeping them up with inflation and taxes. So, be sure to read the rest of the tips in this chapter and make an investment of time to find out more about sound investment options.

Invest in Wealth-Building Assets

During your working years, while you're earning employment income, you probably don't need or want taxable income from your investments because it increases your income tax bill. Real estate, stocks, and small-business investments offer the best long-term growth potential, although you need to be able to withstand downturns in these markets.

Most of the return that you can earn with these wealth-building investments comes from appreciation in their value, making them tax-friendly because you're in control and can decide when to sell and realize your profit. Also, as long as you hold onto these investments for more than one year, your profit is taxed at the lower, long-term capital gains tax rate. (Stock dividends are also subject to these lower tax rates — see Chapter 24.)

Fund "Tax-Reduction" Accounts

When you funnel your savings dollars into retirement accounts, such as a 401(k), 403(b), SEP-IRA, self-employed/i401(k), or IRA, you can earn substantial upfront tax breaks on your contributions. If you think that saving for retirement is boring, consider the tens of thousands of tax dollars these accounts can save you during your working years. Roth accounts — both IRA and employer-based — don't offer upfront tax breaks but present opportunities to grow your money without taxation over time and withdraw investment returns in retirement without taxation.

If you don't use these accounts to save and invest, you may well have to work many more years to accumulate the reserves necessary to retire. Refer to Chapter 22 to find out more, including how recent tax law changes significantly increased the benefits of these accounts.

Make Use of a "Back-Door" Roth IRA

If you're a higher-income earner, you may not be able to contribute to a Roth IRA. In that case, you can make a nondeductible contribution to a regular IRA and then immediately convert that money into your Roth IRA. This is called a "back-door" Roth IRA.

This strategy makes sense to consider when your new contribution to the regular IRA is the only money you would have in regular IRA accounts. Otherwise, if you have additional money in a regular IRA and those investments have generated returns, converting to a Roth IRA will trigger tax on the investment earnings that are transferred. That may still make sense to do for the longer-term tax benefits that a Roth account offers, but you should run some numbers to decide. See Chapter 22 for information on all your retirement plan options.

Work Overseas

When you go to work in some foreign countries, you may be able to save some money on income taxes. For tax year 2021, you can exclude $108,700 of foreign-earned income (whether working for a company or on a self-employed basis) from U.S. income taxes. To qualify for this income tax exclusion, you must work at least 330 days (about 11 months) of the year overseas or be a foreign resident. You claim this income tax exclusion on Form 2555, Foreign Earned Income Exclusion.

If you earn more than $108,700, don't worry about being double-taxed on the income above this amount. You get to claim credits for foreign taxes paid on your U.S. tax return on Form 1116, Foreign Tax Credit. Perhaps to give you more time to fill out this form and others, the IRS gives Americans working abroad two extra months (until June 15) to file their tax returns.

As with many things in life that sound too good to be true, this pot of overseas gold has some catches. First, many of the places you've romanticized about traveling to and perhaps living in — such as England, France, Italy, Sweden, Germany, and Spain — have higher income tax rates than the ones in the United States. Also, this tax break isn't available to U.S. government workers overseas.

TIP

Look at the whole package when deciding whether to work overseas. Some employers throw in a housing allowance and other benefits. And be careful of the allure of supposedly low-cost countries. Be sure to consider all costs and benefits of living overseas, both financial and emotional. And also explore the safety of living in specific countries that you're considering.

Check Whether You Can Itemize

The IRS gives you two methods of determining your total deductions. *Deductions* are just what they sound like: You subtract them from your income before you calculate the tax you owe. So the more deductions you take, the smaller your taxable income — and the smaller your tax bill. You get to pick the method that leads to the largest total deductions — and thus a lower tax bill. But sometimes the choice isn't so clear, so be prepared to do some figuring.

Taking the *standard deduction* usually makes sense if you have a pretty simple financial life — a regular paycheck, a rented apartment, and no large expenses, such as medical bills, or loss due to theft or catastrophe. Single folks qualify for a $12,550 standard deduction, and married couples filing jointly get a $25,100 standard deduction for tax year 2021.

The other method of determining your allowable deductions is to *itemize* them on your tax return. This painstaking procedure is definitely more of a hassle, but if you can tally up more than the standard deduction amounts, itemizing saves you money. Schedule A of your 1040 is the page for summing up your itemized deductions, but you won't know whether you have enough itemized deductions unless you give this schedule a good examination (refer to Chapter 11).

If you currently don't itemize, you may be surprised to discover that your personal property and state income taxes are itemizable. So too are state sales taxes that you pay, especially if your state doesn't have an income tax or your state income tax payments are relatively low.

If you pay a fee to the state to register and license your car, you can itemize the expenditure as a deduction ("Other Taxes" on Schedule A). The IRS allows you to deduct only the part of the fee that relates to the value of your car, however. The state organization that collects the fee should be able to tell you what portion of the fee is deductible. If it's a user-friendly organization, it even shows this figure on your invoice. What service!

When you total your itemized deductions on Schedule A and that amount is equal to or less than the standard deduction, take the standard deduction without fail (unless you're married filing separately, and your spouse is itemizing — then you have to itemize). The total for your itemized deductions is worth checking every year, however, because you may have more deductions in some years than others, and you may occasionally be able to itemize.

TIP

Because you can control when you pay particular expenses for which you're eligible to itemize, you can shift or bunch more of them into selected years when you know that you'll have enough deductions to take full advantage of itemizing. For example, suppose that you're using the standard deduction this year because you just don't have many itemized deductions. Late in the tax year, though, you feel certain that you'll buy a home sometime during the next year. Thanks to the potential write-off of mortgage interest and property taxes, you also know that you'll be able to itemize next year. It makes sense, then, to shift as many deductible expenses as possible into the next year.

Trade Consumer Debt for Mortgage Debt

Suppose that you own real estate and haven't borrowed as much money as a mortgage lender currently allows (given the current market value of the property and your financial situation). And further suppose that you've run up high-interest consumer debt. Well, you may be able to trade one debt for another. You probably can refinance your mortgage and pull out extra cash to pay off your credit card, auto loan, or other expensive consumer credit lines.

You usually can borrow at a lower interest rate for a mortgage, thus lowering your monthly interest bill. Plus, you may get a tax-deduction bonus, because consumer debt — auto loans, credit cards, credit lines — isn't tax-deductible, but mortgage debt generally is. Therefore, the effective borrowing rate on a mortgage is even lower than the quoted rate suggests.

Don't forget, however, that refinancing your mortgage and establishing *home equity lines* involve application fees and other charges (points, appraisals, credit reports, and so on). You must include these fees in the equation to see whether it makes sense to exchange consumer debt for more mortgage debt.

WARNING

Swapping consumer debt for mortgage debt involves one big danger: Borrowing against the equity in your home can be an addictive habit. We've seen cases in which people run up significant consumer debt three or four distinct times and then refinance their homes the same number of times over the years so they can bail themselves out. At a minimum, continued expansion of your mortgage debt handicaps your ability to work toward other financial goals. In the worst case, easy access to borrowing encourages bad spending habits that can lead to bankruptcy or foreclosure on your debt-ridden home.

Consider Charitable Contributions and Expenses

When you itemize your deductions on Schedule A, you can deduct contributions made to charities. For example, most people already know that when they donate money to their favorite church or college, they can deduct it. Yet many taxpayers overlook the fact that they can also deduct expenses on work done for charitable organizations. For example, when you go to a soup kitchen to help prepare and serve meals, you can deduct your transportation costs to get there. You just need to keep track of your bus fares or driving mileage.

You can also deduct the fair market value of donations of clothing, household appliances, furniture, and other goods to charities — many of these charities will even drive to your home to pick up the stuff. Just make sure to keep some documentation: Write a detailed list and get it signed by the charity. Please see Chapter 11 for more on writing off charitable contributions and expenses.

Scour for Self-Employment Expenses

If you're self-employed, you already deduct a variety of expenses from your income before calculating the tax that you owe. When you buy a computer or office furniture, you can deduct those expenses (sometimes they need to be gradually deducted or depreciated over time). Salaries for your employees, office supplies, rent or mortgage interest for your office space, and phone expenses are also generally deductible.

Although more than a few business owners inflate their expenses, some self-employed folks don't take all the deductions they should. In some cases, people simply aren't aware of the wonderful world of deductions. For others, large deductions raise the concern of an audit. Taking advantage of deductions for which you're eligible makes sense and saves you money.

Read This Book, Use Tax Software, Hire a Tax Advisor

Informing yourself better about taxes and possibly hiring tax help is worth the money. You've got this book — read it and use the information in it. Also consider using tax software (see Chapter 2) to help ensure you're leaving no stone unturned. And, you may benefit by hiring a tax preparer/advisor to review your return (even if just for one year).

Chapter **30**

Ten (Plus One) Tax Tips for Military Families

Members of the military and their families have always received special consideration from all branches of the U.S. government, and tax relief is no exception. This chapter highlights important elements of tax relief available to military families together with some other factors you may want to consider if you or your spouse is a member of the armed forces (including the reserves).

This chapter only provides some of the basics. If you or your spouse is in the military, you need to explore further. You can find additional information regarding paying income tax while you're in the military in IRS Publication 3 (*Armed Forces Tax Guide*), which is available online at www.irs.gov or by phone by calling 800-829-3676.

Some Military Wages May Be Tax-Exempt

In fact, if you're serving in a combat zone or a qualified hazardous duty area, all your compensation from active duty while you're stationed there is exempt from taxation unless you're a commissioned officer. Commissioned officers' pay earned while in a combat zone or a qualified hazardous duty area may be partially taxed. In addition, if you're hospitalized due to an injury in a combat zone, or because of disease that you caught there, your pay continues to be tax-exempt.

Even if you're not stationed in a combat zone, much of your military compensation is tax-exempt. For example, living allowances, including the Basic Allowance for Housing and the Basic Allowance for Subsistence, the Overseas Housing Allowance, and other housing costs, whether paid by the U.S. government or a foreign government, are exempt. So are moving allowances and travel allowances, including an annual round-trip for dependent students and leave between consecutive overseas tours of duty.

REMEMBER

Even though you can exclude some or all of the income you've earned while serving in a combat zone or qualified hazardous duty area, you may still use these nontaxable amounts when calculating your Earned Income Credit (EIC), child tax credit, additional child tax credit, or the recovery rebate credit in order to give yourself a bigger credit. Remember, making the election to include nontaxable combat pay when calculating these credits doesn't mean you have to include this income when calculating your tax. This income remains nontaxable!

Rule Adjustments to Home Sales

Chapter 14 covers in great detail the sale of your principal residence and the exclusion of $250,000 of capital gain if single and $500,000 if married filing jointly. One of the requirements to obtain this capital gains break is that you must be living in that house for at least two of the previous five years. Fortunately, someone somewhere realized that this created a hardship for members of the military, and the Military Family Tax Relief Act has addressed this rule.

Now, if you or your spouse serve on qualified official extended duty as a member of the armed forces during any part of the five-year qualifying period, you may choose to exclude your period of service from the five years.

The provisions here are quite extensive, but they're clearly laid out in Publication 3. Check it out if you think this rule may apply to you.

Tax Benefits for Your Family if You're Killed in Action

The Military Family Relief Act increased from $6,000 to $12,000 the amount of benefits paid to the family of any member of the armed forces in the case of that member's death. The full death benefit paid isn't taxed to anyone.

In addition to the $12,000 tax-free payment a family receives when a member of the military is killed in combat, any income tax liability due to that person's income for the year of death and for any earlier tax years that the member served in a combat zone is forgiven. This means that any unpaid tax liability no longer needs to be paid, and any liability for these periods that was already paid will be refunded.

In addition, if the decedent, whether a military or civilian U.S. employee, is killed or later dies from wounds received in a military or terrorist attack, even if it does not happen in a designated combat zone, income tax is forgiven for the year of the attack and the year immediately prior for that person's income tax liability. Refunds will be given for taxes already paid that are later forgiven.

WARNING

For couples filing jointly and surviving spouses, even though the military decedent's tax liability is forgiven, the nonmilitary spouse's isn't. For any income-producing assets that you held jointly with your spouse, only one-half of the income will be excluded, and only one-half of the deductions will be allowed.

SEEK ADVICE

IRS Publication 3920 (*Tax Relief for Victims of Terrorist Attacks*) gives you clear examples of how to calculate the amount of tax forgiveness. It also tells you which income is included in the forgiveness and which isn't. However, the rules are complex; you may want to consult a professional tax preparer before filing the necessary documents to obtain your refunds.

Deadlines Extended During Combat and Qualifying Service

If you're currently stationed in a combat zone or you have qualifying service outside a combat zone, the deadlines for filing your tax returns, paying your taxes, filing claims for refunds, or taking any other actions with the IRS are automatically extended. The deadline for the IRS to take action against you in an audit or in collections is also extended.

WARNING

Extensions are extensions only, not a forgiveness of any tax owed. After you're no longer on active duty in a qualifying area (or no longer hospitalized continuously because of an injury or illness that resulted from duty in one of those areas), the clock begins to run again. You have 180 days after you're no longer stationed in a combat zone or a qualifying hazardous duty area plus the number of days that were left for you to take action with the IRS before you were sent to that combat zone or other qualifying area. For example, if you were deployed on January 5, 2020, and return on November 30, 2021, your 2019 and 2020 income tax returns are automatically extended by 283 days (180 days plus the 103 days from January 6 through April 18, 2020), or September 8, 2022. Your 2021 return is also extended.

Income Tax Payment Deferment Due to Military Service

Even if you're not serving in a combat zone or other qualifying area, you may elect to delay the payment of your income tax that is due either before or during your period of military service. In order to defer payments, though, you must be performing active military service (part-time reserve service doesn't qualify), and you must notify the IRS, in writing, that you can't pay because you're in the military.

This provision is clearly intended for reservists and National Guard members with higher-paying jobs who have been called up for a period of active duty. In order to qualify for this deferral, your period of active service must be longer than 30 consecutive days and must be mandated by either the president or the secretary of defense.

After you're no longer on active duty, you have 180 days to pay the amount of tax you deferred. After that point, the IRS will begin to charge you interest and penalties on any unpaid balance you have.

Travel Expense Deductions for National Guard and Reserves Members

If you fall into this category and you had to travel more than 100 miles from home for a meeting or a drill, you can deduct unreimbursed expenses for transportation, meals, and lodging as a deduction on your Form 1040. You'll need to complete Form 2106 to calculate this deduction, but you'll take it on Schedule 1 of your Form 1040. Look in Chapter 7 for more about this deduction.

No Early Retirement Distribution Penalty for Called Reservists

Qualified military reservists may take retirement account distributions (for example, from their IRA, 401(k), 403(b) plan, and so on) without paying the 10 percent penalty for early distributions. While your distributions are still subject to income tax, you won't be charged the additional 10 percent tax for taking an early distribution from your IRA (whether traditional, nondeductible, or Roth), your 401(k) plan, or your 403(b) plan.

If, after you've completed your military service, you want to recontribute to an IRA all or part of any distribution you took back, you can. Just make that recontribution within two years of the end of your active service.

No Education Account Distribution Penalty for Military Academy Students

If you've been fortunate enough to obtain one of the coveted spots at West Point, the U.S. Naval Academy, the U.S. Air Force Academy, the U.S. Coast Guard Academy, or the Merchant Marine Academy, you're in luck. The taxpayer is paying for all of your tuition, room, board, books, and so on.

But what happens to the money your parents or other friends and relatives scrimped and saved and put into either an ESA or a Section 529 plan? Are you, or they, now going to be penalized because you don't need that money for your education?

In a word, no. Although the investment returns portion of distributions will still be taxed to you, there will be no 10 percent penalty on top of the ordinary income tax, provided that you don't take more in distributions each year than the amount that your qualified educational expenses would cost if you had to pay for them. These amounts should be readily available from the financial offices of the military academy.

Military Base Realignment and Closure Benefits Are Excludable from Income

If you receive payment for moving and storage services due to a permanent change of station, you're entitled to exclude these amounts from your income to the extent that your expenses involved in that move don't exceed the amount of the payment. In addition, don't include in income any amounts you receive as a dislocation allowance, a temporary lodging expense, temporary lodging allowance, or a move-in housing allowance.

Obviously, allowances are never as accurate as reimbursements (but are much easier for the government to administer), so the amounts that you spend on your move may be more or less than the amounts you actually receive. If you receive more than you spent, you must report the excess on your Form 1040. If you received less than the actual costs of your move, you are, of course, entitled to deduct the nonreimbursed portion of your moving costs. Complete Form 3903, Moving Expenses, to determine the total amount of your deduction. This form may only be used by members of the Armed Forces.

State Income Tax Flexibility for Spouses

The Military Spouses Residency Relief Act provided the same state income tax choices for spouses of military members as the military members themselves have had. Thus, military spouses can choose among their original home state of record, their current location where their military spouse is serving, or a prior location. Given the variation in state income rates and terms around the country, having these options can save military families tax dollars.

Deductibility of Some Expenses When Returning to Civilian Life

If the day comes when you elect to leave the military and return to civilian life, your job search, travel, and related moving expenses may be deductible.

Chapter **31**

Ten Interview Questions for Tax Advisors

When you believe that your tax situation warrants outside help, be sure to educate yourself as much as possible beforehand. The more you know, the better able you'll be to evaluate the competence of someone you may hire. That's why you should read the portions of this book that apply to your tax situation even if you're determined to pay for help.

REMEMBER

When all is said and done, make sure that you feel comfortable with a tax advisor. We're not suggesting that you evaluate an advisor the way you would a potential friend or spouse! But if you're feeling uneasy and can't understand what your tax advisor says to you in the early stages of your relationship, trust your instincts and continue your search. Remember that you can be your own best tax advisor — finding out the basics will pay you a lifetime of dividends and can save you tens of thousands of dollars in taxes and tax advisor fees!

Make sure that you ask the right questions to find a competent tax practitioner whose skills match your tax needs. We recommend that you start with the questions discussed in the following sections.

What Tax Services Do You Offer?

Most tax advisors prepare tax returns. We use the term tax advisors because most tax folks do more than simply prepare returns. Many advisors can help you plan and file other important tax documents throughout the year. Some firms can also assist your small business with bookkeeping and other financial reporting, such as income statements and balance sheets. These services can be useful when your business is in the market for a loan, or if you need to give clients or investors detailed information about your business.

TIP

Ask tax advisors to explain how they work with clients. You're hiring the tax advisor because you lack knowledge of the tax system. If your tax advisor doesn't prod and explore your situation, you may experience "the blind leading the blind." A good tax advisor can help you make sure that you aren't overlooking deductions or making other costly mistakes that may lead to an audit, penalties, and interest. Beware of tax preparers who view their jobs as simply plugging into tax forms the information that you bring them.

Do You Have Areas that You Focus On?

This question is important. For example, if a tax preparer works mainly with people who receive regular paychecks from an employer, that tax preparer probably has little expertise in helping small-business owners best complete the blizzard of paperwork that the IRS requires.

TIP

Find out what expertise the tax advisor has in handling whatever unusual financial events you're dealing with this year — or whatever events you expect in future years. For example, if you need help completing an estate tax return for a deceased relative, ask how many of these types of returns the tax preparer has completed in the past year. About 15 percent of estate tax returns are audited, so you don't want a novice preparing one for you.

What Other Services Do You Offer?

Ideally, you want to work with a professional who is 100 percent focused on taxes. We know it's difficult to imagine that some people choose to work at this full time, but they do — and lucky for you!

WARNING

A multitude of problems and conflicts of interest crop up when a person tries to prepare tax returns, sell investments, and appraise real estate — all at the same time. That advisor may not be fully competent or current in any of these areas.

By virtue of their backgrounds and training, some tax preparers also offer consulting and financial planning services for business owners and other individuals. Because they already know a great deal about your personal and tax situation, a competent tax professional may be able to help in these areas. Just make sure that this help is charged on an hourly consulting basis. Avoid tax advisors who sell financial products that pay them a commission — this situation inevitably creates conflicts of interest.

Who Will Prepare My Return?

If you talk to a solo practitioner, the answer to this question should be simple — the person you're talking to should prepare your return. But if your tax advisor has assistants and other employees, make sure that you know what level of involvement these different people will have in the preparation of your return.

It isn't necessarily bad if a junior-level person does the preliminary tax return preparation that your tax advisor will review and finalize. In fact, this procedure can save you money in tax-preparation fees if the firm bills you at a lower hourly rate for a junior-level person. Be wary of firms that charge you a high hourly rate for a senior tax advisor who then delegates most of the work to a junior-level person.

How Aggressive or Conservative Are You Regarding the Tax Law?

Some tax preparers, unfortunately, view their role as enforcement agents for the IRS. This attitude often is a consequence of one too many seminars put on by local IRS folks, who admonish (and sometimes intimidate) preparers with threats of audits.

On the other hand, some preparers are too aggressive and try tax maneuvers that put their clients on thin ice — subjecting them to additional taxes, penalties, interest, and audits.

Assessing how aggressive a tax preparer is can be difficult. Start by asking what percentage of the tax preparer's clients gets audited (see the next question). You can also ask the tax advisor for references from clients for whom the advisor helped unearth overlooked opportunities to reduce tax bills.

What's Your Experience with Audits?

As a benchmark, you need to know that less than 1 percent of all taxpayer returns are audited. For tax advisors working with a more affluent client base or small-business owners, expect a higher audit rate — somewhere in the neighborhood of 1 to 2 percent.

If the tax preparer proudly claims no audited clients, be wary. Among the possible explanations, any of which should cause you to be uncomfortable in hiring such a preparer: The preparer isn't telling you the truth, has prepared few returns, or is afraid of taking some legal deductions, so you'll probably overpay your taxes.

A tax preparer who has been in business for at least a couple of years will have gone through audits. Ask the preparer to explain their recent audits, what happened, and why. This explanation not only sheds light on a preparer's work with clients, but also on their ability to communicate in plain English.

How Does Your Fee Structure Work?

Tax advisor fees, like attorney and financial planner fees, are all over the map — from $50 to $300 or more per hour. Many preparers simply quote you a total fee for preparation of your tax return.

Ultimately, the tax advisor charges you for time, so you should ask what the hourly billing rate is. If the advisor balks at answering this question, try asking what their fee is for a one-hour consultation. You may want a tax advisor to work on this basis if you've prepared your return yourself and want it reviewed as a quality-control check. You also may seek an hourly fee if you're on top of your tax preparation in general but have some very specific questions about an unusual or one-time event, such as the sale of your business.

Clarify whether the preparer's set fee includes follow-up questions that you may have during the year, or if this fee covers IRS audits on the return. Some accountants include these functions in their set fee, but others charge for everything on an as-needed basis. The advantage of the all-inclusive fee is that it removes the psychological obstacle of your feeling that the meter's running every time you call with a question. The drawback can be that you pay for additional services (time) that you may not need or use.

What Qualifies You to Be a Tax Advisor?

Tax advisors come with a variety of backgrounds. The more tax and business experience they have, the better. As we discuss in Chapter 2, tax advisors can earn certifications such as CPAs and EAs. Although gaining credentials takes time and work, these certifications are no guarantee that you get quality, cost-effective tax assistance or that you won't be overcharged.

Generally speaking, more years of experience are better than fewer, but don't rule out a newer advisor who lacks gray hair or who hasn't yet slogged through thousands of returns. Intelligence and training can easily make up for less experience.

Newer advisors also may charge less so they can build up their practices. Be sure, though, that you don't just focus on each preparer's hourly rate. Ask each practitioner that you interview how much total time they expect your tax return to take. Someone with a lower hourly fee can end up costing you more if they're slower than a more experienced and efficient preparer with a higher hourly rate.

Do You Carry Liability Insurance?

If a tax advisor makes a major mistake or gives poor advice, you can lose thousands of dollars. The greater your income, assets, and the importance of your financial decisions, the more financial harm that can be done. We know that you aren't a litigious person, but your tax advisor needs to carry what's known as errors and omissions, or liability insurance. You can, of course, simply sue an uninsured advisor and hope the advisor has enough personal assets to cover a loss, but don't count on it. Besides, you'll have a much more difficult time getting due compensation that way!

You may also ask the advisor whether they have ever been sued and how the lawsuit turned out. It doesn't occur to most people to ask this type of question, so make sure that you tell your tax advisor that you're not out to strike it rich on a lawsuit! Another way to discover whether a tax advisor has gotten into hot water is by checking with appropriate professional organizations to which that preparer may belong. You can also check whether any complaints have been filed with your local Better Business Bureau (BBB), although this is far from a foolproof screening method. Most dissatisfied clients don't bother to register complaints with the BBB, and you should also know that the BBB is loath to retain complaints on file against companies who are members.

Can You Provide References of Clients Similar to Me?

You need to know that the tax advisor has handled cases and problems like yours. For example, if you're a small-business owner, ask to speak with other small-business owners. But don't be overly impressed by tax advisors who claim that they work mainly with one occupational group, such as physicians. Although there's value in understanding the nuances of a profession, tax advisors are ultimately generalists — as are the tax laws.

Appendix

Glossary

Here we provide a list of common tax-related terms that you'll find useful when preparing your taxes or speaking to a tax professional.

A

accelerated depreciation: This depreciation method yields larger deduction amounts for you — as opposed to the straight-line depreciation method. Depreciation amounts are larger in the early years and lesser in the later years. (See *straight-line depreciation*.)

accrual method: This accounting method lets you report income in the year it has been earned, even if not yet received, and expenses when incurred, even if not yet paid. (See *cash method*.)

active participation: This term is used to indicate whether you're eligible to participate in your employer's retirement savings or pension plan. If you're eligible, your ability to deduct a regular Individual Retirement Account (IRA) contribution is based on your income (actually, your adjusted gross income).

adjusted basis: The adjusted basis reflects your cost of property (see *basis*) plus the cost of improvements minus depreciation. You calculate your property's adjusted basis when you sell your property so that you can figure your taxable profit or loss. If you acquire the property by inheritance, the property's adjusted basis is its fair market value on the deceased's date of death. If you acquire the property by gift, the property's adjusted basis is the donor's adjusted basis plus any gift tax paid by the donor on its transfer to the recipient.

adjusted gross income (AGI): AGI consists of all your income (including wages, salaries, tips, and taxable interest) minus allowable adjustments. You calculate your AGI before subtracting itemized deductions and personal exemptions.

after-tax contributions: Some retirement plans (for example, Roth IRAs) allow you to contribute money that has already been taxed. Such contributions are known as after-tax contributions.

alimony: Payments to a divorced or separated spouse that meet a number of IRS requirements and are then deductible by the payer and taxable to the recipient. Receiving alimony qualifies you to make an IRA contribution.

alternative minimum tax (AMT): AMT is a second federal tax system designed to prevent higher-income people from taking too many deductions and paying too little in taxes. Keep calculating!

amended return: Your chance to file another form — 1040X — within three years of the original return, correcting a mistake or making a change in your tax return for that year. Kind of like correcting an exam you've already turned in to the professor — neat, huh?

amortization: Similar to depreciation but relating to the deduction for using up intangible assets (such as goodwill). This is a way of writing off (depreciating) these assets over their projected lives.

annual gift tax exclusion: Each year, you may give up to $15,000 per recipient to as many recipients as your heart desires. The gift isn't taxable to the recipient (also not tax-deductible to the donor, unless given to a qualifying charity).

annuity: An investment product that is essentially a contract backed by an insurance company and is frequently purchased for retirement purposes. Its main benefit is that it allows your money to compound and grow until withdrawal without taxation. Selling annuities is a lucrative source of income for insurance agents and "financial planners" who work on commission, so don't buy one until you're sure that it makes sense for your situation.

assessment: An assessment of tax is a bill for additional tax made when a return is filed that shows a balance due or when the IRS determines, after reviewing your return, that you owe additional tax. Unless the collection of tax is in jeopardy (see *jeopardy assessment*) or a mathematical error has been made, the IRS can't collect an assessment until you have exhausted all your administrative and legal avenues. When the IRS assesses additional tax beyond the amount shown on the original return, it must send you a Statutory Notice of Deficiency. If you choose not to challenge this determination, the IRS may collect the amount of the assessment after 90 days (or 150 days if the notice is sent abroad).

asset: A property or investment, such as real estate, stock, mutual fund, equipment, and so on, that has monetary value that can be realized if sold.

at-risk rules: Rules that limit your loss deductions to the cash amount you have invested.

audit: IRS examination and inquisition, generally at the IRS offices, of your financial records that back up what you declare and claim on portions of or your entire tax return. One of life's ten worst experiences.

Automated Collection System (ACS): The IRS's "collection agency." If, after receiving three notices generated by an IRS service center, you haven't paid what is owed, your delinquent account is sent to the ACS. The ACS has the authority to enter into an installment agreement, and its contact with you is exclusively by telephone (hence the automation portion of its name). If the ACS can't collect from you, a revenue officer at a district office takes over your account.

away from home: Specific IRS guidelines that determine your ability to deduct business travel expenses.

B

backup withholding: When you fail to give your Social Security or other Taxpayer Identification number to the person or organization that pays you interest, dividends, royalties, rents, or a consulting fee, or when you fail to furnish the payer with a statement that you aren't subject to backup withholding, the payer must withhold federal income tax at the rate of 24 percent of the income received. The IRS, for example, notifies the payers of interest and dividends to begin backup withholding when you fail to report and pay tax on interest and dividend income on your tax return.

bad debt: Money that you're owed that you probably won't get. May be tax-deductible.

bankruptcy: Legal action that stops IRS and other creditors' collection actions against you.

basis: The tax basis of property (such as stock and real estate) used for determining the gain or loss on its sale or for claiming a depreciation, casualty loss, or other tax deduction. The tax basis is usually the property's cost to you. (See also *adjusted basis*.)

below-market-rate loan: A loan generally made between family members or friends at an interest rate lower than comparable loans available from financial institutions. The party making the loan, if audited, may be forced to pay income tax on the extra loan income they should have been receiving.

beneficiaries: The people to whom you desire to leave your assets. For each retirement account, for example, you denote beneficiaries.

boot: A term used to describe the receipt of cash, or its equivalent, in the tax-free exchange of investment real estate (known as a 1031 or Starker exchange). A tax-free exchange of real estate allows you, subject to IRS guidelines, to avoid paying tax on your profit when selling a rental property by rolling over that profit into another rental property. Boot is taxable when you're doing such a tax-free exchange, so if you don't want to owe any tax from a tax-free exchange of real estate, don't receive any boot!

business interest: The tax deduction that businesses may take for interest paid on business loans.

business meal: The closest thing to a free lunch you'll get from the IRS. Normally, 50 percent of the cost of IRS-allowable business meals is deductible. For 2021 and 2022, the IRS is allowing restaurant-provided meals that meet certain criteria to be fully deductible.

business use (of an automobile): If you use your car for noncommuting business purposes, you may deduct the actual costs of usage or claim the standard mileage rate. If you work for an employer, you take this deduction on Schedule A (Itemized Deductions).

bypass trust: Also known as *credit shelter* or *exemption equivalent trust.* A trust designed to provide benefits to a surviving spouse, and increased shelter from estate taxes for more of your estate.

C

C Corporation: A business entity taxed according to the corporate, not individual, income tax rate schedule. Income, known as dividends, paid out to the corporation's shareholders is taxed on each shareholder's own tax return.

calendar year: A 12-month period ending on December 31. In contrast, some companies use a fiscal calendar that ends during another time of the year.

capital expenditures or expenses: Expenses that you may not immediately deduct but that you can depreciate over time by adding them to the basis of the property. For example, if you put a new roof on your investment real estate property, that expense is depreciated over time because the roof increases the usefulness/value of the property.

capital gain or loss: A taxable gain or loss effected through the sale of a property or financial asset, such as a stock, bond, or mutual fund held outside of a retirement account. The gain or loss is calculated by subtracting the adjusted basis from the sale price of the asset.

capital gains distribution: Taxable distribution by a mutual fund or a real estate investment trust (REIT) caused by securities that are sold at a profit. This distribution may be either short term (assets held a year or less) or long term (assets held more than 12 months).

capital loss carryover: If you sell stocks, bonds, or other securities with net losses totaling more than $3,000 in a year, for tax purposes you must "carry over" the losses in excess of $3,000 to the subsequent tax year(s). Only $3,000 may be taken as a tax loss on your tax return.

cash method: Business accounting method by which you report income when the income is actually received, and expenses when actually paid. This method gives you more control over when income and expenses are recognized for tax purposes than the accrual method. (See *accrual method.*)

casualty loss: A deductible loss resulting from an unexpected cause, such as an earthquake, fire, or flood. These losses on your personal income tax return are deductible on Schedule A to the extent that they exceed 10 percent of your AGI.

charitable contribution: Allowable deduction taken on Schedule A for donation of cash or property to IRS-approved/qualified charities.

child- and dependent-care credit: Tax credit taken off Form 2441 for expenses you incur for the care of a dependent (a child under the age of 13, or someone who is physically or mentally handicapped) in order to allow you to work.

child support: Payment specifically designated under a divorce decree. Child support payments aren't tax-deductible.

The Code: The Internal Revenue Code, or IRC; the verbiage that makes up the wonderfully complex tax laws.

Cohan Rule: Based on an actual case that George M. Cohan won against the IRS in the 1920s, the Cohan Rule allows deductions based on estimates rather than receipts for certain, primarily smaller, expenses such as taxi fares, tips, and cleaning and maintenance costs.

Collection Information Statement (CIS): A detailed financial and income statement (Form 433-A and Form 433-B) required by individuals and businesses applying for an installment agreement to pay delinquent taxes over a period of time.

community property: Property equally owned by husband and wife for which each spouse must, for state income tax purposes, report one-half of the joint income. Community property states include Arizona, California, Idaho, Louisiana, Nevada, New Mexico, Texas, Washington, and Wisconsin.

consumer interest: The interest incurred on personal and consumer debt (such as credit cards and auto loans). This interest isn't tax-deductible.

correspondence audit: IRS audit conducted entirely by mail. (See *audit*.)

cost of goods sold: In businesses such as retailing and manufacturing, the term applies to the cost of products sold or manufactured. Cost of goods sold includes such items as raw materials, wholesale prices paid for finished goods, labor costs, and so on.

credit: A tax credit reduces your tax bill dollar-for-dollar.

credit for the elderly or the permanently and totally disabled: If you're 65 or older, or if you're disabled, you may be able to claim this credit, but don't count on it. This credit has stringent requirements.

credit shelter trust: See *bypass trust*.

D

declining-balance method: An aggressive depreciation method that allows faster writing off of business assets.

deduction: An expense you may subtract from your income so as to lower your taxable income. Examples include mortgage interest, property taxes (itemized deductions), and most retirement account contributions.

deficiency: The difference between the tax you originally reported as owing on your tax return and the amount of tax you actually owed as determined by the IRS. You may be notified by mail of additional tax that you owe, or this amount may be determined by an audit. (See *assessment*.)

defined-benefit plan: A company-based retirement plan that pays you a monthly income based on how long you worked (your years of service) for that company or nonprofit agency.

defined-contribution plan: Increasingly common type of company-based retirement plan, such as a 401(k) plan, whereby you contribute money into an individual account and the future value of that account depends on how well the investments you choose perform.

dependent: A person whom you support (such as a child) and whom you may claim as an exemption on your tax return, thus saving you tax dollars.

dependent-care credit: See *child- and dependent-care credit*.

depletion: Deduction reflecting the decrease of a depletable natural resource, such as oil and gas, timber, minerals, and so on.

depreciation: Allowable tax deduction for writing off the cost of business assets, such as cars, computers, and cellular phones. Each type of property is depreciated over a certain, IRS-approved number of years. The term also applies to the allowable deduction for the wear and tear on investment real estate over time.

depreciation recapture: That portion of a capital gain attributable to depreciation taken during the years that the untaxed income sheltered by the depreciation deduction was taxed at ordinary income tax rates rather than the potentially more-favorable capital gains rates.

directly related meals and entertainment: Deductions you can take if you're entertaining clients immediately before, during, or after a business discussion.

dividend: Income from your stock and/or mutual fund holdings. For assets held outside retirement accounts or in tax-free money market and tax-free bond funds, dividends are taxable (although stock dividends are taxed at a lower rate than ordinary income).

dividend reinvestment plan: Plan by which you purchase additional shares of stock or mutual funds using dividends. Reinvestment doesn't impact whether or not these dividends are taxable.

double-declining-balance method: An aggressive depreciation method that allows for faster writing off of business assets.

E

earned income: Money that you receive for doing work. Earned income is taxable and qualifies you to make a retirement account contribution that may be tax-deductible.

earned income credit: If your income is in the lower income brackets, you may qualify for this special and not-so-small tax credit.

effective marginal tax rate: See *marginal tax rate*.

enrolled agent: A tax preparer (other than an attorney or a CPA) licensed by the U.S. Department of the Treasury who can represent you before the IRS.

equity: The difference between the market value of an asset and the loan amount owed on that asset. For example, if you own real estate worth $325,000 and have a $200,000 mortgage outstanding on it, your equity is $125,000 ($325,000 – $200,000).

estate: The value, at the time of your death, of your assets minus your loans and liabilities. Estates in excess of certain amounts are taxable at the federal and state level.

estimated tax: Tax payments you make to the IRS either through regular payroll withholding or on a quarterly basis if you're self-employed or retired. For most people, these estimated tax payments must total at least 90 percent of their actual tax bill; otherwise, penalties and interest are incurred.

F

fair market value (FMV): The price at which an asset, such as stock or real estate, is being traded (that is, bought and sold) or is estimated to be worth by an independent, objective third party, such as an appraiser.

federal short-term rate: The interest rate that the IRS uses in computing interest owed on tax underpayments and overpayments. This rate is determined every calendar quarter by computing the average yield on U.S. Treasury bonds having a maturity of less than three years and adding 3 percent for tax underpayments and 2 percent for tax overpayments.

fiduciary: A person or organization (such as an executor, trustee, or administrator) responsible for managing assets for someone else.

field audit: An audit in which the IRS makes a house call, likely at your own business, to examine your records.

filing status: The applicable category, such as single, married filing jointly, married filing separately, head of household, and qualifying widow(er) with dependent child, that determines your tax rates.

fiscal year: Twelve-month accounting period for a business that may end on the last day of any month. Contrast with calendar year, which must end on December 31.

foreign tax credit: Put on your reading glasses to figure this credit. The instructions alone take the better part of a day to wade through. Applies to taxes paid to foreign countries. (This may apply to you — even if you didn't work overseas — if you own international mutual funds outside of a retirement account.)

401(k) plan: Type of retirement savings plan offered by many for-profit companies to their employees. Your contributions are exempt (yes!) from federal and state income taxes until you withdraw the funds, presumably in retirement.

403(b) plan: Similar to a 401(k) plan but for employees of nonprofit organizations.

G

GAO: General Accountability Office (formerly known as the General Accounting Office). Congress's auditing and investigation arm.

goodwill: Purchase price paid for a business in excess of the business's assets minus its liabilities (net worth). Goodwill is depreciated or amortized over the years.

gross income: Your total taxable income before subtracting deductions.

gross receipts: The total revenue received by a business before subtracting cost of goods sold, returns, and so on.

H

half-year convention: A tax law that specifies claiming half a year's worth of depreciation for assets the first year that those assets are used or placed in service in the business.

head of household: Filing status under which you're unmarried — or considered to be unmarried — and are paying for more than 50 percent of the household costs in the place where you live with a relative whom you can claim as a dependent. (Whew!)

hobby losses: Losses arising from enjoyable activities that aren't conducted for profit. These losses can't be used to offset or reduce other taxable income.

holding period: The period of time for which you hold an asset (from date purchased until date sold).

home equity loan: Mortgage loan that allows you to borrow against the equity in your home. Generally, interest on the amount borrowed is tax-deductible so long as your total mortgage debt on your primary home is no more than $750,000.

home office: Tax deductions are allowed if your home is your principal place of business. These deductions lead to a fair number of audits, so make sure that you're entitled to the deduction.

I

IDRS: Integrated Data Retrieval System. Computer system that allows IRS employees instantaneous visual access to a taxpayer's tax account information.

imputed interest: Interest amount considered to have been earned on certain debts whose interest rates are below the applicable federal rate — that is, the rate set by the law. For example, if you get a loan at, say, 3 percent, the IRS says, not surprisingly, this is a below-market interest rate.

incentive stock option: Option allows for key company employees to exercise the right to buy stock in the company, typically at an attractive price. As a company grows and prospers, these options can end up being a significant portion of an employee's total compensation. Tax on the profit on this stock isn't triggered until the stock is sold.

independent contractor: Status defined by (more!) IRS rules, allowing a person to be treated as self-employed. Among other criteria, self-employed people are expected to maintain their own work area, work for multiple employers, and have control over their work and hours. People who qualify are responsible for paying their own estimated taxes.

Individual Retirement Account (IRA): A retirement account into which anyone with sufficient employment income or alimony may contribute. There are two types of IRAs — regular and Roth. Contribution may or may not be tax-deductible on a regular IRA.

information release (IR): The IRS issues these releases to clarify a point of law or an IRS procedure.

information returns: IRS forms (such as 1099, W-2, 1098) that are required to be filed with the IRS by the payers of interest, dividends, pensions, and freelance income stating the amount of income that was paid to a taxpayer in a given year. The IRS uses this "information" to nail people who don't report all of their income.

installment agreement: An arrangement whereby an individual or business can pay delinquent taxes over a period of time. This agreement must be negotiated with the IRS.

installment sale: When property is sold and a portion of the sale price is paid in two different years, the profits from the sale may be taxable over a period of time as well.

intangible assets: Nonphysical property, such as patents and notes receivable. Compare to tangible assets.

Internal Revenue Service (IRS): A service or not, this is the U.S. Treasury agency that enforces the tax laws and collects taxes.

intestate: Means you die without a will. Dying intestate generally isn't a good idea because state law determines what happens to your worldly possessions and assets as well as who cares for your minor children.

investment interest: Yes, investments pay in more ways than one; among them is your ability to borrow against your securities in a (nonretirement) margin account and to claim the interest of that loan as a deduction. A margin account is simply a type of brokerage account in which you may borrow money from the brokerage firm against the value of your securities held in the brokerage account. These write-offs are limited to the amount of investment income you earn.

IRC: Internal Revenue Code of 1986.

IRM: Internal Revenue Manual. Procedural reference guide that IRS employees follow in administering the Internal Revenue Code.

IRS personnel: Revenue agents — that is, IRS employees assigned to the examination division of the IRS who are responsible for auditing tax returns. Revenue officers are responsible for collecting delinquent taxes.

itemized deductions: Expenditures such as mortgage interest, property taxes, state and local taxes, and so on that are deductible on Schedule A.

J

jeopardy assessment: Has nothing to do with the game show. When the Commissioner of the Internal Revenue Service — or their delegate — believes that the collection of tax is in danger of not being collected at all, the IRS may bypass the normal assessment process as required by law and make an immediate assessment. A taxpayer may protest a jeopardy assessment administratively and by court action.

joint return: Filing status for legally married people. This is usually, but not always, cheaper than filing separate returns. In unusual cases where one spouse has high allowable deductions, filing as married-filing-separately may save the couple tax dollars. Filing individually may also make sense when marital problems cause a lack of trust in a spouse's keeping current with taxes.

joint tenants: A method of ownership of property. Each party is considered the co-owner of a one-half interest unless it is specifically stated otherwise. Creditors of one tenant may attach that tenant's interest. Either tenant or their creditors may petition a court to divide the property so it can be sold. (See also *tenants by the entirety.*)

K

Keogh plan: A retirement savings plan available to self-employed individuals, which allows for substantial tax-deductible contributions. These have been declining in usage as more small business owners adopt SEP-IRA and other plans instead.

Kiddie Tax: The relatively low rate of tax on the first $2,200 of unearned income, such as interest and dividends from investments, for children under 18 years of age and dependent college students under the age of 24. Unearned income higher than $2,200 for these children is taxed on the parent's income tax return.

L

levy (Notice of Levy): Means by which a delinquent taxpayer's employment income or property is seized in order to satisfy the amount of tax that is owed to the government. A levy isn't how you want to pay your back taxes.

lien for taxes: A legal claim attaching to property (including bank and other accounts) of an individual who is delinquent in tax payments. The filing of a lien prohibits the sale or transfer of the property without satisfying the amount of the lien.

like-kind exchange: A tax-free exchange of real estate. Normally when you sell an asset (such as stock and mutual funds) that has appreciated in value, you owe tax on the profits realized. As long as you comply with the specific IRS rules, you may defer paying tax on the profits from investment real estate if you purchase another property. These exchanges are called 1031 or Starker exchanges.

long-term capital gain or loss: Gain or loss on the sale or exchange of an asset held for more than 12 months. For your pleasure, the IRS makes you complete Schedule D to report these gains or losses.

lump-sum distribution: The entire amount in your employer's retirement plan that is paid to you within one tax year. Among the qualifications are reaching age 59½, having become disabled or passed away, having left the employer, and so on. Such distributions often may be rolled over into a retirement account so that tax owed on the distribution can be deferred.

M

marginal tax rate: Not all income is treated equally. In fact, the IRS tax laws treat your first dollars of taxable income differently than your last ones. Specifically, lower tax rates apply to lower income amounts. Your marginal tax rate is the combined federal and state tax rates that you paid on your highest or last dollars of earnings.

marital deduction: This deduction allows unlimited asset transfers from one spouse to another without having to pay any estate or gift taxes. If your spouse is a Scrooge or wants to leave someone else a lot of money, you're outta luck to take full advantage of this.

medical expense: A deduction you can take if you itemize your expenses on Schedule A, and your medical expenses exceed 7.5 percent of your AGI. You probably won't qualify, but checking it out may be worthwhile if you have a large amount of unreimbursed medical expenses.

Modified ACRS (MACRS): This term refers to the entire depreciation system, modified in 1986 by Congress. This depreciation is less favorable to businesses than the ACRS and stretches out the number of years during which business assets must be depreciated.

mortgage interest: A tax cut for you, unless the politicians in Congress take it away with a flat tax. Mortgage interest on your primary and secondary residence is deductible on the first $750,000 of mortgage debt.

mutual fund: A professionally managed, diversified fund that enables you to pool your money with that of many other investors. The three major types of funds are money market (which are similar to savings accounts), bond, and stock.

N

negligence: Negligence is a failure to make a reasonable attempt to comply with the tax laws. That portion of a tax underpayment attributable to negligence is subject to the negligence penalty.

net income: Business income left over after all deductions and expenses.

net operating loss (NOL): A loss from your business that exceeds your other income for the year.

nonresident alien: A person who is neither a U.S. citizen nor a permanent resident or green card holder. As far as the IRS is concerned, nonresident aliens usually must pay tax only on income from U.S. sources.

notice status: Reference to those taxpayers who are receiving tax notices demanding payment of unpaid taxes.

O

offer-in-compromise: A formal application that you, or your tax advisor acting on your behalf, make to the IRS requesting that it accept less than full payment for what you owe for taxes, interest, and penalties. Offers may be made if there is doubt as to either collectibility of the tax or liability for the tax.

office audit: This examination of your tax records takes place at a local IRS office. The most common type of audit.

ordinary income: Income, such as from employment or investment interest and dividends, that isn't derived from the sale or exchange of an asset. In other words, income other than that from capital gains.

original issue discount (OID): Debt instruments (that is, bonds) that don't pay interest but that should increase in value over time. The discounted price at which the bond is issued relative to its face value at maturity is considered taxable interest income to be reported on your tax return annually (if you hold the bond outside a retirement account).

P

partnership: An unincorporated business entity that isn't itself taxable. Instead, tax obligations lie with the individual partners to whom the business's net profit (revenue minus expenses) is distributed annually.

passive activity: A business deal or venture in which you're a silent partner (that is, not actively involved in the management of the venture). Losses from these passive activities are limited in their deductibility to offset income from other passive activities.

passive-activity interest: This interest isn't considered investment-interest expense. The cost of this interest for tax purposes can be deducted only from passive-activity income.

payroll withholding: Withholding of taxes from your paycheck that your employer should perform.

pension: See *defined-benefit plan.*

personal interest: See *consumer interest.*

personal property: Includes your boat, plane, and car, but not real estate. Taxes on personal property may be deductible if the assets are used for business purposes. Auto registration fees based on the value of your car and paid to your state are deductible on your personal tax return.

points: The generally deductible prepaid interest that a borrower pays to obtain a mortgage.

probate: The legal process for administering and implementing the directions in your will. Makes probate attorneys wealthy. Minimize their income and maximize your estate by investigating living trusts, which keep your nonretirement assets out of probate.

Q

qualified plan: A government-approved retirement plan (such as a pension plan, Keogh plan, or employee stock ownership plan) that allows for the tax-deferred compounding of your investment dollars over the years until withdrawal.

qualifying widow(er): A special tax filing status that allows a surviving spouse with dependents to use the same tax rates applicable to joint filers in the two years following the year of the first spouse's death.

R

Real Estate Investment Trust (REIT): An investment similar to a mutual fund but that invests in real estate properties. Provides you the benefits of property ownership without the burden of landlording.

real property: Real estate, such as land and buildings.

refund: Great feeling to get money back, isn't it? In this case, though, the money was yours in the first place, and you gave the government too much of it and didn't figure it out until you filed your annual tax return! Take a look at adjusting your withholding (get a copy of Form W-4).

residential rental property: Investment real estate from which at least 80 percent of the total rental income comes from dwelling units. Such property that you own and purchased after May 12, 1993, is depreciated over 39 years.

revenue agents: IRS employees assigned to the Examination Division of the IRS who are responsible for auditing tax returns.

revenue officers: IRS collection agents in the IRS's Collection Division who are responsible for collecting delinquent taxes.

revocable trust: A trust you set up to keep your nonretirement assets out of probate. These trusts can be changed or ended if you so desire.

rollover: The term used to describe moving money from your employer's retirement plan, for example, into your own IRA. Just make sure that you never take personal possession of the money. If you do take possession of the money, your employer is required to withhold 20 percent for federal income tax.

royalty: You may not be a member of the nobility but receiving income from the licensing or sale of intellectual and material property that you own, such as books, movies, patents, natural resources, and so on, is a nice way to make up for that. This income is taxable as ordinary income.

S

S Corporation: A business entity that enjoys the benefits, such as limited legal liability, of being incorporated, but the income from which is taxed on a person's individual income tax return.

salvage value: The estimated value of a depreciable asset at the end of its useful life.

Section 179 deduction: The IRS allows you to write off or deduct a certain amount a year for the cost of tangible business equipment (such as computers and office furniture) in the year it was placed in service.

self-employment tax: The Social Security and Medicare taxes paid by self-employed people. If you work for an employer, your employer pays half of these taxes. If you're self-employed, you get to deduct half of the total self-employment taxes you pay.

separate returns: Individual tax returns filed by married people who aren't filing jointly. Normally, filing separately when you're married doesn't make sense because it leads to the payment of higher total taxes by the couple.

short-term capital gain or loss: The gain or loss that derives from selling or exchanging an asset, such as a stock, bond, mutual fund, or real estate, held for 12 months or less.

SIMPLE: A type of small-business retirement plan.

Simplified Employee Pension (SEP-IRA): An easily established retirement plan for self-employed individuals under which you can put away a significant portion of your income on a tax-deductible basis.

single: Required tax-filing status for a person with no dependents who is not legally married.

standard deduction: Rather than spelling out (itemizing) each individual deduction, the IRS offers you the option of taking a flat deduction amount that depends on your filing status. If you don't own real estate or pay a lot in state income taxes, odds are you'll take the standard deduction.

statute of limitations: The period beyond which the government may not assess or collect a tax. Unless waived in writing, no tax may be assessed after three years from the date a return was filed, nor may the tax be collected more than ten years after the assessment. From your perspective, no refund claims may be made after three years from the filing date or two years after the date the tax was paid, whichever is later.

straight-line depreciation: A method of depreciation in which the deduction is taken in equal amounts each year in the life of an asset.

surviving spouse: A special tax filing status that allows the widow or widower to file a joint income tax return in the year of their spouse's death.

T

tangible assets: Physical property or equipment such as computers, cars, manufacturing assembly-line equipment, and so on. Compare to intangible assets.

tax account: Means by which the IRS records all tax information for a taxpayer. Every taxpayer is assigned a tax account under a Social Security or other Taxpayer Identification number.

tax deferral: The legally allowed delay in paying tax. For example, contributions to retirement accounts may grow and accumulate earnings, and the tax on these earnings is deferred until the money is withdrawn.

tax year: Usually a period of 12 months, beginning on January 1 and ending on December 31, for summarizing your income and expenses. Some businesses use tax years that start and end at some other time of the year, such as October 1 through September 30 or July 1 through June 30.

taxable income: The amount on which you actually pay tax. Not every dollar of your income is taxable. You are taxed on the amount left after having subtracted whatever deductions, exemptions, and credits apply from your AGI.

Taxpayer Bill of Rights: These may not be inalienable rights, but Congress rolled out this bill in 1988 to help you cope with the IRS.

Taxpayer Identification number (TIN): For individuals, this number is their Social Security number; for businesses, it's the Employer Identification number. A TIN is also issued to taxpayers who don't have or aren't qualified to have a Social Security number.

tax-sheltered annuity (TSA): Annuities (offered by insurance companies) that are specific to nonprofit organizations. TSAs offer tax incentives to save and invest for retirement; however, TSAs do carry higher fees than no-load (commission-free) mutual funds, which are a better alternative for nonprofit 403(b) programs.

tenants by the entirety: A method of recording the ownership of property where each party is considered to have an interest in the entire property. Only a husband and wife may hold property in this manner. Without the consent of both parties, a creditor of one can't attach or force the partitioning of the property so that a sale can be made. (See also *joint tenants.*)

tenants in common: Real estate ownership by two or more people; the share of property owned by one of the tenants goes into their estate upon their death.

Totten trust ("in trust for" account): Bank accounts you control during your lifetime but that, upon your death, go to a named beneficiary without having to go through probate. Sometimes referred to as payable-upon-death accounts.

trust: A legal arrangement that passes ownership of your assets to someone else. There are many types of trusts.

200 percent-declining-balance method: An aggressive, fast method of depreciating business assets.

U

unified estate and gift tax credit: A huge tax credit, worth hundreds of thousands of dollars in tax savings, that allows a person to pass substantial assets free of estate taxes on to others. Also known as the applicable credit.

useful life: The amount of time a depreciable asset is expected to be in business use.

W

waiver: A taxpayer's consent to give up a right possessed under the law. A taxpayer can waive or consent to extending the statute of limitations pertaining to when an assessment may be made and the time frame in which a tax may be collected. A taxpayer can also waive the right to a Statutory Notice of Deficiency so that an immediate assessment may be made.

will: A legal document stating your wishes regarding your assets and care of your minor children and requiring that your wishes be heeded when you die.

withholding: Amount withheld during the tax year from your income as a prepayment of your tax liability.

Z

zero-coupon bond: This bond doesn't pay annual interest but is purchased at a discount to its face value, which is paid at maturity. This increased value over time represents income on which taxes must be paid for nonretirement accounts.

Index

local taxes, 39, 221–224

long-term capital gain or loss, 193–194, 308, 313–317, 505, 598

long-term capital loss carry-over, on Form 8949, 317

losses, calculating, 240–241

low-income housing, 535

lump-sum distributions, 99–101, 598–599

lump-sum payments, 109, 482–483

M

mail, filing by, 73

management fees, on Schedule E, 339

mandatory distribution rules, 474

marginal tax rate, 12–20, 599

marital deduction, 599

market discounts, 248–249, 310–311

mark-to-market traders, 331–332

marriage bonus, 59–60

marriage penalty, 56, 59–60

married filing jointly filing status, 53–54

married filing separately filing status, 54–58

medical and dental cost

  about, 213–214

  calculating deduction, 220–221

  checklist for, 214–216

  defined, 599

  home improvements, 220

  insurance premiums, 218–219

  meals and lodging, 218

  nursing home, 220

  recordkeeping for, 39

  reimbursements and damages, 219

  special schooling, 219

  special situations, 217–218

  travel costs, 217

Medicare tax (Form 8959), on Form 1040, Schedule 2, 165, 167

mid-quarter convention, 275, 278–279

military families, 322, 579–583

Military Family Relief Act, 580–581

minimum distributions, 103

minimum payment period, alimony and, 141

minimum retirement age, 104

minor child, as designated beneficiary, 94

misapplied payments, 418

miscellaneous itemized deductions, recordkeeping for, 39

missing tax records, reconstructing, 42–47

mixed-use mortgages, 228

Modified Accelerated Cost Recovery System (MACRS), 276, 280, 284, 599

money market funds, 506–507

mortgage debt, 576–577

mortgage interest

  deduction for, 21

  defined, 599

  paid to banks (Form 1098), 339

  points and, 226–230

  recordkeeping for, 39

  on Schedule C, 285

  write-offs for, 520

mortgage payments, 141, 527–531

moving expenses, 135, 372–374

multiple-support agreement, 217

municipal bonds, 419

Murphy, Kathryn A. (author), 69

mutual funds, 516, 549, 599

Mutual Funds For Dummies (Tyson), 479

N

National Association of Enrolled Agents, 33

negligence, 599

net income, 599

net investment income tax (Form 8960), 167–168

net operating losses (NOLs), 112, 120, 430, 497, 599

net premium tax credit (Form 8962), 182

net profit (or loss), on Schedule C, 292

About the Authors

Eric Tyson, MBA, is a bestselling author, syndicated columnist, and lecturer. He works with and teaches people from myriad income levels and backgrounds, so he knows the financial and tax questions and concerns of real folks.

After toiling away for too many years as a management consultant to behemoth financial-service firms, Eric decided to take his knowledge of the industry and commit himself to making personal financial management accessible to all of us. Despite being handicapped by a joint B.S. in Economics and Biology from Yale and an MBA from Stanford, Eric remains a master at "keeping it simple."

An accomplished freelance personal-finance writer, Eric is the author of other *For Dummies* national bestsellers on Personal Finance, Investing, Real Estate Investing, and Home Buying. His work has been critically acclaimed in hundreds of publications and programs including *Newsweek,* the *Los Angeles Times, Chicago Tribune, Kiplinger's Personal Finance Magazine,* the *Wall Street Journal,* and NBC's *Today Show,* ABC, CNBC, Fox Business Network, PBS's *Nightly Business Report,* CNN, FOX-TV, CBS national radio, Bloomberg Business Radio, and Business Radio Network. You can find his financial insights online at www.erictyson.com.

Margaret Atkins Munro, EA, (who answers to Peggy) is a tax advisor, writer, and lecturer with more than 40 years' experience in various areas of taxation and finance with a mission in life to make taxes understandable. Her practice is concentrated in the areas of family tax, small business, trusts, estates, and charitable foundations.

She is a graduate of The Johns Hopkins University and has also attended University College Cork (Ireland) and the Pontifical Institute of Mediaeval Studies in Toronto, and she feels that her ability to decipher the language in the Internal Revenue Code derives completely from her familiarity with a variety of obscure medieval languages.

Peggy is the author of *529 & Other College Savings Plans For Dummies,* and co-author of *Estate & Trust Administration For Dummies.* Since her move to Costa Rica, she has become more fluent in cross-border issues facing U.S. expatriots living all over the world. She speaks on a variety of tax-related topics and has given numerous interviews to the national and international print and radio media relating her expertise in tax issues, especially with regard to their effects on families. You can reach her through her website at www.taxpanacea.com.

David J. Silverman, EA, has served on the Advisory Group to the Commissioner of Internal Revenue. David has a Certificate in Taxation from New York University and worked in private practice in Manhattan for more than 30 years.

He testified on tax issues before both the Senate Finance Committee and the House of Representatives Committee on Ways and Means. As the result of his suggestions regarding penalty reform that he made while testifying before these committees, legislation was enacted that reduced the amount of penalties that may be assessed in a number of key areas.

Dedication

My deepest and sincerest thanks to my family, friends, clients, and students for their enthusiastic support and encouragement. My wife, Judy, as always, gets special mention for inspiring my love of books and writing.

—Eric Tyson

My family instilled a love of books in all of us from a very early age. This is for you all — my parents, siblings, and especially my husband and my son.

—Margaret Atkins Munro

Authors' Acknowledgments

Special thanks to the people at Wolters Kluwer business — especially Mark Friedlich, who provided the technical review. Every chapter in this book was improved by their knowledge, insights, and experience.

We also want to thank all the good people at Wiley Publishing, Inc. Special recognition goes to Tracy Boggier, Linda Brandon, and Christy Pingleton.

Publisher's Acknowledgments

Senior Acquisitions Editor: Tracy Boggier
Development Editor: Linda Brandon
Copy Editor: Christine Pingleton
Technical Editor: Mark Friedlich, ESQ., CPA

Production Editor: Mohammed Zafar Ali
Cover Image: © karen roach/Shutterstock

Leverage the power

Dummies is the global leader in the reference category and one of the most trusted and highly regarded brands in the world. No longer just focused on books, customers now have access to the dummies content they need in the format they want. Together we'll craft a solution that engages your customers, stands out from the competition, and helps you meet your goals.

Advertising & Sponsorships

Connect with an engaged audience on a powerful multimedia site, and position your message alongside expert how-to content. Dummies.com is a one-stop shop for free, online information and know-how curated by a team of experts.

- Targeted ads
- Video
- Email Marketing
- Microsites
- Sweepstakes sponsorship

20 MILLION PAGE VIEWS EVERY SINGLE MONTH

15 MILLION UNIQUE VISITORS PER MONTH

43% OF ALL VISITORS ACCESS THE SITE VIA THEIR MOBILE DEVICES

700,000 NEWSLETTER SUBSCRIPTIONS TO THE INBOXES OF *300,000* UNIQUE INDIVIDUALS EVERY WEEK

# of dummies

Custom Publishing

Reach a global audience in any language by creating a solution that will differentiate you from competitors, amplify your message, and encourage customers to make a buying decision.

- Apps
- Books
- eBooks
- Video
- Audio
- Webinars

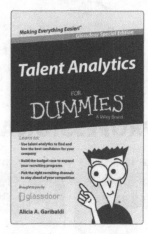

Brand Licensing & Content

Leverage the strength of the world's most popular reference brand to reach new audiences and channels of distribution.

For more information, visit **dummies.com/biz**

PERSONAL ENRICHMENT

Staying Sharp
9781119187790
USA $26.00
CAN $31.99
UK £19.99

Facebook
9781119179030
USA $21.99
CAN $25.99
UK £16.99

Guitar
9781119293354
USA $24.99
CAN $29.99
UK £17.99

Investing
9781119293347
USA $22.99
CAN $27.99
UK £16.99

Beekeeping
9781119310068
USA $22.99
CAN $27.99
UK £16.99

Digital Photography
9781119235606
USA $24.99
CAN $29.99
UK £17.99

Meditation
9781119251163
USA $24.99
CAN $29.99
UK £17.99

Pregnancy
9781119235491
USA $26.99
CAN $31.99
UK £19.99

Samsung Galaxy S7
9781119279952
USA $24.99
CAN $29.99
UK £17.99

iPhone
9781119283133
USA $24.99
CAN $29.99
UK £17.99

Crocheting
9781119287117
USA $24.99
CAN $29.99
UK £16.99

Nutrition
9781119130246
USA $22.99
CAN $27.99
UK £16.99

PROFESSIONAL DEVELOPMENT

Windows 10
9781119311041
USA $24.99
CAN $29.99
UK £17.99

AutoCAD
9781119255796
USA $39.99
CAN $47.99
UK £27.99

Excel 2016
9781119293439
USA $26.99
CAN $31.99
UK £19.99

QuickBooks 2017
9781119281467
USA $26.99
CAN $31.99
UK £19.99

macOS Sierra
9781119280651
USA $29.99
CAN $35.99
UK £21.99

LinkedIn
9781119251132
USA $24.99
CAN $29.99
UK £17.99

Windows 10
9781119310563
USA $34.00
CAN $41.99
UK £24.99

SharePoint 2016
9781119181705
USA $29.99
CAN $35.99
UK £21.99

Fundamental Analysis
9781119263593
USA $26.99
CAN $31.99
UK £19.99

Networking
9781119257769
USA $29.99
CAN $35.99
UK £21.99

Office 2016
9781119293477
USA $26.99
CAN $31.99
UK £19.99

Office 365
9781119265313
USA $24.99
CAN $29.99
UK £17.99

Salesforce.com
9781119239314
USA $29.99
CAN $35.99
UK £21.99

Coding
9781119293323
USA $29.99
CAN $35.99
UK £21.99

dummies.com

dummies
A Wiley Brand

Learning Made Easy

ACADEMIC

9781119293576
USA $19.99
CAN $23.99
UK £15.99

9781119293637
USA $19.99
CAN $23.99
UK £15.99

9781119293491
USA $19.99
CAN $23.99
UK £15.99

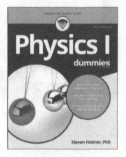

9781119293460
USA $19.99
CAN $23.99
UK £15.99

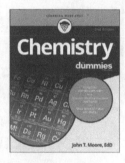

9781119293590
USA $19.99
CAN $23.99
UK £15.99

9781119215844
USA $26.99
CAN $31.99
UK £19.99

9781119293378
USA $22.99
CAN $27.99
UK £16.99

9781119293521
USA $19.99
CAN $23.99
UK £15.99

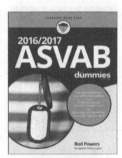

9781119239178
USA $18.99
CAN $22.99
UK £14.99

9781119263883
USA $26.99
CAN $31.99
UK £19.99

Available Everywhere Books Are Sold

dummies.com

Small books for big imaginations

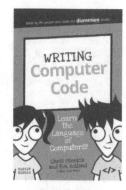